Unit 2 • Animals and Their Habitats

Level 3

Program Authors

Carl Bereiter
Andrew Biemiller
Joe Campione
Iva Carruthers
Doug Fuchs
Lynn Fuchs
Steve Graham
Karen Harris
Jan Hirshberg
Anne McKeough
Peter Pannell
Marsha Roit
Marlene Scardamalia
Marcy Stein
Gerald H. Treadway Jr.
Michael Pressley

SRA

Columbus, OH

Acknowledgments

Grateful acknowledgment is given to the following publishers and copyright owners for permissions granted to reprint selections from their publications. All possible care has been taken to trace ownership and secure permission for each selection included. In case of any errors or omissions, the Publisher will be pleased to make suitable acknowledgments in future editions.

READ ALOUD

"Building Blocks for Survival" from PUDDLER MAGAZINE, Summer 1998, courtesy of Ducks Unlimited.

STUDENT READER

ONE SMALL PLACE IN A TREE by Barbara Brenner, illustrated by Tom Leonard. Copyright © 2004. Used by permission of HarperCollins Publishers.

From MAKE WAY FOR DUCKLINGS by Robert McCloskey, copyright 1941, renewed © 1969 by Robert McCloskey. All rights reserved including the right of reproduction in whole or in part in any form. This edition published by arrangement with Viking Children's Books, a member of Penguin Young Readers Group, a division of Penguin Group (USA) Inc.

WOLF ISLAND by Celia Godkin. Copyright © 1989 Celia Godkin. Used by permission of Fitzhenry and Whiteside.

TWO DAYS IN MAY by Harriet Peck Taylor, pictures by Leyla Torres. Copyright © 1999 by Harriet Peck Taylor, illustrations copyright © 1999 by Leyla Torres. Reprinted by permission of Farrar, Straus & Giroux, LLC.

From CRINKLEROOT'S GUIDE TO KNOWING ANIMAL HABITATS by Jim Arnosky. Text and illustrations copyright © 1986 by Jim Arnosky. All rights reserved. Reprinted by arrangement with the Susan Schulman Agency.

"I have no hatchet" from IF NOT FOR THE CAT by Jack Prelutsky, illustrated by Ted Rand. Copyright © 2004. Used by permission of HarperCollins Publishers.

"We are we are we . . ." from IF NOT FOR THE CAT by Jack Prelutsky, illustrated by Ted Rand. Copyright © 2004. Used by permission of HarperCollins Publishers.

"BEHIND THE REDWOOD CURTAIN" Text copyright © 2000 by Natasha Wing. Published as part of the anthology MY AMERICA: A POETRY ATLAS OF THE UNITED STATES by Simon and Schuster Children's Publishing. All rights reserved. Used with the permission of Sheldon Fogelman Agency, Inc.

"Safe inside my pouch . . ." from IF NOT FOR THE CAT by Jack Prelutsky, illustrated by Ted Rand. Copyright © 2004. Used by permission of HarperCollins Publishers.

SRAonline.com

SRA

Printed in the United States of America.

Send all inquiries to this address:
SRA/McGraw-Hill
4400 Easton Commons
Columbus, OH 43219

ISBN: 978-0-07-616479-0
MHID: 0-07-616479-9

3 4 5 6 7 8 9 WEB 15 14 13 12 11 10 09 08

The McGraw·Hill Companies

National Advisory Board

Patricia Appell
Instructional Interventionist
Annapolis, MD

Christine P. Collins
Former Assistant Superintendent for Instruction and Curriculum
Weymouth, MA

Betsy Degen
Curriculum Director
Shawnee Mission, KS

Bryan Ertsgaard
Teacher
Dayton, OH

James T. Garvin
Assistant Principal
Charlotte, NC

Patsy M. Hall
Title I Professional Development Coordinator
Indianapolis, IN

Michelle L. King
Reading Enhancement Coach
Indianapolis, IN

Deb Owen
Assistant Superintendent for Curriculum and Instruction
Effingham, IL

Patricia Schmella
Curriculum Director
Toppenish, WA

JoAnn Schweda
Teacher
Worley, ID

Sylvia Teahan
Teacher
Medford Lakes, NJ

Joseph Turner
Assistant Principal
Indianapolis, IN

Sue Wennerberg
Teacher
Oak Park, IL

Contributing Author

Michael Milone
Assessment Specialist
Placitas, NM

Literature Consultant

Dr. Laura Apol
Professor, Michigan State University
East Lansing, MI

Program Reviewers

Noemi Arteaga-Gonzales
Teacher
San Antonio, TX

Susan Beede
Consulting Teacher
Nampa, ID

Lisa Beringer
Teacher
Bonita Springs, FL

Paula Bleakley
Teacher
Leesburg, FL

Lisa Bohanan
Instructional Specialist
Pflugerville, TX

Judi Braxton
Reading Coach
Marianna, FL

Benjamin Broadwater
Teacher
Fort Worth, TX

Jodie Broussard
Reading Coach
Pensacola, FL

Jennifer Brown-Mendoza
Reading First Coach
Hominy, OK

Kristine Cain
Teacher
Pensacola, FL

Kellie Campbell
Teacher
Cocoa, FL

Caroline Carithers
Reading Resource Teacher
Pensacola, FL

Jenny Cronan
Literacy Coach
Pittsburg, CA

Margo DiBasio
Reading Specialist
Chelsea, MA

Jennie Eddy
Title I Literacy Coach
Moore, OK

Bryan Ertsgaard
Teacher
Dayton, OH

Tami Ethridge
Instructional Coach
Lancaster, SC

Pamela C. Fendrick
Reading Coach
Tallahassee, FL

Melanie Flores
Teacher
Austin, TX

Tim Francisco
Teacher
Colorado Springs, CO

Kari Franklin
Reading Coach
Pensacola, FL

Rosa Elia Garcia
Reading Specialist
San Antonio, TX

Ashley Garrett
Teacher
Austin, TX

James T. Garvin
Assistant Principal
Charlotte, NC

Dr. Marsha R. Glover
Elementary Reading and Language Arts Developer
Tallahassee, FL

Elaine M. Grohol
Elementary Instructional Specialist
Kissimmee, FL

Patricia Ingles
Teacher
Laguna Niguel, CA

Sarah Jordan
Literacy Specialist
Longview, WA

Cindy Kearney
Teacher
Tulsa, OK

Kim Kempa
Teacher
Santa Ana, CA

Kathy Kindelan
Reading Specialist
Winter Haven, FL

Michelle L. King
Reading Enhancement Coach
Indianapolis, IN

Linda Ann Kosinski
Reading First Coordinator
La Quinta, CA

Sheryl Kurtin
Elementary Specialist, Curriculum and Instruction
Sarasota, FL

Teresa Lopez
Supervisor, Academic Achievement and Accountability
Bakersfield, CA

Jan Maglione
Teacher
Upton, MA

Barbara Maspero
Teacher
San Antonio, TX

Chaitra S. McGrew
Teacher
Austin, TX

Kathy McGuire
Instructional Coach
Roseburg, OR

Becky McPherson
Literacy Coach
Cuthbert, GA

Sheila Menning
Teacher
Largo, FL

Tamarah Michalek
Teacher
Roseburg, OR

Michele Mower
Director of Professional Development
Fontana, CA

Pamela W. Patterson
Instructional Specialist
East Point, GA

Susan Patterson
Reading Coach
Charlotte, NC

Angela Pilcher
Teacher
Stockton, CA

Dr. Jan Rauth
Educational Consultant
Longview, WA

Carlotta Ruiz
Reading Coach
Elk Grove, CA

Dr. Lynda Samons
Curriculum Director
Magnet Cove, AR

Jake Schweikhard
Teacher
Tulsa, OK

Nancy Snyder
Reading Coach
Spring Hill, FL

Dyan Wagner
District Reading Specialist and Intervention Coordinator
Milwaukee, WI

Darlene Watson
Instructional Lead Teacher
Valdosta, GA

Linda Webb
LA Program Specialist
Stockton, CA

Sue Wennerberg
Teacher
Oak Park, IL

Gayle Wilson
Preprimary Department Head
Jacksonville, FL

Linda Wiltz
Instructional Support Teacher
Orlando, FL

Meet the SRA Imagine It! Authors

Carl Bereiter, Ph.D.

A professor emeritus and special advisor on learning technology at the Ontario Institute for Studies in Education, University of Toronto, Dr. Bereiter also invented Computer Supported Intentional Learning Environments, the first networked system for collaborative learning, with Dr. Marlene Scardamalia.

Andrew Biemiller, Ph.D.

A coordinator of elementary teacher education programs at the University of Toronto for thirty-six years, Dr. Biemiller's research on vocabulary development and instruction has had a significant effect on the shape of vocabulary instruction for elementary education in the twenty-first century.

Joe Campione, Ph.D.

A leading researcher on cognitive development, individual differences, assessment, and the design of innovative learning environments, Dr. Campione is a professor emeritus in the School of Education at University of California, Berkeley.

Iva Carruthers, Ph.D.

Equipped with both hands-on and academic experience, Dr. Carruthers serves as a consultant and lecturer in educational technology and matters of multicultural inclusion.

Doug Fuchs, Ph.D.

Dr. Fuchs, the Nicholas Hobbs Professor of Special Education and Human Development at Vanderbilt University, has conducted programmatic research on response-to-intervention as a method for preventing and identifying children with learning disabilities and on reading instructional methods for improving outcomes for students with learning disabilities.

Lynn Fuchs, Ph.D.

A co-director of the Kennedy Center Reading clinic at Vanderbilt University, Dr. Fuchs also conducted research on assessment methods for enhancing instructional planning and instructional methods for improving reading and math outcomes for students with learning disabilities.

Steve Graham, Ph.D.

A professor of literacy at Vanderbilt University, Dr. Graham's research focuses on identifying the factors that contribute to writing development and writing difficulties.

Karen Harris, Ph.D.

The Currey-Ingram Professor of Special Education and Literacy at Vanderbilt University, Dr. Harris's research focuses on theoretical and intervention issues in the development of academic and self-regulation strategies among students who are at risk.

Jan Hirshberg, Ed.D.

Focusing on how children learn to read and write and the logistics of teaching reading and writing in the early grades, Dr. Hirshberg works as a language arts resource coordinator and consultant in Alexandria, Virginia.

Anne McKeough, Ph.D.

A professor in the Division of Applied Psychology at the University of Calgary, Dr. McKeough teaches graduate courses in cognitive development and educational assessment, as well as teacher preparation courses to undergraduates.

Peter Pannell, MA

Principal of Longfellow Elementary School in Pasadena, California, Mr. Pannell has worked to develop the literacy of countless students. To help accomplish this goal, he wrote and implemented a writing project that allowed his students to make great strides in their writing performance.

Marsha Roit, Ed.D.

The Director of Professional Development for SRA/McGraw-Hill, Dr. Roit spends considerable time in classrooms developing reading curricula and working with teachers and administrators in effective instructional practices.

Marlene Scardamalia, Ph.D.

Dr. Scardamalia is the Presidents' Chair in Education and Knowledge Technologies at the University of Toronto and is also the Director of the Institute for Knowledge Innovation and Technology. She received the 2006 World Award of Education from the World Cultural Council for outstanding work in education.

Marcy Stein, Ph.D.

Professor and founding faculty member of the education program at the University of Washington, Tacoma, Dr. Stein teaches At-Risk and Special Education graduate and teacher certification programs.

Gerald H. Treadway Jr, Ph.D.

Chair of the Literacy Education Program and professor of education at San Diego State University, Dr. Treadway teaches classes on reading methods, English Language Learner methods, balanced reading programs, assessment, and reading comprehension. He is also a consultant for the California Reading and Literature Project.

In memoriam

Michael Pressley, Ph.D.

1951–2006

Dr. Pressley was a tireless supporter of education. He championed the rights of all children to a quality education, made seminal contributions in research and practice, and nurtured the development of a host of beginning teachers, young scholars, and editors. While his work and spirit lives on in those he influenced and inspired, there is no substitute for the real thing. We will all miss his wisdom and friendship every day.

Table of Contents

Unit 2

Animals and Their Habitats

Additional Reading

You may wish to provide the following titles to students for additional theme-related reading.

A Log's Life by Wendy Pfeffer

Honeybees by Deborah Heiligman

Raymond's Perfect Present by Therese On Louie

Eliza and the Dragonfly by Susie Caldwell Rinehart

Wildlife Habitats by Emily Stetson

Armadillos Sleep in Dugouts and Other Places Animals Live by Pam Muñoz Ryan

Blue Sky Bluebird by Rick Chrustowski

The Empty Lot by Dale H. Fife

The Moon of the Monarch Butterflies by Jean Craighead George

Forest Fire! by Mary Ann Fraser

Note: You should preview any trade books for appropriateness in your classroom before recommending them to students.

Animals and Their Habitats

OVERVIEW

Do you ever stop to wonder about where animals live? Pets live in our homes, but what about animals in nature? They have their own special habitats. It is important to learn about and respect the homes of the many different animals in our world.

Theme Connection

Look at the photograph. What habitat is portrayed here? What animals do you see? What other animals live in this habitat? How do they share the habitat?

Think BIG

Where do different animals live?

Unit 2

Launching the Theme

Setting Up the Theme

Children are naturally curious about animals. This unit offers students an opportunity to explore not only their curiosity about animals and animal habitats, but also explore the importance of respecting those habitats. This unit encourages students to deepen their understanding of animals, their habitats, and how to create a harmonious relationship between human and animal habitats.

To get students thinking about animals and their habitats, try some of the following ideas:

- Encourage students to talk about animal habitats they already know.
- Have students share stories about encounters with animals in their habitats.
- Have students bring in pictures of animals in their habitats.
- Talk about movies or TV programs that students have seen about animals.
- Play the Unit 2 ***eBackgroundBuilders*** "Animals and Their Habitats."

Students will begin a unit investigation of animals and animal habitats and will continue this investigation over the course of the next six weeks. At the end of the unit, students will publish the results of their investigations.

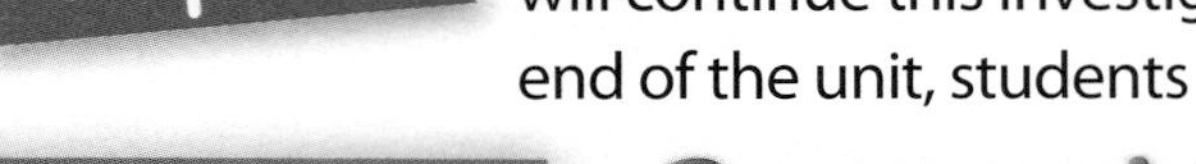

Concept/Question Board

Throughout the unit, students can share their ideas, experiences, and questions by posting them on the **Concept/Question Board.** This will allow the class to become a knowledge-building community, in which questioning and learning are cooperative.

The **Concept/Question Board** can be displayed on a wall, a dry-erase board, or a large poster board. It should be easy for students to access, and they should be given ownership of the board. Consider making teams of students responsible for its maintenance.

Use some of the following materials to generate interest and to encourage students to post their ideas and questions on the **Concept/Question Board:**

- Pictures of wildlife and animal habitats
- Construction paper and markers
- A camera
- Nature magazines for students to cut

In creating knowledge about animals and their habitats, students will need to become active observers of their environment and the various animal habitats within it. They will need to extend their existing knowledge by searching for new facts and explanations.

After discussing the Big Idea question, "Where do different animals live?," ask students the following questions to get them thinking about their Inquiry into animal habitats

- What makes an animal habitat safe?
- Why do different animals have different habitats?
- Why is it important for us to learn more about animals and their habitats?

BIG Idea

Where do different animals live?
Read the Big Idea question to students. Then discuss different places that animals live. Students may point out that jungles, deserts, oceans, and mountains can be habitats. Point out that almost every region on Earth can be a habitat to some type of animal. Explain to students that animal habitats can be as big as the ocean or as small as a spider's web.

Using the Inquiry Planner

Students will research the theme Animals and Their Habitats using the steps below.

	Steps	Models
Week 1	**Step 1** Generate ideas and questions for the **Concept/Question Board.**	**Model 1** *What makes a safe animal habitat? Why are human habitats unsafe for some animals?*
Week 2	**Step 2** Decide on a problem or question to research.	**Model 2** *How should the community protect endangered city animals?*
Week 3	**Step 3** Formulate an idea or a conjecture about the problem or question.	**Model 3** *With a campaign to raise awareness, people will know not to destroy animal habitats.*
	Step 4 Identify needs and make plans.	**Model 4** *I need to learn how many people know about this and how other communities have dealt with this kind of problem. I will interview an expert, make a survey, and research Internet articles and magazines.*
Week 4	**Step 5** Collect facts and use new information to reevaluate the problem or question.	**Model 5** *There are wildlife rescue organizations dedicated to saving and protecting animals.*
Week 5	**Step 6** Continue collecting facts and confirm or revise the conjecture.	**Model 6** *A campaign to raise awareness also needs to convince people to care about the problem.*
Week 6	**Step 7** Create a presentation and share information.	**Model 7** *I will create a pamphlet with visual aids that raises awareness about these animals losing their habitats and present it to the class.*
	Step 8 Identify new questions.	**Model 8** *How can people be convinced to care about animals losing their habitats due to new land development?*

Unit 2

Unit Skills

Week 1

Preparing to Read

Phonics and Fluency ★
- /ī/ Sound/Spellings
- Consonant Blends

Word Structure ★
Regular Plurals

Reading and Responding

Comprehension ★
Strategies
- Asking Questions
- Clarifying
- Visualizing

Skills
- ✓ Author's Purpose
- ✓ Cause and Effect

Fluency ★
Leveled Reader

✓ **Selection Vocabulary** ★

Inquiry

Language Arts

Writing
Summary

Spelling
- ✓ /ī/ Sound/Spellings
- ✓ Plurals

Penmanship
Cursive *m* and *n*

Grammar, Usage, and Mechanics
✓ Possessive Nouns and Pronouns

Study Skills
Note-Taking Skills

Listening/Speaking/Viewing
Asking Questions

Week 2

Preparing to Read

Phonics and Fluency ★
/ō/ Sound/Spellings

Word Structure ★
Irregular Plurals

Reading and Responding

Comprehension ★
Strategies
- Asking Questions
- Predicting

Skills
- ✓ Reality and Fantasy

Fluency ★
Leveled Reader

✓ **Selection Vocabulary** ★

Inquiry

Language Arts

Writing
Nonfiction Book Review

Spelling
- ✓ /ō/ Sound/Spellings
- ✓ Irregular Plurals

Penmanship
Cursive *f* and *h*

Grammar, Usage, and Mechanics
✓ Plurals and Irregular Plurals

Study Skills
Tables and Charts

Listening/Speaking/Viewing
Listen and Respond (to Presentations)

Week 3

Preparing to Read

Phonics and Fluency ★
/ū/ Sound/Spellings

Word Structure ★
Homographs

Reading and Responding

Comprehension ★
Strategies
- Making Connections
- Predicting

Skills
- ✓ Fact and Opinion
- ✓ Making Inferences
- ✓ Reality and Fantasy

Fluency ★
Leveled Reader

✓ **Selection Vocabulary** ★

Inquiry

Language Arts

Writing
Explaining a Process

Spelling
- ✓ Homographs
- ✓ /ū/ Sound/Spellings

Penmanship
Cursive *m*, *n*, *f*, and *h*

Grammar, Usage, and Mechanics
✓ Declarative, Interrogative, Imperative and Exclamatory Sentences

Study Skills
Diagrams

Listening/Speaking/Viewing
Using Visual Aids

★ Phonics ★ Fluency ★ Vocabulary ★ Comprehension

	Week 4	Week 5	Week 6 (Review)
Preparing to Read	**Phonics and Fluency** ★ • /ī/, /ō/, and /ū/ Sound/Spellings • Consonant Blends **Word Structure** ★ Homophones	**Phonics and Fluency** ★ • /ū/ and /o͞o/ Sound/Spellings • Open and Closed Syllables **Word Structure** ★ • Regular Plurals • Irregular Plurals • Homographs • Homophones	**Phonics and Fluency** ★ Unit Review **Word Structure** ★ Unit Review
Reading and Responding	**Comprehension** ★ **Strategies** • Asking Questions • Making Connections • Summarizing **Skills** ✓ Cause and Effect **Fluency** ★ ***Leveled Reader*** ✓ **Selection Vocabulary** ★ **Inquiry**	**Comprehension** ★ **Strategies** • Adjusting Reading Speed • Making Connections • Clarifying **Skills** ✓ Author's Point of View ✓ Classify and Categorize **Fluency** ★ ***Leveled Reader*** ✓ **Selection Vocabulary** ★ **Inquiry**	B ✓ **Vocabulary** ★ **Reading with a Writer's Eye** Unit Review B **Comprehension** ★ **Strategies** Unit Review **Skills** Unit Review B **Fluency** ★ ✓ **Test Strategy** Identifying and Using Important Words **Inquiry**
Language Arts	**Writing** Realistic Story **Spelling** • ✓ /ī/ and /ō/ Sound/Spellings • ✓ Consonant Blends • ✓ Homophones **Penmanship** Cursive *p* and *j* **Grammar, Usage, and Mechanics** • ✓ Nouns and Subjects and Objects • ✓ Pronouns Replacing Nouns **Study Skills** Graphic Organizers **Listening/Speaking/Viewing** Recalling What we Heard	**Writing** Informative Report **Spelling** ✓ /o͞o/ Sound/Spellings **Penmanship** Cursive *c* and *d* **Grammar, Usage, and Mechanics** ✓ Pronouns Replacing Nouns in the Subject **Study Skills** Index **Listening/Speaking/Viewing** Chronological Order	**Writing** Informative Report **Penmanship** Cursive *p, j, c,* and *d*

Key: ★ = five components of Reading ✓ = Lesson Assessment B = Benchmark Assessment

Unit 2

Assessment Plan for Making AYP

is an ongoing cycle.

1 Screen

Administer the initial Benchmark Assessment as a screener to target students who are at risk for failing end of year measures.

Diagnose students' strengths and weaknesses, and differentiate instruction according to their abilities.

2 Diagnose and Differentiate

Diagnosing, differentiating instruction, and monitoring progress is an ongoing cycle.

3 Monitor Progress

Monitor progress weekly, monthly, or any time as needed with both formal and informal assessments.

4 Measure Outcomes

Administer summative Assessments such as Lesson, Benchmark, or state assessments to measure student outcomes.

Screen

For students entering class after the school year has begun, administer ***Benchmark Assessment***, Benchmark 1 to target students at risk for reading failure.

Diagnose and Differentiate

Use the results from the ***Lesson Assessments, Benchmark Assessments***, and informal observation measures to diagnose students' strengths and weaknesses and to differentiate instructions individually and in small groups.

	Approaching Level	On Level	English Learner	Above Level
Leveled Practice	• ***Reteach*** • ***Workshop Kit*** - Activities - Games • ***Intervention*** • ***Curriculum Connections***	• ***Skills Practice 1*** • ***Workshop Kit*** - Activities - Games • ***Intervention Workbook*** • ***Curriculum Connections***	• ***English Learner Support Activities*** • ***Workshop Kit*** - Activities - Games	• ***Challenge Activities*** • ***Workshop Kit*** - Activities - Games
Leveled Readers	• ***Leveled Readers*** • ***Leveled Science Readers***	• ***Leveled Readers*** • ***Leveled Science Readers***	• ***Leveled Readers*** • ***Leveled Science Readers***	• ***Leveled Readers*** • ***Leveled Science Readers***
Technology	• ***eSkills*** • ***eDecodable Stories***	• ***eSkills*** • ***eDecodable Stories***	• ***eSkills*** • ***eDecodable Stories***	

Monitor Progress

Between ***Benchmark Assessments***, use the following to monitor student progress. Regroup student daily or as needed, based on these formative assessment results.

Monitor Progress

Formal Assessment

- Comprehension Rubrics
- Writing Rubrics
- Lesson Assessments
- Oral Fluency Assessments
- ***eAssess***
- Comprehension Observation Logs
- ***Skills Practice 1***
- Research Rubrics

Measure Outcomes

Assess student understanding and mastery of skills by using the ***Lesson Assessments*** or ***Benchmark Assessments.***

Resources to Monitor Progress

	Week 1	Week 2
Skills Practice 1	Phonics, pp. 79–80 Word Structure, pp. 81–82 Selection Vocabulary, pp. 83–84 Writing, pp. 85–86 Spelling, pp. 87–88 Grammar, pp. 89–90 Study Skills, pp. 91–92	Phonics, pp. 93–94 Word Structure, pp. 95–96 Selection Vocabulary, pp. 97–98 Comprehension, pp. 99–100 Inquiry, pp. 101–102 Writing, pp. 103–104 Spelling, pp. 105–106 Grammar, pp. 107–108 Study Skills, pp. 109–110
Decodable Stories, Book 2	Story 17: "Bats"	Story 18: "More Bats"
Leveled Readers	"Savannah Homeland" "Animals in Winter" "Where do Animals Go in the Winter?" "Nothing Grows in the Desert"	"Savannah Homeland" "Animals in Winter" "Where do Animals Go in the Winter?" "Nothing Grows in the Desert"
Lesson Assessment Book 1	Lesson 1, pp. 43–50	Lesson 2, pp. 51–58
Benchmark Assessment		
Technology e-Suite		
Skills & eGames	Skills: Unit 2 Writing	Skills: Unit 2 Writing
Decodable Stories	Decodable 17: "Bats"	Decodable 18: "More Bats"
Fluency	Approaching Level: "Savannah Homeland" On Level: "Animals in Winter" English Learner: "Where do Animals Go in the Winter?" Above Level: "Nothing Grows in the Desert"	Approaching Level: "Savannah Homeland" On Level: "Animals in Winter" English Learner: "Where do Animals Go in the Winter?" Above Level: "Nothing Grows in the Desert"
Assess	***Lesson Assessment Book 1,*** Unit 2, Lesson 1	***Lesson Assessment Book 1,*** Unit 2, Lesson 2

Week 3	Week 4	Week 5	Week 6
Phonics, pp. 111–112 Word Structure, pp. 113–114 Selection Vocabulary, pp. 115–116 Comprehension, pp. 117–118 Inquiry, pp. 119–120 Writing, pp. 121–122 Spelling, pp. 123–124 Grammar, pp. 125–126 Study Skills, pp. 127–128	Phonics, pp. 129–130 Word Structure, pp. 131–132 Selection Vocabulary, pp. 133–134 Inquiry, pp. 135–136 Writing, pp. 137–138 Spelling, pp. 139–140 Grammar, pp. 141–142 Study Skills, pp. 143–144	Phonics, pp. 145–146 Word Structure, pp. 147–148 Selection Vocabulary, pp. 149–150 Comprehension, pp. 151–152 Writing, pp. 153–154 Spelling, pp. 155–156 Grammar, pp. 157–158 Study Skills, pp. 159–160	
Story 19: "Condors"	Story 20: "Strange Stuff"	Story 21: "A Visit"	Story 22: "Migrating Geese"
"Exploring Polar Homes" "Coral Reef Creatures" "Life on a Coral Reef" "Animal Builders"	"Exploring Polar Homes" "Coral Reef Creatures" "Life on a Coral Reef" "Animal Builders"	"Living in a Tropical Rain Forest" "Animals in a High Mountain Habitat" "Mountain Animals" "From Beaches to the Deep Ocean Floor"	"Living in a Tropical Rain Forest" "Animals in a High Mountain Habitat" "Mountain Animals" "From Beaches to the Deep Ocean Floor"
Lesson 3, pp. 59–66	Lesson 4, pp. 67–74	Lesson 5, pp. 75–82	End of Unit Writing Prompt, pp. 83–84
			Unit 2, Benchmark 3
Skills: Unit 2 Phonics Unit 2 Spelling Unit 2 Vocabulary Unit 2 Writing	Skills: Unit 2 Phonics Games: Homophones	Skills: Unit 2 Vocabulary Unit 2 Spelling Games: Homophones	Skills: Unit 2 Spelling Unit 2 Vocabulary Games: Homophones Games: Unit 2 Vocabulary Words
Decodable 19: "Condors"	Decodable 20: "Strange Stuff"	Decodable 21: "A Visit"	Decodable 22: "Migrating Geese"
Approaching Level: "Exploring Polar Homes" On Level: "Coral Reef Creatures" English Learner: "Life on a Coral Reef" Above Level: "Animal Builders"	Approaching Level: "Exploring Polar Homes" On Level: "Coral Reef Creatures" English Learner: "Life on a Coral Reef" Above Level: "Animal Builders"	Approaching Level: "Living in a Tropical Rain Forest" On Level: "Animals in a High Mountain Habitat" English Learner: "Mountain Animals" Above Level: "From Beaches to the Deep Ocean Floor"	Approaching Level: "Living in a Tropical Rain Forest" On Level: "Animals in a High Mountain Habitat" English Learner: "Mountain Animals" Above Level: "From Beaches to the Deep Ocean Floor"
Lesson Assessment Book 1, Unit 2, Lesson 3	***Lesson Assessment Book 1,*** Unit 2, Lesson 4	***Lesson Assessment Book 1,*** Unit 2, Lesson 5	

Lesson Planner

	Day 1	Day 2
Preparing to Read MATERIALS ✦ ***Transparencies*** 44, 48 ✦ ***Skills Practice 1,*** pp. 79–82 ✦ ***Sound/Spelling Card*** 29 ✦ Routines 2–9	**Daily News,** p. T26 ✓ **Phonics and Fluency** Review /ī/ and Consonant Blends, pp. T27–T29	**Daily News,** p. T42 **Phonics and Fluency,** p. T42 **Developing Oral Language,** p. T43 **Dictation,** p. T43
Reading and Responding MATERIALS ✦ ***Student Reader,*** Book 1, pp. 134–157 ✦ ***Transparencies*** 15, 35, 46 ✦ Routines 11, 13, 14, A ✦ ***Skills Practice 1,*** pp. 83–84 ✦ ***Listening Library CDs*** ✦ Writer's Notebook ✦ ***Leveled Reader*** ✦ ***Home Connection,*** pp. 13–16	**Read Aloud,** pp. T30–T35 **Inquiry,** pp. T36–T37	**Build Background,** p. T44 **Preview and Prepare,** p. T45 **Selection Vocabulary,** pp. T46–T47 **Reading the Selection,** pp. T48–T51 1st READ  ✓ **Comprehension Strategies** • Asking Questions, pp. T52, T54 ☆ Clarifying, pp. T49, T53, T55 • Visualizing, p. T54
Language Arts MATERIALS ✦ ***Language Arts Handbook,*** pp. 30–41, 304–307 ✦ ***Skills Practice 1,*** pp. 85–92 ✦ ***Transparencies*** 3, 17, 17A, 45, 47 ✦ Routines 15, 16, 17 ✦ ***Student Reader,*** Book 1, pp. 138–153 ✦ ***Lesson Assessment Book 1,*** pp. 43–50	**Writing** Prewriting, pp. T38–T39 ✓ **Spelling Pretest,** p. T39 **Penmanship,** Cursive Letters *m* and *n,* p. T40	✓ **Writing** Prewriting, pp. T56–T57 **Spelling,** p. T57 ✓ **Grammar, Usage, and Mechanics** Possessive Nouns and Pronouns, pp. T58–T59
Monitor Progress ✓ = **Formal Assessment**	✓ **Phonics and Fluency, p. T29** ✓ **Spelling Pretest, p. T39**	✓ **Comprehension Strategy, p. T49** ✓ **Writing, p. T57** ✓ **Grammar, Usage, and Mechanics, p. T59**

Literature Overview

Read Aloud

Building Blocks for Survival

Student Reader

One Small Place in a Tree

by Barbara Brenner

illustrated by Tom Leonard

Outstanding Science Trade Book for Students K–12 Award

Science Inquiry

Please Feed the Birds

SRA
Imagine It!

★ Phonics ★ Fluency ★ Vocabulary ★ Comprehension

Day 3

Daily News, p. T60
Word Structure
Regular Plurals, pp. T60–T61

Comprehension Strategies
- Asking Questions, pp. T62, T64
- Clarifying, p. T63
- Visualizing, p. T65

Discussing the Selection, p. T66
Review Selection Vocabulary, p. T67
Fluency, p. T67
Theme Connections, p. T68

Writing
Drafting, p. T70
Spelling, p. T71
Study Skills
Taking Notes, p. T72
Grammar, Usage, and Mechanics, p. T73

Word Structure, p. T61
Selection Vocabulary, p. T67
Fluency, p. T67
Spelling, p. T71
Study Skills, p. T72

Day 4

Daily News, p. T74
Word Structure, p. T75
Developing Oral Language, p. T75

2nd READ

Comprehension Skills
- Author's Purpose, p. T76
- Cause and Effect, pp. T78, T80, T82

Reading with a Writer's Eye, pp. T77, T79, T81
Supporting the Reading
- Comprehension Strategy: Clarifying, p. T84

Fluency, p. T85
Science Inquiry, pp. T86–T87
Inquiry, pp. T88–T89

Writing
Revising and Editing/Proofreading, pp. T90–T91
Spelling, p. T91
Study Skills, p. T92
Listening/Speaking/Viewing
Asking Questions, p. T93

Fluency, p. T85
Inquiry, p. T89

Day 5 Review

Phonics and Fluency, p. T94
Word Structure, p. T94

Selection Vocabulary, p. T95
Comprehension Strategies
- Asking Questions, p. T96
- Clarifying, p. T96
- Visualizing, p. T96

Comprehension Skills
- Author's Purpose, p. T96
- Cause and Effect, p. T96

Reading with a Writer's Eye, p. T97
Fluency, p. T97

Writing
Publishing, p. T98
Spelling Test, p. T99
Penmanship, p. T99
Study Skills, p. T100
Listening/Speaking/Viewing, p. T100
Grammar, Usage, and Mechanics, p. T101

Spelling Posttest, p. T99
***Lesson Assessment Book 1,* pp. 43–50**

Student Resources

Genre

Expository Text is nonfiction that is written to inform, to explain, or to persuade.

Comprehension Strategy

Clarifying
As you read, ask yourself questions about things or ideas in the selection that you do not understand.

Focus Questions

How are certain changes in a habitat good for some animals but not for others? How might a tree be a home to many kinds of animals?

One Small Place in a Tree

by Barbara Brenner
illustrated by Tom Leonard

136 137

Student Reader, Book 1, pp. 136–155

Phonics & Fluency

Decodable Stories, Book 3, Story 17, "Bats"

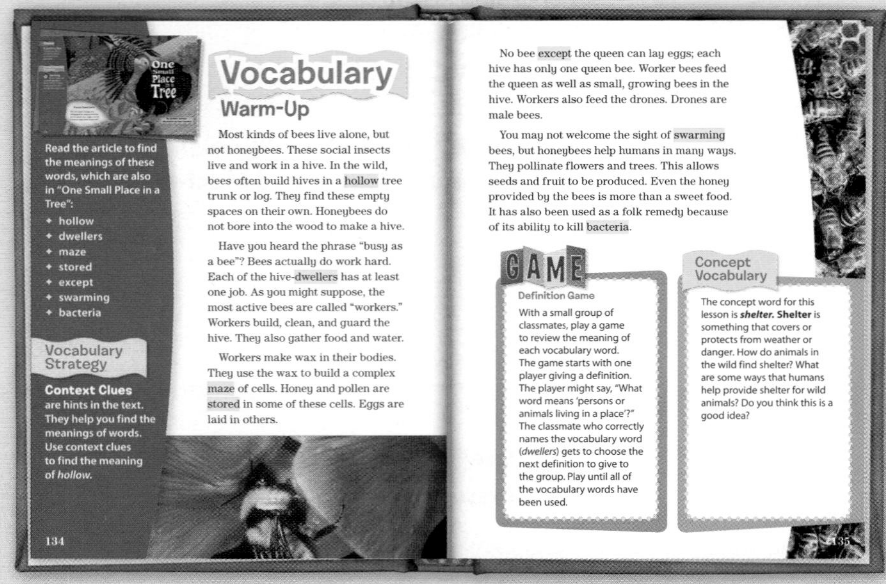

Vocabulary Warm-Up

Read the article to find the meanings of these words, which are also in "One Small Place in a Tree":

- hollow
- dwellers
- maze
- stored
- except
- swarming
- bacteria

Vocabulary Strategy

Context Clues are hints in the text. They help you find the meanings of words. Use context clues to find the meaning of *hollow*.

Most kinds of bees live alone, but not honeybees. These social insects live and work in a hive. In the wild, bees often build hives in a hollow tree trunk or log. They find these empty spaces on their own. Honeybees do not bore into the wood to make a hive.

Have you heard the phrase "busy as a bee"? Bees actually do work hard. Each of the hive-dwellers has at least one job. As you might suppose, the most active bees are called "workers." Workers build, clean, and guard the hive. They also gather food and water.

Workers make wax in their bodies. They use the wax to build a complex maze of cells. Honey and pollen are stored in some of these cells. Eggs are laid in others.

No bee except the queen can lay eggs; each hive has only one queen bee. Worker bees feed the queen as well as small, growing bees in the hive. Workers also feed the drones. Drones are male bees.

You may not welcome the sight of swarming bees, but honeybees help humans in many ways. They pollinate flowers and trees. This allows seeds and fruit to be produced. Even the honey provided by the bees is more than a sweet food. It has also been used as a folk remedy because of its ability to kill bacteria.

GAME

Definition Game

With a small group of classmates, play a game to review the meaning of each vocabulary word. The game starts with one player giving a definition. The player might say, "What word means 'persons or animals living in a place'?" The classmate who correctly names the vocabulary word (*dwellers*) gets to choose the next definition to give to the group. Play until all of the vocabulary words have been used.

Concept Vocabulary

The concept word for this lesson is ***shelter. Shelter*** is something that covers or protects from weather or danger. How do animals in the wild find shelter? What are some ways that humans help provide shelter for wild animals? Do you think this is a good idea?

134 135

Student Reader, Book 1, pp. 134–135

Science

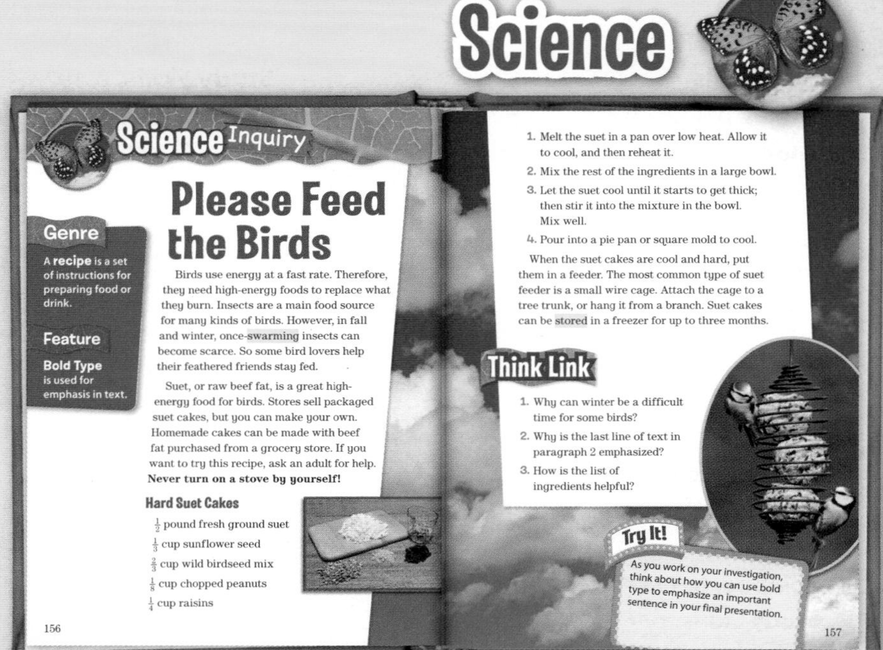
Science Inquiry

Please Feed the Birds

Genre

A **recipe** is a set of instructions for preparing food or drink.

Feature

Bold Type is used for emphasis in text.

Birds use energy at a fast rate. Therefore, they need high-energy foods to replace what they burn. Insects are a main food source for many kinds of birds. However, in fall and winter, once-swarming insects can become scarce. So some bird lovers help their feathered friends stay fed.

Suet, or raw beef fat, is a great high-energy food for birds. Stores sell packaged suet cakes, but you can make your own. Homemade cakes can be made with beef fat purchased from a grocery store. If you want to try this recipe, ask an adult for help. **Never turn on a stove by yourself!**

Hard Suet Cakes

- $\frac{1}{2}$ pound fresh ground suet
- $\frac{1}{3}$ cup sunflower seed
- $\frac{2}{3}$ cup wild birdseed mix
- $\frac{1}{8}$ cup chopped peanuts
- $\frac{1}{4}$ cup raisins

1. Melt the suet in a pan over low heat. Allow it to cool, and then reheat it.
2. Mix the rest of the ingredients in a large bowl.
3. Let the suet cool until it starts to get thick; then stir it into the mixture in the bowl. Mix well.
4. Pour into a pie pan or square mold to cool.

When the suet cakes are cool and hard, put them in a feeder. The most common type of suet feeder is a small wire cage. Attach the cage to a tree trunk, or hang it from a branch. Suet cakes can be stored in a freezer for up to three months.

Think Link

1. Why can winter be a difficult time for some birds?
2. Why is the last line of text in paragraph 2 emphasized?
3. How is the list of ingredients helpful?

Try It!

As you work on your investigation, think about how you can use bold type to emphasize an important sentence in your final presentation.

156 157

Student Reader, Book 1, pp. 156–157

Cross-Curricular Resources

Curriculum Connections

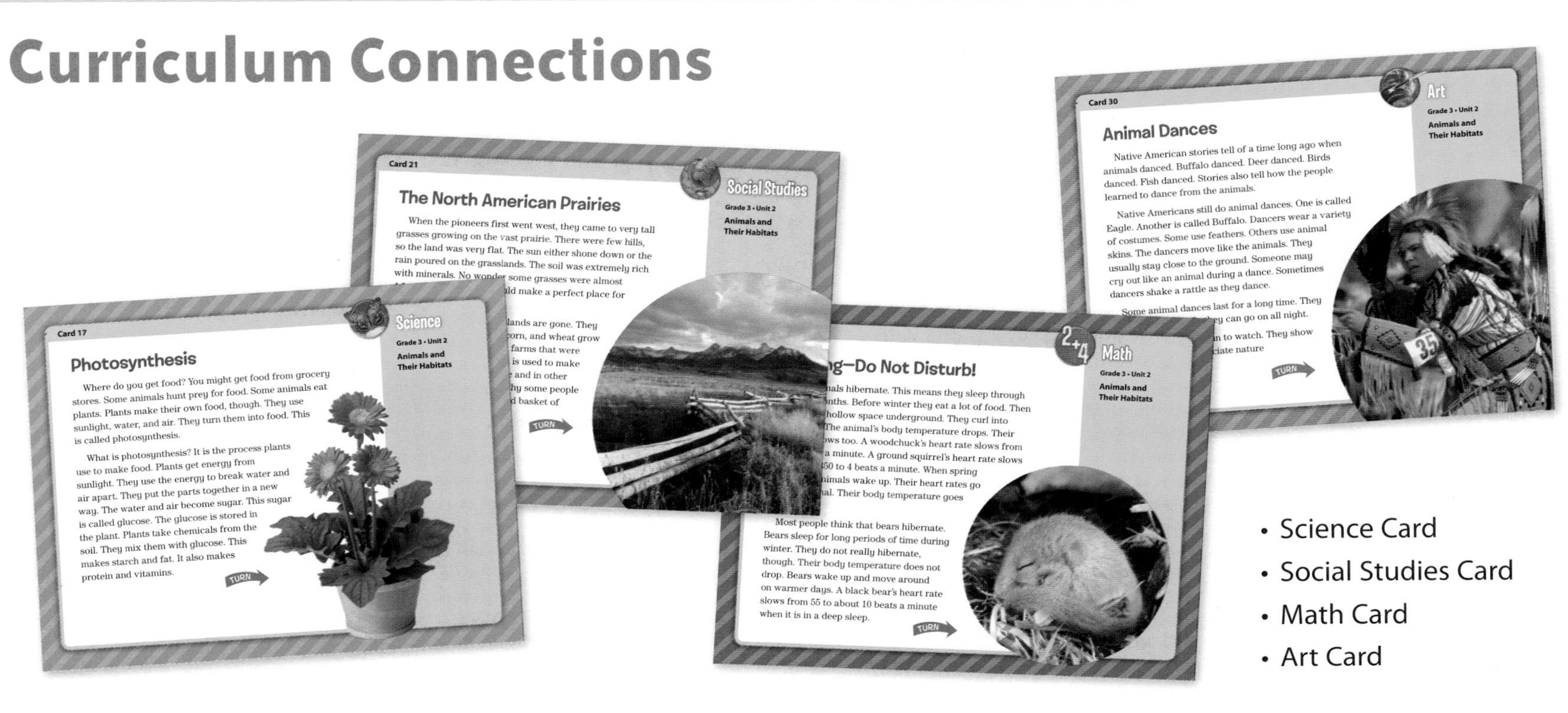

- Science Card
- Social Studies Card
- Math Card
- Art Card

Leveled Readers for Science

Approaching Level

On Level

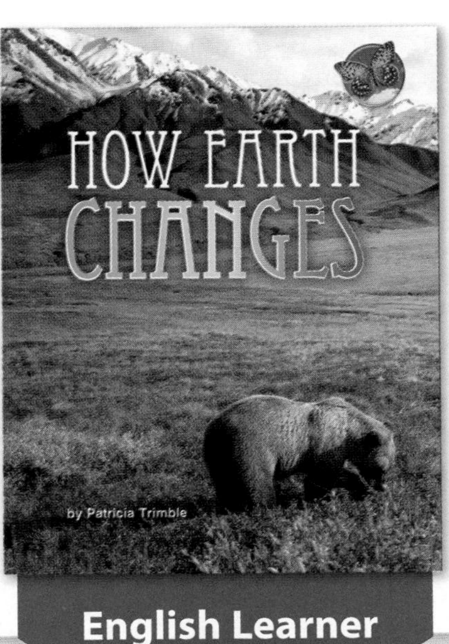

English Learner

Caring for Earth

by Patti Frank

WE RECYCLE

Above Level

Lesson 1 Overview

Differentiating Instruction
for Workshop

Day 1

	Approaching Level	On Level	English Learner	Above Level
Preparing to Read	**Phonics and Fluency:** Help students complete ***Reteach*** page 32, or work with them on the phonics activities in the ***Intervention Workbook*** Unit 2, Lesson 1. Then have students read ***Decodable Stories, Book 3,*** Story 17.	**Phonics and Fluency:** Have students play a game with the ***Sound/Spelling Cards.***	**Phonics and Fluency:** Use ***English Learner Support Guide*** for additional phonics instruction. Then have students read ***Decodable Stories, Book 3,*** Story 17	**Phonics and Fluency:** Have students complete ***Challenge Activities*** page 29
Reading and Responding	**Vocabulary:** Have students add words from *Building Blocks for Survival* that apply to animals and their habitats to their Writer's Notebooks. Help students find the definitions to these words in a dictionary. **Comprehension:** Have students research habitats using print and online references to help build background knowledge. **Inquiry:** Have students work in small groups to generate ideas and questions about animals and animal habitats to place on the **Concept/Question Board.**	**Vocabulary:** Have students add words from *Building Blocks for Survival* that apply to animals and their habitats to their Writer's Notebooks. Have students write the definitions in their own words. **Comprehension:** Have students write a paragraph about a personal connection they have with the selection. **Inquiry:** Have students work in small groups to generate ideas and questions about animals and animal habitats to place on the **Concept/Question Board.**	**Vocabulary:** Have students add words from *Building Blocks for Survival* that apply to animals and their habitats to their Writer's Notebooks. Have students draw small illustrations that will help them remember the meaning of the words. **Comprehension:** Give students an article or poem about animals and their habitats to read to practice visualizing. **Inquiry:** Have students work in small groups to generate ideas and questions about animals and animal habitats to place on the **Concept/Question Board.**	**Vocabulary:** Have students add words from *Building Blocks for Survival* that apply to animals and their habitats to their Writer's Notebooks. Have students write short, informative reports using the words. **Comprehension:** Have students add questions and ideas from the Read Aloud to the **Concept/Question Board.** **Inquiry:** Have students work in small groups to generate ideas and questions about animals and animal habitats to place on the **Concept/Question Board.**
Language Arts	**Writing:** Have students explain the main idea of their books to another student, and then have them work on writing down what was said. **Spelling:** Have students divide three spelling words into separate syllables and try to spell each syllable.	**Writing:** Have students begin to write notes on pieces of information they know they need to include in their summaries. **Spelling:** Have students review the **Sound/Spelling Cards** that correspond to this week's spelling words.	**Writing:** Have students use a translation dictionary to write notes on important information they will want to include in their summaries. **Spelling:** Have students create flash cards to help them study the spelling words.	**Writing:** Have students develop a plan for prewriting, drafting, revising, editing/proofreading, and publishing. **Spelling:** Have students work in pairs to quiz one another on this week's spelling words.

Day 2

	Approaching Level	On Level	English Learner	Above Level
Preparing to Read	**Phonics and Fluency:** Have students listen to the /ī/ sound on the ***Sound/Spelling Card Stories CD.*** Then have students read ***Decodable Stories, Book 3,*** Story 17.	**Phonics and Fluency:** Students can make lists of words to add to the blending lines. In pairs, have students play a game with ***Sound/Spelling Card*** 29.	**Phonics and Fluency:** Have students listen to the /ī/ sound on the ***Sound/Spelling Card Stories CD.*** Then have students read Decodable Stories, Book 3, Story 17.	**Phonics and Fluency:** Have students create sentences with the words from dictation. Students can also list words to add to the blending lines.
Reading and Responding	**Vocabulary:** Have students create illustrations for the selection vocabulary words in their Writer's Notebooks. **Comprehension:** Have students share their visualizations with the rest of the class.	**Vocabulary:** Have students practice using a dictionary by looking up the selection vocabulary words. **Comprehension:** Have students help each other clarify any words or passages while reading the selection.	**Vocabulary:** Use ***English Learner Support Guide*** to review the vocabulary. **Comprehension:** Have students draw an illustration for the selection, based on one of their visualizations.	**Vocabulary:** Have students create flash cards to use as a learning tool for the selection vocabulary words. **Comprehension:** Have students write a descriptive paragraph about one of their visualizations for the selection.
Language Arts	**Writing:** Have students continue to take notes on the main ideas and supporting details in their Writer's Notebooks. **Spelling:** Have students write five spelling words on a piece of paper, leaving one letter blank. Then have them exchange papers with a partner and fill in the blanks. **Grammar, Usage, and Mechanics:** Have students complete ***Reteach*** page 36.	**Writing:** Have students review their notes and add missing details before drafting. **Spelling:** Have students think of four words that rhyme with spelling words and spell them on a sheet of paper. **Grammar, Usage, and Mechanics:** Have students complete a ***Workshop Kit*** activity during Workshop.	**Writing:** Provide nonfiction picture books with minimal text for students to summarize. **Spelling:** Have students slowly read aloud four spelling words, carefully pronouncing each letter or sound spelling in the word. **Grammar, Usage, and Mechanics:** Refer to the ***English Learner Support Guide*** for support activities.	**Writing:** Have students begin drafting after they finish taking notes on their books. **Spelling:** With a partner, have students slowly read two lines of this week's selection aloud and spell the sentence on a piece of paper. **Grammar, Usage, and Mechanics:** Have students complete ***Challenge Activities*** page 36.

Lesson 1 Overview

Differentiating Instruction
for Workshop

Day 3

	Approaching Level	On Level	English Learner	Above Level
Preparing to Read	**Word Structure:** Review the word lines with regular plurals. Then have students complete ***Reteach*** page 33 or work with one of the word structure activities in the ***Intervention Guide,*** Unit 2, Lesson 1.	**Word Structure:** Have students read "One Small Place in a Tree," looking for other regular plural nouns.	**Word Structure:** Review the word lines with regular plurals. Use the ***English Learner Support Guide*** for more word structure instruction.	**Word Structure:** Have students complete ***Challenge Activities*** page 30. Then students can read other materials and look for regular plural nouns.
Reading and Responding	**Vocabulary:** Have students use ***Reteach*** page 34 or work with students using the ***Intervention Guide,*** Unit 2, Lesson 1. **Comprehension:** Have students apply questions and ideas from the selection about animals and their habitats to the Concept/Question Board. **Fluency:** Have students reread a passage from the selection with a partner or individually.	**Vocabulary:** Have students complete a game in the ***Workshop Kit.*** **Comprehension:** Have students visualize forest settings. Have students write a short paragraph describing their visualization. **Fluency:** Have students read into a tape recorder at the beginning and end of the week. Have them listen to themselves at the end of the week so they can hear their progress.	**Vocabulary:** Help students create flash cards for the selection vocabulary words. Have students test themselves with the cards and then use them to quiz a partner. **Comprehension:** Have students use print or online resources to clarify any difficult or unfamiliar words from the selection. **Fluency:** Have students engage in echo reading with passages from the selection.	**Vocabulary:** Have students complete ***Challenge Activities,*** page 31. **Comprehension:** Have students read other articles about animals and their habitats. Have them practice clarifying as they read. **Fluency:** Have students choose a text on their independent level to read silently.
Language Arts	**Writing:** Have students continue to draft their summaries. **Spelling:** Have students complete ***Reteach*** page 35. **Grammar, Usage, and Mechanics:** Have students use the ***Intervention Workbook*** for intervention activities.	**Writing:** Have students continue to draft their summaries. **Spelling:** Have students choose two spelling words and use the letters in those words to think of new words. **Grammar, Usage, and Mechanics:** Have students look for errors in noun/pronoun agreement in a piece of their writing.	**Writing:** Have students leave blanks if they do not know a word. Tell them to use a thesaurus to help them fill in the missing word during revision. **Spelling:** Have students write five words on a piece of paper and read them aloud for a partner to spell. **Grammar, Usage, and Mechanics:** Refer to the ***English Learner Support Guide*** for support activities.	**Writing:** Have students review the information in their graphic organizers to make sure they have included the main ideas and supporting details. **Spelling:** Have students complete ***Challenge Activities*** page 32. **Grammar, Usage, and Mechanics:** Have students work with others to support learning.

Day 4

	Approaching Level	On Level	English Learner	Above Level
Preparing to Read	**Word Structure:** Students can create sentences using words from the word lines.	**Word Structure:** Have students play a game with regular plurals in the ***Workshop Kit.***	**Word Structure:** Students can create sentences using words from the word lines.	**Word Structure:** Have students play a game with regular plurals in the ***Workshop Kit.***
Reading and Responding	**Vocabulary:** Have students write the definitions of three of the selection vocabulary words in their own words. **Comprehension:** Have students read other stories about animals and their habitats. Have students identify the author's point of view used in the stories. **Fluency:** Have students use ***Leveled Readers.*** **Inquiry:** Have students share stories about animals and animal habitats to generate new ideas and questions.	**Vocabulary:** Have students find related words for the selection vocabulary in a thesaurus or dictionary. **Comprehension:** Have students write a paragraph using descriptive language about a habitat of their choice. **Fluency:** Have students complete an activity using ***eSkills & eGames.*** **Inquiry:** Have students share stories about animals and animal habitats to generate new ideas and questions.	**Vocabulary:** Put students in small groups. Assign each group a word, and have students brainstorm other words that are related to the vocabulary word. Have students add the words to their Writer's Notebooks. **Comprehension:** Have students select an illustration from the text and write a short paragraph that explains what is happening. Encourage students to use the text to help them remember the selection. **Fluency:** Have students share their paragraphs with the class. **Inquiry:** Have students share stories about animals and animal habitats to generate new ideas and questions.	**Vocabulary:** Have students research the origin of one of the selection vocabulary words. Have students research the country the word originated from. **Comprehension:** Have students bring in pictures that are close to their visualizations of the forest in the text. Have students explain what the pictures have in common with the forest in the selection. **Fluency:** Have students complete an activity on ***eSkills & eGames.*** **Inquiry:** Have students share stories about animals and animal habitats to generate new ideas and questions.
Language Arts	**Writing:** Have students continue to revise and edit/proofread their summaries. **Spelling:** Working in pairs, have students assist each other in spelling the spelling words.	**Writing:** Have students read their revised summaries to a partner and discuss ideas for further revision. Have them edit/proofread each other's summaries. **Spelling:** Have students carefully proofread their writing activity for spelling errors.	**Writing:** Have students work with a partner to revise and edit/proofread. **Spelling:** Have students review this week's spelling words using the flashcards they made.	**Writing:** Have students read their summaries aloud to proofread their writing. **Spelling:** Have students write a sentence using at least four spelling words on a piece of paper.

Lesson 1 Overview

Differentiating Instruction
for Workshop

Day 5

	Approaching Level	On Level	English Learner	Above Level
Preparing to Read	**Word Structure:** Listen to the /ī/ sound on the ***Sound/Spelling Card Stories CD.*** Then have students read "Bats" from the ***eDecodable Stories.***	**Word Structure:** Review the blending lines. Have pairs of students write clue sentences for words on the blending lines.	**Word Structure:** Listen to the /ī/ sound on the ***Sound/Spelling Card Stories CD.*** Then have students read "Bats" from the ***eDecodable Stories.***	**Word Structure:** Have students create lists of regular plural nouns. Then have them write rhyming poems using the words from their lists.
Reading and Responding	**Vocabulary:** Have students find antonyms and synonyms for the expanding vocabulary words in a thesaurus. **Comprehension:** Have students create review questions for the story and trade questions with a partner. Have students answer each other's questions. **Fluency:** Have students write answers to comprehension questions from ***Leveled Readers.***	**Vocabulary:** Have students create a crossword puzzle using the vocabulary words. **Comprehension:** Have students write a summary of "One Small Place in a Tree." **Fluency:** Have students complete an activity using ***eSkills & eGames.***	**Vocabulary:** Have students read an additional story about the unit theme and add theme-related words from the story to their Writer's Notebooks. **Comprehension:** Have students write a summary of "One Small Place in a Tree." Encourage students to include illustrations if they have trouble expressing themselves. **Fluency:** Have students use vocabulary from ***Leveled Readers*** in extended sentences.	**Vocabulary:** Have students write their own Vocabulary Warm-Ups using the vocabulary words. **Comprehension:** Have students write a descriptive story with the habitat of their choice as the setting. Have students research the habitat to find realistic information to use in their stories. **Fluency:** Have students reread passages from the selection to a partner.
Language Arts	**Writing:** Have students share their summaries in small group activities. **Spelling:** Have students think of four words that are plurals and write them on a piece of paper.	**Writing:** Have students read their summaries orally. **Spelling:** Have students write an imaginary newspaper headline using as many spelling words as possible.	**Writing:** Have students share their summaries with a partner. **Spelling:** Have students practice spelling by saying aloud to a partner each spelling word and write the words as they are heard.	**Writing:** Have students share their summaries with the class. **Spelling:** Have students write two sentences using three spelling words each on a piece of paper.

Resources for

Differentiating Instruction 

Leveled Readers

Approaching Level

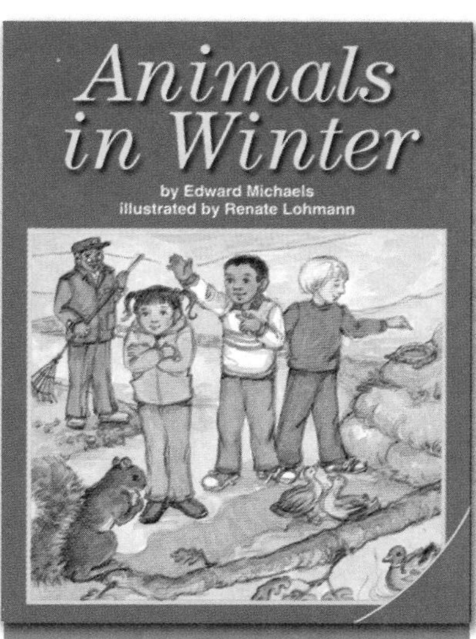

On Level

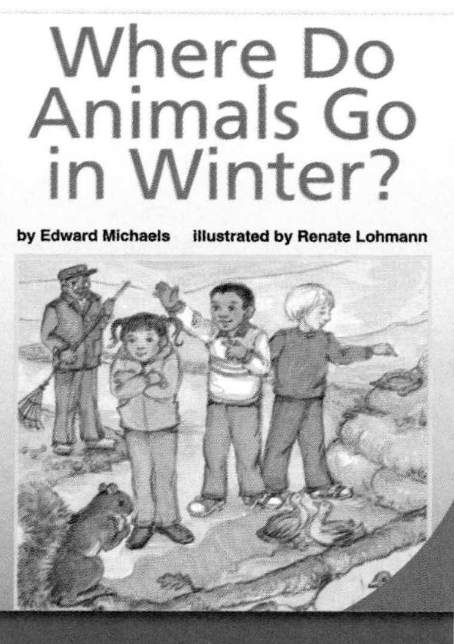

English Learner

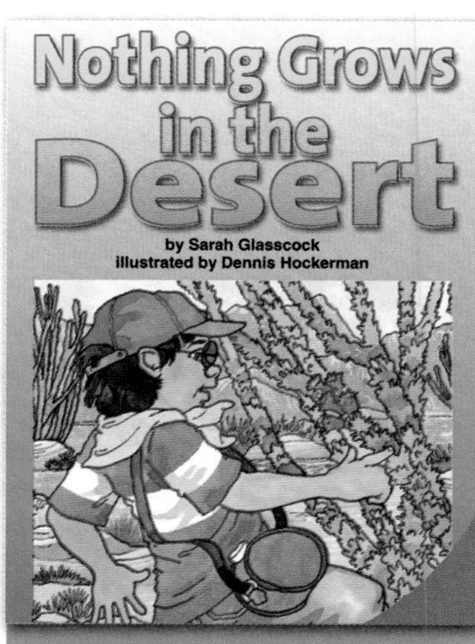

Above Level

Additional Skills Practice

Approaching Level

Reteach

- The /ī/ Sound and Consonant Blends, p. 32
- Regular Plurals, p. 33
- Selection Vocabulary, p. 34
- Spelling, p. 35
- Possessive Nouns and Pronouns, p. 36

On Level

Skills Practice 1

- The /ī/ Sound and Consonant Blends, pp. 79–80
- Regular Plurals, pp. 81–82
- Selection Vocabulary, pp. 83–84
- Writing a Summary, pp. 85–86
- Spelling, pp. 87–88
- Possessive Nouns and Pronouns, pp. 89–90

English Learner

English Learner Support Activities

English Learner Support Activities, Unit 2 Lesson 1

Above Level

Challenge Activities

- The /ī/ Sound and Consonant Blends, p. 29
- Regular Plurals, p. 30
- Selection Vocabulary, p. 31
- Spelling, p. 32
- Possessive Nouns and Pronouns, p. 33

Lesson 1 Overview

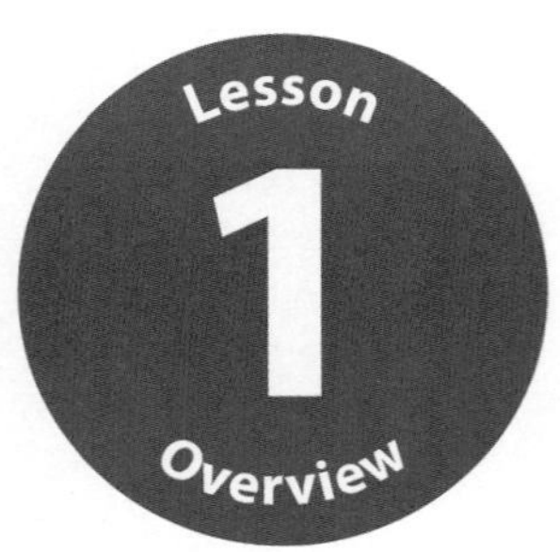

Additional Resources for Differentiating Instruction

RtI

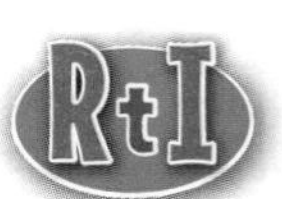

Workshop Kits

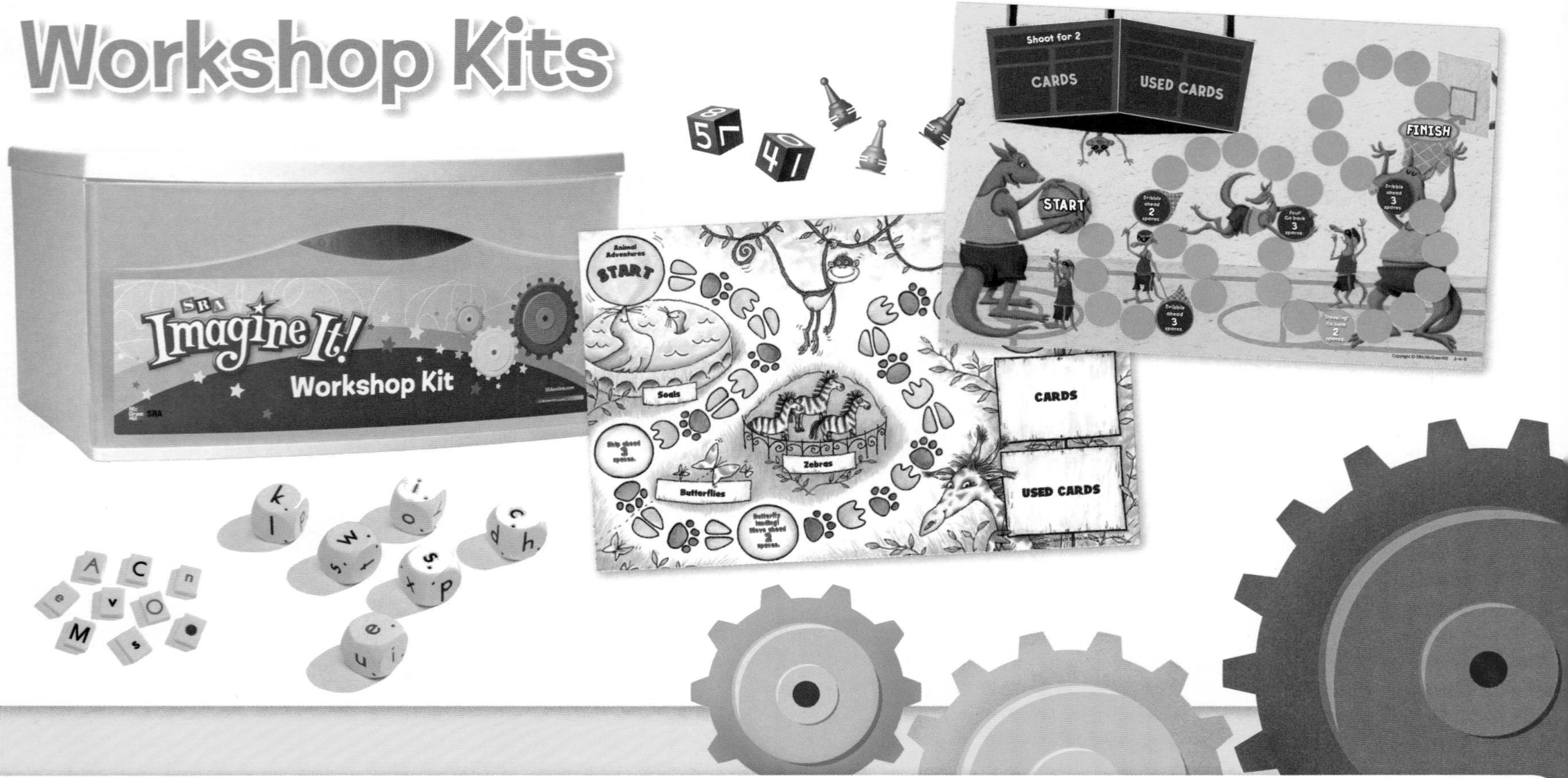

Technology

The following electronic resources are available for students:

- ***eStudent Reader***
- ***eDecodable Stories***
- ***eSkills***
- ***Listening Library***

Electronic resources for the teacher include:

- ***ePlanner***
- ***eTeacher's Edition***
- ***eAssess***
- ***ePresentation***

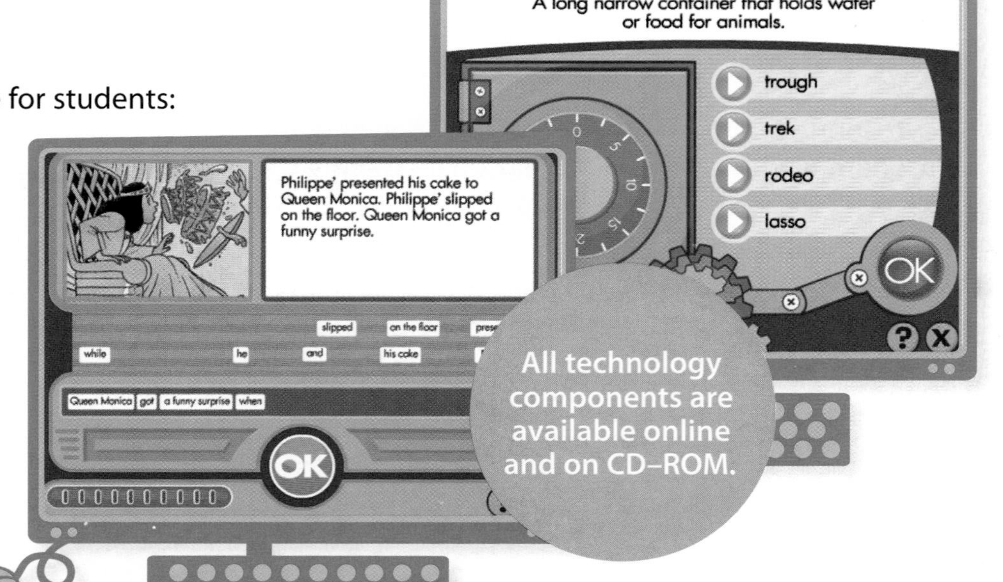

English Learner

Leveled Reader

English Learner Support Activities, Lesson 1

Listening Library Unit 2

English Learner Support Guide, Lesson 1

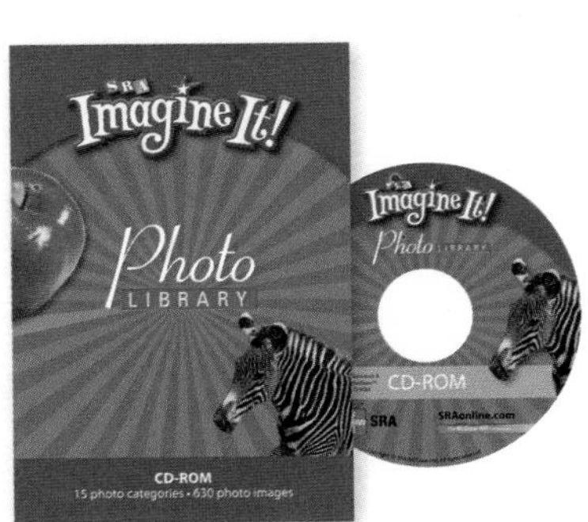

Photo Library

Approaching Level

Intervention

Intervention Workbook

Intervention Teacher's Guide

Lesson 1 Overview

Lesson Assessment

Monitor Progress to Differentiate Instruction

Comprehension Strategies Rubrics

Use the Comprehension Strategies Rubrics to determine whether a student is using the strategies.

- Asking Questions, p. T48
- Clarifying, p. T49
- Visualizing, p. T49

Inquiry Rubrics

Use the Inquiry Rubrics to assess a student's performance throughout the stages of the investigation for each unit. In addition, at the end of the unit you can use the rubrics to assess the groups' collaborative work as well as an individual's participation in that group.

- Generating Ideas and Questions, p. T89

Writing Rubrics

Use the writing rubrics in the Level Appendix to evaluate each student's summary.

- Genre
- Writing Process
- Writing Traits

Lesson Assessments

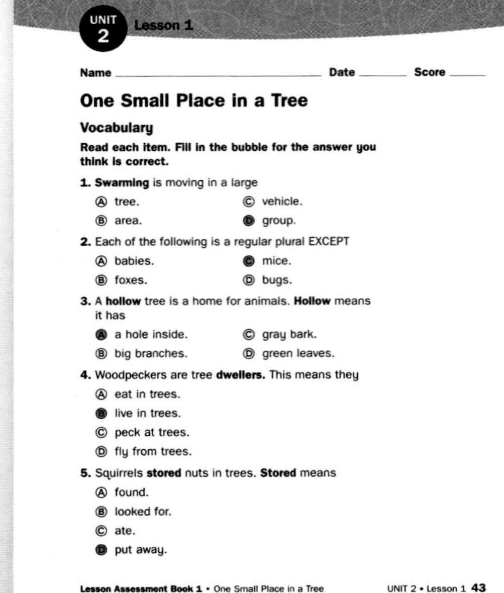

UNIT 2 Lesson 1

Name ______ Date ______ Score ______

One Small Place in a Tree

Vocabulary

Read each item. Fill in the bubble for the answer you think is correct.

1. **Swarming** is moving in a large
   Ⓐ tree. Ⓑ area. Ⓒ vehicle. ● group.
2. Each of the following is a regular plural EXCEPT
   Ⓐ babies. Ⓑ foxes. ● mice. Ⓓ bugs.
3. A **hollow** tree is a home for animals. **Hollow** means it has
   ● a hole inside. Ⓑ big branches. Ⓒ gray bark. Ⓓ green leaves.
4. Woodpeckers are tree **dwellers.** This means they
   Ⓐ eat in trees.
   ● live in trees.
   Ⓒ peck at trees.
   Ⓓ fly from trees.
5. Squirrels **stored** nuts in trees. **Stored** means
   Ⓐ found.
   Ⓑ looked for.
   Ⓒ ate.
   ● put away.

Lesson Assessment Book 1 • One Small Place in a Tree UNIT 2 • Lesson 1 43

Lesson Assessment Book 1, p. 43

UNIT 2 Lesson 1

One Small Place in a Tree (continued)

Comprehension

Read the following questions carefully. Then completely fill in the bubble of each correct answer. You may look back at the selection to find the answer to each of the questions.

1. Which animal in the selection sharpens its claws on a tree?
   Ⓐ owl
   Ⓑ woodpecker
   ● black bear
   Ⓓ squirrel
2. When chips of bark fall off a tree,
   ● timber beetles move into the tree.
   Ⓑ the tree dies right away.
   Ⓒ squirrels play in the bark.
   Ⓓ woodpeckers take the bark for nests.

44 UNIT 2 • Lesson 1 One Small Place in a Tree • **Lesson Assessment Book 1**

Lesson Assessment Book 1, p. 44

Use these summative assessments along with your informal observations to assess student mastery.

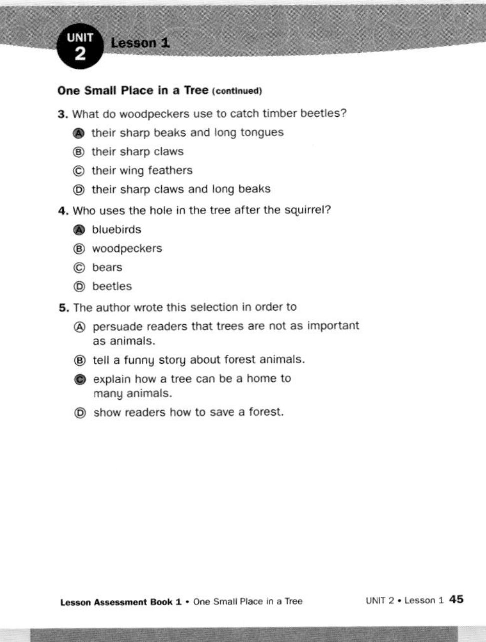

UNIT 2 Lesson 1

One Small Place in a Tree (continued)

3. What do woodpeckers use to catch timber beetles?
   - Ⓐ their sharp beaks and long tongues
   - Ⓑ their sharp claws
   - Ⓒ their wing feathers
   - Ⓓ their sharp claws and long beaks
4. Who uses the hole in the tree after the squirrel?
   - Ⓐ bluebirds
   - Ⓑ woodpeckers
   - Ⓒ bears
   - Ⓓ beetles
5. The author wrote this selection in order to
   - Ⓐ persuade readers that trees are not as important as animals.
   - Ⓑ tell a funny story about forest animals.
   - Ⓒ explain how a tree can be a home to many animals.
   - Ⓓ show readers how to save a forest.

Lesson Assessment Book 1 • One Small Place in a Tree UNIT 2 • Lesson 1 45

Lesson Assessment Book 1, p. 45

UNIT 2 Lesson 1

One Small Place in a Tree (continued)

Read the following questions carefully. Use complete sentences to answer the questions. Possible answers below

6. What do timber beetles do to the tree?
   They bore holes into the tree. They also plant fungi to eat.
7. What sound brings red-bellied woodpeckers to the tree?
   Woodpeckers hear the timber beetles chewing wood and come to the tree.
8. How would a flying squirrel use the hole in the tree?
   A flying squirrel would store nuts in the hole and sleep there in winter.
9. According to the selection, how can trees get tree rot?
   After animals have made a hole, bacteria can come in and cause tree rot.
10. What animals might live in a log after the tree falls?
    Garter snakes, salamanders, and hammock spiders might live there.

46 UNIT 2 • Lesson 1 One Small Place in a Tree • Lesson Assessment Book 1

Lesson Assessment Book 1, p. 46

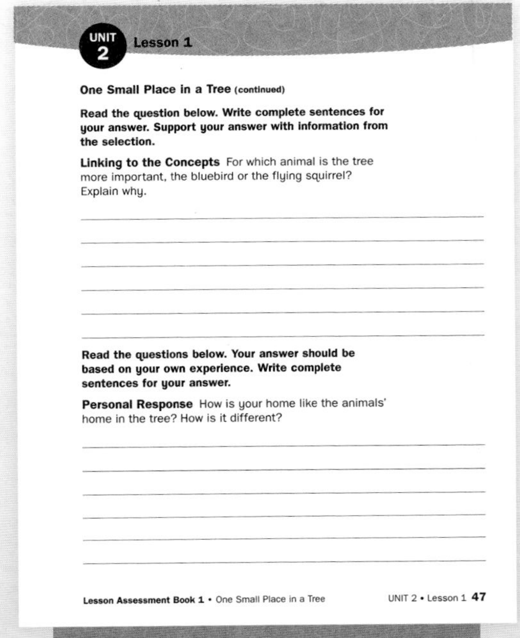

UNIT 2 Lesson 1

One Small Place in a Tree (continued)

Read the question below. Write complete sentences for your answer. Support your answer with information from the selection.

Linking to the Concepts For which animal is the tree more important, the bluebird or the flying squirrel? Explain why.

Read the questions below. Your answer should be based on your own experience. Write complete sentences for your answer.

Personal Response How is your home like the animals' home in the tree? How is it different?

Lesson Assessment Book 1 • One Small Place in a Tree UNIT 2 • Lesson 1 47

Lesson Assessment Book 1, p. 47

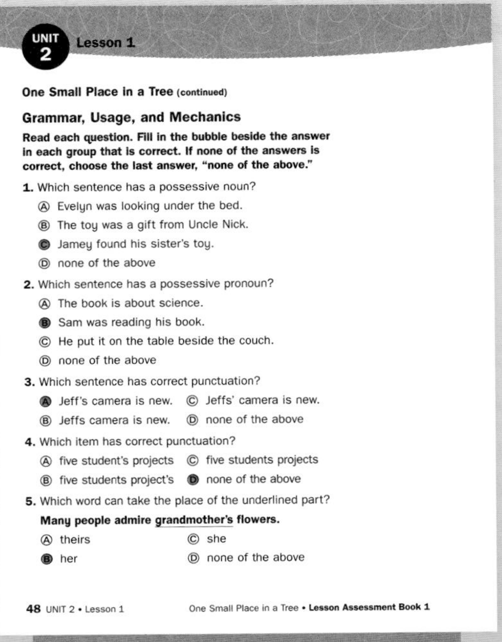

UNIT 2 Lesson 1

One Small Place in a Tree (continued)

Grammar, Usage, and Mechanics

Read each question. Fill in the bubble beside the answer in each group that is correct. If none of the answers is correct, choose the last answer, "none of the above."

1. Which sentence has a possessive noun?
   - Ⓐ Evelyn was looking under the bed.
   - Ⓑ The toy was a gift from Uncle Nick.
   - Ⓒ Jamey found his sister's toy.
   - Ⓓ none of the above
2. Which sentence has a possessive pronoun?
   - Ⓐ The book is about science.
   - Ⓑ Sam was reading his book.
   - Ⓒ He put it on the table beside the couch.
   - Ⓓ none of the above
3. Which sentence has correct punctuation?
   - Ⓐ Jeff's camera is new.
   - Ⓒ Jeffs' camera is new.
   - Ⓑ Jeffs camera is new.
   - Ⓓ none of the above
4. Which item has correct punctuation?
   - Ⓐ five student's projects
   - Ⓒ five students projects
   - Ⓑ five students project's
   - Ⓓ none of the above
5. Which word can take the place of the underlined part?
   Many people admire grandmother's flowers.
   - Ⓐ theirs
   - Ⓒ she
   - Ⓑ her
   - Ⓓ none of the above

48 UNIT 2 • Lesson 1 One Small Place in a Tree • Lesson Assessment Book 1

Lesson Assessment Book 1, p. 48

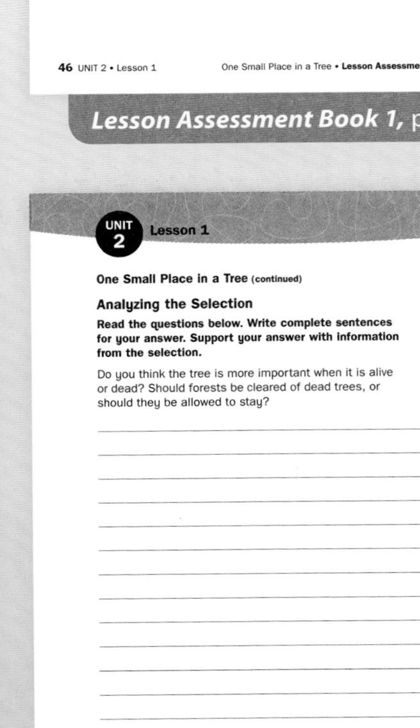

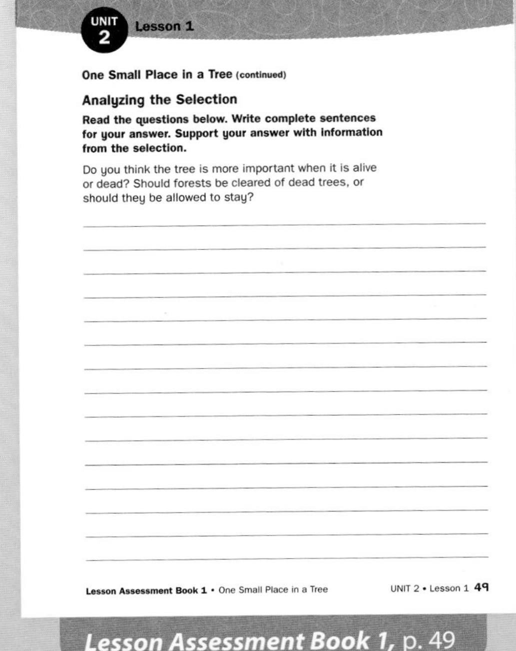

UNIT 2 Lesson 1

One Small Place in a Tree (continued)

Analyzing the Selection

Read the questions below. Write complete sentences for your answer. Support your answer with information from the selection.

Do you think the tree is more important when it is alive or dead? Should forests be cleared of dead trees, or should they be allowed to stay?

Lesson Assessment Book 1 • One Small Place in a Tree UNIT 2 • Lesson 1 49

Lesson Assessment Book 1, p. 49

UNIT 2 Lesson 1

One Small Place in a Tree (continued)

Oral Fluency Assessment

The Watchdog

Ruff wanted to be a watchdog more than anything else. The 1–11
other puppies wanted to be pets, but not Ruff. He wanted to 12–23
find a family to protect. 24–28
One day a family with two children came in to adopt a dog. 29–41
The boy and girl loved Ruff right away. The father said they 42–53
needed a watchdog, and Ruff might grow up to be a big dog. 54–66
Ruff had a new home. 67–71
The family gave Ruff a doghouse, a dish, and a big yard to 72–84
watch. Ruff was as happy as a dog could be. 85–94
Most of the time, Ruff stayed in the house with the family. 95–106
At night, he stayed in his doghouse if the weather was good. 107–118
One night, Ruff sniffed the air and smelled smoke. Ruff 119–128
knew this was dangerous. He barked and barked. He ran to the 129–140
house and jumped on the door and barked again. The people 141–151
came out. They smelled the smoke and saw the fire. They 152–162
were all happy Ruff had kept barking. Ruff had become a real 163–174
watchdog, and his family loved him more than ever. 175–183

EVALUATING CODES FOR ORAL FLUENCY

sky (/) words read incorrectly
blue ^ sky (^) inserted word
( ]) after the last word

READING RATE AND ACCURACY

Total Words Read: ____
Number of Errors: ____
Number of Correct Words Read Per Minute (WPM): ____
Accuracy Rate: ____
(Number of Correct Words Read per Minute ÷ Total Words Read)

READING FLUENCY

	Low	Average	High
Decoding ability	○	○	○
Pace	○	○	○
Syntax	○	○	○
Self-correction	○	○	○
Intonation	○	○	○

Record student rates on the Oral Fluency Scores pages.

50 UNIT 2 • Lesson 1 One Small Place in a Tree • Lesson Assessment Book 1

Lesson Assessment Book 1, p. 50

Preparing to Read

OBJECTIVES

Students will

- ✦ review /ī/ spelled *_igh*, *_y*, and *_ie*.
- ✦ review consonant blends at the beginning or end of words.
- ✦ learn new high-frequency words.
- ✦ build fluency.

MATERIALS

- ✦ ***Transparency*** 44
- ✦ ***Sound/Spelling Card*** 29
- ✦ Routines 3, 4, 5, 6, 9
- ✦ ***Skills Practice 1,*** pp. 79–80

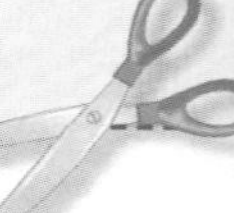

Daily Oral Practice

Daily News

Today!

All living things must have food, water, and shelter to survive. We provide these things for our pets, but how do wild animals survive? Wild animals are very good at creating habitats—or homes. Sometimes people create habitats for them. Let's learn more about how they protect the wildlife of our world.

- ✦ Write the daily news on the board or on chart paper. Then have students read the daily news in unison to practice fluency.
- ✦ As a word structure review from Unit 1, ask a volunteer to identify any compound words in the message. *sometimes, wildlife*

Teacher Tip

SELF-CORRECTING Each day as students read the daily news message and the word lines, have them correct themselves when they notice that the way they pronounced the words doesn't make sense. When they pronounce words incorrectly, have them correct their mistakes by rereading.

Phonics and Fluency

ROUTINE 3 ROUTINE 4

Review: /ī/ spelled _igh, _y, and _ie; consonant blends at the beginning or end of words

Blending

- Write these blending lines and sentences on the board or use ***Transparency*** 44. Show students one line at a time as you go through them by covering up the others. The boldface words are in "One Small Place in a Tree." The underlined words are new high-frequency words.

Line 1	high	tight	bright	lightning
Line 2	shy	fly	dryer	crying
Line 3	lie	pie	tries	untie
Line 4	nest	place	scratch	forest

Sentence 1	From the <u>trees</u>, the bird flies right into the night sky.
Sentence 2	I <u>might</u> <u>even</u> <u>need</u> to dry my clothes in the sunlight.

- Review ***Sound/Spelling Card*** 29 with students. Using Routine 3, follow the whole-word blending process to have students blend the words in Lines 1–4.
- Follow Routine 4, the blending sentences process, to have students blend Sentences 1–2.

Line 1 **/ī/ spelled _*igh***

As you point to each word, have students read it aloud in unison. Ask students to identify /ī/ spelled _*igh* in each word in Line 1. *high, tight, bright, lightning* Ask students to name other words that have /ī/ spelled _*igh*. **Possible Answers** *night, might, thigh, flight, light, right, knight*

Line 2 **/ī/ spelled _*y***

As you point to each word, have students read it aloud in unison. Ask students to identify /ī/ spelled _*y* in each word in Line 2. *shy, fly, dryer, crying* Ask students to name other words that have /ī/ spelled _*y*. **Possible Answers** *try, spy, by, my, reply, sly*

Sound/Spelling Card 29

Teacher Tip

SYLLABICATION To help students blend words and build fluency, demonstrate syllabication using the decodable, multisyllabic words in the word lines.

light • ning
cry • ing
for • est
dry • er
un • tie

Preparing to Read

✦ Use ***Transparency*** 44 with today's blending lines and sentences. Show students the lines one at a time as you go through them by covering up the other lines.

Line 3 **/ī/ spelled _*ie***

As you point to each word in Line 3, have students read it aloud in unison. Have students identify /ī/ spelled _*ie* in each word. */ī/ spelled* _ie *in lie, pie, tries,* and *untie*

Line 4 **Consonant Blends**

Explain to students that consonant blends are two or three consonants that work together to make a sound. In consonant blends, you can hear the sound of each consonant in the blend. For example, in the word *strange,* the letters *str* make a consonant blend, and each consonant—*s, t,* and *r*—can be heard when you say the word. Point out that consonant blends can be at the beginning or end of words. For example, the word *start* has the consonant blend *st* at the beginning and the consonant blend *rt* at the end. Ask students to identify the consonant blends at the beginning or end of the words in Line 4. pl *in* place; scr *in* scratch; st *in* nest *and* forest

Sentences 1–2

Have students point to and read the new high-frequency words in Sentences 1–2. *trees, might, even, need* Ask students to identify words in the sentences with /ī/ spelled _*igh*, _*y*, or _*ie*. *right, night, might, sunlight; sky, dry, my; flies* Ask students to identify any consonant blends at the beginning or end of the words in Sentences 1–2. tr *in* trees, fl *in* flies, sk *in* sky, dr *in* dry, cl *in* clothes, rd *in* bird Have students read the sentences in unison to practice fluency.

Decodable Stories

ROUTINE

Building Fluency

Decodable Stories are used to help develop fluency for students who need extra practice. They are also used to practice the phonics and fluency elements being reviewed. Using Routine 9, reading a ***Decodable Story,*** have students who need additional support read ***Decodable Stories, Book 3,*** Story 17, "Bats."

Decodable Stories, Book 3, Story 17

Syllabication

ROUTINE 5 ROUTINE 6

- To help students recognize common syllable patterns, use Routine 5 for closed syllables and Routine 6 for open syllables to separate the syllables in the multisyllabic words in the word lines. Explain that the syllable routines offer general rules that don't apply to all words.
- Using Routine 5, have students identify the vowel spellings in *lightning* and *untie*. Then have them identify the consonants between the two vowels. Explain that when words have the v-c-c-v spelling pattern, the syllables are usually divided between the two consonants, as in *un • tie*. Explain that when a syllable ends with a consonant sound, the vowel is usually short, and the syllable is a closed syllable. Have students clap for each syllable as they read *lightning* and *untie* aloud. Then have students identify the closed syllables in *forest*.
- Using Routine 6, have students identify the vowel spellings in *dryer* and *crying*. Remind students each vowel sounds adds a syllable to a word. Explain that since *dryer* and *crying* have two vowel sounds in a row, the syllables divide between the two vowel sounds. Explain that when a syllable ends with a vowel sound, the vowel is usually long and the syllable is an open syllable. Have students identify the open syllables in *dryer, crying,* and *untie*. Have students clap for each syllable as they read *dryer* and *crying* aloud.
- Help students start the phonics workbook activities on ***Skills Practice 1,*** pages 79–80. Read the Focus box with them and help them with the first few questions.

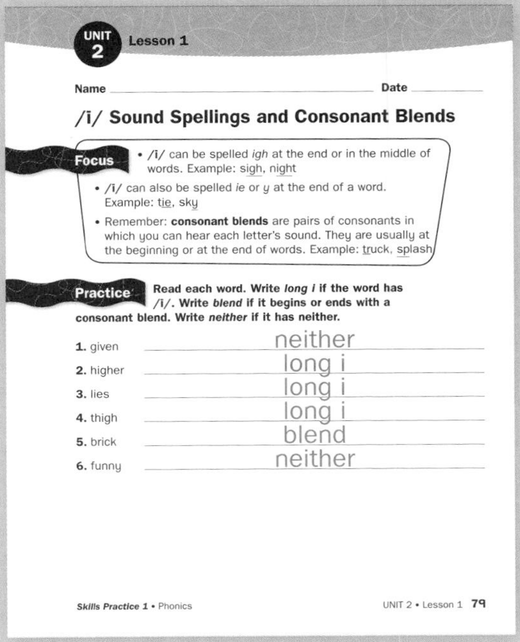

UNIT 2 Lesson 1

Name ______ Date ______

/ī/ Sound Spellings and Consonant Blends

Focus
- /ī/ can be spelled *igh* at the end or in the middle of words. Example: sigh, night
- /ī/ can also be spelled *ie* or *y* at the end of a word. Example: tie, sky
- Remember: **consonant blends** are pairs of consonants in which you can hear each letter's sound. They are usually at the beginning or at the end of words. Example: truck, splash

Practice Read each word. Write *long i* if the word has /ī/. Write *blend* if it begins or ends with a consonant blend. Write *neither* if it has neither.

1. given neither
2. higher long i
3. lies long i
4. thigh long i
5. brick blend
6. funny neither

Skills Practice 1 • Phonics UNIT 2 • Lesson 1 79

Skills Practice 1, p. 79

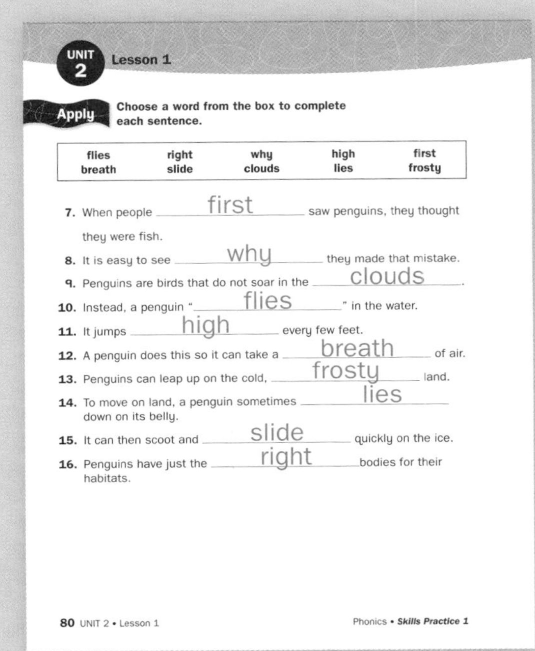

UNIT 2 Lesson 1

Apply Choose a word from the box to complete each sentence.

flies	right	why	high	first
breath	slide	clouds	lies	frosty

7. When people first saw penguins, they thought they were fish.
8. It is easy to see why they made that mistake.
9. Penguins are birds that do not soar in the clouds.
10. Instead, a penguin "flies" in the water.
11. It jumps high every few feet.
12. A penguin does this so it can take a breath of air.
13. Penguins can leap up on the cold, frosty land.
14. To move on land, a penguin sometimes lies down on its belly.
15. It can then scoot and slide quickly on the ice.
16. Penguins have just the right bodies for their habitats.

80 UNIT 2 • Lesson 1 Phonics • Skills Practice 1

Skills Practice 1, p. 80

Monitor Progress to Differentiate Instruction

Formal Assessment 

Phonics and Fluency During the blending activity, note how quickly students are reading the words.

APPROACHING LEVEL	**IF . . .** students need practice with today's sound/spellings for /ī/,	**THEN . . .** work with them on the phonics activities on ***Reteach*** page 32 during Workshop.
	IF . . . students need extra practice with today's sound/spellings for /ī/,	**THEN . . .** work with them on the phonics activities for Unit 2 Lesson 1 in the ***Intervention Guide*** during Workshop.
ON LEVEL	**IF . . .** students understand today's sound/spellings for /ī/,	**THEN . . .** have them play a game with the sound/spelling cards during Workshop.
ABOVE LEVEL	**IF . . .** students are ready for a challenge with today's sound/spellings for /ī/,	**THEN . . .** have them complete the phonics activities on ***Challenge Activities*** page 29 during Workshop.

Day 1

Reading and Responding

OBJECTIVES

Students will

- relate prior knowledge to the theme Animals and Their Habitats.
- listen attentively.
- build vocabulary.

MATERIALS

- *Home Connection,* pp. 13–14

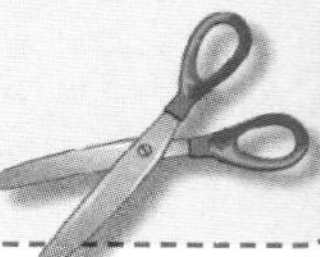

Read Aloud

Activate Prior Knowledge

- Tell students that in this unit they will read and learn about animals and their habitats.
- Ask students the following questions:
  - What do you know about animals and their habitats?
  - Have you ever personally observed animals in their habitats?
  - What books have you read about animals and their habitats? Tell us about these stories.
- Share with students your own experiences with animals and their habitats.

Genre

Building Blocks for Survival is expository text. Explain that in expository text, the information gives facts and real examples.

Comprehension Strategies

It is important to model the comprehension strategies. Modeling is a powerful way to get students to use the comprehension strategies. As you read

- **ask questions** about the events in the selection.
- **visualize** and share the images that pop up in your mind.
- **make connections** between what you know and events in the selection.

Set Purposes

As students listen *to Building Blocks for Survival*, have them think about what is necessary for animals to survive, how animals create habitats, and how people can help create and protect habitats, too. Read the Focus Questions on page T31 and have students suggest possible answers.

Fluency

As you read, model fluent reading by pausing after commas and at end punctuation. Use expression as you read. This helps students appreciate fluency and will help them better understand the story.

Vocabulary Tip

Before reading *Building Blocks for Survival* aloud, introduce the following vocabulary words to students. Say each word and its definition. Then use the word in a sentence.

- habitat (hab′ • i • tat) *n.* the place where an animal or plant naturally lives and grows
- shelter (shel′ • tə r) *n.* something that protects or covers
- disturb (di • stûrb′) *v.* to change the order or arrangement of
- aquatic (ə • kwat′ • ik) *adj.* of, living in, or growing in water
- depend (di • pend′) *v.* to fall back on for help or support

Differentiating Instruction — English Learner

IF . . . students seem confused by the term *building blocks* in this selection's title,
THEN . . . restate the title to make its meaning clear; for example, *Basic Needs for Survival.*

Teacher Tip

BUILDING BACKGROUND Before reading, tell students that this article comes from the children's magazine *Puddler.* This magazine is written to educate youth about the importance of wetlands and the wildlife creatures that inhabit and depend on this type of habitat. The magazine focuses on wildlife, ecology, ecosystems, and animal behavior.

Focus Questions What is a habitat? What are the basic building blocks that animals need to survive?

Building Blocks for Survival

Have you ever seen a polar bear in a desert? How about a killer whale in a forest? Or an elephant in the arctic? Sounds silly, doesn't it? You know these animals don't belong in these places. They're only found where they… um, well…belong!

The place where an animal naturally makes its home is called its habitat. A habitat is made up of plants, animals, land, and water, even the air. It can be any size or any place. For example, it may be the underside of a lily pad, a fallen log, a canyon, or a stretch of ocean. All habitats do have one thing in common: they're places where an animal can find food, water, and shelter—the three basic building blocks it needs to survive. Let's take a closer look at these building blocks.

Shelter

All animals need shelter at times. Shelters are places where animals are protected from weather or danger. They're places animals use to have babies, too. Good habitat provides lots of hiding places or the materials needed to build more permanent homes.

Different species of animals use different kinds of shelters. For example, a field of grass can shelter a mouse trying to hide from a hungry fox. A chipmunk escapes winter's cold by digging an underground burrow. Animals may build their own shelters, or use a sheltered space in their habitat. Animals may use the same shelter year round, for a few weeks, or even for just a few minutes.

Look for wildlife shelters the next time you're outdoors. Remember to keep your distance. Some of these shelters hide young animals, and you don't want to disturb them!

Water

Did you know that most of your body is made of water? All living things need water to survive. In fact, an animal can go many days without food, but it cannot live for more than a few days without water. Good habitat provides an animal with a steady source of water for drinking and bathing. Rainwater and melted snow flow into puddles, ponds, rivers and lakes that animals can visit to drink. Animals can also get the water their bodies need in other ways. For example, plants contain a lot of water. Their leaves collect dew and raindrops, too. Animals that eat plants also get the water that's in and on them. Some aquatic animals can absorb the water they need through their skin.

You can create habitat for more animals in your backyard simply by adding a water source, such as a bird bath, a garbage can lid filled with water, or a small pond. If you decide to try it, keep the water coming…animals will depend on it!

Food

Animals spend most of their waking time eating or trying to find something to eat. Good habitat provides food that matches an animal's diet. Animals that eat other animals are carnivores. Animals that eat plants are herbivores. Animals that eat both plants and other animals are omnivores. Animals that eat dead remains are scavengers.

The more kinds of food an animal can find in its habitat, the better its chances for survival. If one kind of food becomes scarce, an animal will switch to another one. Watch animals gathering food in your area. Do they always choose the same kinds of food? What might make some foods become scarce?

Changes in habitat can cause animal populations to rise and fall. Sometimes, too many animals live in one habitat. For example, lesser snow geese that winter in Texas and Louisiana find so much food there (from farm crops), they easily survive. As a result, their population has grown too large. Now, too many geese look for too few nesting places in their summer habitat. On the other hand, an entire animal species can disappear, or become extinct. Habitat changes may have caused the extinction of the Labrador duck. This duck became extinct in the late 1800's. The Labrador duck's food supply may have disappeared.

Humans need food, shelter, and water to survive, too! Unlike other animals, though, humans can make any area into suitable habitat by building homes, growing food and directing water to where it's needed. Humans also have the ability to protect and provide the habitats animals need. For example, zoos try to re-create animals' natural habitats. The next time you visit a zoo, look for the three building blocks for survival. Sources of food, water, and shelter should be in each animal exhibit.

Discussing the Read Aloud

- ✦ Review the Focus Questions with students: What is a habitat? What are the basic building blocks that animals need to survive?
- ✦ Discuss what students learned about animals and their habitats. Ask them the following questions:
  - How does "Building Blocks for Survival" relate to the theme Animals and Their Habitats? **Possible Answer** *This article teaches readers about the basic requirements of an animal habitat.*
  - What did you learn about animals and the places they inhabit? **Possible Answers** *Animal habitats can be found almost everywhere. Habitats provide animals with food, water, and shelter.*
  - What do animals need to have a suitable habitat? **Possible Answer** *Animal habitats need food, water, and shelter.*
  - What might happen if there is a change in an animal's habitat? **Possible Answer** *If an animal's habitat is changed, it may no longer provide food, water, and shelter for the animal. The animal would have to move to find what it needs, or it possibly would not survive.*
  - How do people help animals with their habitats? How can people help protect animal habitats? *Answers will vary.*
- ✦ Create a Word Bank for students to organize the vocabulary for this unit. Organize the Word Bank by parts of speech: nouns, verbs, adjectives, and adverbs. Write the words or have students write the words on cards and then place them under the appropriate part of speech in the Word Bank. Encourage students to find other words related to the unit theme Animals and Their Habitats and add them to the Word Bank. You may also want to encourage students to find synonyms and antonyms for words in the Word Bank and add them as well. A full explanation of the Word Bank can be found in the Appendix.

Concept/Question Board

✦ Remind students that the **Concept/Question Board** will help them explore the theme Animals and Their Habitats. To get the Board started, have students write about animals and their habitats. Have students post their responses on the Concept side of the Board. Students can post questions after they gain an understanding of the theme.

✦ Brainstorm things that would be appropriate to post on the Animals and Their Habitats **Concept/Question Board.** Suggestions include

- questions about animals and their habitats.
- newspaper and magazine articles about animals and their habitats.
- stories, poems, pictures, or songs about animals and their habitats.

✦ Remind students that they

- may post a question, word, article, illustration, or object related to the theme Animals and Their Habitats any time during the unit. Be sure students include their names or initials on the items they post.
- should feel free to write an answer or a note on someone else's question.
- can read and listen to stories about animals and their habitats at home. They can share their stories with the class and post the title and the author's name on the Board.

Concept/Question Board

To get the **Concept/Question Board** started for this unit, bring in one or two items, such as a newspaper article or a photograph related to animals and their habitats. Post these items on the **Concept/Question Board.**

Distribute page 13 of ***Home Connection***. Students can read books and articles about animals and their habitats with their families. This ***Home Connection*** is also available in Spanish on page 14.

Differentiating Instruction **English Learner**

IF . . . students wish to share information about their native countries, **THEN . . .** encourage them to post materials on the **Concept/Question Board** about animal habitats in their native countries.

Lesson 1 Inquiry Planner

STEP 1: Generating Ideas and Questions

Day 1 Students will discuss initial questions and ideas about the theme Animals and Their Habitats and the Read Aloud.

Day 2 Groups will continue generating ideas about animals and animal habitats.

Day 3 In small groups, discuss ideas about the theme in the Read Aloud *Building Blocks for Survival* and "One Small Place in a Tree."

Day 4 Students will continue generating ideas and sharing stories about the unit theme.

Day 5 Students will work in small groups to generate questions and investigation topics that interest them.

Inquiry Process

Step 1—Generating Ideas and Questions

Whole-Group Time

Whole Group

Students will begin working on their next investigation surrounding the theme Animals and Their Habitats. Remind students that the aim of Inquiry is to learn and explore new things together, and not necessarily to reach final conclusions and correct answers.

- Explain to the class that they will form groups and develop their own questions and conjectures about animals and animal habitats. Tell students they are free to explore anything about animals and animal habitats that interests them.
- To begin the investigation process, conduct an open discussion of questions about animals and animal habitats that interest students. List students' questions on the board. Encourage them to share personal stories about animals and their habitats or stories they know about this theme. These stories may generate questions that students can choose as their unit investigation question.
- Model how stories can evolve into questions. For example, you might tell a story about some wild animals that lost their home due to a new land development. After learning the story about these animals, you may have asked yourself *How can I help these animals? What makes a safe animal habitat? Why are human habitats unsafe for some animals?* As you model, encourage students to ask questions, add ideas, propose how they might form questions from your story, and so on. Remember that any questions you propose are intended to be a model for students, but students should create their own questions for investigation.
- Ask students if the Read Aloud "Building Blocks for Survival" gave them any new ideas about animals and their habitats that they had not thought about before. Encourage discussion of this selection and how it relates to the unit theme. Write students' responses on the board or on chart paper.
- During whole-group discussion, try to categorize and group students' interests in the theme. Help students organize themselves into groups based on similar interests.

Small-Group Time

Small Group

- Have students work in small groups and continue to discuss the different questions and ideas started in the whole-group discussion. Remind them to pursue the ideas and questions that most interest and excite them, because these should lead to a question that they will investigate further.
- Encourage each group to think about how the information about animal habitats in "Building Blocks for Survival" relates to their questions and ideas.
- Allow students to exchange stories they know about animals, reminding them that these stories can lead to more questions they have about animals and animal habitats.

Concept/Question Board

Encourage students to write information, opinions, ideas, or questions on the **Concept/Question Board.** Students might

- post new information they learned from the Read Aloud.
- take and post pictures of wild animals or pets. (Remind students not to disturb the homes of animals as they take their pictures. Encourage them to show respect for the animals and their homes.)
- bring in and post newspaper, magazine, and Internet articles and pictures of animals and their habitats.
- draw pictures that support the theme.
- write the name of a story, book, song, poem, or television program about animals and their habitats and post it on the Board.

To help students support their inquiries or expand their knowledge of a topic, have them read the ***Leveled Science Readers*** for this unit. If students are working in a group, encourage them to share their information with their group members. Use each student's Oral Fluency Assessment score from the previous lesson assessment to diagnose the appropriate ***Leveled Science Reader.***

Language Arts

OBJECTIVES

Students will
- learn to write a summary.
- take the spelling pretest.
- practice cursive *m* and *n*.

MATERIALS

- ***Skills Practice 1,*** p. 85
- ***Transparency*** 45

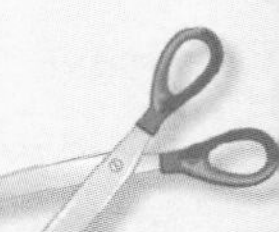

Teacher Tip

PLAN AHEAD Preselect the reading materials, such as nonfiction books, articles, or magazines you would like the students to summarize.

Research in Action

Students should be expected to engage in the following writing activities at all grade levels: story writing, poetry, writing a play, journal writing, summarizing, responding to reading through writing, book review, report writing, writing a description, writing an explanation, learning logs, letter writing, and e-mails.
(Steve Graham and Karen Harris)

Writing Summary

Prewriting

Teach

- Ask a student to give an oral summary of a selection that the class has read. For example, you could have a student summarize "Teammates." As the student talks, jot down on the board as much information as possible. Once that student has completed the summary, have the students look over what you wrote and add to the information details that may have been overlooked.
- Explain to students that a written summary is similar to an oral summary. However, in a written summary the writer has the opportunity to put the summary into proper order, add in details to clarify information, and make the information easier to understand. Like an oral summary, a written summary contains the main idea of the selection being summarized, as well as some supporting details.
- Tell students they will write a summary of the reading materials you have preselected. If necessary, remind students of the stages of the writing process: prewriting, drafting, revising, editing and proofreading, and publishing.
- Discuss audience with students. Explain to students that like the fantasy stories or the autobiographies they wrote, it is important to consider the audience as they plan their summaries. For example, if they are writing summaries about a book they read on fishing, and most of their audience has never gone fishing, they will need to include more specific information than if they had an audience of people who fish often.
- Discuss the purpose of summarizing with students. Summarizing is a strategy that can help condense and organize information and is also a means of informing others in writing or speech.

Writing, continued

Guided Practice

- ✦ Select a book that the entire class has read to discuss. This book may be on bears in their habitats or another book about the theme Animals and Their Habitats. Display the book and discuss the topic based on the title of the book.
- ✦ Once students have selected the books, articles, or magazines they are going to summarize, have students discuss the topics based on the titles and by previewing the articles.
- ✦ Ask students how they will write their summaries based on the discussion of the class. **Possible Answer** *I will need to give some more detailed information because most of the class doesn't know anything about gorillas.*

Apply

Have students identify the purpose and audience on page 85 of ***Skills Practice 1.***

Assessment

You will use the Writing Rubrics found in the Level Appendix to evaluate students' summaries. You may use any of the rubrics for Genre, Writing Process, and Writing Traits. Share with students what you will be looking for when assessing their summaries.

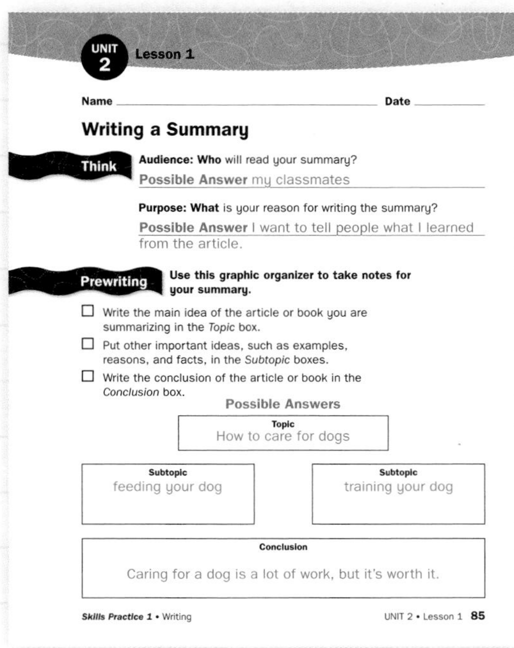

UNIT 2 Lesson 1

Name ______ Date ______

Writing a Summary

Think **Audience:** Who will read your summary?
Possible Answer my classmates

Purpose: What is your reason for writing the summary?
Possible Answer I want to tell people what I learned from the article.

Prewriting **Use this graphic organizer to take notes for your summary.**

- ☐ Write the main idea of the article or book you are summarizing in the *Topic* box.
- ☐ Put other important ideas, such as examples, reasons, and facts, in the *Subtopic* boxes.
- ☐ Write the conclusion of the article or book in the *Conclusion* box.

Possible Answers

Topic: How to care for dogs

Subtopic: feeding your dog

Subtopic: training your dog

Conclusion: Caring for a dog is a lot of work, but it's worth it.

Skills Practice 1 • Writing UNIT 2 • Lesson 1 85

Skills Practice 1, p. 85

Spelling

/ī/ and Regular Plurals Pretest

Teach

- ✦ Students will learn to spell plurals and words with /ī/ spelled *igh*, *_y*, and *_ie*.
- ✦ Say the sentences below. Have students write the spelling words on a separate sheet of paper. When they are finished, have them correct any misspelled words. Give challenge sentences to those students who would like to spell more difficult words.

Pretest Sentences

1. I didn't feel well, so I went to **lie** down.
2. My dad had two **ties** to choose from.
3. Did you see the pretty bird **fly** over our house?
4. That goldfinch **flies** straight to our bird feeder.
5. She split the orange into two **halves.**
6. There are three **cycles** to the process.
7. He did not **reply** to the request.
8. His teacher **replies** to all of his questions.
9. I heard her **sigh,** so I knew she was tired.
10. At the zoo, I like to see the **monkeys.**
11. Henry ate three of his **lunches** outdoors.
12. The hero will **fight** the villain in movie.
13. Three **knights** saved the day in the story.
14. It was about a **spy** and his adventures.
15. How many **spies** were in that novel?

Challenge Sentences

16. Many insects are tree-**dwellers.**
17. The baby was roused by the noisy **outcry.**

Diagnose any misspellings by determining whether students misspelled the plurals, the /ī/, or some other part of the word. Then have students use the pretest as a take-home list to study the spellings of these words.

Teacher Tip

PENMANSHIP If students are having problems forming cursive *m* and *n,* or their letters are floating between the lines, review proper paper position, check to make sure students are holding their pencils correctly, or review letter formation.

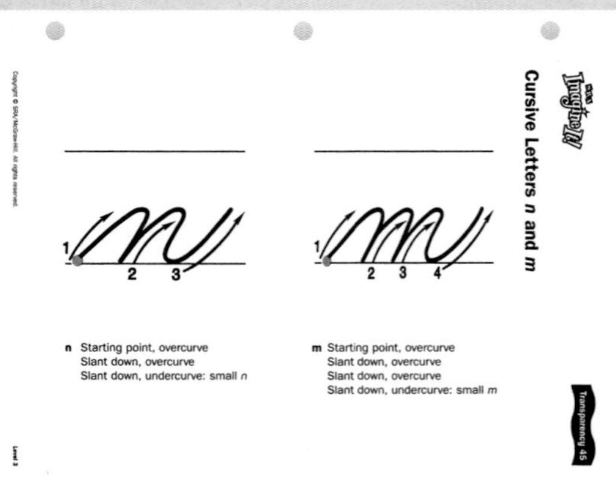

Transparency 45

Penmanship

Cursive Letters *m* and *n*

Teach

- Remind students that all cursive letters are made of four types of strokes (undercurve, overcurve, downcurve, and slant lines).
- Using ***Transparency*** 45, introduce lowercase cursive *m* and *n* as overcurve letters. Trace the letters on the transparency with a pointer to model proper letter formation.
  - **Letter *m*** Starting point, overcurve
Slant down, overcurve
Slant down, overcurve
Slant down, undercurve: small *m*
  - **Letter *n*** Starting point, overcurve
Slant down, overcurve
Slant down, undercurve: small *n*
- On the board, write lowercase cursive *m* and *n,* saying the strokes aloud as you form the letters.
- To model proper letter formation, write the following words on the board: *men, mint, number.*

Guided Practice

Have a student practice writing the letters on the board, and have the class discuss the curve and formation of the letters. Then have another student (or students) practice writing the words on the board. Show students how to connect the letters in the words, if necessary.

Apply

- Have students practice writing each of the letters four times. Ask them to circle the best formation of each of their letters.
- After reviewing the words you wrote on the board, set a timer for three minutes and have students practice writing the words. Have them circle the best formation of each of the words based on the proper formation of *m* and *n*.

Teacher Tip

MODEL Show how to connect *n* to other letters.

Skills Traces

Preparing to Read

Word Structure: Regular Plurals

Introduced in Grade 2, Unit 4, Lesson 1

Grade 3
Reviewed: Unit 2, Lesson 1
Practiced: Unit 2, Lesson 2
Assessed: ***Lesson Assessment Book 1,*** p. 43

Phonics:

See Level Appendix

Reading and Responding

Comprehension Skill: Cause and Effect

Reviewed in Grade 2, Unit 2, Lesson 3

Grade 3
Reviewed: Unit 1, Lesson 1
Practiced: Unit 2, Lesson 1
Assessed: ***Lesson Assessment Book 1,*** pp. 44–47

Reviewed in Grade 4, Unit 1, Lesson 3

Comprehension Skill: Author's Purpose

Introduced in Grade 2, Unit 2, Lesson 1

Grade 3
Reviewed: Unit 1, Lesson 2
Practiced: Unit 2, Lesson 1
Assessed: ***Lesson Assessment Book 1,*** pp. 44–47

Reviewed in Grade 4, Unit 1, Lesson 4

Comprehension Strategy: Asking Questions

Reviewed in Grade 2, Unit 1, Lesson 1

Grade 3
Reviewed: Unit 1, Lesson 1
Practiced: Unit 2, Lesson 1
Assessed: Unit 2, Lesson 1, p. T48

Reviewed in Grade 4, Unit 1, Lesson 2

Comprehension Strategy: Clarifying

Reviewed in Grade 2, Unit 1, Lesson 3

Grade 3
Reviewed: Unit 1, Lesson 5
Practiced: Unit 2, Lesson 1
Assessed: Unit 2, Lesson 1, p. T49

Reviewed in Grade 4, Unit 1, Lesson 4

Language Arts

Writing: Summary

Reviewed in Grade 2, Unit 2, Lesson 3

Grade 3
Reviewed: Unit 2, Lesson 1
Assessed: Unit 2, Lesson 1, p. T98

Reviewed in Grade 4, Unit 4, Lesson 1

Grammar, Usage, and Mechanics: Possessive Nouns and Pronouns

Reviewed in Grade 2, Unit 4, Lesson 2

Grade 3
Reviewed: Unit 2, Lesson 1
Practiced: Unit 6, Lesson 2
Assessed: ***Lesson Assessment Book 1,*** p. 48

Reviewed in Grade 4, Unit 3, Lesson 1

Day 2

Preparing to Read

OBJECTIVES

Students will

- ✦ review /ī/ spelled *_igh*, *_y*, and *_ie*.
- ✦ review consonant blends at the beginning or end of words.
- ✦ build fluency.

MATERIALS

- ✦ ***Transparency*** 44
- ✦ ***Sound/Spelling Card*** 29
- ✦ Routines 2, 3, 4, 7, 8

Daily Oral Practice

Daily News

Today!

What do you know about trees? Tall trees grow high in the sky and sway in the breeze. Trees provide shade that you can lie in to stay cool. Did you know that trees provide homes, too? Who do you think lives in the trees?

Sound/Spelling Card 29

- ✦ Write the daily news on the board or on chart paper. Then have students read the daily news in unison to practice fluency.
- ✦ As a review of yesterday's phonics and fluency lesson, ask a volunteer to identify the words with /ī/ spelled *_igh*, *_y* and *_ie*. *high, sky, lie*

Phonics and Fluency

ROUTINE  ROUTINE 

Review: /ī/ spelled *_igh, _y, and _ie;* and consonant blends at the beginning or end of words

Line 1	high	tight	bright	lightning
Line 2	shy	fly	dryer	crying
Line 3	lie	pie	tries	untie
Line 4	nest	place	scratch	forest

Sentence 1: From the <u>trees</u>, the bird flies right into the night sky.

Sentence 2: I <u>might</u> <u>even</u> <u>need</u> to dry my clothes in the sunlight.

Blending

- ✦ Use ***Transparency*** 44 with the blending lines and sentences from Day 1.
- ✦ Review ***Sound/Spelling Card*** 29 with students. Then use Routine 3, the whole-word blending process, to have students read Lines 1–4.
- ✦ Have students read the sentences using normal intonation and expression. If students have difficulty reading a sentence, stop and use Routine 4, the blending sentences process.

Developing Oral Language

Use one or both of these activities to help students practice reading the words from the blending lines.

- Have one student choose a word from the word lines and choose a classmate to read the word and use the word in a sentence. **Possible Answer** *I taught my little brother how to fly a kite.* Continue for all the words on the blending lines.
- Have students focus on one of the lines. Have a volunteer choose a word and use it in a sentence to begin a story. Have another volunteer continue the story using another word from the line. Continue until all the words are used.

Dictation

- ✦ Follow Routine 7 for whole-word dictation. When dictating words, say the word, use the word in a sentence, and then repeat the word.
- ✦ Follow Routine 8 for sentence dictation. When dictating sentences, say the sentence. Next, dictate one word at a time, following Routine 2 for sounds-in-sequence dictation or Routine 7 whole-word dictation, depending upon your students. Have students proofread for spelling, capitalization, and end punctuation.
- ✦ Dictate the following words and sentence for students to write.

Line 1	sight	sigh	my
Line 2	sky	die	right
Challenge Word	frightful		
Sentence	Did you see the birds fly through the bright sky?		

Teacher Tip

SOUND/SPELLING CARDS With multiple spellings for a sound, it is especially important that students ask "Which spelling?" when they are unsure about which spelling to use in a given word. Remind them to use the ***Sound/Spelling Cards*** and to ask for help when they need it. Remember to define any word that is a homophone so students know which spelling to use.

Differentiating Instruction — English Learner

IF . . . students have difficulty participating in the Developing Oral Language activities, **THEN . . .** define each word and use pictures, objects, or pantomime to help students visualize the words before beginning the activities.

Day 2

Reading and Responding

OBJECTIVES

Students will

- ✦ activate prior knowledge by discussing the theme Animals and Their Habitats.
- ✦ learn selection vocabulary.
- ✦ review the elements of expository text.
- ✦ use the comprehension strategies Asking Questions, Clarifying, and Visualizing.

MATERIALS

- ✦ Routines 11, 13, 14
- ✦ ***Transparencies*** 35, 46
- ✦ ***Student Reader,*** Book 1, pp. 134–145
- ✦ ***Home Connection,*** pp. 15–16

Research in Action

Students need many kinds of knowledge for reading comprehension. Among the types of knowledge they need are background knowledge, knowledge of reading strategies, and genre knowledge. Genre knowledge lets students anticipate how the selection will be written and what its content will be.
(Anne McKeough)

Build Background

Activate Prior Knowledge

- ✦ Discuss contacts students have had with animals and their habitats.
- ✦ Ask students about the animals in *Building Blocks for Survival.*
- ✦ Encourage students to make connections to other books might have read about animals and their habitats.

Background Information

The following information might help students understand the selection they are about to read:

- Bring in photographs or pictures of trees with holes, or with animal or insect activity around it. Discuss and post these on the **Concept/Question Board.**
- Ask students if any of them know what animals might live in a tree.
- Discuss with students what animals might take up residence in a tree and why.

Preview and Prepare 

ROUTINE 13

Browse

Have students read the title and name of the author and take a few minutes to browse the selection. Have students use features such as the selection title and illustrations to predict what this story might have to do with animals and their habitats.

Follow Routine 13, the know, want to know, learned routine, to help students identify and share what they know before reading, what they want to know while reading, and what their purposes are for reading. Students will chart these on a transparency.

Tell students to look for interesting words or pictures as they browse. They may note that many animals appear on the pages of this story.

Use ***Transparency*** 35 to model browsing for students. For example, students may "Know" that the hole in the tree is getting bigger. Under "Want to Know," write *How can different animals use the same tree as a home?* Record students' observations on the transparency as they browse the selection.

Set Purposes

Have students set their own purposes for reading this selection. Remind students that readers can set purposes for reading by picking up clues from the title, illustrations, and genre of the text they are going to read. If students are having trouble, suggest that they look for information about how animals and their habitats are presented in this story.

Where do different animals live?

Before reading the selection, read the Big Idea question. Tell students to keep this question in mind when reading the selection.

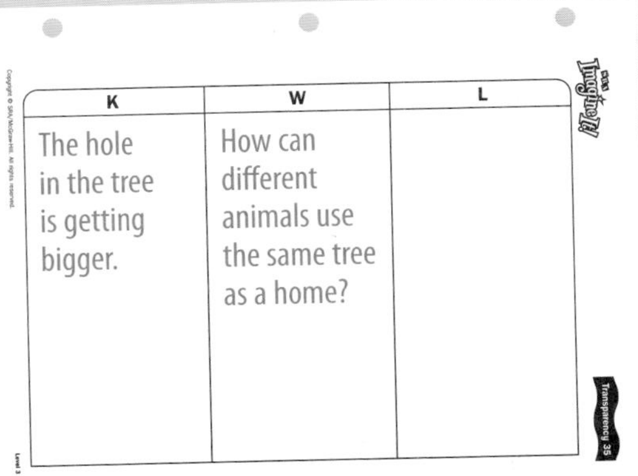

K	W	L
The hole in the tree is getting bigger.	How can different animals use the same tree as a home?	

Transparency 35

Give each student a copy of ***Home Connection*** page 15. The same information is also available in Spanish on ***Home Connection*** page 16. Encourage students to discuss "One Small Place in a Tree" with their families and complete the activity provided.

Selection Vocabulary

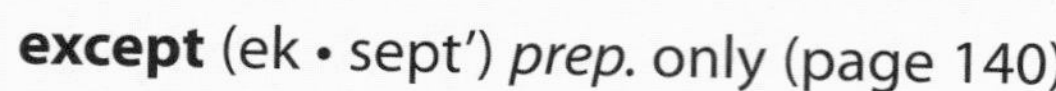

except (ek • sept') *prep.* only (page 140)

maze (māz) *n.* a confusing series of paths or passageways through which people might get lost (page 142)

bacteria (bak • tēr' • ē • ə) *n.* plural form of **bacterium:** a tiny living cell that can be seen only through a microscope. Some cause disease; others help, such as making soil richer (page 146)

hollow (hol' • lō) *adj.* having a hole or an empty space inside (page 146)

stored (stord) *v.* past tense of the verb **store:** to put away for future use (page 147)

dwellers (dwe' • lûrz) *n.* plural form of **dweller:** a person or animal that lives in a certain place (page 150)

swarming (swor' • ming) *adj.* moving in a large group (page 152)

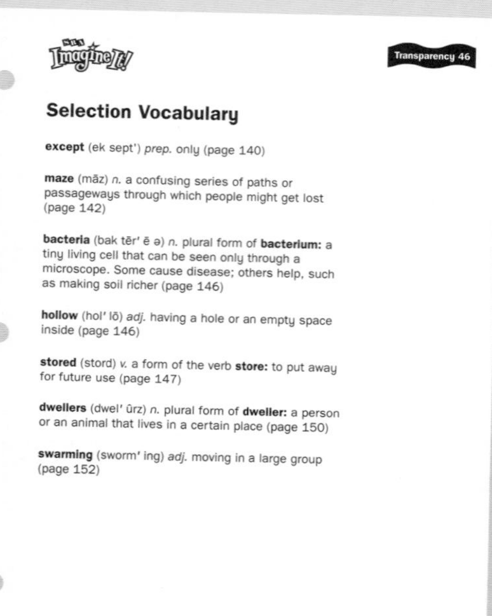

Imagine It! Transparency 46

Selection Vocabulary

except (ek sept') *prep.* only (page 140)

maze (māz) *n.* a confusing series of paths or passageways through which people might get lost (page 142)

bacteria (bak tēr' ē ə) *n.* plural form of **bacterium:** a tiny living cell that can be seen only through a microscope. Some cause disease; others help, such as making soil richer (page 146)

hollow (hol' lō) *adj.* having a hole or an empty space inside (page 146)

stored (stord) *v.* a form of the verb **store:** to put away for future use (page 147)

dwellers (dwel' ûrz) *n.* plural form of **dweller:** a person or an animal that lives in a certain place (page 150)

swarming (sworm' ing) *adj.* moving in a large group (page 152)

Unit 2, Lesson 1 Level 3

Transparency 46

Differentiating Instruction

English Learner

IF . . . students need help understanding the highlighted vocabulary and other words in "One Small Place In a Tree," **THEN . . .** use the ***SRA Imagine It! Photo Library CD,*** other pictures or drawings, or pantomime to help them visualize the words.

Building Vocabulary

ROUTINE 11

Using Routine 11, the selection vocabulary process, have students read aloud the Vocabulary Warm-Up on ***Student Reader,*** Book 1 pages 134–135.

The selection vocabulary words in the ***SRA Imagine It!*** program were selected based on their grade-level appropriateness and their importance to students' comprehension of the story.

As students read, have them stop to blend any difficult or unfamiliar words. Provide students with the pronunciations of words that are not decodable or that they cannot read automatically or fluently.

Guided Vocabulary Practice

Ask students to identify the highlighted vocabulary words they figured out using the vocabulary strategy context clues. **Possible Answers** *maze, except, bacteria* Have students explain how they figured out the meanings of the other vocabulary words as they read the Vocabulary Warm-Up.

Display ***Transparency*** 46, and have students read the words and definitions. Return to the Vocabulary Warm-Up, and have students read the sentences containing the vocabulary words. Then, if necessary, provide a brief in-context explanation of each word.

Read the article to find the meanings of these words, which are also in "One Small Place in a Tree":

- hollow
- dwellers
- maze
- stored
- except
- swarming
- bacteria

Vocabulary Warm-Up

Most kinds of bees live alone, but not honeybees. These social insects live and work in a hive. In the wild, bees often build hives in a hollow tree trunk or log. They find these empty spaces on their own. Honeybees do not bore into the wood to make a hive.

Have you heard the phrase "busy as a bee"? Bees actually do work hard. Each of the hive-dwellers has at least one job. As you might suppose, the most active bees are called "workers." Workers build, clean, and guard the hive. They also gather food and water.

Workers make wax in their bodies. They use the wax to build a complex maze of cells. Honey and pollen are stored in some of these cells. Eggs are laid in others.

No bee except the queen can lay eggs; each hive has only one queen bee. Worker bees feed the queen as well as small, growing bees in the hive. Workers also feed the drones. Drones are male bees.

You may not welcome the sight of swarming bees, but honeybees help humans in many ways. They pollinate flowers and trees. This allows seeds and fruit to be produced. Even the honey provided by the bees is more than a sweet food. It has also been used as a folk remedy because of its ability to kill bacteria.

Vocabulary Strategy

Context Clues are hints in the text. They help you find the meanings of words. Use context clues to find the meaning of *hollow*.

GAME

Definition Game

With a small group of classmates, play a game to review the meaning of each vocabulary word. The game starts with one player giving a definition. The player might say, "What word means 'persons or animals living in a place'?" The classmate who correctly names the vocabulary word (*dwellers*) gets to choose the next definition to give to the group. Play until all of the vocabulary words have been used.

Concept Vocabulary

The concept word for this lesson is ***shelter.*** **Shelter** is something that covers or protects from weather or danger. How do animals in the wild find shelter? What are some ways that humans help provide shelter for wild animals? Do you think this is a good idea?

134

135

Use the vocabulary words on ***Transparency*** 46 to create fill-in-the-blank sentences. Have students fill in the appropriate vocabulary words. For example, "I like to hide toys in the __________ tree in my backyard." *hollow*

Discuss the concept vocabulary word *shelter* with students. Ask students how they think the word *shelter* relates to the theme Animals and Their Habitats. As students read the selections in this unit, encourage them to think about other words that relate to the theme. Students can record these words in the vocabulary section of their Writer's Notebooks.

GAME

Have students play the Definition game during Small-Group Time.

Writer's Notebook

Have students copy the selection vocabulary and concept vocabulary words and definitions into the vocabulary section of their Writer's Notebooks. They can also include other words they think of that relate to the theme.

Concept/Question Board

As students read "One Small Place in a Tree," encourage them to post questions, answers, comments, or other items related to the theme Animals and Their Habitats on the **Concept/ Question Board.**

Reading the Selection

Genre Expository Text

Have students identify the genre of "One Small Place in a Tree." *expository text* If necessary, remind students of the elements of expository text:

- Gives information about something
- Uses facts about real events, people, or animals
- Presents information in a clear way
- Presents events in the order in which they happen
- Might be organized by topics
- Might use diagrams, photographs, or other illustrations
- Contains information that can be checked in sources, such as encyclopedias or newspapers

Comprehension Strategies

Model the use of the following comprehension strategies during the first reading of "One Small Place in a Tree":

- Asking Questions
-  Clarifying
- Visualizing

Comprehension Strategies Rubrics

Use the Informal Comprehension Strategies Rubrics to determine whether a student is using any of the strategies listed below. Note the strategies a student is using, instead of the degree to which a student might be using any particular strategy. In addition, encourage the student to tell of any strategies other than the ones being taught that he or she is using.

Asking Questions

- The student stops to ask questions—any question.
- The student asks questions directly related to the text.
- The student asks *who, what, why, when, where,* or *how* questions as opposed to *yes* or *no* questions.
- The student asks questions that help clarify information in the text.

Focus Questions

Have students read aloud the Focus Questions on page 136. Encourage students to think about the Focus Questions when reading "One Small Place in a Tree."

Clarifying

- The student recognizes when a word or idea is not making sense.
- The student uses decoding skills to read unfamiliar words.
- The student uses structural elements in words to read them.
- The student uses structural elements, context, and questioning to clarify the meanings of unfamiliar words.

Visualizing

- The student recognizes appropriate places in the text to stop and visualize.
- The student visualizes literal ideas or scenes described by the author.
- The student makes inferences while visualizing to show understanding of characters' feelings, mood, and setting. The visualizations go beyond the author's literal words.
- The student uses visualizing differently depending on the type of text (for example, characters, setting, and actions in narratives or a process description in nonfiction).

Monitor Progress to Differentiate Instruction

Formal Assessment 

Comprehension Strategies Note students' understanding of the comprehension strategy Clarifying as they read.

APPROACHING LEVEL

IF . . . students are having difficulty Clarifying as they read,	**THEN . . .** stop and model clarifying whenever students encounter an unfamiliar word. Model think alouds, rereads, and dictionary research. Also allow students to share their own clarifications with the class.

ON LEVEL

IF . . . students are gaining an understanding of Clarifying as they read,	**THEN . . .** have students create a section in the Writer's Notebook of unfamiliar words that they have encountered and successfully clarified.

ABOVE LEVEL

IF . . . students are demonstrating an understanding of Clarifying as they read,	**THEN . . .** have students offer help to those students in the class who are having difficulty with clarifying.

Teacher Tip

DECODING As students read, make sure they use their knowledge of spelling patterns and basic syllabication rules to help decode unfamiliar words.

Technology

eSTUDENT READER Students can access ***SRA Imagine It! Student Reader,*** Book 1 electronically by using the ***eStudent Reader*** online or on CD-ROM.

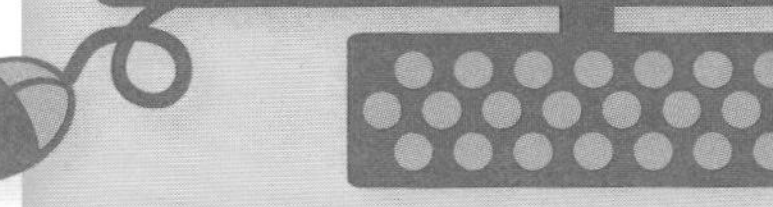

Reading and Responding

Comprehension Skills

Reread "One Small Place in a Tree" using the following comprehension skills:

- Author's Purpose
- Cause and Effect

Reading with a Writer's Eye

Reading with a Writer's Eye focuses on literary elements the author uses to create an enjoyable reading experience. As students read with a writer's eye, they are encouraged to identify such techniques and then use them in their own writing. While rereading "One Small Place in a Tree," explain the following literary elements:

- Text Structure: Technique
- Language Use

Reading Recommendation

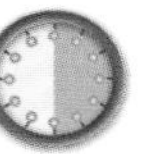

Oral Reading

Use Routine 14, the reading the selection routine, as you read the story. While reading, model strategies and stop to ask and answer questions. Point out how the pictures reflect the story. Share the images that pop up in your mind as you read and how points in the reading relate to ideas you already know. Reread the text by applying comprehension skills. After reading, be sure to discuss the story using the "handing-off" procedure and have students discuss new information they have learned.

"One Small Place in a Tree" lends itself well to oral reading because of its descriptive passages, strong imagery, and conversational style. Encourage students to express their thoughts, ask questions, or give opinions as they read.

Students will read the story twice over a three-day period.

Day 2 **ORAL READ** Have students read the first half of the selection. Model the use of the comprehension strategies.

Day 3 **ORAL READ** Have students finish reading the selection. Continue to model the comprehension strategies.

Day 4 **SILENT READ** Have students reread the selection. Have students focus on the comprehension skills and Reading with a Writer's Eye.

Technology

Have students listen to "One Small Place in a Tree" on the ***Listening Library CD.*** After students have listened, have them discuss what other things such as poetry, songs, or nonfiction they prefer to listen to on the radio or on CDs.

Reading and Responding

A tree hole. One small place in a tree. How does it get there? Who lives inside?

Suppose that you could watch a hole from its beginning. You might see something like this: 1

138

139

Phonics and Fluency

The skills students are reviewing in Phonics and Fluency should help them read the selection. The focuses of this lesson are consonant blends and /ī/ spelled *igh*, *_y*, and *_ie*. Words with these spellings will be found in boxes similar to this one throughout the selection.

Consonant blends: tree, small, place, glimpse, chips, tree

/ī/ spelled *igh*, *_y*, and *_ie*: *by*

Teacher Tip

VOCABULARY STRATEGIES Remind students to use context clues, apposition, or word structure to figure out the meaning of difficult words when reading.

Comprehension Strategies

This selection is broken into two parts. On the first day, read pages 138–145. On the second day, read pages 146–153.

1 Asking Questions Teacher Modeling: *Asking questions is a good way to keep involved with what is happening in a story and to make sure you understand what you're reading. I already have a question. The boy is looking into the hole in the tree. What is he seeing?*

Vocabulary Tip

Point out the word *except* on page 140 in the text. Point out how the author tells the difference between this tree and the others in the forest, and ask students if this helps them understand th meaning of the word. Point out the word *maze* in the text on page 142. Then have students poin the maze on page 143. Have students discuss which vocabulary strategies they would use to figu the meaning of the word *maze*.

2 Clarifying Teacher Modeling: *Remember to clarify any words or ideas that confuse you. I'll stop here because I'm not sure how the bear's scratching relates to the hole in the tree. Remember, to clarify a word or idea, we can reread the text, read further in the text, or consult another source, such as a dictionary or an encyclopedia. I think I'll reread this section. Now I understand. The bear is scratching the bark off of the tree, and that leads to a cut in the tree, which leads to a hole. Does anyone see anything they would like to clarify?*

Comprehension Check

How do you think that timber beetles are going to relate to the theme Animals and Their Habitats? **Possible Answer** *It seems like the timber beetles are going to move into the cut in the tree. That means they might be making that tree their habitat.*

Reading and Responding

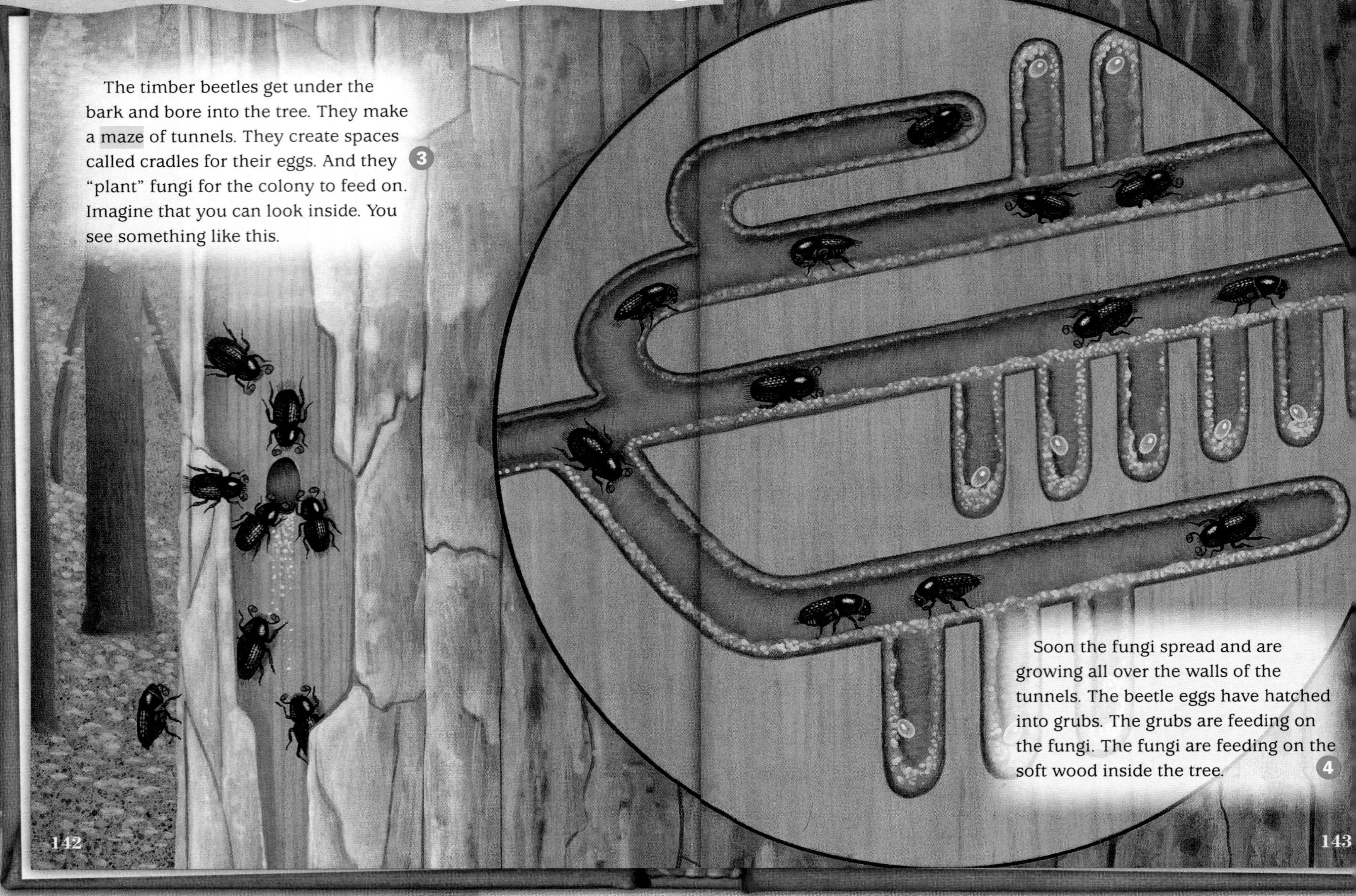

The timber beetles get under the bark and bore into the tree. They make a maze of tunnels. They create spaces called cradles for their eggs. And they "plant" fungi for the colony to feed on. 3
Imagine that you can look inside. You see something like this.

142

Soon the fungi spread and are growing all over the walls of the tunnels. The beetle eggs have hatched into grubs. The grubs are feeding on the fungi. The fungi are feeding on the soft wood inside the tree. 4

143

Phonics and Fluency

Consonant blends: tree, create, spread, growing, spears, cleared
/ī/ spelled *igh, _y,* and *_ie:* flies

Teacher Tip

ASKING QUESTIONS Be alert to students who never ask questions. Spend time with these students and encourage them to discuss selections. Focus on difficulties they might have had and how they solved these problems, and their thoughts about unit concepts.

Comprehension Strategies

3 Answering Questions Teacher Modeling: *I now have an answer to my previous question. I had asked what the boy was seeing when he looked inside the tree. Now I know that timber beetles are living in the tree. They are finding places to lay their eggs.*

4 Visualizing Teacher Modeling: *Visualizing helps readers picture in their minds things they cannot see. The text says that the grubs are feeding on the fungi, and we can see this in the picture. But the text also says that the fungi are feeding on the soft wood inside the tree. We know that* feeding *means "eating," so we can visualize the fungi eating away at the soft wood inside the tree. What part of the text are you visualizing?*

The beetle grubs become full-grown timber beetles.

They eat their way out of the chambers and make more holes in the tree. 5

On your next visit you count more than ten holes. But the first one is the largest.

144

One time when you're near the tree, you actually hear the sound of the beetles chewing wood.

A red-bellied woodpecker hears it, too.

The bird flies to the tree holes. It spears the beetles with its sharp beak, or pulls them out with its long tongue.

Many woodpeckers visit the oak tree to eat. After a summer they've cleared the holes of beetles and beetle grubs. But they've made the big hole even bigger.

145

5 **Clarifying** Teacher Modeling: *I have heard of the word* chambers, *but I am not sure what the author means here. When I think of chambers, I think of rooms. But rooms are in buildings, not trees. Can a tree have rooms? I'm going to reread this section. It says that the beetles are eating their way out of the chambers.* Chambers *must refer to the tunnels in the tree where the beetles have been living. I'll look in the dictionary to double check. The dictionary says that* chambers *can mean "rooms" or "enclosed spaces." Yes, that makes sense. Are there any words or ideas that you need to stop and clarify?*

Comprehension Check

The tree has provided a habitat (shelter and food) for the timber beetles. How is it providing a habitat for the woodpeckers? **Possible Answer** *The woodpeckers are using the tree for food. They eat the beetles to survive.*

Teacher Tip

COMPREHENSION Ask students these questions to make sure they understand what they are reading:

- *Can you summarize what you have read?*
- *Does the story make sense?*

STOP You have read the first half of the story. Continue the story tomorrow on page T62.

OBJECTIVES

Students will
- ✦ learn a note-taking strategy.
- ✦ learn /ī/ and irregular plurals.
- ✦ learn possessive nouns and pronouns.

MATERIALS

- ✦ ***Transparency*** 47
- ✦ ***Routines*** 15, 16
- ✦ ***Skills Practice 1,*** pp. 85, 89–91
- ✦ ***Language Arts Handbook,*** pp. 304–307

Teacher Tip

PLAN AHEAD The graphic organizer in Day 2 is referenced throughout the lesson. Place it somewhere students can access it if necessary.

Summary

A student read a biography about Mae Jemison. Here is her summary.

Mae Jemison was the first African American woman to become an astronaut. She was born in Alabama in 1956, but her family moved to Chicago when she was young. She graduated high school when she was sixteen years old. Then she went to college and became an engineer. She also became a doctor, and she joined the Peace Corps so she could help people. She became an astronaut in 1987. In 1992, she went into space for eight days.

 Level 3

Transparency, 47

Differentiating Instruction English Learner

IF . . . students feel overwhelmed by summarizing large amounts of text, **THEN . . .** provide nonfiction picture books with minimal text for them to summarize.

Traits of Good Writing

IDEAS Writers take notes as they read to organize information.

Writing Summary

ROUTINE  ROUTINE 

Prewriting

Teach—Taking Notes

- ✦ Display ***Transparency*** 47, and have a student read the summary aloud. This is a model summary that the students can follow.
- ✦ Tell students that they will take notes on the information in the book or article they have chosen.
- ✦ If students seem unfamiliar with taking notes, have them read ***Skills Practice 1*** page 91, *Note-Taking Guidelines.*
- ✦ Have students open ***Skills Practice 1*** to page 85. Use Routines 15 and 16. Create a similar graphic organizer either on the board or on chart paper. Use the blank graphic organizer and the book you selected on Day 1 to model taking notes on the main pieces of information. Show students how to organize notes according to main ideas and supporting details.

Guided Practice

- ✦ After you insert information into the Main Topic box, ask students to help you select the most important subtopics or details to put into the Subtopic boxes.
- ✦ Explain that every main idea needs to have supporting details.

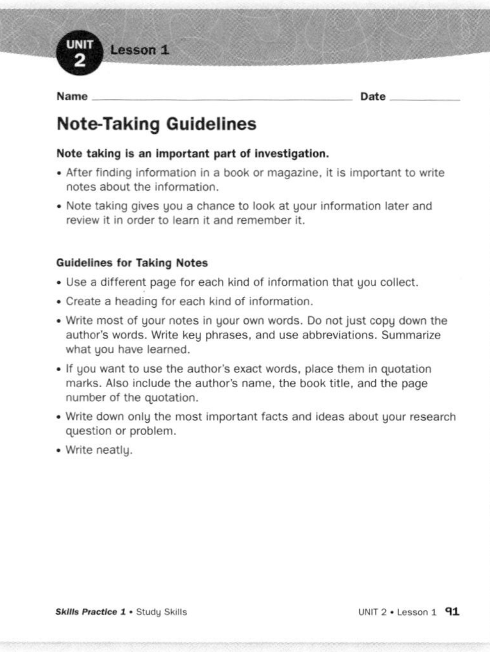

UNIT 2 Lesson 1

Name ______________ Date ________

Note-Taking Guidelines

Note taking is an important part of investigation.
- After finding information in a book or magazine, it is important to write notes about the information.
- Note taking gives you a chance to look at your information later and review it in order to learn it and remember it.

Guidelines for Taking Notes
- Use a different page for each kind of information that you collect.
- Create a heading for each kind of information.
- Write most of your notes in your own words. Do not just copy down the author's words. Write key phrases, and use abbreviations. Summarize what you have learned.
- If you want to use the author's exact words, place them in quotation marks. Also include the author's name, the book title, and the page number of the quotation.
- Write down only the most important facts and ideas about your research question or problem.
- Write neatly.

Skills Practice 1 • Study Skills UNIT 2 • Lesson 1 91

Skills Practice 1, p. 91

Writing, continued

Apply

Composing—Prewriting Have students complete the graphic organizer on ***Skills Practice 1*** page 85.

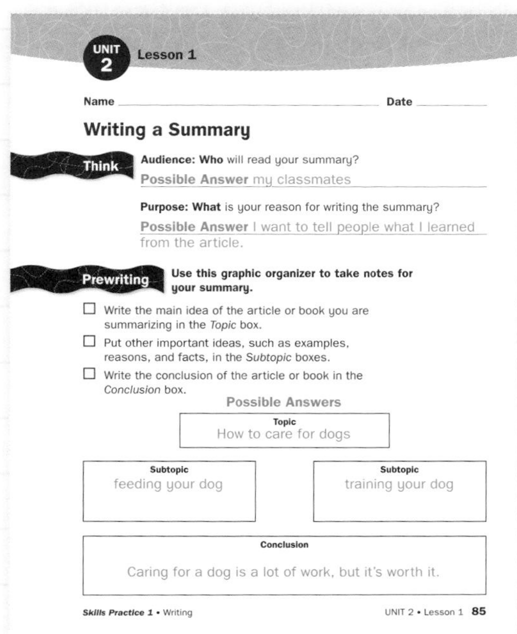
UNIT 2 Lesson 1

Name ______ Date ______

Writing a Summary

Think

Audience: Who will read your summary?
Possible Answer my classmates

Purpose: What is your reason for writing the summary?
Possible Answer I want to tell people what I learned from the article.

Prewriting

Use this graphic organizer to take notes for your summary.

- ☐ Write the main idea of the article or book you are summarizing in the *Topic* box.
- ☐ Put other important ideas, such as examples, reasons, and facts, in the *Subtopic* boxes.
- ☐ Write the conclusion of the article or book in the *Conclusion* box.

Possible Answers

Topic: How to care for dogs

Subtopic: feeding your dog

Subtopic: training your dog

Conclusion: Caring for a dog is a lot of work, but it's worth it.

Skills Practice 1 • Writing UNIT 2 • Lesson 1 85

Skills Practice 1, p. 85

Monitor Progress to Differentiate Instruction

Formal Assessment 

Taking Notes Note whether students are able to transfer information into note form.

APPROACHING LEVEL

IF . . . students need to practice taking notes,	**THEN . . .** have them take notes for their unit investigations.

ON LEVEL

IF . . . students have an understanding of taking notes,	**THEN . . .** have them complete work with another student during Workshop.

ABOVE LEVEL

IF . . . students are ready for a challenge,	**THEN . . .** have them use their notes to create a Roman numeral outline for the unit investigation.

Spelling

/ī/ and Regular Plurals

Teach

✦ Use a word sort to teach students to spell plurals and words with /ī/ spelled *igh, _y,* and *_ie.*

Guided Practice

Write the following headings on the board: *plural* and */ī/.* Then write the word list: *lie, ties, fly, flies, halves, cycles, reply, replies, sigh, monkeys, lunches, fight, knights, spy, spies.* Have volunteers write the words under the correct heading. After the spelling words have all been used, ask volunteers to come to the board and underline the part of each word that reflects the category in which it was placed. If a word fits in more than one category, ask the students to put the word under the heading that they prefer.

Word Sort Answers

Plurals with *-s: ties, cycles, monkeys, knights*
Plurals with *-es: flies, halves, replies, lunches, spies*
Words with */ī/: lie, ties, fly, flies, cycles, reply, replies, sigh, fight, knights, spy, spies*

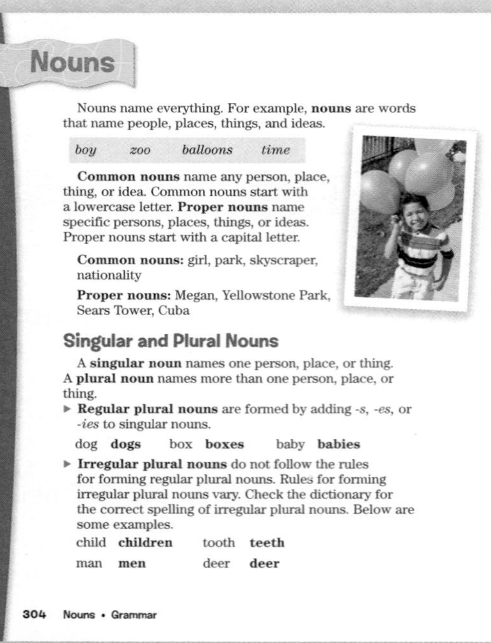

Nouns

Nouns name everything. For example, **nouns** are words that name people, places, things, and ideas.

boy *zoo* *balloons* *time*

Common nouns name any person, place, thing, or idea. Common nouns start with a lowercase letter. **Proper nouns** name specific persons, places, things, or ideas. Proper nouns start with a capital letter.

Common nouns: girl, park, skyscraper, nationality

Proper nouns: Megan, Yellowstone Park, Sears Tower, Cuba

Singular and Plural Nouns

A **singular noun** names one person, place, or thing. A **plural noun** names more than one person, place, or thing.

- **Regular plural nouns** are formed by adding *-s*, *-es*, or *-ies* to singular nouns.

dog **dogs** box **boxes** baby **babies**

- **Irregular plural nouns** do not follow the rules for forming regular plural nouns. Rules for forming irregular plural nouns vary. Check the dictionary for the correct spelling of irregular plural nouns. Below are some examples.

child **children** tooth **teeth**
man **men** deer **deer**

304 Nouns • Grammar

Language Arts Handbook, p. 304

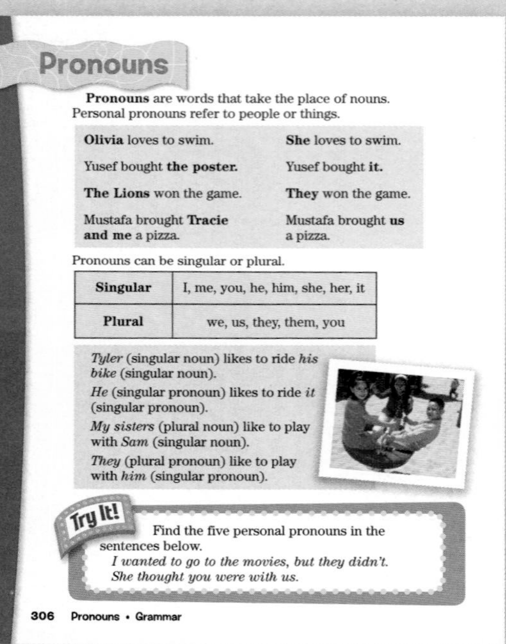

Pronouns

Pronouns are words that take the place of nouns. Personal pronouns refer to people or things.

Olivia loves to swim.	**She** loves to swim.
Yusef bought **the poster.**	Yusef bought **it.**
The Lions won the game.	**They** won the game.
Mustafa brought **Tracie and me** a pizza.	Mustafa brought **us** a pizza.

Pronouns can be singular or plural.

Singular	I, me, you, he, him, she, her, it
Plural	we, us, they, them, you

Tyler (singular noun) likes to ride *his bike* (singular noun).
He (singular pronoun) likes to ride *it* (singular pronoun).
My sisters (plural noun) like to play with *Sam* (singular noun).
They (plural pronoun) like to play with *him* (singular pronoun).

Try It! Find the five personal pronouns in the sentences below.
I wanted to go to the movies, but they didn't.
She thought you were with us.

306 Pronouns • Grammar

Language Arts Handbook, p. 306

Grammar, Usage, and Mechanics

Possessive Nouns and Pronouns

Teach

- ✦ Ask students to provide a sentence for you to write on the board. Suggest that students add an object if the sentence does not have one.
- ✦ Explain that possessive nouns and pronouns show ownership. Using the sentence on the board, demonstrate the different ways possessives can be formed.
  - Demonstrate how to form the possessive of a singular possessive noun by adding an apostrophe and *s* to the noun. For example, *cat* + *'s* = *cat's: the cat's toy*
  - Demonstrate how to form the possessive of a plural noun ending in s by adding an apostrophe. For example, *puppies* + *'* = *puppies': the puppies' food*
  - Demonstrate how to form the possessive of a plural noun not ending in *s* by adding an apostrophe *s*. For example, *children* + *'s* = *children's: the children's books*
- ✦ Explain that possessive pronouns take the place of possessive nouns and can be singular or plural. Possessive pronouns do not add apostrophes. Write the following examples of possessive pronouns on the board: *my, your, her, his, our, their, your.* Have students create sentences using these possessive pronouns.
- ✦ Use ***Language Arts Handbook*** pages 304–307 for rules and examples of possessive nouns and pronouns.

Guided Practice

Have a student read the instruction on ***Skills Practice 1*** page 89. Answer the first Practice question as a class. Clarify and explain as needed.

Apply

Have students complete ***Skills Practice 1*** pages 89–90 to practice recognizing and using possessive nouns and pronouns.

Monitor Progress to Differentiate Instruction

Formal Assessment 

Nouns and Pronouns Note whether students are able to correctly use nouns and their pronoun replacements in speech.

APPROACHING LEVEL

IF . . . students need to practice possessive nouns and pronouns,	**THEN . . .** have them complete ***Reteach*** page 36 during Workshop.
IF . . . students need more practice with possessive nouns and pronouns,	**THEN . . .** have them use ***Intervention Guide*** Unit 2, Lesson 1.

ON LEVEL

IF . . . students have an understanding of possessive nouns and pronouns,	**THEN . . .** have them complete a ***Workshop Kit*** activity during Workshop.

ABOVE LEVEL

IF . . . students need a challenge,	**THEN . . .** have them complete ***Challenge Activities*** page 33 during Workshop.

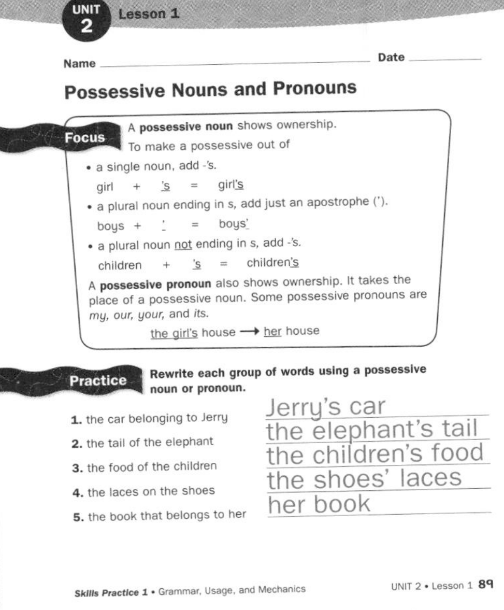

UNIT 2 Lesson 1

Name ______ Date ______

Possessive Nouns and Pronouns

Focus A **possessive noun** shows ownership.

To make a possessive out of

- a single noun, add -'s.
  girl + 's = girl's
- a plural noun ending in s, add just an apostrophe (').
  boys + ' = boys'
- a plural noun not ending in s, add -'s.
  children + 's = children's

A **possessive pronoun** also shows ownership. It takes the place of a possessive noun. Some possessive pronouns are *my, our, your,* and *its.*

the girl's house → her house

Practice Rewrite each group of words using a possessive noun or pronoun.

1. the car belonging to Jerry — Jerry's car
2. the tail of the elephant — the elephant's tail
3. the food of the children — the children's food
4. the laces on the shoes — the shoes' laces
5. the book that belongs to her — her book

Skills Practice 1 • Grammar, Usage, and Mechanics UNIT 2 • Lesson 1 89

Skills Practice 1, p. 89

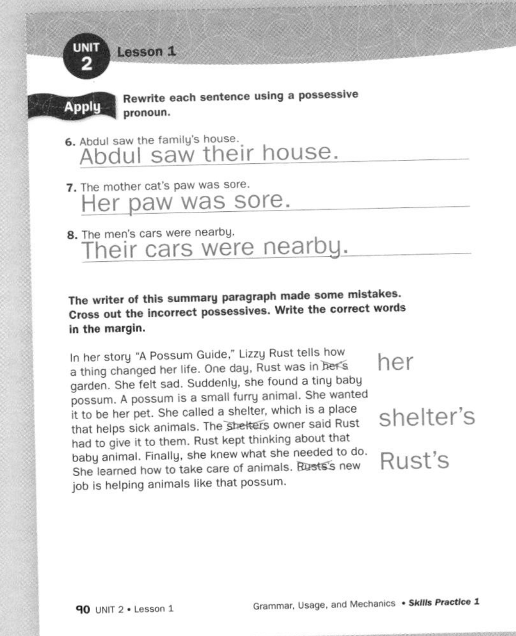

UNIT 2 Lesson 1

Apply Rewrite each sentence using a possessive pronoun.

6. Abdul saw the family's house. — Abdul saw their house.
7. The mother cat's paw was sore. — Her paw was sore.
8. The men's cars were nearby. — Their cars were nearby.

The writer of this summary paragraph made some mistakes. Cross out the incorrect possessives. Write the correct words in the margin.

In her story "A Possum Guide," Lizzy Rust tells how a thing changed her life. One day, Rust was in her's garden. She felt sad. Suddenly, she found a tiny baby possum. A possum is a small furry animal. She wanted it to be her pet. She called a shelter, which is a place that helps sick animals. The shelters owner said Rust had to give it to them. Rust kept thinking about that baby animal. Finally, she knew what she needed to do. She learned how to take care of animals. Rusts's new job is helping animals like that possum. — her; shelter's; Rust's

90 UNIT 2 • Lesson 1 Grammar, Usage, and Mechanics • *Skills Practice 1*

Skills Practice 1, p. 90

Preparing to Read

OBJECTIVES

Students will

- identify and learn how regular plurals are formed.
- build fluency.

MATERIALS

- ***Transparency*** 48
- ***Skills Practice 1,*** pp. 81–82

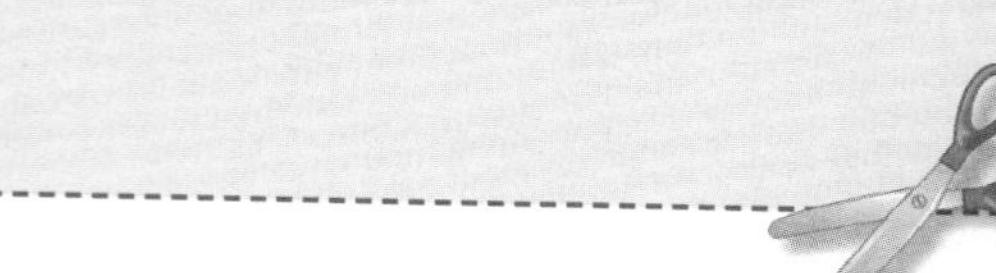

Daily Oral Practice

Daily News

Today!

Have you ever thought about where bugs set up house? Or why birds return to the same nest every year? Or where squirrels go to find shelter? Think about all the trees in the world. Trees provide homes for many kinds of animal life.

- Write the daily news on the board or on chart paper. Then have students read the daily news in unison to practice fluency.
- As a review of yesterday's phonics and fluency lesson, ask a volunteer to identify any words in the message with consonant blends at the beginning or end. gs *in* bugs; rds *in* birds; rn *in* return; st *in* nest; tr *in* trees; rld *in* world; pr *in* provide; nds *in* kinds

Differentiating Instruction **English Learner**

IF . . . students have difficulty pronouncing the plurals, **THEN . . .** say each word, emphasizing the ending /s/ or /z/. Have students repeat the pronunciations several times.

Teacher Tip

SYLLABICATION To help students blend words and build fluency, demonstrate syllabication using the decodable, multisyllabic words in the word lines.

bee • tles	dish • es
spa • ces	ba • bies
fox • es	coun • tries
bran • ches	pup • pies
bush • es	stor • ies

Word Structure

Regular Plurals

- Write the following word lines on the board or use ***Transparency*** 48. Show students one line at time as you go through them by covering up the others. The words in boldface are from "One Small Place in a Tree."

Line 1	claws	bugs	beetles	spaces
Line 2	foxes	branches	bushes	dishes
Line 3	babies	countries	puppies	stories
Line 4	calves	wives	leaves	wolves

Line 1 **Regular plurals**

Explain that there are rules for forming regular plural nouns. Tell students that if a noun ends with a consonant or the letter *e*, then they should add an *s* to make it plural. Have students read the words in Line 1 and tell you the singular form of each. *claw, bug, beetle, space*

Line 2 **Regular plurals**

Tell students that if a noun ends with an *x, ch,* or *sh,* then they should add *es* to make it plural. Have students read the words in Line 2 and tell you the singular form of each. *fox, branch, bush, dish*

Line 3 **Regular plurals**

Tell students that if a noun ends with *y*, then you change the *y* to *i* and add *es* to make it plural. Have students read the words in Line 3 and tell you the singular form of each. *baby, country, puppy, story*

Line 4 **Regular plurals**

- Tell students that if a noun ends with an *f* or *fe*, then you change the *f* to a *v* and add *s* or *es* to make it plural. Have students read the words in Line 4 and tell you the singular form of each. *calf, wife, leaf, wolf*
- Help students start the word structure activities on ***Skills Practice 1*** pages 81–82. Read the Focus box with them and help them with the first few questions. Then have students complete the pages on their own.

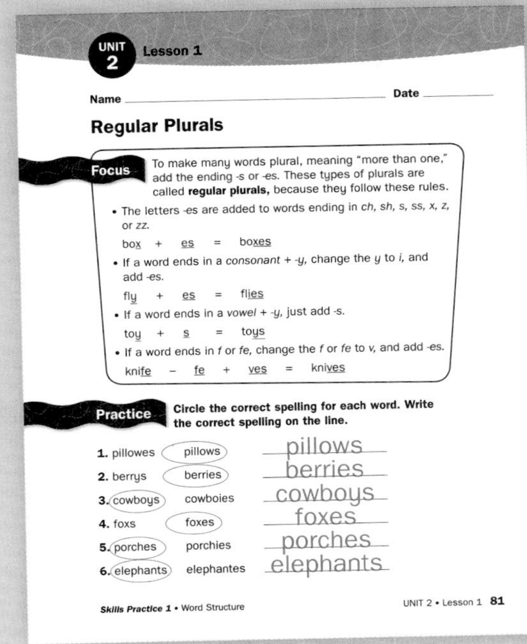

UNIT 2 Lesson 1

Name ______ Date ______

Regular Plurals

Focus To make many words plural, meaning "more than one," add the ending -s or -es. These types of plurals are called **regular plurals,** because they follow these rules.

- The letters -es are added to words ending in *ch, sh, s, ss, x, z,* or *zz.*
  box + es = boxes
- If a word ends in a *consonant* + -y, change the *y* to *i*, and add -es.
  fly + es = flies
- If a word ends in a *vowel* + -y, just add -s.
  toy + s = toys
- If a word ends in *f* or *fe*, change the *f* or *fe* to *v*, and add -es.
  knife − fe + ves = knives

Practice Circle the correct spelling for each word. Write the correct spelling on the line.

1. pillowes (pillows) pillows
2. berrys (berries) berries
3. (cowboys) cowboies cowboys
4. foxs (foxes) foxes
5. (porches) porchies porches
6. (elephants) elephantes elephants

Skills Practice 1 • Word Structure UNIT 2 • Lesson 1 81

Skills Practice 1, p. 81

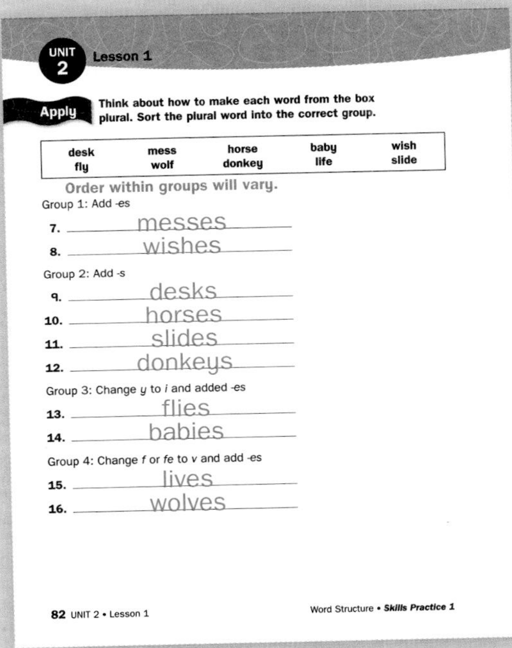

UNIT 2 Lesson 1

Apply Think about how to make each word from the box plural. Sort the plural word into the correct group.

desk	mess	horse	baby	wish
fly	wolf	donkey	life	slide

Order within groups will vary.

Group 1: Add -es

7. messes
8. wishes

Group 2: Add -s

9. desks
10. horses
11. slides
12. donkeys

Group 3: Change *y* to *i* and added -es

13. flies
14. babies

Group 4: Change *f* or *fe* to *v* and add -es

15. lives
16. wolves

82 UNIT 2 • Lesson 1 Word Structure • *Skills Practice 1*

Skills Practice 1, p. 82

Monitor Progress to Differentiate Instruction

Formal Assessment 

Word Structure During the word structure activity, note how well students understand regular plurals.

APPROACHING LEVEL	**IF . . .** students need practice with regular plurals,	**THEN . . .** work with them on the word structure activities on ***Reteach*** page 33 during Workshop.
	IF . . . students need more practice with regular plurals,	**THEN . . .** work with them on the phonics activities for Unit 2 Lesson 1 in the ***Intervention Guide*** during Workshop..
ON LEVEL	**IF . . .** students understand regular plurals,	**THEN . . .** have them make lists of words to add to each word line during Workshop.
ABOVE LEVEL	**IF . . .** students are ready for a challenge with regular plurals,	**THEN . . .** have them complete the word structure activities on ***Challenge Activities*** page 30 during Workshop.

Reading and Responding

Now disease strikes. Bacteria come in through the hole in the tree. You won't see the bacteria—they're too small. But you can see the damage they've done. The tree has heart rot. It's dying inside and out.

Bark begins to loosen and fall off. The hole is now so large that you can actually see inside. It has become a hollow place that looks as if it could be home for something. 6

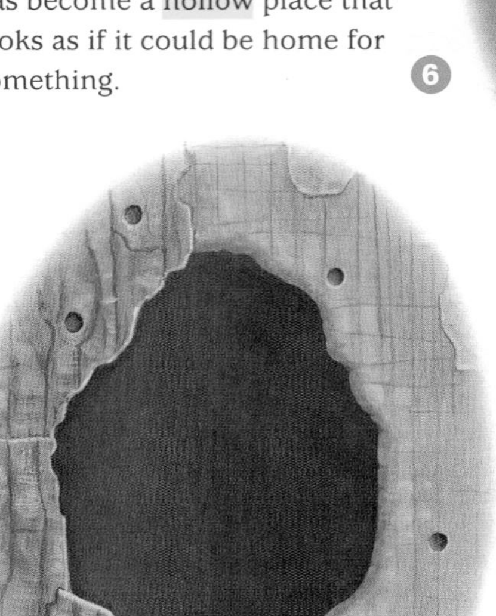

146

The first animal to use it is a flying squirrel. You find the squirrel "holed up" in there one winter day. You notice that it has stored some nuts under the loose bark around the hole. 7

147

OBJECTIVES

Students will

- use the comprehension strategies Asking Questions, Clarifying, and Visualizing.
- discuss the story using the handing-off process.
- review vocabulary, genre, and fluency.

MATERIALS

- ***Student Reader,*** Book 1, pp. 146–155
- Routine A
- ***Skills Practice 1,*** pp. 83–84
- ***Transparencies*** 35, 46

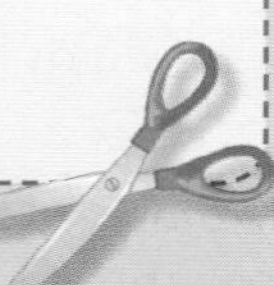

1st READ

Comprehension Strategies

6 Asking Questions Teacher Modeling: *The text says that the hole is getting bigger. It's now a hollow place that looks as if it could be another home. I wonder who is going to move in now. I'll keep reading to find out!*

7 Answering Questions Teaching Modeling: *It didn't take long for me to find out the answer to my question. A flying squirrel has moved into the hollow place in the tree. It stored food there, too. I wonder what is next! What do you think?*

Research in Action

Students enjoy hearing stories read aloud. However, students do not acquire word meanings from hearing a story once. Reading a story once is good entertainment but does little for word meaning acquisition in the primary grades. However, when word stories or expository texts are read repeatedly (two to four times) and meanings are taught, 25 to 40 percent of word meanings are acquired.
(Andy Biemiller)

8 **Clarifying** Teacher Modeling: *I'm going to stop and reread to clarify. The text says that the hole is "just right for bluebirds." I wonder what that means. After I reread the text, I see that it explains that the hole is high enough for the bluebirds' safety. That must mean that there is more danger for them on the ground. Maybe they would be someone else's dinner if they were caught on the ground. I'm glad the bluebirds have a place in the tree.*

Comprehension Check

Why are the bluebird chicks safe in the nest until they're old enough to fly? **Possible Answers** *The chicks are protected from the weather inside the hole. They are also protected from other animals who might want to eat them. Their parents can bring food back to the tree until they are ready to get it for themselves.*

Word Structure

This lesson focuses on regular plurals. These words will be found in boxes similar to this one throughout the selection.

Regular plurals: nuts, bluebirds, weeds, eggs, chicks

Reading and Responding

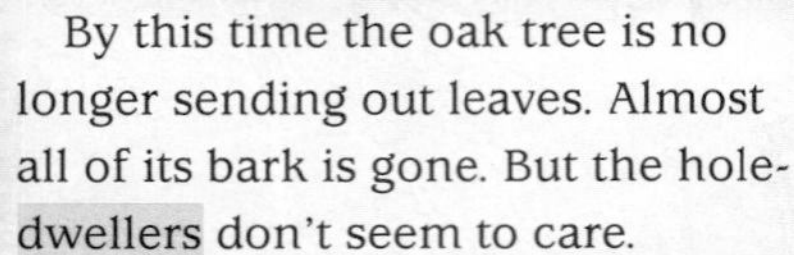

By this time the oak tree is no longer sending out leaves. Almost all of its bark is gone. But the hole-dwellers don't seem to care. 9

For the next three springs, the hole in the tree is a nest for the same pair of bluebirds.

150

For the next three winters, it's home to a family of white-footed mice.

In all those three years, the tree hasn't grown at all. This oak tree is dead. But—the hole is full of life. 10

A hairy woodpecker sometimes comes to roost there.

A gray squirrel often uses the hole as a hiding place.

When the hole has water in it, you can sometimes see a tree frog there.

151

Word Structure

Regular plurals: leaves, hole-dwellers, springs, years, things, eggs, insects

Comprehension Strategies

9 Asking Questions Teacher Modeling: *The oak tree is no longer sending out leaves. That must mean it's not growing leaves. Its bark is almost gone, too. What does this mean to the tree?*

10 Answering Questions Teacher Modeling: *As I continue to read, I found out that the tree is dead. That is what I had suspected. The good news is that there is still a lot of life inside the hole in the tree. Many other animals are coming to take shelter in the hollow place. Even a tree frog makes a home in the tree. Do you have any more questions?*

Differentiating Instruction English Learner

IF . . . students would benefit from a review of the seasons, **THEN . . .** have them use this selection's illustrations to describe aspects of each season. For example, they might use snow and cold to describe the winter scene shown on this page.

11 Visualizing Teacher Modeling: *Now that I have read this story I will look at trees quite differently. Now whenever I look at a tree, I will also know that it is somebody's home. If I close my eyes, I can see all the different forms of life that have lived there and that will someday call this tree their home. Would anyone like to share what they visualize when they think of the tree?*

Comprehension Check

Why are dead trees important? **Possible Answer** *Dead trees are important because they continue to provide a habitat for many kinds of animals and insects. The dead trees help to keep these other animals alive.*

Vocabulary Tip

Point out the word *bacteria* on page 146 in the text. Ask students if knowing that disease has struck the tree helps them understand the meaning of *bacteria*. Point out the word *dwellers* on page 150 in the text. Ask students what context clues help them understand the meaning of this word.

K	W	L
The hole in the tree is getting bigger.	How can different animals use the same tree as a home?	The constant changes in the tree made it useful for all kinds of animals.

Transparency 35

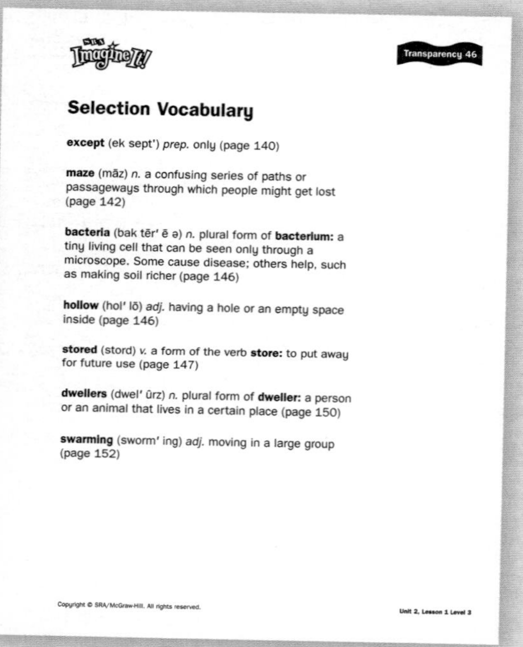

Imagine It! Transparency 46

Selection Vocabulary

except (ek sept') *prep.* only (page 140)

maze (māz) *n.* a confusing series of paths or passageways through which people might get lost (page 142)

bacteria (bak tēr' ē ə) *n.* plural form of **bacterium:** a tiny living cell that can be seen only through a microscope. Some cause disease; others help, such as making soil richer (page 146)

hollow (hol' lō) *adj.* having a hole or an empty space inside (page 146)

stored (stord) *v.* a form of the verb **store:** to put away for future use (page 147)

dwellers (dwel' ûrz) *n.* plural form of **dweller:** a person or an animal that lives in a certain place (page 150)

swarming (sworm' ing) *adj.* moving in a large group (page 152)

Unit 2, Lesson 1 Level 3

Transparency 46

Discussing the Selection

✦ It is important for students to see you as a contributing member of the group. Use Routine A, the handing-off process, to emphasize that you are part of the group. Actively participate in the handing-off process by raising your hand to be called on by the last speaker when you have a contribution to make. Point out unusual and interesting insights verbalized by students so that these insights are recognized and discussed. As the year progresses, students will take more responsibility for the discussion of the selections.

✦ Engage students in a discussion using the handing-off procedure to determine whether they have grasped the following ideas:

- The cut in the tree led to a hole, which became a home for many animals.
- The tree was useful at all stages of its life and death.

✦ Ask students how the story demonstrates the following key concepts:

- Animals of all shapes and sizes can find homes in the same places.
- Nature has a cycle; the tree sheltered animals in life and in death.

✦ Return to the KWL chart on ***Transparency*** 35. Have students discuss whether the selection provided enough information to tell them what they wanted to know, and also have them discuss what they learned by reading the selection. Ask students if the predictions they made while browsing the story were confirmed or not confirmed.

✦ Also, have students return to the Focus Questions on ***Student Reader,*** Book 1 page 136. Select a student to read the questions aloud, and have students answer and discuss the questions. Have them return to the text as necessary.

Genre Review

Review the elements of expository text on page T48 with students. Ask students how they know "One Small Place in a Tree" is expository text.

Where do different animals live?

After reading the selection, read the Big Idea question. Discuss with students how the selection helps answer this question.

Vocabulary Review

Review with students the selection vocabulary words and definitions written in the vocabulary section of the Writer's Notebook. Have students turn to pages 83–84 in ***Skills Practice 1.*** Help students complete the first two questions. Have them complete the rest of the activity on their own. Also, review the concept vocabulary word *shelter*. Ask students whether they can think of other words related to the theme Animals and Their Habitats. **Possible Answers** *homes, protection, life*

Fluency

- While the sentences in "One Small Place in a Tree" are descriptive, they are not lengthy and are ideal for students to practice accuracy. Accuracy, or the number of words identified correctly in a text, is essential for fluency and allows readers to focus their attention on understanding the text instead of merely decoding.
- Read aloud pages 138–139 of "One Small Place in a Tree." Model accuracy for students. For example, read *A tree hole. One small place in a tree. How does it get there?* and point out how you read the lines without long pauses and in a way that sounded like natural conversation. Point out how you paused at the end of each sentence and after the end punctuation. Tell students that it is important to pay attention to end punctuation and commas when reading. Have students follow along in the ***Student Reader*** and tell them to raise their hands when you pause. Tell students that as they reread, they should practice pausing after commas.

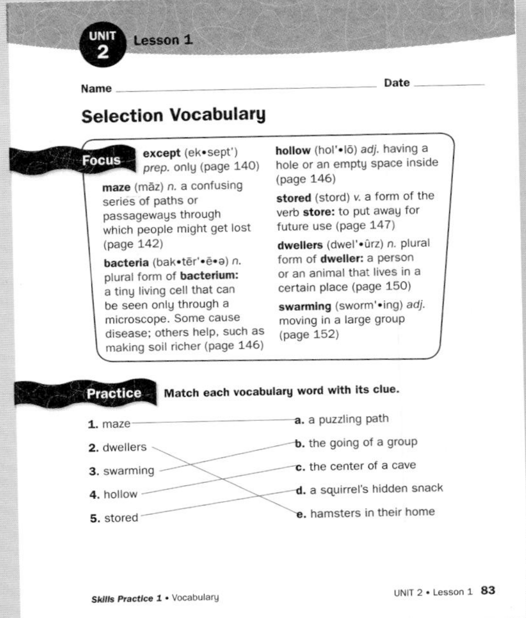
UNIT 2 Lesson 1

Name ______ Date ______

Selection Vocabulary

Focus

except (ek•sept') *prep.* only (page 140)

maze (māz) *n.* a confusing series of paths or passageways through which people might get lost (page 142)

bacteria (bak•tēr'•ē•ə) *n.* plural form of **bacterium:** a tiny living cell that can be seen only through a microscope. Some cause disease; others help, such as making soil richer (page 146)

hollow (hol'•lō) *adj.* having a hole or an empty space inside (page 146)

stored (stord) *v.* a form of the verb **store:** to put away for future use (page 147)

dwellers (dwel'•ûrz) *n.* plural form of **dweller:** a person or an animal that lives in a certain place (page 150)

swarming (sworm'•ing) *adj.* moving in a large group (page 152)

Practice Match each vocabulary word with its clue.

1. maze — a. a puzzling path
2. dwellers — b. the going of a group
3. swarming — c. the center of a cave
4. hollow — d. a squirrel's hidden snack
5. stored — e. hamsters in their home

Skills Practice 1 • Vocabulary UNIT 2 • Lesson 1 83

Skills Practice 1, p. 83–84

Monitor Progress to Differentiate Instruction

Formal Assessment 

Selection Vocabulary Observe students' understanding of the vocabulary words and their definitions.

APPROACHING LEVEL

IF . . . students need extra help with the selection vocabulary,	**THEN . . .** refer to the ***Intervention Guide*** Unit 2, Lesson 1.
IF . . . students need extra help with the selection vocabulary,	**THEN . . .** use ***Reteach,*** page 34.

ON LEVEL

IF . . . students need practice using the selection vocabulary,	**THEN . . .** have students write sentences using the vocabulary words.

ABOVE LEVEL

IF . . . students understand the selection vocabulary,	**THEN . . .** use ***Challenge Activities*** page 31.

Teacher Tips

WORD BANK Remind students to find words from other resources, from their activities, and from family discussions and add them to the Word Bank. Students may also place antonyms and synonyms in the Word Bank.

FLUENCY By this time in Grade 3, good readers should be reading approximately 75 words per minute with fluency and expression. The only way to gain this fluency is by practicing. Have students reread the selection to you and to each other during Workshop to help build fluency. As students read, you may notice that some need work in building fluency. During Workshop, have these students choose a section of the text (a minimum of 160 words) to read several times to build fluency.

Reading and Responding

Teacher Tips

LISTENING During Workshop, have students listen to "One Small Place in a Tree" for a model of oral reading. While students listen, have them keep a list of any new or unfamiliar words they encounter in their Writer's Notebooks, and instruct them to check the words using a dictionary or glossary. Also, instruct students to listen for the lesson's vocabulary words and to check that the words make sense within the reading.

WRITE ABOUT IT! Have students write descriptions of an animal habitat they have seen near their home or school in their Writer's Notebooks.

Meet the Author and Illustrator

After students read the information about the author and illustrator, discuss the following questions with them:

- *How is Barbara Brenner able to connect many of the things she likes in her stories?* **Possible Answer** *By writing about animals and their habitats, she is able to creatively combine many of the things she likes such as science, nature, and animals.*
- *Why do you think Tom Leonard decided to illustrate children's books?* **Possible Answer** *He likes to draw pictures of nature using bright colors. Many children's books use bright colors and are about animals and nature.*

Theme Connections

Within the Selection

1. What different forms of life have lived in the tree? **Possible Answers** *timber beetles, a flying squirrel, bluebirds, mice*
2. What might happen if lightning struck the tree? **Possible Answer** *The tree would probably fall, but the hole would still provide homes for animals for many years to come.*

Beyond the Selection

3. What does "One Small Place in a Tree" tell you about animals and their habitats? **Possible Answer** *"One Small Place in a Tree" teaches us that many types of animals, from small insects to squirrels and birds, can live in a small hole in a tree. The tree provides this shelter even after it dies.*
4. What are some other animal habitats? **Possible Answers** *swamps, forests, oceans, caves*

Meet the Author

Barbara Brenner

Barbara Brenner likes poetry, art, science, animals, and nature. She writes stories that come from both her imagination and from real life. Over the years, Brenner has written over 70 children's books and has won many awards. She and her husband live in Pennsylvania.

Meet the Illustrator

Tom Leonard

Tom Leonard studied art at the Philadelphia College of Art. He has worked as an illustrator for newspapers and magazines, and is now illustrating children's books. He likes to draw pictures of nature using bright colors. Leonard taught art at the Philadelphia University of the Arts and often visits schools to talk about his work.

Animals and Their Habitats

Theme Connections

Within the Selection

1. What different forms of life have lived in the tree?
2. What might happen if lightning struck the tree?

Beyond the Selection

3. What does "One Small Place in a Tree" tell you about animals and their habitats?
4. What are some other animal habitats?

Write about It!

Describe an animal habitat you have seen near your home or school.

Remember to look for pictures of animal habitats to add to the **Concept/Question Board.**

Concept/Question Board

As students discuss "One Small Place in a Tree," encourage them to post ideas on the Board. Students might post questions, answers, comments, or other items related to the theme Animals and Their Habitats on the **Concept/Question Board.**

Teacher Tip

BEYOND THE SELECTION Have students summarize the information they have learned and tell how they might use it in further investigations.

Writer's Notebook

- Have students list in their Writer's Notebooks other nonfiction selections they have read in class or on their own.
- Have students compare the elements found in each selection.

OBJECTIVES

Students will

- learn /ī/ and regular plurals.
- review possessive nouns and pronouns.
- draft their summaries.
- learn note-taking strategies.

MATERIALS

- ***Skills Practice 1,*** pp. 85, 87–88, 91–92
- ***Transparency*** 3

Teacher Tip

VOCABULARY Encourage students to use the high-frequency words and the selection vocabulary words from this lesson in their writing.

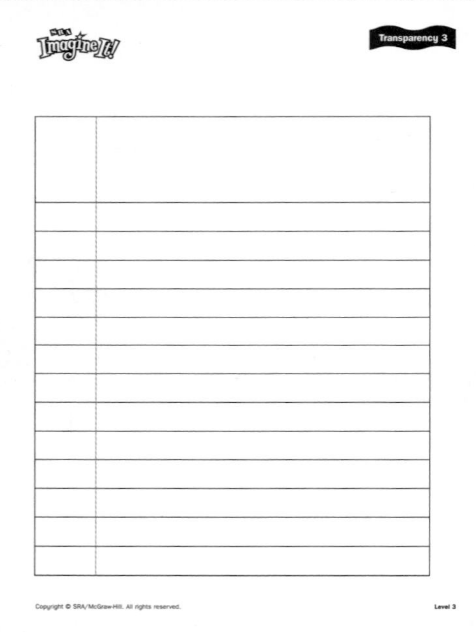

Transparency 3

Writing Summary

Drafting

Teach

- Tell students they will begin drafting their summaries.
- Remind students that during drafting it is most important to get their ideas down on paper. They will have time to revise and edit/proofread later.
- Have students review their graphic organizers in ***Skills Practice 1*** page 85 before they begin.
- Display ***Transparency*** 3, and model drafting your summary using the information from the graphic organizer. Remind students to write on every other line to leave room for revising and editing/proofreading marks.

Guided Practice

- Using the information you wrote on your graphic organizer, ask students to help you write an introductory sentence that includes the main idea. Have them help you create at least one other sentence of your paragraph based on the information in your graphic organizer.

Apply

Composing—Drafting Have students draft their summaries.

Spelling

/ī/, and Regular Plurals Pretest

Teach

- Tell students that to make most words plural, add *-s* or *-es.*
- Tell students that for words that end in:
  - *ch, sh, s, ss, x, z,* or *zz,* add *-es.*
  - consonant + *-y,* change the *y* to *i* and add *-es.*
  - *f,* change the *f* to *v,* and add *-es.*
  - vowel + *-y,* add *-s.*
  - silent *-e,* add *-s.*
- Tell students that /ī/ can be spelled *igh, _y,* and *_ie.*
- Split the class into two groups. Have one group write sentences for the words *fly, reply,* and *spy.* Have the other group write sentences for the words *flies, replies,* and *spies.* Have each group pick one person to come to the board and write each group's sentences.

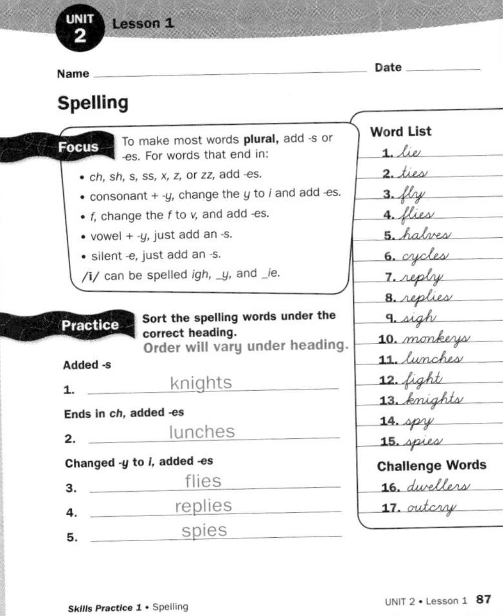

UNIT 2 Lesson 1

Name ______ Date ______

Spelling

Focus To make most words **plural,** add -s or -es. For words that end in:
- ch, sh, s, ss, x, z, or zz, add -es.
- consonant + -y, change the y to i and add -es.
- f, change the f to v, and add -es.
- vowel + -y, just add an -s.
- silent -e, just add an -s.

/ī/ can be spelled igh, _y, and _ie.

Practice Sort the spelling words under the correct heading.
Order will vary under heading.

Added -s
1. knights

Ends in ch, added -es
2. lunches

Changed -y to i, added -es
3. flies
4. replies
5. spies

Word List
1. lie
2. ties
3. fly
4. flies
5. halves
6. cycles
7. reply
8. replies
9. sigh
10. monkeys
11. lunches
12. fight
13. knights
14. spy
15. spies

Challenge Words
16. dwellers
17. outcry

Skills Practice 1 • Spelling UNIT 2 • Lesson 1 87

Skills Practice 1, p. 87

Guided Practice

Have students turn to ***Skills Practice 1*** page 87. Read the instructions with them, and complete the first two questions as a class.

Apply

Have students complete ***Skills Practice 1*** pages 87–88 on their own. Remind students that challenge words are not used in ***Skills Practice*** exercises.

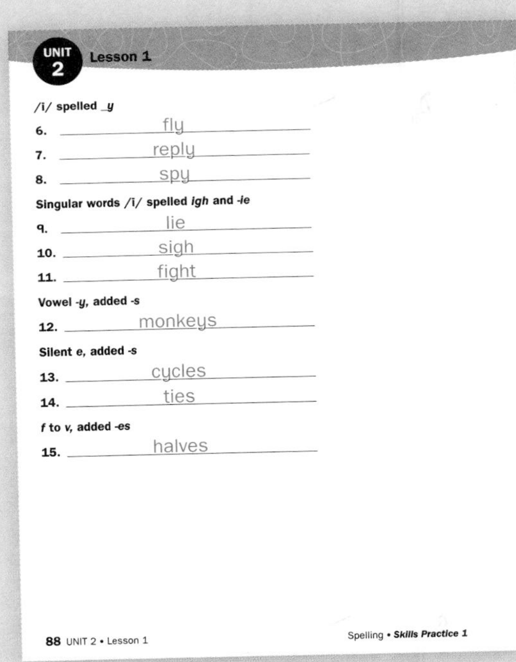

UNIT 2 Lesson 1

/ī/ spelled _y
6. fly
7. reply
8. spy

Singular words /ī/ spelled igh and -ie
9. lie
10. sigh
11. fight

Vowel -y, added -s
12. monkeys

Silent e, added -s
13. cycles
14. ties

f to v, added -es
15. halves

88 UNIT 2 • Lesson 1 Spelling • Skills Practice 1

Skills Practice 1, p. 88

Formal Assessment 

Monitor Progress to Differentiate Instruction

Spelling Note whether students incorporate spelling patterns as they write sentences using the spelling words.

APPROACHING LEVEL

IF . . . students need to practice spelling this week's words,	**THEN . . .** have them complete ***Reteach*** page 35.

ON LEVEL

IF . . . students can spell this week's spelling words,	**THEN . . .** have them write a list of five words with consonant blends that were not on this lesson's spelling list on a separate sheet of paper.

ABOVE LEVEL

IF . . . students are ready for a challenge,	**THEN . . .** have them complete ***Challenge Activities*** page 32.

Monitor Progress 

to Differentiate Instruction
Formal Assessment

Taking Notes Make sure students understand what information to include in notes.

APPROACHING LEVEL

IF . . . students need to practice taking notes, **THEN . . .** have them fill in a chart similar to the one on ***Skills Practice 1*** page 92 for the unit investigation.

ON LEVEL

IF . . . students have an understanding of taking notes, **THEN . . .** have them take notes for the unit investigation.

ABOVE LEVEL

IF . . . students are ready for a challenge, **THEN . . .** have them work with a less proficient student or with an English learner during Workshop.

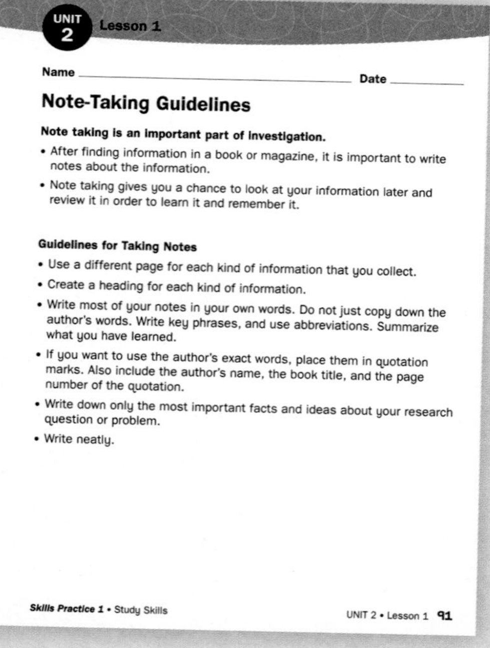

UNIT 2 Lesson 1

Name ______________________ Date ________

Note-Taking Guidelines

Note taking is an important part of investigation.

- After finding information in a book or magazine, it is important to write notes about the information.
- Note taking gives you a chance to look at your information later and review it in order to learn it and remember it.

Guidelines for Taking Notes

- Use a different page for each kind of information that you collect.
- Create a heading for each kind of information.
- Write most of your notes in your own words. Do not just copy down the author's words. Write key phrases, and use abbreviations. Summarize what you have learned.
- If you want to use the author's exact words, place them in quotation marks. Also include the author's name, the book title, and the page number of the quotation.
- Write down only the most important facts and ideas about your research question or problem.
- Write neatly.

Skills Practice 1 • Study Skills   UNIT 2 • Lesson 1 91

Skills Practice 1, p. 91

Study Skills

Note-Taking

Teach

✦ Explain to students that taking notes is an important skill to learn for school and for life. Tell students that people take notes for many reasons. For example people take notes for school or college, they take notes about an informative TV show such as a cooking program, or they take notes when they want to remember what someone said. Have students discuss reasons why they think someone might need to take notes.

✦ Have students turn to ***Skills Practice 1*** page 91. Write the following techniques on the board and explain them to students. Tell students that learning these techniques will be helpful for their investigations and writing assignments.

- Use a different page for each kind of information you encounter.
- Create a heading for each kind of information.
- Summarize the author's ideas in your own words. Use key phrases and abbreviate when possible.
- Use quotation marks when it is important to use the author's exact words. Also, record the author's name, the book's title, and the page number of the quotation.
- Only take notes on the most important and interesting parts.
- Write neatly so that your notes are easy to read.

✦ Explain that the reason it is important to record author and title information is to avoid plagiarism. Explain that plagiarism is taking someone else's words or ideas without that person's permission.

Guided Practice

Work with students to select appropriate books or articles from the Internet, and show them how to create a bibliographical citation using the source copyright information. Have students write their citation on the bottom of ***Skills Practice 1*** page 91.

Apply

Have students complete ***Skills Practice 1*** page 92, either individually or with a partner.

Grammar, Usage, and Mechanics

Possessive Nouns and Pronouns

Teach

- Review the forms of possessive nouns and pronouns by asking students to provide examples. If necessary, remind students that possessive nouns use apostrophes to indicate ownership.
- Write the following sentences on the board, and have students identify the possessive nouns and pronouns.
  - The bunny's ears were white and pink. *bunny's*
  - The ants' home was a maze of tunnels. *ants'*
  - Heidi gave her dog a bath every week. *her*
  - The ducks fed their ducklings in a nest by the pond. *their*

Guided Practice

Have students construct simple sentences using possessive nouns and pronouns. Have them write the sentences on the board.

Apply

For further practice using possessives, have students edit a writing assignment for errors in possession, or have them find sentences in which they can change possessive nouns to possessive pronouns.

Differentiating Instruction **English Learner**

IF . . . students are native Spanish speakers, **THEN . . .** they may be confused by the use of the apostrophe and *s* to show possession, because this construction does not exist in Spanish. Explain to students that *'s* serves the same purpose as the preposition *de* in Spanish.

Day 4

Preparing to Read

OBJECTIVES

Students will

- identify and learn how regular plurals are formed.
- build fluency.

MATERIALS

- ***Transparency*** 48

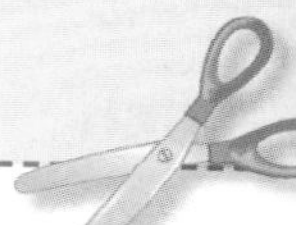

Daily Oral Practice

Daily News

Today!

Oh . . . what is that I see? I see bluebirds in a nest high up in the branches in a tree. Oh . . . what is that I hear? I hear a squirrel digging holes to hide her nuts. I will look and listen, but I will not touch. I will let nature be.

- Write the daily news on the board or on chart paper. Then have students read the daily news in unison to practice fluency.
- As a review of yesterday's word structure lesson, ask a volunteer to identify any regular plural nouns in the message. *bluebirds, branches, holes, nuts*

Differentiating Instruction **English Learner**

IF . . . students have difficulty understanding the possessive pronoun *her* used in the daily news, **THEN . . .** explain that authors sometimes use *her* or *him* to refer to an animal, depending on whether the animal is male or female.

Word Structure

Regular Plurals

✦ Use ***Transparency*** 48 with the word lines from Day 3.

Line 1	claws	bugs	beetles	spaces
Line 2	foxes	branches	bushes	dishes
Line 3	babies	countries	puppies	stories
Line 4	calves	wives	leaves	wolves

✦ Have students tell the rules for forming regular plurals. If necessary, remind them that they should add an *s* to most words that end with a consonant or an *e*, and they should add *es* to words that end in *x*, *ch*, or *sh*. For words that end with a *y*, they must drop the *y* and then add *ies*. Finally, for words that end with /f/ spelled *f*, they need to change the *f* to *v* and add *es*. Tell students the exception to the last rule is for words that end with /f/ spelled *ff* as in *cliff*. They will need to add an *s* to make such words plural.

✦ Have students read the words using normal intonation and expression.

Developing Oral Language

- Create sentences for students to complete using words from the word lines. Ask students to point to and read words from Lines 1–4 to fill in the blanks. For example: We are studying the *countries* of Europe in history class. The *branches* on the trees were blowing in the wind. After modeling a few examples, have students make their own clue sentences.
- Ask a volunteer to give the singular form of a word on the board and use it in a sentence. Then have another volunteer use the plural form in another sentence. **Possible Answer** *bush; A bird in the hand is better than two in the* bush. Bushes *are good hiding places for birds.*
- Have a volunteer choose a word from the word lines, say it, and then use it in a sentence. **Possible Answer** Wolves *are my favorite animal.* Have that student choose another student to extend the sentence by adding to the beginning or end of the original sentence. **Possible Answer** Wolves *are my favorite animal because they run in packs.*

Teacher Tip

BLENDING During Workshop, work with students who have difficulty blending words by using Routine 1 for sound-by-sound blending or Routine 3 for whole-word blending.

Reading and Responding

A tree hole. One small place in a tree. How does it get there? Who lives inside?

Suppose that you could watch a hole from its beginning. You might see something like this:

138

139

OBJECTIVES

Students will

- use the comprehension skill Author's Purpose and Cause and Effect.
- review the comprehension strategy Clarifying.
- review fluency.
- investigate the theme Animals and Their Habitats using the Inquiry process.

MATERIALS

- ***Student Reader,*** Book 1 pp. 138–157
- ***Transparency*** 15

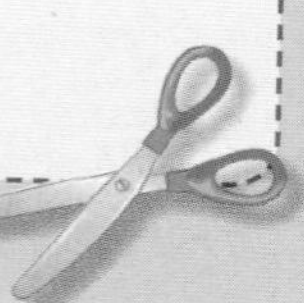

2nd READ

Comprehension Skill

Reread the selection using the comprehension skills Author's Purpose and Cause and Effect.

Author's Purpose

Remind students that authors have many reasons for writing. Tell students to look for clues to the author's purpose for this text while rereading the selection. Understanding the author's purpose helps readers focus on important details in a text, and also helps students make sense of these details. Ask students what they think the author's purpose was for writing "One Small Place in a Tree." **Possible Answer** *The author wants her readers to know how trees provide a habitat for many different life forms.*

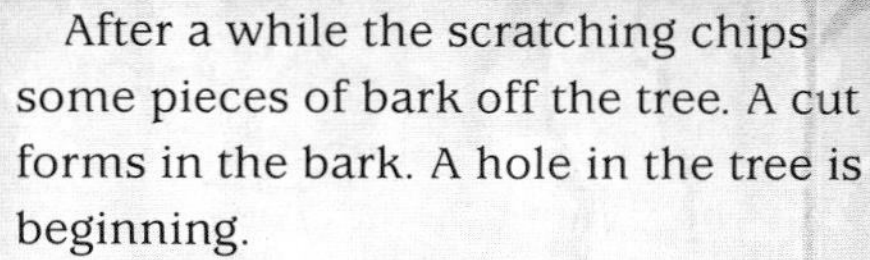

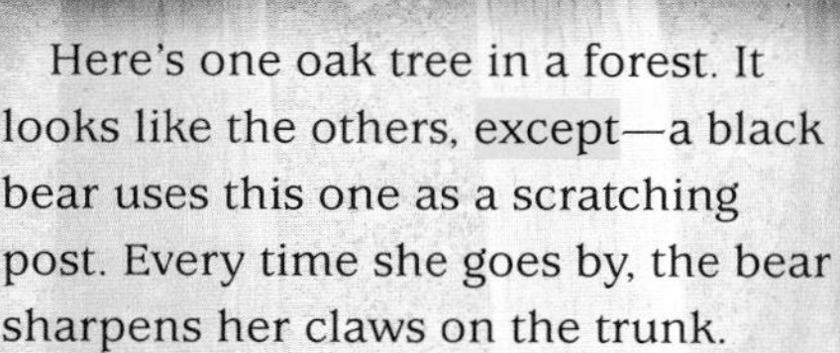

Here's one oak tree in a forest. It looks like the others, except—a black bear uses this one as a scratching post. Every time she goes by, the bear sharpens her claws on the trunk.

You're walking in the woods. You see the tree and notice the scratch marks on the bark. Maybe you even catch a glimpse of the bear!

140

After a while the scratching chips some pieces of bark off the tree. A cut forms in the bark. A hole in the tree is beginning.

Next time you're walking there, you see that tiny bugs have found the cut. They're timber beetles, and they're about to set up housekeeping.

141

Reading with a Writer's Eye

Text Structure: Technique

Explain to students that authors decide on and use certain types of text structure techniques to tell a story. Barbara Brenner tells the story of how one small place in a tree can provide a home to many different animals. She gives facts and examples in her story. She also uses pictures to help tell the story. Ask students:

- *How does the author's use of pictures help tell the story?* **Possible Answer** *The pictures describe the author's words and help the readers see exactly what is happening inside and outside the tree.*

Expanding Vocabulary

You will introduce seven additional vocabulary words to students as the selection is reread.

suppose (sə p • pōz') *v.* to imagine being possible (page 139)
Do you *suppose* there is an owl living in the tree?

Word Structure

Regular plurals: others, claws, woods, marks

Reading and Responding

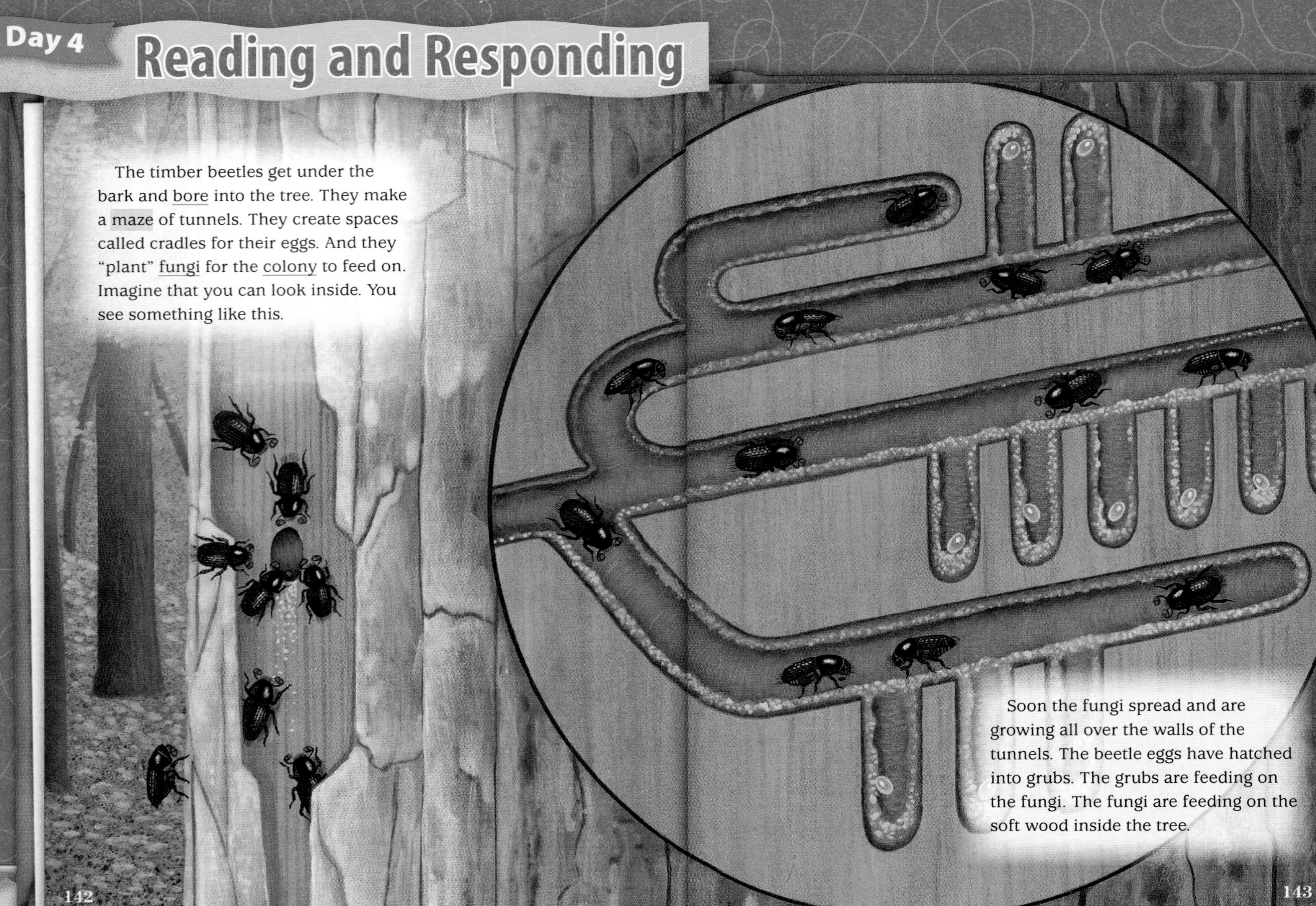

Expanding Vocabulary

bore (bōr) *v.* to make a hole by digging or drilling (page 142)

Some insects *bore* into trees to make homes.

fungi (fun′ • gī) *n.* plural form of **fungus:** a large group of living things that have cell walls similar to those in plants, but that have no flowers, leaves, or green coloring. Fungi live on plant or animal matter. (page 142)

Did you know that mushrooms are *fungi*?

colony (kol′ • ən • ē) *n.* a group of animals or plants of the same kind that live together (page 142)

The ant *colony* nested in the rotten log.

Comprehension Skill

Cause and Effect

Review cause and effect with students by reminding students that "what happened" in a story is called the *effect*. "What prompted it to happen" is the *cause*. Tell students to think about what happened in a story and why it happened when reading. You may want to write a cause-and-effect chart on the board to chart the cause-and-effect relationships throughout the selection. Explain the following cause-and-effect relationships on pages 142–143.

Cause	Effect
Timber beetles bore into trees and create tunnels.	They are able to make spaces to lay their eggs.
The beetles plant fungi.	The grubs feed on the fungi.

The beetle grubs become full-grown timber beetles.

They eat their way out of the chambers and make more holes in the tree.

On your next visit you count more than ten holes. But the first one is the largest.

144

One time when you're near the tree, you actually hear the sound of the beetles chewing wood.

A red-bellied woodpecker hears it, too.

The bird flies to the tree holes. It spears the beetles with its sharp beak, or pulls them out with its long tongue.

Many woodpeckers visit the oak tree to eat. After a summer they've cleared the holes of beetles and beetle grubs. But they've made the big hole even bigger.

145

Reading with a Writer's Eye

Language Use

Tell students that authors are careful when choosing their words. When writing expository text, authors sometimes use descriptive language to describe what they are explaining. By using descriptive language so readers can "see" or "hear" what they are explaining, writers can create vivid pictures that help readers better understand characters, events, and settings. Barbara Brenner uses descriptive language in some of her descriptions of the tree and the animals who inhabit it. If time permits, have students write their own descriptive sentences about animals and their habitats in order to practice using descriptive language. Ask students:

- *What are some vivid descriptions on pages 144–145?* **Possible Answer** *Sometimes you can hear the sound of beetles chewing wood. The woodpecker spears the beetles with its sharp beak or pulls them out with its long tongue. But they've made the hole even bigger.*

Expanding Vocabulary

actually (ak′ • shū • əl • lē′) *adv.* in fact; really (page 145)

I *actually* got to see a lion at the zoo!

Differentiating Instruction — English Learner

IF . . . students have difficulty expressing cause-and-effect relationships, **THEN . . .** have them use the linguistic pattern in the following sentence to describe events in their daily lives: I was late because I missed the bus.

Reading and Responding

Now disease strikes. Bacteria come in through the hole in the tree. You won't see the bacteria—they're too small. But you can see the damage they've done. The tree has heart rot. It's dying inside and out.

Bark begins to loosen and fall off. The hole is now so large that you can actually see inside. It has become a hollow place that looks as if it could be home for something.

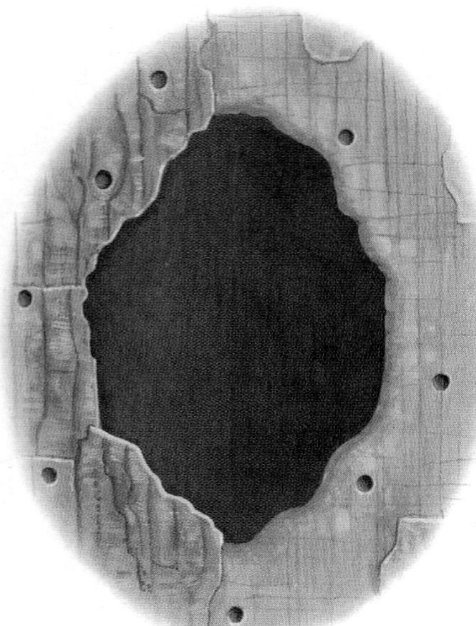

146

The first animal to use it is a flying squirrel. You find the squirrel "holed up" in there one winter day. You notice that it has stored some nuts under the loose bark around the hole.

147

Comprehension Skill

Cause and Effect

Have students continue to read carefully to find out what happened and why it happened. Ask students to identify cause-and-effect relationships on pages 146–147. Add students' findings to the chart on the board.

Cause	Effect
Bacteria enters the tree.	The tree gets heart rot.
Bark loosens and falls from the tree.	The hole grows larger.
The hole grows larger.	The hole becomes a hollow place.

Teacher Tip

WRITING Tell students to think about what they learned in Reading with a Writer's Eye when writing their own stories.

Reading with a Writer's Eye

Text Structure: Techniques

Remind students that authors like Barbara Brenner use specific techniques within the text structure to help tell a story. Barbara's illustrator, Tom Leonard, uses special pictures to help tell the story of the bluebirds on pages 148–149. Barbara also uses examples to elaborate or explain facts to help tell her story. Ask students the following questions:

- *How do the pictures of the bluebirds help tell the story?* **Possible Answers** *Readers can see how the birds build the nest in the hole. We can see how the birds are fed.*
- *How does the author use examples to explain facts?* **Possible Answers** *The author is giving the facts of how the tree is a habitat. Some examples that the author uses are squirrels and bluebirds.*

Expanding Vocabulary

line (līn) *v.* to cover the inside of (page 148)
The college students *line* their drawers with paper before putting their sweaters inside.

Word Structure

Regular plurals: nuts, bluebirds, weeds, eggs, chicks

Reading and Responding

By this time the oak tree is no longer sending out leaves. Almost all of its bark is gone. But the hole-dwellers don't seem to care.

For the next three springs, the hole in the tree is a nest for the same pair of bluebirds.

150

For the next three winters, it's home to a family of white-footed mice.

In all those three years, the tree hasn't grown at all. This oak tree is dead. But—the hole is full of life.

A hairy woodpecker sometimes comes to roost there.

A gray squirrel often uses the hole as a hiding place.

When the hole has water in it, you can sometimes see a tree frog there.

151

Expanding Vocabulary

roost (ro͞ost) *v.* to rest or sleep as a bird does (page 151)

The pigeons *roost* on the window ledges during the day.

Word Structure

Regular plurals: leaves, dwellers, springs, bluebirds, eggs, insects

Comprehension Skill

Cause and Effect

Have students continue to identify the cause-and-effect relationships in the selection. Add their observations under the appropriate headings on the board.

Cause	Effect
Lightning, wind, or rain hit the tree.	The tree falls down.
A hole in a log is all that is left.	The hole continues to provide a home to many living things.

One day lightning, or a high wind, or heavy rain, or snow will bring this dead tree down. Many years later all that may be left will be a log with a hole in it.

But the hole will still be a place for living things. A small garter snake may cool off in there.

A redback salamander may lay its eggs there.

Or maybe a hammock spider will make a web across the hole to catch swarming insects.

Living trees are important. But so are dead and dying trees. A dead tree often has a hole—one small place that is usually home for something.

152

153

Checking Comprehension

Ask students the following questions to check their comprehension of the story:

- *What did you learn about trees from this selection?* **Possible Answers** *They provide shelter to many forms of life both while they are alive and after they die.*
- *What kinds of animals choose a tree as their habitat?* **Possible Answers** *Many types of animals live in a tree: beetles, birds, squirrels, mice, frogs, snakes, and insects.*
- *Why is the tree a good habitat?* **Possible Answers** *It provides shelter from the environment and from predators. It provides food and water.*

Differentiating Instruction **English Learner**

IF . . . students have difficulty with sequence words, **THEN . . .** point to any set of pictures that shows sequence as you review simple order words such as *first, next, last, before,* and *after.*

Supporting the Reading

Comprehension Strategy: Clarifying

Teach

Remind students that Clarifying takes several forms. It can involve clarifying the meanings of words, passages, or ideas. To clarify the meanings of words, students can use context clues, word structure, apposition, or outside sources such as a dictionary. To clarify difficult passages or ideas, students can reread the confusing part of the text to see if they missed something. In some texts, charts or graphics can help clarify confusing passages and ideas.

Guided Practice

Students need to practice clarifying techniques so that they develop the ability to use the techniques automatically. In a whole-group discussion, ask students to share words or passages they needed to clarify while reading "One Small Place in a Tree." Have students share the techniques they used to understand the confusing words and passages. Record their input in a two-column chart on the board or on ***Transparency*** 15. You can use the following as an example to get started:

Confusing Words or Passages	How I Clarified Them
On page 143, I didn't understand how the fungi could feed all of the beetles.	I read the whole page again, and I understood that the fungi spread and grew. That must have been enough for the beetles.

Apply

- Ask students to select three passages or sentences listed on the completed two-column chart. Have students rewrite the passages in their own words. Allow students to share their rewritten passages with the rest of the class.
- Encourage students to experiment with different techniques for coming to an understanding of things that are confusing. Remind students to talk through their clarification processes aloud to help organize their thoughts and become comfortable with the strategy.

Imagine It! Transparency 15

Two-Column Chart

 Level 3

Transparency 15

Fluency

The selection "One Small Place in a Tree" is expository text that reads like a story. Point out its conversational style to students. When reading with students, be sure to emphasize automaticity, or the ability to decode words spontaneously. The boy in the story learns something new on every page, just as the readers might. Ask students to name some of the emotions that should be conveyed during the oral reading of this selection. *excitement, anticipation*

- Model fluency by reading pages 150–151 from "One Small Place in a Tree." Have students follow along in the ***Student Reader.*** Remind students that to read with automaticity, readers sometimes read and then reread in order to learn all of the words in a story.
- After you have read through the passage, call on a volunteer to read the first paragraph. Before the student begins, be sure to clarify any words that may be unfamiliar to the student. Encourage the reader to also use expression, or to read with appropriate excitement and anticipation.
- After the volunteer has finished, have all students chorally read the passage several times until they can read it naturally with good phrasing.
- For additional practice, have students work in pairs reading different passages to each other from this selection. Monitor them to make sure they are reading the passage fluently.

Leveled Readers

To help students build fluency and strengthen their vocabulary and comprehension skills, have them read the ***Leveled Readers*** for this unit. Use each student's Oral Fluency Assessment score from the previous lesson assessment to diagnose the appropriate ***Leveled Readers.***

Fluency Tip

FLUENCY For additional fluency practice, have students read a passage to you independently.

Differentiating Instruction — **English Learner**

IF . . . students need extra help in gaining fluency, **THEN . . .** for partner reading, pair English Learners with proficient English speakers.

Science Inquiry

Genre Recipe

✦ Tell students that a recipe is a set of instructions for preparing food or drink.

Feature Bold Type

Bold type is used for emphasis in text.

Ask students to point to and read the text in bold type. Then ask students why this part of the text is placed in bold type. *to emphasize the fact that this instruction is very important*

Reading "Please Feed the Birds"

Have students take turns reading "Please Feed the Birds" aloud. Ask students what part of this text is a recipe. *the list of ingredients and the instructions on how to prepare them* Ask students how this article relates to the theme Animals and Their Habitats. *Answers will vary.* Make sure students read the bold type in the text.

Think Link

1. Why can winter be a difficult time for some birds? **Possible Answer** *The birds eat insects that cannot be found in the winter.*
2. Why is the last line of text in paragraph 2 emphasized? **Possible Answer** *It is a very important instruction and the bold type emphasizes it so that readers see it and pay attention to the information.*
3. How is the list of ingredients helpful? **Possible Answer** *When someone is going to make a recipe, it is helpful to know in advance what ingredients will be needed.*

Teacher Tip

SELECTION VOCABULARY Review the meaning of the highlighted selection vocabulary words *swarming* and *stored* in "Please Feed the Birds."

Science Inquiry

Please Feed the Birds

Genre

A **recipe** is a set of instructions for preparing food or drink.

Feature

Bold Type is used for emphasis in text.

Birds use energy at a fast rate. Therefore, they need high-energy foods to replace what they burn. Insects are a main food source for many kinds of birds. However, in fall and winter, once-swarming insects can become scarce. So some bird lovers help their feathered friends stay fed.

Suet, or raw beef fat, is a great high-energy food for birds. Stores sell packaged suet cakes, but you can make your own. Homemade cakes can be made with beef fat purchased from a grocery store. If you want to try this recipe, ask an adult for help. **Never turn on a stove by yourself!**

Hard Suet Cakes

$\frac{1}{2}$ pound fresh ground suet
$\frac{1}{3}$ cup sunflower seed
$\frac{2}{3}$ cup wild birdseed mix
$\frac{1}{8}$ cup chopped peanuts
$\frac{1}{4}$ cup raisins

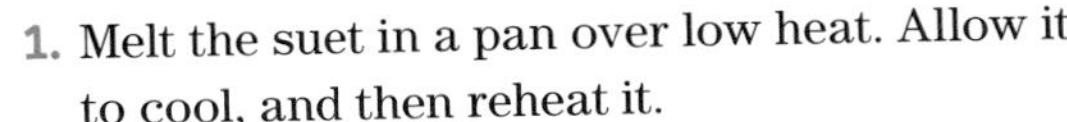

1. Melt the suet in a pan over low heat. Allow it to cool, and then reheat it.
2. Mix the rest of the ingredients in a large bowl.
3. Let the suet cool until it starts to get thick; then stir it into the mixture in the bowl. Mix well.
4. Pour into a pie pan or square mold to cool.

When the suet cakes are cool and hard, put them in a feeder. The most common type of suet feeder is a small wire cage. Attach the cage to a tree trunk, or hang it from a branch. Suet cakes can be stored in a freezer for up to three months.

Think Link

1. Why can winter be a difficult time for some birds?
2. Why is the last line of text in paragraph 2 emphasized?
3. How is the list of ingredients helpful?

Try It!

As you work on your investigation, think about how you can use bold type to emphasize an important sentence in your final presentation.

Inquiry Connection

Have students discuss how using bold type might be helpful in their investigations about animals and their habitats. For example, students might want to put their headings in bold type so readers can easily see the information to be introduced next in the report.

Concept/Question Board

After students read "Please Feed the Birds," encourage them to post questions, answers, comments, photographs, drawings, or other items related to the theme Animals and Their Habitats on the **Concept/Question Board.**

Teacher Tip

GENERATING QUESTIONS Questions with "yes" or "no" answers or questions about facts, which usually begin with *who, what, where,* or *when* are good for starting the questioning process, but typically don't require deep thought, reflection, and research. Good inquiry questions will often be *how* or *why* questions. For example, *How can our city protect the several species of endangered frogs in our area?* is a better inquiry question than *Will the frogs become extinct?* or *Who can help save endangered species?*

Inquiry Process

Step 1—Generating Ideas and Questions

Whole-Group Time

Whole Group

- Remind students that they can post questions and answers about unit selections on the **Concept/Question Board.** They should feel free to respond to others' questions as well.
- Ask students how their understanding of animal habitats has changed since reading the selection "One Small Place in a Tree." Have they learned anything new? What have they found most interesting? Have their ideas about animals or animal habitats changed? Write student responses on the board or on chart paper. Remind students of the note-taking skills they have been practicing, and have them take notes on what they learned in their Writer's Notebook. If they don't mention the idea that animals often have to find new habitats because habitats change, then suggest this in the discussion.
- To help students get ideas for possible investigation topics, conduct a brainstorming session with the class to generate ideas and topics about the theme Animals and Their Habitats. Encourage students to write the ideas and topics on the board. Also have them record the ideas they find most interesting in their Writer's Notebook.
- Continue to model how to turn stories and ideas into questions. Remind students of a question you generated from your story about animals losing their habitats because of new land development: *How can I help these animals?* Ask students if your story makes them think of other stories about animals and animal habitats. Have them share their stories or questions. As they share, model how to turn their stories into questions and write these questions on the board. After modeling a few times, have students start sharing questions that they generated from these stories.

Small-Group Time

Small Group

- Have students break into their small groups. Suggest that students post some of the stories they shared on the **Concept/Question Board.** Remind them that any stories and questions they share will give other students ideas that might help the whole class learn more about the theme.

✦ Using the brainstorming ideas on the board, other notes they have taken, and ideas about animals and animal habitats that they took from "Building Blocks for Survival" and "One Small Place in a Tree," groups should start formulating potential investigation questions.

Concept/Question Board

✦ Have groups post their ideas and questions on the **Concept/ Question Board.**

✦ Help students decide how to organize and arrange the **Concept/Question Board.** Consider separating the board into sections for concepts, questions, articles, pictures, conjectures, and other artifacts.

✦ Continue to encourage use of the **Concept/Question Board** by recognizing and thanking students for their contributions. Incorporate discussion of those items into classroom discussions whenever possible. Remember to also model by posting your own questions and ideas.

Inquiry Rubric

To assess Generating Ideas and Questions, see the Inquiry Rubrics in the Level Appendix.

Teacher Tip

SOURCES FOR IDEAS Remind students that they can use something they learned from reading "One Small Place in a Tree" as an idea for their investigation. They can use ideas from other selections they have read as well.

Monitor Progress

to Differentiate Instruction

Formal Assessment

Generating Questions Note students' ability to generate questions.

APPROACHING LEVEL

IF . . . students are having difficulty generating questions about animals and their habitats,	**THEN . . .** have them reread "One Small Place In a Tree."

ON LEVEL

IF . . . students need to practice generating questions,	**THEN . . .** have them pose questions directly relating to "One Small Place in a Tree."

ABOVE LEVEL

IF . . . students understand how to generate questions,	**THEN . . .** have them start outlining an investigation plan using one of their questions. Remind students that their group may or may not decide to use this question; however, they are free to research questions on their own.

OBJECTIVES

Students will

- ✦ revise and edit/proofread their summaries.
- ✦ learn to spell /ī/ and regular plural words.
- ✦ learn question-asking skills.
- ✦ practice note-taking strategies.

MATERIALS

- ✦ Routine 16
- ✦ ***Transparencies*** 17, 17A
- ✦ ***Skills Practice 1,*** p. 86
- ✦ ***Language Arts Handbook,*** pp. 30–41

Writing Summary

ROUTINE 16

Revising and Editing/Proofreading

Teach

- ✦ Use Routine 16, and ask students to remind you of the stages of the writing process. *prewriting, drafting, revising, editing/proofreading, publishing.*
- ✦ Tell students that writers do not always complete the stages in that order. Writers might revise in the middle of drafting or prewriting when they have a longer activity, such as the fantasy story in Unit 1. Other times, if the writing is shorter, or different skills are involved, writers may combine some of the stages of the writing process. Tell students that this does not mean that writers do not do that stage, but that they work on two stages at one time.
- ✦ Tell students that they will work on revising and editing/proofreading during this lesson.
- ✦ Review the revising and editing/proofreading stages of the writing process in ***Language Arts Handbook*** pages 30–41.
- ✦ Remind students that as they revise they need to make sure they have captured the main points of the information they read. While editing/proofreading, students need to look for spelling, grammar, and punctuation errors.
- ✦ Remind students of the proofreading marks by displaying ***Transparencies*** 17 and 17A.

How Can I Improve My Writing?

When you are done with your draft, it is a good idea to put it aside for a while. You might get some new ideas when you aren't thinking so hard about your writing. You make your writing better during **revising**. If you have written your draft on a computer, you may want to save each new version in a separate file.

Charlie knew that revising also takes a while. She would need to read her writing several times, looking for ways to improve it. She would also let her classmates read her writing. They might spot ways to improve her description that she may have missed. Charlie knew that these questions based on the traits of writing would also help.

Ideas
- Is the main idea clear?
- Do I stay on the topic?

Organization
- Do I follow the order I decided on in prewriting?

Vocabulary Strategies
- Do I repeat some words too often?
- Do I use the best words to describe my face?

Sentence Fluency
- Do my sentences read smoothly?
- Do I use sentences that are too short or too long?

Voice
- Do I show my audience my face with words?

30 How Can I Improve My Writing? • The Writing Process

Language Arts Handbook, p. 30

Transparency 17 17A

Proofreading Marks

¶ Indent.	¶ Dad read nursery rhymes to my sister and me when we were young. Each of us had a favorite rhyme. My sister liked "Jack and Jill." Dad must have read it to her 1,000 times!
∧ Add something.	I also liked it, but my ∧ one was "Three Little Kittens." (favorite)
Take out something.	That rhyme is about ~~the~~ kittens who lost their mittens.
≡ Make a capital letter.	i don't ask dad to read to me anymore.
/ Make a small letter.	Now, I ask if I can read to Him.
sp Check spelling.	What shood I reed to him first?
⊙ Add a period.	I think he will like this one ⊙

 SRA Imagine It! • Level 3 • Transparency 17 • 17A Level 3

Transparencies 17, 17A

Writing, continued

Guided Practice

- Using the summary you created earlier in the lesson, revise your writing. Add a missed detail, and then ask students to help you add another. Using the proofreading marks, correct errors in spelling, grammar, or punctuation. Have students help you make further corrections. Point out a word and ask students if it is spelled correctly based on the spelling rules and patterns they have learned (cvc, cvcc, ccvc, and so on).
- Have students turn to ***Skills Practice 1*** page 86 to read and discuss the revising and editing/proofreading checklist.

Apply

Composing—Revising and Editing/Proofreading Have students revise and edit/proofread their summaries. Have students refer to revising and editing/proofreading checklists on ***Skills Practice 1*** page 86.

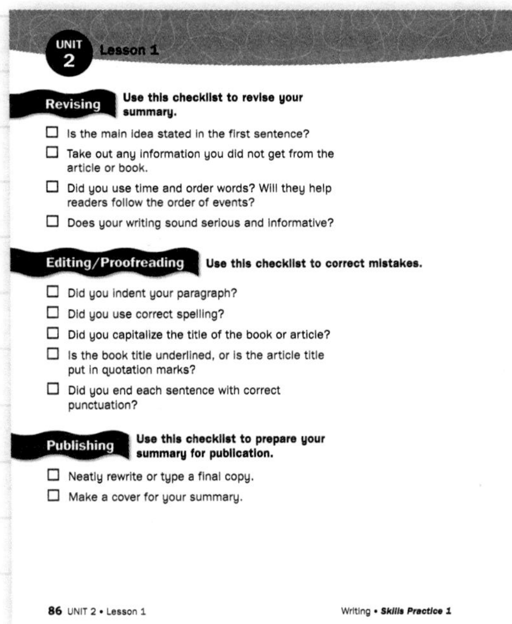
UNIT 2 Lesson 1

Revising — Use this checklist to revise your summary.

- ☐ Is the main idea stated in the first sentence?
- ☐ Take out any information you did not get from the article or book.
- ☐ Did you use time and order words? Will they help readers follow the order of events?
- ☐ Does your writing sound serious and informative?

Editing/Proofreading — Use this checklist to correct mistakes.

- ☐ Did you indent your paragraph?
- ☐ Did you use correct spelling?
- ☐ Did you capitalize the title of the book or article?
- ☐ Is the book title underlined, or is the article title put in quotation marks?
- ☐ Did you end each sentence with correct punctuation?

Publishing — Use this checklist to prepare your summary for publication.

- ☐ Neatly rewrite or type a final copy.
- ☐ Make a cover for your summary.

86 UNIT 2 • Lesson 1 Writing • *Skills Practice 1*

Skills Practice 1, p. 86

Spelling

/ī/ and Regular Plurals

Teach

- Students will learn to spell plurals and words with /ī/ spelled *igh*, *_y*, and *_ie*.
- **Visualizing Strategy** Tell students that sometimes the correct spelling of a word can be determined just by looking at a word to see if it "looks right." Students can use spelling patterns from words they already know to decide whether a new word has used an incorrect pattern even if they have not seen the word before.

Guided Practice

Write the following sentence on the board: *The flie spys as the knites sygh.* Have students circle the misspelled words and rewrite them correctly. The corrected sentence should read: *The fly spies as the knights sigh.*

Study Skills

Taking Notes

Teach

- Remind students that knowing how to take good notes will be helpful as they work on writing projects and unit investigations. Explain that when taking notes, students should record the most important and interesting parts of what they learn. Abbreviating is fine as long as they remember what the abbreviations mean.
- Remind students to use their own words when taking notes and to record the author's name and the page number when they directly quote the author's words.

Guided Practice

Have students listen and take notes as you read a page from "One Small Place in a Tree." Then have students share their notes with the class. Lead a discussion in which students identify which notes are most effective and why.

Apply

Have students revise their notes if necessary, and write a short summary of the page you read based on their notes.

Listening/Speaking/Viewing

Asking Questions

Teach

- Explain that asking and responding to questions is an important skill to learn.
- Tell students we interact with others to learn and to share. However, interactions sometimes take a lot of thought, especially when forming questions or responding to questions. Before we speak, we should carefully think about what we want to say. This will help us clarify ideas and explain information.

Guided Practice

Ask a student a question about "One Small Place in a Tree" or another relevant topic. Have another student summarize the answer the first student provided to your question.

Apply

- Tell students they are going to conduct peer interviews. In pairs, have students take turns asking one another questions about "One Small Place in a Tree" or about the theme Animals and Their Habitats. *Why are trees important to animals? They provide safe habitats for animals. What do animals look for in a habitat? They look for protection, shelter, food, and water.* Remind students to ask questions carefully, and to listen and answer questions thoughtfully.
- As a class, invite students to share what they learned from their partners. Students should be able to paraphrase others' words and comments.

Preparing to Read Review

OBJECTIVES

Students will

- review /ī/spelled *_igh*, *_y*, and *_ie*.
- review consonant blends at the beginning or end of words.
- review regular plural nouns.
- build fluency.

MATERIALS

- ***Sound/Spelling Card*** 29
- ***Transparencies*** 44, 48

Phonics and Fluency

Use ***Transparency*** 44 with the blending lines and sentences from Days 1 and 2 to review /ī/ spelled *_igh*, *_y*, and *_ie;* and consonant blends at the beginning or end of words. Have students read the words and sentences on the blending lines. Then have students name other words with these sound/spellings which could be added to the lines.

Line 1	high	tight	bright	lightning
Line 2	shy	fly	dryer	crying
Line 3	lie	pie	tries	untie
Line 4	nest	place	scratch	forest

Sentence 1	From the trees, the bird flies right into the night sky.
Sentence 2	I might even need to dry my clothes in the sunlight.

Word Structure  

Use ***Transparency*** 48 with the word lines from Days 3 and 4 to review regular plural nouns. Have students read the words on the word lines. Then have students think of new regular plurals to add to each line.

Line 1	claws	bugs	beetles	spaces
Line 2	foxes	branches	bushes	dishes
Line 3	babies	countries	puppies	stories
Line 4	calves	wives	leaves	wolves

Reading and Responding Review

OBJECTIVES

Students will
- review selection vocabulary.
- review the comprehension strategies Asking Questions, Clarifying, and Visualizing.
- review the comprehension skills Author's Purpose and Cause and Effect.

MATERIALS

- ***Student Reader*** Book 1, pp. 134–155
- ***Transparency*** 46

Selection Vocabulary

To review the selection vocabulary with students, organize them into small groups of three or four. Give each group 2 or 3 words. Ask each group to write a definition for each vocabulary word in their own words. When they are finished, have a volunteer from each group share their definitions with the class.

Selection Vocabulary

except (ek • sept') *prep.* only (page 140)

maze (māz) *n.* a confusing series of paths or passageways through which people might get lost (page 142)

bacteria (bak • tēr' • ē • ə) *n.* plural form of **bacterium:** a tiny living cell that can be seen only through a microscope. Some cause disease; others help, such as making soil richer (page 146)

hollow (hol' • lō) *adj.* having a hole or an empty space inside (page 146)

stored (stord) *v.* past tense of **store:** to put away for future use (page 147)

dwellers (dwe' • lûrz) *n.* plural form of **dweller:** a person or an animal that lives in a certain place (page 150)

swarming (swor' • ming) *adj.* moving in a large group (page 152)

Comprehension Strategies 

Review the following comprehension strategies with students. Also, ask student to orally summarize "One Small Place in a Tree."

- **Asking Questions** helps readers focus attention on a text by asking and then finding the answers to questions they have about the text. This strategy is modeled by Barbara Brenner in "One Small Place in a Tree." She begins the story with questions that help readers focus on what they can expect to discover while reading the selection. Have students reread the questions on page 139. Have students find the answers to the questions as they review the story.
- **Clarifying** is used by readers to figure out the meanings of words and difficult ideas. Ask students to find three words or ideas they clarified when reading "One Small Place in a Tree."
- **Visualizing** requires readers to mentally picture the events or characters in a story, resulting in a more vivid and imaginative understanding of the story. Have students review the text and share some of the scenes they visualized as they read "One Small Place in a Tree." Ask students to explain what clues and descriptions they used to form their visualization.

Comprehension Skills

Review the following comprehension skills with students:

- **Author's Purpose** is the purpose the author had for writing the text. Knowing an author's purpose gives readers an idea of what they can expect to find. Review the author's purpose for writing "One Small Place in a Tree." Ask students if they think there were other purposes for the story. If so, have students provide examples to support their ideas.
- **Cause and Effect** is a skill readers use to put together logical explanations in the text once they understand what causes certain events to happen. Ask students to find three examples of cause-and-effect relationships in "One Small Place in a Tree."

Reading with a Writer's Eye

Review the following literary element with students:

Text Structure: Technique is how an author explains and organizes facts and information. Have students return to the text and explain how Barbara Brenner used descriptive examples and a clear sequence of events to tell the story of "One Small Place in a Tree." Remind students to do the same in their own writing.

Language Use is how an author uses words to create colorful scenes and characters in a story. Have students review the text and find descriptive words and passages that Barbara Brenner uses in "One Small Place in a Tree." Ask students to explain how these descriptions helped them better understand the selection.

Fluency

Remind students that automaticity, or reading spontaneously, adds to the meaning of text by making it easier to comprehend and enjoy. Read aloud a passage from pages 137–143 from "One Small Place in a Tree." Make sure that the passage totals at least 160 words to ensure an appropriate practice length. Point out to students that words, sentences, and passages sometimes need to be read more than one time to build automaticity.

Have students read the passage chorally. Encourage students to reread as needed to read with automaticity. Also remind students to pause after commas and end punctuation.

Language Arts

OBJECTIVES

Students will
- publish their summaries.
- take the spelling posttest.
- review cursive *m* and *n.*

MATERIALS
- Routine 17
- ***Language Arts Handbook,*** pp. 42–47
- ***Skills Practice 1***, p. 86
- ***Transparency*** 45
- ***Lesson Assessment Book 1,*** pp. 43–50

Teacher Tip

ASSESSMENT Use the Writing Rubrics in the Level Appendix to evaluate students' summaries.

How Can I Share My Writing?

The last step in the writing process is **publishing.** At this stage, you are ready to share your writing with others. If you haven't already, you need to make a clean copy in your best handwriting or on the computer. The form in which you choose to publish your writing depends on what kind of writing it is and who your audience is. You should choose the best way to share what you have done for the audience that you have chosen.

Ways to Publish

If your writing is a story, you could make it a book and put it in the reading center.

How to Make a Book	
1. Fold some 8½ × 11-inch paper in half.	4. Draw pictures or add charts, tables, or diagrams.
2. Staple it in the middle.	5. Put a construction paper cover on it.
3. Write your story on the pages.	6. Write the title and your name on the cover.

If it is a letter, you should mail it.

If it is a play or a story, you could act it out.

If it is a description, you could illustrate it and put it on a bulletin board. That is what Charlie has decided for now. Later, she will include it in a letter to her pen pal. Then she will mail it to him.

42 How Can I Share My Writing? • The Writing Process

Language Arts Handbook, p. 42

UNIT 2 Lesson 1

Revising Use this checklist to revise your summary.
- ☐ Is the main idea stated in the first sentence?
- ☐ Take out any information you did not get from the article or book.
- ☐ Did you use time and order words? Will they help readers follow the order of events?
- ☐ Does your writing sound serious and informative?

Editing/Proofreading Use this checklist to correct mistakes.
- ☐ Did you indent your paragraph?
- ☐ Did you use correct spelling?
- ☐ Did you capitalize the title of the book or article?
- ☐ Is the book title underlined, or is the article title put in quotation marks?
- ☐ Did you end each sentence with correct punctuation?

Publishing Use this checklist to prepare your summary for publication.
- ☐ Neatly rewrite or type a final copy.
- ☐ Make a cover for your summary.

86 UNIT 2 • Lesson 1 Writing • *Skills Practice 1*

Skills Practice 1, p. 86

Writing Summary

ROUTINE 17

Publishing

Teach

- Use Routine 17, and tell students that they are at the final stage of the writing process: publishing. This means that they will be sharing their summaries with others.
- Students should decide on a method to present their summaries. Since other people will be reading their summaries and each student has a summary to share, a good idea might be to bind all of the summaries into a book. Another idea would be to have students read their summaries orally. Afterwards, the summaries could be bound into the classroom book.
- Before presenting the summaries, each student should make sure his or her summary is ready to be published. Work with students individually or have them work in small groups to make sure all revising and editing/proofreading is completed.
- For further information on publishing, refer to ***Language Arts Handbook*** pages 42–47.

Guided Practice

- Have students turn to ***Skills Practice 1*** page 86 to read and discuss the publishing checklist.

Apply

- **Composing—Publishing** Students should use page 86 in ***Skills Practice 1*** as a guide to put finishing touches on their summaries. This page encourages them to make a clean, neat copy of their summaries.
- Have volunteers make oral presentations of their summaries, and/or have them trade papers and read each others' summaries.
- Encourage students to share their summary books with other classes that are also studying the theme Animals and Their Habitats. Remind them to add their summaries to their writing portfolio.

Spelling

/ī/ and Regular Plurals

Teach

Ask students to write *Spelling* and their names in the top margin of a clean piece of paper. Have them number the first fifteen lines 1–15, then skip a line and number the next two lines 1–2. Read each word, use it in a sentence, and give students time to spell it correctly. Encourage students to try to spell the Challenge words, but assure them that misspelling a Challenge word will not affect their test scores.

Spelling Words		Challenge Words
lie	sigh	dweller
ties	monkeys	outcry
fly	lunches	
flies	fight	
halves	knights	
cycles	spy	
reply	spies	
replies		

Guided Practice

- Have students proofread for any mistakes they made on the posttest. Tell them to categorize the mistakes as
  - careless errors.
  - errors in spelling plurals.
  - errors in spelling words with /ī/.
- Make certain students are spelling plurals and words with /ī/ correctly.

Penmanship

Cursive Letters *m* and *n*

Teach

- Review cursive *m* and cursive *n* with students. Display ***Transparency*** 45 and say the strokes aloud as you use a pointer to trace the letters.
  - **Letter *m*** Starting point, overcurve
Slant down, overcurve
Slant down, overcurve
Slant down, undercurve: small *m*
  - **Letter *n*** Starting point, overcurve
Slant down, overcurve
Slant down, undercurve: small *n*
- To model proper letter formation, write the following sentence on the board: *Many monkeys make many mints.*

Guided Practice

Have a student practice writing the sentence on the board.

Apply

After reviewing the sentence you wrote on the board, set a timer (for three minutes) and have students practice writing the sentence. Have students circle the best sentence based on the correct formation of *m* and *n*.

Teacher Tip

PENMANSHIP If students are not using proper spacing between words, check to make sure they are positioning their papers correctly, are holding their pencils correctly, and understand how to lift the pencil at the end of the word and reposition it for the next word.

Day 5

Language Arts

Review

OBJECTIVES

Students will

- review possessive nouns and pronouns.
- review the reasons for taking notes.
- review listening and speaking skills.

MATERIALS

- ***Student Reader,*** Book 1, pp. 138–153
- ***Lesson Assessment Book 1,*** pp. 43–50

Study Skills

Note-Taking

- Remind students that knowing how to take good notes will be beneficial for writing assignments and unit investigations, in this or any other school subject. Ask students when they might take notes. **Possible Answers** *when writing a summary, researching a book or an encyclopedia for an investigation project*
- For additional practice with note taking skills, have students take notes while others present their unit investigations.

Listening/Speaking/Viewing

Asking Questions

Remind students that it is important to ask and answer questions clearly and appropriately.

- In pairs, have students turn to "One Small Place in a Tree" to ask and answer questions about the text.
- Have students create questions they would ask a guest speaker about the theme Animals and Their Habitats.

Grammar, Usage, and Mechanics

Possessive Nouns and Pronouns

Write the following sentences on the board. Then have students underline the possessive nouns and circle the possessive pronouns.

- The sun's rays were bright. *sun's*
- The flowers' petals were yellow and white. *flowers'*
- We're going to the children's baseball game on Saturday. *children's*
- Our backyard is home to a family of cardinals, squirrels, and chipmunks. *our*
- Her birthday is in April. *her*

For further practice using possessive nouns and pronouns, have students create five sentences each. Tell them to write the sentences about friends and some of the toys, animals, or siblings the friends have. Then have the students trade papers and edit the sentences by inserting possessive pronouns.

Monitor Progress

Formal Assessment

Use pages 43–50 in ***Lesson Assessment,*** Book 1 to assess students' understanding of the skills taught in this lesson. Intervene with ***Reteach, Challenge Activities, Intervention Guide, eSkills, Leveled Readers,*** or activities in the ***Workshop Kit*** as needed.

Lesson Planner

Preparing to Read

MATERIALS

- ***Transparencies*** 49, 53
- ***Sound/Spelling Card*** 30
- Routines 2, 3, 4, 5, 6, 7, 8, 9
- ***Skills Practice 1,*** pp. 93–96

Day 1

Daily News, p. T116
Phonics and Fluency
Review /ō/, pp. T117–T119

Day 2

Daily News, p. T136
Phonics and Fluency, pp. T136–T137
Developing Oral Language, p. T137
Dictation, p. T137

Reading and Responding

MATERIALS

- ***Student Reader,*** Book 1, pp. 158–173
- ***Transparencies*** 5, 15, 35, 50
- ***Home Connection,*** pp. 17–18
- Routines 11, 12, 14, A
- ***Skills Practice 1,*** pp. 97–102
- ***Listening Library CDs***
- Writer's Notebook
- ***Leveled Readers***

Day 1

Build Background, p. T120
Preview and Prepare, p. T121
Selection Vocabulary, pp. T122–T123
Reading the Selection, pp. T124–T127
Comprehension Skill
☆ Reality and Fantasy, p. T126
Comprehension Strategy
Asking Questions, pp. T128–T129
Inquiry, pp. T130–T131

1st READ

Day 2

Comprehension Strategy
Predicting, pp. T138–T139
Discussing the Selection, p. T140
Review Selection Vocabulary, p. T141
Fluency, p. T141
Theme Connections, p. T142

Language Arts

MATERIALS

- ***Transparencies*** 3, 17, 17A, 51, 52, 58, 58A
- ***Skills Practice 1,*** pp. 103–110
- ***Language Arts Handbook,*** pp. 92–97, 218–219
- Routines 15, 16, 17
- ***Student Reader,*** Book 1, pp. 162–169
- ***Lesson Assessment Book 1,*** pp. 51–58

Day 1

Writing
Prewriting, pp. T132–T133
Spelling Pretest, p. T133
Penmanship, Cursive Letters *f* and *h,* p. T134

Day 2

Writing
Drafting, pp. T144–T145
Spelling, p. T145
Grammar, Usage, and Mechanics
Regular and Irregular Plurals, pp. T146–T147

Monitor Progress

✓ = **Formal Assessment**

Day 1

✓ **Phonics and Fluency, p. T119**
✓ **Comprehension Skill, p. T125**
✓ **Spelling Pretest, p. T133**

Day 2

✓ **Selection Vocabulary, p. T141**
Fluency, p. T141
✓ **Grammar, Usage, and Mechanics, p. T147**

Literature Overview

Student Reader

Make Way for Ducklings

written and illustrated by Robert McCloskey

Caldecott Medal

Science Inquiry

Frozen Frogs

SRA
Imagine It!

★ Phonics ★ Fluency ★ Vocabulary ★ Comprehension

Day 3

Daily News, p. T148
Word Structure
Irregular Plurals, p. T149

Comprehension Skill
2nd READ
Reality and Fantasy, p. T150
Reading with a Writer's Eye, p. T151
Supporting the Reading
Reality and Fantasy, p. T152
Fluency, p. T153
Inquiry, p. T153

Writing
Revising, p. T154
Spelling, p. T155
Study Skills
Tables and Charts, p. T156
Grammar, Usage, and Mechanics, p. T157

Word Structure, p. T149
Comprehension Skill, p. T152
Fluency, p. T153
Spelling, p. T155
Study Skills, p. T156

Day 4

Daily News, p. T158
Word Structure, p. T159
Developing Oral Language, p. T159

Comprehension Skill
Reality and Fantasy, p. T160
Science Inquiry, pp. T162–T163
Inquiry, pp. T164–T165

Writing
Editing/Proofreading, pp. T166–T167
Spelling, p. T167
Study Skills, p. T168
Listening/Speaking/Viewing
Listen and Respond, p. T169

Writing, p. T167

Day 5 Review

Phonics and Fluency, p. T170
Word Structure, p. T170

Selection Vocabulary, p. T171
Comprehension Strategies
- Asking Questions, p. T172
- Predicting, p. T172

Comprehension Skill
Reality and Fantasy, p. T172
Reading with a Writer's Eye, p. T173
Fluency, p. T173

Writing
Publishing, p. T174
Spelling Test, p. T175
Penmanship, p. T175
Study Skills, p. T176
Listening/Speaking/Viewing, p. T176
Grammar, Usage, and Mechanics, p. T177

Spelling Posttest, p. T175
***Lesson Assessment Book,* pp. 51–58**

Student Resources

Genre

A **fantasy** is a fictional story that could not happen in real life. Fantasy stories may have characters that do things or tell of things that could not happen in real life.

Comprehension Skill

Reality and Fantasy

As you read, identify examples of reality and fantasy in the story.

Make Way for Ducklings

by Robert McCloskey

Focus Questions

How do various types of city wildlife adapt to their environments? What roles do people play in protecting the natural environment?

160

161

Student Reader, Book 1, pp. 160–171

Phonics & Fluency

Decodable Stories, Book 3, Story 18, "More Bats"

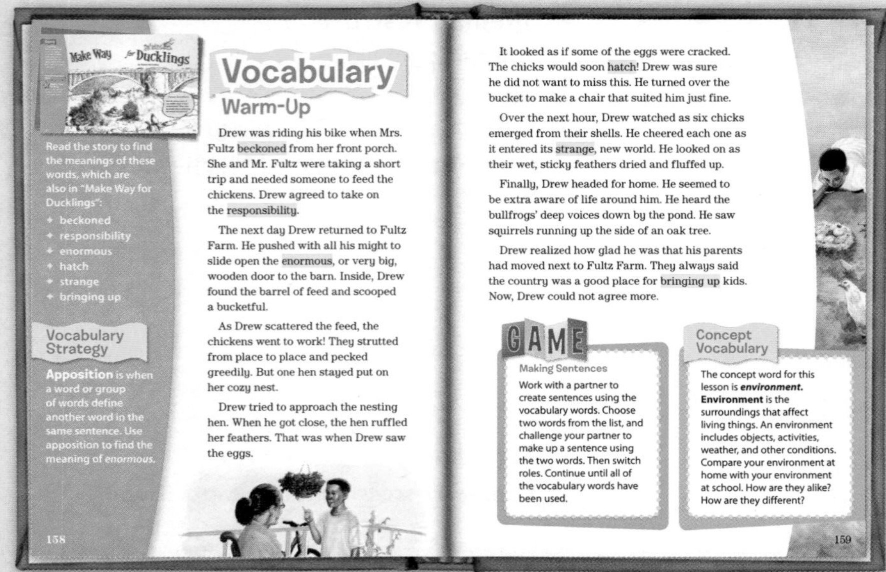

Make Way for Ducklings

Read the story to find the meanings of these words, which are also in "Make Way for Ducklings":

- beckoned
- responsibility
- enormous
- hatch
- strange
- bringing up

Vocabulary Strategy

Apposition is when a word or group of words define another word in the same sentence. Use apposition to find the meaning of *enormous.*

Vocabulary Warm-Up

Drew was riding his bike when Mrs. Fultz beckoned from her front porch. She and Mr. Fultz were taking a short trip and needed someone to feed the chickens. Drew agreed to take on the responsibility.

The next day Drew returned to Fultz Farm. He pushed with all his might to slide open the enormous, or very big, wooden door to the barn. Inside, Drew found the barrel of feed and scooped a bucketful.

As Drew scattered the feed, the chickens went to work! They strutted from place to place and pecked greedily. But one hen stayed put on her cozy nest.

Drew tried to approach the nesting hen. When he got close, the hen ruffled her feathers. That was when Drew saw the eggs.

158

It looked as if some of the eggs were cracked. The chicks would soon hatch! Drew was sure he did not want to miss this. He turned over the bucket to make a chair that suited him just fine.

Over the next hour, Drew watched as six chicks emerged from their shells. He cheered each one as it entered its strange, new world. He looked on as their wet, sticky feathers dried and fluffed up.

Finally, Drew headed for home. He seemed to be extra aware of life around him. He heard the bullfrogs' deep voices down by the pond. He saw squirrels running up the side of an oak tree.

Drew realized how glad he was that his parents had moved next to Fultz Farm. They always said the country was a good place for bringing up kids. Now, Drew could not agree more.

GAME

Making Sentences

Work with a partner to create sentences using the vocabulary words. Choose two words from the list, and challenge your partner to make up a sentence using the two words. Then switch roles. Continue until all of the vocabulary words have been used.

Concept Vocabulary

The concept word for this lesson is ***environment.*** **Environment** is the surroundings that affect living things. An environment includes objects, activities, weather, and other conditions. Compare your environment at home with your environment at school. How are they alike? How are they different?

159

Student Reader, Book 1, pp. 158–159

Science

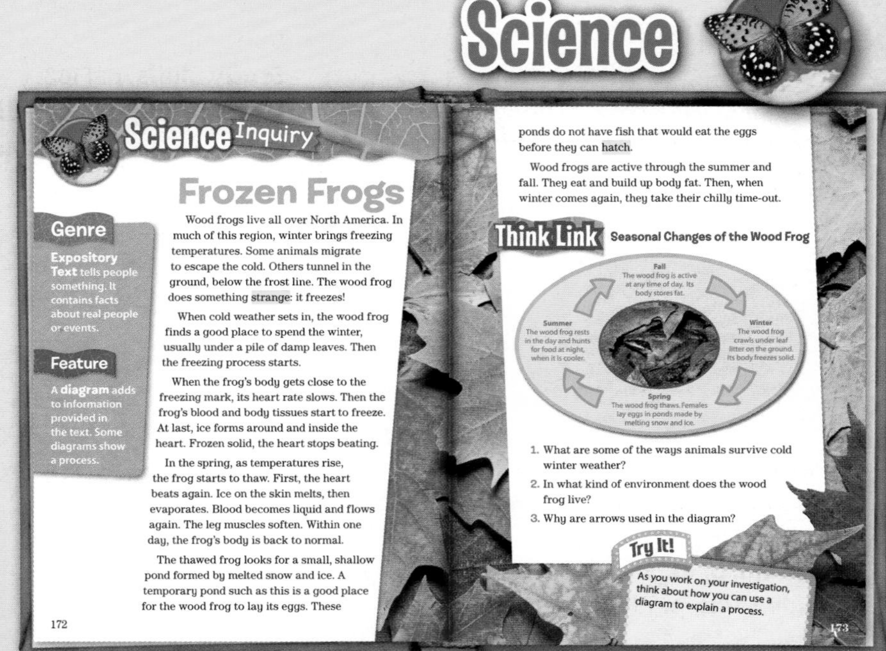

Science Inquiry

Frozen Frogs

Genre

Expository Text tells people something. It contains facts about real people or events.

Feature

A **diagram** adds to information provided in the text. Some diagrams show a process.

Wood frogs live all over North America. In much of this region, winter brings freezing temperatures. Some animals migrate to escape the cold. Others tunnel in the ground, below the frost line. The wood frog does something strange: it freezes!

When cold weather sets in, the wood frog finds a good place to spend the winter, usually under a pile of damp leaves. Then the freezing process starts.

When the frog's body gets close to the freezing mark, its heart rate slows. Then the frog's blood and body tissues start to freeze. At last, ice forms around and inside the heart. Frozen solid, the heart stops beating.

In the spring, as temperatures rise, the frog starts to thaw. First, the heart beats again. Ice on the skin melts, then evaporates. Blood becomes liquid and flows again. The leg muscles soften. Within one day, the frog's body is back to normal.

The thawed frog looks for a small, shallow pond formed by melted snow and ice. A temporary pond such as this is a good place for the wood frog to lay its eggs. These

172

ponds do not have fish that would eat the eggs before they can hatch.

Wood frogs are active through the summer and fall. They eat and build up body fat. Then, when winter comes again, they take their chilly time-out.

Think Link Seasonal Changes of the Wood Frog

Fall
The wood frog is active at any time of day. Its body stores fat.

Winter
The wood frog crawls under leaf litter on the ground. Its body freezes solid.

Spring
The wood frog thaws. Females lay eggs in ponds made by melting snow and ice.

Summer
The wood frog rests in the day and hunts for food at night, when it is cooler.

1. What are some of the ways animals survive cold winter weather?
2. In what kind of environment does the wood frog live?
3. Why are arrows used in the diagram?

Try It!

As you work on your investigation, think about how you can use a diagram to explain a process.

173

Student Reader, Book 1, pp. 172–173

Cross-Curricular Resources

Curriculum Connections

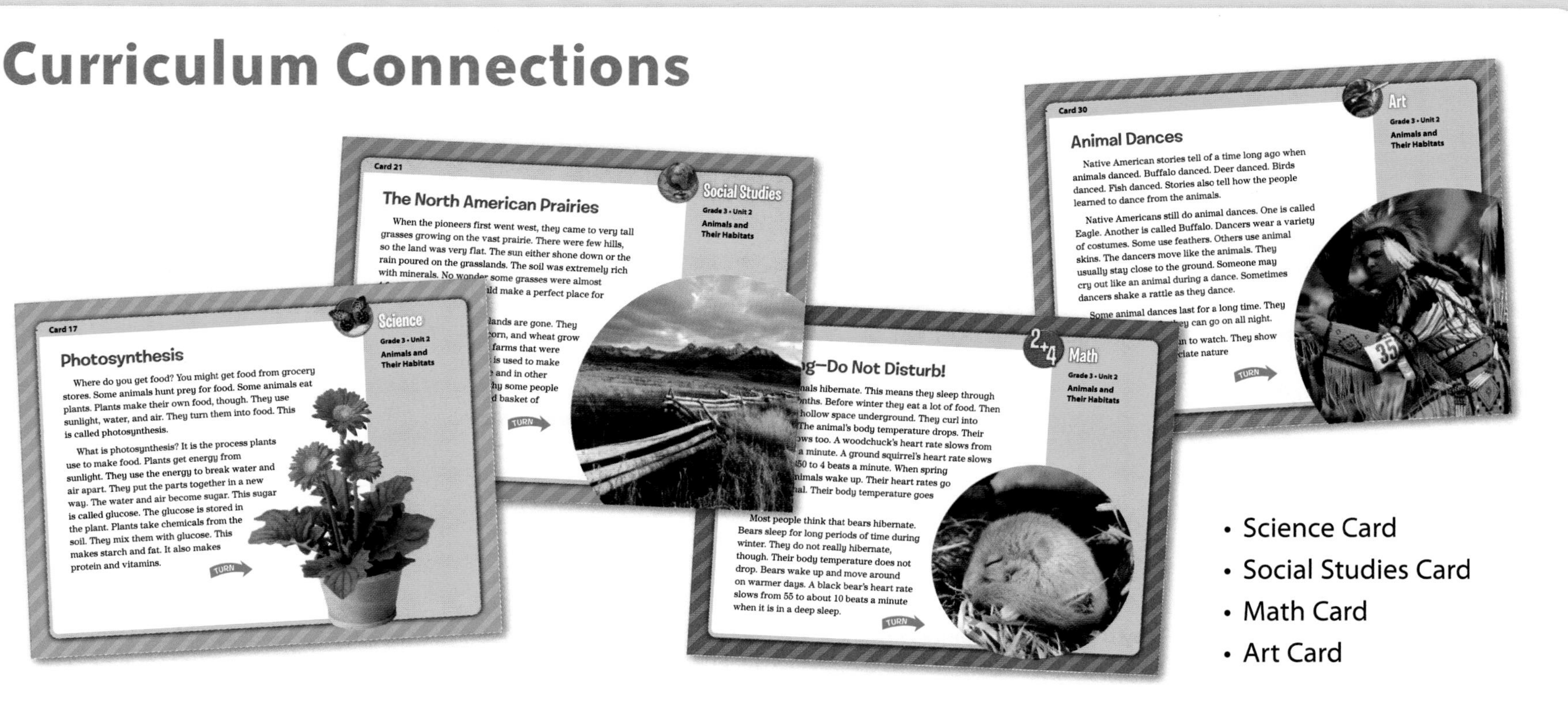

- Science Card
- Social Studies Card
- Math Card
- Art Card

Leveled Readers for Science

Approaching Level

On Level

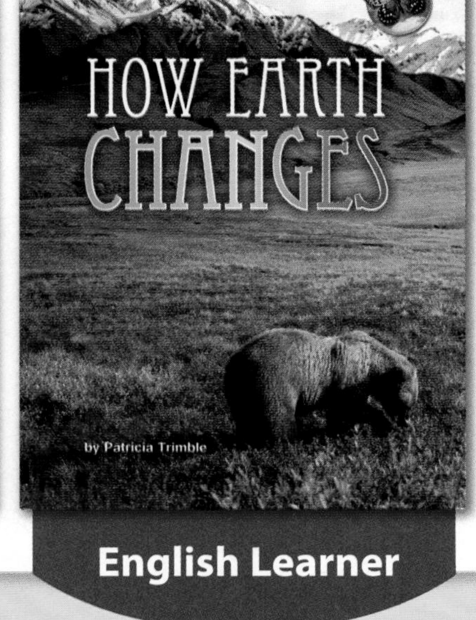

English Learner

Above Level

Differentiating Instruction for Workshop

Day 1

	Approaching Level	On Level	English Learner	Above Level
Preparing to Read	**Phonics and Fluency:** Help students complete ***Reteach*** page 37, or work with them on the phonics activities in the ***Intervention Guide*** for Unit 2, Lesson 2. Then have students read ***Decodable Stories, Book 3,*** Story 18.	**Phonics and Fluency:** Have students make lists of words to add to the word lines.	**Phonics and Fluency:** Use the ***English Learner Support Guide*** for more phonics instruction. Then have students read ***Decodable Stories, Book 3,*** Story 18.	**Phonics and Fluency:** Have students complete ***Challenge Activities*** page 34. Students can then read other materials, looking for other words to add to the word lines.
Reading and Responding	**Vocabulary:** Have students create illustrations for the selection vocabulary words in their Writer's Notebooks. **Comprehension:** Have students discuss any questions they have about the story with the rest of the class. **Inquiry:** Have students work in groups to discuss questions and things they wonder about related to the theme.	**Vocabulary:** Have students play the Charades game with the selection vocabulary words. **Comprehension:** Have students write a list of questions they have about the story and friendship. Add questions to the **Concept/Question Board.** **Inquiry:** Have students work in groups to discuss questions and things they wonder about related to the theme.	**Vocabulary:** Use ***English Learner Support Guide*** to review vocabulary. **Comprehension:** Have students find a passage in the story where they needed to adjust their reading speed to understand the story. Give students time to reread the passage with a partner. **Inquiry:** Have students work in groups to discuss questions and things they wonder about related to the theme.	**Vocabulary:** Have students write three examples for three of the selection vocabulary words. For example, *What are three things that are strange? What are three things that are enormous?* **Comprehension:** Have students begin a list of ideas about how this story might relate to the unit theme. Place new ideas on the **Concept/ Question Board.** **Inquiry:** Have students work in groups to discuss questions and things they wonder about related to the theme.
Language Arts	**Writing:** Have students continue to take notes and create an outline for their book reviews. **Spelling:** Have pairs of students study the spelling words in this lesson.	**Writing:** Have students work with a peer to add, change, or delete information in their outlines before drafting. **Spelling:** Have students proofread their book review for spelling errors.	**Writing:** Have students work with a peer to add, change, or delete information in their outlines before drafting. **Spelling:** Have students rewrite one paragraph from their selections, carefully spelling the words.	**Writing:** Have students begin drafting after they have organized their notes and outlines. **Spelling:** Have students pick five spelling words and use the letters from those words to correctly spell new words.

Day 2

	Approaching Level	On Level	English Learner	Above Level
Preparing to Read	**Phonics and Fluency:** Students can listen to the /ō/ sound on the ***Sound/Spelling Cards Story CD.*** Have students read ***Decodable Stories, Book 3,*** Story 18.	**Phonics and Fluency:** Students can read the ***High-Frequency Flash Cards*** with a partner. Have students read other materials, looking for words to add to the blending lines.	**Phonics and Fluency:** Use the ***English Learner Support Guide*** for today's sound and spellings. Have students read ***Decodable Stories, Book 3,*** Story 18.	**Phonics and Fluency:** Have students write poems with words that rhyme with the words on the word lines.
Reading and Responding	**Vocabulary:** Have students use ***Reteach*** page 39 or work with students using the ***Intervention Guide,*** Unit 2, Lesson 2. **Comprehension:** Review the **Concept/Question Board** with students. Add any new ideas learned from reading the story. **Fluency:** Have students reread a passage from the story with a partner.	**Vocabulary:** Have students complete a game in the ***Workshop Kit.*** **Comprehension:** Have students write a paragraph about a prediction they made about the story. Remind students to include details from the story that they used to form their predictions. **Fluency:** Have students read into a tape recorder at the beginning and end of the week. Have them listen to themselves at the end of the week so they can hear their progress.	**Vocabulary:** Help students find the selection vocabulary words in the story. Have students rewrite the sentences in the story using their own words in their Writer's Notebook. **Comprehension:** Place students into small groups, and allow them to discuss the story. Encourage students to discuss their favorite parts of the story. **Fluency:** Have students listen to ***Listening Library CD,*** Unit 2.	**Vocabulary:** Have students complete ***Challenge Activities*** page 36. **Comprehension:** Have students write a short play based on the story. **Fluency:** Have students perform their short plays by using Reader's Theater.
Language Arts	**Writing:** Have students continue to draft their book reviews. **Spelling:** Have students work in groups to review this week's spelling word list. **Grammar, Usage, and Mechanics:** Have students complete ***Reteach*** page 43.	**Writing:** Have students review what they wrote and refer to their outlines to make sure they have included all necessary information. **Spelling:** Have students write the irregular plurals on a piece of paper and write the corresponding singular next to each one. **Grammar, Usage, and Mechanics:** Have students work with the ***Workshop Kit.***	**Writing:** Have students review what they wrote and refer to their outlines to make sure they have included all necessary information. **Spelling:** Have students work in pairs to brainstorm for ideas to help them with their spelling. **Grammar, Usage, and Mechanics:** Refer to the ***English Learner Support Guide*** for support activities.	**Writing:** Have students work on distinguishing facts from opinions in their writing. **Spelling:** Have students think of and spell two other spelling words that contain the /ō/ sound spellings. **Grammar, Usage, and Mechanics:** Have students complete ***Challenge Activities*** page 37.

Differentiating Instruction
for Workshop

Day 3

	Approaching Level	On Level	English Learner	Above Level
Preparing to Read	**Word Structure:** Review the word lines with irregular plurals. Then have students complete ***Reteach*** page 38 or work with them on the word structure activities in the ***Intervention Guide,*** Unit 2, Lesson 2.	**Word Structure:** Have students write sentences using the singular and plural forms of the words on the word lines. Students can use an activity with irregular plurals in the ***Workshop Kit.***	**Word Structure:** Review the word lines with irregular plurals. Then use the ***English Learner Support Guide*** for more word structure instruction.	**Word Structure:** Have students complete ***Challenge Activities*** page 35. Students can use an activity with irregular plurals in the ***Workshop Kit.***
Reading and Responding	**Vocabulary:** Have students write the definitions of three of the expanding vocabulary words using their own words. **Comprehension:** Have students draw a map of the ducks' journey from their spot near the water to the island. Have them use their text to make the map as detailed as possible. **Fluency:** Have students use ***Leveled Readers.***	**Vocabulary:** Have students add words they already know that are related to the selection vocabulary words in their Writer's Notebooks. **Comprehension:** Have students write a list of details from the story that could happen in a realistic fiction text. **Fluency:** Have students reread a passage from the text with a partner.	**Vocabulary:** Have students play the Charades game with the expanding vocabulary words. **Comprehension:** Have students list the events in the story that prove that "Make Way for Ducklings" is a fantasy. **Fluency:** Have students reread a passage with a partner or individually.	**Vocabulary:** Have students select three vocabulary words, research print and online dictionaries to find additional information, and record it in their Writer's Notebooks. **Comprehension:** Have students list elements of fantasy found in the story, and then list other stories, movies, or books that have similar elements. **Fluency:** Have students read a text on their independent level.
Language Arts	**Writing:** Have students work with a partner to revise their book reviews. **Spelling:** Have students complete Reteach page 42. **Grammar, Usage, and Mechanics:** Refer to the Intervention Guide, Unit 2, Lesson 2.	**Writing:** Have students conference with a partner before they revise their reviews. **Spelling:** Have students write five sentences using the spelling words. **Grammar, Usage, and Mechanics:** Have students edit a piece of writing for irregular plural nouns.	**Writing:** Have students conference with a partner before they revise their reviews. **Spelling:** Working in small groups, have students help one another study their spelling list. **Grammar, Usage, and Mechanics:** Refer to the ***English Learner Support Guide*** for support activities.	**Writing:** Have students read their reviews to at least two other students. **Spelling:** Have students complete ***Challenge Activities*** page 38 **Grammar, Usage, and Mechanics:** Have students edit their book reviews for irregular plural nouns.

Day 4

	Approaching Level	On Level	English Learner	Above Level
Preparing to Read	**Word Structure:** Use the irregular plural activity in the ***Workshop Kit.***	**Word Structure:** In pairs, have students create clue sentences for the irregular plurals on the word lines.	**Word Structure:** Use the irregular plural activity in the ***Workshop Kit.***	**Word Structure:** Have students play word detective and look for compound words in other reading materials.
Reading and Responding	**Vocabulary:** Have students write sentences using the expanding vocabulary words. **Comprehension:** Have students create three review questions for the story beginning with *why* and *how* and trade questions with a partner. Have students answer each other's questions. **Inquiry:** Have students read one of the ***Leveled Readers*** about animal habitats, and have them share what questions they have about the reading.	**Vocabulary:** Have students write their own functional definitions for the selection vocabulary words. **Comprehension:** Have students read another fantasy story. Have students compare and contrast the story to "Make Way for Ducklings" on a two-column chart. **Inquiry:** Have students read one of the ***Leveled Readers*** about animal habitats, and have them share what questions they have about the reading.	**Vocabulary:** Have students place the vocabulary words into categories. Categories might include actions, objects, or places. **Comprehension:** Have students write a summary of "Make Way for Ducklings." Encourage students to include illustrations if they have trouble expressing themselves. **Inquiry:** Have students read one of the ***Leveled Readers*** about animal habitats, and have them share what questions they have about the reading.	**Vocabulary:** Have students write a story using the selection vocabulary words. **Comprehension:** Have students write a story using one of the ducklings as the main character. **Inquiry:** Have students read one of the ***Leveled Readers*** about animal habitats, and have them share what questions they have about the reading.
Language Arts	**Writing:** Have students work with a partner to edit/proofread their book reviews. **Spelling:** Have students proofread their writing activity for spelling errors.	**Writing:** Have students begin working on their final drafts after they finish editing/proofreading. **Spelling:** Have students write five words that rhyme with spelling words on a piece of paper.	**Writing:** Have students use the ***Language Arts Handbook*** as they edit/proofread their book reviews. **Spelling:** Have students circle the spelling words with the /ō/ sound and underline the part of the word that makes that sound.	**Writing:** Have students revise, edit/proofread, and publish their book reviews that will be submitted to the school newspaper. **Spelling:** Have students pick two spelling words and write four words each that rhyme with those words.

Lesson 2 Overview

Differentiating Instruction for Workshop

Day 5

	Approaching Level	On Level	English Learner	Above Level
Preparing to Read	**Word Structure:** Review the word lines. Then have students read "More Bats" from the ***eDecodable Stories***. Have the students read the ***High-Frequency Flash Cards*** with a partner.	**Word Structure:** Have students read other materials, looking for irregular plural nouns. With a partner, students can scramble words from the word lines.	**Word Structure:** Have students listen to the /ō/ sound on ***Sound/Spelling Cards Stories CD.*** Review the word lines. Then have students read "More Bats" from ***eDecodable Stories.***	**Word Structure:** Have students read other materials, looking for irregular plural nouns.
Reading and Responding	**Vocabulary:** Have students write sentences related to the unit theme Animals and Their Habitats with the vocabulary words. **Comprehension:** Have students read a book or story and practice making predictions while reading. **Fluency:** Have students write answers to comprehension questions from ***Leveled Readers.***	**Vocabulary:** Have students create riddles for three of the selection vocabulary words to share with the class. **Comprehension:** Have students write a short play using the story. **Fluency:** Have students reread passages from the text with a partner.	**Vocabulary:** Have students research articles and stories about Animals and Their Habitats to find additional concept vocabulary words to add to the Word Bank. **Comprehension:** Have students write a short play based on the story. **Fluency:** Have students use vocabulary from ***Leveled Readers*** in extended sentences.	**Vocabulary:** Have students write their own Vocabulary Warm-Ups using the vocabulary words. **Comprehension:** Have students write their own story that uses Animals and Their Habitats as the theme. **Fluency:** Have students create a play from the story to use with Reader's Theater.
Language Arts	**Writing:** Have students create a list of books they would like to read based on the book reviews. **Spelling:** Have students carefully rewrite a paragraph from their selection, while keeping an eye on spelling the words correctly.	**Writing:** Have students create a list of books they would like to read based on the book reviews. **Spelling:** Have students make a list of five spelling words with one letter missing and trade papers with a partner to fill in the blanks.	**Writing:** Have students create a list of books they would like to read based on the book reviews. **Spelling:** Have students choose five spelling words for a partner to spell on a piece of paper.	**Writing:** Have students create a list of books they would like to read based on the book reviews. **Spelling:** Have students write an imaginary letter to someone using at least six spelling words.

Resources for Differentiating Instruction

Leveled Readers

Approaching Level

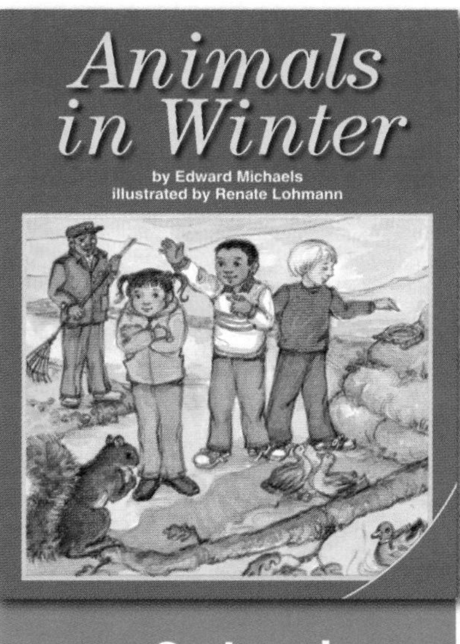

On Level

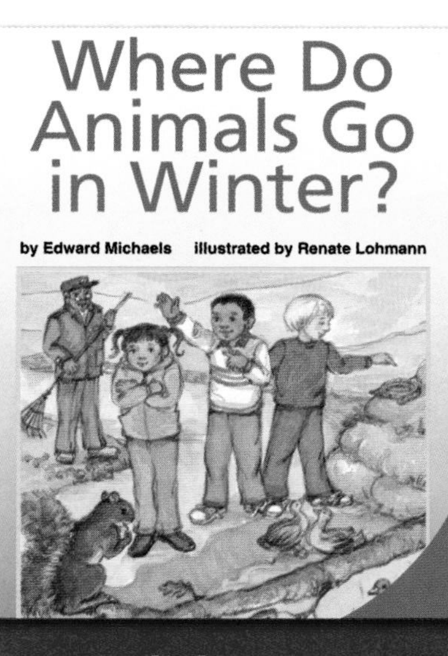

English Learner

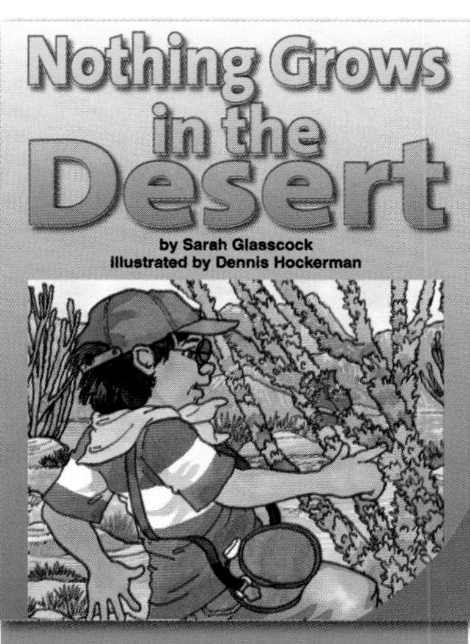

Above Level

Additional Skills Practice

Approaching Level

Reteach

- The /ō/ Sound/ Spellings, p. 37
- Irregular Plurals, p. 38
- Selection Vocabulary, p. 39
- Reality and Fantasy, pp. 40–41
- Spelling, p. 42
- Plural Nouns, p. 43

On Level

Skills Practice 1

- The /ō/ Sound/Spellings, pp. 93–94
- Irregular Plurals, pp. 95–96
- Selection Vocabulary, pp. 97–98
- Reality and Fantasy, pp. 99–100
- Inquiry, pp. 101–102
- Writing a Nonfiction Book Review, pp. 103–104
- Spelling, pp. 105–106
- Plural Nouns, pp. 107–108

English Learner

English Learner Support Activities

English Learner Support Activities, Unit 2 Lesson 2

Above Level

Challenge Activities

- The /ō/ Sound/ Spellings, p. 34
- Irregular Plurals, p. 35
- Selection Vocabulary, p. 36
- Reality and Fantasy, p. 37
- Spelling, p. 38
- Plural Nouns, p. 39

Lesson 2 Overview

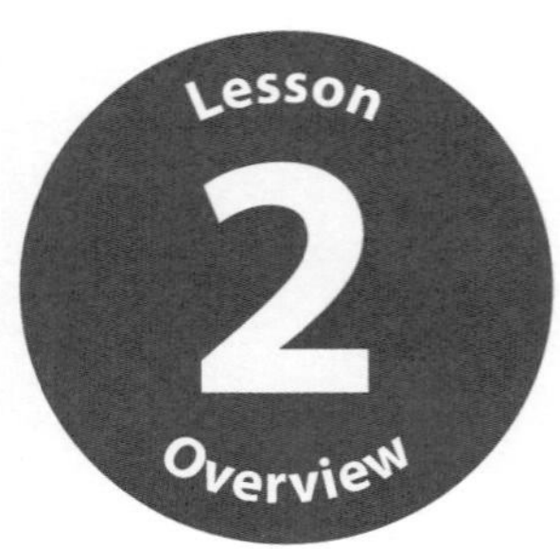

Additional Resources for Differentiating Instruction

RtI

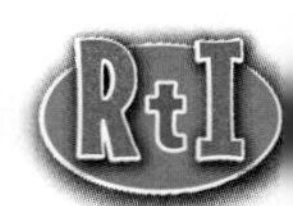

Workshop Kits

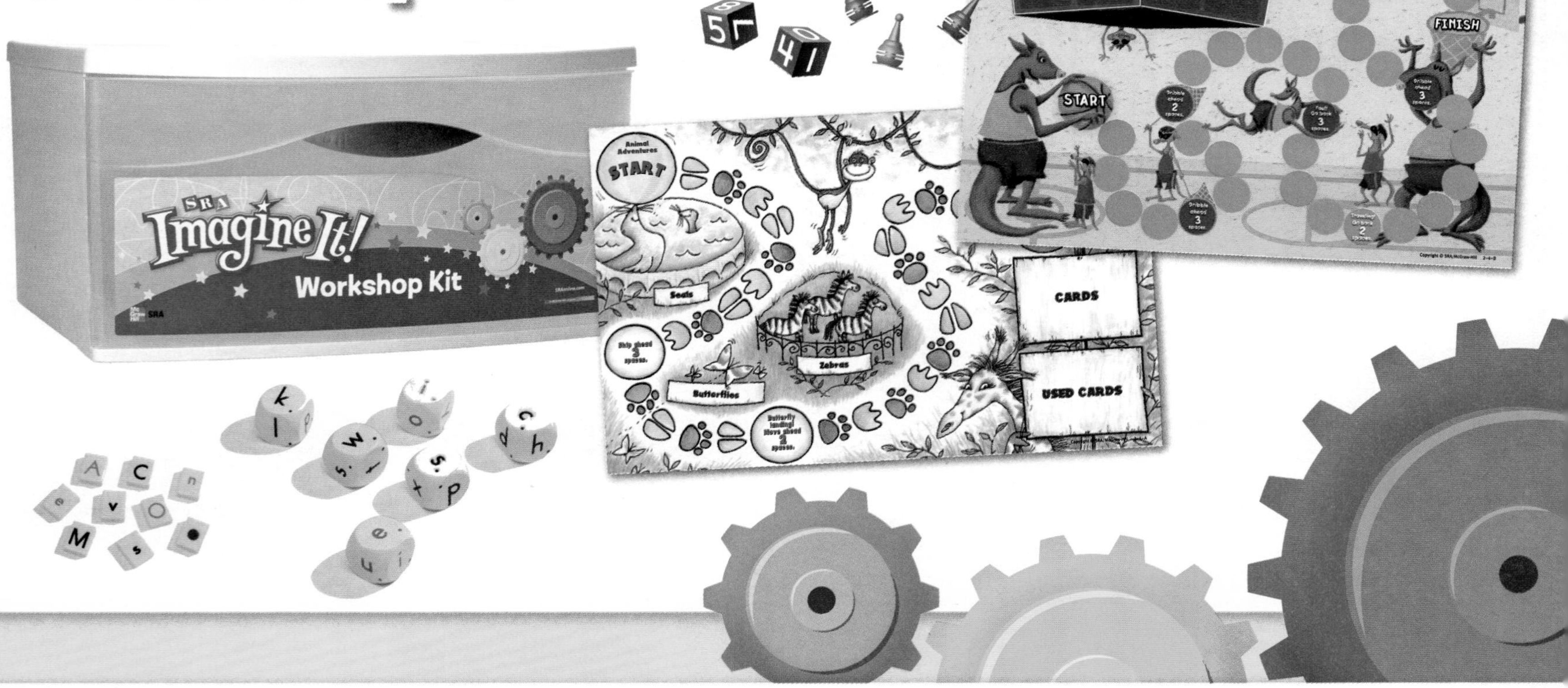

Technology

The following electronic resources are available for students:

- ***eStudent Reader***
- ***eDecodable Stories***
- ***eSkills***
- ***Listening Library***

Electronic resources for the teacher include:

- ***ePlanner***
- ***eTeacher's Edition***
- ***eAssess***
- ***ePresentation***

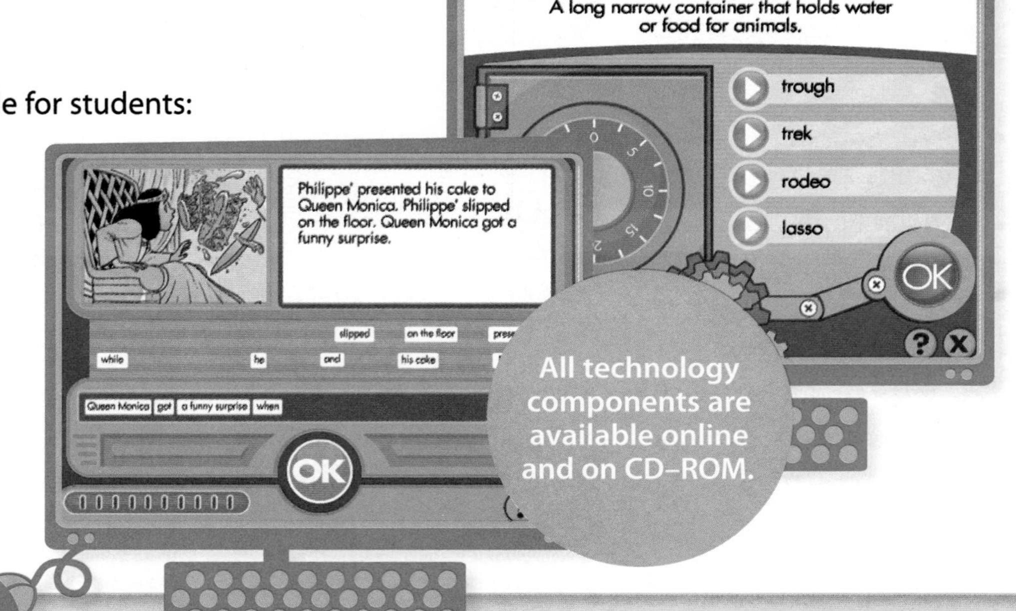

English Learner

Leveled Reader

English Learner Support Activities, Lesson 2

Listening Library Unit 2

English Learner Support Guide, Lesson 2

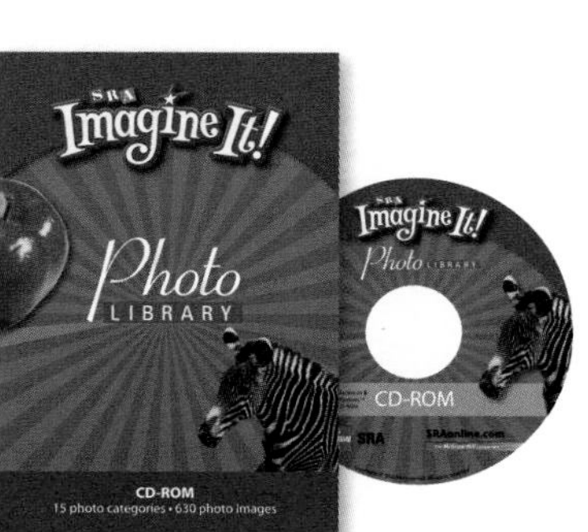

Photo Library

Approaching Level

Intervention

Intervention Workbook

Intervention Guide

Lesson 2 Overview

Lesson Assessment

Monitor Progress to Differentiate Instruction

Comprehension Strategies Rubrics

Use Comprehension Strategies Rubrics to determine whether a student is using the strategies.

- Asking Questions, p. T125
- Predicting, p. T125

Inquiry Rubrics

Use the Inquiry Rubrics to assess a student's performance throughout the stages of the investigation for each unit. In addition, at the end of the unit you can use the rubrics to assess the groups' collaborative work as well as an individual's participation in that group.

- Identifying a Question to Investigate, p. T165

Writing Rubrics

Use the writing rubrics in the Level Appendix to evaluate each student's nonfiction book review.

- Genre
- Writing Process
- Writing Traits

Lesson Assessments

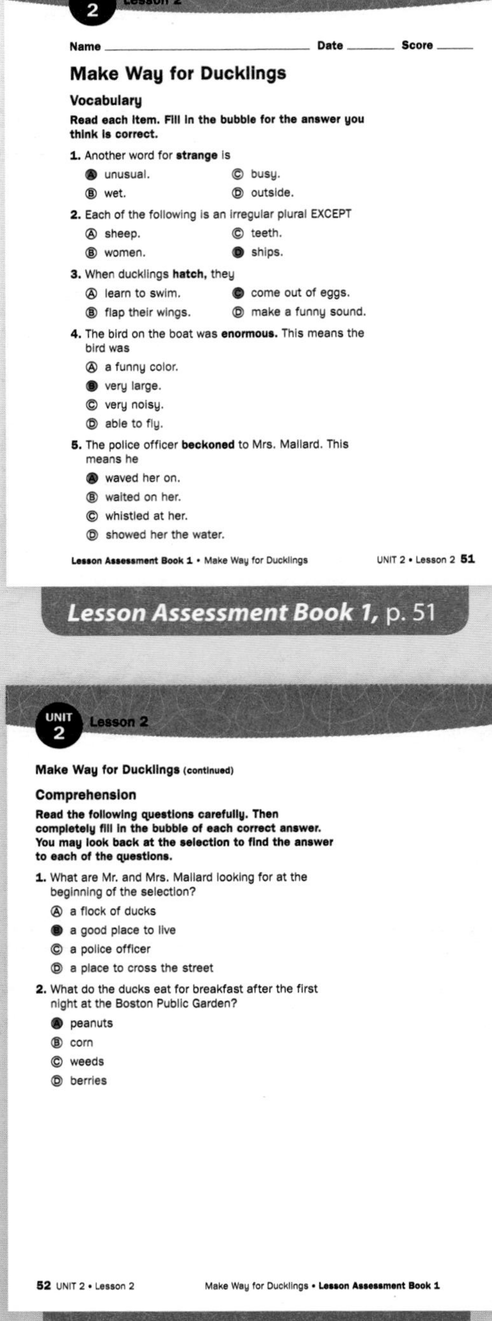

UNIT 2 Lesson 2

Name ______ Date ______ Score ______

Make Way for Ducklings

Vocabulary

Read each item. Fill in the bubble for the answer you think is correct.

1. Another word for **strange** is
   - (A) unusual.
   - (B) wet.
   - (C) busy.
   - (D) outside.
2. Each of the following is an irregular plural EXCEPT
   - (A) sheep.
   - (B) women.
   - (C) teeth.
   - (D) ships.
3. When ducklings **hatch,** they
   - (A) learn to swim.
   - (B) flap their wings.
   - (C) come out of eggs.
   - (D) make a funny sound.
4. The bird on the boat was **enormous.** This means the bird was
   - (A) a funny color.
   - (B) very large.
   - (C) very noisy.
   - (D) able to fly.
5. The police officer **beckoned** to Mrs. Mallard. This means he
   - (A) waved her on.
   - (B) waited on her.
   - (C) whistled at her.
   - (D) showed her the water.

Lesson Assessment Book 1 • Make Way for Ducklings UNIT 2 • Lesson 2 51

Lesson Assessment Book 1, p. 51

UNIT 2 Lesson 2

Make Way for Ducklings (continued)

Comprehension

Read the following questions carefully. Then completely fill in the bubble of each correct answer. You may look back at the selection to find the answer to each of the questions.

1. What are Mr. and Mrs. Mallard looking for at the beginning of the selection?
   - (A) a flock of ducks
   - (B) a good place to live
   - (C) a police officer
   - (D) a place to cross the street
2. What do the ducks eat for breakfast after the first night at the Boston Public Garden?
   - (A) peanuts
   - (B) corn
   - (C) weeds
   - (D) berries

52 UNIT 2 • Lesson 2 Make Way for Ducklings • Lesson Assessment Book 1

Lesson Assessment Book 1, p. 52

Use these summative assessments along with your informal observations to assess student mastery.

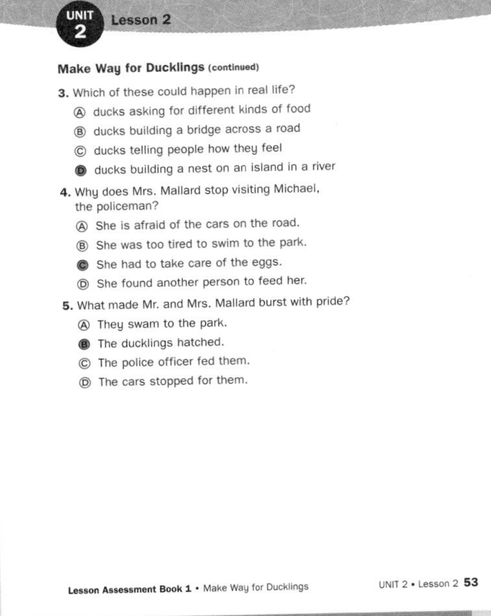

UNIT 2 Lesson 2

Make Way for Ducklings (continued)

3. Which of these could happen in real life?
   (A) ducks asking for different kinds of food
   (B) ducks building a bridge across a road
   (C) ducks telling people how they feel
   ● ducks building a nest on an island in a river
4. Why does Mrs. Mallard stop visiting Michael, the policeman?
   (A) She is afraid of the cars on the road.
   (B) She was too tired to swim to the park.
   ● She had to take care of the eggs.
   (D) She found another person to feed her.
5. What made Mr. and Mrs. Mallard burst with pride?
   (A) They swam to the park.
   ● The ducklings hatched.
   (C) The police officer fed them.
   (D) The cars stopped for them.

Lesson Assessment Book 1 • Make Way for Ducklings UNIT 2 • Lesson 2 53

Lesson Assessment Book 1, p. 53

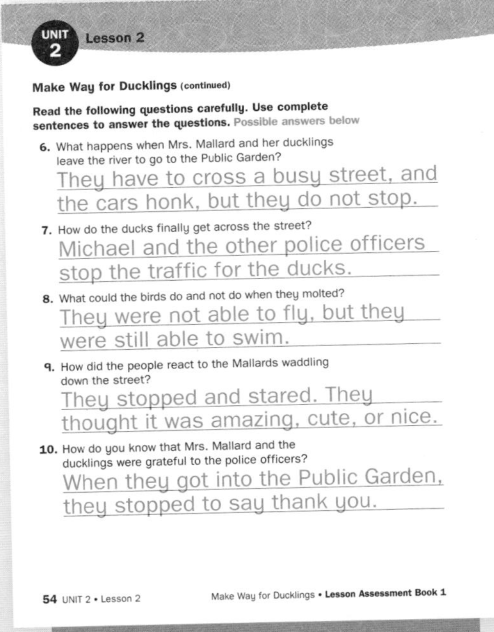

UNIT 2 Lesson 2

Make Way for Ducklings (continued)

Read the following questions carefully. Use complete sentences to answer the questions. Possible answers below

6. What happens when Mrs. Mallard and her ducklings leave the river to go to the Public Garden?
   They have to cross a busy street, and the cars honk, but they do not stop.
7. How do the ducks finally get across the street?
   Michael and the other police officers stop the traffic for the ducks.
8. What could the birds do and not do when they molted?
   They were not able to fly, but they were still able to swim.
9. How did the people react to the Mallards waddling down the street?
   They stopped and stared. They thought it was amazing, cute, or nice.
10. How do you know that Mrs. Mallard and the ducklings were grateful to the police officers?
   When they got into the Public Garden, they stopped to say thank you.

54 UNIT 2 • Lesson 2 Make Way for Ducklings • Lesson Assessment Book 1

Lesson Assessment Book 1, p. 54

UNIT 2 Lesson 2

Make Way for Ducklings (continued)

Read the question below. Write complete sentences for your answer. Support your answer with information from the selection.

Linking to the Concepts Why is the island a good city home for the Mallards?

Read the questions below. Your answer should be based on your own experience. Write complete sentences for your answer.

Personal Response Is there a place near where you live that would make a good home for mallards? Why?

Lesson Assessment Book 1 • Make Way for Ducklings UNIT 2 • Lesson 2 55

Lesson Assessment Book 1, p. 55

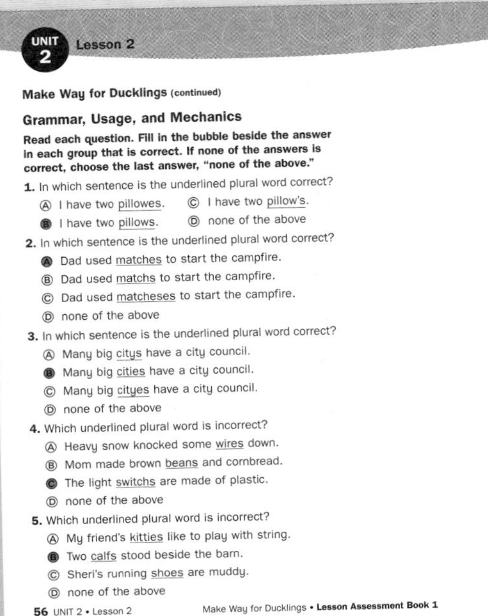

UNIT 2 Lesson 2

Make Way for Ducklings (continued)

Grammar, Usage, and Mechanics

Read each question. Fill in the bubble beside the answer in each group that is correct. If none of the answers is correct, choose the last answer, "none of the above."

1. In which sentence is the underlined plural word correct?
   (A) I have two pillowes. (C) I have two pillow's.
   ● I have two pillows. (D) none of the above
2. In which sentence is the underlined plural word correct?
   ● Dad used matches to start the campfire.
   (B) Dad used matchs to start the campfire.
   (C) Dad used matcheses to start the campfire.
   (D) none of the above
3. In which sentence is the underlined plural word correct?
   (A) Many big citys have a city council.
   ● Many big cities have a city council.
   (C) Many big cityes have a city council.
   (D) none of the above
4. Which underlined plural word is incorrect?
   (A) Heavy snow knocked some wires down.
   (B) Mom made brown beans and cornbread.
   ● The light switchs are made of plastic.
   (D) none of the above
5. Which underlined plural word is incorrect?
   (A) My friend's kitties like to play with string.
   ● Two calfs stood beside the barn.
   (C) Sheri's running shoes are muddy.
   (D) none of the above

56 UNIT 2 • Lesson 2 Make Way for Ducklings • Lesson Assessment Book 1

Lesson Assessment Book 1, p. 56

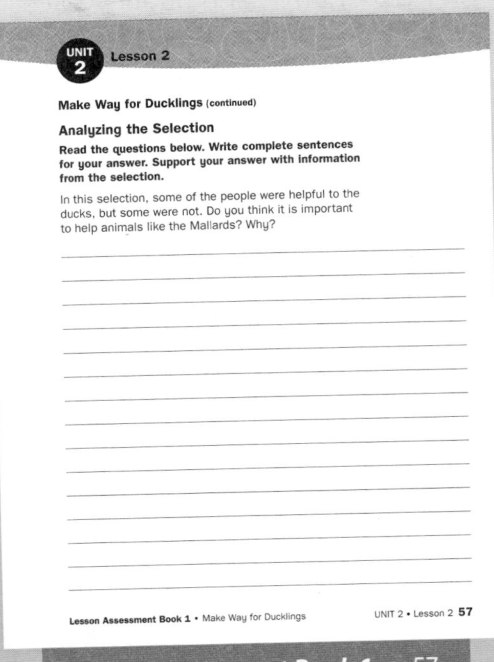

UNIT 2 Lesson 2

Make Way for Ducklings (continued)

Analyzing the Selection

Read the questions below. Write complete sentences for your answer. Support your answer with information from the selection.

In this selection, some of the people were helpful to the ducks, but some were not. Do you think it is important to help animals like the Mallards? Why?

Lesson Assessment Book 1 • Make Way for Ducklings UNIT 2 • Lesson 2 57

Lesson Assessment Book 1, p. 57

UNIT 2 Lesson 2

Make Way for Ducklings (continued)

Oral Fluency Assessment

The Jacket

Tim looked at his younger sister and sighed. Sammie had 1–10
taken off her coat again. Now she was running around the 11–21
playground wearing just a sweater. It had been hard to get 22–32
the coat on her in the first place. Tim was not looking forward 33–45
to doing it again. But since he was babysitting, it was his job. 46–58
"Sammie, you need your jacket," Tim said. 59–65
"I don't want to!" Sammie answered, slowly walking back 66–74
to him. 75–76
Tim stayed calm. "Look at me. I'm wearing my jacket to 77–87
stay warm." 88–89
"But I'm not cold," Sammie pouted. "Feel my skin." Tim put 90–100
his hand against her arm. He had to admit she was warm. 101–112
Tim wondered if Sammie did not get cold as easily as he did. 113–125
Plus, she was running around a lot. Maybe she was warm from 126–137
all the exercise. 138–140
Tim asked, "What if you do get cold?" 141–148
Sammie quickly said, "I'll come put my coat on." 149–157
"Okay," said Tim, and he watched Sammie go climb on 158–167
the bars. Then Tim smiled and thought, "Hey, I used to hate 168–179
wearing my jacket too!" 180–183

EVALUATING CODES FOR ORAL FLUENCY

sky (/) words read incorrectly
blue ^ sky (^) inserted word
( ]) after the last word

READING RATE AND ACCURACY

Total Words Read: ______
Number of Errors: ______
Number of Correct Words Read Per Minute (WPM): ______
Accuracy Rate: ______
(Number of Correct Words Read per Minute ÷ Total Words Read)

READING FLUENCY

	Low	Average	High
Decoding ability	○	○	○
Pace	○	○	○
Syntax	○	○	○
Self-correction	○	○	○
Intonation	○	○	○

Record student rates on the Oral Fluency Scores pages.

58 UNIT 2 • Lesson 2 Make Way for Ducklings • Lesson Assessment Book 1

Lesson Assessment Book 1, p. 58

Preparing to Read

OBJECTIVES

Students will
- review /ō/ spelled _*ow* and *oa*_.
- learn new high-frequency words.
- build fluency.

MATERIALS

- ***Transparency*** 49
- ***Sound/Spelling Card*** 30
- Routines 3, 4, 5, 6, 9
- ***Skills Practice 1,*** pp. 93–94

Daily Oral Practice

Daily News

Today!

Do ducks live in the country or the city? They can live in both. Sometimes it's harder for animals to live in the city. Animals living in cities must be careful to protect themselves. People can also do their part to help protect animal habitats in the city.

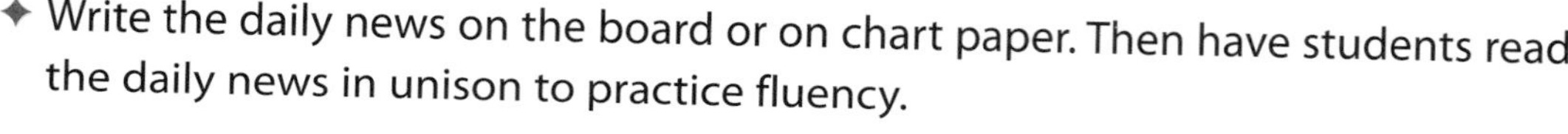

- Write the daily news on the board or on chart paper. Then have students read the daily news in unison to practice fluency.
- As a phonics and fluency review from Lesson 1, ask a volunteer to identify any words in the daily news with consonant blends at the beginning or end of the words. st *in* must; rt *in* part; pr *and* ct *in* protect; lp *in* help

Phonics and Fluency

ROUTINE 3 ROUTINE 4

Review: /ō/ spelled _ow and oa_

Blending

- Write the following blending lines and sentences on the board or use ***Transparency*** 49. Show students one line at a time as you go through the lines by covering up the others. The boldface words are from "Make Way for Ducklings." The underlined words are new high-frequency words.

Line 1	flow	grow	throw	know
Line 2	follow	yellow	**blowing**	mower
Line 3	boat	road	coast	groan
Line 4	toaster	floating	boasting	overcoat

Sentence 1	The snow blows slowly against the <u>side</u> of the <u>house</u>.
Sentence 2	The <u>same</u> loaf of oat bread will make good toast.

- Review ***Sound/Spelling Card*** 30 with students. Using Routine 3, follow the whole-word blending process to have students blend the words in Lines 1–4.
- Follow Routine 4, the blending sentences process, to have students blend Sentences 1–2.

Lines 1–2 **/ō/ spelled _ow**

As you point to each word in Lines 1–2, have students read the word aloud in unison. Then ask students to identify /ō/ spelled _ow in each word. */ō/ spelled _ow in* flow, grow, throw, know, follow, yellow, blowing *and* mower Ask students to name other words that have /ō/ spelled _ow. Challenge students to come up with multisyllabic words, such as *below, overthrow,* and *undertow*. **Possible Answers** *low, bow, mow, row, crow, show, snow, mellow, slow*

Sound/Spelling Card 30

Teacher Tip

SYLLABICATION To help students blend words and build fluency, demonstrate syllabication using the decodable, multisyllabic words in the word lines.

fol • low	toa • ster
yel • low	floa • ting
blow • ing	boa • sting
mow • er	o • ver • coat

Preparing to Read

✦ Use ***Transparency*** 49 with today's blending lines and sentences. Show students the lines one at a time as you go through them by covering up the other lines.

Lines 3–4 **/ō/ spelled *oa_***

Point to each word in Lines 3–4 individually and have students read the word aloud in unison. Then ask students to identify /ō/ spelled *oa_* in each word. */ō/ spelled* oa_ *in* boat, road, coast, groan, toaster, floating, boasting, overcoat Ask students to name any other words they can think of that have /ō/ spelled *oa_*. **Possible Answers** *toad, load, coal, foal, foam, roam, throat, roast*

Sentences 1–2

Have students point to and read the new high-frequency words in Sentences 1–2. *side, house, same* Ask students to identify any words in Sentence 1 with /ō/ spelled *_ow*. */ō/ spelled* _ow *in* snow, blows, *and* slowly Ask students to identify any words in Sentence 2 with /ō/ spelled *oa_*. */ō/ spelled* oa_ *in* loaf, oat, *and* toast Have students read the sentences in unison to practice fluency.

Decodable Stories

Building Fluency

Decodable Stories are used to help develop fluency for students who need extra practice. They are also used to practice the phonics and fluency elements they are reviewing. Using Routine 9, reading a ***Decodable Story,*** have students who need additional support read ***Decodable Stories, Book 3,*** Story 18, "More Bats."

Decodable Stories, Book 3, Story 18

Syllabication

- To help students recognize common syllable patterns, use Routine 5 for closed syllables and Routine 6 for open syllables to separate the syllables in the multisyllabic words in the word lines. Explain that the syllable routines offer general rules that don't apply to all words.

- Using Routine 5, have students identify the vowel spellings in *follow* and *yellow*. Then have them identify the consonants between the two vowels. Explain that the syllables are usually divided between the consonants in words with the v-c-c-v spelling pattern, as in *fol • low*. Remind students that when a syllable ends with a consonant sound, the vowel is usually short, and the syllable is a closed syllable. Have students read *follow* and *yellow* aloud, clapping for each syllable.

- Using Routine 6, have students identify the vowel spellings in *toaster, floating, boasting,* and *overcoat*. Then have them identify the consonant between the first two vowel spellings. Explain that the syllables are usually divided before the consonant in words with the v-c-v spelling pattern, as in *toa • ster*. Remind students that when a vowel spelling is not followed by a consonant spelling, the vowel is usually long, and the syllable is open. Point out that *overcoat* has three syllables because it has three vowel sounds. Have students clap for each syllable as they read *toaster, floating, boasting,* and *overcoat* aloud. Have students identify the initial open syllables in *blowing* and *mower* and then read these words aloud, clapping for each syllable.

- Help students start the phonics activities on ***Skills Practice 1*** pages 93–94. Read the Focus box with them and help them with the first few questions.

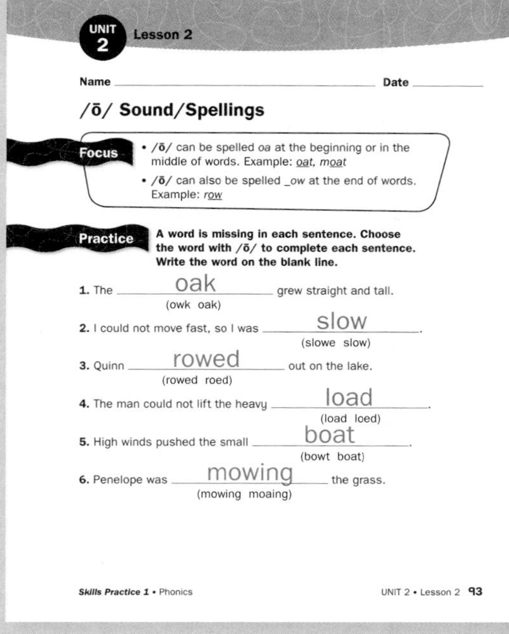
UNIT 2 Lesson 2

Name ________ Date ________

/ō/ Sound/Spellings

Focus
- /ō/ can be spelled *oa* at the beginning or in the middle of words. Example: oat, moat
- /ō/ can also be spelled _*ow* at the end of words. Example: row

Practice A word is missing in each sentence. Choose the word with /ō/ to complete each sentence. Write the word on the blank line.

1. The oak grew straight and tall. (owk oak)
2. I could not move fast, so I was slow. (slowe slow)
3. Quinn rowed out on the lake. (rowed roed)
4. The man could not lift the heavy load. (load loed)
5. High winds pushed the small boat. (bowt boat)
6. Penelope was mowing the grass. (mowing moaing)

Skills Practice 1 • Phonics UNIT 2 • Lesson 2 93

Skills Practice 1, p. 93

UNIT 2 Lesson 2

Apply Part of a word containing /ō/ is missing in each sentence below. Read the clue about the missing word. Write the missing letters to complete the word.

7. There is a Vietnamese story about a t oa d. (Clue: a small green animal)
8. In the story, there had been no rain or s n ow for years. (Clue: frozen white water)
9. The toad and a group of animals walked the r oa d to the Sky King's home. (Clue: a kind of path)
10. All he saw was a toad, so Sky King sent Thunder to b l ow it away. (Clue: what the wind does)
11. But all the animals fought Thunder; they made Sky King g r ow tired. (Clue: what a plant does when it gets taller)
12. Sky King said, "I give up. Now whenever toad grinds his teeth, I'll make rain f l ow again. (Clue: what a river does)

94 UNIT 2 • Lesson 2 Phonics • Skills Practice 1

Skills Practice 1, p. 94

Monitor Progress to Differentiate Instruction

Formal Assessment

Phonics and Fluency During the blending activity, note how quickly students are reading the words.

APPROACHING LEVEL	**IF . . .** students need practice with today's sound/spellings for /ō/,	**THEN . . .** work with them on the phonics activities on ***Reteach*** page 37 during Workshop.
	IF . . . students need extra practice with today's sound/spellings for /ō/,	**THEN . . .** work with them on the phonics activities for Unit 2 Lesson 2 Day 1 in the ***Intervention Guide*** during Workshop.
ON LEVEL	**IF . . .** students understand today's sound/spellings for /ō/,	**THEN . . .** have them make lists of words to add to the word lines during Workshop.
ABOVE LEVEL	**IF . . .** students are ready for a challenge with today's sound/spellings for /ō/,	**THEN . . .** have them complete the phonics activities on ***Challenge Activities*** page 34 during Workshop.

Reading and Responding

OBJECTIVES

Students will

- activate prior knowledge to prepare for the story.
- learn selection vocabulary.
- learn the elements of a fantasy.
- use the comprehension strategy Asking Questions.
- investigate animals and their habitats using the Inquiry process.

MATERIALS

- ***Student Reader,*** Book 1, pp. 158–166
- Routines 11, 12, 14
- ***Transparencies*** 5, 50
- ***Skills Practice 1,*** p. 101
- ***Home Connections,*** pp. 17–18

Build Background

Activate Prior Knowledge

- Introduce "Make Way for Ducklings" by determining students' prior knowledge. Ask students to talk about times they have seen ducks or other birds in the city. Ask students to tell you about what the ducks or birds did and how people acted around them.
- Discuss what city life might be like for ducks or other birds. What might be easier for them? What might be more difficult?
- Ask students how people can help ducks or other animals that live in the city.
- Discuss with students whether they have read other fantasy stories about animals.
- Encourage students to make connections to other fantasy stories they have read or other books or stories about animals living in cities.

Background Information

The following information might help students understand the story they are about to read:

- Bring in some pictures of ducks, including pictures of ducks in public places such as a park. Discuss why the ducks might live in such an area. Post the pictures on the **Concept/Question Board.**
- Remind students that this story is a fantasy. Although the situation could be real, the talking ducks in the story are not real. Sometimes fantasies take place in locations that do not really exist. In this particular story, however, the city and places within the city are real.

Preview and Prepare 

ROUTINE 12

Browse

Have students read the title, and give them a few minutes to browse the first few pages of the story. Have students use features such as the story's title and illustrations to predict what this story might have to do with animals and their habitats.

Use Routine 12, the clues, problems, and wonderings routine, to help students identify what they know before reading, what problems they may encounter while reading, and what their purposes are for reading. Students will chart these on a transparency.

Tell students to look for interesting words in the story. These words could be fun words to read or words that are unfamiliar to them. They may note the names of the characters, Mr. and Mrs. Mallard. Students might find this humorous, and it might also tell them that this story is a fantasy.

Display ***Transparency*** 5 and model browsing for students. For example, a "Clue" to the story might be that the ducks talk like people. Under "Problems," point out *dither* as an unfamiliar word. Write *Why are the ducks in the city?* under "Wonderings." Record students' observations on the transparency as they browse the story.

Set Purposes

Encourage students to set their own purposes for reading the story. Remind students that readers can set purposes for reading by picking up clues from the title, illustrations, and genre of the text they are going to read. If students need help, tell them that fantasies are often written to entertain readers, but sometimes readers learn something, too. To connect the theme, tell students that when reading they should think about how this story illustrates both the advantages and disadvantages faced by wildlife that live in the city.

BIG Idea

Where do different animals live?

Before reading the story, read the Big Idea question. Tell students to keep this question in mind as they read the story.

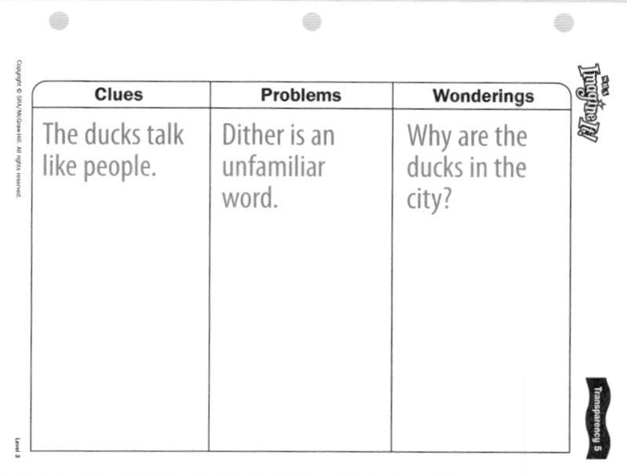

Clues	Problems	Wonderings
The ducks talk like people.	Dither is an unfamiliar word.	Why are the ducks in the city?

Transparency 5

Give each student a copy of ***Home Connection*** page 17. The same information is also available in Spanish on ***Home Connection*** page 18. Encourage students to discuss "Make Way for Ducklings" with their families and complete the activity provided.

Selection Vocabulary

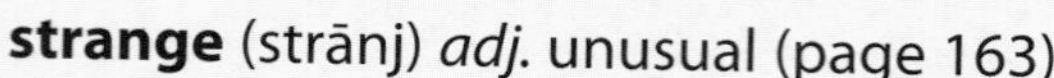

strange (strānj) *adj.* unusual (page 163)

enormous (ē • nor′ • mə s) *adj.* very big (page 163)

hatch (hach) *v.* to come out of an egg (page 164)

responsibility (ri • spon′ • sə • bi′ • li • tē) *n.* a duty (page 166)

bringing up (bring′ • ing up) *v.* raising, as in children (page 166)

beckoned (bek′ • ə nd) *v.* past tense of **beckon:** to call someone by waving (page 168)

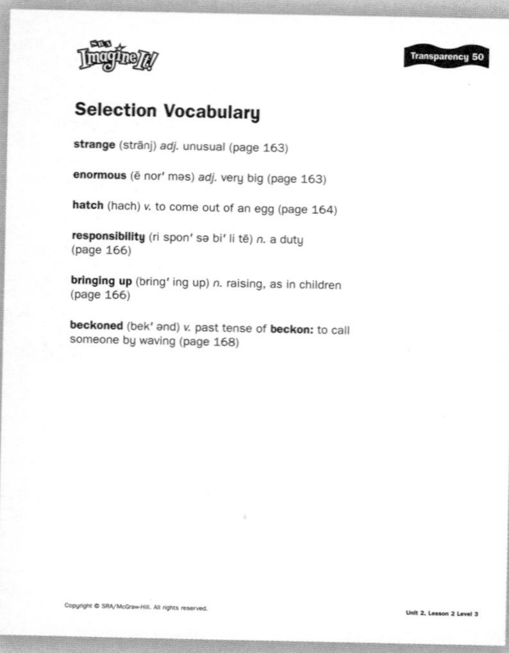

Imagine It! Transparency 50

Selection Vocabulary

strange (strānj) *adj.* unusual (page 163)

enormous (ē nor′ məs) *adj.* very big (page 163)

hatch (hach) *v.* to come out of an egg (page 164)

responsibility (ri spon′ sə bi′ li tē) *n.* a duty (page 166)

bringing up (bring′ ing up) *n.* raising, as in children (page 166)

beckoned (bek′ ənd) *v.* past tense of **beckon:** to call someone by waving (page 168)

Copyright © SRA/McGraw-Hill. All rights reserved. Unit 2, Lesson 2 Level 3

Transparency 50

Building Vocabulary

Using Routine 11, the selection vocabulary process, have students read aloud the Vocabulary Warm-Up on ***Student Reader,*** Book 1 pages 158–159.

As students read, have them stop to blend any difficult or unfamiliar words. Provide students with the pronunciations of words that are not decodable or that they cannot read fluently.

Guided Vocabulary Practice

Ask students to identify the highlighted vocabulary words they figured out using the vocabulary strategy apposition. **Possible Answer** *enormous* Have students explain how they figured out the meanings of the other vocabulary words as they read the Vocabulary Warm-Up.

Display ***Transparency*** 50, and have students read the words and definitions. Return to the Vocabulary Warm-Up, and read the sentences containing the vocabulary words with students. Then, if necessary, provide a brief in-context explanation of each word.

Use the vocabulary words on ***Transparency*** 50 to create fill-in-the-blank sentences. Have students fill in the appropriate vocabulary words. For example, When it was my turn to practice pitching, the coach ________ me to the pitcher's mound. *beckoned*

Read the story to find the meanings of these words, which are also in "Make Way for Ducklings":

- beckoned
- responsibility
- enormous
- hatch
- strange
- bringing up

Vocabulary Strategy

Apposition is when a word or group of words define another word in the same sentence. Use apposition to find the meaning of *enormous*.

Vocabulary Warm-Up

Drew was riding his bike when Mrs. Fultz beckoned from her front porch. She and Mr. Fultz were taking a short trip and needed someone to feed the chickens. Drew agreed to take on the responsibility.

The next day Drew returned to Fultz Farm. He pushed with all his might to slide open the enormous, or very big, wooden door to the barn. Inside, Drew found the barrel of feed and scooped a bucketful.

As Drew scattered the feed, the chickens went to work! They strutted from place to place and pecked greedily. But one hen stayed put on her cozy nest.

Drew tried to approach the nesting hen. When he got close, the hen ruffled her feathers. That was when Drew saw the eggs.

158

It looked as if some of the eggs were cracked. The chicks would soon hatch! Drew was sure he did not want to miss this. He turned over the bucket to make a chair that suited him just fine.

Over the next hour, Drew watched as six chicks emerged from their shells. He cheered each one as it entered its strange, new world. He looked on as their wet, sticky feathers dried and fluffed up.

Finally, Drew headed for home. He seemed to be extra aware of life around him. He heard the bullfrogs' deep voices down by the pond. He saw squirrels running up the side of an oak tree.

Drew realized how glad he was that his parents had moved next to Fultz Farm. They always said the country was a good place for bringing up kids. Now, Drew could not agree more.

GAME

Making Sentences

Work with a partner to create sentences using the vocabulary words. Choose two words from the list, and challenge your partner to make up a sentence using the two words. Then switch roles. Continue until all of the vocabulary words have been used.

Concept Vocabulary

The concept word for this lesson is ***environment.*** **Environment** is the surroundings that affect living things. An environment includes objects, activities, weather, and other conditions. Compare your environment at home with your environment at school. How are they alike? How are they different?

159

Discuss the concept vocabulary word *environment* with students. Ask students how they think the word *environment* relates to the theme Animals and Their Habitats. As students read the selections in this unit, encourage them to think about other words that relate to the theme. Students can record these words in the vocabulary section of the Writer's Notebooks.

GAME

Have students play the Making Sentences game during Small-Group Time.

Writer's Notebook

Have students copy the selection vocabulary and concept vocabulary words and definitions into the vocabulary section of their Writer's Notebooks. They can also include other words that relate to the theme as they think of them.

Concept/Question Board

As students read "Make Way for Ducklings," encourage them to post questions, answers, comments, or other items related to the theme Animals and Their Habitats on the **Concept/Question Board.**

Reading the Selection

Genre Fantasy

Have students identify the genre of "Make Way for Ducklings." *fantasy* If necessary tell students the elements of a fantasy.

- People, animals, or objects can do things that they cannot do in real life.
- Events occur that could not happen in the real world.
- A story takes place that could not occur in the real world.
- The story has creatures that do not exist in the real world.

Comprehension Strategies

Model and prompt the use of the following comprehension strategies during the first reading of "Make Way for Ducklings."

- Asking Questions
- Predicting

Comprehension Strategies Rubrics

Use the Informal Comprehension Strategies Rubrics to determine whether a student is using any of the strategies listed below. Note the strategies a student is using, instead of the degree to which a student might be using any particular strategy. In addition, encourage the student to tell of any strategies other than the ones being taught, that he or she is using.

Technology

Students can access ***SRA Imagine It! eStudent Reader*** electronically by using the ***eStudent Reader*** online or on CD-ROM.

Asking Questions

- ✦ The student stops to ask questions—any question.
- ✦ The student asks questions directly related to the text.
- ✦ The student asks *who, what, why, when, where,* or *how* questions as opposed to *yes* or *no* questions.
- ✦ The student asks questions that help clarify information in the text.

Predicting

- ✦ The student stops to make a prediction about the text.
- ✦ The student identifies the clues in the text used to make a prediction.
- ✦ The student uses clues in the text and prior knowledge to make a prediction.
- ✦ The student recognizes when a prediction is or is not confirmed by the text.

Formal Assessment 

Monitor Progress to Differentiate Instruction

Comprehension Skill Note students' understanding of the comprehension skill Reality and Fantasy.

APPROACHING LEVEL

IF . . . students are having difficulty with reality and fantasy as they read,

THEN . . . begin telling students any appropriate, well-known children's story that contains elements of fantasy. When you tell students a part of the story that could never happen, stop and ask *Could that ever really happen?* If the students' answer is "no," write the instance on the board. Continue modeling this question throughout "Make Way for Ducklings."

ON LEVEL

IF . . . students are gaining an understanding of reality and fantasy as they read,

THEN . . . have students create a two-column chart in the Writer's Notebook to list the elements of reality and the elements of fantasy they find while reading.

ABOVE LEVEL

IF . . . students are demonstrating an understanding of reality and fantasy as they read,

THEN . . . have students write a short fantasy story of their own, using a real-life location as the setting of their story.

Day 1

Reading and Responding

Differentiating Instruction **English Learner**

IF . . . students do not seem to understand the Focus Questions on page 161, **THEN . . .** restate the questions using simpler language. For example, *How do different wild animals live in cities? How do people help protect nature?*

Comprehension Skills

Reread "Make Way for Ducklings" using the following comprehension skill:

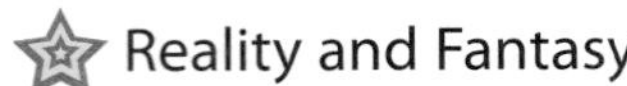

Reality and Fantasy

Reading with a Writer's Eye

When rereading "Make Way for Ducklings," explain the following literary element:

- Setting

Focus Questions

Have students read aloud the Focus Questions on page 161. Encourage students to think about the Focus Questions as they read "Make Way for Ducklings."

Reading Recommendation

Oral Reading

Use Routine 14, the reading the selection routine, as you read the story. While reading, model strategies and stop to ask and answer questions. Point out how the pictures reflect the story. Share the images that pop up in your mind as you read and how points in the reading relate to ideas you already know. Reread the text by applying comprehension skills. After reading, be sure to discuss the story using the "handing-off" procedure, and have students discuss new information they have learned.

This story lends itself to oral reading because of its descriptive language, use of dialogue, and the dramatic emphasis inherent in the story's various characterizations.

Technology

Have students listen to "Make Way for Ducklings" on the ***Listening Library CD.*** After students have listened, have them discuss what other things such as poetry, songs, or nonfiction they prefer to listen to on the radio or on CDs.

Genre

A **fantasy** is a fictional story that could not happen in real life. Fantasy stories may have characters that do things or tell of things that could not happen in real life.

Comprehension Skill

Reality and Fantasy

As you read, identify examples of reality and fantasy in the story.

Make Way *for* Ducklings

by Robert McCloskey

Focus Questions

How do various types of city wildlife adapt to their environments? What roles do people play in protecting the natural environment?

160

161

Students will read the story twice over a four-day period.

Day 1 **ORAL READ** Have students read the first half of the story. Model the comprehension strategies.

Day 2 **ORAL READ** Have students finish reading the story. Continue to model the comprehension strategies.

Day 3 **SILENT READ** Have students reread the first half of the story, focusing on the comprehension skill and Reading with a Writer's Eye.

Day 4 **SILENT READ** Have students finish rereading the story.

Reading and Responding

Mr. and Mrs. Mallard were looking for a place to live. But every time Mr. Mallard saw what looked like a nice place, Mrs. Mallard said it was no good. There were sure to be foxes in the woods or turtles in the water, and she was not going to raise a family where there might be foxes or turtles. So they flew on and on. 1

When they got to Boston, they felt too tired to fly any further. There was a nice pond in the Public Garden, with a little island on it. "The very place to spend the night," quacked Mr. Mallard. So down they flapped.

Next morning they fished for their breakfast in the mud at the bottom of the pond. But they didn't find much.

162

Just as they were getting ready to start on their way, a strange enormous bird came by. It was pushing a boat full of people, and there was a man sitting on its back. "Good morning," quacked Mr. Mallard, being polite. The big bird was too proud to answer. But the people on the boat threw peanuts into the water, so the Mallards followed them all round the pond and got another breakfast, better than the first.

"I like this place," said Mrs. Mallard as they climbed out on the bank and waddled along. "Why don't we build a nest and raise our ducklings right in this pond? There are no foxes and no turtles, and the people feed us peanuts. What could be better?"

"Good," said Mr. Mallard, delighted that at last Mrs. Mallard had found a place that suited her. But—

163

Phonics and Fluency

The skills students are reviewing in Phonics and Fluency should help them read the story. This lesson focuses on /ō/ spelled *_ow* and *oa_*. Words with these spellings will be found in boxes similar to this one throughout the story.

/ō/ spelled *oa_*: boat

Comprehension Strategies

This story is broken into two parts. On the first day, read pages 162–165. On the second day, read pages 166–169.

1 **Asking Questions** Teacher Modeling: *Asking questions as we read helps us to make sense of the story. I have a question. The story says that Mrs. Mallard is unhappy with places to raise her family. I wonder why. Maybe I'll find out if I keep reading. Oh, I see. It says that Mrs. Mallard is concerned about the foxes and turtles. Would anyone like to ask a question about the story at this time?*

Teacher Tip

GENRE Remind students that this story is a fantasy. However, even though there are elements of fantasy, like the talking ducks, other elements are real, such as the setting.

"Look out!" squawked Mrs. Mallard, all of a dither. "You'll get run over!" And when she got her breath she added: "*This* is no place for babies, with all those horrid things rushing about. We'll have to look somewhere else." ❷

So they flew over Beacon Hill and round the State House, but there was no place there.

They looked in Louisburg Square, but there was no water to swim in.

Then they flew over the Charles River. "This is better," quacked Mr. Mallard. "That island looks like a nice quiet place, and it's only a little way from the Public Garden." "Yes," said Mrs. Mallard, remembering the peanuts. "That looks like just the right place to hatch ducklings."

164

So they chose a cozy spot among the bushes near the water and settled down to build their nest. And only just in time, for now they were beginning to molt. All their old wing feathers started to drop out, and they would not be able to fly again until the new ones grew in.

But of course they could swim, and one day they swam over to the park on the river bank, and there they met a policeman called Michael. Michael fed them peanuts, and after that the Mallards called on Michael every day.

After Mrs. Mallard had laid eight eggs in the nest she couldn't go to visit Michael any more, because she had to sit on the eggs to keep them warm. She moved off the nest only to get a drink of water, or to have her lunch, or to count the eggs and make sure they were all there.

One day the ducklings hatched out. First came Jack, then Kack, and then Lack, then Mack and Nack and Ouack and Pack and Quack. Mr. and Mrs. Mallard were bursting with pride. It was a great

165

❷ **Asking Questions** Teacher Modeling: *I have another question. Why is Mrs. Mallard squawking? She seems so upset. Why does she want to look for a new home? Okay, I think I understand. I think Mrs. Mallard is upset about the "horrid things" that rush around. She thinks it's unsafe for her to raise a family so near to them. Be sure to let the class know if you have a question or an answer to a question.*

Comprehension Check

Why are the Mallards so particular about where they make their home? **Possible Answer** *To raise their ducklings, their home needs to be in a safe spot away from traffic, near water, and close to food.*

Vocabulary Tip

Point out the words *strange* and *enormous* on page 163 in the text. Then have students point to the picture of the strange and enormous bird on page 163. Ask students to explain how the illustration helps them understand the meaning of the word. Ask students to identify other strategies they use to figure out the meanings of unfamiliar words.

STOP You have read the first half of the story. You will continue the story tomorrow on page T138.

Lesson 2

Inquiry Planner

STEP 2: Choosing an Investigation Question

Day 1 With the whole group and in small-group discussions, students will generate possible investigation questions.

Day 2 Student will continue asking new questions.

Day 3 With the whole group, discuss ideas about the theme in "Make Way for Ducklings."

Day 4 Groups will choose one question to research and investigate.

Day 5 Students can post items on the **Concept/Question Board** and continue thinking about investigation topics and generating ideas.

Research in Action

Inquiry builds on the innate curiosity of the very young and nurtures and supports children on their developmental trajectory towards developing the increasingly metacognitive skills of proficient knowledge creation. In inquiry, "questions of wonderment become the driving force in designing the what and how of instruction"

(Murray, Shea & Shea, 2004)

Teacher Tip

CHOOSING AN INVESTIGATION QUESTION Some students may decide on their investigation question quickly. If so, have them start making conjectures. Because Inquiry is not a lock-step process, allow groups to progress through the steps of their investigations in the ways that are most effective for them.

Inquiry Process

Step 2—Choosing an Investigation Question

Whole-Group Time

Whole Group

- By this point, students have formed groups and explored possible investigation questions and ideas.
- Explain that each group's ideas and questions may be helpful to the other groups. Ask students to share some of the ideas they discussed in their small groups. Using the note-taking skills they learned in Lesson 1, have students practice taking notes about the main ideas presented by each group.
- Model how to choose good investigation questions. For example, return to the story you presented earlier. The problem in the story involved how to save animals who lost their habitat due to land development. This led to the question, *How can I help these animals?* Model how this question can develop into other research questions, saying something like this: *Now I realize that I can't protect all these animals all by myself. So this made me think of these other questions, which might be good investigation questions: Why do people disturb animal habitats? How can I convince others to help protect these animals habitats? How should the community protect these animals? Ask students what other questions this story might lead to, and write their answers on the board.*
- If students need help getting started, continue modeling general questions: Why do animals need habitats? What makes an animal habitat safe? How do animals choose their habitats? How are animal habitats destroyed, or how do they become unsafe? Why should we try to protect some animal habitats? How can people help protect animals and their habitats? Why do people only keep some kinds of animals as pets? How can similar animals live in different habitats? If groups are interested in specific kinds of animals, reflect this in the questions you model.
- Explain that groups are free to pursue any investigation question they want related to the unit theme Animals and Their Habitats. Remind students to choose questions that particularly interest them and those that they are excited to explore and learn more about.

Small-Group Time

Small Group

- Have students break into their groups. As students share stories and discuss ideas for their investigation, have them practice asking questions after each person tells a story. Remind them to listen carefully to the answers.
- Students should review the questions they recorded earlier in their Writer's Notebooks to remind them of the ideas and potential investigation questions they formed.
- Help each group with ***Skills Practice 1*** page 101 to help them develop good investigation questions.
- As you circulate among the groups, help them think through why the initial questions they have are interesting or valuable.

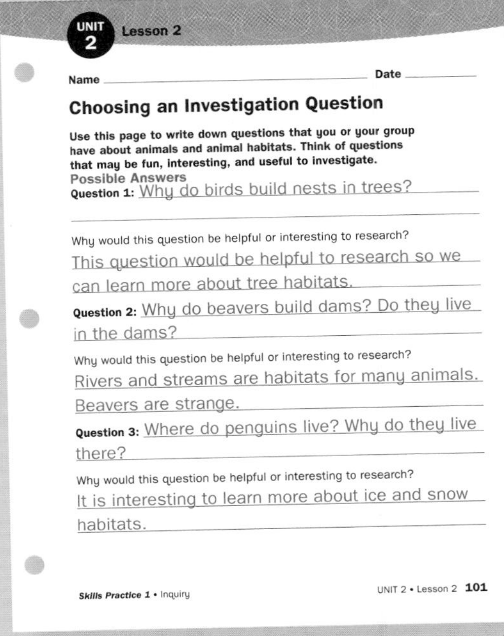

UNIT 2 Lesson 2

Name ______ Date ______

Choosing an Investigation Question

Use this page to write down questions that you or your group have about animals and animal habitats. Think of questions that may be fun, interesting, and useful to investigate.

Possible Answers

Question 1: Why do birds build nests in trees?

Why would this question be helpful or interesting to research?
This question would be helpful to research so we can learn more about tree habitats.

Question 2: Why do beavers build dams? Do they live in the dams?

Why would this question be helpful or interesting to research?
Rivers and streams are habitats for many animals. Beavers are strange.

Question 3: Where do penguins live? Why do they live there?

Why would this question be helpful or interesting to research?
It is interesting to learn more about ice and snow habitats.

Skills Practice 1 • Inquiry UNIT 2 • Lesson 2 101

Skills Practice 1, p. 101

Concept/Question Board

Encourage students to write facts, opinions, ideas, or questions on the **Concept/Question Board.** Students might

- post new ideas learned from whole-group or small-group discussions.
- bring in and post magazine articles and pictures of animals and their habitats.
- take and post pictures of pets or wild animals in their habitats. (Remind students not to disturb the homes of animals if they take their pictures. Encourage them to show respect for the animals and their homes.)
- draw pictures that support the theme.
- post titles and summaries of books, articles, or TV shows about animals and their habitats.
- respond to questions others have raised.

Remember that a good way to encourage use of the **Concept/ Question Board** is to model using it yourself.

Teacher Tips

CONCEPT/QUESTION BOARD Have students bring in photographs they have taken or pictures collected from the Internet or magazines that show animals and their habitats.

ASKING QUESTIONS Students might first ask questions about facts which usually begin with *who, what, when,* or *where*. Encourage students to ask *how* or *why* questions, which typically require more thought, reflection, and research. For example, *How do people make wild animals pets?* or *Why did the sabertooth tiger become extinct, but not other kinds of tigers?* are good investigation questions.

OBJECTIVES

Students will
- take notes and develop an outline for their book reviews.
- take spelling pretest.
- practice cursive *f* and *h*.

MATERIALS

- Routine 15
- ***Transparencies*** 51, 52
- ***Skills Practice 1,*** p. 103
- ***Language Arts Handbook,*** pp. 218–219

Teacher Tip

PLAN AHEAD Have students select and read a nonfiction book about the theme Animals and Their Habitats prior to beginning this writing assignment. Select a book that you can use to model writing a book review.

Nonfiction Book Review

Review of *Crinkleroot's Book of Animal Tracking* by Jim Arnosky

Crinkleroot's Book of Animal Tracking explains how you can tell where an animal has been by the tracks and other signs that they leave. The book starts with beavers and tells how they make dams. Then, it tells about river otters. It shows what the otter's tail-print and footprints look like. Raccoons, whitetail deer, snowshoe rabbits, bobcats, and red foxes are also covered in the book. There are special things to learn about each animal. For example, the red fox makes a funny little dog yip.

This book was great! Crinkleroot is a funny character. Even though Crinkleroot is funny, I learned a lot. There are drawings on every page. One thing that surprised me was the picture of the raccoon's tracks. They look like a person's hands! At the end of the book, there are even more pictures of animals' tracks. The book made me want to go hunting for animal tracks right away!

 Level 3

Transparency 51

Writing Nonfiction Book Review

ROUTINE 15

Prewriting

Teach—Taking Notes and Outlining

- Use Routine 15 as a guide for modeling writing strategies.
- Display ***Transparency*** 51. Read the book review aloud. Explain to students that people write book reviews to help others decide whether they should read the same book. The writer gives a brief description of the book and explains what he or she liked or disliked and why.
- Discuss the audience of a book review with students. Ask them who will most likely be their audience. **Possible Answer** *other students in the class who may want to read the book*
- Point out sentences on ***Transparency*** 51 that contain the summary of the book or that contain the writer's opinion. Explain that a good book review will contain facts about the book as well as the writer's opinion.
- Tell students that they will begin the writing process by taking notes on important information from the book they plan to review. Remind students that in Study Skills Unit 2 Lesson 1, they learned note-taking skills. Have students refer to page 91 in ***Skills Practice 1*** to review the note-taking guidelines.
- Tell students that after they complete their notes, they will be putting the notes into outline form. Explain that outlining is a way to organize notes in a format that will be easy to follow once the writer is ready to begin drafting sentences and paragraphs.
- Show students a basic outline on the board or on chart paper, and explain that the Roman numerals are the main topics. The capital letters are the main ideas of the paragraphs, and the numbers under the capitals are the details that should be included in each paragraph.
- For more information about outlining, see ***Language Arts Handbook*** pages 218–219.

Writing, continued

Guided Practice

- Using the book you selected, show students how to take notes on main topics and supporting details, and then show students how to convert those notes into outline form, using an outline form similar to the one found on page 103 in ***Skills Practice 1.***
- Ask a student to give the title of his or her book. Write the title on the board. Using a basic outline format, ask the student for the main topic of the book and some of the details about that topic. Show students how to add the details to the outline.

Apply

Composing—Prewriting Have students take notes on their individual books. Then, have students turn to ***Skills Practice 1*** page 103 and complete the Think section and the outline.

Traits of Good Writing

Ideas and Organization The writer's tone is informative.

Assessment

You will use the Writing Rubrics found in the Level Appendix to evaluate students' book reviews. You may use any of the rubrics for Genre, Writing Process, and Writing Traits. Share with students what you will be looking for when assessing their book reviews.

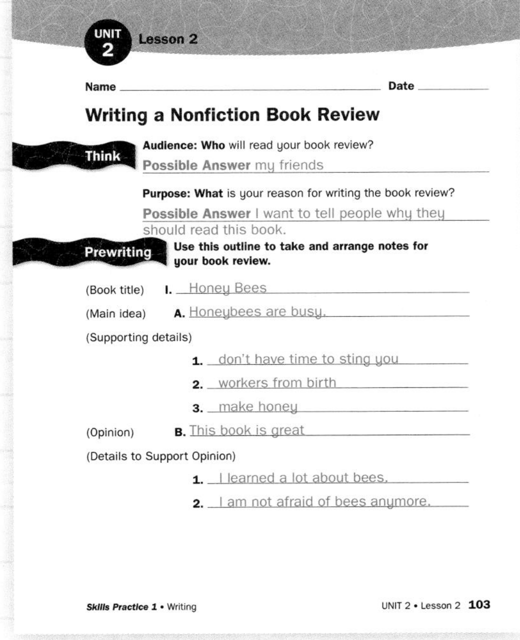
UNIT 2 Lesson 2

Name ______ Date ______

Writing a Nonfiction Book Review

Think

Audience: Who will read your book review?
Possible Answer my friends

Purpose: What is your reason for writing the book review?
Possible Answer I want to tell people why they should read this book.

Prewriting **Use this outline to take and arrange notes for your book review.**

(Book title) I. Honey Bees
(Main idea) A. Honeybees are busy.
(Supporting details)
1. don't have time to sting you
2. workers from birth
3. make honey
(Opinion) B. This book is great
(Details to Support Opinion)
1. I learned a lot about bees.
2. I am not afraid of bees anymore.

Skills Practice 1 • Writing UNIT 2 • Lesson 2 103

Skills Practice 1, p. 103

Spelling

/ō/ and Irregular Plurals Pretest

Teach

Say the sentences below. Have students write the spelling words on a separate sheet of paper. When they are finished, have them correct any misspelled words.

Pretest Sentences

1. Please tape a **bow** on the gift.
2. The **mice** scurried through the field.
3. The men and **women** gathered in the room.
4. My baseball **coach** is also my math teacher.
5. I saw four **deer** in the woods.
6. **Throw** the football to me!
7. We are going to **roast** chestnuts in the winter.
8. My little brother lost his two front **teeth.**
9. I see the **crow** flying overhead in the evenings.
10. The **oxen** pulled the plow.
11. The birds are flying **low** to the ground.
12. We went to the bank to get a **loan.**
13. My aunt is going to **grow** tomatoes.
14. Hannah likes to swim and **float** in the lake.
15. Can you see the **fish** swimming in the lake?

Challenge Sentences

16. Many beautiful **cacti** grow in the desert.
17. Remember to pack your **pillow.**

Diagnose any misspellings by determining whether students misspelled the irregular plurals, the /ō/ spellings, or some other part of the word. Then have students use the pretest as a take-home list to study irregular plurals and the /ō/ spellings.

Teacher Tips

PRACTICE Encourage students to practice these letter formations as they draft and revise their book reviews.

PENMANSHIP If students are having problems forming cursive *f* and *h*, or their letters are floating between the lines, review proper paper position, check to make sure students are holding their pencils correctly, and review letter formation.

Research in Action

In addition to learning how to write the letters of the alphabet correctly, students must be able to produce them quickly. Penmanship fluency generally develops as a consequence of writing frequently. As a result, we need to provide students with plenty of opportunities to write.
(Steve Graham and Karen Harris)

Differentiating Instruction English Learner

IF . . . English Learners need help understanding your descriptions of the cursive strokes, **THEN . . .** use arrows, drawings, objects, or pantomime to help students understand the meanings of *under, over, back, forward, down, loop,* and *slant.*

Penmanship

Cursive Letters *f* and *h*

Teach

- Remind students that cursive letters are made of four types of strokes (undercurve, overcurve, downcurve, and slant lines).
- Introduce lowercase cursive *f* and *h* as slant line letters with loops. Display ***Transparency*** 52. Using a pointer, trace the letter saying the formations aloud.

Letter *f*	Starting point, undercurve Loop back, slant down Loop forward into undercurve: small *f*
Letter *h*	Starting point, undercurve Loop back, slant down Overcurve, slant down Undercurve: small *h*

- Tell students that the loops in *f* and *h* should touch the top line.
- To model proper letter formation, write the following words on the board: *fan, hat, father.*

Guided Practice

Have volunteers practice writing the letters on the board.

Apply

- Have students practice writing each of the letters four times on a piece of paper. Ask them to circle the best formation of each of their letters.
- After reviewing the words you wrote on the board, ask students to write the words on a sheet of paper to practice letter formation. Have them circle the best formation of each letter.

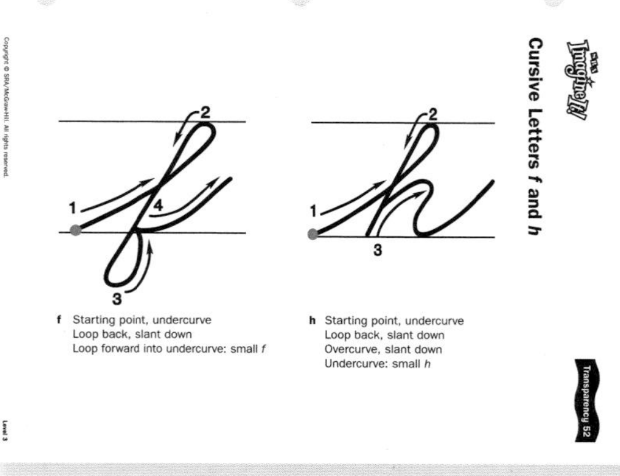

Transparency 52

Lesson 2

Skills Traces

Preparing to Read

Word Structure: Plurals

Introduced in Grade 2, Unit 4, Lesson 5

Reviewed: Unit 2, Lesson 1
Practiced: Unit 2, Lesson 2
Unit 2, Lesson 5
Assessed: ***Lesson Assessment Book 2,*** p. 51

Reviewed in Grade 4, Unit 1, Lesson 3

Phonics:

See Level Appendix

Reading and Responding

Comprehension Skill: Reality and Fantasy

Reviewed in Grade 2, Unit 1, Lesson 4

Grade 3
Reviewed: Unit 2, Lesson 2
Practiced: Unit 2, Lesson 3
Assessed: ***Lesson Assessment Book 1,*** pp. 52–54

Comprehension Strategy: Asking Questions

Reviewed in Grade 2, Unit 1, Lesson 1

Grade 3
Reviewed: Unit 1, Lesson 1
Practiced: Unit 2, Lesson 1
Assessed: Unit 2, Lesson 2 , p. T125

Reviewed in Grade 4, Unit 1, Lesson 2

Comprehension Strategy: Predicting

Reviewed in Grade 2, Unit 1, Lesson 3

Grade 3
Reviewed: Unit 1, Lesson 1
Practiced: Unit 2, Lesson 2
Assessed: Unit 2, Lesson 2, p. T125

Reviewed in Grade 4, Unit 1, Lesson 1

Language Arts

Writing: Book Review

Reviewed in Grade 2, Unit 4, Lesson 3

Grade 3
Reviewed: Unit 2, Lesson 2
Assessed: Unit 2, Lesson 2, p. T174

Reviewed in Grade 4, Unit 5, Lesson 3

Grammar, Usage, and Mechanics: Plurals and Irregular Plurals

Grade 3
Introduced: Unit 2, Lesson 2
Practiced: Unit 6, Lesson 2
Assessed: ***Lesson Assessment Book 1,*** p. 56

Reviewed in Grade 4, Unit 1, Lesson 3

Preparing to Read

OBJECTIVES

Students will
- review /ō/ spelled _*ow* and *oa*_.
- build fluency.

MATERIALS

- ***Transparency*** 49
- ***Sound/Spelling Card*** 30
- Routines 2, 3, 4, 7, 8

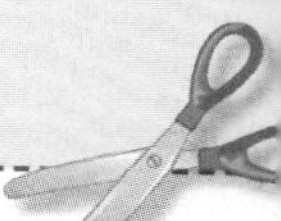

Daily Oral Practice

Daily News

Honk! Honk! Beep! Beep! Animals roam through the noisy city roads looking for safe homes. Many city animals know where to look for good homes, but we should also help protect these animal habitats in the city.

- Write the daily news on the board or on chart paper. Then have students read the daily news in unison to practice fluency.
- As a review of yesterday's phonics and fluency lesson, ask a volunteer to identify any words in the message with /ō/ spelled _*ow* or *oa*_. */ō/ spelled _ow in* know; */ō/ spelled oa_ in* roam, roads

Phonics and Fluency

ROUTINE  ROUTINE 

Review : /ō/ spelled _*ow* and *oa*_

Blending

Line 1	flow	grow	throw	know
Line 2	follow	yellow	blowing	mower
Line 3	boat	road	coast	groan
Line 4	toaster	floating	boasting	overcoat

Sentence 1 The snow blows slowly against the <u>side</u> of the <u>house</u>.

Sentence 2 The <u>same</u> loaf of oat bread will make good toast.

Blending

✦ Use ***Transparency*** 49 with the blending lines and sentences from Day 1.

✦ Review ***Sound/Spelling Card*** 30 with students. Then use Routine 3, the whole-word blending process, to have students read Lines 1–4.

✦ Have students read the sentences using normal intonation and expression. If students have difficulty reading a sentence, stop and use Routine 4, the blending sentences process.

Developing Oral Language

Use one or both of these activities to help students practice reading the word from the blending lines.

- Choose a student to point to a word, pronounce it, and use it in a sentence. **Possible Answer** Yellow *is my favorite color.* Then have the student choose a new word and select another student to continue the activity. Repeat until all words have been used.
- Create sentences for students to complete using words from the word lines. Ask students to point to and read words from Lines 1–4 to fill in the blanks. For example, He had to put gas in the *mower* . The more you *know*, the smarter you will be. After modeling a few examples, have students make their own clue sentences.

Dictation

ROUTINE 2 ROUTINE 7 ROUTINE 8

✦ Follow Routine 7 for whole-word dictation. When dictating words, say the word, use the word in a sentence, and then repeat the word.

✦ Follow Routine 8 for sentence dictation. When dictating sentences, say the sentence. Next, dictate one word at a time, following Routine 2 for sounds-in-sequence dictation or Routine 7 for whole-word dictation, depending on your students. Have students proofread for spelling, capitalization, and end punctuation.

✦ Dictate the following words and sentence for students to write.

Line 1	crow	elbow	slow
Line 2	soap	toad	throat
Challenge Word	oatmeal		
Sentence	Do you soak your oatmeal in milk?		

Sound/Spelling Card 30

Teacher Tip

BLENDING During Workshop, work with students who have difficulty blending words by using Routine 1 for sound-by-sound blending or Routine 3 for whole-word blending.

Differentiating Instruction English Learner

IF . . . students have difficulty writing the dictated words, **THEN . . .** before you dictate the words, write them on the board, emphasize /ō/ as you pronounce them, and then have students repeat the pronunciations.

responsibility taking care of so many ducklings, and it kept them very busy.

One day Mr. Mallard decided he'd like to take a trip to see what the rest of the river was like, further on. So off he set. "I'll meet you in a week, in the Public Garden," he quacked over his shoulder. "Take good care of the ducklings."

"Don't you worry," said Mrs. Mallard. "I know all about bringing up children." And she did.

She taught them how to swim and dive.

She taught them to walk in a line, to come when they were called, and to keep a safe distance from bikes and scooters and other things with wheels.

166

When at last she felt perfectly satisfied with them, she said one morning: "Come along, children. Follow me." Before you could wink an eyelash Jack, Kack, Lack, Mack, Nack, Ouack, Pack, and Quack fell into line, just as they had been taught. Mrs. Mallard led the way into the water and they swam behind her to the opposite bank.

There they waded ashore and waddled along till they came to the highway.

Mrs. Mallard stepped out to cross the road. "Honk, honk!" went the horns on the speeding cars. "Qua-a-ack!" went Mrs. Mallard as she tumbled back again. "Quack! Quack! Quack! Quack!" went Jack, Kack, Lack, Mack, Nack, Ouack, Pack, and Quack, just as loud as their little quackers could quack. The cars kept speeding by and honking, and Mrs. Mallard and the ducklings kept right on quack-quack-quacking. 3

167

OBJECTIVES

Students will

- use the comprehension strategy Predicting.
- discuss the story using the handing-off process.
- review vocabulary, genre, and fluency.

MATERIALS

- ***Student Reader***, Book 1, pp. 166–171
- Routine A
- ***Skills Practice 1,*** pp. 97–98
- ***Transparencies*** 5, 50

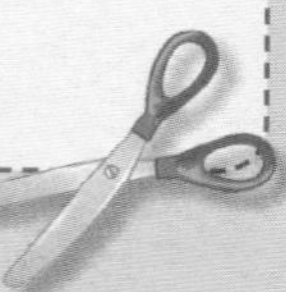

Comprehension Strategies

3 Predicting Teacher Modeling: *Predictions based on details from the story help readers think about what might happen next. Thinking about what I've read so far will help me. I know that the title is "Make Way for Ducklings." I think that Mrs. Mallard will teach her ducklings to cross the street, and that people will help them get safely across. I think that's where the title of the story comes from. As we read, we can check to see if my prediction is confirmed. Do you have any predictions you would like to make?*

Vocabulary Tip

Point out the phrase *bringing up* on page 166 in the text. Ask students whether comparing ducklings to children helps them understand the phrase *bringing up*. Point out the word *beckoned* in the text on page 168. Ask students to look at the picture of the policeman on page 168. Check to see whether looking at the illustration helps them understand the word *beckoned.*

They made such a noise that Michael came running, waving his arms and blowing his whistle.

He planted himself in the center of the road, raised one hand to stop the traffic, and then beckoned with the other, the way policemen do, for Mrs. Mallard to cross over.

As soon as Mrs. Mallard and the ducklings were safe on the other side and on their way down Mount Vernon Street, Michael rushed back to his police booth.

He called Clancy at headquarters and said: "There's a family of ducks walkin' down the street!" Clancy said: "Family of *what?*" *"Ducks!"* yelled Michael. "Send a police car, quick!"

Meanwhile Mrs. Mallard had reached the Corner Book Shop and turned into Charles Street, with Jack, Kack, Lack, Mack, Nack, Ouack, Pack, and Quack all marching in line behind her.

Everyone stared. An old lady from Beacon Hill said: "Isn't it

168

amazing!" and the man who swept the streets said: "Well, now, ain't that nice!" and when Mrs. Mallard heard them she was so proud she tipped her nose in the air and walked along with an extra swing in her waddle.

When they came to the corner of Beacon Street there was the police car with four policemen that Clancy had sent from headquarters. The policemen held back the traffic so Mrs. Mallard and the ducklings could march across the street, right on into the Public Garden.

Inside the gate they all turned round to say thank you to the policemen. The policemen smiled and waved good-by.

When they reached the pond and swam across to the little island, there was Mr. Mallard waiting for them, just as he had promised. 4

The ducklings liked the new island so much that they decided to live there. All day long they follow the swan boats and eat peanuts.

And when night falls they swim to their little island and go to sleep.

169

4 Confirming Predictions Teacher Modeling: *Remember that when you make predictions, you should verify whether your prediction was confirmed or not. My earlier prediction was confirmed. I predicted that Mrs. Mallard would teach her ducks to cross the road and that people would help them get across safely. Michael, the policeman, stopped the traffic to make way for the ducklings to cross the street. The policeman did his part to keep the ducks safe. Now the Mallards are safe on their island home.*

Comprehension Check

Why did Michael the policeman call headquarters? **Possible Answer** *He wanted Clancy to send other police officers and cars to help Mrs. Mallard and her ducklings safely get home to their island.*

Differentiating Instruction English Learner

IF . . . students are confused by the use of the word *quack* on page 167 in the story, **THEN . . .** point out that it is used as a verb, to indicate the sound a duckling makes, and as the name of one of the ducklings. Ask students what word from their own language means "the sound a duck makes."

Teacher Tip

PREDICTING Remind students that clues in the text help form predictions. Predicting is not a guessing game, but rather a way to think critically about what is being read.

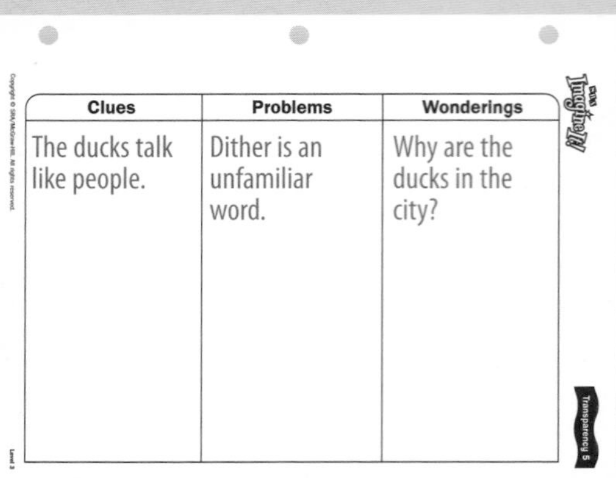

Clues	Problems	Wonderings
The ducks talk like people.	Dither is an unfamiliar word.	Why are the ducks in the city?

Transparency 5

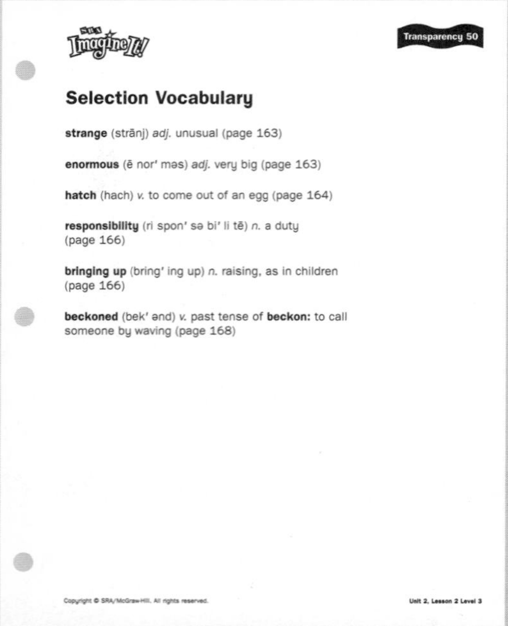

Transparency 50

Selection Vocabulary

strange (strānj) *adj.* unusual (page 163)

enormous (ē nor' məs) *adj.* very big (page 163)

hatch (hach) *v.* to come out of an egg (page 164)

responsibility (ri spon' sə bi' li tē) *n.* a duty (page 166)

bringing up (bring' ing up) *n.* raising, as in children (page 166)

beckoned (bek' ənd) *v.* past tense of **beckon:** to call someone by waving (page 168)

Unit 2, Lesson 2 Level 3

Transparency 50

Differentiating Instruction **English Learner**

IF . . . students need extra help to participate in the discussion, **THEN . . .** rephrase the questions, using simpler language. For example: *What were the good things and bad things about city life for the Mallards?*

Discussing the Selection

- It is important for students to see you as a contributing member of the group. Use Routine A, the handing-off process, to emphasize that you are part of the group. Actively participate in the handing-off process by raising your hand to be called on by the last speaker when you have a contribution to make. Point out unusual and interesting insights verbalized by students so that these insights are recognized and discussed. As the year progresses, students will take more responsibility for the discussion of the selections.
- Engage students in a discussion using the handing-off procedure to determine whether they have grasped the following ideas:
  - Animals have specific requirements for suitable and safe habitats.
  - Human beings can help protect animals and their habitats.
- Ask students how the story demonstrates the following key concepts:
  - Animals face many challenges in finding suitable habitats.
  - There were many advantages and disadvantages of city life for the Mallards.
- Return to the Clues, Problems, and Wonderings chart on ***Transparency*** 5. Have students discuss which clues were useful, how they resolved their problems, and how they answered their questions. Also, ask students if the predictions they made while browsing the story were confirmed or not confirmed.
- Have students return to the Focus Questions on ***Student Reader,*** Book 1 page 161. Select a student to read the questions aloud, and have students answer and discuss the questions. Have them return to the text as necessary.

Genre Review

Review the elements of fantasy with students on page T124. Ask students how they know "Make Way for Ducklings" is a fantasy.

Where do different animals live?

After reading the story, read the Big Idea question. Discuss with students how the story helps answer this question.

Vocabulary Review

Review with students the selection vocabulary words and definitions they wrote in the vocabulary section of their Writer's Notebook. Then refer students turn to pp. 97–98 in ***Skills Practice 1.*** Help students complete the first two questions. Have students complete the rest on their own. Also, review the concept word *environment*. Ask students whether they can think of other words related to the theme Animals and their Habitats. **Possible Answers** *homes, surroundings, protection, compassion*

Fluency

"Make Way for Ducklings" features lighthearted and funny dialogue and is ideal for practicing intonation. Intonation, or the rise and fall in pitch and volume of the voice, is essential to fluency because students can read the words and phrases of a story in the same manner that the author of the story intended the words to sound. Careful attention to intonation helps readers "hear" the words of the story correctly, which aids in both understanding and enjoyment of the text.

- Read aloud pages 162–163 of "Make Way for Ducklings." Model intonation for students. For example, after reading *Why don't we build a nest and raise our ducklings right in this pond?* point out how you lifted your voice at the end of the sentence because of the question mark. Tell students to lift their voices at the end of a sentence that contains a question mark and to add special emphasis to words that are followed by an exclamation point. Have students follow along in the ***Student Reader*** and tell them to raise their hands when you pause.

Formal Assessment 

Monitor Progress to Differentiate Instruction

Selection Vocabulary Note students' understanding of the vocabulary words and their definitions.

APPROACHING LEVEL

IF . . . students need extra help with the selection vocabulary,	**THEN . . .** use ***Intervention Guide*** Unit 2, Lesson 2.
IF . . . students need extra help with the selection vocabulary,	**THEN . . .** use ***Reteach,*** page 39.

ON LEVEL

IF . . . students need practice using the selection vocabulary,	**THEN . . .** have students write sentences using the vocabulary words.

ABOVE LEVEL

IF . . . students understand the selection vocabulary,	**THEN . . .** use ***Challenge Activities*** page 36.

Teacher Tip

WORD BANK If you created a Word Bank of key words related to the theme Animals and Their Habitats, remind students to add to the Word Bank as they find words from other resources, from their activities, and from family discussions. Organize the words according to parts of speech.

Fluency Tip

FLUENCY By this time in Grade 3, good readers should be reading approximately 99 words per minute with fluency and expression. The only way to gain this fluency is through practice. Have students reread the selection to you and to each other during Workshop to help build fluency. As students read, you may notice that some need work in building fluency. During Workshop, have these students choose a section of the text (a minimum of 160 words) to read several times to build fluency.

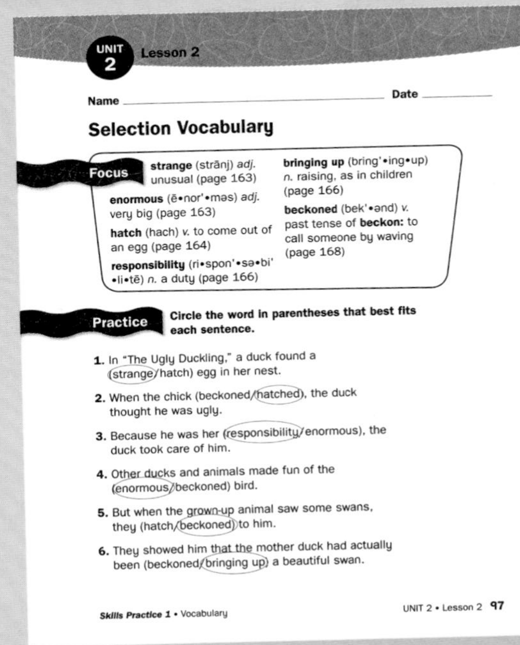

UNIT 2 Lesson 2

Name ______ Date ______

Selection Vocabulary

Focus

strange (strānj) *adj.* unusual (page 163)

enormous (ē•nor'•məs) *adj.* very big (page 163)

hatch (hach) *v.* to come out of an egg (page 164)

responsibility (ri•spon'•sə•bi'•li•tē) *n.* a duty (page 166)

bringing up (bring'•ing•up) *n.* raising, as in children (page 166)

beckoned (bek'•ənd) *v.* past tense of **beckon:** to call someone by waving (page 168)

Practice **Circle the word in parentheses that best fits each sentence.**

1. In "The Ugly Duckling," a duck found a (strange/hatch) egg in her nest.
2. When the chick (beckoned/hatched), the duck thought he was ugly.
3. Because he was her (responsibility/enormous), the duck took care of him.
4. Other ducks and animals made fun of the (enormous/beckoned) bird.
5. But when the grown-up animal saw some swans, they (hatch/beckoned) to him.
6. They showed him that the mother duck had actually been (beckoned/bringing up) a beautiful swan.

Skills Practice 1 • Vocabulary UNIT 2 • Lesson 2 97

Skills Practice 1, p. 97

Reading and Responding

Teacher Tips

LISTENING During Workshop, have students listen to "Make Way for Ducklings" for a model of oral reading. While students listen, have them keep a list in their Writer's Notebooks of any new or unfamiliar words they encounter, and instruct them to check the words using a dictionary or glossary. Also, instruct students to listen for the lesson's vocabulary words and to check that the words make sense within the reading.

WRITE ABOUT IT! Have students write about a time when they helped an animal in their Writer's Notebooks.

Meet the Author and Illustrator

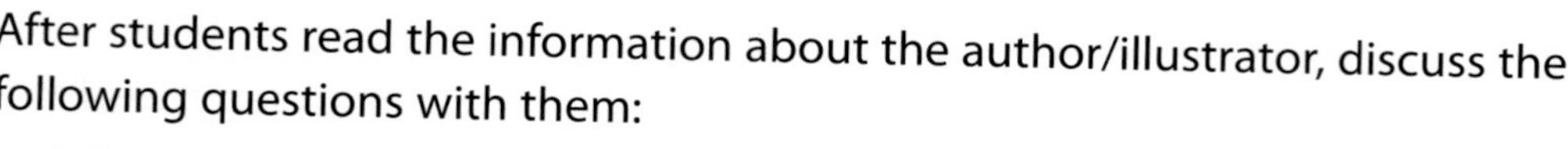

After students read the information about the author/illustrator, discuss the following questions with them:

- Robert McCloskey thought he wanted to be an inventor when he was a child. What does being an inventor have in common with being a writer and illustrator? **Possible Answer** *One must be creative in all three situations. They all require imagination to create new ideas.*
- *Winning a Caldecott Medal is an important honor for illustrators. Robert McCloskey has won two Caldecott awards. How might winning an award affect an illustrator?* **Possible Answer** *An award lets an illustrator know others appreciate and enjoy looking at his or her illustrations. It is a nice honor.*

Theme Connections

Within the Selection

1. What was important to Mr. and Mrs. Mallard as they looked for a home in the city? **Possible Answer** *The Mallards wanted to find a safe place where they could raise their family, have food, and have water in which to swim.*
2. How did the people in the story help protect Mr. and Mrs. Mallard and their family? **Possible Answers** *The police officers helped the Mallards cross the streets. Many people provided food for them, too.*

Across Selections

3. How is this selection like "One Small Place in a Tree"? **Possible Answer** *Both stories are about animals seeking safe habitats where they can find food and shelter.*
4. How is it different? *Answers will vary.*

Beyond the Selection

5. What does "Make Way for Ducklings" tell you about animals and their habitats? **Possible Answers** *"Make Way for Ducklings" tells us that it isn't always easy for animals to find the perfect home. People must sometimes help animals stay safe in their habitats.*
6. What can you do to help protect the animals that live in your neighborhood? *Answers will vary.*

Meet the Author and Illustrator

Robert McCloskey

Robert McCloskey changed his mind many times before he settled on a career. He learned to play several instruments in the hopes of being a musician. He later thought he would be an inventor because he liked to work with mechanical things. Then he began drawing and became very good at it. To prepare for writing *Make Way for Ducklings*, McCloskey bought four mallard ducks, which he kept in his apartment to observe and sketch. It took him two years to plan what he wanted to write about, and another two years to write and draw the story. His hard work and patience paid off. He won a Caldecott Medal, an important award for Children's books, for *Make Way for Ducklings*.

170

Animals and Their Habitats

Theme Connections

Within the Selection

1. What was important to Mr. and Mrs. Mallard as they looked for a home in the city?
2. How did the people in the story help protect Mr. and Mrs. Mallard and their family?

Across Selections

3. How is this selection like "One Small Place in a Tree"?
4. How is it different?

Beyond the Selection

5. What does "Make Way for Ducklings" tell you about animals and their habitats?
6. What can you do to help protect animals that live in your neighborhood?

Write about It!

Describe a time you helped an animal.

Remember to look for articles about people helping animals in their habitats to add to the **Concept/Question Board.**

171

Concept/Question Board

As students discuss "Make Way for Ducklings," encourage them to post questions, answers, comments, or other items related to the theme Animals and Their Habitats on the **Concept/Question Board.**

Teacher Tip

BEYOND THE SELECTION Have students summarize what they have learned, and tell how they might use this information in further investigations.

Writer's Notebook

- Have students list other fiction stories they have read in class or on their own in their Writer's Notebooks.
- Have students compare the elements found in each story.

OBJECTIVES

Students will

- learn to spell words with /ō/ and irregular plurals.
- learn regular and irregular plural nouns.
- draft book reviews.

MATERIALS

- ***Language Arts Handbook,*** pp. 92–97
- ***Skills Practice 1,*** pp. 107–108
- ***Transparency*** 3

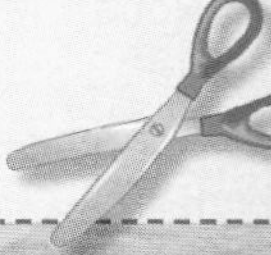

Writing Nonfiction Book Review

Drafting

Teach

- Students are going to draft their book reviews using their outlines and the notes they have taken.
- Tell students that their reviews will contain an introductory paragraph and a conclusion. Explain that the number of capital letters they have on their outlines will match the number of paragraphs in their reviews. For example, if the outline has capital *A* and *B* with detail numbers under each, then the book review should contain four paragraphs total. Paragraph 1 contains the introduction, including the book title, author, and basic summary of the information in the book review. Paragraphs 2 and 3 are the capital *A* and *B* paragraphs with the numbered details. Paragraph 4 is the conclusion, in which students will sum up what they stated in the previous paragraphs and write their final opinion (why they do or do not recommend the book).
- Tell students that during drafting, they should concentrate on writing their ideas on paper. They will have time to go back and revise and edit/proofread their papers later.
- For further information about book reviews, see ***Language Arts Handbook*** pages 92–97.

Research in Action

Skilled writing does not take place in a vacuum. What and how well students write is influenced by a host of social factors, including the amount of time devoted to writing, the creation of a supportive writing environment, and interactions with peers and teachers as audience and collaborators.
(Steve Graham and Karen Harris)

Book Review for Nonfiction

Nonfiction means that the story or information is about a real person, place, or event. The purpose of nonfiction is usually to inform, explain, or persuade. Begin with the title of the book and the author. Write a paragraph that tells what the book was about and what you learned from it. Then include a paragraph about what you thought about the book. It is okay if you don't like a book, but you should remember to give good reasons.

Ali used this graphic organizer for the nonfiction book *One Small Place in a Tree* by Barbara Brenner.

Title: One Small Place in a Tree
Author: Barbara Brenner
Summary
What was it about?
things that live in trees
What did I learn?
many animals live in trees
holes make good habitats for small animals
holes make a tree die
animals can live in dead trees
My Opinion
a good book with good pictures

Expository Writing • Book Review 95

Language Arts Handbook, p. 95

Writing, continued

Guided Practice

Using a student's outline or the model you created earlier, draft a first paragraph on Transparency 3. Once you have created the first paragraph, ask students to explain what information should follow the introductory paragraph based on the outline.

Apply

Composing—Drafting Have students draft their book reviews. Tell students to write on every other line so that they can easily revise and edit marks later. Remind students to refer to their outlines and notes as they draft.

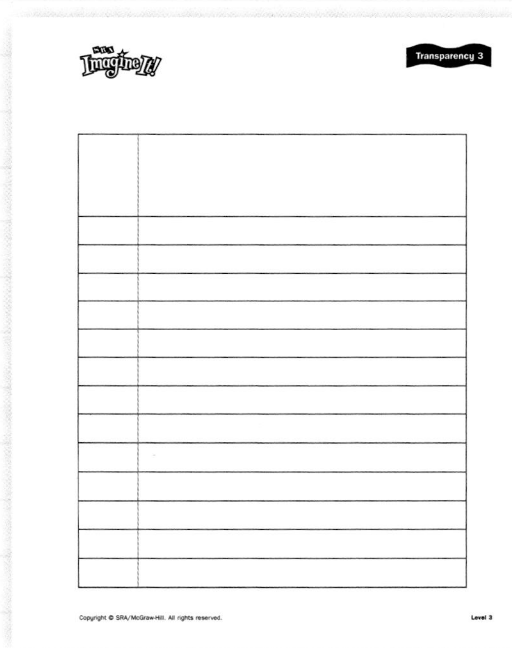

Transparency 3

Spelling

/ō/ and Irregular Plurals

Teach

Use a word sort to teach irregular plurals and words with /ō/ spelled *_ow* and *oa_*.

Guided Practice

Write the following headings on the board: *irregular plurals, /ō/*. Then write the word list: *bow, mice, women, coach, deer, throw, roast, teeth, crow, oxen, low, loan, grow, float,* and *fish*. Have volunteers write the words under the correct heading. Once the spelling words have all been used, ask for students to come to the board and underline the part of each word that reflects the category in which it was placed. If a word fits in more than one category, ask the students to put the word under the heading that they prefer.

Word Sort Answers

Irregular Plurals: *mice, women, deer, teeth, oxen, fish*
Words with /ō/ spelled *_ow: bow, throw, crow, low, grow*
Words with /ō/ spelled *oa_: coach, roast, loan, float*

Differentiating Instruction **English Learner**

IF . . . students are native Spanish speakers, **THEN . . .** they might have trouble pronouncing /v/ when a noun that ends in *f* is used as a plural. They might pronounce /v/ as a /b/ or an /f/. Provide extra time for students to practice these pronunciations.

Grammar, Usage, and Mechanics

Regular Plural Nouns and Irregular Plural Nouns

Teach

✦ Start a chart for Regular and Irregular Plurals on chart paper. For example:

Noun	Regular Plural	Irregular Plural
ant	ants	
fox	foxes	
country	countries	
wolf	wolves	

✦ Make the chart accessible to students so they can add examples to the list throughout the lesson.

✦ Explain that plural nouns name more than one person, place, thing, or idea.

✦ Explain the rules for making regular nouns plural. As you explain each rule, ask students for a corresponding example to add to the chart.

- The plural of most regular nouns is formed by adding *-s.*
- For regular nouns ending in *s, ch, sh, ss, z, zz,* or *x,* the plural is formed by adding *-es.*
- For regular nouns ending with a consonant and *y,* the plural is formed by changing the *y* to *i* and adding *-es.*
- Regular nouns that end with an *f* sound like /v/ sound when used as a plural. Therefore, change the *f* to *v* and add *-es.*

✦ Explain that some nouns are irregular and do not follow these rules. Students need to memorize the plural forms of these words or use a dictionary for the correct spelling.

Guided Practice

Have students turn to ***Skills Practice 1,*** page 107. Read the directions aloud. Complete the first two Practice questions as a class.

Apply

Have students complete ***Skills Practice 1*** pages 107–108 to practice forming plural nouns and irregular plural nouns.

Monitor Progress to Differentiate Instruction

Formal Assessment

Regular and Irregular Plurals Note whether students understand irregular plurals.

APPROACHING LEVEL

IF . . . students need to practice regular and irregular plurals,	**THEN . . .** have them complete ***Reteach*** page 43 during Workshop.
IF . . . students need more practice with regular and irregular plurals,	**THEN . . .** refer to Unit 2 Lesson 2 in the ***Intervention Guide***.

ON LEVEL

IF . . . students have an understanding of regular and irregular plurals,	**THEN . . .** have them work with the ***Workshop Kits*** during Workshop.

ABOVE LEVEL

IF . . . students are ready for a challenge,	**THEN . . .** have them complete ***Challenge Activities*** page 39 during Workshop.

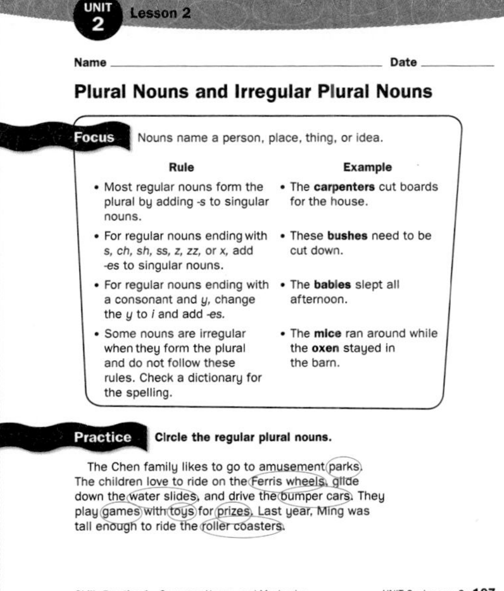

UNIT 2 Lesson 2

Name ______ Date ______

Plural Nouns and Irregular Plural Nouns

Focus Nouns name a person, place, thing, or idea.

Rule	Example
• Most regular nouns form the plural by adding *-s* to singular nouns.	• The **carpenters** cut boards for the house.
• For regular nouns ending with *s, ch, sh, ss, z, zz,* or *x,* add *-es* to singular nouns.	• These **bushes** need to be cut down.
• For regular nouns ending with a consonant and *y,* change the *y* to *i* and add *-es.*	• The **babies** slept all afternoon.
• Some nouns are irregular when they form the plural and do not follow these rules. Check a dictionary for the spelling.	• The **mice** ran around while the **oxen** stayed in the barn.

Practice **Circle the regular plural nouns.**

The Chen family likes to go to amusement parks. The children love to ride on the Ferris wheels, glide down the water slides, and drive the bumper cars. They play games with toys for prizes. Last year, Ming was tall enough to ride the roller coasters.

Skills Practice 1 • Grammar, Usage, and Mechanics UNIT 2 • Lesson 2 **107**

Skills Practice 1, p. 107

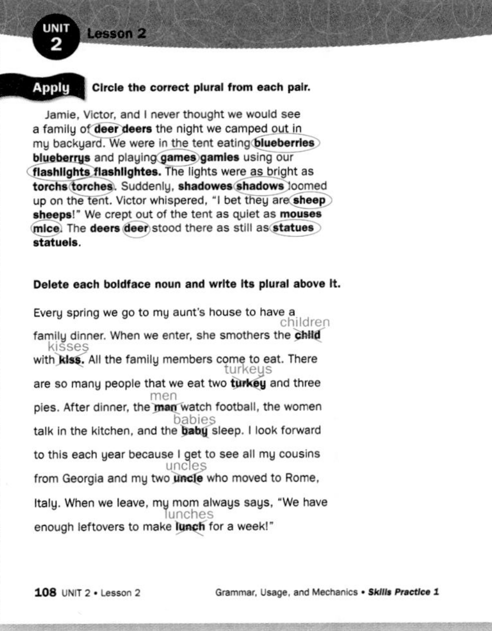

UNIT 2 Lesson 2

Apply **Circle the correct plural from each pair.**

Jamie, Victor, and I never thought we would see a family of **deer deers** the night we camped out in my backyard. We were in the tent eating **blueberries blueberrys** and playing **games gamies** using our **flashlights flashlightes.** The lights were as bright as **torchs torches**. Suddenly, **shadowes shadows** loomed up on the tent. Victor whispered, "I bet they are **sheep sheeps**!" We crept out of the tent as quiet as **mouses mice**. The **deers deer** stood there as still as **statues statuels**.

Delete each boldface noun and write its plural above it.

Every spring we go to my aunt's house to have a family dinner. When we enter, she smothers the **child** (children) with **kiss.** (kisses) All the family members come to eat. There are so many people that we eat two **turkey** (turkeys) and three pies. After dinner, the **man** (men) watch football, the women talk in the kitchen, and the **baby** (babies) sleep. I look forward to this each year because I get to see all my cousins from Georgia and my two **uncle** (uncles) who moved to Rome, Italy. When we leave, my mom always says, "We have enough leftovers to make **lunch** (lunches) for a week!"

108 UNIT 2 • Lesson 2 Grammar, Usage, and Mechanics • ***Skills Practice 1***

Skills Practice 1, p. 108

Preparing to Read

OBJECTIVES

Students will

- identify and learn irregular plurals.
- build fluency.

MATERIALS

- ***Transparency*** 53
- ***Skills Practice 1,*** pp. 95–96

Daily Oral Practice

Daily News Today!

Look at the cute little ducklings floating on the pond. The little ones are in school, learning from their parents. The babies follow everything their parents do. Why are they soaking their heads in the water? Oh, they're taking a bath.

- Write the daily news on the board or on chart paper. Then have students read the daily news in unison to practice fluency.
- As a review of yesterday's phonics and fluency lesson, ask a volunteer to identify any words in the message with /ō/ spelled *_ow* or *oa_*. */ō/ spelled* _ow *in* follow; */ō/ spelled* oa_ *in* floating *and* soaking

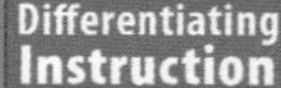

Differentiating Instruction: English Learner

IF . . . students need extra help with irregular plurals, **THEN . . .** organize the words into categories and discuss the plural pattern in each. For example: *foot/feet, tooth/teeth, goose/geese; deer/deer, moose/moose, fish/fish, sheep/sheep; child/children, woman/women, policeman/policemen, ox/oxen*

Word Structure

Irregular Plurals

✦ Write the following word lines on the board or use ***Transparency*** 53. Show students one line at time as you go through them by covering up the others. The words in boldface are from "Make Way for Ducklings."

Line 1	**people**	**children**	cacti	policemen
Line 2	women	deer	feet	teeth
Line 3	moose	mice	fish	fungi
Line 4	sheep	geese	oxen	bacteria

Lines 1–4 Irregular Plurals

✦ Explain that irregular plural nouns do not follow the rules for forming regular plural nouns. Because there are so many exceptions, these words and their spellings must be memorized. Tell students to check the dictionary for correct spelling of a plural noun when in doubt.

✦ Point to the words in Lines 1–4, and ask students to read the words together.

✦ Ask students to tell you the singular forms of the nouns on the word lines. **Possible Answers** *person, child, cactus, woman, deer, foot, mouse, fish, crisis, ox* If students do not know the singular form of *bacteria*, have them look up the word in a dictionary.

✦ Help students start the word structure activities on ***Skills Practice 1*** pages 95–96. Read the Focus box, and help them with the first few questions. Then have students complete the page on their own.

Teacher Tip

SYLLABICATION To help students blend words and build fluency, demonstrate syllabication using the decodable, multisyllabic words in the word lines.

peo • ple	wo • men
chil • dren	fun • gi
cac • ti	bac • ter • i • a
po • lice • men	ox • en

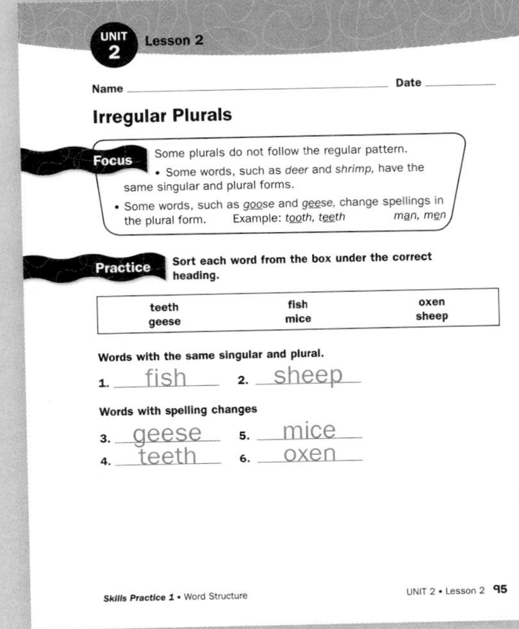

UNIT 2 Lesson 2

Name ______ Date ______

Irregular Plurals

Focus: Some plurals do not follow the regular pattern.
• Some words, such as *deer* and *shrimp*, have the same singular and plural forms.
• Some words, such as *goose* and *geese*, change spellings in the plural form. Example: *tooth, teeth* *man, men*

Practice: Sort each word from the box under the correct heading.

teeth geese	fish mice	oxen sheep

Words with the same singular and plural.
1. fish 2. sheep

Words with spelling changes
3. geese 5. mice
4. teeth 6. oxen

Skills Practice 1 • Word Structure UNIT 2 • Lesson 2 95

Skills Practice 1, pp. 95–96

Monitor Progress to Differentiate Instruction

Formal Assessment 

Word Structure During the word structure activity, note how well students understand irregular plurals.

APPROACHING LEVEL	IF . . . students need practice with irregular plurals,	THEN . . . work with them on the word structure activities on ***Reteach*** page 38 during Workshop.
	IF . . . students need extra practice with irregular plurals,	THEN . . . work with them on the word structure activities for Unit 2 Lesson 2 in the ***Intervention Guide*** during Workshop.
ON LEVEL	IF . . . students understand irregular plurals,	THEN . . . have them write sentences using the singular and plural forms of the words on the word lines during Workshop.
ABOVE LEVEL	IF . . . students are ready for a challenge with irregular plurals,	THEN . . . have them complete the word structure activities on ***Challenge Activities*** page 35 during Workshop.

Reading and Responding

Mr. and Mrs. Mallard were looking for a place to live. But every time Mr. Mallard saw what looked like a nice place, Mrs. Mallard said it was no good. There were sure to be foxes in the woods or turtles in the water, and she was not going to raise a family where there might be foxes or turtles. So they flew on and on.

When they got to Boston, they felt too tired to fly any further. There was a nice pond in the Public Garden, with a little island on it. "The very place to spend the night," quacked Mr. Mallard. So down they flapped.

Next morning they fished for their breakfast in the mud at the bottom of the pond. But they didn't find much.

162

Just as they were getting ready to start on their way, a strange enormous bird came by. It was pushing a boat full of people, and there was a man sitting on its back. "Good morning," quacked Mr. Mallard, being polite. The big bird was too proud to answer. But the people on the boat threw peanuts into the water, so the Mallards followed them all round the pond and got another breakfast, better than the first.

"I like this place," said Mrs. Mallard as they climbed out on the bank and waddled along. "Why don't we build a nest and raise our ducklings right in this pond? There are no foxes and no turtles, and the people feed us peanuts. What could be better?"

"Good," said Mr. Mallard, delighted that at last Mrs. Mallard had found a place that suited her. But—

163

OBJECTIVES

Students will

- use comprehension skill Reality and Fantasy.
- build fluency.

MATERIALS

- ***Student Reader***, Book 1, pp. 162–165
- ***Transparency*** 15
- ***Skills Practice 1***, pp. 99–100

2nd READ

Comprehension Skill

Reread the story using the comprehension skill Reality and Fantasy.

Reality and Fantasy

Remind students that a fantasy tells about something that could not happen in real life. Unlike fantasy, realistic fiction tells about something that could happen in real life, and expository texts give factual information about real people or events. Ask students to find examples of the fantastical elements in this story.

Possible Answer *On page 162, the story says, "Mrs. Mallard said it was no good." Talking animals are characteristic of fantasy stories.*

Expanding Vocabulary

pond (pond) *n.* a small lake (page 162) The ducks swam in the *pond*. **flapped** (flapt) *v.* past tense of **flap:** to move up and down, as in wings (page 162) The bird *flapped* its wings. **waddled** (wä′ • dəld) *v.* past tense of **waddle:** to walk with short steps, swaying the body from side to side (page 163) The geese *waddled*. **suited** (so͞o′ • təd) *v.* past tense of **suit:** to meet the needs of (page 163) The pond *suited* the ducks.

"Look out!" squawked Mrs. Mallard, all of a dither. "You'll get run over!" And when she got her breath she added: "*This* is no place for babies, with all those horrid things rushing about. We'll have to look somewhere else."

So they flew over Beacon Hill and round the State House, but there was no place there.

They looked in Louisburg Square, but there was no water to swim in.

Then they flew over the Charles River. "This is better," quacked Mr. Mallard. "That island looks like a nice quiet place, and it's only a little way from the Public Garden." "Yes," said Mrs. Mallard, remembering the peanuts. "That looks like just the right place to hatch ducklings."

164

So they chose a cozy spot among the bushes near the water and settled down to build their nest. And only just in time, for now they were beginning to molt. All their old wing feathers started to drop out, and they would not be able to fly again until the new ones grew in.

But of course they could swim, and one day they swam over to the park on the river bank, and there they met a policeman called Michael. Michael fed them peanuts, and after that the Mallards called on Michael every day.

After Mrs. Mallard had laid eight eggs in the nest she couldn't go to visit Michael any more, because she had to sit on the eggs to keep them warm. She moved off the nest only to get a drink of water, or to have her lunch, or to count the eggs and make sure they were all there.

One day the ducklings hatched out. First came Jack, then Kack, and then Lack, then Mack and Nack and Ouack and Pack and Quack. Mr. and Mrs. Mallard were bursting with pride. It was a great

165

Reading with a Writer's Eye

Setting

Robert McCloskey, the author of "Make Way for Ducklings," was very careful when he wrote the setting for his story. Although this story is a fantasy, he wanted the setting to be realistic. Ask students:

- *What details did the author include to make the setting in the story realistic?* **Possible Answer** *He includes places that exist in real life. Beacon Hill, Louisburg Square, the State House, the Public Gardens, and the Charles River are all real places in Boston, Massachusetts. Michael, the policeman, could be real.*
- *What does Robert McCloskey include in his story to tell about the challenges that animals face when looking for homes in the city?* **Possible Answer** *He lets the reader know about the dangers of traffic, turtles, and foxes.*

Expanding Vocabulary

dither (dith′• ûr) *n.* a confused, upset feeling (page 164)

The lost puppy was all of a *dither*.

cozy (cō′ • zē) *adj.* warm and comfortable (page 165)

The duck's *cozy* nest was safe and warm.

settled down (set′ • təld doun′) *v.* past tense of **settle down:** to make one's home (page 165)

The deer *settled down* before winter came.

molt (mōlt) *v.* to lose or shed hair, feathers, skin, or a shell (page 165)

As the snake grows, it will *molt*.

STOP You have reread the first half of the story. You will continue the story tomorrow on page T160.

Imagine It! Transparency 15

Two-Column Chart

 Level 3

Transparency 15

UNIT 2 Lesson 2

Name ______ Date ______

Fantasy and Reality

Focus An author may write a story that is based on reality or on fantasy.

- **Fantasy** stories are stories that could not happen in real life. A fantasy story may have make-believe characters, such as genies or fairies.
- A story based on **reality** is realistic. It tells of something that could happen in real life.

Practice **Read the list of story topics. Write an *F* beside each topic that is a fantasy story. Write an *R* beside a topic that is realistic.**

1. Ali, Juan, and Sue go to school. R
2. A cat speaks in poems. F
3. A giant eats the trees in your backyard. F
4. A girl's family moves to a new town. R
5. A boy breaks a window with a football. R
6. Three girls fly out of their bedroom windows at night. F
7. Cali's pig can fly around his farm. F
8. Kevin gets a toy truck for his birthday. R

Skills Practice 1 • Comprehension Skill UNIT 2 • Lesson 2 99

Skills Practice 1, pp. 99–100

Supporting the Reading

Comprehension Skill: Reality and Fantasy

Teach

Explain that learning to identify different types of writing helps students anticipate or predict the content of texts they read, increase their comprehension of those texts, and choose what type of reading they want to do. Experiencing many different types of texts also allows students to develop their own personal preferences for reading material. Remind students that fantasies and realistic stories are two different types of stories. Fantasy stories have elements that cannot happen in real life. Realistic stories have characters, events, and settings that could be real and might happen in real life.

Guided Practice

Use the two-column chart on ***Transparency*** 15 to show information about fantasy and reality. Label the chart columns *Fantasy* and *Reality*. Have students reread the story and record events from the story that are strictly fantasy under the "Fantasy" heading. Under the "Reality" heading, have students record how events would have been treated in a realistic fiction or nonfiction story. You can use the following example to get started:

Fantasy	Reality
Mr. and Mrs. Mallard looked for a good place to live.	The two ducks flew around the city searching for a place to live.

Apply

Have students turn to pages 99–100 in ***Skills Practice 1.*** Have students read aloud the Focus section of the lesson. Work through the Practice section of the lesson with students. Have them look through the story to find more examples of fantasy. They can refer to these examples when working on Practice and Apply. Have students complete the Apply section of ***Skills Practice 1*** on their own. Encourage students to consider the characteristics of fantasy and reality as they write fantasy and reality stories during Language Arts.

Monitor Progress to Differentiate Instruction

Formal Assessment

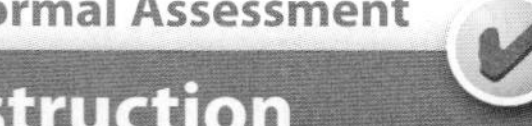

Comprehension Skill Note students' understanding of Reality and Fantasy.

APPROACHING LEVEL

IF . . . students need extra help with reality and fantasy, **THEN . . .** use ***Reteach*** pages 40–41.

IF . . . students need practice with reality and fantasy, **THEN . . .** have students play a game in the Workshop Kit.

ABOVE LEVEL

IF . . . students understand Author's reality and fantasy, **THEN . . .** use ***Challenge Activities*** page 37.

Differentiating Instruction: English Learner

IF . . . students have difficulty describing the elements of fantasy and reality in the story, **THEN . . .** ask them *yes or no* questions about those aspects and then lead students to use their answers to fill in the chart. For example, *Do ducks really live in cities? Do ducks really get married?*

Fluency

"Make Way for Ducklings" should be a fun story for students to read. The language is lively and fun. The many "noise" sounds make the reading interesting. Students should find the names of the ducks amusing and fun to say. Reading with proper intonation, or the rise and fall in pitch and volume of the voice, will make the ducks' dialogue humorous and will also make the story easier to understand.

- Tell students that when they see the quotation marks in "Make Way for Ducklings" they know that someone is talking. They should read these lines with proper intonation and expression.
- Encourage students to have fun with the language, as it is a light-hearted story. Remind students that there are some serious elements to this story, and those sections should be treated as such.
- Model intonation by reading pages 166–167 from "Make Way for Ducklings." Have students follow along in ***Student Reader,*** Book 1. Change your voice for each character, demonstrating how the tone of your voice would be different for the different characters. Accentuate the sounds such as "honk" and "quack" as they occur.
- After you have read through the passage, call on a volunteer to read the first three complete paragraphs. Before the student begins, make sure the student understands that the voice of each character will have a unique sound.

Fluency Tip

FLUENCY For additional fluency practice, students can read passages in small groups during Small-Group Time, or they can read to you.

To help students build fluency and strengthen their vocabulary and comprehension skills, have them read the ***Leveled Readers*** for this unit. Use each student's Oral Fluency Assessment score from the previous lesson assessment to diagnose the appropriate ***Leveled Readers.***

Inquiry

Choosing an Investigation Question

- Students have been sharing stories and questions they have about animals and animal habitats. These stories and questions should lead to one investigation question or topic they want to research further.
- Ask students to share any new questions they have about animals or animal habitats after reading "Make Way for Ducklings." Explain that if any of these new questions they have are more interesting to them than previous questions, then they can use one as their group's investigation question.

OBJECTIVES

Students will
- ✦ revise their book reviews.
- ✦ learn to spell words with /ō/ and irregular plurals.
- ✦ review regular and irregular plural nouns.
- ✦ understand and create charts, tables, and graphs.

MATERIALS

- ✦ ***Skills Practice 1,*** pp. 104–106, 109–110
- ✦ ***Transparencies*** 58, 58A
- ✦ Routine 16

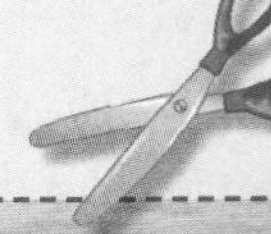

Imagine It! Transparency 58 58A

Revising: Rearranging Information

We thought our ride was about the most exciting thing we'd ever done. Courtney and I nervously prepared for our very first plane ride. The engines were revving as we sat down and fastened our seat belts. The plane began backing up, and we were soon zooming down the runway. Up in the air and over the clouds we flew. Our ears plugged up and it was hard to hear. All too soon, though, our ride was over.

Copyright © SRA/McGraw-Hill. All rights reserved. Level 3

Transparencies 58, 58A

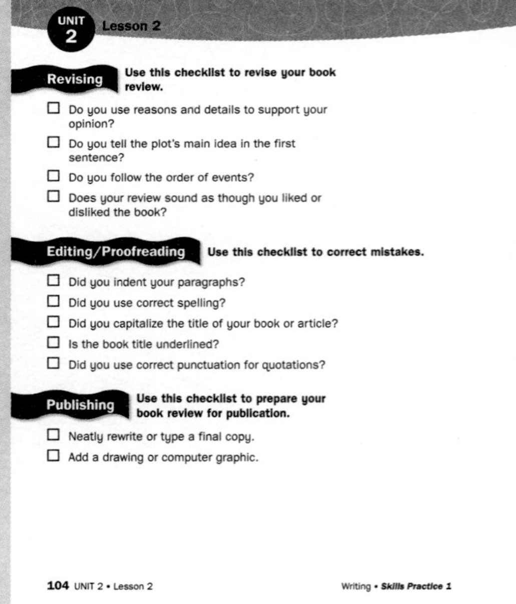

UNIT 2 Lesson 2

Revising Use this checklist to revise your book review.

- ☐ Do you use reasons and details to support your opinion?
- ☐ Do you tell the plot's main idea in the first sentence?
- ☐ Do you follow the order of events?
- ☐ Does your review sound as though you liked or disliked the book?

Editing/Proofreading Use this checklist to correct mistakes.

- ☐ Did you indent your paragraphs?
- ☐ Did you use correct spelling?
- ☐ Did you capitalize the title of your book or article?
- ☐ Is the book title underlined?
- ☐ Did you use correct punctuation for quotations?

Publishing Use this checklist to prepare your book review for publication.

- ☐ Neatly rewrite or type a final copy.
- ☐ Add a drawing or computer graphic.

104 UNIT 2 • Lesson 2 Writing • *Skills Practice 1*

Skills Practice 1, p. 104

Writing Nonfiction Book Review

Revising

Teach

- ✦ Use Routine 16 and tell students that they will now revise their book reviews to clarify sentences and paragraphs. Tell students that just as sentences should flow smoothly from one to the next, so should paragraphs.
- ✦ Tell students that one way to make sure their ideas are clearly stated is to read the review aloud. Many times we will stumble over incorrectly written sentences when we say them aloud or will realize that ideas or words have been misplaced.

Guided Practice

- ✦ Display ***Transparency*** 58. Have a student read the paragraph aloud. Have students discuss sentences or words they think should be changed or moved. Then display ***Transparency*** 58a and discuss the revisions. Ask students why they think the first sentence was moved to become the last sentence. **Possible Answer** *It sounds more like a conclusion and did not fit with the rest of the paragraph.*
- ✦ Have students turn to ***Skills Practice 1,*** page 104 to read and discuss the revising checklist.

Apply

- ✦ Have students quietly read their book reviews aloud to a partner or to themselves. Tell students that if they have a problem reading a section or certain words, they should work on revising those areas. They may also discover that a piece of information is missing or a sentence seems out of place.
- ✦ Have students refer to the revising checklist on ***Skills Practice 1*** page 104 as they revise their book reviews.

Differentiating Instruction English Learner

IF . . . students tend to repeat words too often in their book reviews, **THEN . . .** have them work with a proficient English speaker partner to identify repeated words. Ask the partners to suggest synonyms or different ways to express the same ideas.

Spelling

/ō/, and Irregular Plurals

Teach

- ✦ Tell students that the spellings of some words do not change when the plural is formed. The spellings of some words change altogether.
- ✦ Tell students that /ō/ can be spelled *_ow* and *oa_*.
- ✦ Divide the class into two teams. Write the following word pairs on the board: *bow/boa, mouses/mice, womans/women, coach/cowch, deers/deer, throw/throa, rost/roast, tooths/teeth, croe/crow, oxen/oxens, loe/low, lown/loan, grow/groa, flowt/float, fish/fishs.* Call on one student from each team to find the correctly spelled spelling word on the board and pronounce it. For the /ō/ spelling words, have the student circle the letters that spell /ō/. If the student is correct, give that student's team a point. The team with the most points wins.

Guided Practice

Have students turn to ***Skills Practice 1*** page 105. Read the instructions with them, and complete the first two questions as a class.

Apply

Have students complete ***Skills Practice 1*** pages 105–106 on their own. Remind students that challenge words are not used in ***Skills Practice*** exercises.

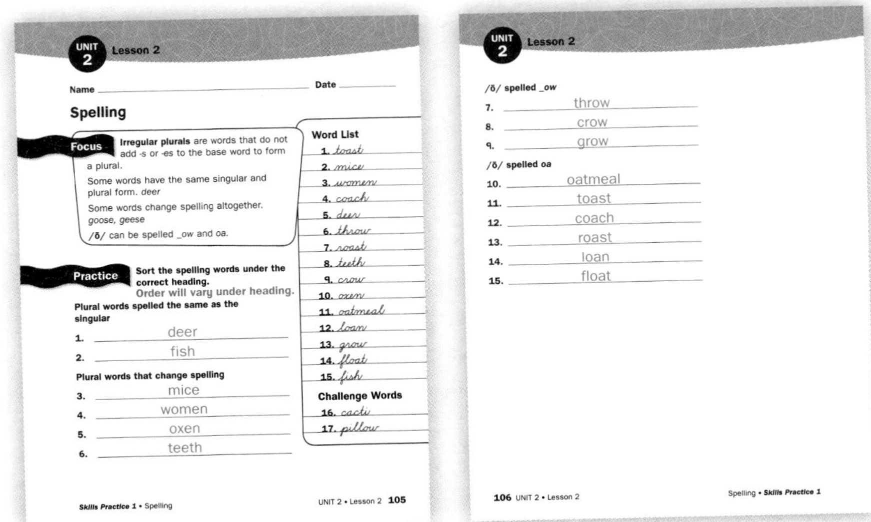
UNIT 2 Lesson 2

Name ______ Date ______

Spelling

Focus Irregular plurals are words that do not add -s or -es to the base word to form a plural.
Some words have the same singular and plural form. deer
Some words change spelling altogether. goose, geese
/ō/ can be spelled _ow and oa.

Word List
1. toast
2. mice
3. women
4. coach
5. deer
6. throw
7. roast
8. teeth
9. crow
10. oxen
11. oatmeal
12. loan
13. grow
14. float
15. fish

Challenge Words
16. cacti
17. pillow

Practice Sort the spelling words under the correct heading. Order will vary under heading.

Plural words spelled the same as the singular
1. deer
2. fish

Plural words that change spelling
3. mice
4. women
5. oxen
6. teeth

Skills Practice 1 • Spelling — UNIT 2 • Lesson 2 105

UNIT 2 Lesson 2

/ō/ spelled _ow
7. throw
8. crow
9. grow

/ō/ spelled oa
10. oatmeal
11. toast
12. coach
13. roast
14. loan
15. float

106 UNIT 2 • Lesson 2 — Spelling • Skills Practice 1

Skills Practice 1, pp. 105–106

Monitor Progress

to Differentiate Instruction
Formal Assessment

Spelling Note whether students are using the correct spellings of plurals as they practice using the spelling words.

APPROACHING LEVEL

IF . . . students need to practice spelling this week's words,	**THEN . . .** have them complete ***Reteach*** page 42.

ON LEVEL

IF . . . students can spell this week's spelling words,	**THEN . . .** tell them to write five sentences using the spelling words. Have them leave the spelling words out of the sentences, and then trade sentences with a partner and have the partner fill in the blanks with the correct spelling words.

ABOVE LEVEL

IF . . . students are ready for a challenge,	**THEN . . .** have them complete ***Challenge Activities*** page 38.

Monitor Progress 

to Differentiate Instruction

Tables and Charts Note whether students understand the difference between columns and rows.

APPROACHING LEVEL

IF . . . students need to practice tables and charts,	**THEN . . .** have them interpret information in a table or chart they are using for the unit investigation during Workshop.

ON LEVEL

IF . . . students have an understanding of tables and charts,	**THEN . . .** have them work on creating a chart during Workshop to use in the unit investigation.

ABOVE LEVEL

IF . . . students need a challenge,	**THEN . . .** have them use multimedia to create a chart for the unit investigation during Workshop.

UNIT 2 Lesson 2

Name ______ Date ______

Tables and Charts

Information can sometimes be presented in charts or tables. Charts and tables show a lot of information in a small amount of space. Information is listed in columns and rows to help you easily and quickly find specific information.

Favorite Wildlife in Our Neighborhood				
Class	Tree	Insect	Animal	Wildflower
Grade 1	white oak	ant	raccoon	goldenrod
Grade 2	maple	praying mantis	squirrel	violet
Grade 3	live oak	caterpillar	hawk	purple aster
Grade 4	blue spruce	praying mantis	raccoon	milkweed
Grade 5	sycamore	honeybee	mouse	violet

Using the chart above, answer the following questions.

1. What is the title of the chart? Favorite Wildlife in Our Neighborhood
2. What classes gave information for the chart? Grades 1–5
3. What is Grade 3's favorite animal? hawk

Skills Practice 1 • Study Skills UNIT 2 • Lesson 2 109

Skills Practice 1, pp. 109–110

Study Skills

Tables and Charts

Teach

✦ Ask students to describe what they know about tables and charts. Have them give examples of which kind they have seen or used. Tell students that:

- tables and charts show a lot of information in a small amount of space.
- tables and charts list information in columns and rows to help readers easily find specific information.

✦ Present the following guidelines for making a chart or table:

- Use a chart or table if you are presenting similar information about several items.
- Choose a title for your chart or table that sums up the information.
- Write headings down the left side of the chart or table. The heading gives information about the items in the chart or table. These headings are called row headings.
- Write short headings across the top of the chart or table to tell the information you will give about each item. These headings are called column headings.

Guided Practice

Have students open to page 109 in ***Skills Practice 1.*** Have a student read the directions and Focus box. Then help students complete the first Practice question.

Apply

Have students individually complete ***Skills Practice 1*** pages 109–110.

Grammar, Usage, and Mechanics

Regular and Irregular Plural Nouns

Teach

- Have students review regular and irregular plural nouns. If necessary, remind students of the special plural spellings of some nouns.

Guided Practice

Have students generate a sentence for you to write on the board. Have students identify the nouns, and then edit the sentences to change singular nouns to plural nouns. Ask a student to read the sentence aloud to see if any other changes need to be made.

Apply

- Have students write the plural forms of selection vocabulary words.
- Have students look for regular plurals and irregular plurals in their own writing. Tell them to correct any errors they find.

OBJECTIVES

Students will
- ✦ identify and learn irregular plurals.
- ✦ build fluency.

MATERIALS

- ✦ ***Transparency*** 53

Daily Oral Practice

Daily News

Today!

Ducks nestle into their nests for the night. Deer go to sleep under the stars. Spiders are snug in their webs. All is quiet in these animal habitats as night falls. What is that we hear? Ah . . . the owls and bats are coming out to play!

- ✦ Write the daily news on the board or on chart paper. Then have students read the daily news in unison to practice fluency.
- ✦ As a review of yesterday's word structure lesson, ask a volunteer to identify any irregular plurals in the message. *deer*

Differentiating Instruction **English Learner**

IF . . . students would benefit from extra practice with plurals, **THEN . . .** have them identify the regular plurals in the daily news. Use the word *falls* to emphasize that an *s* ending does not necessarily mean the word is a plural noun.

Research in Action

Fluent reading involves three key elements: reading accurately, reading at a suitable rate, and reading with appropriate prosody. In the early grades, young readers are often focused on reading accurately as they apply their knowledge of phonics and high-frequency sight words to reading decodable text. Rate gradually increases with pratice.
(*Marsha Roit*)

Word Structure

Irregular Plurals

✦ Use ***Transparency*** 53 with the word lines from Day 3.

Line 1	people	children	cacti	policemen
Line 2	women	deer	feet	teeth
Line 3	moose	mice	fish	fungi
Line 4	sheep	geese	oxen	bacteria

✦ Review irregular plurals. Remind students that there are no rules for forming irregular plurals, so they need to memorize irregular plural nouns or look them up in a dictionary.

✦ Have students read the words using normal intonation and expression.

Developing Oral Language

Use any of these activities to help students practice reading the words.

- Have a student volunteer select one word from the word lines and use it to begin a story. Have another volunteer continue the story by supplying another sentence using a different word from the board. Continue until all words are used.
- Have a volunteer choose one word from the word lines. Have that student use the singular form in one sentence and the plural form in another sentence. Continue for all words. **Possible Answer** *On one* foot *she wore a blue sock. On both of her* feet *she wore sandals.*
- Create sentences for students to complete using words from the word lines. Ask students to identify the words they used to fill in the blanks. For example, I saw three spotted *deer* running into the woods. Last month, one tooth fell out; and this month two more *teeth* fell out. After modeling a few examples, have volunteers create their own clue sentences.

Teacher Tip

BLENDING During Workshop, work with students who have difficulty blending words by using Routine 1 for sound-by-sound blending or Routine 3 for whole-word blending.

responsibility taking care of so many ducklings, and it kept them very busy.

One day Mr. Mallard decided he'd like to take a trip to see what the rest of the river was like, further on. So off he set. "I'll meet you in a week, in the Public Garden," he quacked over his shoulder. "Take good care of the ducklings."

"Don't you worry," said Mrs. Mallard. "I know all about bringing up children." And she did.

She taught them how to swim and dive.

She taught them to walk in a line, to come when they were called, and to keep a safe distance from bikes and scooters and other things with wheels.

166

When at last she felt perfectly satisfied with them, she said one morning: "Come along, children. Follow me." Before you could wink an eyelash Jack, Kack, Lack, Mack, Nack, Ouack, Pack, and Quack fell into line, just as they had been taught. Mrs. Mallard led the way into the water and they swam behind her to the opposite bank.

There they waded ashore and waddled along till they came to the highway.

Mrs. Mallard stepped out to cross the road. "Honk, honk!" went the horns on the speeding cars. "Qua-a-ack!" went Mrs. Mallard as she tumbled back again. "Quack! Quack! Quack! Quack!" went Jack, Kack, Lack, Mack, Nack, Ouack, Pack, and Quack, just as loud as their little quackers could quack. The cars kept speeding by and honking, and Mrs. Mallard and the ducklings kept right on quack-quack-quacking.

167

OBJECTIVES

Students will

- use the comprehension skill Reality and Fantasy.
- check comprehension.
- investigate the unit theme Animals and Their Habitats by using the Inquiry process.

MATERIALS

- ***Student Reader,*** Book 1, pp. 166–173
- ***Skills Practice 1,*** p. 102

Comprehension Skill

Reality and Fantasy

Have students continue to locate examples of fantasy.

- Michael beckoned the ducks to cross the street, just as if they were people.
- Mrs. Mallard understood the praises of the people on the street and was proud. She tipped her nose in response.
- Mrs. Mallard and the ducklings said "thank you" to Michael the police officer.

They made such a noise that Michael :ame running, waving his arms and ›lowing his whistle.

He planted himself in the center of he road, raised one hand to stop the raffic, and then beckoned with the other, he way policemen do, for Mrs. Mallard to :ross over.

As soon as Mrs. Mallard and the ducklings were safe on the other side and on their way lown Mount Vernon Street, Michael rushed back o his police booth.

He called Clancy at headquarters and said: 'There's a family of ducks walkin' down the street!" Clancy said: "Family of *what?*" *"Ducks!"* yelled Michael. "Send a police car, quick!"

Meanwhile Mrs. Mallard had reached the Corner Book Shop and turned into Charles Street, with Jack, Kack, Lack, Mack, Nack, Ouack, Pack, and Quack all marching in line ›ehind her.

Everyone stared. An old lady rom Beacon Hill said: "Isn't it

168

amazing!" and the man who swept the streets said: "Well, now, ain't that nice!" and when Mrs. Mallard heard them she was so proud she tipped her nose in the air and walked along with an extra swing in her waddle.

When they came to the corner of Beacon Street there was the police car with four policemen that Clancy had sent from headquarters. The policemen held back the traffic so Mrs. Mallard and the ducklings could march across the street, right on into the Public Garden.

Inside the gate they all turned round to say thank you to the policemen. The policemen smiled and waved good-by.

When they reached the pond and swam across to the little island, there was Mr. Mallard waiting for them, just as he had promised.

The ducklings liked the new island so much that they decided to live there. All day long they follow the swan boats and eat peanuts.

And when night falls they swim to their little island and go to sleep.

169

Checking Comprehension

Ask students the following questions to check their comprehension of the story:

- *Why is the city habitat so important in this story?* **Possible Answer** *This is a story about a family of ducks who settle in the pond near the Public Garden in Boston. The story tells about some of the challenges the ducks face living in the city.*
- *What do the events in the story have to do with the title?* **Possible Answer** *The policeman helps Mrs. Mallard and her ducklings cross the busy streets so they can get to the Public Garden. He and the other police officers stop the traffic so the cars "make way" for the ducklings.*
- *Fantasies can sometimes inform as well as entertain. What did you learn from this story?* **Possible Answers** *Ducks need food, water, and a safe and cozy place to live. The ducklings learn by watching their parents. Sometimes people need to help protect animals in some situations.*

Word Structure

Irregular plurals: traffic, policemen, children

Teacher Tip

AUTHOR'S PURPOSE Tell students that fantasy can inform as well as entertain. Ask them what the author has told them about the true habits of mallard ducks.

Science Inquiry

Genre Expository Text 

Review the elements of expository text. If necessary, remind students that expository text

- gives information.
- contains facts about real events or people.
- presents information in a straightforward way.
- may be organized by topics.
- may contain diagrams, photographs, and other illustrations.
- contains information that can be checked by looking at other sources.

Feature Diagram

Diagrams add to information provided in the text. Some diagrams show a process.

Ask students to point to the diagram in the story. Then ask students why they think the diagram was included with the story.

Reading "Frozen Frogs"

Have students take turns reading "Frozen Frogs" aloud. Ask students how this article relates to the story "Make Way for Ducklings." Make sure students read and understand the diagram.

Think Link

1. What are some of the ways animals survive cold winter weather? **Possible Answer** *Some animals migrate to escape the cold. Some tunnel underground below the frost line. Some animals, like wood frogs, freeze.*
2. In what kind of environment does the wood frog live? **Possible Answer** *Wood frogs live in North America where it is cold much of the time. In the winter they find a cozy spot under piles of damp leaves. In the spring, wood frogs lay their eggs in shallow ponds.*
3. Why are arrows used in the diagram? **Possible Answer** *The arrows show the direction of the seasonal changes.*

Teacher Tip

SELECTION VOCABULARY Review the meaning of the highlighted selection vocabulary words *strange* and *hatch* in "Frozen Frogs."

Differentiating Instruction English Learner

IF . . . students are confused by the use of *freeze, freezing*, and *frozen* in the Science Inquiry, **THEN . . .** explain that *freeze* is a verb meaning "to turn to ice." *Frozen* is an adjective meaning "turned into ice." And in this selection, *freezing* is an adjective meaning "icy."

Science Inquiry

Frozen Frogs

Genre

Expository Text tells people something. It contains facts about real people or events.

Feature

A **diagram** adds to information provided in the text. Some diagrams show a process.

Wood frogs live all over North America. In much of this region, winter brings freezing temperatures. Some animals migrate to escape the cold. Others tunnel in the ground, below the frost line. The wood frog does something strange: it freezes!

When cold weather sets in, the wood frog finds a good place to spend the winter, usually under a pile of damp leaves. Then the freezing process starts.

When the frog's body gets close to the freezing mark, its heart rate slows. Then the frog's blood and body tissues start to freeze. At last, ice forms around and inside the heart. Frozen solid, the heart stops beating.

In the spring, as temperatures rise, the frog starts to thaw. First, the heart beats again. Ice on the skin melts, then evaporates. Blood becomes liquid and flows again. The leg muscles soften. Within one day, the frog's body is back to normal.

The thawed frog looks for a small, shallow pond formed by melted snow and ice. A temporary pond such as this is a good place for the wood frog to lay its eggs. These ponds do not have fish that would eat the eggs before they can hatch.

Wood frogs are active through the summer and fall. They eat and build up body fat. Then, when winter comes again, they take their chilly time-out.

Think Link Seasonal Changes of the Wood Frog

Fall
The wood frog is active at any time of day. Its body stores fat.

Winter
The wood frog crawls under leaf litter on the ground. Its body freezes solid.

Spring
The wood frog thaws. Females lay eggs in ponds made by melting snow and ice.

Summer
The wood frog rests in the day and hunts for food at night, when it is cooler.

1. What are some of the ways animals survive cold winter weather?
2. In what kind of environment does the wood frog live?
3. Why are arrows used in the diagram?

Try It!

As you work on your investigation, think about how you can use a diagram to explain a process.

Inquiry Connection

Have students discuss how diagrams might be helpful in their investigations about animals and their habitats. For example, if students are investigating where ducks live, they might use a diagram to show the ducks' migration patterns.

Teacher Tip

CONCEPT/QUESTION BOARD After students read "Frozen Frogs," encourage them to post questions, answers, comments, photographs, drawings, or other items related to the theme Animals and Their Habitats on the **Concept/Question Board.**

Inquiry Process

Step 2—Choosing an Investigation Question

Whole-Group Time

Whole Group

- Explain that students can get ideas and new questions from the selections they read. Ask the class what they learned about the theme from the story, "Make Way for Ducklings." Have students take notes in their Writer's Notebooks. If they don't mention that people working together can help protect animals, then suggest this idea.

- To continue guiding students through the process of choosing an investigation question, lead a class discussion about students' interests in animals and animal habitats. For example, students might initially wonder: *Why do some wild animals avoid humans? Why are some animals are losing their habitats but not others? Why are some animals moving closer to human habitats? How can animals and humans peacefully live in the same places?*

- To help students choose their investigation question, model how initial questions and wonderings can lead to a good investigation question. Say something like the following: *After wondering How I can help these animals, I realized that I need others to help too. So, I thought of other questions like* Why do people disturb animal habitats? *and* How should the community protect these animals? *I've decided, after all, to make my investigation question* How should the community protect these animals? *because I'm most interested in making a difference. This question will also help me to learn more about a problem that matters to me.*

- Explain how a good investigation question will require students to gather information from sources or other people, and then form opinions based on the information gathered.

Small-Group Time

Small Group

- Have students break into their investigation groups. To help groups narrow their inquiry to one investigation question, have groups complete ***Skills Practice 1*** page 102. Assist groups as necessary if they are having difficulty narrowing down their investigation choices or finding a question on which they all agree.
- As groups work on ***Skills Practice 1*** page 102, help them think about why and how their investigation topic could be useful to others.
- Once each group has selected its question, have them post their investigation question on the **Concept/Question Board.** Remind students that they can update or change their questions as they encounter new information.

Concept/Question Board

- Remind students that they can consult the **Concept/Question Board** at any time for ideas to help them decide which question to investigate.
- Ask students to think about what they can add to the **Concept/Question Board.** Continue to encourage use of the Board by recognizing and thanking students for their contributions. Incorporate discussion of those items into classroom discussions whenever possible. Remember to also model by posting your own questions and ideas.

Inquiry Rubric

To assess Identifying a Question to Investigate, see the Inquiry Rubrics in the Level Appendix.

Teacher Tip

SOURCES FOR IDEAS Remind students that they can use something they learned from reading "Make Way for Ducklings" as an idea for their investigation. They can use ideas from other selections about animals and animal habitats as well.

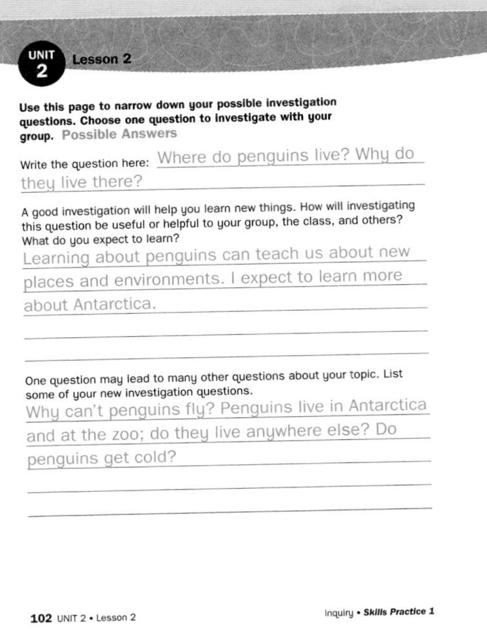

UNIT 2 Lesson 2

Use this page to narrow down your possible investigation questions. Choose one question to investigate with your group. Possible Answers

Write the question here: Where do penguins live? Why do they live there?

A good investigation will help you learn new things. How will investigating this question be useful or helpful to your group, the class, and others? What do you expect to learn?

Learning about penguins can teach us about new places and environments. I expect to learn more about Antarctica.

One question may lead to many other questions about your topic. List some of your new investigation questions.

Why can't penguins fly? Penguins live in Antarctica and at the zoo; do they live anywhere else? Do penguins get cold?

102 UNIT 2 • Lesson 2 Inquiry • Skills Practice 1

Skills Practice 1, p. 102

OBJECTIVES

Students will

- edit/proofread their book reviews.
- spell words with /ō/ and irregular plurals.
- learn to listen and respond to information.
- create a chart.

MATERIALS

- Routine 16
- ***Skills Practice 1,*** p. 104
- ***Transparencies*** 17, 17A, 82, 82A
- ***Student Reader,*** Book 1, pp. 162–169

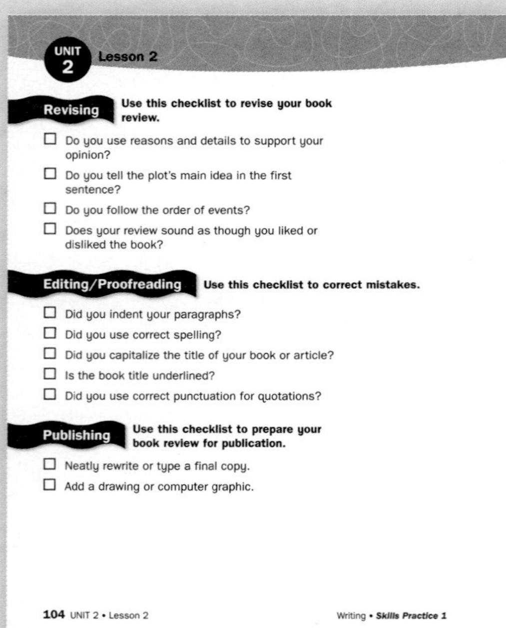

UNIT 2 Lesson 2

Revising **Use this checklist to revise your book review.**

- ☐ Do you use reasons and details to support your opinion?
- ☐ Do you tell the plot's main idea in the first sentence?
- ☐ Do you follow the order of events?
- ☐ Does your review sound as though you liked or disliked the book?

Editing/Proofreading **Use this checklist to correct mistakes.**

- ☐ Did you indent your paragraphs?
- ☐ Did you use correct spelling?
- ☐ Did you capitalize the title of your book or article?
- ☐ Is the book title underlined?
- ☐ Did you use correct punctuation for quotations?

Publishing **Use this checklist to prepare your book review for publication.**

- ☐ Neatly rewrite or type a final copy.
- ☐ Add a drawing or computer graphic.

104 UNIT 2 • Lesson 2 Writing • *Skills Practice 1*

Skills Practice 1, p.104

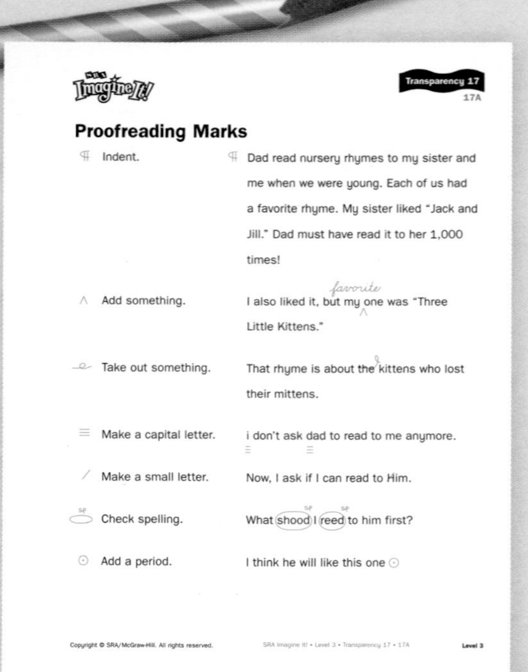

Imagine It! Transparency 17 17A

Proofreading Marks

¶ Indent.	¶ Dad read nursery rhymes to my sister and me when we were young. Each of us had a favorite rhyme. My sister liked "Jack and Jill." Dad must have read it to her 1,000 times!
∧ Add something.	I also liked it, but my ^favorite^ one was "Three Little Kittens."
Take out something.	That rhyme is about the kittens who lost their mittens.
≡ Make a capital letter.	i don't ask dad to read to me anymore.
/ Make a small letter.	Now, I ask if I can read to Him.
○ Check spelling.	What (shood) I (reed) to him first?
⊙ Add a period.	I think he will like this one ⊙

 SRA Imagine It! • Level 3 • Transparency 17 • 17A Level 3

Transparencies 17, 17A

Writing Nonfiction Book Review

ROUTINE 16

Editing/Proofreading

Teach

- Use Routine 16 and tell students that they will now edit/proofread their book reviews.
- Display ***Transparency*** 17 and 17A to remind students of the editing marks they will use.
- Tell students that as part of the editing/proofreading process, they should go back through their papers and quietly read the final version to themselves to make sure they have written what they intended to write and to ensure they have made all necessary corrections.

Guided Practice

- Display ***Transparency*** 82. Have a student read the paragraph aloud. Ask students to suggest corrections that need to be made. Write a list on the board. Then, display ***Transparency*** 82A, and compare the edits that were made to the list of corrections.
- Have students turn to ***Skill Practice 1*** page 104 to read and discuss the editing/proofreading checklist.

Editing: Grammar, Punctuation, Capitalization

frederick Lorz ran and won the boston Marathon on april 19th 1905. Frederick was born in Bay Ridge, new york on december 18th 1880. He began running in small races as a young boy he loved to run. he ran on the track team in school competed in his first race when he was fifteen. in 1904 Frederick ran in the summer Olympic Games in st Louis Missouri. He became too tired to finish therace and he asked his couch to drive him back to the stadium. The coaches car broke down on the way back to the statium. frederick had to walk the rest of the way and was the first runer to cross the finish line. everyone thought he one the race but he told them the truth. that year thomas j Hicks won the Summer Olympic race. when a local reporter asked a judge about the race results, the judge said, "Todays race was the most confusing spectacle ive ever seen. It was so puzzling that I thought I had won the race.

 SRA Imagine It! • Level 3 • Transparency 82 • 82A Level 3

Transparencies 82, 82A

Writing, continued

Apply

Composing—Editing/Proofreading Have students edit/proofread their book reviews. Have students refer to the checklist on ***Skills Practice 1*** page 104.

Monitor Progress to Differentiate Instruction

Formal Assessment

Editing/Proofreading Note whether students are able to edit/proofread their own writing.

APPROACHING LEVEL

IF . . . students need to practice editing/proofreading,	**THEN . . .** have them work with a partner to edit/proofread their book reviews during Workshop.

ON LEVEL

IF . . . students have an understanding of editing/proofreading,	**THEN . . .** have them use workshop time to work on publishing once they have proofread their book reviews.

ABOVE LEVEL

IF . . . students need a challenge,	**THEN . . .** use workshop time to revise, edit/proofread and publish their book reviews. Then suggest they submit their work to school newspapers.

Spelling

/ō/ and Irregular Plurals

Teach

Meaning Strategy Tell students that when they use a word, it is important to make sure that the word is spelled properly and that they are using the correct meaning.

Guided Practice

Write the following sentences on the board, and have students circle the correct plural form.

1. I saw three (deer, deers) jump over the fence in the field. *deer*
2. My mom told me to brush my (tooths, teeth) after every meal. *teeth*
3. Many varieties of (fishes, fish) live in the sea. *fish*
4. (Mouses, Mice) have tails. *Mice*
5. The (oxes, oxen) have been working in the field for hours. *oxen*

Study Skills

Tables and Charts

Teach

- Tell students that tables and charts are used to add information to written reports, to display information in oral presentations, and to restate information in a more concise way in reports and presentations.
- Draw a chart on the board with the heading "Ducks and Frogs." Make three columns and three rows. In the middle column write "Ducks," and in the right column, write "Frogs." On the first column of the second row, write "Sleep." In the first column of the third row, write "Lay Eggs."

Guided Practice

Help students fill in the appropriate columns with information they have learned in "Make Way for Ducklings" and "Frozen Frogs." **Possible Answers** *Frogs sleep in the day in the summer. Ducks sleep at night. Frogs lay their eggs in shallow ponds. Ducks build nests near water.* Ask students how this chart might add to a report or presentation. **Possible Answer** *This chart gives a visual representation of the information.*

Apply

Have students turn to "Make Way for Ducklings" in ***Student Reader*** Book 1. Then, have them make a chart of what Mrs. Mallard wanted in a good home and what she thought made a bad home. Remind students to title their charts and to write column headings such as, "Good Home for Ducks" and "Bad Home for Ducks."

Listening/Speaking/Viewing

Listen and Respond

Teach

- Explain that presenting information in front of a group of people is a very important skill to learn. When we present, we share our knowledge of a topic with others.
- List the following rules on the board and explain that these rules will serve as a guide for presenting information.
    - Speak clearly so everyone understands the presentation.
    - Speak loudly enough for all in the room to hear.
    - Speak slowly and do not rush through the information.
    - Recognize clues the audience gives, such as facial expressions, indicating when someone does not understand.
- Explain that the audience has an equally important job during a presentation. The job of the audience is to listen to the presentation so that they can learn from the presenter.
- List the following rules for listening and discuss each one.
    - Listeners must pay careful attention to get the most information from the speaker. They should face the speaker and make eye contact.
    - Listeners also need to pay attention and ask insightful questions.
    - Listeners should be able to summarize the information conveyed during the presentation.
    - Listeners should make connections to experiences in their own lives.

Guided Practice

Ask a student to volunteer to stand in front of the class and give a brief summary of "Make Way for Ducklings." Tell the rest of the class that they need to practice good listening skills. Coach the presenter on voice control and body language. Have the audience ask questions at the end of the summary.

Apply

Have students work with a partner. Give one of the partners five minutes to talk about what he or she likes to do during summer vacation. Next, have the other partner paraphrase what was learned and present this information to the class. Remind students to speak clearly and practice voice control. Remind listeners to pay careful attention and to summarize what is being said. Have students switch roles and repeat the activity.

Preparing to Read Review

OBJECTIVES

Students will
- ✦ review /ō/ spelled _*ow* and *oa*_.
- ✦ review irregular plural nouns.
- ✦ build fluency.

MATERIALS

- ✦ ***Sound/Spelling Card*** 30
- ✦ ***Transparencies*** 49, 53

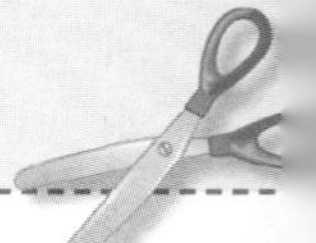

Phonics and Fluency

Use ***Transparency*** 49 with the blending lines and sentences from Days 1 and 2 to review /ō/ spelled _*ow* and *oa*_. Have students read the words and sentences on the blending lines. Then have volunteers choose two words from the lines and use them in a single sentence.

Line 1	flow	grow	throw	know
Line 2	follow	yellow	blowing	mower
Line 3	boat	road	coast	groan
Line 4	toaster	floating	boasting	overcast

Sentence 1: The snow blows slowly against the side of the house.

Sentence 2: The same loaf of oat bread will make good toast.

Word Structure

Use ***Transparency*** 53 with the word lines from Days 3 and 4 to review irregular plural nouns. Have students read the words on the word lines. Then have volunteers choose two words from the lines and use them in a single sentence.

Line 1	people	children	cacti	policemen
Line 2	women	deer	feet	teeth
Line 3	moose	mice	fish	fungi
Line 4	sheep	geese	oxen	bacteria

Reading and Responding Review

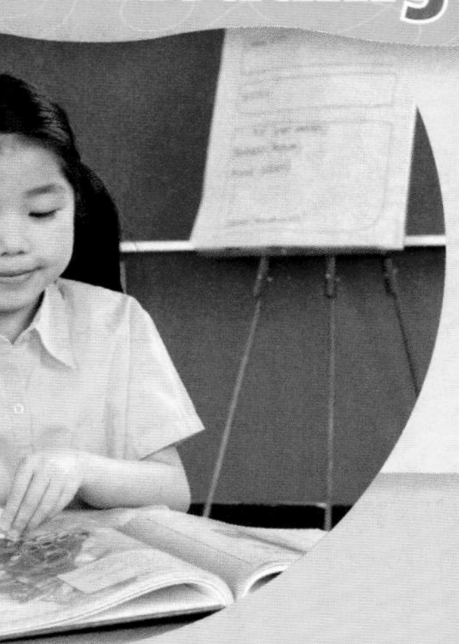

OBJECTIVES

Students will
- ✦ review selection vocabulary.
- ✦ review the comprehension strategies Asking Questions and Predicting.
- ✦ review the comprehension skill Reality and Fantasy.

MATERIALS

- ✦ ***Student Reader,*** Book 1, pp. 158–171
- ✦ ***Transparency*** 50

Selection Vocabulary  

To review the selection vocabulary, organize students into groups and give each group a vocabulary word. Each group should keep the word a secret. Have the groups decide how they will act out the definition of their vocabulary word. Then have each group act out their word while the other groups guess the word. After each group has acted out their word and another group has guessed it, have students return to the text and chorally read the sentence in which the word appears.

Selection Vocabulary

strange (strānj) *adj.* unusual (page 163)

enormous (ē • nor′ • məs) *adj.* very big (page 163)

hatch (hach) *v.* to come out of an egg (page 164)

responsibility (ri • spon′ • sə • bi′ • li • tē) *n.* a duty (page 166)

bringing up (bring′ • ing up) *v.* raising, as in children (page 166)

beckoned (bek′ • ənd) *v.* past tense of **beckon:** to call someone by waving (page 168)

Comprehension Strategies

Review the following comprehension strategies with students. Then ask studen to orally summarize "Make Way for Ducklings."

- **Asking Questions** helps readers focus attention on what they are reading by asking and then finding the answers to questions they have about the text. Have students review "Make Way for Ducklings" to find answers to questions about Animals and Their Habitats from the **Concept/Question Board.** What did the story teach them about animals and their habitats? Did students lear something new about habitats by reading this story?
- **Predicting** is when readers analyze information about story events and characters in the context of how it may logically connect to the story's conclusion. Have students review the story and the predictions that they made while reading. Ask students whether they enjoyed making predictions when reading, and whether their predictions were confirmed later in the text

Comprehension Skill

Review the following comprehension skill with students:

Reality and Fantasy is the readers' awareness of the differences between a text that is a fantasy, which includes events, characters, or settings that cann be real; and reality, which includes events, characters, or settings that could b real. Have students find examples of fantasy in "Make Way for Ducklings." Writ these examples on the board. Then ask students if they can think of any othe stories that have these qualities.

ʀeading with a Writer's Eye

ɛview the following literary element with students:

ɛtting is the time and place or places where the story takes place. Ask students find descriptive details of the setting of "Make Way for Ducklings" in the text. so, have students explain why the setting was so important in "Make Way for ucklings."

Fluency

ɛview fluency by modeling intonation for students. Remind students that tonation, or reading with the correct pitch and volume, adds to the meaning text by making it easier to comprehend and enjoy. Read a passage from pages 52–165 from "Make Way for Ducklings" to students. Be sure to model intonation hile reading. Also, make sure that the passage totals at least 160 words to nsure an appropriate practice length.

ave students read the passage chorally. Encourage students to use intonation nd to pause after commas and end punctuation.

OBJECTIVES

Students will

- publish their book reviews.
- take the spelling posttest.
- practice cursive *f* and *h*.

MATERIALS

- ***Skills Practice 1,*** p. 104
- ***Transparency*** 52
- Routine 17
- ***Lesson Assessment, Book 1,*** pp. 51–58

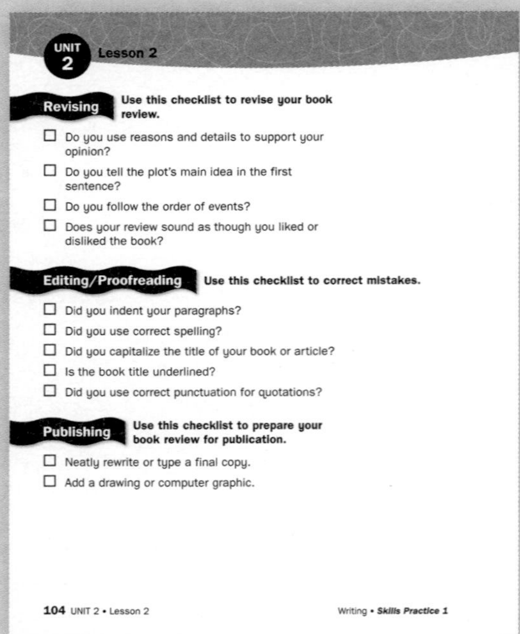

UNIT 2 Lesson 2

Revising Use this checklist to revise your book review.

- ☐ Do you use reasons and details to support your opinion?
- ☐ Do you tell the plot's main idea in the first sentence?
- ☐ Do you follow the order of events?
- ☐ Does your review sound as though you liked or disliked the book?

Editing/Proofreading Use this checklist to correct mistakes.

- ☐ Did you indent your paragraphs?
- ☐ Did you use correct spelling?
- ☐ Did you capitalize the title of your book or article?
- ☐ Is the book title underlined?
- ☐ Did you use correct punctuation for quotations?

Publishing Use this checklist to prepare your book review for publication.

- ☐ Neatly rewrite or type a final copy.
- ☐ Add a drawing or computer graphic.

104 UNIT 2 • Lesson 2 Writing • *Skills Practice 1*

Skills Practice 1, p. 104

Teacher Tips

ASSESSMENT Use the Writing Rubrics found in the Level Appendix to evaluate students' book reviews. You may use any of the rubrics for Genre, Writing Process, and Writing Traits.

PORTFOLIOS Suggest that students put their book reviews into their writing portfolio.

Writing Nonfiction Book Review

ROUTINE 17

Publishing

Teach

- Use Routine 17 during this lesson. Tell students they are at the final stage of the writing process: publishing. This means they will be sharing their book reviews. Discuss different methods of publishing and presentation with students.
- After students have written their final drafts, have volunteers give oral presentations of their book reviews. Also, have volunteers discuss how the reviews can help them decide whether they want to read the books.

Guided Practice

- Have students discuss how they used the stages of the writing process to complete the book review. Then have them discuss how following an outline simplified the drafting process.
- Have students read and discuss the publishing checklist on ***Skills Practice 1*** page 104.

Apply

Composing—Publishing Have students create a clean copy of their book reviews. Have students share their reviews with the class or in groups. Have students refer to ***Skills Practice 1*** page 104, the publishing checklist.

Spelling

/ō/ and Irregular Plurals

Teach

Have students write Spelling and their names in the top margin of a clean piece of paper. Have them number the first fifteen lines 1–15 then skip a line and number the next two lines 1–2. Read each word, use it in a sentence, and give students time to spell it correctly. Encourage students to try to spell the Challenge words, but assure them that mispelling a Challenge word will not affect their test scores.

Spelling Words		Challenge Words
bow	crow	cacti
mice	oxen	pillow
women	low	
coach	loan	
deer	grow	
throw	float	
roast	fish	
teeth		

Guided Practice

✦ Have students proofread for any mistakes they made on the posttest. Tell them to categorize the mistakes as

- careless errors
- errors in spelling irregular plurals
- errors in spelling words with /ō/ spelled *_ow* or *oa_*.

✦ Make certain students are correctly spelling irregular plurals and words with /ō/ spelled *_ow* and *oa_*.

Penmanship

Cursive Letters *f* and *h*

Teach

✦ Display ***Transparency*** 52, and review lowercase cursive *f* and cursive *h* with students.

Letter f Starting point, undercurve
Loop back, slant down
Loop forward, into undercurve: small *f*

Letter h Starting point, undercurve
Loop back, slant down
Overcurve, slant down
Undercurve: small *h*

✦ To model proper letter formation, write the following sentence on the board: *The hen's feathers fluttered.*

Guided Practice

✦ Have volunteers practice writing each of the letters on the board. Then, have students practice wiritng the sentence.

Apply

✦ Have students practice writing each of the letters twice.

✦ After reviewing the sentence you wrote on the board, set a timer for three minutes, and have students practice writing the sentence. Have them circle the best sentence based on the correct formation of *f* and *h*.

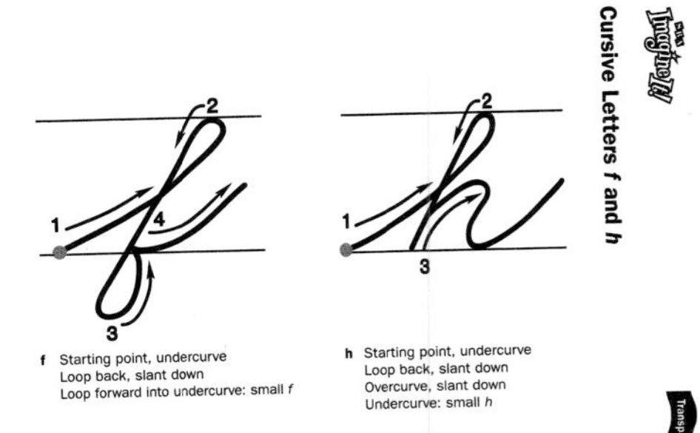

Transparency 52

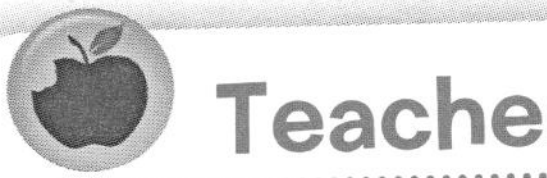

Teacher Tip

PENMANSHIP If students are not using proper spacing between words, check to make sure they are positioning their papers correctly and understand how to lift the pencil at the end of the word and reposition it for the next word.

Language Arts

Review

OBJECTIVES

Students will:

- review the use of tables and charts.
- review listening and speaking skills during presentations.
- review regular and irregular plural nouns.

MATERIALS

- ***Student Reader,*** Book 1, pp. 162–169
- ***Lesson Assessment Book 1,*** pp. 51–58

Study Skills

Tables and Charts

Remind students that using tables and charts might be a helpful tool for the unit investigation. Ask students where they might find tables and charts. **Possible Answers** *books, magazine articles, how-to manuals, directions*

For further practice, have students create a list of the different tables and charts that are used in the classroom or in the school. Have them create a two-column chart. Suggest they title one column "the table or chart" and the other "the use or reason for the table or chart."

After students complete this task, discuss all of the different reasons why we chart information.

Listening/Speaking/Viewing

Listen and Respond

Remind students that it is important to speak clearly and listen carefully during presentations.

Ask volunteers to give a brief summary of what they learned from reading "Make Way for Ducklings." Remind students to speak clearly, slowly, and loudly.

Remind the student audience to listen carefully and summarize what is being said.

Ask other volunteers to paraphrase what was said by the student presenters.

Repeat this process using other topics or selections.

Grammar, Usage, and Mechanics

Regular and Irregular Plural Nouns

Write the following sentences on the board. Have students underline the regular plurals and circle the irregular plurals.

- The flowers blossomed next to the bushes. *regular: flowers, bushes*
- The children were amazed when the mice and the cats became friends. *regular: cats, friends; irregular: children, mice*
- The ducks stayed away from the turtles and the foxes. *regular: ducks, turtles, foxes*

Have students add new plurals to the Regular and Irregular Plurals chart. Have them add decoration to the chart, and then display the chart in the classroom.

Have students select a piece of writing, such as the fantasy story they wrote in Unit 1, and edit it for regular and irregular plural nouns.

Monitor Progress

Formal Assessment

Use pages 51–58 in ***Lesson Assessment*** to assess students' understanding of the skills taught in this lesson. Intervene with ***Reteach, Challenge Activities, Intervention Guide, eSkills, Leveled Readers,*** or activities in the ***Workshop Kit*** as needed.

Lesson Planner

	Day 1	Day 2
Preparing to Read MATERIALS ✦ ***Transparencies*** 54, 57 ✦ ***Sound/Spelling Card*** 31 ✦ Routines 2, 3, 4, 5, 6, 7, 8, 9 ✦ ***Skills Practice 1,*** pp. 111–114	**Daily News,** p. T192 **Phonics and Fluency** Review /ū/, pp. T193–T195	**Daily News,** p. T214 **Phonics and Fluency,** pp. T214–T215 **Developing Oral Language,** p. T215 **Dictation,** p. T215
Reading and Responding MATERIALS ✦ ***Student Reader,*** Book 1, pp. 174–193 ✦ ***Transparencies*** 9, 23, 35, 55 ✦ Routines 11, 13, 14, A ✦ Writer's Notebook ✦ ***Skills Practice 1,*** pp. 101–102, 115–120 ✦ ***Home Connection,*** pp. 19–20 ✦ ***Listening Library CDs*** ✦ ***Leveled Reader***	**Build Background,** p. T196 **Preview and Prepare,** p. T197 **Selection Vocabulary,** pp. T198–T199 **Reading the Selection,** pp. T200–T203 **Comprehension Skill** ☆ Making Inferences, p. T202 1st READ **Comprehension Strategies** • Making Connections, pp. T204, T206–T207 • Predicting, pp. T204–T207 **Inquiry,** pp. T208–T209	**Comprehension Strategies** • Making Connections, p. T216 • Predicting, pp. T216–T217 **Discussing the Selection,** p. T218 **Review Selection Vocabulary,** p. T219 **Fluency,** p. T219 **Theme Connections,** p. T220
Language Arts MATERIALS ✦ ***Transparencies*** 45, 52, 64, 64A ✦ ***Skills Practice 1,*** pp. 121–128 ✦ ***Language Arts Handbook,*** pp. 98–100 ✦ Routines 15, 16 ✦ ***Student Reader,*** Book 1, pp. 178–189 ✦ ***Lesson Assessment Book 1,*** pp. 59–66	**Writing** Prewriting, p. T210–T211 **Spelling Pretest,** p. T211 **Penmanship,** Cursive Letters *f, h, m,* and *n,* p. T212	**Writing** Prewriting, p. T222 **Spelling,** p. T223 **Grammar, Usage, and Mechanics** Types of Sentences, pp. T224–T225
Monitor Progress ✔ = **Formal Assessment**	✔ **Phonics and Fluency, p. T195** ✔ **Comprehension Strategy, p. T200** ✔ **Comprehension Skill, p. T201** ✔ **Spelling Pretest, p. T211**	✔ **Selection Vocabulary, p. T219** **Fluency, p. T219** ✔ **Grammar, Usage, and Mechanics, p. T151**

Literature Overview

Student Reader

Wolf Island

written and illustrated by Celia Godkin

Children's Literature Roundtable of Canada Information Book Award

Science Inquiry

Ancient Wolves

SRA
Imagine It!

Day 3

Daily News, p. T226
Word Structure
Homographs, p. T226–T227

2nd READ

Comprehension Skills
- Fact and Opinion, p. T230
- Making Inferences, pp. T228, T231

Reading with a Writer's Eye, p. T229
Supporting the Reading
- Comprehension Skill: Making Inferences, p. T232

Fluency, p. T233
Inquiry, p. T233

Writing
Drafting, p. T234
Spelling, p. T235
Study Skills
Diagrams, p. T236
Grammar, Usage, and Mechanics, p. T237

Word Structure, p. T227
Comprehension Skill, p. T232
Fluency, p. T233
Spelling, p. T235
Study Skills, p. T236

Day 4

Daily News, p. T238
Word Structure, p. T239
Developing Oral Language, p. T239

Comprehension Skill
- Reality and Fantasy, p. T240

Science Inquiry, p. T242–T243
Inquiry, pp. T244–T245

Writing
Revising and Editing/Proofreading, pp. T246–T247
Spelling, p. T247
Study Skills, p. T248
Listening/Speaking/Viewing
Using Visual Aids, p. T249

Writing, p. T247

Day 5 Review

Phonics and Fluency, p. T250
Word Structure, p. T250

Selection Vocabulary, p. T251
Comprehension Strategies
- Making Connections, p. T252
- Predicting, p. T252

Comprehension Skills
- Fact and Opinion, p. T252
- Making Inferences, pp. T252
- Reality and Fantasy, p. T252

Reading with a Writer's Eye, p. T253
Fluency, p. T253

Writing
Publishing, p. T255
Spelling Posttest, p. T255
Penmanship, p. T255
Study Skills, p. T256
Listening/Speaking/Viewing, p. T256
Grammar, Usage, and Mechanics, p. T257

Spelling Posttest, p. T255
***Lesson Assessment Book 1,* pp. 59–66**

Student Resources

Genre

Narrative Nonfiction blends elements of fiction with elements of nonfiction to make a more exciting story. Facts about real people, places, and events are included in narrative nonfiction.

Comprehension Skill

Making Inferences
As you read, make inferences by connecting information from the story to what you already know.

Focus Questions

What are ways that different animals help make a habitat successful? How might your habitat be affected if an important part was removed?

176

Wolf Island

by Celia Godkin

177

Student Reader, Book 1, pp. 176–191

Phonics & Fluency

Decodable Stories, Book 3, Story 19, "Condors"

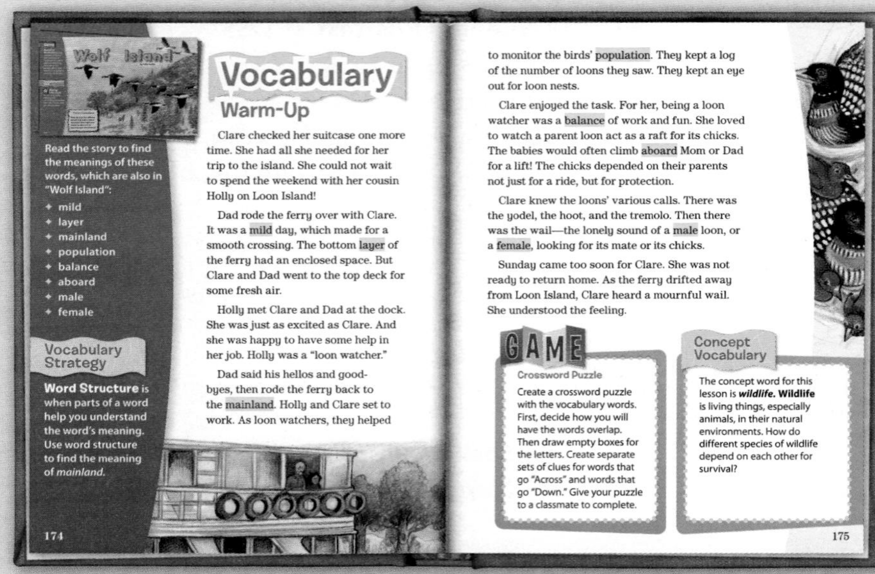
Wolf Island

Vocabulary
Warm-Up

Read the story to find the meanings of these words, which are also in "Wolf Island":

- mild
- layer
- mainland
- population
- balance
- aboard
- male
- female

Vocabulary Strategy

Word Structure is when parts of a word help you understand the word's meaning. Use word structure to find the meaning of *mainland.*

Clare checked her suitcase one more time. She had all she needed for her trip to the island. She could not wait to spend the weekend with her cousin Holly on Loon Island!

Dad rode the ferry over with Clare. It was a mild day, which made for a smooth crossing. The bottom layer of the ferry had an enclosed space. But Clare and Dad went to the top deck for some fresh air.

Holly met Clare and Dad at the dock. She was just as excited as Clare. And she was happy to have some help in her job. Holly was a "loon watcher."

Dad said his hellos and good-byes, then rode the ferry back to the mainland. Holly and Clare set to work. As loon watchers, they helped to monitor the birds' population. They kept a log of the number of loons they saw. They kept an eye out for loon nests.

Clare enjoyed the task. For her, being a loon watcher was a balance of work and fun. She loved to watch a parent loon act as a raft for its chicks. The babies would often climb aboard Mom or Dad for a lift! The chicks depended on their parents not just for a ride, but for protection.

Clare knew the loons' various calls. There was the yodel, the hoot, and the tremolo. Then there was the wail—the lonely sound of a male loon, or a female, looking for its mate or its chicks.

Sunday came too soon for Clare. She was not ready to return home. As the ferry drifted away from Loon Island, Clare heard a mournful wail. She understood the feeling.

GAME

Crossword Puzzle

Create a crossword puzzle with the vocabulary words. First, decide how you will have the words overlap. Then draw empty boxes for the letters. Create separate sets of clues for words that go "Across" and words that go "Down." Give your puzzle to a classmate to complete.

Concept Vocabulary

The concept word for this lesson is ***wildlife. Wildlife*** is living things, especially animals, in their natural environments. How do different species of wildlife depend on each other for survival?

174 175

Student Reader, Book 1, pp. 174–175

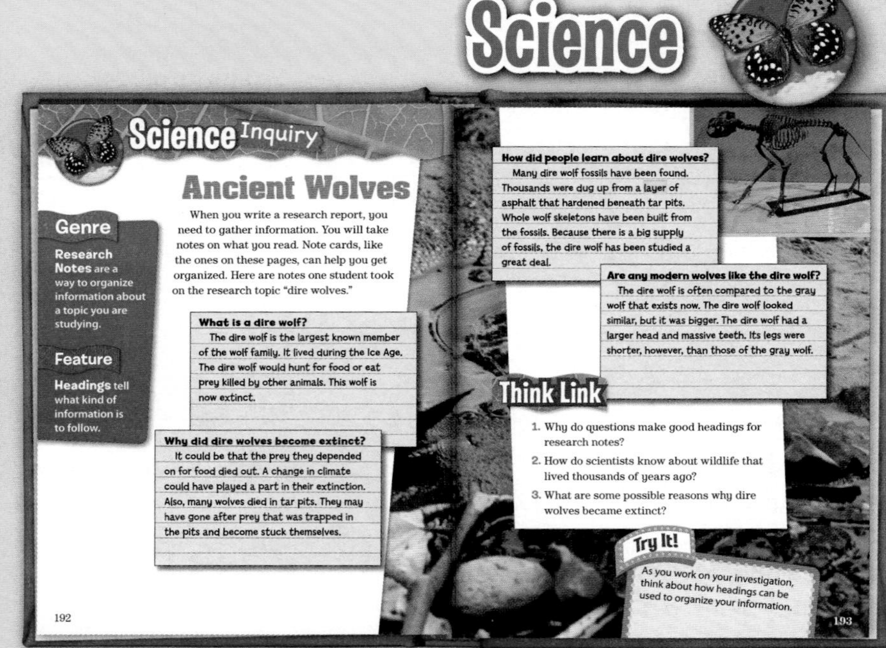
Science

Science Inquiry

Ancient Wolves

Genre

Research Notes are a way to organize information about a topic you are studying.

Feature

Headings tell what kind of information is to follow.

When you write a research report, you need to gather information. You will take notes on what you read. Note cards, like the ones on these pages, can help you get organized. Here are notes one student took on the research topic "dire wolves."

What is a dire wolf?
The dire wolf is the largest known member of the wolf family. It lived during the Ice Age. The dire wolf would hunt for food or eat prey killed by other animals. This wolf is now extinct.

Why did dire wolves become extinct?
It could be that the prey they depended on for food died out. A change in climate could have played a part in their extinction. Also, many wolves died in tar pits. They may have gone after prey that was trapped in the pits and become stuck themselves.

How did people learn about dire wolves?
Many dire wolf fossils have been found. Thousands were dug up from a layer of asphalt that hardened beneath tar pits. Whole wolf skeletons have been built from the fossils. Because there is a big supply of fossils, the dire wolf has been studied a great deal.

Are any modern wolves like the dire wolf?
The dire wolf is often compared to the gray wolf that exists now. The dire wolf looked similar, but it was bigger. The dire wolf had a larger head and massive teeth. Its legs were shorter, however, than those of the gray wolf.

Think Link

1. Why do questions make good headings for research notes?
2. How do scientists know about wildlife that lived thousands of years ago?
3. What are some possible reasons why dire wolves became extinct?

Try It!

As you work on your investigation, think about how headings can be used to organize your information.

192 193

Student Reader, Book 1, pp. 192–193

Cross-Curricular Resources

Curriculum Connections

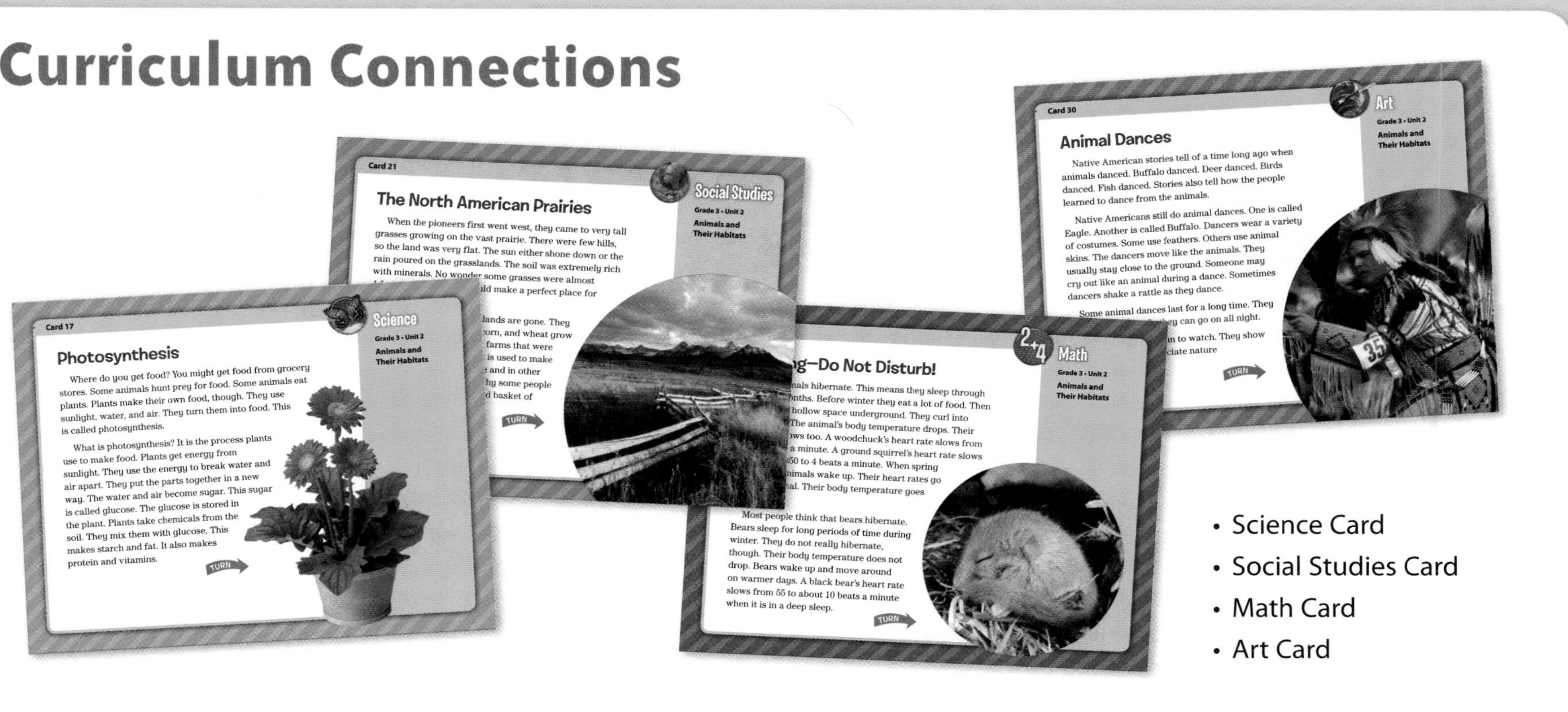

- Science Card
- Social Studies Card
- Math Card
- Art Card

Leveled Readers for Science

Approaching Level

On Level

English Learner

Living in a Tropical Rain Forest

by Dan Katsuyama

Above Level

Differentiating Instruction
for Workshop

Day 1

	Approaching Level	On Level	English Learner	Above Level
Preparing to Read	**Phonics and Fluency:** Help students complete ***Reteach*** page 44, or work with them on the phonics activities in the ***Intervention Guide*** Unit 2, Lesson 3. Then have students read ***Decodable Stories, Book 3,*** Story 19.	**Phonics and Fluency:** Have students use ***eSkills*** for extra phonics practice.	**Phonics and Fluency:** Use the ***English Learner Support Guide*** for additional phonics instruction. Then have students read ***Decodable Stories, Book 3,*** Story 19.	**Phonics and Fluency:** Have students complete ***Challenge Activities*** page 40.
Reading and Responding	**Vocabulary:** Place students in small groups. Assign each group a vocabulary word, and have each group create a list of similar or related words for their assigned word. **Comprehension:** Have students share any connections they can make to the story with the rest of the class. **Inquiry:** Have groups of students compare conjectures they made about their investigation questions.	**Vocabulary:** Have students use the selection vocabulary words to write riddles. Encourage students to share the riddles with the rest of the class. **Comprehension:** Have students write a journal entry about a personal connection they can make to the story in their Writer's Notebooks. **Inquiry:** Have groups of students compare conjectures they made about their investigation questions.	**Vocabulary:** Use ***English Learner Support Guide*** to review vocabulary. **Comprehension:** Have students write a short paragraph about a personal connection they can make to the story. If students have difficulty expressing themselves, encourage them to illustrate their ideas. **Inquiry:** In groups, have students compare conjectures they made about their investigation question.	**Vocabulary:** Have students select three vocabulary words and write a paragraph explaining when they have used the words in their own writing or discussions. If students have not used any of the words, have them explain how they can use the words in the future. **Comprehension:** Have students add questions and ideas about animals and their habitats to the **Concept/ Question Board.** **Inquiry:** In groups, have students compare conjectures they made about their investigation questions.
Language Arts	**Writing:** Have students work with the librarian to select reading materials. **Spelling:** Have students work on ***eSkills*** spelling activities.	**Writing:** Have students discuss topic ideas with peers. **Spelling:** Have students work in small groups to scramble the spelling words and trade papers with another group and unscramble them.	**Writing:** Provide short How-To books for students to understand process. **Spelling:** Have students write the spelling words in alphabetical order.	**Writing:** Have students share their ideas with their classmates. **Spelling:** Have students write the spelling words that are homographs and ask a partner to pronounce each word. Remind students that each word has at least two pronunciations.

Day 2

	Approaching Level	On Level	English Learner	Above Level
Preparing to Read	**Phonics and Fluency:** Students can listen to the /ū/ sound on the ***Sound/Spelling Cards Stories CD.*** Have students read ***Decodable Stories, Book 3,*** Story 19.	**Phonics and Fluency:** Have students create lists of words to add to the word lines and use them in sentences.	**Phonics and Fluency:** Use ***eSkills*** for extra phonics practice. Then have students read ***Decodable Stories, Book 3,*** Story 19.	**Phonics and Fluency:** Use ***eSkills & eGames*** for extra phonics practice.
Reading and Responding	**Vocabulary:** Use ***Intervention Guide,*** Unit 2, Lesson 3, or have students complete ***Reteach*** page 46. **Comprehension:** Have students write a paragraph about a prediction they made while reading the story. Remind them to include the details they used to base their predictions. **Fluency:** Have students listen to ***Listening Library CD,*** Unit 2.	**Vocabulary:** Have students complete a game in the ***Workshop Kit.*** **Comprehension:** Have students research ecological issues, such as the balance of nature, using print and online references to help them understand "Wolf Island." **Fluency:** Have students reread a passage from the selection with a partner or individually.	**Vocabulary:** Help students create flash cards for the selection vocabulary words. **Comprehension:** Have students create a checklist of the predictions that they made for the story. Have students check off the predictions that have been confirmed. **Fluency:** Have students listen to ***Listening Library CD,*** Unit 2.	**Vocabulary:** Have students complete ***Challenge Activities*** page 42. **Comprehension:** Have students write a journal entry about a prediction that they made about the story. Tell students to include the details that supported their prediction. **Fluency:** Have students discuss the books they are reading independently in a book chat.
Language Arts	**Writing:** Have students add information to their graphic organizers. **Spelling:** Have students rewrite a paragraph from their selection, carefully spelling each word. **Grammar, Usage, and Mechanics:** Have students complete ***Reteach*** page 50.	**Writing:** Have students continue to add details to their organizers. **Spelling:** Have students work on ***eSkills & eGames*** spelling activities. **Grammar, Usage, and Mechanics:** Refer to the ***Workshop Kit*** for Workshop activities.	**Writing:** Have students continue to add details to their organizers. **Spelling:** Have students think of three pairs of homographs that were not in this lesson and write them on a piece of papers. **Grammar, Usage, and Mechanics:** Refer to the ***English Learner Support Guide*** for support activities.	**Writing:** Have students begin drafting. **Spelling:** Have students write three sentences that use three spelling words each on a piece of paper. **Grammar, Usage, and Mechanics:** Have students complete ***Challenge Activities*** page 45.

Differentiating Instruction for Workshop

Day 3

	Approaching Level	On Level	English Learner	Above Level
Preparing to Read	**Word Structure:** Review the word lines with homographs. Then have students complete ***Reteach*** page 45, or work with them on the word structure activities in the ***Intervention Guide,*** Unit 2, Lesson 3.	**Word Structure:** Have students write sentences using the different meaning of homographs from the word lines.	**Word Structure:** Review the word lines with homographs. Then use the ***English Learner Support Guide*** for additional word structure instruction.	**Word Structure:** Have students complete ***Challenge Activities*** page 41. Then have students look for homographs while reading other materials.
Reading and Responding	**Vocabulary:** Have students write the definitions of three of the selection vocabulary words in their own words. **Comprehension:** Have students find facts and opinions in other articles based on animals and their habitats. **Fluency:** Have students complete an activity using ***eSkills & eGames.***	**Vocabulary:** Have students complete a vocabulary activity on ***eSkills & eGames.*** **Comprehension:** Have students find facts and opinions in news articles and on Web sites. **Fluency:** Have students read ***Leveled Readers.***	**Vocabulary:** Have students create clue words that help them remember the meanings of the selection vocabulary words. List the clue words in their Writer's Notebooks. **Comprehension:** Use ***English Learner Support Guide*** for additional help with fact and opinion. **Fluency:** Have students read ***Leveled Readers.***	**Vocabulary:** Have students select three of the vocabulary words and create lists of words that are similar or related to the words they have chosen. **Comprehension:** Have students select a topic related to animals and their habitats, research the topic using print and online references, and list any facts and opinions they find. **Fluency:** Have students complete an activity using ***eFluency.***
Language Arts	**Writing:** Have students review their organizers and add details they may have missed. **Spelling:** Have students complete ***Reteach*** page 49. **Grammar, Usage, and Mechanics:** Refer to the ***Intervention Guide,*** Unit 2, Lesson 3.	**Writing:** Have students review their drafts and add information as needed. **Spelling:** Have students change one consonant in each spelling word on a piece of paper and correct a partner's paper. **Grammar, Usage, and Mechanics:** Have students create skits that include each type of sentence.	**Writing:** Have students review their paragraphs and add transition words. **Spelling:** Have students work on ***eSkills & eGames*** spelling activities. **Grammar, Usage, and Mechanics:** Refer to the ***English Learner Support Guide*** for support activities.	**Writing:** Have students review their drafts for precise word choices. **Spelling:** Have students complete ***Challenge Activities*** page 44. **Grammar, Usage, and Mechanics:** Have students edit a piece of their writing to include each type of sentence.

Day 4

	Approaching Level	On Level	English Learner	Above Level
Preparing to Read				
	Word Structure: Use the homograph activity in the ***Workshop Kit.***	**Word Structure:** Have students reread "Wolf Island" looking for homographs.	**Word Structure:** Use the homograph activity in the ***Workshop Kit.***	**Word Structure:** Have students reread "Wolf Island" and look for homographs.
Reading and Responding				
	Vocabulary: Have students complete a vocabulary activity on ***eSkills.*** **Comprehension:** Have students add new information and ideas learned about animals and their habitats to the Concept/Question Board. **Inquiry:** Have students discuss how they will research their topic. Have them make a research plan based on their investigation needs.	**Vocabulary:** Have students write their own Vocabulary Warm-Ups using the expanding vocabulary words. **Comprehension:** Place students in small groups to find elements of narrative nonfiction in the text. **Inquiry:** Have students discuss how they will research their topic. Have them make a research plan based on their investigation needs.	**Vocabulary:** Put students into pairs and research any vocabulary words that might still need clarification using a print or an online dictionary. **Comprehension:** Place students in small groups to clarify any passages or ideas that are still unfamiliar or confusing. **Inquiry:** Have students discuss how they will research their topic. Have them make a research plan based on their investigation needs.	**Vocabulary:** Have students write sentences that relate to the unit theme Animals and Their Habitats using vocabulary words. **Comprehension:** Have students write about how "Wolf Island" applies to the unit theme Animals and Their Habitats. **Inquiry:** Have students discuss how they will research their topic. Have them make a research plan based on their investigation needs.
Language Arts				
	Writing: Have students use a thesaurus or a dictionary as they work on revising and editing/proofreading. **Spelling:** Working in pairs, have students help each other study this week's spelling words.	**Writing:** Have students work on ***eSkills & eGames.*** **Spelling:** Have students sort this week's spelling words into two categories: homographs and words with the /ū/ sound spellings.	**Writing:** Have students act out the process for an English-Speaking partner. **Spelling:** Have students take turns reading spelling words aloud to a partner, while the partner spells the words on paper.	**Writing:** Have students work on adding different sentence patterns to their drafts. **Spelling:** Have students work on ***eSkills & eGames*** spelling activities.

Differentiating Instruction for Workshop

Day 5

	Approaching Level	On Level	English Learner	Above Level
Preparing to Read	**Word Structure:** Review the word lines. Then have students read "Condors" from the ***eDecodable Stories.*** Have the students read the ***High-Frequency Flash Cards*** with a partner. Students also can use ***eSkills*** for extra phonics practice.	**Word Structure:** Have students read other materials while looking for homographs to add to the word lines.	**Word Structure:** Review the word lines. Then have students read "Condors" from ***eDecodable Stories.*** Have the students read the ***High-Frequency Flash Cards*** with a partner. Students also can use ***eSkills*** for extra phonics practice.	**Word Structure:** Have students read other materials while looking for homographs.
Reading and Responding	**Vocabulary:** Have students write three questions containing three of the vocabulary words and exchange them with a partner. Have students write their answers. **Comprehension:** Have students create review questions beginning with how and why. Have students answer each other's questions. **Fluency:** Have students write answers to comprehension questions from ***Leveled Readers.***	**Vocabulary:** Help students create a list of writing prompts using the vocabulary words on the board. Have students write a response to the prompt of their choice. **Comprehension:** Have students write a summary of "Wolf Island." **Fluency:** Have students complete an activity using ***eFluency.***	**Vocabulary:** Help students review and categorize the vocabulary words. **Comprehension:** Have students write a summary of "Wolf Island." Encourage students to include illustrations if they have trouble expressing themselves. **Fluency:** Have students use vocabulary from ***Leveled Readers*** in extended sentences.	**Vocabulary:** Have students add any useful, interesting new words from "Wolf Island" to the vocabulary information in their Writer's Notebooks. **Comprehension:** Have students write a paragraph that compares and contrasts "Wolf Island" to "One Small Place in a Tree." **Fluency:** Place students in small groups, and have them discuss this selection by comparing it to the other selections read so far in the unit.
Language Arts	**Writing:** Have students switch papers and read other students' process papers. **Spelling:** Have students copy this week's spelling list on paper and circle the sound spellings from this lesson.	**Writing:** Have students share the reasons why they chose to explain their process with peers. **Spelling:** Have students write the spelling words into alphabetical order on a piece of paper.	**Writing:** Refer to the ***English Learner Support Guide*** for support activities. Have students share their process papers with peers. **Spelling:** Have students write three sentences using two spelling words each.	**Writing:** Have students share their process papers with the class. **Spelling:** Have students write six words that were not in this lesson that have the /ū/ sound spellings on a piece of paper.

Resources for

Differentiating Instruction 

Leveled Readers

Approaching Level

On Level

English Learner

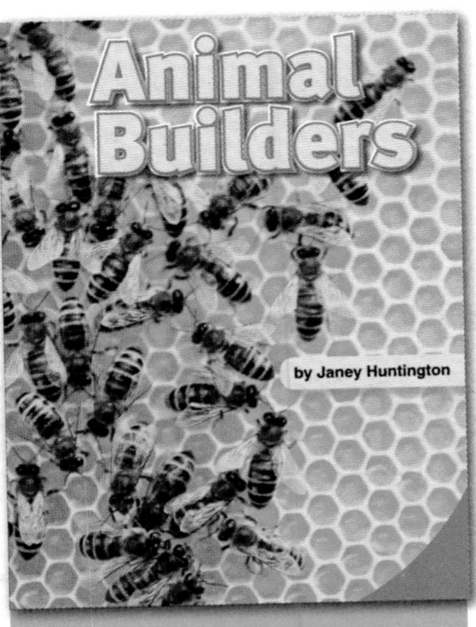

Above Level

Additional Skills Practice

Approaching Level

Reteach

- The /ū/ Sound/ Spellings, p. 44
- Homographs, p. 45
- Vocabulary, p. 46
- Making Inferences, pp. 47–48
- Spelling, p. 49
- Types of Sentences, p. 50

On Level

Skills Practice 1

- The /ū/ Sound/Spellings, pp. 111–112
- Homographs, pp. 113–114
- Vocabulary, pp. 115–116
- Making Inferences, pp. 117–118
- Explaining a Process, pp. 121–122
- Spelling, pp. 123–124
- Types of Sentences, pp. 125–126

English Learner

English Learner Support Activities

English Learner Support Activities, Unit 2 Lesson 3

Above Level

Challenge Activities

- The /ū/ Sound/ Spellings, p. 40
- Homographs, p. 41
- Vocabulary, p. 42
- Making Inferences, p. 43
- Spelling, p. 44
- Types of Sentences, p. 45

Additional Resources for Differentiating Instruction

Workshop Kits

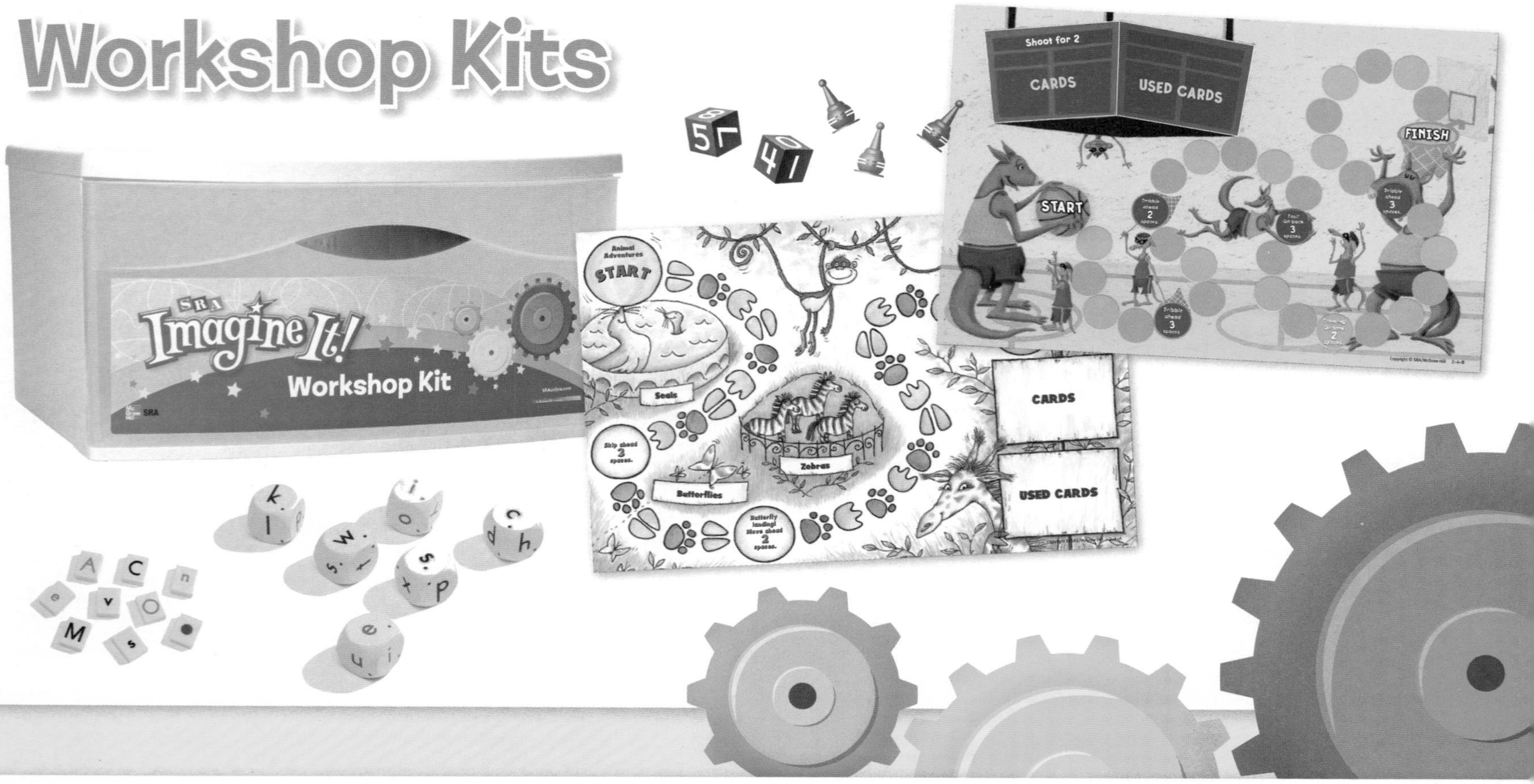

Technology

The following electronic resources are available for students:

- ***eStudent Reader***
- ***eDecodables***
- ***eSkills***
- ***Listening Library CD***

Electronic resources for the teacher include:

- ***ePlanner***
- ***eTeacher's Edition***
- ***eAssess***
- ***ePresentation***

English Learner

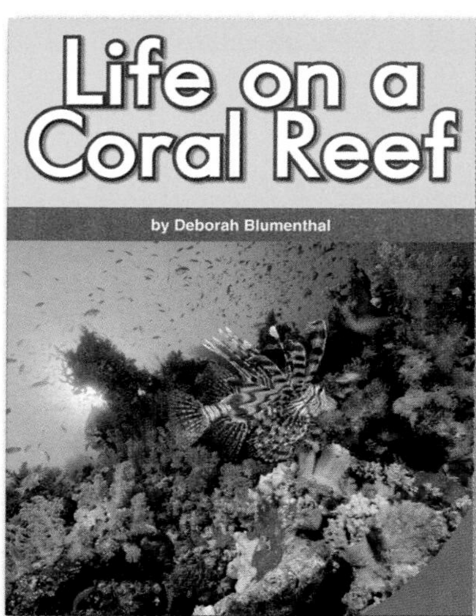

Leveled Reader

English Learner Support Activities, Lesson 3

English Learner Support Guide, Lesson 3

Listening Library Unit 2

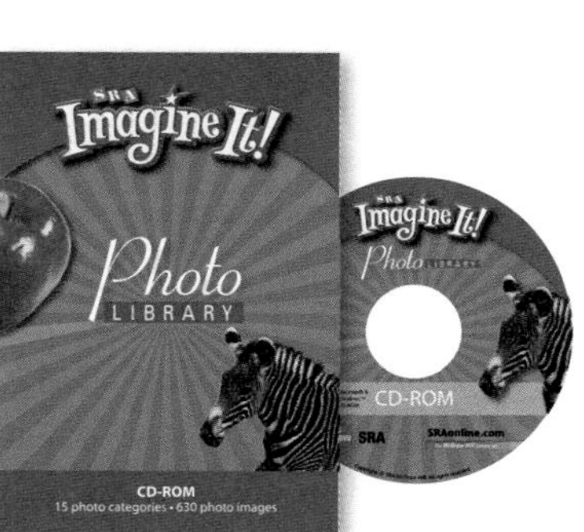

Photo Library

Approaching Level

Intervention

Intervention Workbook

Intervention Guide

Lesson 3 Overview

Lesson Assessment

Monitor Progress to Differentiate Instruction

Comprehension Strategies Rubrics

Use the Comprehension Strategies Rubrics to determine whether a student is using the strategies.

- Making Connections, p. T200
- Predicting, p. T201

Inquiry Rubrics

Use the Inquiry Rubrics to assess a student's performance throughout the stages of the investigation for each unit. In addition, at the end of the unit you can use the rubrics to assess the groups' collaborative work as well as an individual's participation in that group.

- Making Conjectures, p. T209
- Identifying Information Needs, p. T245

Writing Rubrics

Use the writing rubrics in the Level Appendix to evaluate each student's ability to explain a process.

- Genre
- Writing Process
- Writing Traits

Lesson Assessments

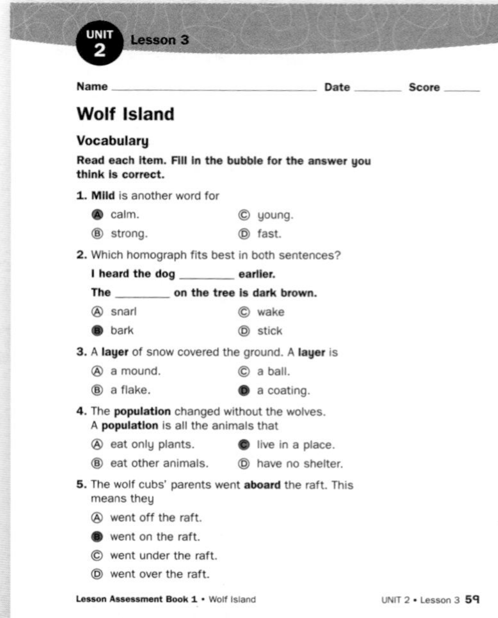

UNIT 2 Lesson 3

Name ______ Date ______ Score ______

Wolf Island

Vocabulary

Read each item. Fill in the bubble for the answer you think is correct.

1. **Mild** is another word for
   Ⓐ calm. Ⓒ young.
   Ⓑ strong. Ⓓ fast.
2. Which homograph fits best in both sentences?
   I heard the dog ______ earlier.
   The ______ on the tree is dark brown.
   Ⓐ snarl Ⓒ wake
   Ⓑ bark Ⓓ stick
3. A **layer** of snow covered the ground. A **layer** is
   Ⓐ a mound. Ⓒ a ball.
   Ⓑ a flake. Ⓓ a coating.
4. The **population** changed without the wolves. A **population** is all the animals that
   Ⓐ eat only plants. Ⓒ live in a place.
   Ⓑ eat other animals. Ⓓ have no shelter.
5. The wolf cubs' parents went **aboard** the raft. This means they
   Ⓐ went off the raft.
   Ⓑ went on the raft.
   Ⓒ went under the raft.
   Ⓓ went over the raft.

Lesson Assessment Book 1 • Wolf Island UNIT 2 • Lesson 3 59

Lesson Assessment Book 1, p. 59

UNIT 2 Lesson 3

Wolf Island (continued)

Comprehension

Read the following questions carefully. Then completely fill in the bubble of each correct answer. You may look back at the selection to find the answer to each of the questions.

1. Which of these is a real thing wolves do?
   Ⓐ make rafts to float on a lake
   Ⓑ hunt deer for food
   Ⓒ talk to people or other animals
   Ⓓ raise crops for other animals
2. When the cubs howled from the raft, their parents
   Ⓐ howled back to them.
   Ⓑ swam out to them.
   Ⓒ did not hear them.
   Ⓓ kept on eating.

60 UNIT 2 • Lesson 3 Wolf Island • Lesson Assessment Book 1

Lesson Assessment Book 1, p. 60

Use these summative assessments along with your informal observations to assess student mastery.

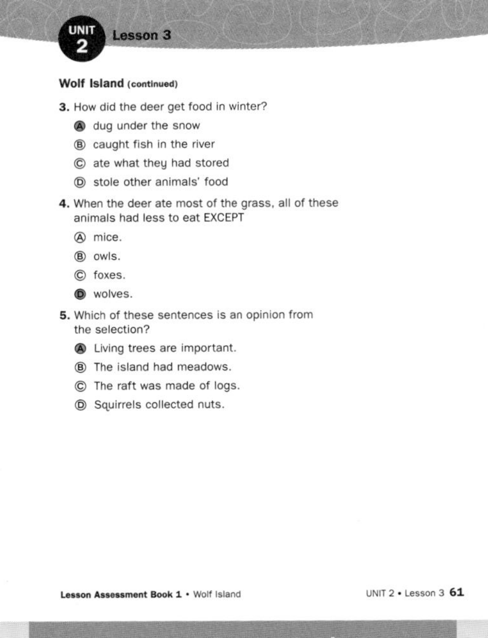

UNIT 2 Lesson 3

Wolf Island (continued)

3. How did the deer get food in winter?
   - Ⓐ dug under the snow (filled in)
   - Ⓑ caught fish in the river
   - Ⓒ ate what they had stored
   - Ⓓ stole other animals' food
4. When the deer ate most of the grass, all of these animals had less to eat EXCEPT
   - Ⓐ mice.
   - Ⓑ owls.
   - Ⓒ foxes.
   - Ⓓ wolves. (filled in)
5. Which of these sentences is an opinion from the selection?
   - Ⓐ Living trees are important. (filled in)
   - Ⓑ The island had meadows.
   - Ⓒ The raft was made of logs.
   - Ⓓ Squirrels collected nuts.

Lesson Assessment Book 1 • Wolf Island UNIT 2 • Lesson 3 61

Lesson Assessment Book 1, p. 61

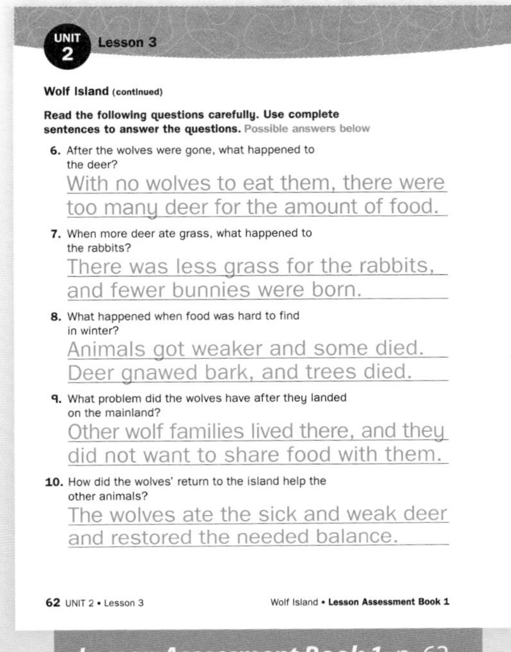

UNIT 2 Lesson 3

Wolf Island (continued)

Read the following questions carefully. Use complete sentences to answer the questions. Possible answers below

6. After the wolves were gone, what happened to the deer?
   With no wolves to eat them, there were too many deer for the amount of food.
7. When more deer ate grass, what happened to the rabbits?
   There was less grass for the rabbits, and fewer bunnies were born.
8. What happened when food was hard to find in winter?
   Animals got weaker and some died. Deer gnawed bark, and trees died.
9. What problem did the wolves have after they landed on the mainland?
   Other wolf families lived there, and they did not want to share food with them.
10. How did the wolves' return to the island help the other animals?
    The wolves ate the sick and weak deer and restored the needed balance.

62 UNIT 2 • Lesson 3 Wolf Island • Lesson Assessment Book 1

Lesson Assessment Book 1, p. 62

UNIT 2 Lesson 3

Wolf Island (continued)

Read the question below. Write complete sentences for your answer. Support your answer with information from the selection.

Linking to the Concepts What happens to a habitat when an important animal is removed?

____

Read the questions below. Your answer should be based on your own experience. Write complete sentences for your answer.

Personal Response How did you feel when the adult wolves got on the raft and it landed on the mainland? What made you feel that way?

____

Lesson Assessment Book 1 • Wolf Island UNIT 2 • Lesson 3 63

Lesson Assessment Book 1, p. 63

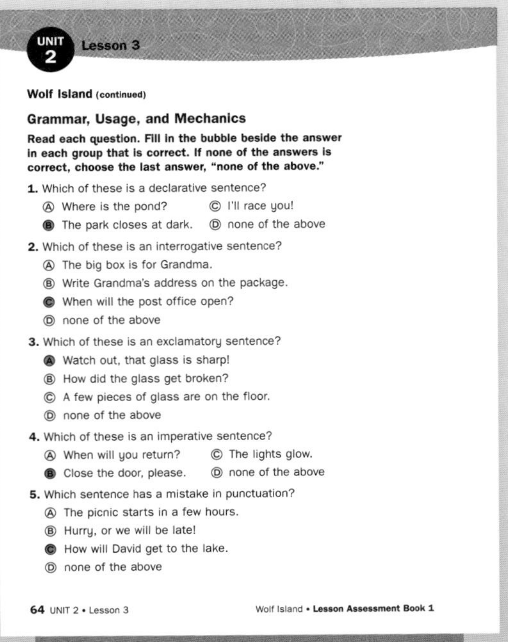

UNIT 2 Lesson 3

Wolf Island (continued)

Grammar, Usage, and Mechanics

Read each question. Fill in the bubble beside the answer in each group that is correct. If none of the answers is correct, choose the last answer, "none of the above."

1. Which of these is a declarative sentence?
   - Ⓐ Where is the pond?
   - Ⓑ The park closes at dark. (filled in)
   - Ⓒ I'll race you!
   - Ⓓ none of the above
2. Which of these is an interrogative sentence?
   - Ⓐ The big box is for Grandma.
   - Ⓑ Write Grandma's address on the package.
   - Ⓒ When will the post office open? (filled in)
   - Ⓓ none of the above
3. Which of these is an exclamatory sentence?
   - Ⓐ Watch out, that glass is sharp! (filled in)
   - Ⓑ How did the glass get broken?
   - Ⓒ A few pieces of glass are on the floor.
   - Ⓓ none of the above
4. Which of these is an imperative sentence?
   - Ⓐ When will you return?
   - Ⓑ Close the door, please. (filled in)
   - Ⓒ The lights glow.
   - Ⓓ none of the above
5. Which sentence has a mistake in punctuation?
   - Ⓐ The picnic starts in a few hours.
   - Ⓑ Hurry, or we will be late!
   - Ⓒ How will David get to the lake. (filled in)
   - Ⓓ none of the above

64 UNIT 2 • Lesson 3 Wolf Island • Lesson Assessment Book 1

Lesson Assessment Book 1, p. 64

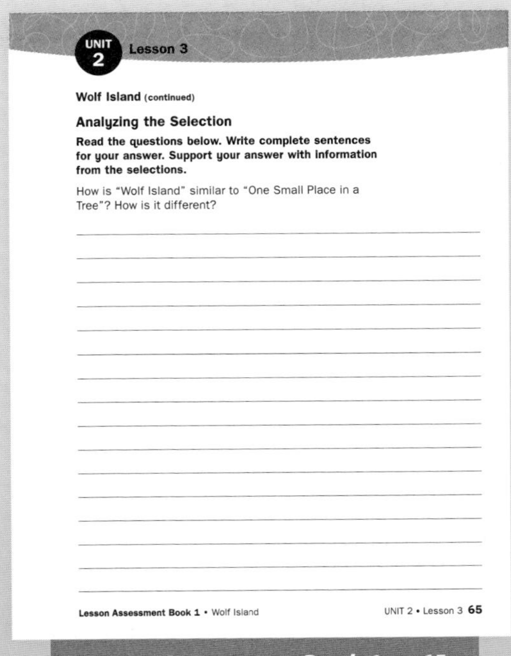

UNIT 2 Lesson 3

Wolf Island (continued)

Analyzing the Selection

Read the questions below. Write complete sentences for your answer. Support your answer with information from the selections.

How is "Wolf Island" similar to "One Small Place in a Tree"? How is it different?

____

Lesson Assessment Book 1 • Wolf Island UNIT 2 • Lesson 3 65

Lesson Assessment Book 1, p. 65

UNIT 2 Lesson 3

Wolf Island (continued)

Oral Fluency Assessment

The Cloud Artist

"Look!" said Uncle Chuck. "Skywriting!" He pointed up into 1–9
the blue sky. 10–12
Todd was spending the day in New York City with his 13–23
favorite uncle. It was a Saturday in February, and they were 24–34
seeing the sights. The two felt like ants surrounded by such 35–45
tall buildings. 46–47
"I read about this in the newspaper," said Uncle Chuck. "For 48–58
the next couple of days, an airplane will be creating cloud 59–69
shapes in the sky." 70–73
"Wow," said Todd. He watched as the outline of the cloud 74–84
started to fade. Uncle Chuck grabbed Todd's hand and began 85–94
racing from corner to corner. He started peering up and down 95–105
the crowded streets. 106–108
"What are you looking for?" asked Todd. 109–115
"The cloud artist," Uncle Chuck explained, "he's down here 116–124
somewhere." 125
Todd was puzzled. "You mean the artist isn't the pilot of the 126–137
plane?" he asked. 138–140
Uncle Chuck shook his head. "No, his name is Tad Muniz. He 141–152
takes photographs of things. He designed the clouds the plane 153–162
is making." Uncle Chuck paused. "He sounds like an interesting 163–172
artist. Maybe we can find a place that is showing his work." 173–184

EVALUATING CODES FOR ORAL FLUENCY

sky (/) words read incorrectly
blue ^ sky (^) inserted word
( ]) after the last word

READING RATE AND ACCURACY

Total Words Read: ______
Number of Errors: ______
Number of Correct Words Read Per Minute (WPM): ______
Accuracy Rate: ______
(Number of Correct Words Read per Minute ÷ Total Words Read)

READING FLUENCY

	Low	Average	High
Decoding ability	○	○	○
Pace	○	○	○
Syntax	○	○	○
Self-correction	○	○	○
Intonation	○	○	○

Record student rates on the Oral Fluency Scores pages.

66 UNIT 2 • Lesson 3 Wolf Island • Lesson Assessment Book 1

Lesson Assessment Book 1, p. 66

Day 1

Preparing to Read

OBJECTIVES

Students will
- ✦ review /ū/ spelled _*ew* and _*ue*.
- ✦ learn new high-frequency words.
- ✦ build fluency.

MATERIALS

- ✦ ***Transparency*** 54
- ✦ ***Sound/Spelling Card*** 31
- ✦ Routines 3, 4, 5, 6, 9
- ✦ ***Skills Practice 1,*** pp. 111–112

Daily Oral Practice

Daily News

Today!

Do you know what is meant by a balance of nature? When nature is in balance, living things have plenty to eat, and homes in which to sleep. When nature is out of balance, animals find surviving hard. A balance in nature is best, and it is something we can all work toward.

- ✦ Write the daily news on the board or on chart paper. Then have students read the daily news in unison to practice fluency.
- ✦ As a phonics and fluency review from Lesson 2, have volunteers find any words in the message with /ō/ spelled _*ow*. *know*

Technology

PHONICS eSKILLS Have students use the phonics activity for this unit to practice long-vowel sound/spellings for /ī/, /ō/, and /ū/.

Phonics and Fluency

ROUTINE 3 ROUTINE 4

Review: /ū/ spelled _ew and _ue

Blending

- Write the following blending lines and sentences on the board or use ***Transparency*** 54. Show students one line at a time as you go through them by covering up the others. The boldface words are in "Wolf Island." The underlined words are new high-frequency words.

Line 1	**few**	**fewer**	fewest	curfew
Line 2	pew	mew	skew	nephew
Line 3	cue	hue	rescue	argue
Line 4	value	continue	barbeque	tissue

Sentence 1	I <u>often</u> want to view the <u>world</u> from outer space.
Sentence 2	<u>Without</u> its cover, the issue was valued at only ten dollars.

- Review ***Sound/Spelling Card*** 31 with students. Using Routine 3, follow the whole-word blending process to have students blend the words in Lines 1–4.
- Follow Routine 4, the blending sentences process, to have students blend Sentences 1–2.

Lines 1–2 **/ū/ spelled _*ew***

As you point to each word in Lines 1–2, have students read the word aloud in unison. Ask students to identify /ū/ spelled _*ew* in each word. */ū/ spelled _ew in* few, fewer, fewest, curfew, pew, mew, skew, nephew Students may not know all of these words, such as *pew, mew,* or *skew.* If necessary, look up some of these words in the dictionary with students and use them in sentences that demonstrate their meaning.

Sound/Spelling Card 31

Teacher Tip

SYLLABICATION To help students blend words and build fluency, demonstrate syllabication using the decodable, multisyllabic words in the word lines.

few • er	neph • ew	val • ue
few • est	res • cue	con • tin • ue
cur • few	ar • gue	bar • be • que
		tis • sue

Preparing to Read

✦ Use ***Transparency*** 54 with today's blending lines and sentences. Show students the lines one at a time as you go through them by covering up the other lines.

Lines 3–4 **/ū/ spelled _*ue***

As you point to each word, have students read the word aloud in unison. Ask students to identify /ū/ spelled _*ue* in each word in Lines 3–4. */ū/ spelled* _ue *in* cue, hue, rescue, argue, value, continue, barbeque, tissue Students may not know what all these words mean, for example, *cue* or *hue.* If necessary, help students look up these words in a dictionary. Then use the words in sentences to demonstrate their meaning.

Sentences 1–2

Have students point to and read the new high-frequency words in Sentences 1–2. *often, world, Without* Ask students to identify words in the sentences with /ū/ spelled _*ew* or _*ue.* */ū/ spelled* _ew *in* view; */ū/ spelled* _ue *in* issue, valued Have students read the sentences in unison to practice fluency.

Differentiating Instruction **English Learner**

IF . . . students have difficulty pronouncing the words in the blending lines, **THEN . . .** write each word on the board, and below it, write a simple phonetic spelling for /ū/ in each word. For example: *few/fyoo, value/valyou, continue/continyoo*

Decodable Stories

Building Fluency

Decodable Stories are used to help develop fluency for students who need extra practice. They are also used to practice the phonics and fluency elements being reviewed. Using Routine 9, reading a ***Decodable Story,*** have students who need additional support read ***Decodable Stories, Book 3,*** Story 19, ***"****Condors."*

Decodable Stories, Book 3, Story 19

Syllabication

- To help students recognize common syllable patterns, use Routine 5 for closed syllables and Routine 6 for open syllables to separate the syllables in the multisyllabic words in the word lines. Explain that the syllable routines offer general rules that don't apply to all words.
- Using Routine 5, have students identify the vowel spellings in *curfew, rescue, argue, continue, barbeque,* and *tissue.* Then have them identify the consonants between the two vowels. Remind students that the syllables are usually divided between the consonants in words with the v-c-c-v spelling pattern, as in *res • cue.* Explain that syllables that end in consonant sounds usually have short vowels and are closed. Remind students that there is a separate syllable for each vowel sound, so *continue* and *barbeque* have three syllables. Have students read *curfew, rescue, argue, continue, barbeque,* and *tissue* aloud, clapping for each syllable. Then have students identify the closed syllables at the beginning of *nephew* and *value.*
- Using Routine 6, have students identify the vowel spellings in *fewer* and *fewest.* Remind students that /ū/ spelled _*ew* is a vowel spelling even though it ends in a consonant. Explain that when a word has two vowel sounds in a row, like *fewer* and *fewest*, the syllables are divided between the vowels because each syllable can only have one vowel sound. Remind students that syllables with long vowel sounds are usually open. Have students identify the initial open syllables in *fewer* and *fewest* and then read these words aloud, clapping for each syllable.
- Help students start the phonics activities in ***Skills Practice 1,*** pages 111–112. Read the Focus box with them and help them with the first few questions. Then have students complete the pages on their own.

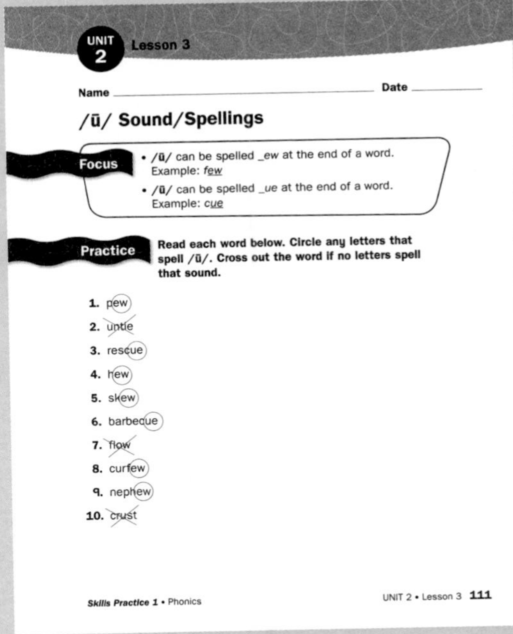
UNIT 2 Lesson 3

Name ______ Date ______

/ū/ Sound/Spellings

Focus
- /ū/ can be spelled _ew at the end of a word. Example: few
- /ū/ can be spelled _ue at the end of a word. Example: cue

Practice Read each word below. Circle any letters that spell /ū/. Cross out the word if no letters spell that sound.

1. pew
2. untie
3. rescue
4. hew
5. skew
6. barbeque
7. flow
8. curfew
9. nephew
10. crust

Skills Practice 1 • Phonics

UNIT 2 • Lesson 3 111

Skills Practice 1, p. 111

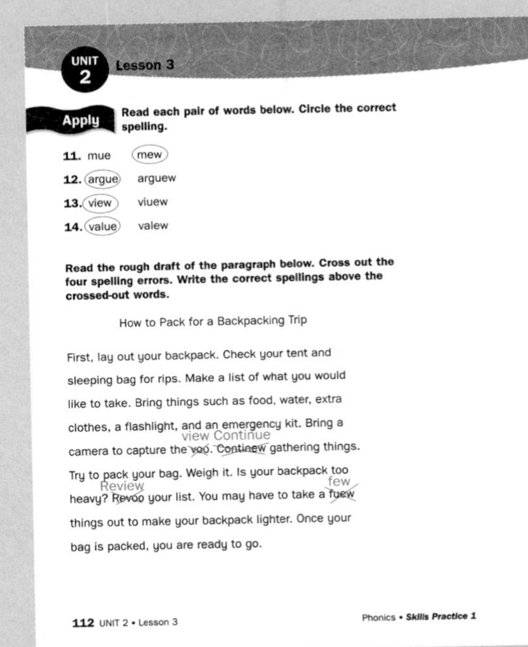
UNIT 2 Lesson 3

Apply Read each pair of words below. Circle the correct spelling.

11. mue mew
12. argue arguew
13. view viuew
14. value valew

Read the rough draft of the paragraph below. Cross out the four spelling errors. Write the correct spellings above the crossed-out words.

How to Pack for a Backpacking Trip

First, lay out your backpack. Check your tent and sleeping bag for rips. Make a list of what you would like to take. Bring things such as food, water, extra clothes, a flashlight, and an emergency kit. Bring a camera to capture the vuo. Continew gathering things. Try to pack your bag. Weigh it. Is your backpack too heavy? Revuo your list. You may have to take a fuew things out to make your backpack lighter. Once your bag is packed, you are ready to go.

112 UNIT 2 • Lesson 3

Phonics • Skills Practice 1

Skills Practice 1, p. 112

Monitor Progress to Differentiate Instruction

Formal Assessment 

Phonics and Fluency During the blending activity, note how quickly students are reading the words.

APPROACHING LEVEL	**IF . . .** students need practice with today's sound/spellings for /ū/,	**THEN . . .** work with them on the phonics activities on ***Reteach*** page 44 during Workshop.
	IF . . . students need extra practice with today's sound/spellings for /ū/,	**THEN . . .** work with them on the phonics activities for Unit 2 Lesson 3 in the ***Intervention Guide*** during Workshop.
ON LEVEL	**IF . . .** students understand today's sound/spellings for /ū/,	**THEN . . .** have them use ***eSkills*** during Workshop.
ABOVE LEVEL	**IF . . .** students are ready for a challenge with today's sound/spellings for /ū/,	**THEN . . .** have them complete the phonics activities on ***Challenge Activities*** page 40 during Workshop.

Day 1

Reading and Responding

OBJECTIVES

Students will

- activate prior knowledge to prepare to read the selection.
- learn selection vocabulary.
- learn the elements of narrative nonfiction.
- use the comprehension strategies Making Connections and Predicting.
- investigate the theme Animals and Their Habitats using the Inquiry process.

MATERIALS

- Routines 11, 13, 14
- ***Transparencies*** 9, 35, 55
- ***Student Reader,*** Book 1 pp. 174–185
- ***Skills Practice 1,*** pp. 101–102
- ***Home Connection,*** pp. 19–20

Build Background

Activate Prior Knowledge

- Discuss experiences students have had with various animals living in the same habitats, such as a forest or a jungle.
- Ask students to discuss the many animals that shared a habitat in "One Small Place in a Tree." Have students tell how some of the animals depended on the actions of others for their survival.
- Ask students what other stories they have read about animals sharing a habitat in the wild.

Background Information

The following information might help students understand the story they are about to read:

- Discuss the balance of nature. Explain that the phrase describes a harmonious, equal balance of existence. If something happens to change one element, such as human actions or weather, then the entire system is changed and is in danger of being upset.
- Students may have heard news reports of endangered animals. Explain that animal species are endangered when the entire species is in danger of dying and becoming extinct. This happens when animals' habitats change or are removed.
- Habitats are often lost through competition with humans. Some examples of this are deforestation (logging and the clearing of trees for wood and plantations), hunting, poaching (illegal hunting), pollution, and housing and commercial developments moving further into animal territories.
- Explain that environmental and conservation groups are working to see that lost habitats are reestablished. They help establish protected areas of land for animals, educate those who live in forests to farm the land more wisely without such a loss of trees, encourage consumers to buy wood and paper products from protected forests where new trees are planted, encourage

recycling, and discourage hunting and poaching. Conservation efforts can help bring nature back into balance.

- Habitats can change due to natural occurrences such as animal behavior, weather changes, and so on. This is what takes place in "Wolf Island." If the population of a certain animal or plant species decreases due to human intervention or otherwise, then that decrease will affect the life cycle of other animal and plant species.
- Tell students that this is a true story. The author demonstrates an imbalance in nature and how it corrected itself.

K	W	L
Wolves and other animals live on the island.	How do all of the animals get along on the island?	

Transparency 35

Preview and Prepare 

ROUTINE 13

Browse

Have students read the title and author, and take a few minutes to browse the selection. Have students use features such as the story's title and illustrations to predict how this story might relate to animals and their habitats.

Follow Routine 13, the know, want to know, learned routine, to help students identify and share what they know before reading, what they want to know while reading, and what their purposes are for reading. Students will chart these on a transparency.

Display ***Transparency*** 35 and model browsing. For example, by browsing the illustrations, students may "Know" that wolves and other animals live on the island. Under "Want to Know," write *How do all of the animals get along on the island?* Record students' observations on the transparency as they browse the selection.

Set Purposes

Have students set their own purposes for reading this selection. Remind students that readers can set purposes for reading by picking up clues from the title, illustrations, and genre of the text they are going to read. If students have trouble, suggest that they look for information about how changes in the habitat of one species affect the changes in the habitat for all species living on the island as they read.

Where do different animals live?

Before reading the selection, read the Big Idea question. Tell students to keep this question in mind when reading the selection.

Differentiating Instruction — English Learner

IF . . . students are unfamiliar with the word *species,* **THEN . . .** explain to them that *species* is a term used to categorize a group of living creatures that share similar features.

Give each student a copy of ***Home Connection*** page 19. The information is also available in Spanish on ***Home Connection*** page 20. Encourage students to discuss "Wolf Island" with their families and complete the activity provided.

Selection Vocabulary

male (māl) *adj.* of or having to do with men or boys (page 178)

female (fē′ • māl) *n.* a woman or girl (page 178)

aboard (ə • bord′) *adv.* on or into a ship, train, or an airplane (page 181)

mainland (mān′ • lənd) *n.* the chief landmass of a country, or continent, as different from an island (page 181)

mild (mīld) *adj.* gentle or calm; not harsh or sharp (page 182)

layer (lā′ • ûr) *n.* one thickness of something (page 182)

population (pop′ • ū • lā′ • shən) *n.* the people or animals living in a place (page 182)

balance (bal′ • əns) *n.* a steady, secure position (page 189)

Transparency 55

Selection Vocabulary

male (māl) *adj.* of or having to do with men or boys (page 178)

female (fē′ māl) *n.* a woman or girl (page 178)

aboard (ə bord′) *adv.* on or into a ship, train, or air-plane (page 181)

mainland (mān′ lənd) *n.* the chief landmass of a country, or continent, as different from an island (page 181)

mild (mīld) *adj.* gentle or calm; not harsh or sharp (page 182)

layer (lā′ ûr) *n.* one thickness of something (page 182)

population (pop′ ū lā′ shən) *n.* the people or animals living in a place (page 182)

balance (bal′ əns) *n.* a steady, secure position (page 188)

Unit 2, Lesson 3 Level 3

Transparency 55

Writer's Notebook

Have students copy the selection vocabulary and concept vocabulary words and definitions into the vocabulary section of their Writer's Notebooks. They can also include other words they think of that relate to the theme.

Building Vocabulary

ROUTINE 11

Using Routine 11, the selection vocabulary process, have students read aloud the Vocabulary Warm-Up on ***Student Reader,*** Book 1 pages 174–175.

As students read, have them stop to blend any difficult or unfamiliar words. Provide students with the pronunciations of words that are not decodable or that they cannot read automatically or fluently.

Guided Vocabulary Practice

Ask students to identify the highlighted vocabulary words they figured out using the vocabulary strategy word structure. **Possible Answer** *mainland* Have students explain how they figured out the meanings of the other vocabulary words as they read the Vocabulary Warm-Up.

Display ***Transparency*** 55, and have students read the words and definitions. Return to the Vocabulary Warm-Up, and read the sentences containing the vocabulary words with students. Then, if necessary, provide a brief in-context explanation of each word.

Read the story to find the meanings of these words, which are also in "Wolf Island":

- mild
- layer
- mainland
- population
- balance
- aboard
- male
- female

Vocabulary Strategy

Word Structure is when parts of a word help you understand the word's meaning. Use word structure to find the meaning of *mainland*.

Vocabulary Warm-Up

Clare checked her suitcase one more time. She had all she needed for her trip to the island. She could not wait to spend the weekend with her cousin Holly on Loon Island!

Dad rode the ferry over with Clare. It was a mild day, which made for a smooth crossing. The bottom layer of the ferry had an enclosed space. But Clare and Dad went to the top deck for some fresh air.

Holly met Clare and Dad at the dock. She was just as excited as Clare. And she was happy to have some help in her job. Holly was a "loon watcher."

Dad said his hellos and good-byes, then rode the ferry back to the mainland. Holly and Clare set to work. As loon watchers, they helped to monitor the birds' population. They kept a log of the number of loons they saw. They kept an eye out for loon nests.

Clare enjoyed the task. For her, being a loon watcher was a balance of work and fun. She loved to watch a parent loon act as a raft for its chicks. The babies would often climb aboard Mom or Dad for a lift! The chicks depended on their parents not just for a ride, but for protection.

Clare knew the loons' various calls. There was the yodel, the hoot, and the tremolo. Then there was the wail—the lonely sound of a male loon, or a female, looking for its mate or its chicks.

Sunday came too soon for Clare. She was not ready to return home. As the ferry drifted away from Loon Island, Clare heard a mournful wail. She understood the feeling.

GAME

Crossword Puzzle

Create a crossword puzzle with the vocabulary words. First, decide how you will have the words overlap. Then draw empty boxes for the letters. Create separate sets of clues for words that go "Across" and words that go "Down." Give your puzzle to a classmate to complete.

Concept Vocabulary

The concept word for this lesson is ***wildlife.*** **Wildlife** is living things, especially animals, in their natural environments. How do different species of wildlife depend on each other for survival?

174

175

Use the vocabulary words on ***Transparency*** 55 to create fill-in-the-blank sentences. Have students fill in the appropriate vocabulary words. For example, "The warm, soft breeze outside was calm and ________." *mild*

Discuss the concept vocabulary word *wildlife* with students. Ask students how they think the word *wildlife* relates to the theme Animals and Their Habitats. As students read the selections in this unit, encourage them to think about other words that relate to the theme. Students can record these words in the vocabulary section of their Writer's Notebooks.

GAME

Have students play the Crossword Puzzle game during Small-Group Time.

Technology

VOCABULARY Use ***eSkills*** for additional vocabulary practice.

Reading the Selection

Genre

Narrative Nonfiction

Have students identify the genre of "Wolf Island." *narrative nonfiction* If necessary, tell students that narrative nonfiction

- blends elements of fiction with nonfiction to make a more exciting story.
- includes facts about real people, places, and events.

Comprehension Strategies

Model the use of the following comprehension strategies during the first reading of "Wolf Island."

- Making Connections
- Predicting

Comprehension Strategies Rubrics

Use the Informal Comprehension Strategies Rubrics to determine whether a student is using any of the strategies listed below. Note the strategies a student is using, instead of the degree to which a student might be using any particular strategy. In addition, encourage the student to tell of any strategies other than the ones being taught that he or she is using.

Making Connections

- ✦ The student makes connections between prior knowledge and information in the text.
- ✦ The student makes connections between or relates personal experiences to what is read in the text (text-to-self connections).
- ✦ The student makes connections across or relates information from different selections (text-to-self connections).
- ✦ The student makes connections or relates information between what is happening in the text to what is happening in the world today (text-to-self connections).

Concept/Question Board

As students read "Wolf Island," encourage them to post questions, answers, comments, or other items related to the theme Animals and Their Habitats on the **Concept/Question Board.**

Monitor Progress

Formal Assessment

Comprehension Observation Log Observe individual students as they read, and use the Comprehension Observation Log, located in ***Lesson Assessment Book 1,*** to record anecdotal information about each student's strengths and weaknesses.

Predicting

- ✦ The student stops to make a prediction about the text.
- ✦ The student identifies the clues in the text used to make a prediction.
- ✦ The student uses clues in the text and prior knowledge to make a prediction.
- ✦ The student recognizes when a prediction is or is not confirmed by the text.

Monitor Progress to Differentiate Instruction

Formal Assessment 

Comprehension Skill Note students' understanding of the comprehension skill Making Inferences as they read.

APPROACHING LEVEL

IF . . .	THEN . . .
IF . . . students are having difficulty making inferences as they read,	**THEN . . .** have students read sample sentences gathered about activities and characters. Have students read these sample sentences, and help them infer as much information using their own personal knowledge and experience as possible. Ask questions such as *What do you think is going to happen? What do you think this character is going to do? Why do you think so?*

ON LEVEL

IF . . .	THEN . . .
IF . . . students are gaining an understanding of making inferences as they read,	**THEN . . .** have students keep a list of the inferences that they made from the selection. Have students write a journal entry about a personal experience that helped them infer what would happen next in the story.

ABOVE LEVEL

IF . . .	THEN . . .
IF . . . students are demonstrating an understanding of making inferences as they read,	**THEN . . .** have students write a paragraph about a character preparing for an activity. Have students keep the actual activity a secret. Allow students to switch paragraphs, and see if they can correctly guess the activity in their partner's paragraph.

Technology

eSTUDENT READER Students can access ***SRA Imagine It! Student Reader,*** Book 1 electronically by using the ***eStudent Reader*** online or on CD-ROM.

Comprehension Skills

Reread "Wolf Island" using the following comprehension skills:

- Making Inferences
- Fact and Opinion
- Reality and Fantasy

Reading with a Writer's Eye

While rereading "Wolf Island," explain the following literary element: Author's Purpose

Focus Questions

Have students read aloud the Focus Questions on page 176. Encourage students to think about the Focus Questions as they read "Wolf Island."

Teacher Tip

WORD STRUCTURE As they read, make sure students are recognizing and using their word structure and basic syllabication rules to help decode unfamiliar words.

Reading Recommendation

ROUTINE 14

Oral Reading

Use Routine 14, the reading the selection routine, as you read the story. While reading, model strategies and stop to ask and answer questions. Point out how the pictures reflect the story. Share the images that pop up in your mind as you read and how points in the reading relate to ideas you already know. Reread the text by applying the comprehension skills. After reading, be sure to discuss the story using the "handing-off" procedure and have students discuss new information that they have learned.

This story is ideal for oral reading because of its direct, simple, and yet descriptive and fluid language.

Differentiating Instruction — English Learner

IF . . . students need extra help with the comprehension strategy Making Connections, **THEN . . .** see ***English Learner Support Guide*** Unit 2 Lesson 3 for additional instruction and practice.

Genre

Narrative Nonfiction blends elements of fiction with elements of nonfiction to make a more exciting story. Facts about real people, places, and events are included in narrative nonfiction.

Comprehension Skill

Making Inferences
As you read, make inferences by connecting information from the story to what you already know.

Wolf Island

by Celia Godkin

Focus Questions

What are ways that different animals help make a habitat successful? How might your habitat be affected if an important part was removed?

176 177

Students will read the story twice over a four-day period.

Day 1 **ORAL READ** Have students read the first half of the selection. Model the use of the comprehension strategies.

Day 2 **ORAL READ** Have students finish reading the selection. Continue to model the comprehension strategies.

Day 3 **SILENT READ** Have students reread the first half of the selection silently. Have students focus on the comprehension skills and Reading with a Writer's Eye.

Day 4 **SILENT READ** Have students finish rereading the selection.

Technology

Have students listen to "Wolf Island" on the ***Listening Library CD.*** After students have listened, have them discuss what other things such as poetry, songs, or nonfiction they prefer to listen to on the radio or on CDs.

Reading and Responding

Once there was an island. It was an island with trees and meadows, and many kinds of animals. There were mice, rabbits and deer, squirrels, foxes and several kinds of birds.

All the animals on the island depended on the plants and the other animals for their food and well-being. Some animals ate grass or other plants; some ate insects; some ate other animals. The island animals were healthy. There was plenty of food for all. 1

A family of wolves lived on the island, too, a male wolf, a female, and their five cubs.

178

One day the wolf cubs were playing on the beach while their mother and father slept. The cubs found a strange object at the edge of the water.

It was a log raft, nailed together with boards. The cubs had never seen anything like this before. They were very curious. They climbed onto it and sniffed about. Everything smelled different. 2

179

Teacher Tip

INQUIRY Remind students that the things they wonder about as they read can be valid topics for further research or investigation.

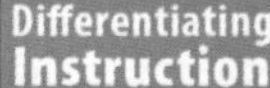

Differentiating Instruction English Learner

IF . . . students need help understanding the descriptions of the island and animals, **THEN . . .** use the illustrations to point out the island, deer, birds, wolves, and cubs. As you point to each animal, say, "This is a(n) ______. The ______ lives on the island."

1st READ

Comprehension Strategies

This selection is broken into two parts. On the first day, read pages 178–185. On the second day, read pages 186–189.

1 Making Connections Teacher Modeling: *Making connections between the text and your own experiences helps you enjoy and understand a story. When a story reminds you of things that have happened to you, share them with the class. This story reminds me of "One Small Place in a Tree." In that story, the animals also depended on each other for their well-being. Can anyone else make a connection to this part of the story?*

2 Predicting Teacher Modeling: *When reading, make predictions about what might happen next based on the clues in the story. I'm going to predict that the cubs will get into trouble. They have left their parents and climbed onto a raft. I'll keep reading; I want to know what happens to the wolf cubs. Do you have a prediction you would like to make?*

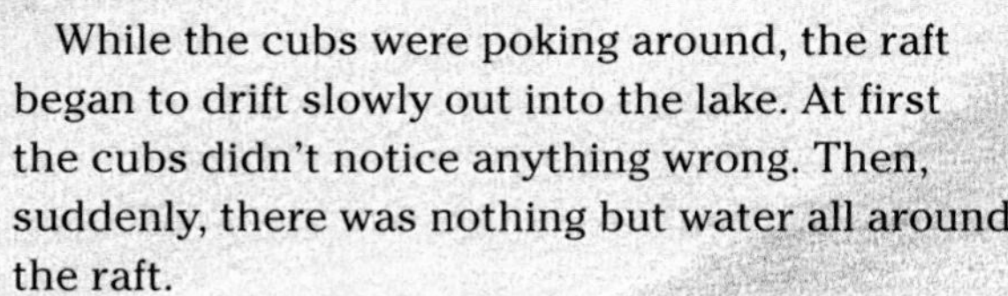

While the cubs were poking around, the raft began to drift slowly out into the lake. At first the cubs didn't notice anything wrong. Then, suddenly, there was nothing but water all around the raft.

The cubs were scared. They howled. The mother and father wolf heard the howling and came running down to the water's edge. 3

180

They couldn't turn the raft back, and the cubs were too scared to swim, so the adult wolves swam out to the raft and climbed aboard. The raft drifted slowly and steadily over to the mainland. Finally it came to rest on the shore and the wolf family scrambled onto dry land. 4

There were no longer wolves on the island.

181

3 **Confirming Predictions** Teacher Modeling: *My first prediction has been confirmed. The wolf cubs did get into a little bit of trouble. The mom and dad are going to try and save them. I'll keep reading to see what happens next.*

4 **Predicting** Teacher Modeling: *The mom and dad wolves weren't able to stop the raft or turn it around. But they did get aboard so the whole family could be together. I'm going to make another prediction. The wolf family is no longer on the island, so I think they will set up a new home on the mainland.*

Comprehension Check

Why didn't the cubs get off the raft? **Possible Answer** *The raft was surrounded by water, and the cubs were too afraid to swim.* ***Why did the mom and dad swim to and get aboard the raft?*** **Possible Answer** *They didn't want the cubs to be alone, so the parents got on the raft with the cubs.*

Vocabulary Tip

Point out the words *aboard* and *mainland* on page 181 in the text. Ask students whether seeing the picture of the wolves on the raft helps them understand the meaning of the word *aboard*. Ask students to give the meanings of the two smaller words, *main* and *land*, and then tell you the definition of the word *mainland*.

Reading and Responding

Time passed. Spring grew into summer on the island, and summer into fall. The leaves turned red. Geese flew south, and squirrels stored up nuts for the winter.

Winter was mild that year, with little snow. The green plants were buried under a thin white layer. Deer dug through the snow to find food. They had enough to eat. 5

Next spring, many fawns were born.

There were now many deer on the island. They were eating large amounts of grass and leaves. The wolf family had kept the deer population down, because wolves eat deer for food. Without wolves to hunt the deer, there were now too many deer on the island for the amount of food available.

182

Spring grew into summer and summer into fall. More and more deer ate more and more grass and more and more leaves.

Rabbits had less to eat, because the deer were eating their food. There were not many baby bunnies born that year.

Foxes had less to eat, because there were fewer rabbits for them to hunt.

Mice had less to eat, because the deer had eaten the grass and grass seed. There were not many baby mice born that year.

Owls had less to eat, because there were fewer mice for them to hunt. Many animals on the island were hungry. 6

183

Differentiating Instruction

English Learner

IF . . . students are native speakers of Vietnamese, Hmong, or Cantonese, **THEN . . .** they will need extra help forming and understanding compound words as these do not exist in their native languages.

Teacher Tip

USING STRATEGIES Remind students to use all the reading strategies they have learned so far in order to better understand and appreciate the story.

Comprehension Strategies

5 **Making Connections** Teacher Modeling: *I remember once when we had a warm winter with not much snow. The squirrels were very fat that year. They had plenty to eat all winter long. In the winters that are colder and we have more snow, I feed the birds and the other wildlife in my backyard so they don't go hungry. Can anyone else share a connection to this part of the story?*

6 **Predicting** Teacher Modeling: *Since the wolves left, the island has changed. Now that there are more deer, there is less food for the rabbits, which means there is less food for the foxes, mice, and owls. I predict that many animals on the island will die because they don't have enough to eat. I feel bad for the animals.*

Comprehension Check

How does this selection relate to the unit theme Animals and Their Habitats?

Possible Answer *This selection tells about one animal habitat for many species, and how one event changes the habitat for all species who live there.*

The first snow fell. Squirrels curled up in their holes, wrapped their tails around them for warmth, and went to sleep. The squirrels were lucky. They had collected a store of nuts for winter. 7

Other animals did not have winter stores. They had to find food in the snow. Winter is a hard time for animals, but this winter was harder than most. The snow was deep and the weather cold. Most of the plants had already been eaten during the summer and fall. Those few that remained were hard to find, buried deep under the snow.

184

Rabbits were hungry. Foxes were hungry. Mice were hungry. Owls were hungry. Even the deer were hungry. The whole island was hungry.

The owls flew over to the mainland, looking for mice. They flew over the wolf family walking along the mainland shore. The wolves were thin and hungry, too. They had not found a home, because there were other wolf families on the mainland. The other wolves did not want to share with them. 8

185

7 **Making Connections** Teacher Modeling: *I know that squirrels store nuts for the winter. I've seen them in my backyard and in the yard at school. They scurry around looking for nuts in the fall and then they bury them to eat in the winter. I wish the other animals could have been that fortunate. Do you have any connections to make?*

8 **Confirming Predictions** Teacher Modeling: *One of my predictions was not confirmed. I predicted that the wolf family would find a new home on the mainland. Unfortunately, the wolves aren't doing any better than most of the animals on the island. They are thin and hungry, too. Have any of the predictions you have made been confirmed or not confirmed?*

Phonics and Fluency

the /ū/ sound: fewer, few

Teacher Tip

COMPREHENSION Ask students the following questions to make sure they understand what they are reading:

- *Can you summarize what you have read?*
- *Does what you are reading make sense?*

STOP You have read the first half of the story. You will continue the story tomorrow on page T216.

Lesson 3 Inquiry Planner

STEP 3: Making Conjectures

Day 1 In groups, students will make conjectures about their investigation questions.

Day 2 Students will read "Wolf Island" for more ideas about the theme.

Day 3 As a whole group, students will discuss how ideas in "Wolf Island" relate to students' conjectures.

STEP 4: Identifying Needs and Making Plans

Day 4 With their groups, students will discuss things their group needs to know about their investigation topic and make plans for their investigation.

Day 5 Groups will begin collecting sources and carrying out investigation plans.

Teacher Tip

MAKING CONJECTURES Conjecturing may seem like a difficult concept for some students. Remind them that a conjecture is a possible answer to their investigation question based on what they know. They should make conjectures in order to continue investigating their question. Explain that as they continue to investigate, they may find that their conjecture no longer applies to the question. Or, they may find that they need to change their conjecture in some way. Tell students that this is alright and that this is what the investigation process is all about. Students should continually revise their questions and answers as they continue to investigate.

Inquiry Process

Step 3—Making Conjectures

Whole-Group Time

Whole Group

✦ At this point, student groups have chosen their investigation questions. Now they will begin making conjectures about their questions.

✦ Remind students that a conjecture is a statement about what they think the answer to their question is based on what they know now. After they collect information, they will review their conjectures in light of new information. Explain that their ideas about their investigation question may change after they do more research.

✦ Return to the investigation question you modeled earlier: *How should the community protect these animals?* Model making a conjecture about this question. *I think that too many people are unaware of this problem, so my conjecture is: There needs to be a campaign to raise awareness about the problem, and then people will know not to destroy animal habitats.* Remind students that this is just an example and that they are free to propose their own conjectures about questions that interest them. Have students discuss their ideas and conjectures about the question you modeled.

✦ If necessary, model making conjectures about some of the questions raised so far in the unit and in discussions. For example: *Where do animals live? What makes an animal habitat safe? Why do different animals have different habitats?* Example conjectures: *Animals live in homes and in wild places. A habitat is safe if animals have food, water, shelter, and a place to raise their young. Different animals eat different things, so they need habitats that have the things they eat.*

✦ If time permits, students might want to arrange for a wildlife expert in your area to talk to the class. You should assist students in contacting the local humane society, rehabilitation center, state department of forestry, parks and recreation department, or local colleges and universities. Before the expert visits, review ***Transparency*** 9 with students and the interviewing skills learned in Unit 1. Help students prepare good interview questions, especially ones that relate to their topics.

Small-Group Time

Small Group

- ✦ In their small groups, students should refer to the question they chose, how that question will be helpful, and other questions related to their investigation on ***Skills Practice 1*** pages 101–102.
- ✦ As you circulate among the groups, continue modeling conjectures with students. Keep in mind, however, that the investigations are student-driven. Groups should develop their own questions, conjectures, and presentations based on their own interests.
- ✦ Remind students that conjectures should be based on what they already know about their topic. Have groups discuss what they know about their topic and make a conjecture. Have students discuss which conjectures are more reasonable, likely, or helpful answers to their question. Students should record their conjectures in their Writer's Notebooks and post them on the ***Concept/Question Board.***

Transparency 9

Interviewing Guidelines and Questions

Here are some guidelines to help you with your interview.

1. **Always ask permission to interview the person.** You can do this face to face, by phone, or by letter. Explain what you're doing and why. Be sure to tell him or her how much time you think you'll need.
2. **Decide ahead of time what you want to know.**
3. **Make up questions that will help you get the information you need.**
4. **Write your questions down in an organized order, leaving space between each one for taking notes.**
5. **Speak clearly, and be polite.** Pay attention as the person answers.
6. **Take notes on the answers.** Jot down only enough to help you remember what the person said. You might find it helpful to use a tape recorder if one is available. Always ask the person's permission before you record his or her voice.
7. **Read over your notes as soon after you leave the interview as possible, while the conversation is still fresh in your mind.** Make additional notes to help you clarify ideas where necessary.

 Level 3

Transparency 9

Concept/Question Board

Encourage students to continue to write information on the **Concept/Question Board.** Students might

- share findings or questions they encountered as they discussed investigation ideas and possible conjectures.
- bring in articles and/or pictures from magazines, the Internet, and newspapers of animals and their habitats.
- draw pictures that support the theme.
- write a summary of a television program or film they have seen about animals and their habitats.

Teacher Tip

CONCEPT/QUESTION BOARD Have students download articles about animal habitats to post on the **Concept/Question Board.** Encourage students to write summaries of what they learned about the theme from any articles they post and include these summaries with the article.

Inquiry Rubric

To assess Making Conjectures, see the Inquiry Rubrics in the Level Appendix.

Language Arts

OBJECTIVES

Students will

- ✦ complete a web organizer for a process paper.
- ✦ take the spelling pretest.
- ✦ review cursive *f, h, m,* and *n.*

MATERIALS

- ✦ Routine 15
- ✦ ***Language Arts Handbook,*** pp. 98–100
- ✦ ***Skills Practice 1,*** p. 121
- ✦ ***Transparencies*** 45, 52

Teacher Tip

PLAN AHEAD Save this list of processes for students to reference.

Explaining a Process

When you tell someone how to do something or how to get somewhere, your purpose is to explain. Giving directions or explaining how to do something takes some practice. You must choose your words and write your sentences carefully. It's very important to keep your audience in mind when you explain something. A first grader will not be able to read the same words as an adult. You will also need to use shorter sentences for a first grader. No matter who your audience is, you must use words they will understand. You must explain step-by-step so your reader will be able to follow along.

Putting Things in Order

When you explain a process, you tell someone how to do something. You might explain how to tie a shoe, wash the dog, or wrap a present. To get started, imagine how to do the task in your mind.

Nick thought about how he planted seeds in his garden last summer. Here are the notes he made as he thought about what he'd had to do.

1. break up the ground
2. make a hole
3. put in the seed
4. cover it
5. water it

98 Explaining a Process • Expository Writing

Language Arts Handbook, p. 98

Differentiating Instruction

English Learner

IF . . . students need help to understanding the writing project, **THEN . . .** tell them that a process is a system for doing something. Provide short How-To picture books for students to browse in order to understand the concept.

Writing

Explaining a Process

Prewriting

ROUTINE 15

Teach

- ✦ Ask a student to explain what he or she does in the morning to get ready to go to school. After the description, tell students that a process was just explained to them.
- ✦ Tell students that any time they give directions, the purpose is to explain. In order for others to follow the directions, they need to be written very carefully.
- ✦ Use Routine 15. Tell students that they will be explaining a process for this writing lesson. In the process, they will have to give step-by-step directions, and will have to think very carefully about word choice and audience.
- ✦ Discuss with students why word choice and audience will be very important in this writing lesson. If necessary, explain that the person or persons receiving the information will determine the words that are used. For example, if the writer is explaining how to make a fruit smoothie to someone who has never made one before, the writer will need to use specific ingredients and measurements.
- ✦ For further information on explaining a process, see ***Language Arts Handbook*** pages 98–100.

Guided Practice

- ✦ Have students help you create a list of possible processes that they can explain on the board. **Possible Answers** how to make a sandwich, how to wash a dog, how to wrap a present, how to do homework, how to set the table, and so on
- ✦ Have students turn to ***Skills Practice 1*** page 121. Read the Think section with the students and discuss possible answers.

Vriting, continued

Apply

- Have students continue to brainstorm ideas either individually or with a partner.
- Have students individually complete the top of ***Skills Practice 1,*** page 121.

ssessment

ou will use the Writing Rubrics found in the Level Appendix o evaluate students' process papers. You may use any of the ubrics for Genre, Writing Process, and Writing Traits. Share vith students what you will be looking for when assessing heir process papers.

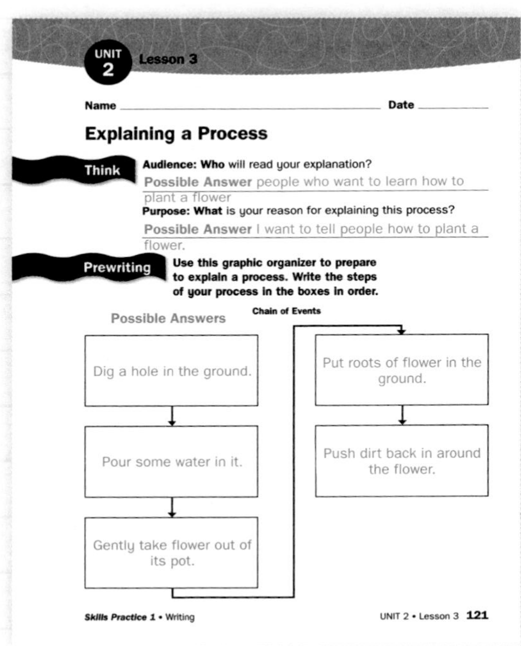
UNIT 2 Lesson 3

Name ______ Date ______

Explaining a Process

Think
Audience: Who will read your explanation?
Possible Answer people who want to learn how to plant a flower
Purpose: What is your reason for explaining this process?
Possible Answer I want to tell people how to plant a flower.

Prewriting
Use this graphic organizer to prepare to explain a process. Write the steps of your process in the boxes in order.

Possible Answers
Chain of Events
Dig a hole in the ground.
Pour some water in it.
Gently take flower out of its pot.
Put roots of flower in the ground.
Push dirt back in around the flower.

Skills Practice 1 • Writing   UNIT 2 • Lesson 3 121

Skills Practice 1, p. 121

Spelling

/ū/ and Homographs Pretest

Teach

- Say the sentences below. Have students write the spelling words on a separate sheet of paper. When they are finished, have them correct any misspelled words.

Pretest Sentences

1. Follow my **cue** and stand up when I do.
2. After the party, a **few** apples were left.
3. Sandy saw the doctor because she did not feel **well.**
4. The bride wanted one more **rose** in her bouquet.
5. The teacher didn't want her students to **argue.**
6. I need a new **tire** for my bicycle.
7. The **hue** of the leaf was beautiful.
8. The bell is going to **ring** in five minutes.
9. Do you know the **value** of the bicycle?
10. The country is a nice **change** of scenery for me.
11. The sprinkler began to **spew** water.
12. My family will **rescue** a dog from the shelter.
13. The **park** is across the street from our house.
14. I have a nice **view** of the river from my home.
15. Please turn off the **light** when you leave.

Challenge Sentences

16. The **pitcher** looks like it has a crack.
17. My **nephew** Taylor is a college sophomore.

Diagnose any misspellings by determining whether students misspelled the homographs, the /ū/ spellings, or other parts of the word. Then have students use the pretest as a take-home list to study the spellings of homographs and words with /ū/.

Teacher Tip

PENMANSHIP If students are having problems forming cursive *f, h, m,* and *n*, or their letters are floating between the lines, review proper paper position, check to make sure students are holding their pencils correctly, or review letter formation.

Penmanship 

Review Cursive Letters *f, h, m,* and *n*

Teach

- Remind students that cursive letters are made of four types of strokes (undercurve, overcurve, downcurve, and slant lines).
- Review lowercase cursive *f* and *h* as slant letters with loops. Review lowercase cursive *m* and *n as* overcurve letters. For instruction on letter formation, refer to Unit 2 lessons 1 and 2; ***Transparencies*** 45 and 52; and the Level Appendix.
- On the board, write lowercase cursive *f, h, m,* and *n* saying the strokes aloud as you form the letters.
- To model proper letter formation, write the following words on the board: *half, hoof, mane, manor.*

Guided Practice

- Using a pointer or your fingertip, show students how to write in the air to practice letter formation.
- Tell students to hold their index fingers in the air in front of them. Say the strokes aloud as you trace the letters, and have students mimic your movements as if they were writing in the air.

Apply

- Have students practice writing each of the letters twice.
- After reviewing the words you wrote on the board, set a timer for three minutes and have students write the words on a sheet of notebook paper to practice letter formation. Have them circle the best formation of each word according to the proper letter formation of *f, h, m,* and *n.*

Skills Traces

Preparing to Read

Word Structure: Homographs

Introduced in Grade 2, Unit 5, Lesson 4

Reviewed: Unit 2, Lesson 3
Practiced: Unit 2, Lesson 4
Unit 2, Lesson 5
Assessed: ***Lesson Assessment Book 1,*** p. 59

Reviewed in Grade 4, Unit 2, Lesson 5

Phonics:

See Level Appendix

Reading and Responding

Comprehension Skill: Fact and Opinion

Reviewed in Grade 2, Unit 3, Lesson 3

Grade 3
Reviewed: Unit 1, Lesson 1
Practiced: Unit 2, Lesson 4
Assessed: ***Lesson Assessment Book 1,*** pp. 60–62

Reviewed in Grade 4, Unit 2, Lesson 4

Comprehension Skill: Reality and Fantasy

Reviewed in Grade 2, Unit 1, Lesson 4

Grade 3
Reviewed: Unit 2, Lesson 2
Practiced: Unit 2, Lesson 3
Assessed: ***Lesson Assessment Book 1,*** pp. 60–62

Comprehension Skill: Making Inferences

Reviewed in Grade 2, Unit 1, Lesson 5

Grade 3
Reviewed: Unit 2, Lesson 3
Practiced: Unit 4, Lesson 2
Assessed: ***Lesson Assessment Book 1,*** pp. 60–62

Reviewed in Grade 4, Unit 1, Lesson 5

Comprehension Strategy: Making Connections

Reviewed in Grade 2, Unit 1, Lesson 1

Grade 3
Reviewed: Unit 1, Lesson 1
Practiced: Unit 2, Lesson 3
Assessed: Unit 2, Lesson 3, p. T200

Reviewed in Grade 4, Unit 1, Lesson 1

Language Arts

Writing: Explaining a Process

Reviewed in Grade 2, Unit 3, Lesson 3

Grade 3
Reviewed: Unit 2, Lesson 3
Assessed: ***Skill Practice 1,*** pp. 121–122

Reviewed in Grade 4, Unit 2, Lesson 1

Grammar, Usage, and Mechanics: Plurals and Irregular Plurals

Grade 3
Introduced: Unit 2, Lesson 3
Practiced: Unit 6, Lesson 2
Assessed: Unit 2, Lesson 3, p. T254

Reviewed in Grade 4, Unit 2, Lesson 2

Preparing to Read

OBJECTIVES

Students will
- review /ū/ spelled _*ew* and _*ue*.
- build fluency.

MATERIALS

- ***Transparency*** 54
- ***Sound/Spelling Card*** 31
- Routines 2, 3, 4, 7, 8

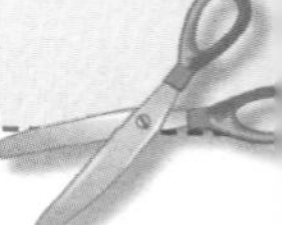

Differentiating Instruction

English Learner

IF . . . students confuse the pronunciations of *few* and *dew* in the daily news, **THEN . . .** write a simple phonetic spelling of the words on the board and have students practice the different pronunciations; for example, *few/fyoo, dew/doo, hue/hyoo*

Daily Oral Practice

Daily News

Today!

It was a few hours before dawn in the forest. The dew seemed cool to the squirrels as they crawled around the trees. The birds woke as the first hues of sunlight struck the leaves. It's a peaceful morning in this wildlife forest.

- Write the daily news on the board or on chart paper. Then have students read the daily news in unison to practice fluency.
- As a review of yesterday's phonics and fluency lesson, ask a volunteer to identify any words in the message with /ū/ spelled _*ew* or _*ue*. */ū/ spelled* _ew *in* few; */ū/ spelled* _ue *in* hue

Phonics and Fluency

ROUTINE 3 ROUTINE 4

Review: /ū/ spelled _*ew* and _*ue*

Line 1	few	fewer	fewest	curfew
Line 2	pew	mew	skew	nephew
Line 3	cue	hue	rescue	argue
Line 4	value	continue	barbeque	tissue

Sentence 1 I <u>often</u> want to view the <u>world</u> from outer space.

Sentence 2 <u>Without</u> its cover, the issue was valued at only ten dollars.

Blending

- ✦ Use ***Transparency*** 54 with the blending lines and sentences from Day 1.
- ✦ Review ***Sound/Spelling Card*** 31 with students. Then use Routine 3, the whole-word blending process, to have students read Lines 1–4.
- ✦ Have students read the sentences using normal intonation and expression. If students have difficulty reading a sentence, stop and use Routine 4, the blending sentences process.

Developing Oral Language

Use one or both of these activities to help students practice reading the words from the blending lines.

- Ask a student to choose a word, identify the sound/spelling, and then use the word in a sentence. **Possible Answer** /ū/ *spelled* _ew *in* curfew; *I have to be home before my* curfew. Continue for all the words in the lines.
- Let students take turns choosing a word, reading it, and using it in a sentence. **Possible Answer** *Every 4th of July we have a* barbeque. Then have a classmate extend the sentences. Encourage students to extend sentences by adding words to the beginning and end of the sentence. **Possible Answer** *At my uncle's house, every 4th of July we have a* barbeque *before we go see fireworks.*

Dictation

ROUTINE 2 ROUTINE 7 ROUTINE 8

- ✦ Follow Routine 7 for whole-word dictation. When dictating words, say the word, use the word in a sentence, and then repeat the word.
- ✦ Follow Routine 8 for sentence dictation. When dictating sentences, say the sentence. Next, dictate one word at a time, following Routine 2 for sounds-in-sequence dictation or Routine 7 for whole-word dictation, depending on your students. Have students proofread for spelling, capitalization, and end punctuation.
- ✦ Dictate the following words and sentence for students to write.

Line 1	review	fewest
Line 2	argued	valued
Challenge Word	discontinue	
Sentence	I need a few pieces of tissue paper.	

Sound/Spelling Card 31

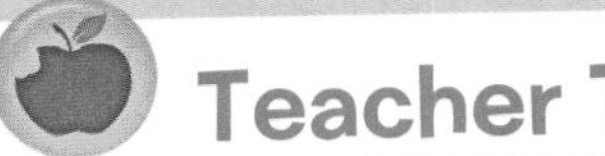

Teacher Tip

SOUND/SPELLING CARDS If students do not note the various features of the ***Sound/Spelling Cards,*** tell them about the information on these cards, such as the color bands, the picture, the blanks that are part of the spellings, and so on. ***Sound/Spelling Cards*** are an important resource for both reading and spelling.

Snow fell for many weeks. The drifts became deeper and deeper. It was harder and harder for animals to find food. Animals grew weaker, and some began to die. The deer were so hungry they gnawed bark from the trees. Trees began to die. 9

Snow covered the island. The weather grew colder and colder. Ice began to form in the water around the island, and along the mainland coast. It grew thicker and thicker, spreading farther and farther out into the open water. One day there was ice all the way from the mainland to the island.

186

The wolf family crossed the ice and returned to their old home. 10 11

187

OBJECTIVES

Students will

- use the comprehension strategies Predicting and Making Connections.
- discuss the story using the handing-off procedure.
- review vocabulary, genre, and fluency.

MATERIALS

- Routine A
- ***Transparencies*** 35, 55
- ***Student Reader,*** Book 1, pp. 186–191
- ***Skills Practice 1,*** pp. 117–118

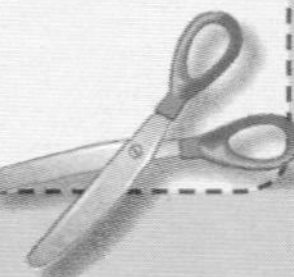

Comprehension Strategies

9 **Confirming Predictions** Teacher Modeling: *Unfortunately, my prediction about some of the animals dying was confirmed. They didn't have enough food and then the weather turned even colder. It must be very hard for the animals to survive. I hope their situation gets better soon.*

10 **Making Connections** Teacher Modeling: *When I was young, sometimes in the winter it would get so cold that a pond in our neighborhood would freeze all the way through. If we were very careful and adults went with us, we were allowed to ice skate on the pond. I've seen birds and other animals run and skid across the ice too. In the story, I'm glad the ice formed far enough across that the wolf family was able to return to their home.*

11 **Predicting** Teacher Modeling: *I'm going to make another prediction. Now that the wolf family is returning home, I predict that the habitat will change back to what it was before.*

The wolves were hungry when they eached the island, and there were many veak and sick deer for them to eat. The wolves left the healthy deer alone.

Finally, spring came. The snow melted, and grass and leaves began to grow. The wolves emained in their island home, hunting deer. No longer would there be too many deer on he island. Grass and trees would grow again. Rabbits would find enough food. The mice would find enough food. There would be ood for the foxes and owls. And there would be food for the deer. The island would have ood enough for all.

88

Life on the island was back in balance. 12

189

12 **Confirming Predictions** Teacher Modeling: *My prediction was confirmed! The sland is back to the way it used to be. There is enough food for all of the animals and nature is back in balance again!*

Comprehension Check

Why is the arrival of spring important to the animals on the island? **Possible Answer** *Plants, grass, and trees will begin to grow again. The snow will soon be gone and all of the animals will be able to find plenty of food.*

Vocabulary Tip

oint out the word *balance* in the text. Ask students how knowing that the animals were ealthy once again helps them understand the meaning of life being in *balance?*

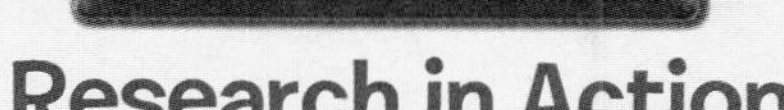

Research in Action

Remember to discuss with the students difficulties that occur during reading. While problems that arise during reading should be addressed as they occur, it is important to reflect on the problems and how they were solved. After reading, have students identify the difficulties. Probe with questions that foster metacognition, or thinking about thinking, such as *What did you find difficult here? How did you try to figure it out? Did that work? What else might work?*

(Michael Pressley)

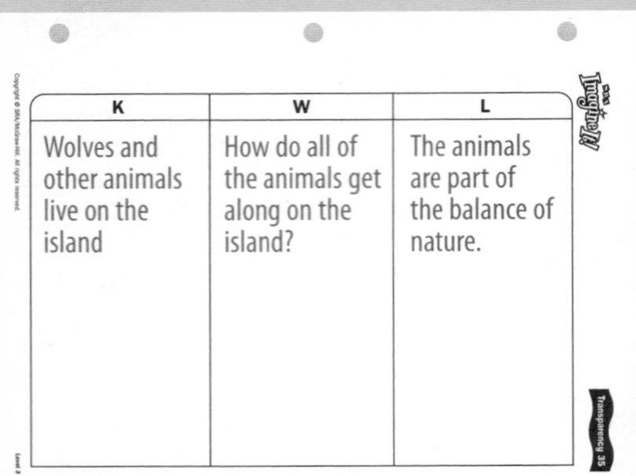

K	W	L
Wolves and other animals live on the island	How do all of the animals get along on the island?	The animals are part of the balance of nature.

Transparency 35

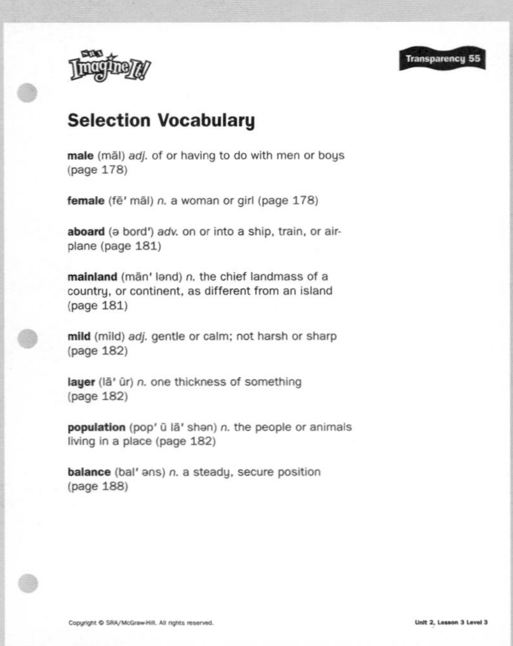

Transparency 55

Selection Vocabulary

male (māl) *adj.* of or having to do with men or boys (page 178)

female (fē' māl) *n.* a woman or girl (page 178)

aboard (ə bord') *adv.* on or into a ship, train, or airplane (page 181)

mainland (mān' land) *n.* the chief landmass of a country, or continent, as different from an island (page 181)

mild (mīld) *adj.* gentle or calm; not harsh or sharp (page 182)

layer (lā' ûr) *n.* one thickness of something (page 182)

population (pop' ū lā' shən) *n.* the people or animals living in a place (page 182)

balance (bal' əns) *n.* a steady, secure position (page 188)

Unit 2, Lesson 3 Level 3

Transparency 55

Discussing the Selection

✦ It is important for students to see you as a contributing member of the group. Use Routine A, the handing-off process, to emphasize that you are part of the group. Actively participate in the handing-off process by raising your hand to be called on by the last speaker when you have a contribution to make. Point out unusual and interesting insights verbalized by students so that these insights are recognized and discussed. As the year progresses, students will take more responsibility for the discussion of the selections.

✦ Engage students in a discussion using the handing-off procedure to determine whether they have grasped the following ideas:

- At the beginning of the story, life on the island was in balance. The animals were healthy.
- When the wolf family left, life on the island changed.

✦ Ask students how the story demonstrates the following key concepts:

- When nature is in balance, life for its inhabitants is healthy.
- Animal habitats are delicate and fragile. One small change can bring many changes for life in a habitat.

✦ Return to the KWL chart on ***Transparency*** 35. Have students discuss whether the selection provided enough information to tell them what they wanted to know, and also have them discuss what they learned by reading the selection. Ask students if the predictions they made while browsing the story were confirmed or not confirmed.

✦ Have students return to the Focus Questions on ***Student Reader,*** Book 1 page 176. Select a student to read the questions aloud, and have students answer and discuss the questions. Have them return to the text as necessary.

Genre Review

Review the elements of narrative nonfiction with students on page T200. Ask students how they know "Wolf Island" is narrative nonfiction.

Where do different animals live?

After reading the selection, read the Big Idea question. Discuss with students how the selection helps answer this question.

Vocabulary Review

Review the selection vocabulary words and definitions students wrote in the vocabulary section of the Writer's Notebook. Have students refer to pages 115–116 in ***Skills Practice 1.*** Read the first two questions aloud, and help students find the answers. Let students complete the rest on their own. Review the concept word *wildlife*. Ask students whether they can think of other words related to the theme Animals and Their Habitats. **Possible Answers** *environment, conservation, shelter, protection, balance, compassion, dependent*

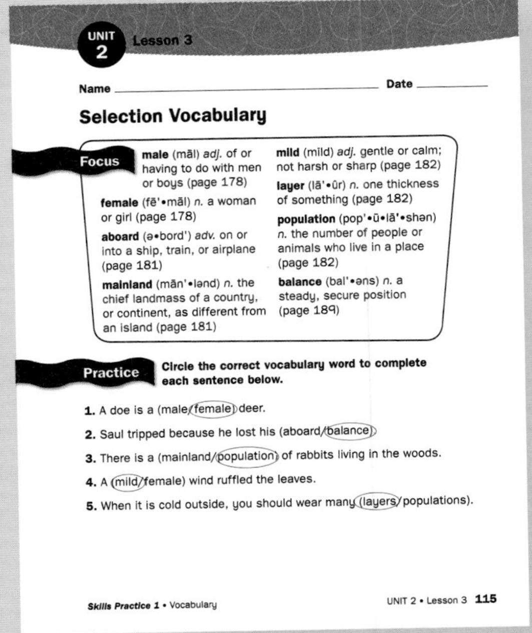

UNIT 2 Lesson 3

Name ______ Date ______

Selection Vocabulary

Focus

male (māl) *adj.* of or having to do with men or boys (page 178)

female (fē'•māl) *n.* a woman or girl (page 178)

aboard (ə•bord') *adv.* on or into a ship, train, or airplane (page 181)

mainland (mān'•lənd) *n.* the chief landmass of a country, or continent, as different from an island (page 181)

mild (mīld) *adj.* gentle or calm; not harsh or sharp (page 182)

layer (lā'•ûr) *n.* one thickness of something (page 182)

population (pop'•ū•lā'•shən) *n.* the number of people or animals who live in a place (page 182)

balance (bal'•əns) *n.* a steady, secure position (page 189)

Practice **Circle the correct vocabulary word to complete each sentence below.**

1. A doe is a (male/female) deer.
2. Saul tripped because he lost his (aboard/balance).
3. There is a (mainland/population) of rabbits living in the woods.
4. A (mild/female) wind ruffled the leaves.
5. When it is cold outside, you should wear many (layers/populations).

Skills Practice 1 • Vocabulary UNIT 2 • Lesson 3 115

Skills Practice 1, p. 115

Fluency

Focus on accuracy when reading "Wolf Island." Accuracy is essential to fluency because readers are able to focus on comprehending text. In order to help students with accuracy, a passage of unfamiliar words may need to be read several times in order for students to read the passage with accuracy.

- Read aloud pages 178–179 of "Wolf Island." Model fluency for students. For example, after reading *All the animals on the island depended on the plants and other animals for their food and well being,* point out how you read the sentence with careful attention to each word. Model rereading for students as well, and stress the fact that all readers sometimes have to read and reread in order to read with accuracy. Point out how you paused at the end of each sentence and after the end punctuation. Have students follow along in the ***Student Readers,*** and tell them to raise their hands when you pause. Tell students that as they reread, they should practice rereading all unfamiliar words in order to read with accuracy.

Teacher Tip

WORD BANK If you created a Word Bank of key words related to the theme Animals and Their Habitats, remind students to find words from other resources, their activities, and family discussions and add them to the Word Bank. Organize the words according to parts of speech.

Fluency Tip

FLUENCY By this time in Grade 3, good readers should be reading approximately 99 words per minute with fluency and expression. The only way to gain this fluency is by practicing. Have students reread the selection to you and to each other during Workshop to help build fluency. As students read, you may notice that some need work in building fluency. During Workshop, have these students choose a section of the text (a minimum of 160 words) to read several times to build fluency.

Formal Assessment

Monitor Progress to Differentiate Instruction

Selection Vocabulary Observe students' understanding of the vocabulary words and their definitions.

APPROACHING LEVEL

IF . . . students need extra help with the selection vocabulary,	**THEN . . .** use ***Intervention Guide,*** Unit 2 Lesson 3.
IF . . . students need extra help with the selection vocabulary,	**THEN . . .** use ***Reteach*** page 46.

ON LEVEL

IF . . . students need practice using the selection vocabulary words,	**THEN . . .** have students complete vocabulary activities on ***eSkills.***

ABOVE LEVEL

IF . . . students understand the selection vocabulary,	**THEN . . .** use ***Challenge Activities*** page 42.

Teacher Tips

LISTENING During Workshop, have students listen to "Wolf Island" for a model of oral reading. While students listen, have them keep a list of any new or unfamiliar words they encounter in the Writer's Notebook, and instruct them to check the words using a dictionary or glossary. Also, instruct students to listen for the lesson's vocabulary words and to check that the words make sense within the reading.

WRITE ABOUT IT! Have students write about how the animals on the island lived after the wolves left in their Writer's Notebooks.

Meet the Author and Illustrator

After students read the information about the author and illustrator, discuss the following questions with them:

- *Why do you think Celia Godkin wrote "Wolf Island"?* **Possible Answer** *Godkin may have written "Wolf Island" because she is concerned about animals and their habitats.*
- *Celia Godkin has lived in three different countries. How do you think these experiences have helped her writing and her illustrating?* **Possible Answer** *She has seen and lived in areas with different plants and animals. These experiences helped form her love of nature and science.*

Theme Connections

Within the Selection

1. How did the habitat change on the island? **Possible Answer** *In the beginning of "Wolf Island," the animal habitat was in balance. The animals were healthy.*
2. What finally brought the habitat back into balance? **Possible Answer** *The habitat returned to balance when the wolf family returned home to the island.*

Across Selections

3. How is the animal habitat in "Wolf Island" like the animal habitat in "One Small Place in a Tree"? **Possible Answer** *The animal habitat in "Wolf Island" is like the animal habitat in "One Small Place in a Tree" because the plants and animals depend on each other for survival.*
4. How are the habitats different? **Possible Answer** *In "One Small Place in a Tree," nothing happened to upset the balance.*

Beyond the Selection

5. How might you cause change in an animal habitat? **Possible Answer** Animal habitats can be changed by removing or adding trees, grass, plants, or water.
6. How could you tell if you are causing change? **Possible Answer** You can tell if you are causing change by observing wildlife in its habitat. Depending upon the changes you make, animals might have to leave or more animals might thrive in the habitat.

Meet the Author and Illustrator

Celia Godkin

Celia Godkin grew up in Brazil and England and now lives in an old farmhouse in Eastern Canada. Science has always fascinated her. While working at a zoo, Godkin got the chance to help make a book about Canada's endangered wildlife. She has since worked on many projects that combine her talents as a writer and illustrator with her love of science.

190

Animals and Their Habitats

Theme Connections

Within the Selection

1. How did the habitat change on the island?
2. What finally brought the habitat back into balance?

Across Selections

3. How is the animal habitat in "Wolf Island" like the animal habitat in "One Small Place in a Tree"?
4. How is it different?

Beyond the Selection

5. How might you cause change in an animal habitat?
6. How could you tell that you are causing change?

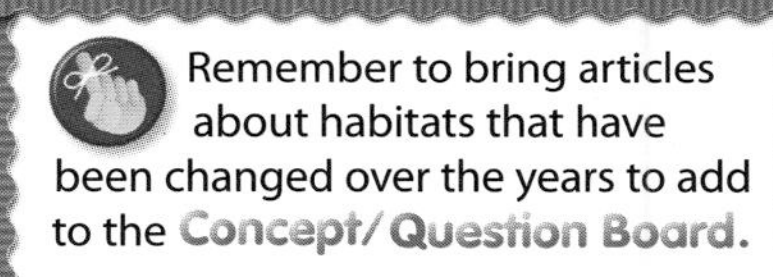

Write about It!

Describe how the animals on the island lived after the wolves left.

Remember to bring articles about habitats that have been changed over the years to add to the **Concept/Question Board.**

191

Concept/Question Board

As students discuss "Wolf Island," encourage them to post questions, answers, comments, or other items related to the theme Animals and Their Habitats on the **Concept/Question Board.**

Teacher Tip

BEYOND THE SELECTION Have students summarize what they have learned and tell how they might use this information in further investigations.

Writer's Notebook

- Have students list other nonfiction selections they have read in class or on their own in their Writer's Notebooks.
- Have students compare the elements found in each selection.

OBJECTIVES

Students will

- ✦ complete a graphic organizer.
- ✦ spell words with /ū/ and homographs.
- ✦ learn different types of sentences.
- ✦ create a cause-and-effect graphic organizer.

MATERIALS

- ✦ Routine 16
- ✦ ***Skills Practice 1,*** pp. 121, 125–126
- ✦ ***Language Arts Handbook,*** p. 303

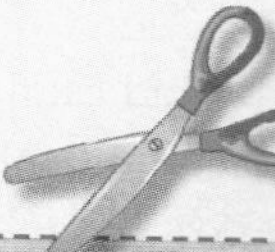

Writing Explaining a Process

ROUTINE 16

Prewriting

Teach

- ✦ Remind students that they should have selected a process to explain and then answered the two questions at the top of ***Skills Practice 1*** page 121.
- ✦ Use Routine 16. Tell students that they will now fill in the graphic organizer on that same page.

Guided Practice

Draw the chain of events graphic organizer on the board or on large chart paper.

- ✦ Model putting information about a process onto the chart. For example, you may want to explain how to add double-digit numbers or how to perform a simple task. Select a process that the students will know so that they can help you add pieces of information to the graphic organizer.
- ✦ Discuss whether any pieces of information have been left out of the process, and if so, where they should be added.

Apply

- ✦ **Composing—Prewriting** Have students complete the graphic organizer in ***Skills Practice 1*** page 121.

Teacher Tip

PLAN AHEAD Place your chain of events graphic organizer in a location that can be referenced throughout the lesson.

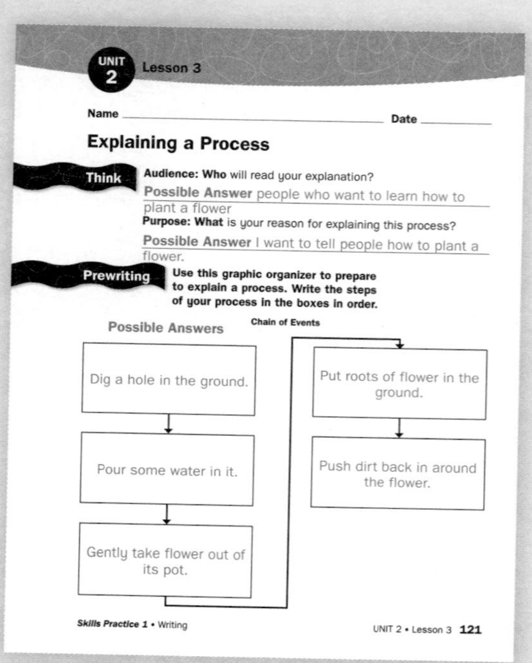

UNIT 2 Lesson 3

Name ______ Date ______

Explaining a Process

Think **Audience:** Who will read your explanation?
Possible Answer people who want to learn how to plant a flower

Purpose: What is your reason for explaining this process?
Possible Answer I want to tell people how to plant a flower.

Prewriting **Use this graphic organizer to prepare to explain a process. Write the steps of your process in the boxes in order.**

Possible Answers — Chain of Events

Dig a hole in the ground. → Pour some water in it. → Gently take flower out of its pot. → Put roots of flower in the ground. → Push dirt back in around the flower.

Skills Practice 1 • Writing — UNIT 2 • Lesson 3 121

Skills Practice 1, p. 121

Spelling

/ū/ and Homographs

Teach

Use a word sort to teach homographs and words with /ū/ spelled *_ew, _ue*.

Guided Practice

Write the following headings on the board: *homographs* and /ū/. Then write the word list: *cue, few, well, rose, argue, tire, hue, ring, value, change, spew, rescue, park, view,* and *light*. Have volunteers write the words under the correct heading. Once the spelling words have all been used, ask for students to come to the board and underline the part of each word that reflects the category in which it was placed.

Word Sort Answers

Homographs: *well, rose, tire, ring, change, park, light*
Words with /ū/ spelled *_ew: few, spew, view*
Words with /ū/ spelled *_ue: cue, argue, hue, value, rescue*

Grammar, Usage, and Mechanics 

Types of Sentences

Teach

✦ Write the following four sentences on the board.

- The animals in the forest were healthy and happy.
- Did Candice adopt a dog or a cat from the shelter?
- Please pass the green beans.
- Brian and Chris both made the team!

✦ Explain that there are four types of sentences.

- A declarative sentence makes a statement, tells facts, and ends with a period.
- An interrogative sentence asks questions, and ends with a question mark.
- An imperative sentence gives commands or makes requests and ends with a period.
- An exclamatory sentence shows strong feelings and ends with an exclamation point.

✦ Go back to the first four sentences and ask students to identify each type. *Sentence 1, declarative; sentence 2, interrogative; sentence 3, imperative; sentence 4, exclamatory*

✦ Explain that using the different types of sentences will make their writing more interesting to read.

✦ Use ***Language Arts Handbook*** page 303 for definitions and examples of types of sentences.

Differentiating Instruction **English Learner**

IF . . . students are native Spanish speakers,
THEN . . . remind them that in English, question marks and exclamation points appear only at the end of a sentence.

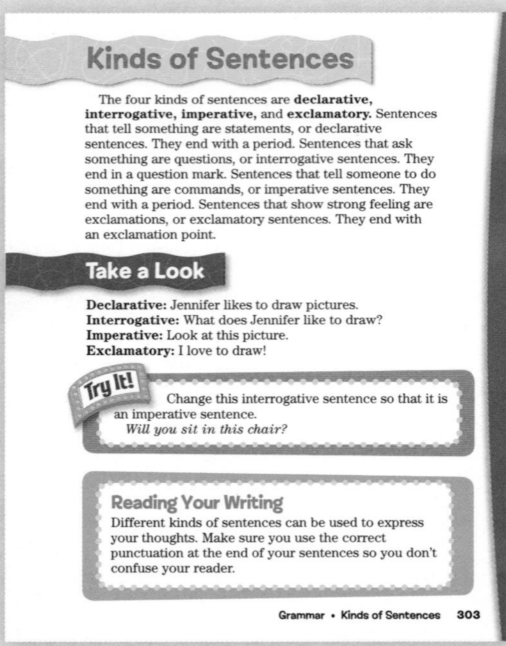

Kinds of Sentences

The four kinds of sentences are **declarative, interrogative, imperative,** and **exclamatory.** Sentences that tell something are statements, or declarative sentences. They end with a period. Sentences that ask something are questions, or interrogative sentences. They end in a question mark. Sentences that tell someone to do something are commands, or imperative sentences. They end with a period. Sentences that show strong feeling are exclamations, or exclamatory sentences. They end with an exclamation point.

Take a Look

Declarative: Jennifer likes to draw pictures.
Interrogative: What does Jennifer like to draw?
Imperative: Look at this picture.
Exclamatory: I love to draw!

Try It! Change this interrogative sentence so that it is an imperative sentence.
Will you sit in this chair?

Reading Your Writing
Different kinds of sentences can be used to express your thoughts. Make sure you use the correct punctuation at the end of your sentences so you don't confuse your reader.

Grammar • Kinds of Sentences 303

Language Arts Handbook, p. 303

Guided Practice

- ✦ Have students provide several sentences of each type to be written on the board.
- ✦ Read the directions at the top of ***Skills Practice 1*** page 125. Help students answer the first two questions in the Practice section as a class.

Apply

Use ***Skills Practice 1,*** pages 125–126 to practice recognizing and using the four different types of sentences.

Monitor Progress to Differentiate Instruction

Formal Assessment 

Types of Sentences Note whether students are using correct end punctuation.

APPROACHING LEVEL

IF . . . students need to practice recognizing and creating different sentence types,	**THEN . . .** have them complete ***Reteach*** page 50 during Workshop.
IF . . . students need more practice with recognizing and creating different sentence types,	**THEN . . .** refer to Unit 2 Lesson 3 in the ***Intervention Guide*** during Workshop.

ON LEVEL

IF . . . students have an understanding of recognizing and creating different sentence types,	**THEN . . .** have them use ***Workshop Kits*** during Workshop.

ABOVE LEVEL

IF . . . students need a challenge,	**THEN . . .** have them complete ***Challenge Activities*** page 45 during Workshop.

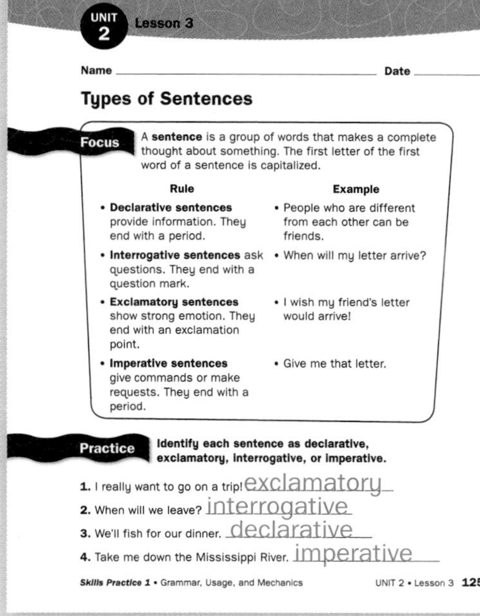

UNIT 2 Lesson 3

Name ______ Date ______

Types of Sentences

Focus A **sentence** is a group of words that makes a complete thought about something. The first letter of the first word of a sentence is capitalized.

Rule	Example
• **Declarative sentences** provide information. They end with a period.	• People who are different from each other can be friends.
• **Interrogative sentences** ask questions. They end with a question mark.	• When will my letter arrive?
• **Exclamatory sentences** show strong emotion. They end with an exclamation point.	• I wish my friend's letter would arrive!
• **Imperative sentences** give commands or make requests. They end with a period.	• Give me that letter.

Practice **Identify each sentence as declarative, exclamatory, interrogative, or imperative.**

1. I really want to go on a trip! exclamatory
2. When will we leave? interrogative
3. We'll fish for our dinner. declarative
4. Take me down the Mississippi River. imperative

Skills Practice 1 • Grammar, Usage, and Mechanics UNIT 2 • Lesson 3 **125**

Skills Practice 1, p. 125

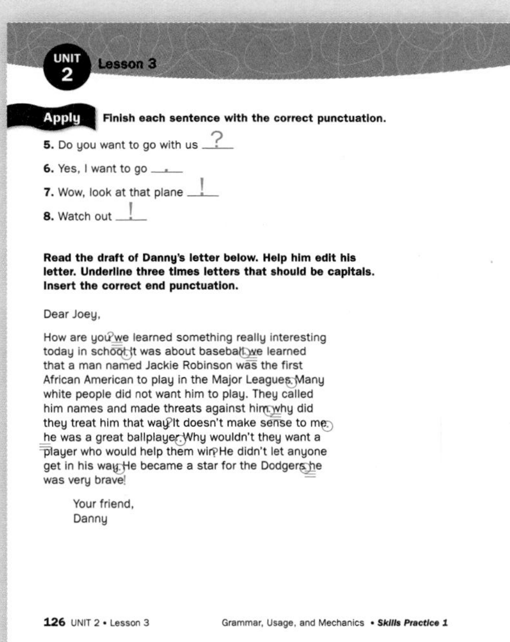

UNIT 2 Lesson 3

Apply **Finish each sentence with the correct punctuation.**

5. Do you want to go with us ?
6. Yes, I want to go .
7. Wow, look at that plane !
8. Watch out !

Read the draft of Danny's letter below. Help him edit his letter. Underline three times letters that should be capitals. Insert the correct end punctuation.

Dear Joey,

How are you? we learned something really interesting today in school. It was about baseball. we learned that a man named Jackie Robinson was the first African American to play in the Major Leagues. Many white people did not want him to play. They called him names and made threats against him. why did they treat him that way? It doesn't make sense to me. he was a great ballplayer. Why wouldn't they want a player who would help them win? He didn't let anyone get in his way. He became a star for the Dodgers. he was very brave!

Your friend,
Danny

126 UNIT 2 • Lesson 3 Grammar, Usage, and Mechanics • *Skills Practice 1*

Skills Practice 1, p. 126

Day 3

Preparing to Read

OBJECTIVES

Students will

- ✦ identify and know the meaning of homographs.
- ✦ build fluency.

MATERIALS

- ✦ ***Transparency*** 57
- ✦ ***Skills Practice 1,*** pp. 113–114

Daily Oral Practice

Daily News

Today!

I hear the birds singing in the trees outside my window. I see a few squirrels and chipmunks chewing on seeds. It is springtime and new bunnies are hopping about. My backyard is their animal habitat. I will do whatever I can to make it a peaceful one.

- ✦ Write the daily news on the board or on chart paper. Then have students read the daily news in unison to practice fluency.
- ✦ As a review of yesterday's phonics and fluency lesson, ask a volunteer to identify any words in the daily news with /ū/ spelled _*ew*. *few*

Word Structure

Homographs

- ✦ Write the following word lines on the board or use ***Transparency*** 57. Show students one line at time as you go through them by covering up the others. The words in boldface are in the selection, "Wolf Island."

Line 1	well	mine	sink	fall
Line 2	store	bark	pass	fly
Line 3	wind	tear	bow	close
Line 4	dove	live	present	lead

Lines 1–2 Homographs

✦ Tell students that some words can have more than one meaning or part of speech. A homograph is a word with one spelling but more than one meaning or part of speech. For example, the word *bat* could be a flying mammal or it could mean "to hit."

✦ As you point to each word in Lines 1–2, have students read it aloud. Ask students what the possible meanings are for each word. If necessary, help them with the possible definitions, or have them use a dictionary.

Lines 3–4 Homographs with Different Pronunciations

✦ Explain that some homographs will be pronounced differently depending upon which meaning is intended. For example, the word *does* is a homograph that is pronounced /dōz/ for "many female deer" and /duz/ when it is used as a form of the verb "to do."

✦ Read the words in Lines 3–4 aloud for students, and accentuate both pronunciations. Ask students what the word means for each pronunciation. **Possible Answers** Dove *refers to a kind of bird or the past tense of* dive. Present *could be a gift or a verb that means* "to display."

✦ Help students start the word structure activities on ***Skills Practice 1*** on pages 113–114. Read the Focus box with them, and help them with the first few questions. Then have students complete the pages on their own.

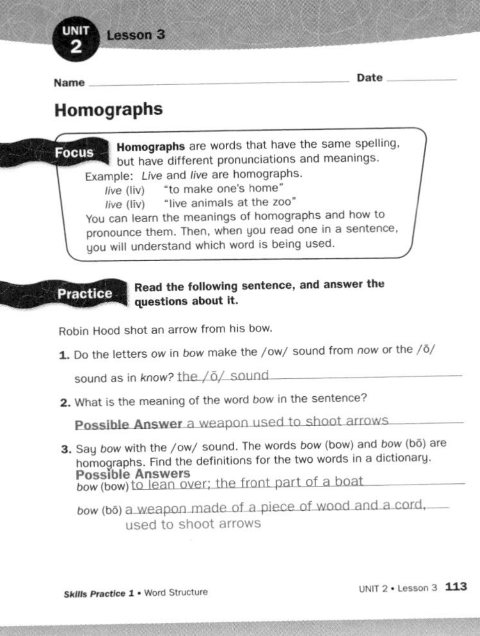
UNIT 2 Lesson 3

Name ______ Date ______

Homographs

Focus **Homographs** are words that have the same spelling, but have different pronunciations and meanings.
Example: *Live* and *live* are homographs.
live (liv) "to make one's home"
live (līv) "live animals at the zoo"
You can learn the meanings of homographs and how to pronounce them. Then, when you read one in a sentence, you will understand which word is being used.

Practice **Read the following sentence, and answer the questions about it.**

Robin Hood shot an arrow from his bow.

1. Do the letters *ow* in *bow* make the /ow/ sound from *now* or the /ō/ sound as in *know*? the /ō/ sound
2. What is the meaning of the word *bow* in the sentence?
Possible Answer a weapon used to shoot arrows
3. Say *bow* with the /ow/ sound. The words *bow* (bow) and *bow* (bō) are homographs. Find the definitions for the two words in a dictionary.
Possible Answers
bow (bow) to lean over; the front part of a boat
bow (bō) a weapon made of a piece of wood and a cord, used to shoot arrows

Skills Practice 1 • Word Structure UNIT 2 • Lesson 3 113

Skills Practice 1, p. 113

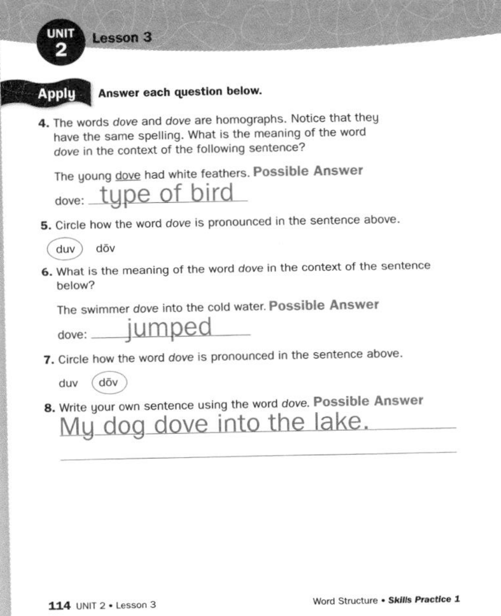
UNIT 2 Lesson 3

Apply **Answer each question below.**

4. The words *dove* and *dove* are homographs. Notice that they have the same spelling. What is the meaning of the word *dove* in the context of the following sentence?
The young dove had white feathers. **Possible Answer**
dove: type of bird
5. Circle how the word *dove* is pronounced in the sentence above.
(duv) dōv
6. What is the meaning of the word *dove* in the context of the sentence below?
The swimmer *dove* into the cold water. **Possible Answer**
dove: jumped
7. Circle how the word *dove* is pronounced in the sentence above.
duv (dōv)
8. Write your own sentence using the word *dove*. **Possible Answer**
My dog dove into the lake.

114 UNIT 2 • Lesson 3 Word Structure • *Skills Practice 1*

Skills Practice 1, p. 114

Monitor Progress to Differentiate Instruction

Formal Assessment

Word Structure During the word structure activity, note how well students understand homographs.

APPROACHING LEVEL	**IF . . .** students need practice with homographs,	**THEN . . .** work with them on the word structure activities on ***Reteach*** page 45 during Workshop.
	IF . . . students need extra practice with homographs,	**THEN . . .** work with them on the word structure activities for Unit 2 Lesson 3 in the ***Intervention Guide*** during Workshop.
ON LEVEL	**IF . . .** students understand homographs,	**THEN . . .** have them write sentences using the different meanings of the words in the word lines during Workshop.
ABOVE LEVEL	**IF . . .** students are ready for a challenge with homographs,	**THEN . . .** have them complete the word structure activities on ***Challenge Activities*** page 41 during Workshop.

Reading and Responding

Once there was an island. It was an island with trees and meadows, and many kinds of animals. There were mice, rabbits and deer, squirrels, foxes and several kinds of birds.

All the animals on the island depended on the plants and the other animals for their food and well-being. Some animals ate grass or other plants; some ate insects; some ate other animals. The island animals were healthy. There was plenty of food for all.

A family of wolves lived on the island, too, a male wolf, a female, and their five cubs.

178

One day the wolf cubs were playing on the beach while their mother and father slept. The cubs found a strange object at the edge of the water.

It was a log raft, nailed together with boards. The cubs had never seen anything like this before. They were very curious. They climbed onto it and sniffed about. Everything smelled different.

179

OBJECTIVES

Students will

- use the comprehension skills Making Inferences and Fact and Opinion.
- build fluency.
- investigate Animals and Their Habitats using the Inquiry process.

MATERIALS

- ***Student Reader, Book 1*** pp. 178–185
- ***Transparency*** 23
- ***Skills Practice 1,*** pp. 117–118

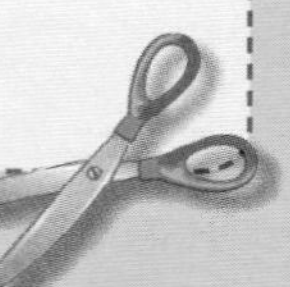

2nd READ

Comprehension Skill

Reread the selection using the comprehension skills Making Inferences, and Fact and Opinion.

Making Inferences

Tell students that readers make inferences when they take pieces of information from the selection and then use that information for better understanding. Students may also use background knowledge and personal experiences to help them understand. Ask students:

- *What clues have you read in the story so far that help you infer what might happen next?* **Possible Answer** *The cubs were curious. They climbed on the raft and smelled new things. Something is going to happen or change.*

While the cubs were poking around, the raft began to drift slowly out into the lake. At first the cubs didn't notice anything wrong. Then, suddenly, there was nothing but water all around the raft.

The cubs were scared. They howled. The mother and father wolf heard the howling and came running down to the water's edge.

180

They couldn't turn the raft back, and the cubs were too scared to swim, so the adult wolves swam out to the raft and climbed aboard. The raft drifted slowly and steadily over to the mainland. Finally it came to rest on the shore and the wolf family scrambled onto dry land.

There were no longer wolves on the island.

181

Reading with a Writer's Eye

Author's Purpose

Remind students that when authors write a story, they think about the purpose for writing that story. By focusing on purpose, authors can clearly convey their reasons for writing the story. Purposes for writing include writing to entertain, to teach a lesson, to record and reflect on experience, to make readers feel emotion, to give facts and information, and to communicate a message. Remind students that sometimes an author has more than one purpose in mind. Ask students the following question:

- *Celia Godkin wrote an enjoyable story. Do you think that was her only reason for writing "Wolf Island"?* **Possible Answer** *Celia Godkin also gives facts and information about animal behaviors and habitats in her story. She makes readers feel emotions toward the animals.*

Expanding Vocabulary

meadows (med′ • ōz) *n.* plural form of **meadow:** a field of grassy land used as a pasture for animals (page 178)

The *meadow* is bursting with flowers.

several (sev′ • ər • əl) *adj.* more than two, but not many (page 178)

Melita read *several* books last summer.

depended (də • pend′ • əd) *v.* past tense of **depend:** to rely on; to trust (page 178)

The cub *depended* on its mother for food.

raft (raft) *n.* a kind of flat boat made of logs or boards fixed firmly together (page 179)

I floated on a *raft* with my friends.

boards (bordz) *n.* plural form of **board:** a long, flat piece of sawed wood (page 179)

The fence was made with *boards.*

Reading and Responding

Time passed. Spring grew into summer on the island, and summer into fall. The leaves turned red. Geese flew south, and squirrels stored up nuts for the winter.

Winter was mild that year, with little snow. The green plants were buried under a thin white layer. Deer dug through the snow to find food. They had enough to eat.

Next spring, many fawns were born.

There were now many deer on the island. They were eating large amounts of grass and leaves. The wolf family had kept the deer population down, because wolves eat deer for food. Without wolves to hunt the deer, there were now too many deer on the island for the amount of food available.

182

Spring grew into summer and summer into fall. More and more deer ate more and more grass and more and more leaves.

Rabbits had less to eat, because the deer were eating their food. There were not many baby bunnies born that year.

Foxes had less to eat, because there were fewer rabbits for them to hunt.

Mice had less to eat, because the deer had eaten the grass and grass seed. There were not many baby mice born that year.

Owls had less to eat, because there were fewer mice for them to hunt. Many animals on the island were hungry.

183

Word Structure

Homographs: spring, fall, leaves, plants, find, down, fell, store, stores

Teacher Tip

FACT AND OPINION While studying fact and opinion, discuss the difference between fact and opinion for different media. For example, discuss how to differentiate fact and opinion in newspapers, in magazines, on television, on the radio, and in films. Have students share examples.

Comprehension Skill

Fact and Opinion

Explain that writers use both facts and opinions when writing a story. Facts can be verified or tested. Opinions are the writers' own ideas which might be supported but not proven. Tell students that although both facts and opinion can be found in one story, sometimes stories have strictly one or the other. Ask students the following question:

- *Are there any opinions expressed on pages 182–182? If yes, what are they? If no, why do you think not?* **Possible Answer** *The writer does not give any personal opinions. Everything she writes about is the facts that are happening in the story.*

Comprehension Skill

Making Inferences

Tell students that making inferences is an ongoing process. Readers make inferences as they gather additional information from a story. Ask students:

- *What inferences can you make about the animals on the island?* **Possible Answer** *The animals are all hungry. Even the wolves are hungry. I think they are in trouble and might die.*
- *How did you make these inferences?* **Possible Answer** *Because the animals are hungry, they will probably starve. Unless something happens to change their condition, they will probably starve to death.*

Expanding Vocabulary

collected (kəl • lekt′ • əd) *v.* a form of the verb **collect:** to gather together (page 184)
The students *collected* aluminum cans as a recycling project.

remained (rē • mānd′) *v.* past tense of **remain:** to be left (page 184)
The bakery's bread that *remained* unsold at the end of the day was sent to a homeless shelter.

STOP You have reread the first half of the story. You will continue the story tomorrow on page T240.

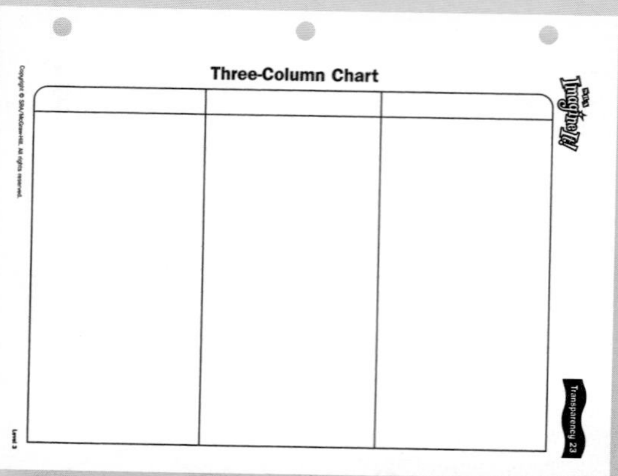

Transparency 23

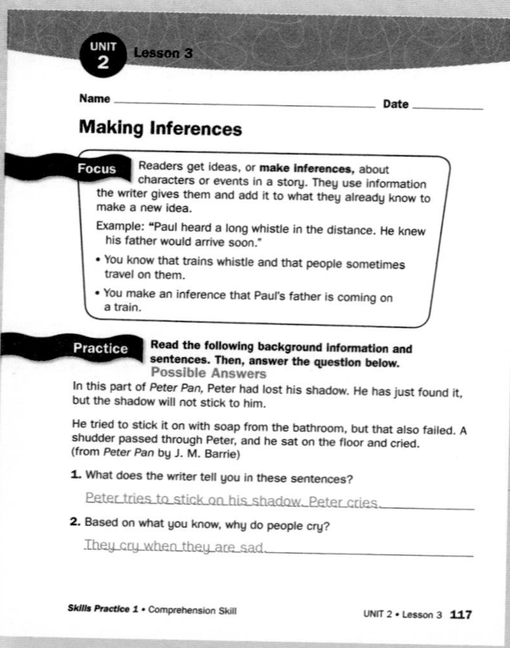
UNIT 2 Lesson 3

Name ______ Date ______

Making Inferences

Focus Readers get ideas, or **make inferences,** about characters or events in a story. They use information the writer gives them and add it to what they already know to make a new idea.

Example: "Paul heard a long whistle in the distance. He knew his father would arrive soon."

- You know that trains whistle and that people sometimes travel on them.
- You make an inference that Paul's father is coming on a train.

Practice **Read the following background information and sentences. Then, answer the question below.**

Possible Answers

In this part of *Peter Pan,* Peter had lost his shadow. He has just found it, but the shadow will not stick to him.

He tried to stick it on with soap from the bathroom, but that also failed. A shudder passed through Peter, and he sat on the floor and cried. (from *Peter Pan* by J. M. Barrie)

1. What does the writer tell you in these sentences?

Peter tries to stick on his shadow. Peter cries.

2. Based on what you know, why do people cry?

They cry when they are sad.

Skills Practice 1 • Comprehension Skill   UNIT 2 • Lesson 3 117

Skills Practice 1, pp. 117–118

Supporting the Reading

Comprehension Skill: Making Inferences

Teach

Tell students that writers do not always state everything about a topic, character, or event in their stories. They do, however, provide many details and clues about which students may note. As students read, they should pay attention to details and should use the information to help make inferences about topics, events, or characters in the story. Students can also use their own background knowledge and personal experiences to make inferences about what they read.

Guided Practice

Have students reflect on their wonderings from what they recorded before reading the story. In a three-column chart using ***Transparency*** 23, have students record wonderings and other questions they asked themselves while reading in the first column. In the second column, have them give the clues they read in the story or information they have from their own background and experiences. In the last column, students should note the inferences they made.

Apply

Have students turn to pages 117–118 in ***Skills Practice 1.***

- Have students read aloud the Focus section of the lesson.
- Work through the Practice section of the lesson with students. Have students look through the story "Wolf Island" to find more clues that lead them to inferences. Students can also use background information and personal experiences to make inferences. Have them record examples to refer to as they work on the Practice and Apply sections of the lesson. Have students complete the Apply section on their own.

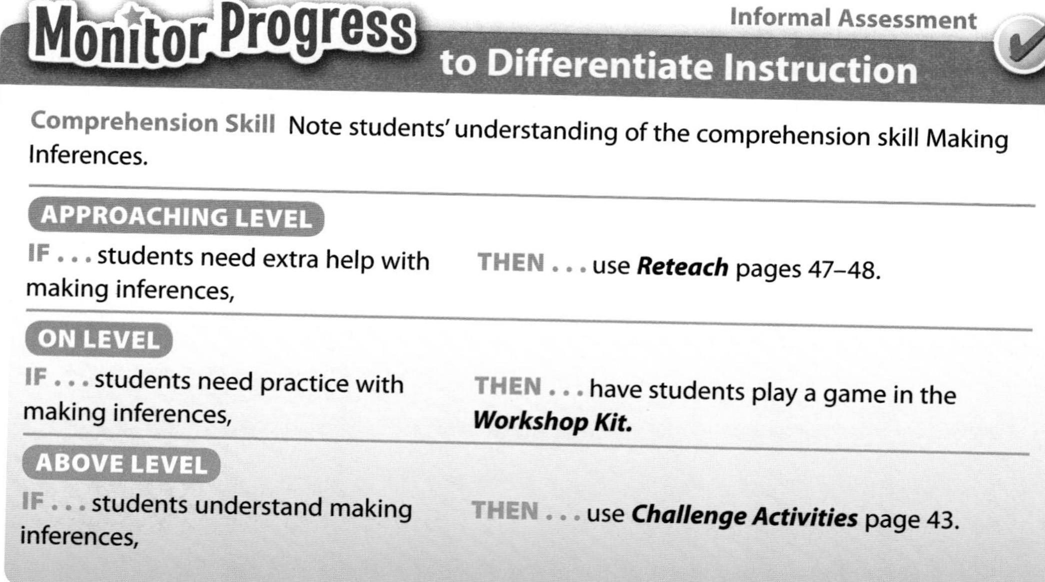
Monitor Progress to Differentiate Instruction — Informal Assessment

Comprehension Skill Note students' understanding of the comprehension skill Making Inferences.

APPROACHING LEVEL

IF . . . students need extra help with making inferences,	**THEN . . .** use ***Reteach*** pages 47–48.

ON LEVEL

IF . . . students need practice with making inferences,	**THEN . . .** have students play a game in the ***Workshop Kit.***

ABOVE LEVEL

IF . . . students understand making inferences,	**THEN . . .** use ***Challenge Activities*** page 43.

Fluency

"Wolf Island" has simple and direct language. Emotional and some vivid descriptions accompany this direct style. Focus on accuracy when modeling this story for students. Tell students that reading with accuracy is especially important when reading nonfiction. Accuracy helps readers gain knowledge and remember what they have read.

- Let students know that there are emotional elements to this story. Even though the events are matter-of-fact, the subject is emotional. Tell students they should convey this emotion as they read the story.
- Model fluency by reading pages 184–185 from "Wolf Island." Have students follow along in ***Student Reader,*** Book 1. Ask them to raise their hands if they hear an unfamiliar word or passage.
- After you have read through the passage, call on a volunteer to read the first paragraph. Before the student begins, review any words that the student may need help pronouncing. Review definitions if necessary.
- After the volunteer has finished, have all students chorally read the passage several times until they can read it naturally with good phrasing.

Inquiry

Conjectures

- ✦ Remind students that they have made conjectures about their research question, but they may change their conjectures based on new things they learn from the unit selections.
- ✦ Have students think about what they learned from reading "Wolf Island" and how it might relate to their conjectures. Remind students that new information they learn can confirm their conjectures, but it can also challenge or complicate them. Ask students to share how their conjectures have been affected by their understanding of "Wolf Island."
- ✦ Write any ideas students share on the board or chart paper. Keep a record of these ideas, and use them later to help groups confirm or revise their conjectures. Have students write any ideas they have about how the selection relates to their conjectures in their Writer's Notebooks.

LEVELED READERS To help students build fluency and strengthen their vocabulary and comprehension skills, have them read the ***Leveled Readers*** for this unit. Use each student's Oral Fluency Assessment score from the previous lesson assessment to diagnose the appropriate ***Leveled Readers.***

Fluency Tip

FLUENCY For additional fluency practice, students can take turns reading different pages of "Wolf Island" to each other during Small-Group Time.

OBJECTIVES

Students will
- ✦ draft process papers.
- ✦ spell words with /ū/ and homographs.
- ✦ review sentence types.
- ✦ review how diagrams are used.

MATERIALS

- ✦ ***Skills Practice 1,*** pp. 123–124, 127–128

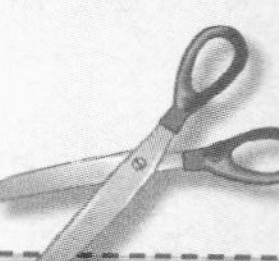

Writing Explaining a Process

Drafting

Teach

- ✦ Remind students of the writing process: prewriting, drafting, revising, editing/proofreading, and publishing.
- ✦ Tell students that they will now draft their process papers. Tell students to use the graphic organizers they created to write their draft. Remind them that what is most important is getting all of the information down on paper in order. Tell them they can revise and edit their papers later.
- ✦ Tell students to use transition words such as *first, next,* or *lastly* as they draft their processes.
- ✦ Ask students to name the four types of sentences. *declarative, imperative, interrogative, exclamatory* Ask students what sentence types they may use for their process papers. **Possible Answer** *declarative, exclamatory* Tell students to try to use at least two types of sentences as they draft their process papers.

Guided Practice

Using the chain of events graphic organizer on the board, have a student write an introductory sentence beside it. Have other students add to the sentence. Then have them complete the paragraph. Save this paragraph for later revision.

Apply

Composing—Drafting Have students refer to their graphic organizers as they write a draft of their process papers.

Spelling

/ū/ and Homographs

Teach

- Tell students that homographs are words that have the same spelling but different pronunciations and meanings.
- Tell students that /ū/ may be spelled _*ew* or _*ue*.
- Write the homographs from the word list on the board: *well, rose, tire, ring, change, park, light*. Choose a volunteer to use one of the words in a sentence and write that sentence on the board. Then have that student choose a volunteer to use the word's homograph in another sentence and write it on the board. Repeat until all words are used.
- Write the following sets of words on the board: *cue/hue, few/spew*. Organize the class into two groups and assign each group one set of words. Have students in each group write rhyming words using the same spelling patterns under each set; for example: *due/Sue/blue/glue, dew/knew/new/chew*.
- Write the following words on the board: *argue, value, rescue*. Have volunteers come to the board and write a sentence using each word.

Guided Practice

Have students turn to ***Skills Practice 1*** page 123. Read the instructions with them, and complete the first two questions as a class.

Apply

Have students complete ***Skills Practice 1*** pages 123–124 on their own. Remind students that challenge words are not used in ***Skills Practice*** exercises

Monitor Progress

to Differentiate Instruction
Formal Assessment

Spelling Note how well students are able to spell the lesson words correctly.

APPROACHING LEVEL

IF . . . students need to practice spelling this week's words, **THEN . . .** tell them to complete ***Reteach*** page 49.

ON LEVEL

IF . . . students can spell this week's spelling words, **THEN . . .** have them think of words that were not in this week's lesson but use the same skills that were reviewed. Have them write the words on a separate sheet of paper.

ABOVE LEVEL

IF . . . students are ready for a challenge, **THEN . . .** have them complete ***Challenge Activities*** page 44.

UNIT 2 Lesson 3

Name ________ Date ________

Spelling

Focus **Homographs** are words that have the same spelling, but have different pronunciations and meanings.
/ū/ can be spelled _ew and _ue.

Practice **Sort the spelling words under the correct heading.**
Order will vary under heading.

Homographs

1. well
2. rose
3. tire
4. ring
5. change
6. park
7. light

/ū/ spelled _ew

8. few
9. spew
10. view

Word List

1. cue
2. few
3. well
4. rose
5. argue
6. tire
7. hue
8. ring
9. value
10. change
11. spew
12. rescue
13. park
14. view
15. light

Challenge Words

16. pitcher
17. nephew

Skills Practice 1 • Spelling UNIT 2 • Lesson 3 123

Skills Practice 1, pp. 123–124

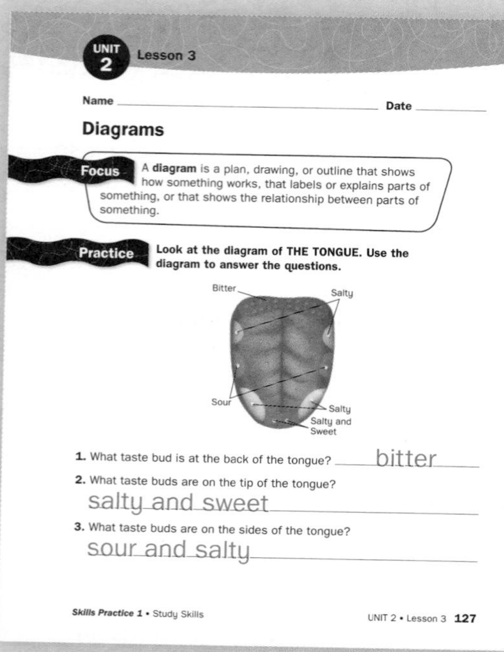
UNIT 2 Lesson 3

Name ____________ Date ________

Diagrams

Focus A **diagram** is a plan, drawing, or outline that shows how something works, that labels or explains parts of something, or that shows the relationship between parts of something.

Practice **Look at the diagram of THE TONGUE. Use the diagram to answer the questions.**

1. What taste bud is at the back of the tongue? bitter
2. What taste buds are on the tip of the tongue? salty and sweet
3. What taste buds are on the sides of the tongue? sour and salty

Skills Practice 1 • Study Skills UNIT 2 • Lesson 3 **127**

Skills Practice 1, p. 127

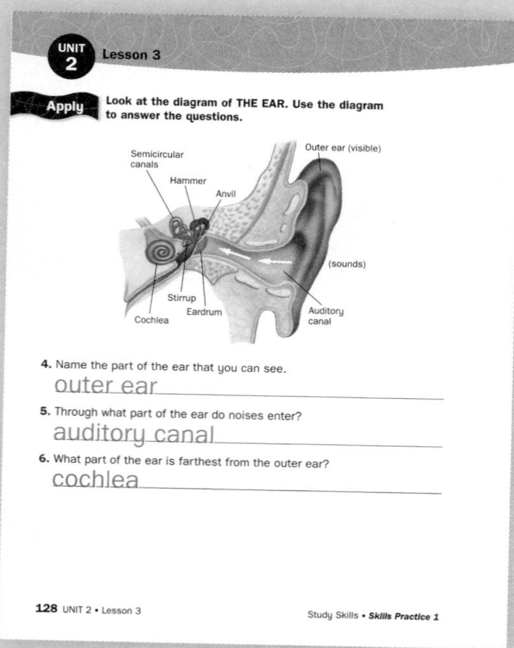
UNIT 2 Lesson 3

Apply **Look at the diagram of THE EAR. Use the diagram to answer the questions.**

4. Name the part of the ear that you can see. outer ear
5. Through what part of the ear do noises enter? auditory canal
6. What part of the ear is farthest from the outer ear? cochlea

128 UNIT 2 • Lesson 3 Study Skills • *Skills Practice 1*

Skills Practice 1, p. 128

Study Skills

Diagrams

Teach

✦ Have students review the use of tables and charts. Explain that diagrams are another special visual that shows the arrangement or parts of something. These parts are often labeled to make the diagram easy to understand.

✦ Tell students that diagrams are used in textbooks, instruction manuals, floor plans, and assembly instructions. They also have many other uses. Diagrams provide a model so we can identify parts and learn their names. They also help us determine parts that need to be connected, and they are used to help us understand the relationship between different parts.

Guided Practice

Have students turn to page 127 in ***Skills Practice 1.*** Have a student read the directions aloud. Work with students to complete the first two Practice questions.

Apply

Have students complete ***Skills Practice 1*** pages 127–128.

Monitor Progress to Differentiate Instruction

Formal Assessment 

Diagrams Note whether students understand how to read a diagram.

APPROACHING LEVEL

IF . . . students need to practice diagrams,	**THEN . . .** have them work independently on simple diagrams, paying careful attention to the labeled parts, during Workshop.

ON LEVEL

IF . . . students have an understanding of diagrams,	**THEN . . .** have them complete their own diagram for the unit investigation during Workshop.

ABOVE LEVEL

IF . . . students are ready for a challenge,	**THEN . . .** have them use multimedia to create a diagram for their unit investigation during Workshop.

Grammar, Usage, and Mechanics

Types of Sentences

Teach

- Have students review the four types of sentences: declarative, interrogative, imperative, and exclamatory. If necessary, review the punctuation at the end of each type of sentence.

Guided Practice

- Write *declarative*, *imperative*, *interrogative*, and *exclamatory* in a column on one side of the board. Ask for volunteers to write a corresponding sentence beside each word. Discuss the sentences with the class and have students make any necessary corrections.
- Next, have students create definitions for each sentence type based on the sentences on the board and any subsequent discussions.

Apply

- Have students individually create a sentence for each sentence type. Then, have the students switch with a partner and review the partner's sentences. Have them discuss any revisions that need to be made.
- Have students edit their writing for sentence types and correct end punctuation.

OBJECTIVES

Students will
- ✦ identify and know the meaning of homographs.
- ✦ build fluency.

MATERIALS

- ✦ ***Transparency*** 57

Daily Oral Practice

Daily News

Today!

The animals are happy in their habitats. Nature has a way of taking care of itself. Some times are difficult, but then there are moments of wonder and joy. Natural wonders are all around you to see, hear, and feel. Respect nature and it will stay beautiful and last much longer.

- ✦ Write the daily news on the board or on chart paper. Then have students read the daily news in unison to practice fluency.
- ✦ As a review of yesterday's word structure lesson, ask a volunteer to identify any homographs in the message. *care, own, wonders* If students have a hard time recognizing these as homographs, point out how they can be used as different parts of speech. For example, use *care* and *wonder* in two different sentences, one using the noun form of the word and the other using the verb form.

Word Structure

Homographs

✦ Use ***Transparency*** 57 with the word lines from Day 3.

Line 1	well	mine	sink	fall
Line 2	store	bark	pass	fly
Line 3	wind	tear	bow	close
Line 4	dove	live	present	lead

✦ Review the meaning of homographs. If necessary, remind students that homographs are words that are spelled the same but have different meanings, like *fan*, which refers to a machine that moves air, or someone who cheers for a person or team.

✦ Have students read the words using normal intonation and expression.

Developing Oral Language

Use either of these activities to help students practice reading the words.

- To review homographs, have a volunteer choose one homograph from the blending lines and use it in a sentence that demonstrates one of its meanings. **Possible Answer** Bark *is what is on the outside of a tree trunk.* Then have that student choose a classmate to use the same word in a sentence demonstrating its other definition. **Possible Answer** *A* bark *is a sound that a dog makes.* Ask the volunteer to identify the homograph in that sentence. Continue for all the words on the lines.
- Select a word from Lines 3–4 and have a student give both pronunciations for the word. Then have the student use the word in two sentences, one for each meaning and pronunciation. **Possible Answer** *A* tear *rolled down her cheek. Hey, don't* tear *up that paper!* Continue this process for all the words from Lines 3–4.

Teacher Tip

BLENDING During Workshop, work with students who have difficulty blending words by using Routine 1 for sound-by-sound blending or Routine 3 for whole-word blending.

Differentiating Instruction English Learner

IF . . . students think that all homographs are pronounced differently for different meanings,

THEN . . . use pictures or pantomime to illustrate the noun and verb meanings of *fly* and *bark*. Use each word in a sentence emphasizing the same pronunciation but different meaning.

Reading and Responding

Snow fell for many weeks. The drifts became deeper and deeper. It was harder and harder for animals to find food. Animals grew weaker, and some began to die. The deer were so hungry they gnawed bark from the trees. Trees began to die.

Snow covered the island. The weather grew colder and colder. Ice began to form in the water around the island, and along the mainland coast. It grew thicker and thicker, spreading farther and farther out into the open water. One day there was ice all the way from the mainland to the island.

186

The wolf family crossed the ice and returned to their old home.

187

OBJECTIVES

Students will

- use the comprehension skill Reality and Fantasy.
- check comprehension.
- investigate Animals and Their Habitats using the Inquiry process.

MATERIALS

- ***Student Reader,*** Book 1, pp. 186–193
- ***Skills Practice 1,*** pp. 119–120

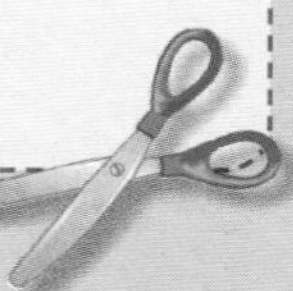

Comprehension Skill

Reality and Fantasy

Remind students that a fantasy tells about something that could not happen. A realistic story is about something that could really happen. In realistic fiction, the story may or may not have happened just as it is presented; however, the characters, settings, and events could all be real. Ask students:

- Ask students whether "Wolf Island" is fantasy or reality. *"Wolf Island" is a realistic story. The animals, the setting, and the events could all exist.*
- Ask students to name a fantasy story read so far in Unit 2. *"Make Way for Ducklings."*
- Ask students how "*Make Way for Ducklings*" is similar to and different from "*Wolf Island.*" **Possible Answer** *The stories are similar because they are both about animal habitats and the settings in both stories are real. They are different because the animals in "Make Way for Ducklings" can talk—it is a fantasy story.*

Checking Comprehension

Ask students the following questions to check their comprehension of the story:

- *What is the problem of the story?* **Possible Answer** *The animal habitat is upset and the animals start to die.*
- *Why does this happen?* **Possible Answer** *When the wolf family leaves, it changes the balance of the habitat. The weather also affects the ability of the animals to get food.*
- *How does balance return to the habitat?* **Possible Answer** *The wolf family comes back to the island and the weather gets warmer. The animals' lives are healthy again.*

Word Structure

Homographs: fell, find, bark, coast, spring, leaves

Differentiating Instruction English Learner

IF . . . students are native Spanish speakers, **THEN . . .** you might need to review the comparison *-er* ending, as it does not exist in Spanish. To help students understand, restate those comparison sentences in the selection, using the word *more*. For example, *The weather grew more cold and more cold.*

Science Inquiry

Genre Research Notes

Tell students that research notes are a way to organize information about a topic they are studying.

Feature Headings

Point to the headings in "Ancient Wolves." Tell students that **headings** are titles within the text of a selection. Explain that headings tell what kind of information is about to be given.

Ask students to point to and read each heading aloud. Then ask students what they think the headings might be about.

Reading "Ancient Wolves"

Have students take turns reading "Ancient Wolves" aloud. Ask students how this story is similar to "Wolf Island" and how it relates to the theme Animals and Their Habitats. Make sure students read the heading of each paragraph before reading the information.

Think Link

1. Why do questions make good headings for research notes? **Possible Answer** *Questions make good headings because when you look through your notes, you know exactly what information and what kind of answers you'll find under each heading.*
2. How do scientists know about wildlife that lived thousands of years ago? **Possible Answer** *One way scientists know about extinct wildlife is fossils, the remains of an animal or plant that has been embedded in rock or earth. Scientists can study fossils to learn about wildlife that no longer exists.*
3. What are some possible reasons why dire wolves became extinct? **Possible Answer** *The dire wolf may have become extinct because their prey died out or because of weather and climate changes, and some may have become stuck in tar pits while chasing prey.*

Teacher Tip

SELECTION VOCABULARY Review the meaning of the highlighted selection vocabulary word *layer* in "Ancient Wolves."

Differentiating Instruction English Learner

IF . . . students have trouble understanding the passive voice used in the notes,
THEN . . . restate those sentences in active voice. For example: *People found many dire wolf fossils. People built whole wolf skeletons from the fossils.*

Science Inquiry

Ancient Wolves

Genre

Research Notes are a way to organize information about a topic you are studying.

Feature

Headings tell what kind of information is to follow.

When you write a research report, you need to gather information. You will take notes on what you read. Note cards, like the ones on these pages, can help you get organized. Here are notes one student took on the research topic "dire wolves."

What is a dire wolf?

The dire wolf is the largest known member of the wolf family. It lived during the Ice Age. The dire wolf would hunt for food or eat prey killed by other animals. This wolf is now extinct.

Why did dire wolves become extinct?

It could be that the prey they depended on for food died out. A change in climate could have played a part in their extinction. Also, many wolves died in tar pits. They may have gone after prey that was trapped in the pits and become stuck themselves.

192

How did people learn about dire wolves?

Many dire wolf fossils have been found. Thousands were dug up from a layer of asphalt that hardened beneath tar pits. Whole wolf skeletons have been built from the fossils. Because there is a big supply of fossils, the dire wolf has been studied a great deal.

Are any modern wolves like the dire wolf?

The dire wolf is often compared to the gray wolf that exists now. The dire wolf looked similar, but it was bigger. The dire wolf had a larger head and massive teeth. Its legs were shorter, however, than those of the gray wolf.

Think Link

1. Why do questions make good headings for research notes?
2. How do scientists know about wildlife that lived thousands of years ago?
3. What are some possible reasons why dire wolves became extinct?

Try It!

As you work on your investigation, think about how headings can be used to organize your information.

193

Inquiry Connection

Have students discuss how headings might be helpful in their investigations about animals and their habitats. For example, if students are investigating how people can help save an animal habitat, then a possible main heading might be *How People Can Save and Protect an Animal Habitat.*

Teacher Tip

CONCEPT/QUESTION BOARD After students read "Ancient Wolves," encourage them to post questions, answers, comments, photographs, drawings, or other items related to the theme Animals and Their Habitats on the **Concept/ Question Board.**

Teacher Tip

IDENTIFYING NEEDS AND MAKING PLANS Remind students that identifying needs and then making a plan helps them organize their thoughts. A good plan will also help them decide how to organize the information they collect. As new information comes in throughout the investigation, they can incorporate it into their plan.

Inquiry Process

Step 4—Identifying Needs and Making Plans

Whole-Group Time

Whole Group

- Ask students to consult the **Concept/Question Board** for ideas to help them identify needs, find sources, and make plans. Remind them to post articles, book titles, summaries, and respond to others' questions and ideas.
- Each group should have produced a conjecture and discussed it in their investigation groups. Conduct a whole-class discussion of each group's conjectures. Have groups briefly present their conjectures and allow the class to offer suggestions, constructive criticisms, questions, and sources for more information about a topic. These contributions should help each group as they identify needs and make plans for their investigations.
- Remind students that they can use what they learn about animal habitats from the unit selections in their investigations. Discuss what students learned from "Wolf Island" and how this changes their understanding of animals and animal habitats. Have students take notes in their Writer's Notebooks during the discussion.
- Explain that each group needs to construct a plan for their investigation. This plan should include the things they need to find out and where they will get information about their question and conjecture. Have students identify and search for different kinds of reference materials, including photos, maps, charts, graphs, and time lines.
- To help groups get started with identifying their needs, explain that they should be asking themselves such questions as: *What information will we need to help us decide whether our conjectures are correct? Where can we find this information? What do we need to understand to make our conjecture better? What would an expert on this problem know that we don't know? What experts could we contact or interview?*
- Students should use these questions to help them decide which sources they can use in their investigations. Model identifying research needs and making plans by answering these questions. You might say: *I know that I need to find out how many people know about these animals losing their habitats. And I also need some information on how successful awareness campaigns are. I could interview an expert who could give me some of this information. I could also make a survey asking how many people know and care about this problem. I can look for articles about other communities that are having a problem like this to see what they're doing.*

Small-Group Time

Small Group

- ✦ In their groups, students should review their questions and conjectures as well as any notes they have taken or ideas they have learned from reading the unit selections. These should help them as they identify their needs and make a plan.
- ✦ Students should work in their groups on ***Skills Practice 1*** pages 119–120. As you circulate among the groups, help them identify what information they need and possible sources they can use. Groups should refer to these pages throughout their investigations. Explain that they can update or make changes to their at plan any time during the investigation.
- ✦ After identifying their needs and where they can get information, groups need to assign tasks fairly to each group member. Encourage teamwork and monitor how groups distribute and assign tasks. Have students practice making tables and charts by creating a chart labeling which tasks are being completed by each group member.

Concept/Question Board

Continue to encourage use of the **Concept/Question Board** by recognizing and thanking students for their contributions. Incorporate discussion of those items into classroom discussions whenever possible. Remember to post your own questions, articles, pictures, book titles, and ideas.

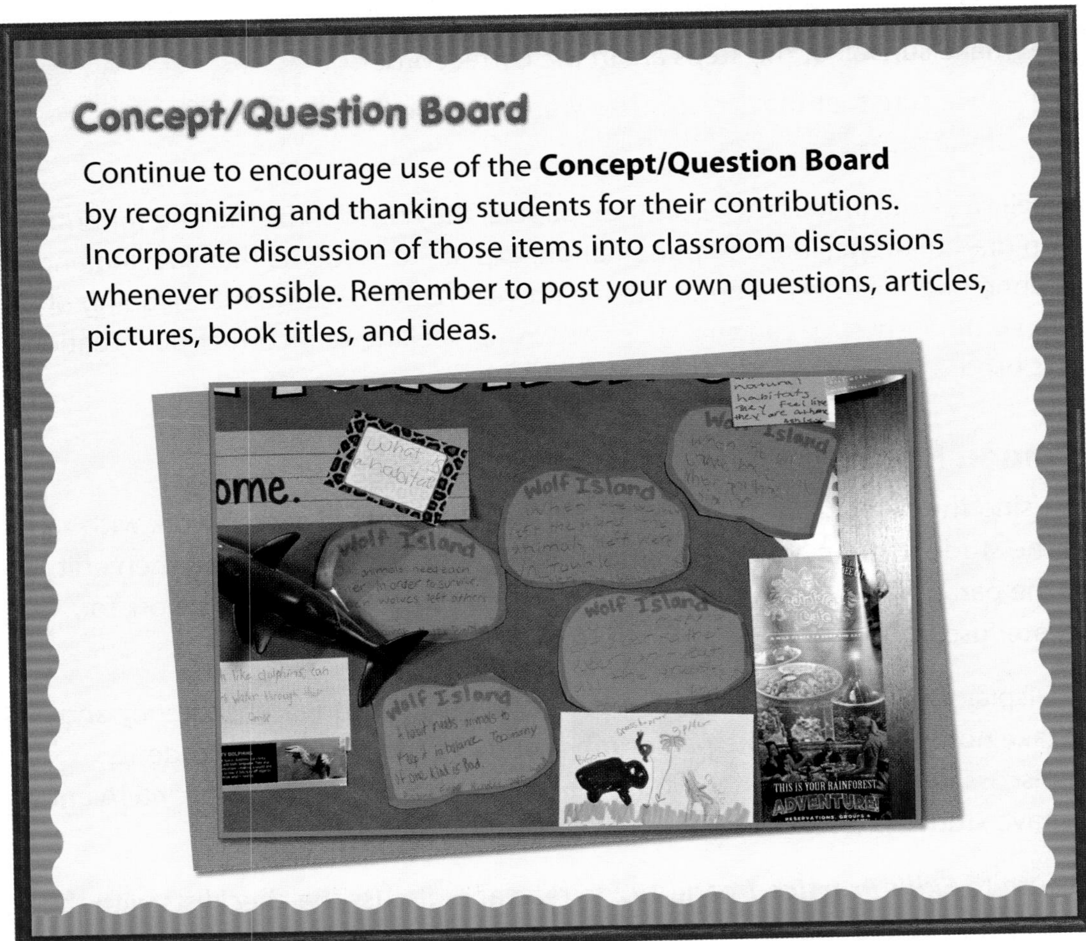

Inquiry Rubric

To assess Identifying Information Needs, see the Inquiry Rubrics in the Level Appendix.

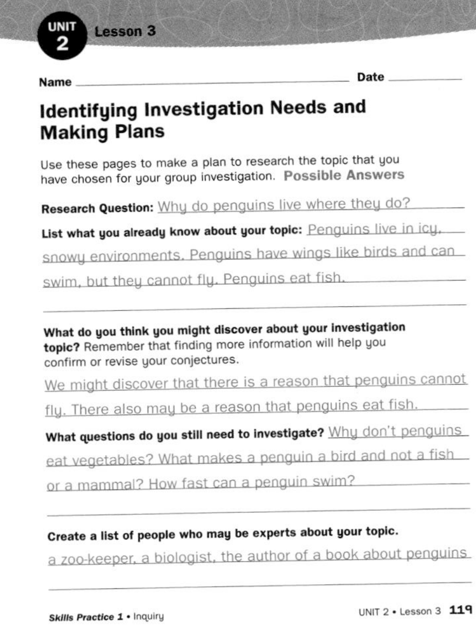

UNIT 2 Lesson 3

Name ______ Date ______

Identifying Investigation Needs and Making Plans

Use these pages to make a plan to research the topic that you have chosen for your group investigation. **Possible Answers**

Research Question: Why do penguins live where they do?

List what you already know about your topic: Penguins live in icy, snowy environments. Penguins have wings like birds and can swim, but they cannot fly. Penguins eat fish.

What do you think you might discover about your investigation topic? Remember that finding more information will help you confirm or revise your conjectures.

We might discover that there is a reason that penguins cannot fly. There also may be a reason that penguins eat fish.

What questions do you still need to investigate? Why don't penguins eat vegetables? What makes a penguin a bird and not a fish or a mammal? How fast can a penguin swim?

Create a list of people who may be experts about your topic.

a zoo-keeper, a biologist, the author of a book about penguins

Skills Practice 1 • Inquiry UNIT 2 • Lesson 3 **119**

Skills Practice 1, p. 119

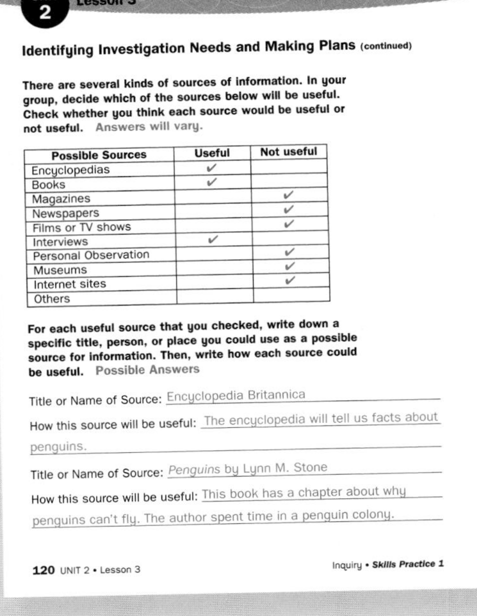

UNIT 2 Lesson 3

Identifying Investigation Needs and Making Plans (continued)

There are several kinds of sources of information. In your group, decide which of the sources below will be useful. Check whether you think each source would be useful or not useful. Answers will vary.

Possible Sources	Useful	Not useful
Encyclopedias	✓	
Books	✓	
Magazines		✓
Newspapers		✓
Films or TV shows		✓
Interviews	✓	
Personal Observation		✓
Museums		✓
Internet sites		✓
Others		

For each useful source that you checked, write down a specific title, person, or place you could use as a possible source for information. Then, write how each source could be useful. Possible Answers

Title or Name of Source: Encyclopedia Britannica

How this source will be useful: The encyclopedia will tell us facts about penguins.

Title or Name of Source: *Penguins* by Lynn M. Stone

How this source will be useful: This book has a chapter about why penguins can't fly. The author spent time in a penguin colony.

120 UNIT 2 • Lesson 3 Inquiry • ***Skills Practice 1***

Skills Practice 1, p. 120

OBJECTIVES

Students will
- ✦ spell words with /ū/ and homographs.
- ✦ understand the use of visual aids.
- ✦ create a diagram.
- ✦ revise and edit/proofread their process papers.

MATERIALS
- ✦ ***Transparencies*** 64, 64A
- ✦ ***Skills Practice 1,*** p. 122

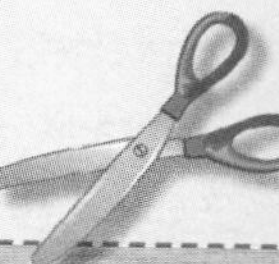

Transparency 64
64A

Revising: Word Choice

One ~~nice~~ evening, Dona was watching television. A ~~short~~ message ~~was~~ on the screen. It said: "Great auroras tonight." Dona ~~put~~ on her warm ~~jacket~~ and ~~went~~ outside. Twin pathways of ~~colorful~~ light ~~went across~~ the dark sky. As Dona watched the ~~pretty~~ trail, a red border grew along its bottom edge. Then, the ball of light ~~seemed to burst~~, putting rays all over the night sky.

 SRA Imagine It! • Level 3 • Transparency 64 • 64A Level 3

Transparencies 64, 64A

UNIT 2 Lesson 3

Revising Use this checklist to revise your explanation of a process.
- ☐ Did you include all the necessary steps?
- ☐ Are the sentences in the best order to help readers understand the process?
- ☐ Are your words clear and specific?
- ☐ Is your writing easy to understand?

Editing/Proofreading Use this checklist to correct mistakes.
- ☐ Did you use correct spelling?
- ☐ Did you use correct punctuation?
- ☐ Did you capitalize the title of your explanation?
- ☐ Are words such as *First, Next,* and *Finally* in order?

Publishing Use this checklist to prepare for publication.
- ☐ Neatly rewrite or type a final copy.
- ☐ Make a chart to show the steps in your process.

122 UNIT 2 • Lesson 3 Writing • *Skills Practice 1*

Skills Practice 1, p. 122

Writing Explaining a Process

ROUTINE 16

Revising and Editing/Proofreading

Teach—Revising for Precise Word Choice

✦ Use Routine 16. Tell students that now it is time to revise and edit their process paper.

✦ Tell students that as they revise they need to
- make sure all of the steps of the process are followed.
- make sure all of the steps are in the correct order.
- make sure that they use precise words in describing each step of the process.

✦ Tell students that as they edit their papers, they need to be looking for errors in grammar, spelling, and punctuation. Explain to students that spelling and punctuation are very important in a process paper because the meaning of an entire sentence can change if the wrong spelling or incorrect punctuation is used.

Guided Practice

✦ Using the paragraph and the graphic organizer created earlier, work with the students to revise the paragraph for concise word choice and then edit the paragraph for grammar, spelling, and punctuation. Keep this work for later use.

✦ Display ***Transparency*** 64. Have students silently read the transparency and take notes on editing the paragraph for precise wording. Have students discuss what changes they would make. Then, display Transparency 64A and have students discuss the changes.

✦ Turn to ***Skills Practice 1*** page 122 to read and discuss the checklists with the students before they begin revising and editing.

Writing, continued

Apply

Composing—Revising and Editing/Proofreading Have students revise and edit their process papers. Have them refer to the checklists in ***Skills Practice 1*** page 122.

Traits of Good Writing

Vocabulary The writer uses knowledge of vocabulary and makes precise word choices when revising and editing manuscript.

Differentiating Instruction English Learner

IF . . . students need guidance for revising their process papers, **THEN . . .** have them act out the process for a proficient English-speaking partner to observe. The partner should compare the actions to the writing and point out any parts of the process that are not explained.

Monitor Progress to Differentiate Instruction

Formal Assessment

Revising for Precise Wording Note whether students have the vocabulary knowledge to create precise sentences.

APPROACHING LEVEL

IF . . . students need to practice precise word choice,	**THEN . . .** have them use a Thesaurus or Dictionary as a tool for revision during Workshop.

ON LEVEL

IF . . . students have an understanding of precise word choice,	**THEN . . .** have them use ***eSkills*** during Workshop.

ABOVE LEVEL

IF . . . students need a challenge,	**THEN . . .** have them work on adding different sentence patterns during Workshop.

Spelling

/ū/ and Homographs

Teach

Visualizing Strategy Tell students that sometimes the correct spelling of a word can be determined by looking at a word to see if it "looks right." Students can use spelling patterns from words that they already know to decide whether a new word has used an incorrect pattern even if they have not seen the word before.

Guided Practice

Write the following sentence on the board: *The roas will groh wel at the parc, as long as it gets enough lite.* Have students circle the misspelled words and rewrite them correctly. The corrected sentence should read: *The rose will grow well at the park, as long as it gets enough light.*

Study Skills

Diagrams

Teach

Remind students that diagrams are special drawings that show the arrangements and labels of the parts of something.

Guided Practice

Draw a simple line drawing of a wolf on the board, and write the following words next to it: *head, body, legs, ears, tail*. Ask for volunteers to draw a line from the word to the part of the wolf it names, and have them write the names of the parts on the lines. When all parts have been identified, tell students they have just made a diagram.

Apply

On the board or an overhead transparency, draw an island, a body of water, and a mainland. Tell students to copy this drawing on their own paper. Then tell students to look through "Wolf Island" and draw pictures of the animals mentioned in the story and where they might be on the island, in the water, or on the mainland. Tell students to remember to label the animal groupings as well as other elements of the story they would like to include on the diagram. Have students explain what purpose this diagram would serve. **Possible Answer** *The diagram gives a visual representation of all the different animals in their habitats.*

Listening/Speaking/Viewing

Using Visual Aids

Teach

- Explain that visual aids can be diagrams, tables, charts, graphics, pictures, photographs, drawings, maps, objects, or other items that can be displayed during oral presentations.
- Tell students that visual aids make oral presentations more informative and exciting. Visual aids give the audience more information and something on which they can focus their attention.
- Discuss the fact that visual aids should be appropriate for the subject material of the presentations and should enhance the meaning of the presentations.

Guided Practice

Draw a simple diagram on the board. This can be of a house, tree, car, or bicycle, for example. Have students label the various parts.

Apply

Organize the class into small groups. Each group will discuss which type of visual aid they would use for a presentation about wolves. Provide example topics for students: *Where Wolves Live; Extinct Wolf Species and Why; Wolf Characteristics and Behaviors.* Write a list on the board of types of visual aids on the board for students to reference. Have each group present their visual aid and explain why they chose it and why it would be helpful.

Differentiating Instruction

English Learner

IF . . . students need help understanding the different kinds of visual aids, **THEN . . .** show them examples of each visual aid and identify it in a simple sentence, such as "This is a map." Ask students to echo your sentence in response to the question "What is this?"

Day 5

Preparing to Read

Review

OBJECTIVES

Students will

- review /ū/ spelled _*ew* and _*ue*.
- review homographs.
- build fluency.

MATERIALS

- ***Sound/Spelling Card*** 31
- ***Transparencies*** 54 and 57

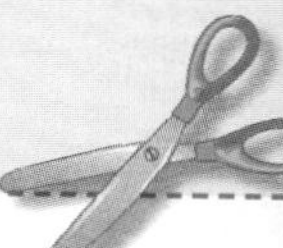

Phonics and Fluency

Use ***Transparency*** 54 with the blending lines and sentences from Days 1 and 2 to review /ū/ spelled _*ew* and _*ue*. Have students read the words and sentences on the blending lines. Then have volunteers choose words from the lines and use them in sentences.

Line 1	few	fewer	fewest	curfew
Line 2	pew	mew	skew	nephew
Line 3	cue	hue	rescue	argue
Line 4	value	continue	barbeque	tissue

Sentence 1 I <u>often</u> want to view the <u>world</u> from outer space.

Sentence 2 <u>Without</u> its cover, the issue was valued at only ten dollars.

Word Structure

Use ***Transparency*** 57 with the word lines from Days 3 and 4 to review homographs. Have students read the words on the word lines. Then have students give two definitions for each word on the lines.

Line 1	well	mine	sink	fall
Line 2	store	bark	pass	fly
Line 3	wind	tear	bow	close
Line 4	dove	live	present	lead

OBJECTIVES

Students will

- review selection vocabulary.
- review the comprehension strategies Making Connections and Predicting.
- review the comprehension skills Fact and Opinion, Making Inferences, and Reality and Fantasy.
- review fluency.

MATERIALS

- ***Student Reader, Book 1,*** pp. 176–191
- ***Transparency*** 55

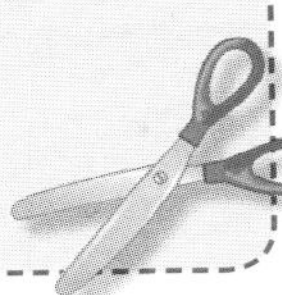

Selection Vocabulary

To review the selection vocabulary with students, organize them into 3–4 teams, depending on the size of the class. Give the class one vocabulary word at a time. Tell students that the first team to use the word correctly in an original sentence and read it aloud will score a point for their team. Repeat this exercise until all of the vocabulary words have been reviewed.

Selection Vocabulary

male (māl) *adj.* of or having to do with men or boys (page 178)

female (fē′ • māl) *n.* a woman or girl (page 178)

aboard (ə • bord′) *adv.* on or into a ship, train, or an airplane (page 181)

mainland (mān′ • lənd) *n.* the chief landmass of a country, or continent, as different from an island (page 181)

mild (mīld) *adj.* gentle or calm; not harsh or sharp (page 182)

layer (lā′ • ûr) *n.* one thickness of something (page 182)

population (pop′ • ū • lā′ • shən) *n.* the people or animals living in a place (page 182)

balance (bal′ • əns) *n.* a steady, secure position (page 189)

Comprehension Strategies  

Review the following comprehension strategies with students.

- **Making Connections** helps readers use their own experiences to understand what is happening in a story. Have students turn to page 179, and ask them if they can make any personal connections with the wolf cubs and their curiosity. Have students share tales of times when curiosity got the best of them.
- **Predicting** is when readers analyze information about events and characters in the context of how these may logically connect to the story's conclusion. Have students discuss the predictions they made throughout "Wolf Island." Ask students whether their predictions were confirmed later in the text.

Comprehension Skills   

Review the following comprehension skills with students:

- **Fact and Opinion** is the readers' ability to determine whether text is a fact or an opinion. In order to do this, students must understand the differences between facts and opinions. Facts can be verified or tested. Opinions, however, are the writer's own judgments which cannot be tested and may vary between sources. Ask students to find examples of facts in "Wolf Island."
- **Making Inferences** helps readers use clues and suggestions from the text and their own background knowledge to form a more complete picture of the story. Have students go back to "Wolf Island" and ask them if they applied their own background knowledge to help them understand the meaning of the text. For example, were students able to infer that the wolf cubs were headed for trouble when they wandered onto the raft? What inferences could they make about the wolf family and its move to another island?
- **Reality and Fantasy** is the readers' awareness of the differences between a text that is a fantasy, which includes events, characters, or settings that cannot be real; and reality, which includes events, characters, or settings that could be real. Ask students to review "Wolf Island" and find examples of reality. List these examples on the board. Then ask students what might have happened in the story to make it a fantasy instead.

Reading with a Writer's Eye  

eview the following literary element with students:

uthor's Purpose is the reason an author writes a story. Ask students what the uthor's purpose was for writing "Wolf Island." Have students review the story nd find examples of the ways the author is able to accomplish that purpose.

luency 

emind students that accuracy, or reading words correctly, adds to the meaning text by making it easier to comprehend and enjoy. Remind students that ading with accuracy is especially important when reading nonfiction, because allows readers to understand and remember the information being taught by e author. Read aloud a passage from pages 182–185 from "Wolf Island." Make re that the passage totals at least 160 words to ensure an appropriate practice ngth.

ave students read the passage chorally. Remind students to pay attention to curacy. Also remind students to pause after commas and end punctuation.

OBJECTIVES

Students will

- publish their process papers.
- take the spelling posttest.
- review cursive *f, h, m,* and *n.*

MATERIALS

- Routine 17
- ***Transparencies*** 45, 52
- ***Skills Practice 1,*** p. 122

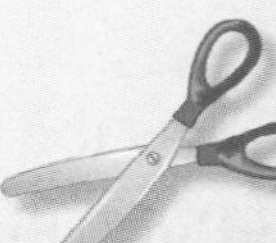

UNIT 2 Lesson 3

Revising Use this checklist to revise your explanation of a process.

- ☐ Did you include all the necessary steps?
- ☐ Are the sentences in the best order to help readers understand the process?
- ☐ Are your words clear and specific?
- ☐ Is your writing easy to understand?

Editing/Proofreading Use this checklist to correct mistakes.

- ☐ Did you use correct spelling?
- ☐ Did you use correct punctuation?
- ☐ Did you capitalize the title of your explanation?
- ☐ Are words such as *First, Next,* and *Finally* in order?

Publishing Use this checklist to prepare for publication.

- ☐ Neatly rewrite or type a final copy.
- ☐ Make a chart to show the steps in your process.

122 UNIT 2 • Lesson 3 Writing • *Skills Practice 1*

Skills Practice 1, p. 122

Teacher Tip

ASSESSMENT Use the Writing Rubrics found in the Level Appendix to evaluate students' process papers. You may use any of the rubrics for Genre, Writing Process, and Writing Traits.

Writing Explaining a Process

ROUTINE 17

Publishing

Teach

- Use Routine 17. Tell students that they are at the final stage of the writing process: publishing. This means students will be sharing their writing.
- Discuss ways that students can publish their work. For instance, they might decide to bind their processes into a "How-to" book.
- This is an ideal assignment for oral presentations. Set aside time for volunteers to give oral presentations to the class. If giving oral presentations, encourage students to use visual aids such as diagrams, tables, or charts to enhance their presentations.
- If students are not making oral presentations, have students form small groups and read each other's papers.

Guided Practice

Read with students the publishing checklist in ***Skills Practice 1*** page 122.

Apply

Composing—Publishing Have students create an error-free copy of their process papers. Encourage them to add a chart to the process. Also, have them refer to the publishing checklist on ***Skills Practice 1*** page 122. Have volunteers give oral presentations.

Spelling

/ū/ and Homographs

Teach

Have students write Spelling and their names in the top margin of a clean piece of paper. Have them number the first fifteen lines 1–15, then skip a line and number the next two lines 1–2. Read each word, use it in a sentence, and give students time to spell it correctly. Encourage students to try to spell the challenge words, but assure them that misspelling a challenge word will not affect their test scores.

Spelling Words

cue
few
well
rose
argue
tire
hue
ring
value
change
spew
rescue
park
view
light

Challenge Words

pitcher
nephew

Guided Practice

- Have students proofread for any mistakes they made on the posttest. Tell them to categorize the mistakes as
  - careless errors.
  - errors in spelling homographs.
  - errors in spelling words with /ū/ spelled _*ew* or _*ue*.
- Make certain students are correctly spelling homographs and words with /ū/ spelled _*ew* and _*ue*.

Penmanship

Cursive Letters *f, h, m,* and *n*

Teach

- Remind students that all cursive letters are made of four types of strokes (undercurve, overcurve, downcurve, and slant lines).
- Review lowercase *f, h, m,* and *n* using ***Transparency*** 52 and 45. For further information see Unit 2 Lessons 1 and 2 and the Level Appendix.
- Write each letter on the board, saying the strokes aloud.
- To model proper letter formation, write the following sentence on the board: *The moon is farther north.*

Guided Practice

Have students practice writing the sentence on the board.

Apply

- After reviewing the sentence on the board, have students practice writing the sentence. Have them circle the best formation of the sentence.
- For further cursive writing practice, have students write their final process draft in cursive.

Differentiating Instruction — English Learner

IF . . . students have difficulty following your directions for handwriting, **THEN . . .** demonstrate the meanings of the words *top, bottom, up,* and *down*. Give students an opportunity to practice saying and demonstrating the words.

Language Arts

OBJECTIVES

Students will
- review and create diagrams.
- review and create visual aids.
- review types of sentences.

MATERIALS

- ***Student Reader,*** Book 1 pp. 198–211
- ***Lesson Assessment Book 1,*** pp. 59–66
- ***Home Connection,*** pp. 21–22

Study Skills

Diagrams

Remind students that diagrams are special drawings that show the parts of an object. The parts are usually labeled. Ask student where they might find a diagram. **Possible Answers** *textbooks, instruction manuals, encyclopedias, technical books, how-to manuals*

Ask students to share information from the unit investigations that could be used in a diagram.

If applicable, have students complete the diagrams for their unit investigations.

Listening/Speaking/Viewing

Using Visual Aids

Remind students that using visual aids enhances oral presentations. They give more information and can clarify the information given in a presentation.

Have students turn to ***Student Reader,*** Book 1 page 178. Have them review the selection and then ask students what type of visual aids they might use if they were presenting a book review of "Wolf Island." **Possible Answers** *a map of the island and the mainland, a graphic of the food chain of the animals on the island, a weather map*

Have students make a list of the types of visual aids they could create to accompany their unit investigations.

They should include a diagram as part of the visual aids they choose.

Grammar, Usage, and Mechanics

Types of Sentences

Write the following sentences on the board. Then have students identify which sentence is declarative, interrogative, imperative, or exclamatory.

- Jane is a scientist who studies chimpanzees in Africa. *declarative*
- Diane won the conservation scholarship! *exclamatory*
- Can Francis join us on our field trip to the wildlife rehabilitation center? *interrogative*
- Log on to the Internet to find out more information about the volunteer vacation program. *imperative*

Have students look for the four types of sentences in "Wolf Island." Have them copy each type of sentence, label it, and then share their findings with classmates.

Have students work with a partner to write a short skit that incorporates each of the four sentence types. Have the pairs practice and then perform their skits.

Monitor Progress

Formal Assessment

Use pages 59–66 in ***Lesson Assessment Book 1*** to assess students' understanding of the skills taught in this lesson. Intervene with ***Reteach, Challenge Activities, Intervention Guide, eSkills, Leveled Readers,*** or activities in the ***Workshop Kit*** as needed.

Lesson Planner

	Day 1	Day 2
Preparing to Read MATERIALS ✦ ***Transparencies*** 59, 63 ✦ ***Sound/Spelling Cards*** 29–31 ✦ Routines 2–9 ✦ ***Skills Practice 1,*** pp. 129–132	**Daily News,** p. T272 ✔ **Phonics and Fluency** Review /ī/, /ō/, /ū/, and Consonant Blends, pp. T273–T275	**Daily News,** p. T294 **Phonics and Fluency,** p. T294–T295 **Developing Oral Language,** p. T295 **Dictation,** p. T295
Reading and Responding MATERIALS ✦ ***Student Reader,*** Book 1, pp. 194–215 ✦ ***Transparencies*** 5, 15, 60 ✦ Routines 11, 12, 14, A ✦ ***Skills Practice 1,*** pp. 133–136 ✦ Writer's Notebook ✦ ***Home Connection,*** pp. 21–22 ✦ ***Listening Library CDs*** ✦ ***Leveled Reader***	**Build Background,** p. T276 **Preview and Prepare,** p. T277 **Selection Vocabulary,** pp. T278–T279 **Reading the Selection,** pp. T280–T283 (1st READ) ✔ **Comprehension Strategies** • Asking Questions, pp. T284–T286 ☆ Making Connections, pp. T281, T285 • Summarizing, p. T287 **Inquiry,** pp. T288–T289	✔ **Comprehension Strategies** • Asking Questions, pp. T297, T298 ☆ Making Connections, pp. T296, T298 • Summarizing, p. T299 **Discussing the Selection,** p. T300 ✔ **Review Selection Vocabulary,** p. T301 **Fluency,** p. T301 **Theme Connections,** pp. T302–T303
Language Arts MATERIALS ✦ ***Transparencies*** 3, 17, 17A, 61, 62 ✦ ***Skills Practice 1,*** pp. 137–144 ✦ ***Language Arts Handbook,*** pp. 42, 126–129 ✦ ***Student Reader,*** Book 1, pp. 214–215 ✦ ***Lesson Assessment Book 1,*** pp. 67–74 ✦ Routines 15, 16, 17	**Writing** Prewriting, pp. T290–T291 ✔ **Spelling Pretest,** p. T291 **Penmanship,** p. T292	**Writing** Drafting, p. T304–T305 **Spelling,** p. T305 ✔ **Grammar, Usage, and Mechanics** Subjects and Direct Objects, pp. T306–T307
Monitor Progress ✔ = **Formal Assessment**	✔ **Phonics and Fluency, p. T275** ✔ **Comprehension Strategy, p. T281** ✔ **Spelling Pretest, p. T291**	✔ **Selection Vocabulary, p. T301** **Fluency, p. T301** ✔ **Grammar, Usage, and Mechanics, p. T307**

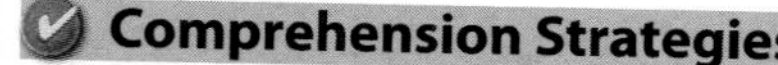

Literature Overview

Student Reader

Two Days in May

by Harriet Peck Taylor

illustrated by Leyla Torres

Parent's Choice Recommendation

Science Inquiry

A National Pleasure

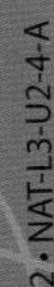

SRA
Imagine It!

★ Phonics ★ Fluency ★ Vocabulary ★ Comprehension

Day 3

Daily News, p. T308
Word Structure
Homophones, p. T308–T309

2nd READ

Comprehension Skill
- Cause and Effect, pp. T310, T312

Reading with a Writer's Eye, pp. T311, T313
Supporting the Reading
☆ Comprehension Strategy: Making Connections, p. T314
Fluency, p. T315
Inquiry, p. T315

Writing
Revising, p. T316
Spelling, p. T317
Study Skills
Graphic Organizers, p. T318
Grammar, Usage, and Mechanics, p. T319

Word Structure, p. T309
Fluency, p. T315
Spelling, p. T317
Study Skills, p. T318

Day 4

Daily News, p. T320
Word Structure, p. T321
Developing Oral Language, p. T321

Comprehension Skill
- Cause and Effect, pp. T322, T324

Reading with a Writer's Eye, p. T323
Science Inquiry, pp. T326–T327
Inquiry, pp. T328–T329

Writing
Proofreading and Editing, p. T330–T331
Spelling, p. T331
Study Skills, p. T332
Listening/Speaking/Viewing
Recalling Information Presented Orally, p. T333

Writing, p. T331

Day 5 Review

Phonics and Fluency, p. T334
Word Structure, p. T334

Selection Vocabulary, p. T335
Comprehension Strategies
- Asking Questions, p. T336
- ☆ Making Connections, p. T336
- Summarizing, p. T336

Comprehension Skill
- Cause and Effect, p. T336

Reading with a Writer's Eye, p. T337
Fluency, p. T337

Writing
Publishing, p. T338
Spelling Posttest, p. T339
Penmanship, p. T339
Study Skills, p. T340
Listening/Speaking/Viewing, p. T340
Grammar, Usage, and Mechanics, p. T341

Spelling Posttest, p. T339
***Lesson Assessment Book 1*, pp. 67–74**

Student Resources

Genre

Realistic Fiction involves stories about people and events that are true to life and that could really happen.

Comprehension Strategy

Making Connections As you read, make connections between what you already know about habitats and what you are reading.

Focus Questions

How do you think deer find their way into the city? What can be done to protect the deer in the city?

196

Two Days in May

by Harriet Peck Taylor
illustrated by Leyla Torres

197

Student Reader, Book 1, pp. 196–213

Phonics & Fluency

Decodable Stories, Book 3, Story 20, "Strange Stuff"

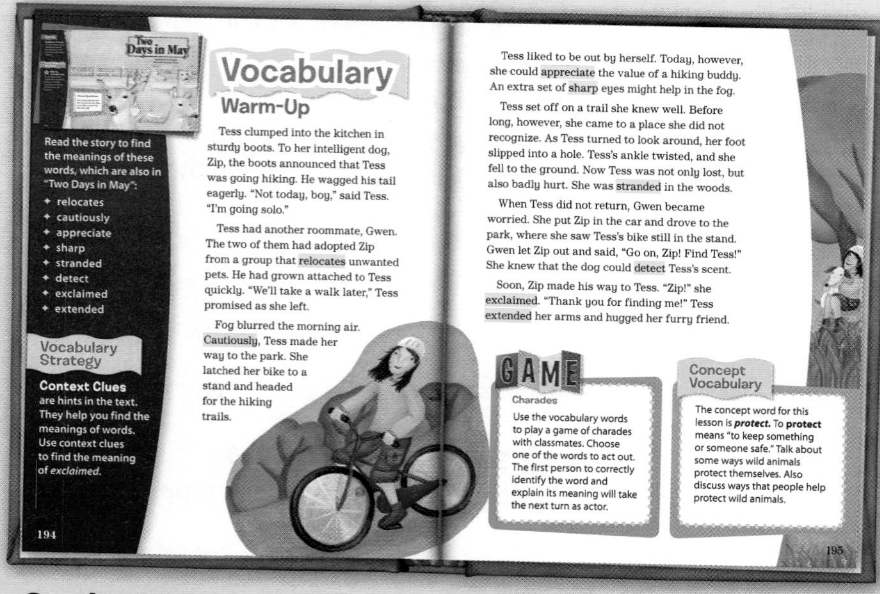
Two Days in May

Read the story to find the meanings of these words, which are also in "Two Days in May":
- relocates
- cautiously
- appreciate
- sharp
- stranded
- detect
- exclaimed
- extended

Vocabulary Strategy

Context Clues are hints in the text. They help you find the meanings of words. Use context clues to find the meaning of *exclaimed.*

Vocabulary Warm-Up

Tess clumped into the kitchen in sturdy boots. To her intelligent dog, Zip, the boots announced that Tess was going hiking. He wagged his tail eagerly. "Not today, boy," said Tess. "I'm going solo."

Tess had another roommate, Gwen. The two of them had adopted Zip from a group that relocates unwanted pets. He had grown attached to Tess quickly. "We'll take a walk later," Tess promised as she left.

Fog blurred the morning air. Cautiously, Tess made her way to the park. She latched her bike to a stand and headed for the hiking trails.

Tess liked to be out by herself. Today, however, she could appreciate the value of a hiking buddy. An extra set of sharp eyes might help in the fog.

Tess set off on a trail she knew well. Before long, however, she came to a place she did not recognize. As Tess turned to look around, her foot slipped into a hole. Tess's ankle twisted, and she fell to the ground. Now Tess was not only lost, but also badly hurt. She was stranded in the woods.

When Tess did not return, Gwen became worried. She put Zip in the car and drove to the park, where she saw Tess's bike still in the stand. Gwen let Zip out and said, "Go on, Zip! Find Tess!" She knew that the dog could detect Tess's scent.

Soon, Zip made his way to Tess. "Zip!" she exclaimed. "Thank you for finding me!" Tess extended her arms and hugged her furry friend.

GAME

Charades

Use the vocabulary words to play a game of charades with classmates. Choose one of the words to act out. The first person to correctly identify the word and explain its meaning will take the next turn as actor.

Concept Vocabulary

The concept word for this lesson is ***protect.*** To **protect** means "to keep something or someone safe." Talk about some ways wild animals protect themselves. Also discuss ways that people help protect wild animals.

194

195

Student Reader, Book 1, pp. 194–195

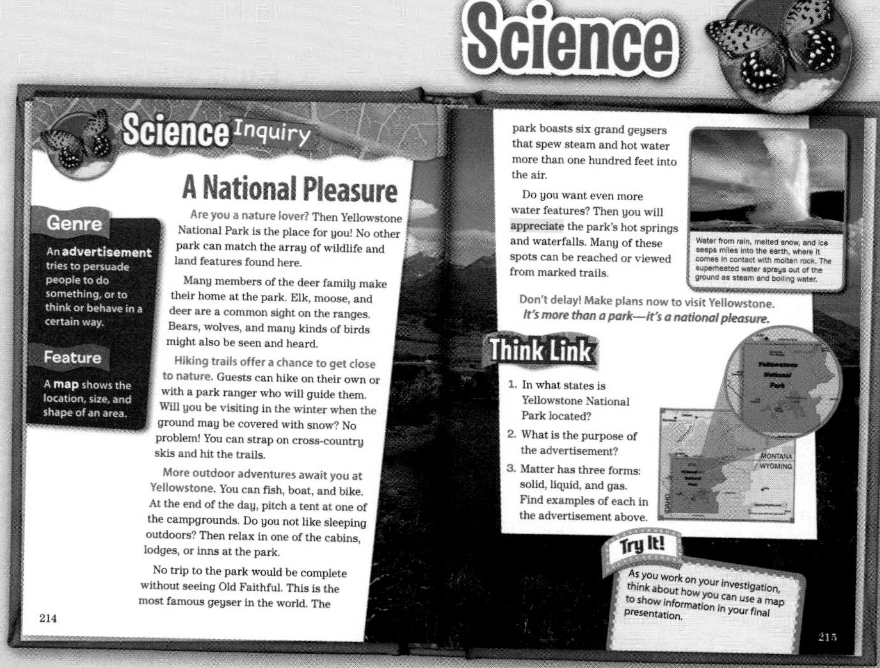
Science

Science Inquiry

A National Pleasure

Genre

An **advertisement** tries to persuade people to do something, or to think or behave in a certain way.

Feature

A **map** shows the location, size, and shape of an area.

Are you a nature lover? Then Yellowstone National Park is the place for you! No other park can match the array of wildlife and land features found here.

Many members of the deer family make their home at the park. Elk, moose, and deer are a common sight on the ranges. Bears, wolves, and many kinds of birds might also be seen and heard.

Hiking trails offer a chance to get close to nature. Guests can hike on their own or with a park ranger who will guide them. Will you be visiting in the winter when the ground may be covered with snow? No problem! You can strap on cross-country skis and hit the trails.

More outdoor adventures await you at Yellowstone. You can fish, boat, and bike. At the end of the day, pitch a tent at one of the campgrounds. Do you not like sleeping outdoors? Then relax in one of the cabins, lodges, or inns at the park.

No trip to the park would be complete without seeing Old Faithful. This is the most famous geyser in the world. The park boasts six grand geysers that spew steam and hot water more than one hundred feet into the air.

Do you want even more water features? Then you will appreciate the park's hot springs and waterfalls. Many of these spots can be reached or viewed from marked trails.

Water from rain, melted snow, and ice seeps miles into the earth, where it comes in contact with molten rock. The superheated water sprays out of the ground as steam and boiling water.

Don't delay! Make plans now to visit Yellowstone. *It's more than a park—it's a national pleasure.*

Think Link

1. In what states is Yellowstone National Park located?
2. What is the purpose of the advertisement?
3. Matter has three forms: solid, liquid, and gas. Find examples of each in the advertisement above.

Try It!

As you work on your investigation, think about how you can use a map to show information in your final presentation.

214

215

Student Reader, Book 1, pp. 214–215

Cross-Curricular Resources

Curriculum Connections

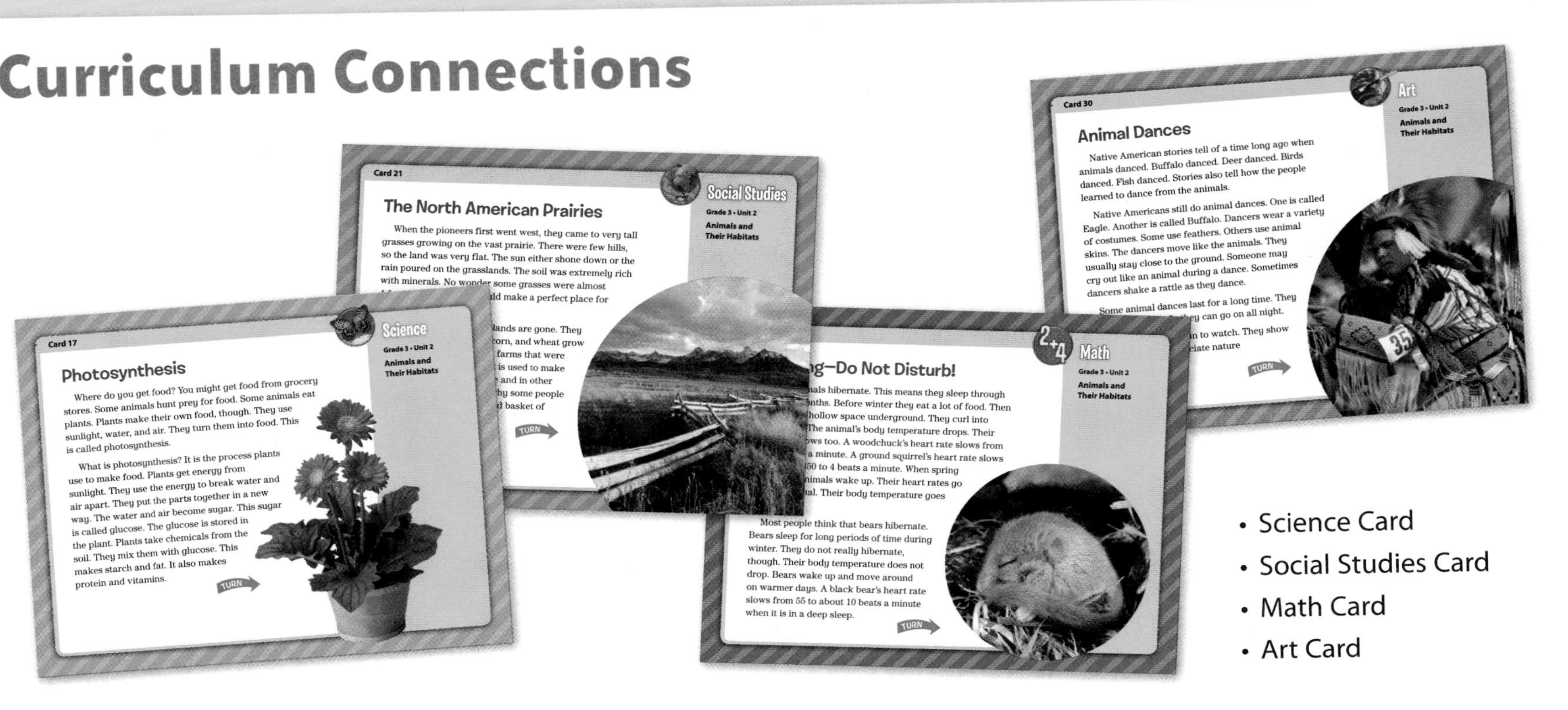

- Science Card
- Social Studies Card
- Math Card
- Art Card

Leveled Readers for Science

Approaching Level

On Level

English Learner

Above Level

Differentiating Instruction for Workshop

Day 1

	Approaching Level	On Level	English Learner	Above Level
Preparing to Read	**Phonics and Fluency:** Help students complete ***Reteach*** page 51 or work with them on the phonics activities for Unit 2 Lesson 4 in the ***Intervention Guide***. Then have students read ***Decodable Stories, Book 3,*** Story 20.	**Phonics and Fluency:** Have students make lists of words to add to the word lines.	**Phonics and Fluency:** Use the ***English Learner Support Guide*** for more phonics instruction. Then have students read ***Decodable Stories, Book 3,*** Story 20.	**Phonics and Fluency:** Have students complete ***Challenge Activities*** page 46. Students can play a game with ***Sound/Spelling Cards*** 29–31.
Reading and Responding	**Vocabulary:** Have students use a thesaurus to find words that are similar to the selection vocabulary words. Have students add these words to their Writer's Notebooks. **Comprehension:** Have students add questions about how this selection might relate to animals and their habitats to the ***Concept/Question Board***. **Inquiry:** Have students record information from a research source.	**Vocabulary:** Have students make a crossword puzzle with the vocabulary words. **Comprehension:** Have students write a short summary for the first half of the story. **Inquiry:** Have students record information from a research source.	**Vocabulary:** Place students in small groups. Have them select three vocabulary words and brainstorm related words. Let students use a dictionary or a thesaurus if needed **Comprehension:** Have students write a short paragraph about a connection they can make with the story. If students have difficulty expressing themselves, encourage them to illustrate their ideas. **Inquiry:** Have students record information from a research source.	**Vocabulary:** Have students list synonyms and antonyms for the vocabulary words in their Writer's Notebooks. Let students use print and online resources if needed. **Comprehension:** Have students research references such as local newspapers and telephone directories to find local organizations that help animals. **Inquiry:** Have students record information from a research source.
Language Arts	**Writing:** Have students read other examples of realistic fiction. **Spelling:** Have students write the meaning of consonant blends and homophones on a piece of paper.	**Writing:** Have students take notes on character, setting, and plot on their story maps. **Spelling:** Have students proofread their writing activity for spelling errors.	**Writing:** Review the elements of realistic fiction using ***Transparency*** 61. **Spelling:** Have students check a partner's writing activity for errors in spelling.	**Writing:** Have students create character webs to develop characters. **Spelling:** Have students write a two-sentence story using as many spelling words as possible.

Day 2

	Approaching Level	On Level	English Learner	Above Level
Preparing to Read	**Phonics and Fluency:** Students can listen to /ī/, /ō/, and /ū/ on the ***Sound/Spelling Cards Stories CD.*** Students can also use ***eSkills*** for extra phonics practice.	**Phonics and Fluency:** Have students extend the sentences from the blending lines. Encourage them to add to the beginning and end of sentences.	**Phonics and Fluency:** Students can listen to the /ī/, the /ō/, and the /ū/ sounds on the ***Sound/Spelling Cards Stories CD.*** Have students write sentences using words from the blending lines.	**Phonics and Fluency:** Have students write rhyming poems using words from the blending lines.
Reading and Responding	**Vocabulary:** Have students use ***Reteach*** page 53 or work with them using ***Intervention Guide,*** Unit 2, Lesson 4. **Comprehension:** Have students apply questions asked about the story to the **Concept/Question Board.** **Fluency:** Have students choose a text on their independent level to read silently.	**Vocabulary:** Have students complete a game in the ***Workshop Kit.*** **Comprehension:** Have students create a checklist of the questions that they have about the story. Have students check off the questions as they are answered. **Fluency:** Have students read into a tape recorder at the beginning and end of the week. Have them listen to themselves at the end of the week so they can hear their progress.	**Vocabulary:** Help students create flash cards for the selection vocabulary words. Have students test themselves with the cards and then quiz a partner. **Comprehension:** Have students write a short paragraph summarizing the story so far. **Fluency:** Have students engage in echo reading with passages from the selection.	**Vocabulary:** Have students complete ***Challenge Activities*** page 48. **Comprehension:** Have students create a character web for their favorite character in the story. **Fluency:** Have students choose a text on their independent level to read silently.
Language Arts	**Writing:** Have students practice dialogue with a partner and then draft. **Spelling:** Have students work in pairs to review the sounds that the consonant blends make in each spelling word. **Grammar, Usage, and Mechanics:** Have students complete ***Reteach*** page 55.	**Writing:** Have student continue to draft using character dialogue. **Spelling:** Have students write the spelling words that are homophones in pairs on a piece of paper. **Grammar, Usage, and Mechanics:** Have students pay attention to the nouns they use as subjects and direct objects as they continue to draft their stories.	**Writing:** Have students practice using speaking tags. **Spelling:** Have students write three consonant blends on a piece of paper, trade with a partner, and write the words that contain each blend. **Grammar, Usage, and Mechanics:** Refer to the ***English Learner Support Guide*** for support activities.	**Writing:** Have students pay attention to punctuation as they draft their dialogue. **Spelling:** Have students write five pairs of homophones that were not in this lesson on a piece of paper. **Grammar, Usage, and Mechanics:** Have students complete ***Challenge Activities*** page 50.

Differentiating Instruction for Workshop

Day 3

	Approaching Level	On Level	English Learner	Above Level
Preparing to Read	**Word Structure:** Review the word lines with homophones. Have students complete ***Reteach*** page 52, or work with them on the word structure activities in the ***Intervention Guide,*** Unit 2, Lesson 4.	**Word Structure:** Have students use the word structure activities in ***eSkills*** for more practice with homographs and homophones.	**Word Structure:** Review the word lines with homophones. Use the ***English Learner Support Guide*** for more word structure instruction.	**Word Structure:** Have students complete ***Challenge Activities*** page 47. Have students use the word structure activities in ***eSkills*** for more practice with homographs and homophones.
Reading and Responding	**Vocabulary:** Have students find antonyms for the vocabulary words in a thesaurus. Have students list the antonyms in their Writer's Notebooks. **Comprehension:** Have students use graphic organizers to organize character details from the story. **Fluency:** Have students use ***Leveled Readers.***	**Vocabulary:** Have students play Charades using the vocabulary words. **Comprehension:** Have students read other stories about animals and their habitats. Have them keep track of the cause-and-effect relationships they find by using a two-column chart. **Fluency:** Have students select a book on their independent level to read.	**Vocabulary:** Have students find words that are related to the selection vocabulary words in a thesaurus or a dictionary. **Comprehension:** Have students write a paragraph describing their favorite character in the story. Encourage students to use clues from the story to help with their descriptions. **Fluency:** Have students whisper read with you as you read passages from the text.	**Vocabulary:** Have students find additional concept vocabulary words by researching an online thesaurus or dictionary. **Comprehension:** Have students write a journal entry comparing Mr. Smiley and the Pigeon Lady. **Fluency:** Have students use ***Leveled Readers.***
Language Arts	**Writing:** Have students check punctuation as they add dialogue during revision. **Spelling:** Have students complete ***Reteach*** page 54. **Grammar, Usage, and Mechanics:** Have students review their writing for the correct use of pronouns.	**Writing:** Have students continue to revise their stories. **Spelling:** Have students write two sentences that include four of this week's spelling words each. **Grammar, Usage, and Mechanics:** Have students check their work to make sure they use the correct pronouns when replacing nouns.	**Writing:** Have students continue to revise their stories. **Spelling:** Have students write an imaginary news story using spelling words. **Grammar, Usage, and Mechanics:** Refer to the ***English Learner Support Guide*** for support activities.	**Writing:** Have students make sure the dialogue matches the character's personality. **Spelling:** Have students complete ***Challenge Activities*** page 49. **Grammar, Usage, and Mechanics:** Have students look for noun/pronoun agreement in a previous piece of writing.

Day 4

	Approaching Level	On Level	English Learner	Above Level
Preparing to Read	**Word Structure:** Have students write sentences using words from the word lines. Have students use the word structure activities in ***eSkills*** for more practice with homographs and homophones.	**Word Structure:** Have students scramble words from the word lines and give them to a partner to unscramble.	**Word Structure:** Have students write sentences using words from the word lines. Have students use the word structure activities in ***eSkills*** for more practice with homographs and homophones.	**Word Structure:** Have students scramble words from the word lines and give them to a partner to unscramble.
Reading and Responding	**Vocabulary:** Have students add additional words from the text related to the unit theme to the Word Bank. **Comprehension:** Pair students into small groups to discuss a book they have read. **Inquiry:** Assist students in organizing information by making graphic organizers.	**Vocabulary:** Have students write examples for three of the selection vocabulary words in their Writer's Notebooks. **Comprehension:** Have students compare and contrast "Two Days in May" with "Make Way for Ducklings." **Inquiry:** Assist students in organizing information by making graphic organizers.	**Vocabulary:** Have students find and explain idiomatic expressions in other stories and articles. Have students add the idioms and their meanings to their Writer's Notebooks. **Comprehension:** Have students find cause-and-effect relationships in other stories. **Inquiry:** Assist students in organizing information by making graphic organizers.	**Vocabulary:** Help students brainstorm writing prompts containing the vocabulary words. Have students select a prompt and write a response in their Writer's Notebooks. **Comprehension:** Have students use a graphic organizer to dissect the story. **Inquiry:** Assist students in organizing information by making graphic organizers.
Language Arts	**Writing:** Have students continue to edit/proofread. Have them begin the final draft. **Spelling:** Have students write six spelling words on a piece of paper spelled incorrectly, trade papers with a partner, and correct them.	**Writing:** Have students type their final drafts after they have completed proofreading. **Spelling:** Working in pairs, have students write some rules that they think will help each other learn to spell the spelling words.	**Writing:** Have students read their stories aloud to proofread for grammar errors. **Spelling:** Have students write an imaginary news story between two and three sentences long.	**Writing:** Have students begin typing their final version after they complete editing/proofreading. Tell them to look for illustrations to add to their stories. **Spelling:** Have students use the letters from their spelling words of their choice to create new words that use the same skills.

Differentiating Instruction
for Workshop

Day 5

	Approaching Level	On Level	English Learner	Above Level
Preparing to Read	**Word Structure:** Review the word lines. Then have students read "Strange Stuff" from ***eDecodable Stories.*** Have the students read the ***High-Frequency Flash Cards*** with a partner.	**Word Structure:** Have students write clue sentences for words in the word lines, and have a partner guess the words.	**Word Structure:** Review the word lines. Then have students read "Strange Stuff" from ***eDecodable Stories.*** Have the students read the ***High-Frequency Flash Cards*** with a partner.	**Word Structure:** Have students write clue sentences for words in the word lines, and have a partner guess the words.
Reading and Responding	**Vocabulary:** Have students use print or online dictionaries to learn more information about the selection vocabulary. **Comprehension:** Have students create review questions and trade with a partner. Have students answer each other's questions. **Fluency:** Have students write answers to comprehension questions from ***Leveled Readers.***	**Vocabulary:** Put students into small groups, and have them find the selection vocabulary words in the story. Have them list the vocabulary strategy that can be used to determine the words' meanings. **Comprehension:** Have students write a summary of "Two Days in May." **Fluency:** Have students write answers to comprehension questions from ***Leveled Readers.***	**Vocabulary:** Have students review vocabulary using the ***English Learner Support Guide.*** **Comprehension:** Have students write a summary of "Two Days in May." Encourage students to include illustrations if they have trouble expressing themselves. **Fluency:** Put students in groups to discuss a book or story they are reading independently.	**Vocabulary:** Have students add interesting words from the story to their Writer's Notebooks for future use. **Comprehension:** Use online and print resources to research the effects that humans have on animals' habitats. **Fluency:** Have students create a play based on the story to use with Reader's Theater.
Language Arts	**Writing:** Have students share their stories with the class. **Spelling:** Have students write two pairs of homophones on a piece of paper.	**Writing:** Have students publish their stories using multimedia. **Spelling:** Have students work in pairs to review the /ī/ sound spellings in this lesson.	**Writing:** Have students publish their stories using multimedia. **Spelling:** Have students copy the list of spelling words onto a piece of paper, then circle the homophones, underline the consonant blends, and draw a box around the words with /ī/ sound spellings.	**Writing:** Have students publish their stories using multimedia and present them to the class. **Spelling:** Have students think of as many words as they can with constant blends and write a list of these words.

Resources for

Differentiating Instruction 

Leveled Readers

Approaching Level

On Level

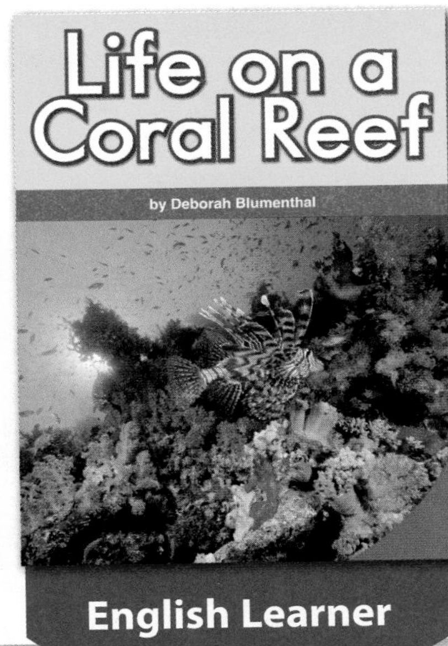

English Learner

Above Level

Additional Skills Practice

Approaching Level

Reteach

- The /ī/, /ō/, and /ū/ Sounds and Consonant Blends, p. 51
- Homophones, p. 52
- Vocabulary, p. 53
- Spelling, p. 54
- Nouns and Replacement Nouns, p. 55

On Level

Skills Practice 1

- The /ī/, /ō/, and /ū/ Sounds and Consonant Blends, pp. 129–130
- Homophones, pp. 131–132
- Vocabulary, pp. 133–134
- Writing a Realistic Story, pp. 137–138
- Spelling, pp. 139–140
- Nouns and Replacement Nouns, pp. 141–142

English Learner

English Learner Support Activities

English Learner Support Activities, Unit 2, Lesson 4

Above Level

Challenge Activities

- The /ī/, /ō/, and /ū/ Sounds and Consonant Blends, p. 46
- Homophones, p. 47
- Vocabulary, p. 48
- Spelling, p. 49
- Nouns and Replacement Nouns, p. 50

Lesson 4 Overview

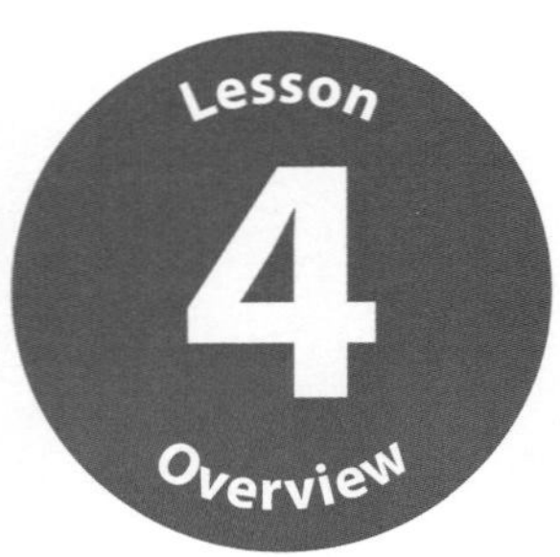

Additional Resources for Differentiating Instruction

RtI

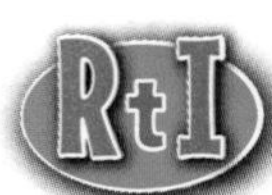

Workshop Kits

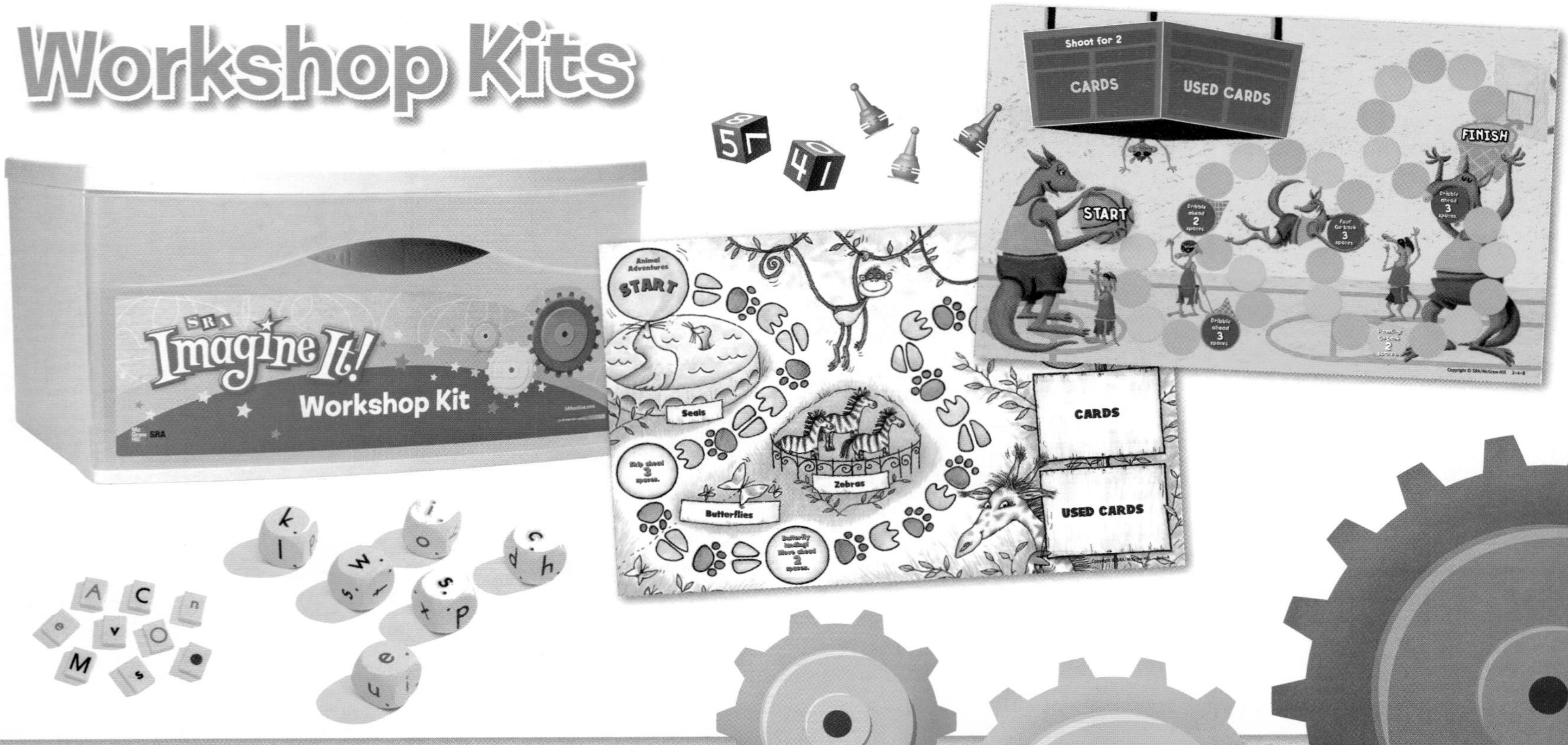

Technology

The following electronic resources are available for students:

- ***eStudent Reader***
- ***eDecodables***
- ***eSkills***
- ***eGames***
- ***Listening Library CD***

Electronic resources for the teacher include:

- ***ePlanner***
- ***eTeacher's Edition***
- ***eAssess***
- ***ePresentation***

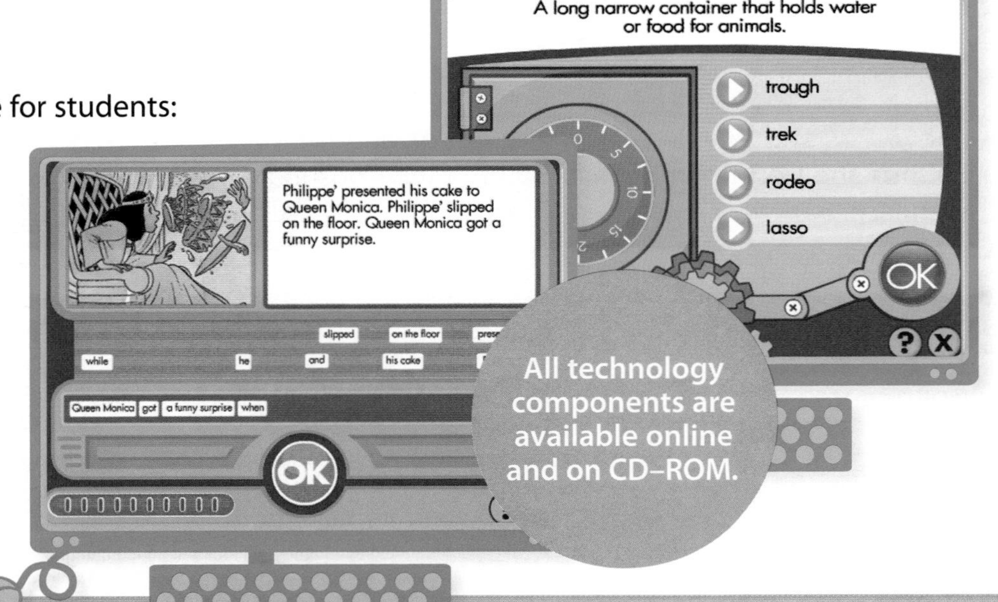

English Learner

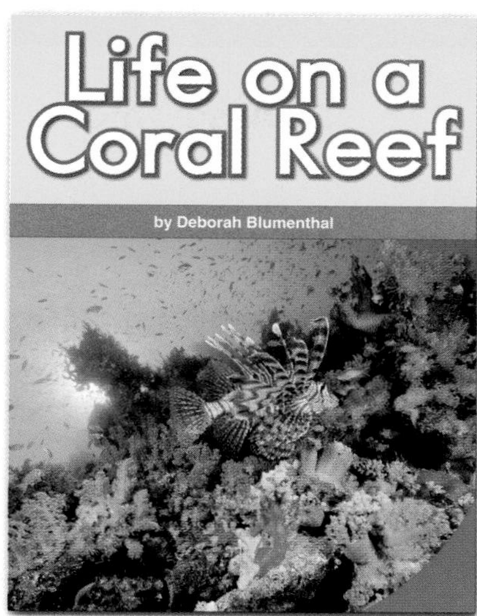

Leveled Reader

English Learner Support Activities, Lesson 4

Listening Library Unit 2

English Learner Support Guide, Lesson 4

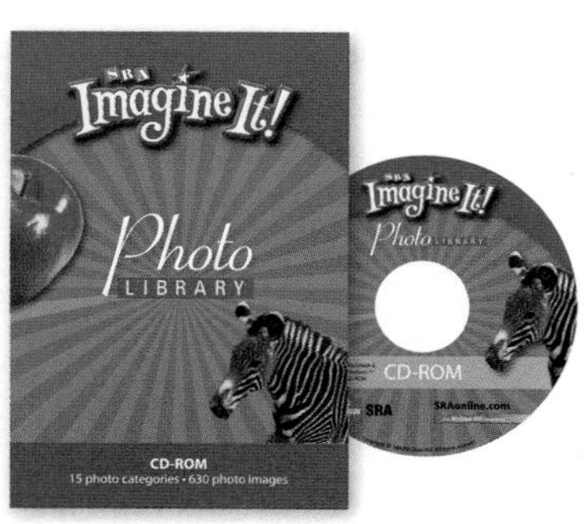

Photo Library

Approaching Level

Intervention

Intervention Workbook

Intervention Guide

Lesson 4 Overview

Lesson Assessment

Monitor Progress to Differentiate Instruction

Comprehension Strategies Rubrics

Use the Comprehension Strategies Rubrics to determine whether a student is using the strategies.

- Asking Questions, p. T280
- Making Connections, p. T281
- Summarizing, p. T281

Inquiry Rubrics

Use the Inquiry Rubrics to assess a student's performance throughout the stages of the investigation for each unit. In addition, at the end of the unit you can use the rubrics to assess the groups' collaborative work as well as an individual's participation in that group.

- Collecting Information, p. T329

Writing Rubrics

Use the Writing Rubrics in the Level Appendix to evaluate each student's realistic story.

- Genre
- Writing Process
- Writing Traits

Lesson Assessments

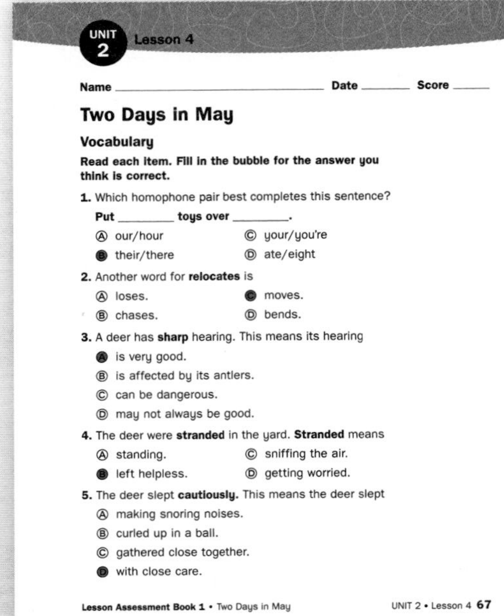

UNIT 2 Lesson 4

Name ______________________ Date ________ Score ________

Two Days in May

Vocabulary

Read each item. Fill in the bubble for the answer you think is correct.

1. Which homophone pair best completes this sentence?
   Put ________ toys over ________.
   - Ⓐ our/hour
   - ● their/there
   - Ⓒ your/you're
   - Ⓓ ate/eight
2. Another word for **relocates** is
   - Ⓐ loses.
   - Ⓑ chases.
   - ● moves.
   - Ⓓ bends.
3. A deer has **sharp** hearing. This means its hearing
   - ● is very good.
   - Ⓑ is affected by its antlers.
   - Ⓒ can be dangerous.
   - Ⓓ may not always be good.
4. The deer were **stranded** in the yard. **Stranded** means
   - Ⓐ standing.
   - ● left helpless.
   - Ⓒ sniffing the air.
   - Ⓓ getting worried.
5. The deer slept **cautiously.** This means the deer slept
   - Ⓐ making snoring noises.
   - Ⓑ curled up in a ball.
   - Ⓒ gathered close together.
   - ● with close care.

Lesson Assessment Book 1 • Two Days in May UNIT 2 • Lesson 4 67

Lesson Assessment Book 1, p. 67

UNIT 2 Lesson 4

Two Days in May (continued)

Comprehension

Read the following questions carefully. Then completely fill in the bubble of each correct answer. You may look back at the selection to find the answer to each of the questions.

1. The deer could not stay in the city. Why not?
   - Ⓐ There was not enough food.
   - ● The city was not a safe place.
   - Ⓒ People wanted them for pets.
   - Ⓓ It was too noisy in the city.
2. Why do deer sometimes wander into cities?
   - Ⓐ The new roads make it easy.
   - Ⓑ The cities seem interesting.
   - ● The forests are disappearing.
   - Ⓓ The city people are nice to them.

68 UNIT 2 • Lesson 4 Two Days in May • Lesson Assessment Book 1

Lesson Assessment Book 1, p. 68

Use these summative assessments along with your informal observations to assess student mastery.

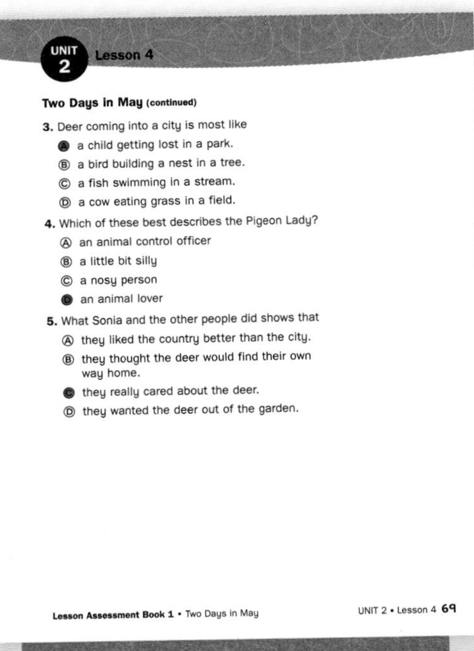

UNIT 2 Lesson 4

Two Days in May (continued)

3. Deer coming into a city is most like
   - ● a child getting lost in a park.
   - Ⓑ a bird building a nest in a tree.
   - Ⓒ a fish swimming in a stream.
   - Ⓓ a cow eating grass in a field.
4. Which of these best describes the Pigeon Lady?
   - Ⓐ an animal control officer
   - Ⓑ a little bit silly
   - Ⓒ a nosy person
   - ● an animal lover
5. What Sonia and the other people did shows that
   - Ⓐ they liked the country better than the city.
   - Ⓑ they thought the deer would find their own way home.
   - ● they really cared about the deer.
   - Ⓓ they wanted the deer out of the garden.

Lesson Assessment Book 1 • Two Days in May   UNIT 2 • Lesson 4 69

Lesson Assessment Book 1, p. 69

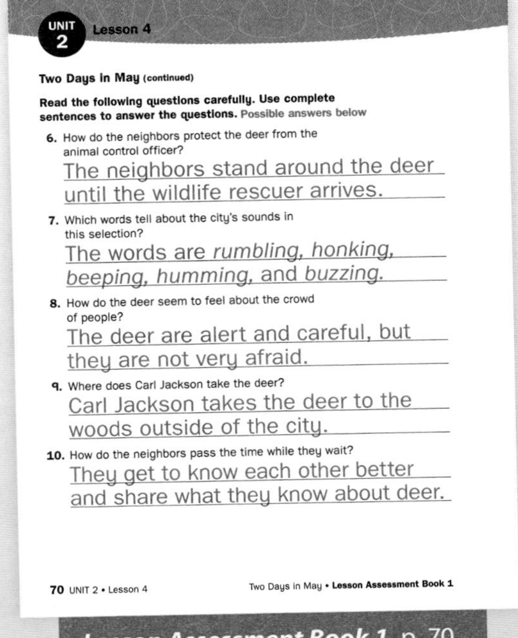

UNIT 2 Lesson 4

Two Days in May (continued)

Read the following questions carefully. Use complete sentences to answer the questions. Possible answers below

6. How do the neighbors protect the deer from the animal control officer?
   The neighbors stand around the deer until the wildlife rescuer arrives.
7. Which words tell about the city's sounds in this selection?
   The words are *rumbling, honking, beeping, humming,* and *buzzing.*
8. How do the deer seem to feel about the crowd of people?
   The deer are alert and careful, but they are not very afraid.
9. Where does Carl Jackson take the deer?
   Carl Jackson takes the deer to the woods outside of the city.
10. How do the neighbors pass the time while they wait?
    They get to know each other better and share what they know about deer.

70 UNIT 2 • Lesson 4   Two Days in May • Lesson Assessment Book 1

Lesson Assessment Book 1, p. 70

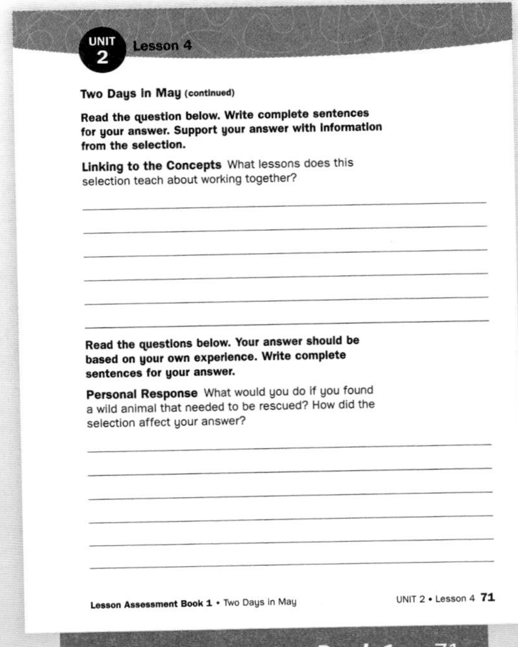

UNIT 2 Lesson 4

Two Days in May (continued)

Read the question below. Write complete sentences for your answer. Support your answer with information from the selection.

Linking to the Concepts What lessons does this selection teach about working together?

Read the questions below. Your answer should be based on your own experience. Write complete sentences for your answer.

Personal Response What would you do if you found a wild animal that needed to be rescued? How did the selection affect your answer?

Lesson Assessment Book 1 • Two Days in May   UNIT 2 • Lesson 4 71

Lesson Assessment Book 1, p. 71

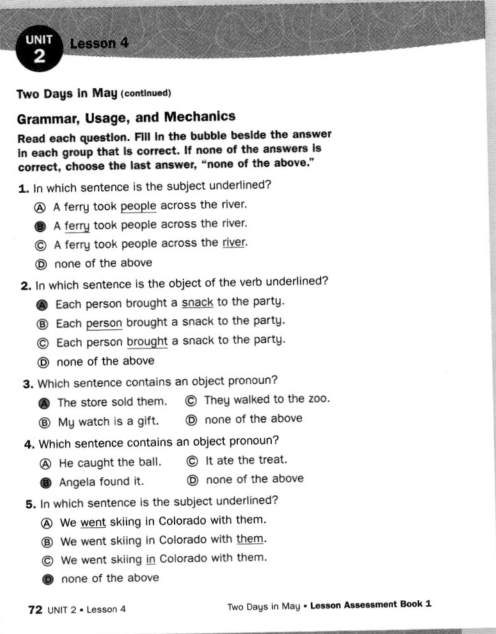

UNIT 2 Lesson 4

Two Days in May (continued)

Grammar, Usage, and Mechanics

Read each question. Fill in the bubble beside the answer in each group that is correct. If none of the answers is correct, choose the last answer, "none of the above."

1. In which sentence is the subject underlined?
   - Ⓐ A ferry took <u>people</u> across the river.
   - ● A <u>ferry</u> took people across the river.
   - Ⓒ A ferry took people across the <u>river</u>.
   - Ⓓ none of the above
2. In which sentence is the object of the verb underlined?
   - ● Each person brought a <u>snack</u> to the party.
   - Ⓑ Each <u>person</u> brought a snack to the party.
   - Ⓒ Each person <u>brought</u> a snack to the party.
   - Ⓓ none of the above
3. Which sentence contains an object pronoun?
   - ● The store sold them.
   - Ⓒ They walked to the zoo.
   - Ⓑ My watch is a gift.
   - Ⓓ none of the above
4. Which sentence contains an object pronoun?
   - Ⓐ He caught the ball.
   - Ⓒ It ate the treat.
   - ● Angela found it.
   - Ⓓ none of the above
5. In which sentence is the subject underlined?
   - Ⓐ We <u>went</u> skiing in Colorado with them.
   - Ⓑ We went skiing in Colorado with <u>them</u>.
   - Ⓒ We went skiing <u>in</u> Colorado with them.
   - ● none of the above

72 UNIT 2 • Lesson 4   Two Days in May • Lesson Assessment Book 1

Lesson Assessment Book 1, p. 72

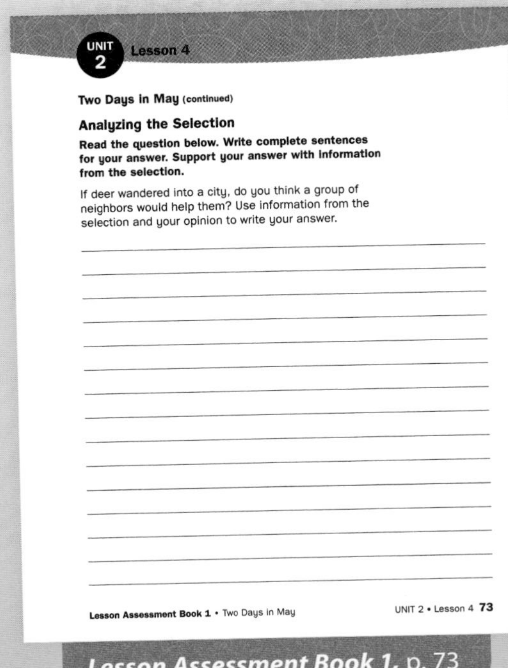

UNIT 2 Lesson 4

Two Days in May (continued)

Analyzing the Selection

Read the question below. Write complete sentences for your answer. Support your answer with information from the selection.

If deer wandered into a city, do you think a group of neighbors would help them? Use information from the selection and your opinion to write your answer.

Lesson Assessment Book 1 • Two Days in May   UNIT 2 • Lesson 4 73

Lesson Assessment Book 1, p. 73

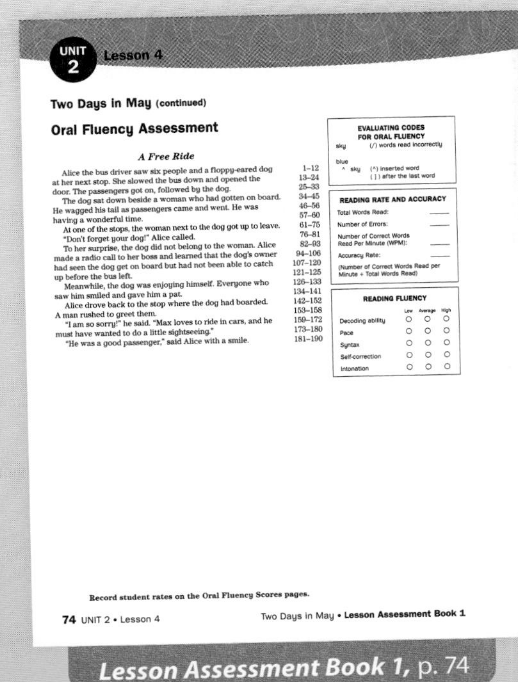

UNIT 2 Lesson 4

Two Days in May (continued)

Oral Fluency Assessment

A Free Ride

Alice the bus driver saw six people and a floppy-eared dog 1–12
at her next stop. She slowed the bus down and opened the 13–24
door. The passengers got on, followed by the dog. 25–33
The dog sat down beside a woman who had gotten on board. 34–45
He wagged his tail as passengers came and went. He was 46–56
having a wonderful time. 57–60
At one of the stops, the woman next to the dog got up to leave. 61–75
"Don't forget your dog!" Alice called. 76–81
To her surprise, the dog did not belong to the woman. Alice 82–93
made a radio call to her boss and learned that the dog's owner 94–106
had seen the dog get on board but had not been able to catch 107–120
up before the bus left. 121–125
Meanwhile, the dog was enjoying himself. Everyone who 126–133
saw him smiled and gave him a pat. 134–141
Alice drove back to the stop where the dog had boarded. 142–152
A man rushed to greet them. 153–158
"I am so sorry!" he said. "Max loves to ride in cars, and he 159–172
must have wanted to do a little sightseeing." 173–180
"He was a good passenger," said Alice with a smile. 181–190

EVALUATING CODES FOR ORAL FLUENCY

sky (/) words read incorrectly

blue ^ sky (^) inserted word

( ]) after the last word

READING RATE AND ACCURACY

Total Words Read: ____

Number of Errors: ____

Number of Correct Words Read Per Minute (WPM): ____

Accuracy Rate: ____

(Number of Correct Words Read per Minute ÷ Total Words Read)

READING FLUENCY

	Low	Average	High
Decoding ability	○	○	○
Pace	○	○	○
Syntax	○	○	○
Self-correction	○	○	○
Intonation	○	○	○

Record student rates on the Oral Fluency Scores pages.

74 UNIT 2 • Lesson 4   Two Days in May • Lesson Assessment Book 1

Lesson Assessment Book 1, p. 74

Preparing to Read

OBJECTIVES

Students will

- review /ī/ spelled _igh, _y, and _ie; /ō/ spelled _ow and oa_; and /ū/ spelled _ew and _ue.
- review consonant blends at the beginning or end or words.
- learn new high-frequency words.
- build fluency.

MATERIALS

- ***Transparency*** 59
- ***Sound/Spelling Cards*** 29–31
- Routines 3, 4, 5, 6, 9
- ***Skills Practice 1,*** pp. 129–130

Daily Oral Practice

The deer were grazing in the woods. The mother, father, and baby deer were eating the grass and leaves around them. Their fur shone in the sun rays as they bounded off to find a new grazing spot.

- Write the daily news on the board or on chart paper. Then have students read the daily news in unison to practice fluency.
- As a word structure review from Lesson 3, ask a volunteer to identify any homographs in the message. *leaves, spot*

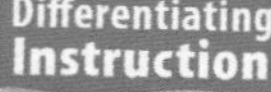

English Learner

IF . . . students have difficulty understanding the verb tenses used in the daily news, **THEN . . .** restate the paragraph using simple past tense. Examples: *The deer* grazed *in the woods. The mother, father and baby deer* ate *the grass and leaves.*

Phonics and Fluency

Review: /ī/ spelled _igh, _y, and _ie; /ō/ spelled _ow and oa_; /ū/ spelled _ew and _ue; consonant blends

Blending

✦ Write the following blending lines and sentences on the board or use ***Transparency*** 59. Show students one line at a time as you go through them by covering up the others. The boldface words are from "Two Days in May." The underlined words are new high-frequency words.

Line 1	highways	moonlight	identify	replies
Line 2	aglow	window	throat	coastline
Line 3	**few**	pewter	**rescuer**	**continued**
Line 4	streets	slept	**except**	**protest**

Sentence 1: The glowing bright light <u>almost</u> made my <u>eyes</u> water.

Sentence 2: They rescued a few sheep and <u>part</u> of the lost goat herd.

✦ Review ***Sound/Spelling Cards*** 29–31 with students. Using Routine 3, follow the whole-word blending process to have students blend the words in Lines 1–4.

✦ Follow Routine 4, the blending sentences process, to have students blend Sentences 1–2.

Line 1 /ī/ spelled *_igh, _y,* and *_ie*

As you point to each word in Line 1, have students read it aloud. Then ask students to identify /ī/ spelled *_igh, _y,* or *_ie* in each word. */ī/ spelled* _igh *in* highways, moonlight; */ī/ spelled* _y *in* identify; */ī/ spelled* _ie *in* replies

Line 2 /ō/ spelled *_ow* and *oa_*

Have students read the words in Line 2 in unison as you point to them. Then ask students to identify /ō/ spelled *_ow* or *oa_* in each word. */ō/ spelled* _ow *in* aglow, window; */ō/ spelled* oa_ *in* throat, coastline

Sound/Spelling Cards
29, 30, and 31

Teacher Tip

SYLLABICATION To help students blend words and build fluency, demonstrate syllabication using the decodable, multisyllabic words in the word lines.

high • ways	a • glow	res • cu • er
moon • light	win • dow	con • tin • ued
i • den • ti • fy	coast • line	ex • cept
re • plies	pew • ter	pro • test

✦ Use ***Transparency*** 59 with today's blending lines and sentences. Show students the lines one at a time as you go through them by covering up the other lines.

Line 3 **/ū/ spelled _*ew* and _*ue***

As you point to each word in Line 3, have students read it in unison. Then ask students to identify /ū/ spelled _*ew* or _*ue in* each word. */ū/ spelled* _ew *in* few *and* pewter; */ū/ spelled* _ue *in* rescuer *and* continued

Line 4 **Consonant Blends**

Ask students what consonant blends are. If necessary, remind them that consonant blends are strings of consonants that work together to make a sound. Each consonant in a consonant blend will also contribute its own sound to the blend as the *p* and *l* do in *play*. Have students read the words in Line 4 in unison. Ask students to identify any consonant blends at the beginning or end of the words. str *and* ts *in* streets; sl *and* pt *in* slept, pt *in* except, pr *and* st *in* protest

Sentences 1–2

Have students point to and read the new high-frequency words in Sentences 1–2. *almost, eyes, part* Ask students to identify words in the sentences with /ī/ spelled _*igh* or _*y*, /ō/ spelled _*ow* or *oa*_, or /ū/ spelled _*ew* or _*ue*. */ī/ spelled* _igh *in* bright, light; */ī/ spelled* _y *in* my; */ō/ spelled* _ow *in* glowing *and* oa_ *in* goat; */ū/ spelled* _ew *in* few *and* _ue *in* rescued. Ask students to identify any consonant blends in the sentences. gl *in* glowing; br *in* bright; st *in* almost, lost; rt *in* part; rd *in* herd Have students read the sentences in unison to practice fluency.

Decodable Stories, Book 3, Story 20

Decodable Stories

Building Fluency

Decodable Stories are used to help develop fluency for students who need extra practice. They are also used to practice the phonics and fluency elements being reviewed. Using Routine 9, reading a ***Decodable Story,*** have students who need additional support read ***Decodable Stories, Book 3,*** Story 20, "Strange Stuff."

ROUTINE 5 ROUTINE 6

Syllabication

✦ To help students recognize common syllable patterns, use Routine 5 for closed syllables and Routine 6 for open syllables to separate the syllables in the multisyllabic words in the word lines. Explain that the syllable routines offer general rules that don't apply to all words.

✦ Using Routine 5, have students identify the vowel spellings in *moonlight*, *window*, and *except*. Then have them identify the consonants spellings between the two vowels. Remind students that the syllables are usually divided between the consonants in words with the v-c-c-v spelling pattern, as in *moon • light*. Explain that syllables that end in consonant sounds usually have short vowels and are closed. Have students read *moonlight, window,* and *except* aloud, clapping for each syllable. Then have students identify the closed syllables in *rescuer* and *continued* and clap the three syllables as they read these words.

✦ Using Routine 6, have students identify the vowel spellings in *replies, pewter,* and *protest*. Then have students identify the consonant spellings between the two vowels. Remind students that the syllables are usually divided before the consonant in words with the v-c-v spelling pattern, as in *re • plies*. Remind students that syllables that end with vowels are usually open syllables with long vowels. Have students read *replies, pewter,* and *protest* aloud, clapping for each syllable. Then have students identify the open syllables at the end of *identify, aglow,* and *window*.

✦ Help students start the phonics workbook activities in ***Skills Practice 1,*** pages 129–130. Read the Focus box with them and help them with the first few questions.

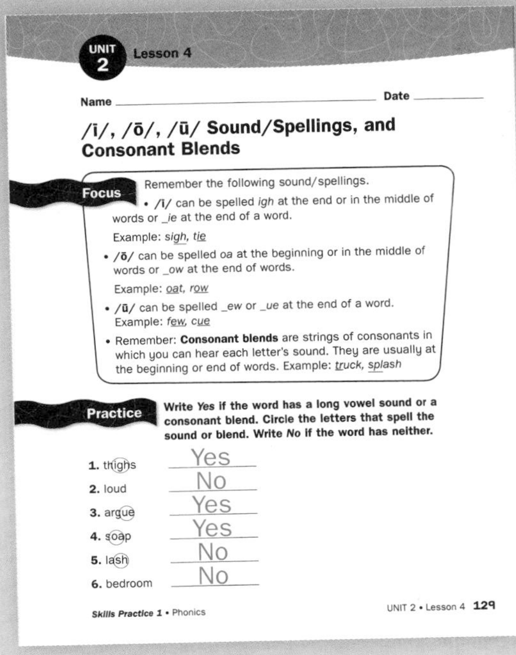

UNIT 2 Lesson 4

Name ______ Date ______

/ī/, /ō/, /ū/ Sound/Spellings, and Consonant Blends

Focus Remember the following sound/spellings.

- /ī/ can be spelled *igh* at the end or in the middle of words or *_ie* at the end of a word. Example: *sigh, tie*
- /ō/ can be spelled *oa* at the beginning or in the middle of words or *_ow* at the end of words. Example: *oat, row*
- /ū/ can be spelled *_ew* or *_ue* at the end of a word. Example: *few, cue*
- Remember: **Consonant blends** are strings of consonants in which you can hear each letter's sound. They are usually at the beginning or end of words. Example: *truck, splash*

Practice **Write *Yes* if the word has a long vowel sound or a consonant blend. Circle the letters that spell the sound or blend. Write *No* if the word has neither.**

1. thighs Yes
2. loud No
3. argue Yes
4. soap Yes
5. lash No
6. bedroom No

Skills Practice 1 • Phonics UNIT 2 • Lesson 4 129

Skills Practice 1, pp. 129–130

Monitor Progress to Differentiate Instruction **Formal Assessment**

Phonics and Fluency During the blending activity, note how quickly students are reading the words.

APPROACHING LEVEL	**IF . . .** students need practice with today's sound/spellings for /ī/, /ō/, or /ū/,	**THEN . . .** work with them on the phonics activities on ***Reteach*** page 51 during Workshop.
	IF . . . students need extra practice with today's sound/spellings for /ī/, /ō/, or /ū/,	**THEN . . .** work with them on the phonics activities for Unit 2 Lesson 4 in the ***Intervention Guide*** during Workshop.
ON LEVEL	**IF . . .** students understand today's sound/spellings for /ī/, /ō/, and /ū/,	**THEN . . .** have them make lists of words to add to the word lines during Workshop.
ABOVE LEVEL	**IF . . .** students are ready for a challenge with today's sound/spellings for /ī/, /ō/, and /ū/,	**THEN . . .** have them complete the phonics activities on ***Challenge Activities*** page 46 during Workshop.

Reading and Responding

OBJECTIVES

Students will

- activate prior knowledge to prepare to read the story.
- learn selection vocabulary.
- review the elements of realistic fiction.
- use the comprehension strategies Asking Questions, Making Connections, and Summarizing.
- investigate the theme Animals and Their Habitats using the Inquiry Process.

MATERIALS

- Routines 11, 12, 14
- ***Transparencies*** 5, 60
- ***Home Connection,*** pp. 21–22
- ***Student Reader,*** Book 1, pp. 194–205
- ***Skills Practice 1,*** pp. 135–136

Build Background

Activate Prior Knowledge

- Introduce "Two Days in May" by first determining students' prior knowledge. Ask them the following questions:
  - Have you ever seen deer up close?
  - Have you ever seen other types of large wildlife?
- Ask students how disappearing natural habitats and expanding cities might be affecting wildlife.
- Discuss how people can help wild animals that are stranded in urban places by taking the animals to wildlife rehabilitation centers or calling local humane agencies.

Background Information

The following information might help students understand the story they are about to read:

- Tell students that the story they will be reading is a fictionalized account of a true story. This means the basic events in the story are true, but the characters, names, and dialogue have been fictionalized by the writer. This is why the story is considered fiction.
- Explain to students that urban and suburban development increases every year. As development increases, wildlife habitats are impacted. Scientists, developers, landowners, businesses, and conservationists debate about the effects of development on wildlife and what to do about it.
- The discussion of development versus conservation is currently an important and much debated subject in this country, and the debate will continue as the rate of development continues to increase.

Preview and Prepare 

ROUTINE 12

Browse

Have students read the title, and take a few minutes to browse the first few pages of the story. Have students use features such as the story's title and illustrations to predict what this story might have to do with animals and their habitats.

Follow Routine 12, the clues, problems, and wonderings routine, to help students identify what they know before reading, what problems they may encounter while reading, and what their purposes are for reading. Students will chart these on a transparency.

Tell students to look for interesting words when reading. These words could be fun words to read, or words that are unfamiliar to them. Students may be familiar with the story but unfamiliar with some of the vocabulary. Some of the character names may also be unfamiliar; you may want to preview some of the names before reading the story.

Display ***Transparency*** 5 and model browsing for students. For example, a "Clue" to the story might be that deer are grazing in a city garden. Under "Problems," point out *courtyard* as an unfamiliar word. Write *How did the deer get there?* under "Wonderings." Record students' observations on the transparency as they browse the story.

Set Purposes

Encourage students to set their own purposes for reading this story. Remind students that readers can set purposes for reading by picking up clues from the title, illustrations, and genre of the text they are going to read. As students read, have them think about questions concerning wildlife living in the city that this story might help to answer.

Where do different animals live?

Before reading the story, read the Big Idea question. Tell students to keep this question in mind as they read the story.

Clues	Problems	Wonderings
The deer are grazing in a city garden.	courtyard	How did the deer get there?

Transparency 5

Give each student a copy of ***Home Connection*** page 21. The same information is also available in Spanish on ***Home Connection*** page 22. Encourage students to discuss "Two Days in May" with their families and complete the activity provided.

Selection Vocabulary

relocates (rē • lō′ • kāts) *v.* a form of the verb **relocate:** to move to a new place (page 204)

stranded (strand′ • əd) *v.* a form of the verb **strand:** to leave in a helpless position (page 204)

exclaimed (eks • klāmd′) past tense of **exclaim:** to speak out (page 205)

sharp (sharp) *adj.* alert (page 205)

detect (də • tekt′) *v.* to find out (page 205)

cautiously (kosh′ • əs • lē′) *adv.* with close care (page 205)

appreciate (əp • prē′ • shē • āt′) *v.* to understand the value of (page 205)

extended (eks • tend′ • əd) *v.* past tense of **extend:** to reach out (page 210)

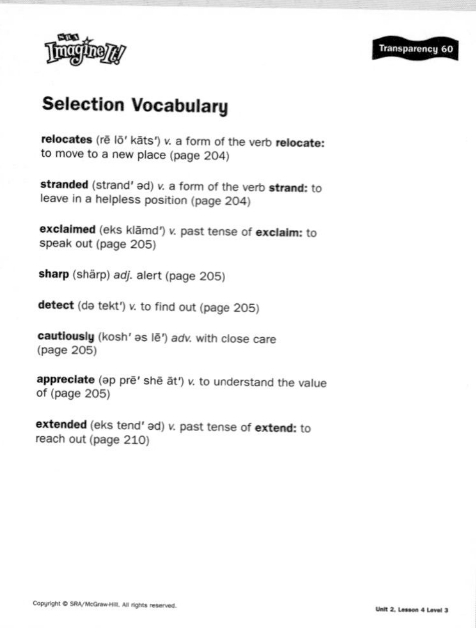
Imagine It! Transparency 60

Selection Vocabulary

relocates (rē lō′ kāts′) *v.* a form of the verb **relocate:** to move to a new place (page 204)

stranded (strand′ əd) *v.* a form of the verb **strand:** to leave in a helpless position (page 204)

exclaimed (eks klāmd′) *v.* past tense of **exclaim:** to speak out (page 205)

sharp (shärp) *adj.* alert (page 205)

detect (də tekt′) *v.* to find out (page 205)

cautiously (kosh′ əs lē′) *adv.* with close care (page 205)

appreciate (əp prē′ shē āt′) *v.* to understand the value of (page 205)

extended (eks tend′ əd) *v.* past tense of **extend:** to reach out (page 210)

Copyright © SRA/McGraw-Hill. All rights reserved. Unit 2, Lesson 4 Level 3

Transparency 60

Building Vocabulary

Using Routine 11, the selection vocabulary process, have students read aloud the Vocabulary Warm-Up on ***Student Reader,*** Book 1 pages 194–195. As students read, have them stop to blend any difficult or unfamiliar words. Provide students with the pronunciations of words that are not decodable or that they cannot read automatically or fluently.

Guided Vocabulary Practice

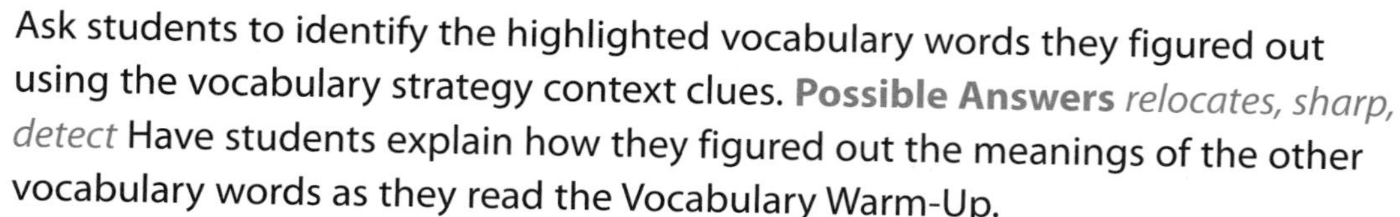

Ask students to identify the highlighted vocabulary words they figured out using the vocabulary strategy context clues. **Possible Answers** *relocates, sharp, detect* Have students explain how they figured out the meanings of the other vocabulary words as they read the Vocabulary Warm-Up.

Display ***Transparency*** 60, and have students read the words and definitions. Return to the Vocabulary Warm-Up, and read the sentences containing the vocabulary words with students. Then, if necessary, provide a brief in-context explanation of each word.

Writer's Notebook

Have students copy the selection vocabulary and concept vocabulary words and definitions into the vocabulary section of their Writer's Notebooks. They can also include other words they think of that relate to the theme.

Read the story to find the meanings of these words, which are also in "Two Days in May":

- relocates
- cautiously
- appreciate
- sharp
- stranded
- detect
- exclaimed
- extended

Vocabulary Strategy

Context Clues are hints in the text. They help you find the meanings of words. Use context clues to find the meaning of *exclaimed.*

Vocabulary Warm-Up

Tess clumped into the kitchen in sturdy boots. To her intelligent dog, Zip, the boots announced that Tess was going hiking. He wagged his tail eagerly. "Not today, boy," said Tess. "I'm going solo."

Tess had another roommate, Gwen. The two of them had adopted Zip from a group that relocates unwanted pets. He had grown attached to Tess quickly. "We'll take a walk later," Tess promised as she left.

Fog blurred the morning air. Cautiously, Tess made her way to the park. She latched her bike to a stand and headed for the hiking trails.

Tess liked to be out by herself. Today, however, she could appreciate the value of a hiking buddy. An extra set of sharp eyes might help in the fog.

Tess set off on a trail she knew well. Before long, however, she came to a place she did not recognize. As Tess turned to look around, her foot slipped into a hole. Tess's ankle twisted, and she fell to the ground. Now Tess was not only lost, but also badly hurt. She was stranded in the woods.

When Tess did not return, Gwen became worried. She put Zip in the car and drove to the park, where she saw Tess's bike still in the stand. Gwen let Zip out and said, "Go on, Zip! Find Tess!" She knew that the dog could detect Tess's scent.

Soon, Zip made his way to Tess. "Zip!" she exclaimed. "Thank you for finding me!" Tess extended her arms and hugged her furry friend.

GAME

Charades

Use the vocabulary words to play a game of charades with classmates. Choose one of the words to act out. The first person to correctly identify the word and explain its meaning will take the next turn as actor.

Concept Vocabulary

The concept word for this lesson is ***protect.*** To **protect** means "to keep something or someone safe." Talk about some ways wild animals protect themselves. Also discuss ways that people help protect wild animals.

194 195

Use the vocabulary words on ***Transparency*** 60 to create fill-in-the-blank sentences. Have students fill in the appropriate vocabulary words. For example, "The animal rights group ________ animals that wander into the city." *relocates*

Discuss the concept vocabulary word *protect* with students. Ask students how they think the word *protect* relates to the theme Animals and Their Habitats. As students read the selections in this unit, encourage them to think about other words that relate to the theme. Students can record these words in the vocabulary section of their Writer's Notebooks.

GAME

Have students play the Charades game during Small-Group Time.

Reading the Selection

Genre Realistic Fiction

Have students identify the genre of "Two Days in May." *realistic fiction* If necessary, tell students of the elements of realistic fiction:

- The characters or animals behave as people or animals do in real life.
- The setting of the story is a real place or could be a real place.
- The events in the story could happen in real life.

Silent Reading

This realistic fiction story lends itself to silent reading because of the interesting characters and the unusual problems they face. You may want to stop periodically or wait until students have finished the story to discuss the reading strategies. Have students practice reading on their own for at least 10 minutes at a time. Preview the strategies below, and have students use the strategies to understand the story. For example, have them ask questions about the story as they read. Also have students make connections to the story's plot, setting, and characters. Encourage students to occasionally stop to summarize what they have read. As they become better readers, students will read silently with increasing ease over longer periods of time.

Comprehension Strategies

Model the use of the following comprehension strategies during the first reading of "Two Days in May."

- Asking Questions
- Making Connections
- Summarizing

Comprehension Strategies Rubrics

Use the Informal Comprehension Strategies Rubrics to determine whether a student is using any of the strategies listed below. Note the strategies a student is using, instead of the degree to which a student might be using any particular strategy. In addition, encourage the student to tell of any strategies other than the ones being taught that he or she is using.

Asking Questions

- The student stops to ask questions—any question.
- The student asks questions directly related to the text.
- The student asks *who, what, why, when, where,* or *how* questions as opposed to *yes* or *no* questions.
- The student asks questions that help clarify information in the text.

Concept/Question Board

As students read "Two Days in May," encourage them to post questions, answers, comments, or other items related to the theme Animals and Their Habitats on the **Concept/Question Board.**

Monitor Progress
Formal Assessment

Comprehension Observation Log Observe individual students as they read, and use the Comprehension Observation Log, located in ***Lesson Assessment Book 1,*** to record anecdotal information about each student's strengths and weaknesses.

Making Connections

- The student makes connections between prior knowledge and information in the text.
- The student makes connections between or relates personal experience to what is read in the text (text-to-self connections).
- The student makes connections across or relates information from different selections (text-to-text connections).
- The student makes connections or relates information between what is happening in the text to what is happening in the world today (text-to-world connections).

Summarizing

- The student retells information from the story.
- The student paraphrases or puts the main ideas and details in his or her own words.
- The student gives a summary that includes only the important or main ideas.
- The student recognizes when the same ideas are included more than once in a summary and deletes them.

Monitor Progress to Differentiate Instruction

Formal Assessment 

Comprehension Strategy Note students' understanding of the comprehension strategy Making Connections as they read.

APPROACHING LEVEL

IF . . .	THEN . . .
IF . . . students are having difficulty making connections as they read,	THEN . . . demonstrate a real life example, such as how you use personal experience to connect to a story.

ON LEVEL

IF . . .	THEN . . .
IF . . . students are gaining an understanding of making connections as they read,	THEN . . . have them make connections to other selections you are reading in class.

ABOVE LEVEL

IF . . .	THEN . . .
IF . . . students are demonstrating an understanding of making connections as they read,	THEN . . . have them write a journal entry about how they are making connections to this selection.

Technology

eSTUDENT READER Students can access ***SRA Imagine It! Student Reader*** electronically by using the ***eStudent Reader*** online or on CD-ROM.

Reading and Responding

Comprehension Skills

Reread "Two Days in May" using the following comprehension skill:

- Cause and Effect

Reading with a Writer's Eye

When rereading "Two Days in May," explain the following literary elements:

- Characterization
- Plot

Focus Questions

Have students read aloud the Focus Questions on page 196. Encourage students to think about the Focus Questions as they read "Two Days in May."

DECODING Make sure students are recognizing and using word structure and basic syllabication rules to help decode unfamiliar words as they read.

Reading Recommendation

Silent Reading

Use Routine 14, the reading the selection routine, as you read the story. While reading, model strategies and stop to ask and answer questions. Point out how the pictures reflect the story. Share the images that pop up in your mind as you read and how points in the reading relate to ideas you already know. Reread the text by applying comprehension skills. After reading, be sure to discuss the story using the "handing-off" procedure and have students discuss new information that they have learned.

This story is ideal for silent reading because of the interesting conversational characters, the beautiful descriptions, and the intriguing plot.

Genre

Realistic Fiction involves stories about people and events that are true to life and that could really happen.

Comprehension Strategy

Making Connections As you read, make connections between what you already know about habitats and what you are reading.

Two Days in May

by Harriet Peck Taylor
illustrated by Leyla Torres

Focus Questions

How do you think deer find their way into the city? What can be done to protect the deer in the city?

196 197

Students will read the story twice over a four-day period.

Day 1 **SILENT READ** Have students read the first half of the story. Remind them to use the comprehension strategies.

Day 2 **SILENT READ** Have students finish reading the story. Have them continue to use the comprehension strategies.

Day 3 **SILENT READ** Have students reread the first half of the story silently. Have students focus on the comprehension skill and Reading with a Writer's Eye.

Day 4 **SILENT READ** Have students finish rereading the story.

Technology

Have students listen to "Two Days in May" on the ***Listening Library CD.*** After students have listened, have them discuss what other things, such as poetry, songs, or nonfiction, they prefer to listen to on the radio or on CDs.

Day 1

Reading and Responding

Early one Saturday morning in May, I went to our fire escape window and rubbed the sleep from my eyes. I looked down at the small garden I had planted behind our apartment building. Five animals were grazing on the new lettuce in my garden! 1

"Mama! Mama!" I called. "Come see what's in our yard!"

Mama hurried over to the window and gasped. "Sonia, those animals are deer, but how did they get here?" she asked. "I'll run and tell Mr. Donovan."

198

By the time Papa and I got out to the courtyard, a small crowd was gathering.

"Papa, why are there deer in the city?" I asked.

"The deer may have come all this way looking for food. They probably smelled your garden," he explained. 2

I thought I had never seen such an amazing sight. Their fur was a golden brown, and they balanced on tiny hooves. They had nervous tails, and eyes that were big and black and gentle.

Down the block a train rumbled by, but here life seemed to stand still. Pigeons and squirrels were almost the only birds or animals we ever saw in our neighborhood.

199

Phonics and Fluency

One of the focuses of this lesson is /ī/ spelled *igh*, *_y*, and *_ie*. Words with these spellings will be found in boxes similar to this one throughout the story.

/ī/ spelled *igh*, *_y*, and *_ie*: my, by, why, sight, brightly

Teacher Tip

STRATEGIES Although Asking Questions is the strategy being modeled, encourage students to use any strategy they have learned as they read the story.

Comprehension Strategies

This story is broken into two parts. On the first day, read pages 198–205. On the second day, read pages 206–211.

1 **Asking Questions** Teacher Modeling: *Remember to ask questions as you read and then keep reading to find the answers. I wonder why the deer got into Sonia's garden. Maybe this story doesn't take place in the city. However, fire escapes and apartment buildings are usually found in the city. Is this a big city or a small town near the country? I'll keep reading to find out.*

2 **Answering Questions** Teacher Modeling: *I kept reading and my question was answered. It says in the text that the story is set in the city. That's exactly what I thought. Sonia's father tells her that the deer may have come to her garden because they were looking for food.*

Looking around, I recognized many neighbors. There was Isidro Sánchez and his sister, Ana. Standing near me were Mr. Smiley, owner of Smiley's Laundromat, and my best friend, Peach, and Chester and Clarence Martin and the Yasamura sisters from down the hall. I saw Mr. Benny, the taxi driver, and the old Pigeon Lady, who was smiling brightly. I noticed that even neighbors who were almost strangers were standing close to each other and whispering in a friendly way. Well, everyone except Mr. Smiley and the Pigeon Lady, who were not on speaking terms. Mr. Smiley was angry because the Pigeon Lady fed her pigeons in front of his Laundromat, and he thought that was bad for business. 3

200

Mr. Donovan, our landlord, approached Papa. They spoke in hushed voices, but I was all ears.

"Luis, I, too, think the deer are really beautiful, but we both know they can't stay here," whispered Mr. Donovan. "They could be hit by a car. They belong in the woods, not in the city. I think we'd better call the animal control officers."

Papa nodded solemnly, and they walked off.

The Pigeon Lady came up to Peach and me and said, "Oh, girls, aren't they wonderful!"

"Yes!" we both answered together.

"I think two of the deer may be smaller. Those are probably females, or does. The males are called bucks. I used to see deer many years ago when I lived in the country."

201

3 **Making Connections** Teacher Modeling: *This scene reminds me of something that happened once in my neighborhood. Most of the people of the neighborhood got together to form a neighborhood watch. At the first meeting, everyone started talking to each other, even if they didn't know each other very well.*

Comprehension Check

Why are Mr. Donovan and the landlord concerned for the deer? **Possible Answer** *They don't think the deer will be safe in the city. They want to protect them, so they want to find a way for them to go back to the woods where they will be safe.*

Teacher Tip

MAKING CONNECTIONS Remind students that when reading, they should be aware of how ideas in the text remind them of things they have experienced. Tell students that when they make connections, they should share them with the class.

Soon, Papa and Mr. Donovan returned with worried looks on their faces. They gathered the group together.

"The animal control office wants to shoot the deer," said Papa. "It's the law. The city is afraid the deer will starve." 4

"There aren't enough woods left for all the deer to find a home," added Mr. Donovan. "That's why the young deer wander far away. They're looking for territory of their own." 5

Everyone was so quiet that all you could hear was street sounds: honking and beeping, rumbling and humming.

202

Mr. Benny was the first to speak. "We can't let them shoot the deer. There must be another way."

"Yeah! That's right!" said Teresa Yasamura.

All around, people were nodding in agreement.

Then Chester spoke up. "They wouldn't shoot the deer in front of this many people. It would be too dangerous."

"It's true!" exclaimed Papa. "We can form a human wall around the deer without getting too close."

"Right on!" said Isidro. "We'll stay here until we can figure out what to do."

And that was the beginning of our peaceful protest.

203

Phonics and Fluency

/ī/ spelled *igh*, *_y*, and *_ie*: right, bright, right, night, headlights

Differentiating Instruction: English Learner

IF . . . students are native speakers of Spanish, **THEN . . .** point out that adverbs in English that end in *-ly*, such as *cautiously*, usually end in *-mente* in Spanish.

Comprehension Strategies

4 Asking Questions Teacher Modeling: *I don't understand why the animal control officer has to shoot the deer. I read just a little farther and found out that the officer wants to shoot them because he is afraid they will starve. Isn't there something else they can do to keep the deer safe and alive? I'll keep reading to find out.*

5 Answering Questions Teacher Modeling: *I found an answer to one of my earlier questions. The deer have come to the city to find food because there aren't enough woods left for all of the deer to have homes.*

Comprehension Check

What does Sonia mean when she says, "And that is the beginning of our peaceful protest"? **Possible Answer** *The people didn't want the deer to die. They wanted to find another way to take care of the problem. They are going to protest, or strongly object to, animal control harming the deer by not letting the officer near them.*

Mr. Benny wrinkled his brow. "I remember reading a few months back about an organization that rescues and relocates animals that are stranded or injured. A fox had been hit by a car but wasn't badly hurt. This outfit took it in until it healed and then found a new home for it far from busy streets. I'll go see if I can find the number." 6

A little while later, Mr. Benny returned and announced, "The wildlife rescuer isn't in at the moment, but I left a message for him to call. I said it was an emergency."

When the animal control officer arrived, he saw the crowd surrounding the deer and decided not to take any chances. "If you don't mind, folks," he said, "I'll just hang around until you've all had enough and gone home." But we weren't leaving. 7

We stayed all afternoon, waiting anxiously, hoping to hear from the rescue organization. We got to know one another better, and we learned more about the deer.

Peach's eyes were wide and bright. "Look how they rotate their big soft ears to the left and right," she exclaimed.

Clarence said, "We studied deer in science. Their hearing is very sharp. It helps them detect enemies approaching from far away."

Mr. Benny nodded as he walked over to us. "I sometimes see this kind of deer at night, in the headlights, when I drive way past the city limits. When they're startled by the taxi's lights, their tails go up like flags. The tails are white underneath, which means the animals are white-tailed deer."

The deer grazed and slept cautiously, always alert to danger. They watched us with curious, intelligent eyes. I could see that the people made them uncomfortable, and it helped me appreciate that these really were wild animals. We tried to keep our distance and not make any sudden movements.

6 Answering Questions Teacher Modeling: *I read just a little bit farther and I found the answer I was looking for. There is another solution to the problem of the deer that doesn't involve harming them. Mr. Benny knows about an organization that rescues and finds better homes for animals in this same situation. He's going to contact them. I'm glad they are going to find a way to save and protect the deer.*

7 Summarizing Teacher Modeling: *I'm going to summarize all the important things that have happened so far in order to better understand the story. Deer came into the city to find food. Animal control was called but the only solution they had was to kill the deer. Sonia's neighbors surrounded the deer to keep them from being killed. An organization that helps find homes is being contacted to help the deer.*

Vocabulary Tip

Point out the word *relocates* on page 204 in the text. Ask students how knowing that a rescue organization found a new home for the deer helps them remember the meaning of the word *relocates*. Ask students how the words *alert* and *danger* help them remember how the word *cautiously* is used in that sentence on page 205.

Teacher Tip

COMPREHENSION Ask students the following questions to make sure they understand the story:

- *Can you summarize what you have read?*
- *Does what you are reading make sense?*

STOP You have read the first half of the story. You will continue the story tomorrow on page T296.

Lesson 4 Inquiry Planner

STEP 5: Collecting Information

Day 1 Students will be collecting resources and information about their investigation questions and topics. They can use information from the unit selections.

Day 2 Groups will continue collecting information for their investigations.

Day 3 Students can post new items on the **Concept/Question Board.** They can also look for new ideas and sources of information on the Board.

Day 4 Groups will continue collecting information and finalize their presentation ideas.

Day 5 With their groups, students will continue collecting information to use for their group presentation.

Teacher Tip

COLLECTING INFORMATION As students begin collecting information, review how different sources are used. For example, tell students that the titles of nonfiction books, chapters, and articles should give them an idea of the kind of information contained in the book and whether the book will provide the information they need.

Research in Action

The students are reading all day every day. Encourage them to bring to class examples of intriguing characters, interesting ways authors have presented characters, and effective passages of dialogue from things they read outside of class.

(Marsha Roit)

Inquiry Process

Step 5—Collecting Information

Whole-Group Time

Whole Group

- Remind students that their groups should now have a question, a conjecture, a plan for their investigation, and some information from the unit selections. Now they should continue collecting information to evaluate their conjectures and to use in a presentation.
- Remind students that they can use different sources from which to collect information. Encourage them to use or revise the list of sources they created on page 120 of ***Skills Practice 1*** for their investigation.
- To encourage students to practice the study skills they've learned in this unit, have them take notes from their sources. Also recommend that they make tables, charts, and diagrams of information they collect. These will help them as they assemble and arrange information for their presentation.
- If time permits, arrange for an animal expert give a presentation to the class. For this presentation, have students practice the listening, speaking, and viewing skills they learned in Lessons 1 and 2 for asking questions as well as listening and responding to a presentation.
- Groups should start thinking about the presentations they want to give at the end of the unit. For each group, suggest possibilities for the kinds of presentations they could give, but allow them to choose how they want to present the results of their investigation. Some presentation possibilities include making posters with pictures, charts, graphs, and diagrams; oral presentations with visuals; displaying a model of an animal habitat; giving a slide show; creating a picture book; or making an informational pamphlet or booklet about an animal habitat.
- Model choosing a presentation method: *Since I want to help these animals who are losing their habitats, I think that I should create a pamphlet highlighting important things about these animal habitats and how to protect them. Then I can share this information with others and also help convince them to protect these animals.*

✦ Throughout the remaining time in this unit, meet with each group to arrange schedules, discuss problems that groups are encountering, hear preliminary presentation ideas, and discuss interesting findings.

Small-Group Time

Small Group

✦ Meet with each group individually to provide guidance and to ensure that they are obtaining information, meeting or revising their needs and plans, and developing final presentation ideas.

✦ Each group should review page 119 in ***Skills Practice 1*** as a reminder of any information they still might need to acquire for their conjectures.

✦ Help groups by showing them where to go and how to collect any sources of information they need for their inquiries. Consider having a librarian give students tutorials about finding and using sources.

✦ As groups collect information from their sources, have them record information on ***Skills Practice 1*** pages 135–136. Remind them that they can use selections from the unit as sources.

Concept/Question Board

Encourage students to write information, ideas, or questions on the **Concept/Question Board.** Students might

- bring in pictures of animals and wildlife in their own backyard. (Remind students not to disturb the habitats of the animals while they are observing or photographing them.)
- bring in articles and/or pictures from magazines, newspapers, and the Internet of animals and their habitats.
- respond to questions or conjectures on the board.
- write a summary of a television program or film they have seen about animals and their habitats.

Teacher Tip

PRESENTATIONS Students may have fun making a model of animals in their habitats. Suggest this as a presentation possibility. If they make a model, they could give a presentation explaining its various parts and what they mean.

UNIT 2 Lesson 4

Name ______ Date ______

Collecting Information for Inquiry

Use these pages to record new information that you gather for your group's research investigation. List your sources, any new information, and any new questions about your topic below. Possible Answers

Title or name of source: *Animal Fact File* by Tony Hare

New information about your topic: Penguins can swim 10 to 15 kilometers an hour. They stay warm with feathers and a layer of fat called blubber.

Does any information in this source change your ideas about your topic at all? How? Yes. I thought penguins were slow and wobbled around on the ice.

New questions that you need to answer: What makes penguins swim so fast? Do any animals hunt penguins?

Title or name of source: *Penguin* by Claire Robinson

New information about your topic: Most penguins build nests like other birds. The nests are made of rocks, branches, and grass.

Does any information in this source change your ideas about your topic at all? How? Yes. I thought all penguins lived in the snow.

Skills Practice 1 • Inquiry UNIT 2 • Lesson 4 **135**

Skills Practice 1, pp. 135–136

Day 1 **Language Arts**

OBJECTIVES

Students will
- ✦ brainstorm ideas for their realistic stories.
- ✦ take the spelling pretest.
- ✦ practice cursive *p* and *j*.

MATERIALS

- ✦ Routines 15–16
- ✦ ***Language Arts Handbook,*** pp. 126–129
- ✦ ***Skills Practice 1,*** p. 137
- ✦ ***Transparencies*** 61, 62

Research in Action

Support students as they begin to apply the knowledge, skills, or strategies you teach them. This can include reteaching, providing hints and reminders, giving useful feedback, and initially helping students apply what was taught.
(Steve Graham and Karen Harris)

Realistic Story

A **realistic story** contains people, places, and events that are made up, but could be real. A story about a boy who wants a puppy for his birthday would be realistic. The boy and the puppy are not real, but they seem real.

When you write a realistic story, you use your imagination to write a story that entertains your audience. Your story can have funny characters, exciting places, or strange events that could be true. That's what makes it different from a fantasy. In fantasy, things happen that could never really happen.

Which of the ideas below could you use to write a realistic story?
- ▸ Two friends try out for a team.
- ▸ A girl meets a singing turtle by a pond.
- ▸ Your neighbor's dog wins the spelling bee at school.
- ▸ A boy gets a brand-new bicycle for his birthday.

Parts of a Realistic Story

A realistic story has a plot, one or more characters, and a setting. The plot of a realistic story has events that could happen in real life. The characters act like real people or animals would. The setting is a place that is real or could be real.

126 Realistic Story • Narrative Writing

Language Arts Handbook, p. 126

Writing Realistic Story

ROUTINE  ROUTINE 

Prewriting

Teach

- ✦ Follow Routine 15. Remind students of the stages of the writing process: prewriting, drafting, revising, editing/proofreading, and publishing. Tell students they will be writing a realistic story. If necessary, discuss the meaning of *realistic*.
- ✦ Display ***Transparency*** 61. Have a student read the paragraph aloud. Discuss the elements that make this a realistic story.
- ✦ Tell students that a realistic story contains people, places, and events that are made up but could be real. In "Two Days in May" for example, the events really happened, but the characters and setting were made up by the author of the story.
- ✦ Tell students that when writing a realistic story, the writer uses his or her imagination to tell a story. Remind students that their stories will have a plot, a setting or settings, and characters. The settings and characters should seem real.
- ✦ Tell students another important element of their stories is to have a clear beginning, middle, and end. A story map graphic organizer will help with these important elements. Tell students the story map will help them organize story ideas into an easy-to-follow story line.
- ✦ For further information about writing a realistic story, refer to ***Language Arts Handbook*** pages 126–129.

Realistic Story

Nate got to school early on Friday morning. He was excited about Games Day. Nate saw his friend Brad on the playground.

"Are you nervous?" asked Brad.

"A little," said Nate.

Nate was one of the fastest runners in third grade. Today he might win a blue ribbon. He had a dream about winning a blue ribbon.

It was time for the race. The runners lined up. At the signal, they all started to run.

Nate got a good start, but Tina was ahead of him. He thought about the ribbon. He ran faster and faster. He passed Tina and crossed the finish line. He won!

Later, Nate walked home. He looked at his blue ribbon. He smiled and thought, "I guess dreams do come true, sometimes."

 Level 3

Transparency 61

Writing, continued

Guided Practice

- Model gathering ideas for your own realistic story. Explain to students that they can get ideas from their surroundings, such as school and school friends, family and family members, a community or neighborhood event, and so on. Brainstorm ideas with the class, and write them on the board.

- Use Routine 16. Create a story map graphic organizer on the board for your own story. Stress the importance of having realistic characters and settings and having a clear beginning, middle, and end to the story.

Have students turn to ***Skills Practice 1*** page 137 and help them complete the Think section. Review the story map graphic organizer.

Apply

- Have students work independently to brainstorm their own ideas for a realistic story.

- Then have students complete page 137 in ***Skills Practice 1,*** which includes the Think section and the graphic organizer.

Assessment

You will use the Writing Rubrics found in the Level Appendix to evaluate students' realistic stories. You may use any of the rubrics for Genre, Writing Process, and Writing Traits. Share with students what you will be looking for when assessing their realistic stories.

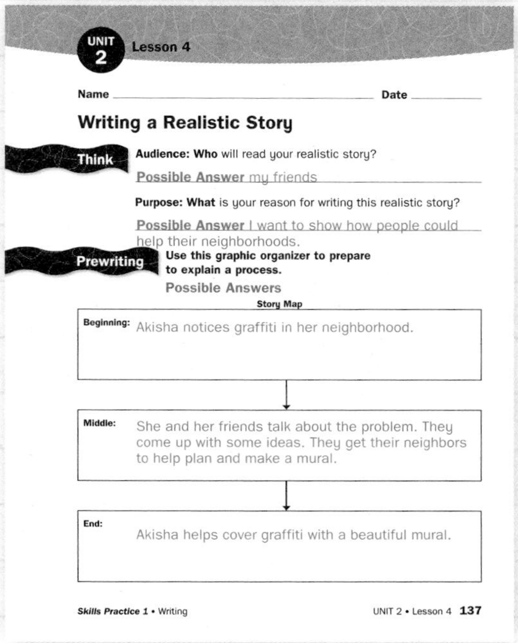
UNIT 2 Lesson 4

Name ______ Date ______

Writing a Realistic Story

Think

Audience: Who will read your realistic story?

Possible Answer my friends

Purpose: What is your reason for writing this realistic story?

Possible Answer I want to show how people could help their neighborhoods.

Prewriting **Use this graphic organizer to prepare to explain a process.**

Possible Answers

Story Map

Beginning: Akisha notices graffiti in her neighborhood.

Middle: She and her friends talk about the problem. They come up with some ideas. They get their neighbors to help plan and make a mural.

End: Akisha helps cover graffiti with a beautiful mural.

Skills Practice 1 • Writing UNIT 2 • Lesson 4 **137**

Skills Practice 1, p. 137

Spelling

Lesson Review and Homophones Pretest

- Students will learn homophones and review words with /ī/, /ō/, and consonant blends.

- Say the sentences below. Have students write the spelling words on a sheet of paper. When they are finished, have them correct any misspelled words.

Pretest Sentences

1. The tired man let out a **groan.**
2. The puppy has really **grown** since I saw him last.
3. The **seam** on my shirt is ripped.
4. It movie did not **seem** very long.
5. Who ate the last **piece** of pizza?
6. The dove is a symbol of **peace.**
7. Place this book on the table **by** the bookshelf.
8. Would you like to **buy** a notebook?
9. My **toe** was broken, so I had to use crutches.
10. I enjoy watching huge boats **tow** smaller boats.
11. The **horse** had a beautiful mane.
12. The cold made my throat feel sore and my voice sounded **hoarse.**
13. The parents will **meet** the new teachers.
14. Turkey is my favorite kind of **meat.**
15. My brother told a scary **tale** at the campfire.

Challenge Sentences

16. We can recycle our **waste.**
17. The pants fit neatly around her **waist.**

Diagnose any misspellings by determining whether students misspelled the homophones, long vowels, consonant blends, or some other part of the word. Then have students use the pretest as a take-home list to study the spellings of words with these homophones, long vowel spellings, and consonant blends.

Penmanship

Cursive Letters *p* and *j*

Teach

✦ Remind students that cursive letters are made of four types of strokes (undercurve, overcurve, downcurve, and slant lines). Draw them on the board.

✦ Display ***Transparency*** 62. Introduce lowercase cursive *p* and *j* as undercurve letters. Using your fingertip or a pointer, trace the letters while saying the formations aloud.

- ***Letter p*** Starting point, undercurve
Slant, loop back
Overcurve
Curve back, undercurve: small *p*
- ***Letter j*** Starting point, undercurve
Slant down
Loop back
Overcurve to endpoint
Dot exactly above: small *j*

✦ On the board, write lowercase cursive *p* and *j*. Say the strokes aloud as you form the letters.

✦ To model proper letter formation, write the following words on the board: *paper, jam, jump, pajamas.*

Guided Practice

Tell students to hold up their index fingers in front of them. Say the strokes aloud as you trace the letters, and have students mimic your movements as if they were writing in the air.

Apply

✦ Have students practice writing each of the letters four times. Ask them to circle the best formation of each of their letters.

✦ After reviewing the words you wrote on the board, have students practice writing the words. Check for proper letter formation. Have them circle the best formation of each word based on the proper letter formation of *p* and *j*.

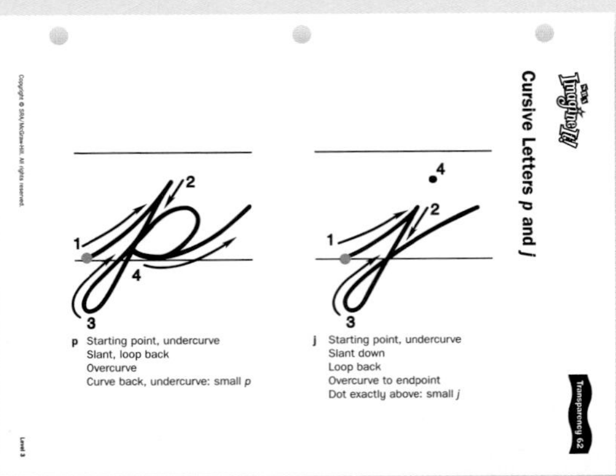

Transparency 62

Teacher Tips

PENMANSHIP If students are having problems forming cursive *p* and *j* or their letters are floating between the lines, review proper paper position, check to make sure students are holding their pencils correctly, or review letter formation.

MODEL Show how to connect *p* to other letters.

Differentiating Instruction English Learner

IF . . . students are native speakers of Arabic or Hebrew, **THEN . . .** keep in mind that they are used to writing from right to left across a page. Be alert for students who need extra help with handwriting.

Skills Traces

Preparing to Read

Word Structure: Homophones

Introduced in Grade 2, Unit 5, Lesson 4

Reviewed: Unit 2, Lesson 4
Practiced: Unit 2, Lesson 5
Unit 3, Lesson 1
Assessed: ***Lesson Assessment Book 1,*** p. 67

Reviewed in Grade 4, Unit 3, Lesson 1

Phonics:

See Level Appendix

Reading and Responding

Comprehension Skill: Cause and Effect

Reviewed in Grade 2, Unit 2, Lesson 3

Grade 3
Reviewed: Unit 1, Lesson 1
Practiced: Unit 2, Lesson 4
Assessed: ***Lesson Assessment Book 1,*** pp. 68–70

Reviewed in Grade 4, Unit 1, Lesson 3

Comprehension Strategy: Asking Questions

Reviewed in Grade 2, Unit 1, Lesson 1

Grade 3
Reviewed: Unit 1, Lesson 1
Practiced: Unit 1, Lesson 2
Assessed: Unit 2, Lesson 4 , p. T280

Reviewed in Grade 4, Unit 1, Lesson 2

Comprehension Strategy: Making Connections

Reviewed in Grade 2, Unit 1, Lesson 2

Grade 3
Reviewed: Unit 1, Lesson 2
Practiced: Unit 2, Lesson 4
Assessed: Unit 2, Lesson 4, p. T281

Reviewed in Grade 4, Unit 1, Lesson 1

Comprehension Strategy: Summarizing

Reviewed in Grade 2, Unit 1, Lesson 2

Grade 3
Reviewed: Unit 1, Lesson 2
Practiced: Unit 2, Lesson 4
Assessed: Unit 2, Lesson 4, p. T281

Reviewed in Grade 4, Unit 1, Lesson 2

Language Arts

Writing: Realistic Story

Reviewed in Grade 2, Unit 6, Lesson 4

Grade 3
Reviewed: Unit 2, Lesson 4
Assessed: Unit 2, Lesson 4, p. T338

Reviewed in Grade 4, Unit 1, Lesson 1

Grammar, Usage, and Mechanics: Nouns as Subject and Objects

Grade 3
Introduced: Unit 2, Lesson 4
Practiced: Unit 6, Lesson 1
Assessed: ***Lesson Assessment Book 1,*** p. 72

Reviewed in Grade 4, Unit 1, Lesson 4

Grammar, Usage, and Mechanics: Prounous as Subjects and Objects

Grade 3
Introduced: Unit 2, Lesson 4
Reviewed: Unit 2, Lesson 4
Practiced: Unit 6, Lesson 2
Assessed: ***Lesson Assessment Book 1,*** p. 72

Reviewed in Grade 4, Unit 1, Lesson 4

Day 2

Preparing to Read

OBJECTIVES

Students will

- review /ī/ spelled *_igh*, *_y*, and *_ie;* /ō/ spelled *_ow* and *oa_;* and /ū/ spelled *_ew* and *_ue.*
- review consonant blends at the beginning or end or words.
- build fluency.

MATERIALS

- ***Transparency*** 59
- ***Sound/Spelling Cards*** 29–31
- Routines 2, 3, 4, 7, 8

Daily Oral Practice

Daily News

Today!

It would be fun to visit a wildlife rehabilitation center. There experts care for all types of injured and orphaned wild animals. When the animals are healthy and old enough, they're released back into their natural habitats.

- Write the daily news on the board or on chart paper. Then have students read the daily news in unison to practice fluency.
- As a review of yesterday's phonics and fluency lesson, ask a volunteer to identify any consonant blends in the words. rts *in* experts, ld *in* wild, ls *in* animals

Phonics and Fluency

ROUTINE 3 ROUTINE 4

Review: /ī/ spelled *_igh, _y,* and *_ie;* /ō/ spelled *_ow* and *oa_;* /ū/ spelled *_ew* and *_ue;* and consonant blends at the beginning or end of words

Line 1	highways	moonlight	identify	replies
Line 2	aglow	window	throat	coastline
Line 3	few	pewter	rescuer	continued
Line 4	streets	slept	except	protest

Sentence 1 The glowing bright light <u>almost</u> made my <u>eyes</u> water.

Sentence 2 They rescued a few sheep and <u>part</u> of the lost goat herd.

Differentiating Instruction — English Learner

IF . . . students are confused by the *-ed* ending of some words in the daily news, **THEN . . .** remind them that some *-ed* ending words are the past tense of a verb, such as *cared* and *released*. Others, such as *injured* and *orphaned*, are often used as adjectives. Teach students how to use context to identify a word with an *-ed* ending as a verb or an adjective.

Blending

✦ Use ***Transparency*** 59 with the blending lines and sentences from Day 1.

✦ Review ***Sound/Spelling Cards*** 29–31 with students. Then use Routine 3, the whole-word blending process, to have students read Lines 1–4.

✦ Have students read the sentences using normal intonation and expression. If students have difficulty reading a sentence, stop and use Routine 4, the blending sentences process.

Developing Oral Language

Use one or both of these activities to help students practice reading the words from the blending lines.

- Have one student choose a word from the word lines and choose a classmate to read the word and use it in a sentence. **Possible Answer** *The people staged a peaceful* protest *to save the deer.* Have that student choose a classmate to continue the activity. Continue for all words.
- Have a volunteer choose a word and use it in a sentence to begin a story. Have another volunteer continue the story by supplying a sentence that uses another word from the lines. Continue until all the words have been used.

Dictation

ROUTINE 2 ROUTINE 7 ROUTINE 8

✦ Follow Routine 7 for whole-word dictation. When dictating words, say the word, use the word in a sentence, and then repeat the word.

✦ Follow Routine 8 for sentence dictation. When dictating sentences, say the sentence. Next, dictate one word at a time, following Routine 2 for sounds-in-sequence dictation or Routine 7 for whole-word dictation, depending on your students. Have students proofread for spelling, capitalization, and end punctuation.

✦ Dictate the following words and sentence for students to write.

Line 1	midnight	rely	cries	groan
Line 2	own	snowman	rescued	view
Challenge Word	approach			
Sentence	The fence protected the goat from the highway.			

Differentiating Instruction — English Learner

IF . . . students are native speakers of Vietnamese, Hmong, Cantonese, or other tonal languages in which intonation determines word meaning, **THEN . . .** they will need extra help understanding the role of intonation in English and in producing correct sentence intonation.

Sound/Spelling Cards 29–31

Teacher Tip

BLENDING During Workshop, work with students who have difficulty blending words by using Routine 1 for sound-by-sound blending or Routine 3 for whole-word blending.

When evening came, the crowd grew. We talked quietly and told jokes as we kept watch over our silent friends. We ordered pizza from Giuseppe's.

Ana Sánchez spoke to the animal control officer. "Would you like a slice of pizza?" she asked.

"Thanks so much," he said. "My name is Steve Scully, and I understand how hard this must be for all of you. This is the part of my job I dislike.

"The problem is population growth. We've built towns and highways where there were once forests and streams. Now there is very little habitat left for the deer. There is no easy solution." He shook his head sadly.

206

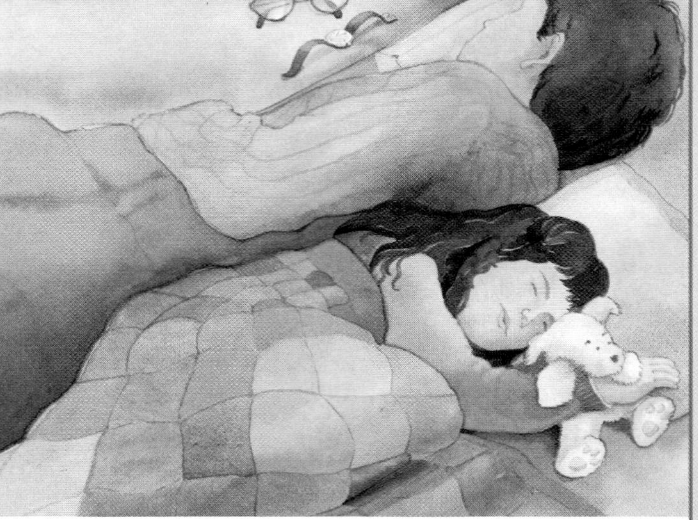

I begged Papa to let me sleep outside all night, since almost everyone was staying. Mama came out with my baby brother, Danny. She brought blankets, a quilt, a jacket, and even my stuffed dog, Hershey.

Mama sat close and draped her arm across my shoulders. "Are you sure you'll be warm enough, Sonia?" she asked.

"I'm sure," I said.

We sat silently together, admiring the deer.

Finally she said, "I have to go put Danny to bed." She kissed me on the top of my head. "Sweet dreams, pumpkin."

I slept like a bear cub, curled in a ball against Papa's broad back. 8

207

OBJECTIVES

Students will

- use comprehension strategies Making Connections, Asking Questions, and Summarizing.
- discuss the selection using the handing-off process.
- review vocabulary, genre, and fluency.

MATERIALS

- ***Student Reader,*** Book 1, pp. 206–213
- Routine A
- ***Transparencies*** 5, 60
- ***Skills Practice 1,*** pp. 133–134

Comprehension Strategies

8 **Making Connections** Teacher Modeling: *This scene reminds me of something that happened to me. It reminds me of the time I went camping with my family in the fall. Mom brought lots of quilts and blankets for us because it was chilly outside at night. We all slept snuggled under the blankets outside. My nose was cold, but I didn't care. It was fun being together.*

Research in Action

Students need multiple exposures to words. Multiple exposures can occur through different learning experiences. Often the word may be used only one or two times in text in a grade level, so additional experiences need to be created. Preteaching and post-teaching vocabulary words, using vocabulary words during discussion and for writing, posting and revisiting vocabulary words on a regular basis, and making vocabulary words a part of a personal dictionary that students can refer to throughout the year will give students multiple exposures to new words.
(Marsha Roit)

Next morning, I awoke with the sun in my eyes and city sounds buzzing in my ears. Papa hugged me and asked how I liked camping out.

"I dreamed I was sleeping with the deer in cool forests under tall trees."

"You were, Sonia!" he said, laughing. "But not in the forest."

I looked at the deer. "Has the wildlife rescuer called back?" I asked.

"Yes, Sonia. The organization called late last night and hopes to get someone out here this morning."

The group was quiet as we all continued to wait.

208

Later that morning, a rusty orange truck pulled up. The man who got out had a friendly, open face. All eyes were on him.

"Hi, folks. My name is Carl Jackson, and I'm with the wildlife rescue organization," he said. "I need to put the deer in crates in order to take them to our center. Don't be alarmed—I'm going to shoot them with a small amount of tranquilizer to make them sleep for a little while." Then, as they wobbled on unsteady legs, he grabbed them gently and guided them toward the wooden crates. 9

209

9 **Asking Questions** Teacher Modeling: *I have another question. Where will the wildlife rescue organization take the deer?*

Comprehension Check

How does this story relate to the theme Animals and Their Habitats? **Possible Answer** *This story is about a family of deer who were forced to leave their habitat. Towns and highways are taking the place of forests and streams and the deer have to move to have food and water. How do the people of this city protect the deer?* **Possible Answer** *They don't want the deer to be harmed, but they also know they wouldn't be safe in the city. The wildlife rescue organization will help relocate them.*

Phonics and Fluency

/ī/ spelled *_igh:* highways, night

Teacher Tip

REALISTIC FICTION Remind students that this is a fictionalized account of a true event. Have students find text segments that indicate this event is realistic.

Carl turned to the crowd and smiled. "I'm an animal lover, too, and all of you should feel proud for helping save these deer. I'll find a home for them in the woods, where they'll be safe and happy and have plenty to eat." 10

Steve Scully came forward and extended his hand to Carl. "Glad you came, man."

A cheer went up from the crowd. People slapped each other on the back. Isidro high-fived everyone, including Mr. Donovan and the Pigeon Lady. Peach and I hugged each other, and Papa shook hands with Carl and Steve. I said goodbye to Teresa and Sandy Yasamura and to Mr. Benny.

I even saw Mr. Smiley shake the Pigeon Lady's hand. "Maybe you can feed the pigeons *behind* my Laundromat," he said. "I have a little space back there."

The Pigeon Lady smiled. 11

210

A few days later, Papa got a call from Carl. One of the does had given birth to two fawns! And Carl had found a home for all seven deer in a wooded area northwest of the city.

Sometimes, when I'm sitting on the fire escape, watching the flickering city lights, I think of the deer. In my mind, they're gliding silently across tall grass meadows all aglow in silver moonlight. 12

211

Vocabulary Tip

Point out the word *extended* on page 210 in the text. Ask students how they know what the author means when she says that Steve Scully "*extended* his hand." Point out how the context clues *came forward* and *hand* help them figure out the meaning.

Differentiating Instruction English Learner

IF . . . students have difficulty with the idiomatic expression *high-fived*, **THEN . . .** write the expression on the board, demonstrate its meaning, and explain how the noun *five* has been made into a verb.

Comprehension Strategies

10 Answering Questions Teacher Modeling: *My question about where the wildlife rescue organization would take the deer was answered. They're going to find the deer a home in the woods where they'll be safe, happy, and have plenty to eat. Like the people in the story, I'm glad to know the deer will be safe.*

11 Making Connections Teacher Modeling: *The neighbors were so happy when they found out the deer would be safe. Saving the deer really brought the people together. I remember once when an older lady in our neighborhood got sick. She was always really nice to the kids, so we all got together and wrote her a card and our parents made her meals. She was so happy. When she got better, all of the kids and the parents in the neighborhood were happy, too.*

⑫ **Summarizing** Teacher Modeling: *We're at the end of the story, so I'll summarize. Sonia saw deer in her garden. The deer weren't safe in the city, so Sonia's dad called animal control. Animal control felt that the deer would starve and wanted to shoot the deer. To save the deer, a wildlife rescue organization was called. Sonia's neighbors surrounded the deer all night to keep them safe. Then, the rescue group came and took all of the deer to the woods. Everyone was happy that they were able to work together and save the deer.*

Comprehension Check

Why do you think Mr. Smiley shook the Pigeon Lady's hand and offered her space behind his business to feed the pigeons? **Possible Answer** *He probably felt good about doing something that helped the deer and he wanted to continue helping and feeling good. He came up with a good compromise that would please the Pigeon Lady, as well as himself.*

Phonics and Fluency

/ī/ spelled *_igh:* high, lights, moonlight

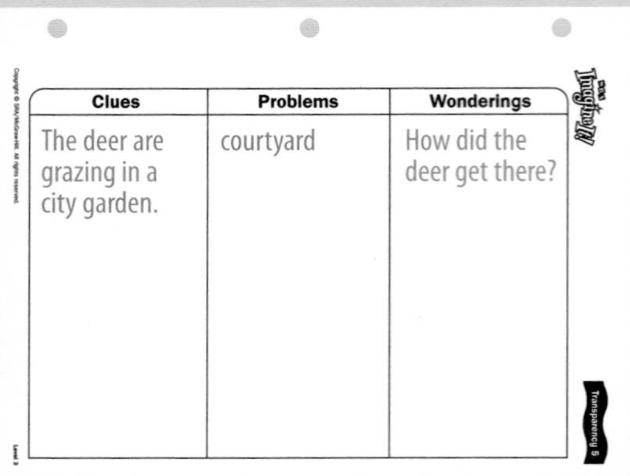

Clues	Problems	Wonderings
The deer are grazing in a city garden.	courtyard	How did the deer get there?

Transparency 5

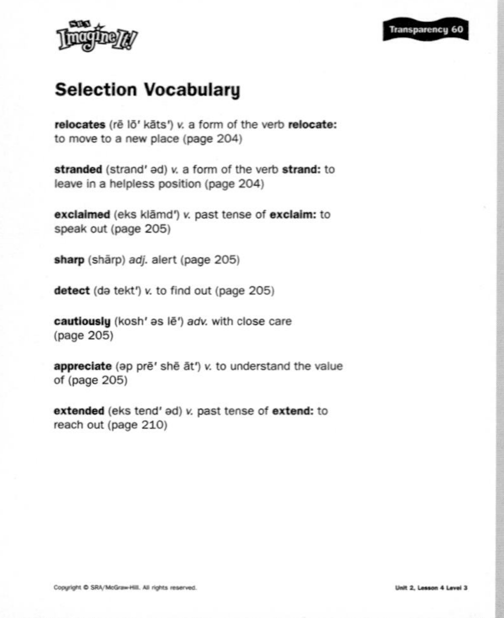

Transparency 60

Selection Vocabulary

relocates (rē lō' kāts') *v.* a form of the verb **relocate:** to move to a new place (page 204)

stranded (strand' əd) *v.* a form of the verb **strand:** to leave in a helpless position (page 204)

exclaimed (eks klāmd') *v.* past tense of **exclaim:** to speak out (page 205)

sharp (shärp) *adj.* alert (page 205)

detect (də tekt') *v.* to find out (page 205)

cautiously (kosh' əs lē') *adv.* with close care (page 205)

appreciate (əp prē' shē āt') *v.* to understand the value of (page 205)

extended (eks tend' əd) *v.* past tense of **extend:** to reach out (page 210)

Transparency 60

Teacher Tip

SILENT READ Ask students about the comprehension strategies they used to understand the story. Have them share which strategies they used, as well as give examples of where they used them.

Discussing the Selection

- It is important for students to see you as a contributing member of the group. Use Routine A, the handing-off process, to emphasize that you are part of the group. Actively participate in the handing-off process by raising your hand to be called on by the last speaker when you have a contribution to make. Point out unusual and interesting insights verbalized by students so that these insights are recognized and discussed. As the year progresses, students will take more responsibility for the discussion of the selections.
- Engage students in a discussion using the handing-off procedure to determine whether they have grasped the following ideas:
  - The deer were losing their habitat in the forests and had to look for areas closer to the city.
  - The deer would not be able to find enough food to survive in the city.
- Ask students how the story demonstrates the following key concepts:
  - Animals are losing habitats all over the world.
  - It is up to people to see that some areas of the world are protected to ensure the safety of animal habitats.
- Return to the Clues, Problems, and Wonderings chart on ***Transparency*** 5. Have students discuss which clues were useful, how they resolved their problems, and how they answered their questions. Ask students if predictions made about friendship before the story was read were confirmed or not confirmed.
- Also, have students return to the Focus Questions on ***Student Reader,*** Book 1 page 196. Select a student to read the questions aloud, and have students answer and discuss the questions. Have them return to the text as necessary.

Genre Review

Review the elements of realistic fiction with students on page T280. Then ask students how they know "Two Days in May" is realistic fiction.

Where do different animals live?

After reading the story, read the Big Idea question. Discuss with students how the story helps answer this question.

Vocabulary Review

Review the selection vocabulary words and definitions students wrote in the Vocabulary section of their Writer's Notebook. Have students refer to 133–134 in ***Skills Practice 1.*** Read the first two questions aloud, and help students find the answers. Let students complete the rest on their own. Also, review the concept word *protect*. Ask students whether they can think of other words related to the theme Animals and Their Habitats. **Possible Answers** *compassion, kindness, thoughtfulness, shelter, safe, sanctuary*

Fluency

- Focus on expression when reading "Two Days in May." Expression, or using tone of voice to indicate feelings and emotions when reading, is essential to fluency. Have students note the feelings of Sonia and her neighbors while they try to save the deer in the story.
- Read aloud pages 198–199 of "Two Days in May." Model expression for students. For example, point out the sentence *I thought I had never seen such an amazing sight*. Tell students that by reading this sentence with the feeling of amazement that Sonia feels, the sentence tells the reader even more about her feelings towards the deer. Have students follow along in the ***Student Readers,*** and tell them to raise their hands when you pause. Tell students that they should practice expressing emotions as they reread.

Monitor Progress to Differentiate Instruction

Formal Assessment 

Selection Vocabulary Observe students' understanding of the vocabulary words and their definitions.

APPROACHING LEVEL

IF . . . students need extra help with the selection vocabulary,	**THEN . . .** use ***Intervention Guide,*** Unit 2 Lesson 4.
IF . . . students need extra help with the selection vocabulary,	**THEN . . .** use ***Reteach*** page 53.

ON LEVEL

IF . . . students need practice using the selection vocabulary,	**THEN . . .** have students write sentences using the vocabulary words.

ABOVE LEVEL

IF . . . students understand the selection vocabulary,	**THEN . . .** use ***Challenge Activities*** page 48.

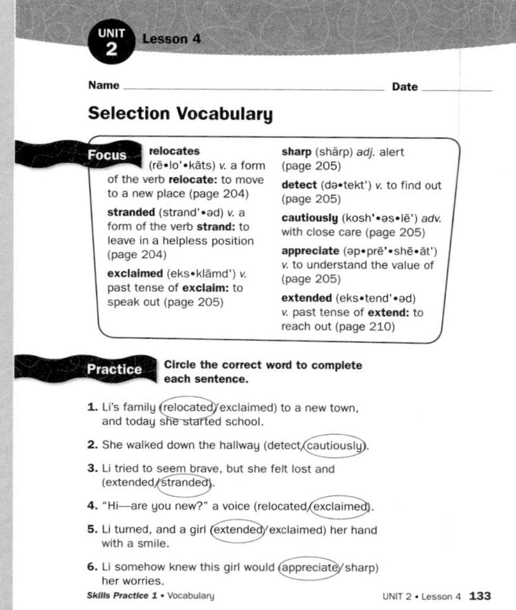

UNIT 2 Lesson 4

Name ____________ Date ______

Selection Vocabulary

Focus

relocates (rē•lo'•kāts) *v.* a form of the verb **relocate:** to move to a new place (page 204)

stranded (strand'•əd) *v.* a form of the verb **strand:** to leave in a helpless position (page 204)

exclaimed (eks•klāmd') *v.* past tense of **exclaim:** to speak out (page 205)

sharp (shärp) *adj.* alert (page 205)

detect (də•tekt') *v.* to find out (page 205)

cautiously (kosh'•əs•lē') *adv.* with close care (page 205)

appreciate (əp•prē'•shē•āt') *v.* to understand the value of (page 205)

extended (eks•tend'•əd) *v.* past tense of **extend:** to reach out (page 210)

Practice **Circle the correct word to complete each sentence.**

1. Li's family (relocated/exclaimed) to a new town, and today she started school.
2. She walked down the hallway (detect/cautiously).
3. Li tried to seem brave, but she felt lost and (extended/stranded).
4. "Hi—are you new?" a voice (relocated/exclaimed).
5. Li turned, and a girl (extended/exclaimed) her hand with a smile.
6. Li somehow knew this girl would (appreciate/sharp) her worries.

Skills Practice 1 • Vocabulary UNIT 2 • Lesson 4 **133**

Skills Practice 1, p. 133

Teacher Tip

WORD BANK If you created a Word Bank of key words related to the theme Animals and Their Habitats, remind students to find words from other sources, their activities, and family discussions and add them to the Word Bank. Organize the words according to parts of speech.

Fluency Tip

FLUENCY By this time in Grade 3, good readers should be reading approximately 99 words per minute with fluency and expression. The only way to gain this fluency is by practicing. To help build fluency have students reread the selection to you and to each other during Workshop to help build fluency. As students read, you may notice that some need work in building fluency. During Workshop, have these students choose a section of the text (a minimum of 160 words) to read several times to build fluency.

Reading and Responding

Teacher Tips

LISTENING During Workshop, have students listen to "Two Days in May" for a model of oral reading. While students listen, have them keep a list in their Writer's Notebooks of any new or unfamiliar words they encounter, and instruct them to check the words using a dictionary or glossary. Also, instruct students to listen for the lesson's vocabulary words and to check that the words make sense within the reading.

WRITE ABOUT IT! Have students use their Writer's Notebooks to write about how they have helped animals in their neighborhood.

Differentiating Instruction — English Learner

IF . . . students have difficulty expressing their answers in complete sentences,
THEN . . . rephrase the questions so that they can be answered *yes* or *no* or with a word or phrase. For example: *Is Sonia's garden in the city? Do deer live in the city or in the woods?*

Meet the Author and Illustrator

After students read the information about the author and illustrator, discuss the following questions with them:

- *Why do you think Harriet Peck Taylor chooses animals as the subjects of her stories?* **Possible Answer** *She has had many pets in her life and she likes writing about them.*
- *How could the writers of other children's books have been "like teachers" to Torres?* **Possible Answer** *By reading their work, she learned how to write and illustrate books.*

Theme Connections

Within the Selection

1. Why would Sonia's garden in the city not make a good home for the deer? **Possible Answer** *The deer could not find enough food to eat. The city is a dangerous place for deer, because they would not have very good shelter.*
2. "Two Days in May" is based on a true story. Why are more deer and other wildlife coming to the city? **Possible Answer** *Deer and wildlife are coming to the city because they are losing their own habitats. Cities are growing closer to the forests and the woods and are taking over the animals' habitats.*

Across Selections

3. How is this story like "Make Way for Ducklings"? **Possible Answer** *This story is like "Make Way for Ducklings" because the animals in both stories were looking for a habitat of their own in a city. Also, in both stories, people helped the animals.*
4. How is it different? **Possible Answer** *It is not like "Make Way for Ducklings" because "Two Days in May" is realistic fiction and "Make Way for Ducklings" is a fantasy story.*

Beyond the Selection

5. What does "Two Days in May" tell you about animals and their habitats? **Possible Answer** *"Two Days in May" tells us that animals are losing their habitats and are moving closer to cities, which is dangerous for them. People must find ways to help protect and save the animal habitats.*
6. How can your community get involved to help animals in your neighborhood? *Answers will vary.*

Meet the Author

Harriet Peck Taylor

Harriet Peck Taylor has loved two things her entire life: painting and nature. She also loves animals, both wild and tame. She once had a coyote follow her and her two dogs on a number of walks. Whether she is writing or walking in the woods, Taylor is careful to both enjoy and respect nature and its animals.

Leyla Torres

As a child in South America, Leyla Torres spent a lot of time making rag dolls, painting, or reading books. After college, she became involved with a group of puppeteers. Creating puppet shows inspired Torres to make books. Six years after moving to New York City and learning English, Torres completed her first book. She now lives in Vermont with her husband and enjoys painting in her workshop.

212

Theme Connections

Within the Selection

1. Why would Sonia's garden in the city not make a good home for the deer?
2. "Two Days in May" is based on a true story. Why are more deer and other wildlife coming to the city?

Across Selections

3. How is this story like "Make Way for Ducklings"?
4. How is it different?

Beyond the Selection

5. What does "Two Days in May" tell you about animals and their habitats?
6. How can your community get involved to help animals in your neighborhood?

Write about It!

Describe how you or someone you know helped an animal in your neighborhood.

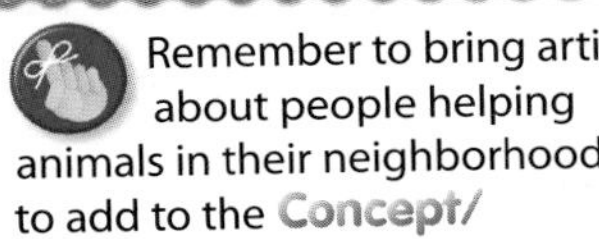

Remember to bring articles about people helping animals in their neighborhoods to add to the **Concept/Question Board.**

213

Concept/Question Board

As students discuss "Two Days in May," encourage them to post questions, answers, comments, or other items related to the theme Animals and Their Habitats on the **Concept/Question Board.**

Teacher Tip

BEYOND THE SELECTION Have students summarize what they have learned and tell how they might use this information in further investigations.

Writer's Notebook

- Have students use their Writer's Notebooks to list other fiction stories they have read in class or on their own.
- Have students compare the elements found in each story.

OBJECTIVES

Students will
- ✦ spell homophones and review previous spelling skills.
- ✦ learn subjects and direct objects.
- ✦ draft their realistic stories.

MATERIALS
- ✦ ***Transparency*** 3
- ✦ ***Skills Practice 1,*** pp. 141–142

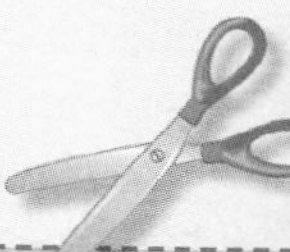

Teacher Tip

PLAN AHEAD Plan your draft so that you can revise and edit it for dialogue.

CONFERENCING Have students conference during drafting.

Writing Realistic Story

Drafting

Teach—Using Dialogue

- ✦ Tell students that they will use their story map graphic organizers to draft their realistic stories. The story map will also help them organize their ideas into an easy-to-follow story line.
- ✦ Have students list the four types of sentences. *declarative, imperative, exclamatory, interrogative* Tell students to try to use each type of sentence in the draft of their stories.
- ✦ Tell students that as they draft their realistic stories they should ask themselves the following:
  - Does the story have a plot, well-developed characters, and a setting?
  - Does the story have a clear beginning, middle, and end?
  - Does the story have details that make it seem real?
  - Does the story have a problem and a solution?
  - Is the story line easy to follow?
- ✦ Tell students that another important aspect of a realistic story is dialogue. Show them examples of dialogue in "Two Days in May." Explain that using dialogue makes characters more interesting and more real. Encourage students to use dialogue in their stories. Point out the punctuation used for dialogue, and remind students that different types of sentences require different punctuation.

Writing, continued

Guided Practice

- Model using a story-map graphic organizer as notes for your story draft. Use the story map you created during prewriting and ***Transparency*** 3. Have students suggest which piece of information should be in each paragraph based on your story map.

Apply

Composing—Drafting Have students follow their story maps as they draft their realistic stories. Tell students to use "Two Days in May" as a guide and to remember to add the correct punctuation for dialogue.

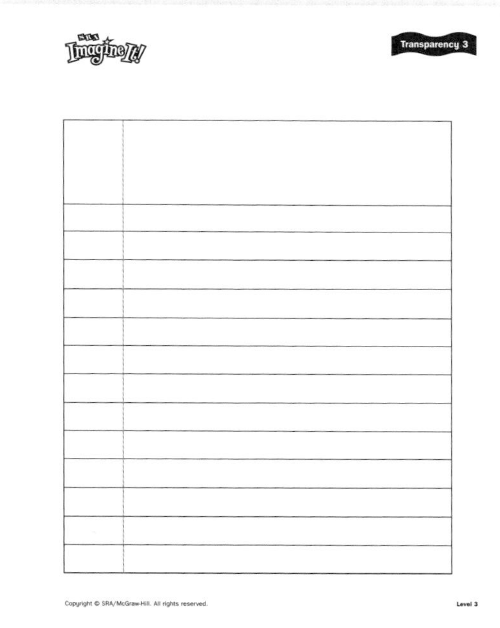

Transparency 3

Spelling

Lesson Review and Homophones

Teach

- Tell students that homophones are words that sound the same but are written differently and mean different things.
- Use a word sort to teach homophones, and review words with /ī/, /ō/, and consonant blends.

Guided Practice

Write the following headings on the board: *homophones, /ī/, /ō/,* and *consonant blends.* Then write the following word list: *groan, grown, seam, seem, piece, peace, by, buy, toe, tow, horse, hoarse, meet, meat,* and *tale.* Have volunteers write the words under the correct heading. Once the spelling words have all been used, ask for students to come to the board and underline the part of each word that reflects the category in which it was placed. If a word fits in more than one category, ask the students to put the word under the heading that they prefer.

Word Sort Answers

Homophones: *groan/grown, seam/seem, piece/peace, by/buy, toe/tow, horse/hoarse, meet/meat*
Words with /ī/: *by, buy*
Words with /ō/: *groan, grown, toe, tow*
Words with consonant blends: *groan, grown*

Grammar, Usage, and Mechanics

Subjects and Direct Objects

Teach

- Write the following sentences on the board:
  a. The sun burned Robby.
  b. The sun burned him.
  c. Kendra bought flowers.
  d. Kendra bought them.
- Have students compare both sentence pairs. Ask students to explain the difference between sentences a and b. **Possible Answer** *The word* him *replaced the word Robby.*
- Explain that in the first sentence *sun* is the subject noun and *Robby* is the direct object noun. In the second sentence, the noun *Robby* is replaced by the object pronoun *him*.
- Explain that in the third sentence, *Kendra* is the subject noun and *flowers* is the direct object noun. In the fourth sentence, the direct object noun *flowers* is replaced by the object pronoun *them*.
- Discuss reasons why we replace nouns with pronouns.
- Explain to students that the direct object of a sentence is the noun or pronoun which receives the action from the subject.

Guided Practice

- Have students think of one more sentence for you to write on the board. Have students identify the subject and the direct object. Then have students replace the direct object with an appropriate object pronoun.
- Have students turn to page 141 in ***Skills Practice 1.*** Read the directions, and help the students complete the Practice section.

Apply

Have students complete ***Skills Practice 1*** pages 141–142.

Differentiating Instruction — English Learner

IF . . . students have difficulty with the subject-verb-object word order shown in these examples, **THEN . . .** keep in mind that this is not the standard order in all languages. In Japanese and Korean, for example, the standard order is subject-object-verb.

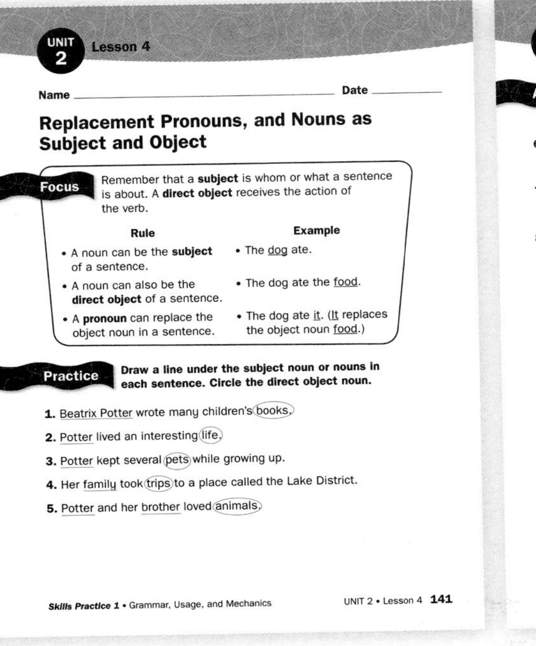

UNIT 2 Lesson 4

Name ______________________ Date ________

Replacement Pronouns, and Nouns as Subject and Object

Focus Remember that a **subject** is whom or what a sentence is about. A **direct object** receives the action of the verb.

Rule	Example
• A noun can be the **subject** of a sentence.	• The dog ate.
• A noun can also be the **direct object** of a sentence.	• The dog ate the food.
• A **pronoun** can replace the object noun in a sentence.	• The dog ate it. (It replaces the object noun food.)

Practice Draw a line under the subject noun or nouns in each sentence. Circle the direct object noun.

1. Beatrix Potter wrote many children's books.
2. Potter lived an interesting life.
3. Potter kept several pets while growing up.
4. Her family took trips to a place called the Lake District.
5. Potter and her brother loved animals.

Skills Practice 1 • Grammar, Usage, and Mechanics UNIT 2 • Lesson 4 141

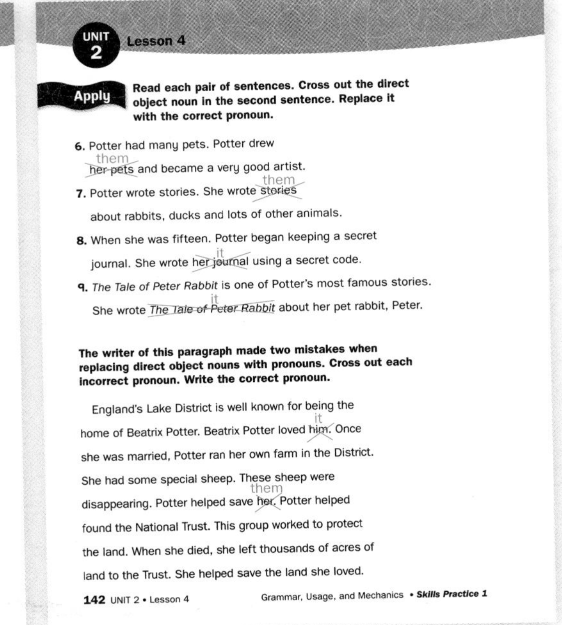

UNIT 2 Lesson 4

Apply Read each pair of sentences. Cross out the direct object noun in the second sentence. Replace it with the correct pronoun.

6. Potter had many pets. Potter drew ~~her pets~~ them and became a very good artist.
7. Potter wrote stories. She wrote ~~stories~~ them about rabbits, ducks and lots of other animals.
8. When she was fifteen, Potter began keeping a secret journal. She wrote ~~her journal~~ it using a secret code.
9. *The Tale of Peter Rabbit* is one of Potter's most famous stories. She wrote ~~*The Tale of Peter Rabbit*~~ it about her pet rabbit, Peter.

The writer of this paragraph made two mistakes when replacing direct object nouns with pronouns. Cross out each incorrect pronoun. Write the correct pronoun.

England's Lake District is well known for being the home of Beatrix Potter. Beatrix Potter loved ~~him~~ it. Once she was married, Potter ran her own farm in the District. She had some special sheep. These sheep were disappearing. Potter helped save ~~her~~ them. Potter helped found the National Trust. This group worked to protect the land. When she died, she left thousands of acres of land to the Trust. She helped save the land she loved.

142 UNIT 2 • Lesson 4 Grammar, Usage, and Mechanics • Skills Practice 1

Skills Practice 1, p. 141–142

Monitor Progress to Differentiate Instruction

Formal Assessment 

Subjects and Direct Objects Note whether students grasp the concept of subjects and direct objects as well as object pronouns.

APPROACHING LEVEL

IF . . . students need practice with subjects and direct objects, **THEN . . .** have them complete ***Reteach*** page 55 during Workshop.

IF . . . students need more practice with subjects and direct objects, **THEN . . .** use Unit 2 Lesson 4 in the ***Intervention Guide.***

ON LEVEL

IF . . . students have an understanding of subjects and direct objects, **THEN . . .** have them pay attention to subjects and direct objects as they draft their stories during Workshop.

ABOVE LEVEL

IF . . . students need a challenge, **THEN . . .** have them complete ***Challenge Activities*** page 50 during Workshop.

Preparing to Read

OBJECTIVES

Students will
- identify and know the meaning of homophones.
- build fluency.

MATERIALS
- ***Transparency*** 63
- ***Skills Practice 1***, pp. 131–132

Daily Oral Practice

Daily News

Today!

Have you ever protected an animal habitat? A town can protect a family of deer, an organization can protect a rainforest, and one student can protect animals at a local animal shelter or in a backyard habitat. You have the power to protect our world.

- Write the daily news on the board or on chart paper. Then have students read the daily news in unison to practice fluency.
- As a word structure review from Lesson 3, ask a volunteer to identify any homographs in the daily news. *can* If the students don't identify *can* as a homograph, point it out and ask them to give two definitions of the word.

Word Structure

Homophones

- Write the following word lines on the board or use ***Transparency*** 63. Show students one line at time as you go through them by covering up the others. The words in boldface are from "Two Days in May."

Line 1	deer	dear	one	won
Line 2	knew	new	tails	tales
Line 3	know	no	two	too
Line 4	there	their	blue	blew

Technology

WORD STRUCTURE Have students use the ***eSkills*** word structure activity for this unit for practice with homographs and homophones.

Lines 1–4 **Homophones**

- Explain that homophones are words that sound the same but have different meanings and different spellings. For example, the words *hair* and *hare* are pronounced the same, but they mean different things. *Hair* is what grows on a person's head, and a *hare* is a rabbit.
- Point to the words in Lines 1–2, and have students read the words in unison together. After reading each pair of homophones, have students give a definition of each word. **Possible Answers** Knew *is the past tense of* know; new *is the opposite of* old. Tails *are what some animals have;* tales *are stories.*
- Ask students to give examples of other homophones they know. If they cannot think of any, give them extra examples. **Possible Answers** Hear *is what ears do;* here *is a place.* Right *means correct;* write *means to spell out words.*
- Help students start the word structure activities in ***Skills Practice 1*** pages 131–132. Read the Focus box, and help them with the first few questions. Then have students complete the pages on their own.

Differentiating Instruction **English Learner**

IF . . . students need additional help with the homophones in the blending lines, **THEN. . .** write and say each word in each homophone pair in a sentence that emphasizes their same sounds but different spellings and meanings. Write the pair on the board.

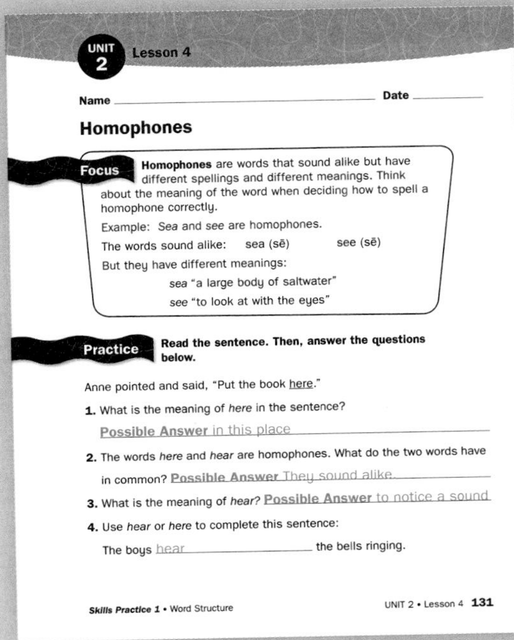
UNIT 2 Lesson 4

Name ______ Date ______

Homophones

Focus **Homophones** are words that sound alike but have different spellings and different meanings. Think about the meaning of the word when deciding how to spell a homophone correctly.

Example: *Sea* and *see* are homophones.

The words sound alike: sea (sē) see (sē)

But they have different meanings:

sea "a large body of saltwater"

see "to look at with the eyes"

Practice **Read the sentence. Then, answer the questions below.**

Anne pointed and said, "Put the book here."

1. What is the meaning of *here* in the sentence? Possible Answer in this place
2. The words *here* and *hear* are homophones. What do the two words have in common? Possible Answer They sound alike.
3. What is the meaning of *hear*? Possible Answer to notice a sound
4. Use *hear* or *here* to complete this sentence: The boys hear the bells ringing.

Skills Practice 1 • Word Structure UNIT 2 • Lesson 4 131

Skills Practice 1, pp. 131–132

Monitor Progress to Differentiate Instruction

Formal Assessment 

Word Structure During the word structure activity, note how well students understand homophones.

APPROACHING LEVEL	**IF . . .** students need practice with homophones,	**THEN . . .** work with them on the word structure activities on ***Reteach*** page 52 during Workshop.
	IF . . . students need extra practice with homophones,	**THEN . . .** work with them on the word structure activities for Unit 2 Lesson 4 in the ***Intervention Guide*** during Workshop.
ON LEVEL	**IF . . .** students understand homophones,	**THEN . . .** have them use ***eSkills*** during Workshop.
ABOVE LEVEL	**IF . . .** students are ready for a challenge with homophones,	**THEN . . .** have them complete the word structure activities on ***Challenge Activities*** page 47 during Workshop.

Reading and Responding

Early one Saturday morning in May, I went to our fire escape window and rubbed the sleep from my eyes. I looked down at the small garden I had planted behind our apartment building. Five animals were grazing on the new lettuce in my garden!

"Mama! Mama!" I called. "Come see what's in our yard!"

Mama hurried over to the window and gasped. "Sonia, those animals are deer, but how did they get here?" she asked. "I'll run and tell Mr. Donovan."

198

By the time Papa and I got out to the courtyard, a small crowd was gathering.

"Papa, why are there deer in the city?" I asked.

"The deer may have come all this way looking for food. They probably smelled your garden," he explained.

I thought I had never seen such an amazing sight. Their fur was a golden brown, and they balanced on tiny hooves. They had nervous tails, and eyes that were big and black and gentle.

Down the block a train rumbled by, but here life seemed to stand still. Pigeons and squirrels were almost the only birds or animals we ever saw in our neighborhood.

199

OBJECTIVES

Students will

- use the comprehension skill Cause and Effect.
- review the comprehension strategy Making Connections.
- build fluency.

MATERIALS

- ***Student Reader,*** Book 1, pp. 198–205
- ***Transparency*** 15

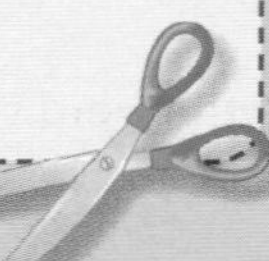

Comprehension Skill

Reread the selection using the comprehension skill Cause and Effect.

Cause and Effect

When rereading the story, tell students to look for relationships between causes and effects. Remind students that the *cause* is why something happened and the *effect* is what happened. Use a two-column chart on the board to keep track of causes and effects students find as they read the story. Ask students to find examples of cause and effect on ***Student Reader,*** Book 1 pages 198–199.

Cause	Effect
Sonia saw deer eating the lettuce in her garden.	Sonia called for her mother to come and look out the window.
The deer smelled the garden.	They came to Sonia's garden to eat the lettuce.

Looking around, I recognized many neighbors. There was Isidro Sánchez and his sister, Ana. Standing near me were Mr. Smiley, owner of Smiley's Laundromat, and my best friend, Peach, and Chester and Clarence Martin and the Yasamura sisters from down the hall. I saw Mr. Benny, the taxi driver, and the old Pigeon Lady, who was smiling brightly. I noticed that even neighbors who were almost strangers were standing close to each other and whispering in a friendly way. Well, everyone except Mr. Smiley and the Pigeon Lady, who were not on speaking terms. Mr. Smiley was angry because the Pigeon Lady fed her pigeons in front of his Laundromat, and he thought that was bad for business.

200

Mr. Donovan, our landlord, approached Papa. They spoke in hushed voices, but I was all ears.

"Luis, I, too, think the deer are really beautiful, but we both know they can't stay here," whispered Mr. Donovan. "They could be hit by a car. They belong in the woods, not in the city. I think we'd better call the animal control officers."

Papa nodded solemnly, and they walked off.

The Pigeon Lady came up to Peach and me and said, "Oh, girls, aren't they wonderful!"

"Yes!" we both answered together.

"I think two of the deer may be smaller. Those are probably females, or does. The males are called bucks. I used to see deer many years ago when I lived in the country."

201

Reading with a Writer's Eye

Characterization

Tell students that characters have specific traits, feelings, and relationships that make each story unique and help tell the story. Harriet Peck Taylor has descriptive, strong characters with a purpose for being in the story. Ask students to find details used by Taylor to make each of the following characters unique:

- Mr. Smiley **Possible Answer** *He is angry at the Pigeon Lady for feeding pigeons in front of his business. He seems to be a serious businessman who isn't as sensitive to animal issues like the Pigeon Lady is.*
- Pigeon Lady **Possible Answer** *Pigeon Lady smiles brightly and is kind to Sonia and Peach, so she is probably a kind person. She likes the deer and seems to know about animals, maybe because she lived in the country.*
- Mr. Donovan **Possible Answer** *He seems like a good person because he likes the deer and wants to keep them safe.*

Expanding Vocabulary

hooves (ho͞ovz) *n.* plural form of **hoof:** a hard covering on the feet of animals such as horses and cows (page 199)

Horses' *hooves* can be protected by horseshoes.

solemnly (sol' • əm • lē) *adv.* seriously page 201)

My team reacted *solemnly* after losing the game.

Word Structure

Homophones: one (won), new (knew), see (sea), by (buy), hall (haul)

Soon, Papa and Mr. Donovan returned with worried looks on their faces. They gathered the group together.

"The animal control office wants to shoot the deer," said Papa. "It's the law. The city is afraid the deer will starve."

"There aren't enough woods left for all the deer to find a home," added Mr. Donovan. "That's why the young deer wander far away. They're looking for territory of their own."

Everyone was so quiet that all you could hear was street sounds: honking and beeping, rumbling and humming.

202

Mr. Benny was the first to speak. "We can't let them shoot the deer. There must be another way."

"Yeah! That's right!" said Teresa Yasamura.

All around, people were nodding in agreement.

Then Chester spoke up. "They wouldn't shoot the deer in front of this many people. It would be too dangerous."

"It's true!" exclaimed Papa. "We can form a human wall around the deer without getting too close."

"Right on!" said Isidro. "We'll stay here until we can figure out what to do."

And that was the beginning of our peaceful protest.

203

Word Structure

Homophones: right (write), not (knot), night (knight), way (weigh), past (passed), tails (tales), made (maid)

Differentiating Instruction — English Learner

IF . . . students are native speakers of Spanish, **THEN . . .** point out that adverbs in English that end in *-ly*, such as *cautiously*, usually end in *-mente* in Spanish.

Comprehension Skill

Cause and Effect

Have students continue to look for cause-and-effect relationships throughout the story. Tell students that certain words can be used to show these relationships. These words include *because, so, that, then,* and *since*. Even if the writer does not use these words in the story, students can use the words to explain cause and effect. Ask students to practice writing sentences illustrating cause-and-effect relationships:

- *The neighbors would not leave the deer* so *the deer were not harmed.*
- *The deer slept cautiously* because *being so close to the people made them feel uncomfortable.*
- Since *they are wildlife and not used to being around people, the deer were uncomfortable.*

Mr. Benny wrinkled his brow. "I remember reading a few months back about an organization that rescues and relocates animals that are stranded or injured. A fox had been hit by a car but wasn't badly hurt. This outfit took it in until it healed and then found a new home for it far from busy streets. I'll go see if I can find the number."

A little while later, Mr. Benny returned and announced, "The wildlife rescuer isn't in at the moment, but I left a message for him to call. I said it was an emergency."

When the animal control officer arrived, he saw the crowd surrounding the deer and decided not to take any chances. "If you don't mind, folks," he said, "I'll just hang around until you've all had enough and gone home." But we weren't leaving.

204

We stayed all afternoon, waiting anxiously, hoping to hear from the rescue organization. We got to know one another better, and we learned more about the deer.

Peach's eyes were wide and bright. "Look how they rotate their big soft ears to the left and right," she exclaimed.

Clarence said, "We studied deer in science. Their hearing is very sharp. It helps them detect enemies approaching from far away."

Mr. Benny nodded as he walked over to us. "I sometimes see this kind of deer at night, in the headlights, when I drive way past the city limits. When they're startled by the taxi's lights, their tails go up like flags. The tails are white underneath, which means the animals are white-tailed deer."

The deer grazed and slept cautiously, always alert to danger. They watched us with curious, intelligent eyes. I could see that the people made them uncomfortable, and it helped me appreciate that these really were wild animals. We tried to keep our distance and not make any sudden movements.

205

Reading with a Writer's Eye

Plot

Remind students that the plot of the story includes the events of the story, the problem that arises, and how it is solved. When creating a plot, writers must work these elements into a beginning, middle, and end, just as students are doing in their writing assignments. Ask students the following question:

What events, or problems, does Harriet Peck Taylor present in her story to create the plot? **Possible Answer** *The deer that are in Sonia's garden cannot stay there, and animal control officers feel they have no choice but to shoot the deer. The neighbors do not want this to happen and are going to hold a peaceful protest until they can figure out how to save the deer.*

STOP You have reread the first half of the story. You will continue the story tomorrow on page T322.

Expanding Vocabulary

territory (ter′ • rit • or′ • ē) *n.* any large area of land, usually owned by someone or by a country. (page 202)

A family of robins set up *territory* in the tree.

announced (ə • nounst) *v.* past tense of **announce:** to make known (page 204)

The coach *announced* the beginning of the race.

surrounding (sûr • round′ • ing) *adj.* forming a circle around (page 204)

The fence was *surrounding* the yard.

city limits (sit′ • ē lim′ • its) *n.* the points at which the city ends (page 205)

My sister lives outside of the *city limits*.

grazed (grāzd) *v.* past tense of **graze:** to feed on grass or other plants (page 205)

The cattle *grazed* on the grass.

Supporting The Reading

Comprehension Strategy: Making Connections

Teach

Remind students that when they are making connections, they are noticing how their own experiences and knowledge relate to the text. Thinking about how a text reminds us of our own experiences helps readers to more fully understand and appreciate what is being read.

Guided Practice

Students should have been making connections to the story "Two Days in May" as you read it the first time. Have students reflect on the story while paging through it again. Encourage them to tell the class about any connections they can make to any part of the story. Record students' responses on the board or on a two-column chart on ***Transparency*** 15. You can use the following as an example to get started.

Example from Story	Student Connection
Sonia saw deer in her city garden.	I saw deer at my brother's house. But he lives in the country and has acres of woods in his backyard. I think the deer are safe there.

Apply

Have students look through the story "Two Days in May" to find more examples of connections they can make to the story. Have them record examples they can refer to.

Encourage students to think about the realistic stories they are writing during Language Arts. Using personal experiences when writing will help their stories seem real. It's also possible that the readers will make their own connections to what the writers experienced.

Differentiating Instruction **English Learner**

IF . . . students have difficulty expressing their connections to the story, **THEN . . .** ask simple questions to help them participate in the discussion. For example: *Have you ever seen a deer? Where did you see the deer? What do deer eat?*

Imagine It! Transparency 15

Two-Column Chart

 Level 3

Transparency 15

Fluency

Students should not have difficulty reading "Two Days in May." It has a conversational tone. The characters are sympathetic and friendly. Certain scenes are exciting and full of anticipation. You may want to review some of the pronunciations of characters' names before reading aloud. Remind students that as they read, they should keep the personalities of the characters in mind. Focus on expression, or using tone of voice to indicate feelings and emotions.

- Model reading with expression as you read pages 210–211 from "Two Days in May." Have students follow along in the ***Student Reader.*** Ask them to raise their hands if they hear an unfamiliar word or passage.
- After you have read the passage, call on a volunteer to read the first three paragraphs. Before the student begins, make sure the student understands the excitement and good feelings that the neighbors are experiencing, as well as the significance of the relationship between Mr. Smiley and the Pigeon Lady.
- After the volunteer has finished, have all students chorally read the passage several times until they can read it naturally with good phrasing.

To help students build fluency and strengthen their vocabulary and comprehension skills, have them read the ***Leveled Readers*** for this unit. Use each student's Oral Fluency Assessment score from the previous lesson assessment to diagnose the appropriate ***Leveled Reader***.

Teacher Tip

FLUENCY For additional fluency practice, students can read this passage and others in the story with a partner during Small-Group Time.

Inquiry

Collecting Information

- For their investigations, students should be working with their groups to gather information from various sources to help them evaluate their conjectures.
- Remind students that they can use articles from the **Concept/Question Board** as sources of information. They can also find titles and summaries of other useful sources of information about animals and animal habitats.
- Periodically post articles and summaries on the **Concept/Question Board** to encourage students to do the same. Remind the students that the Board belongs to the whole class and should benefit everyone.

Language Arts

OBJECTIVES

Students will

- revise their realistic stories.
- spell homophones and review previous spelling skills.
- practice subjects and direct objects.
- practice using graphic organizers.

MATERIALS

- Routine 16
- ***Skills Practice 1,*** pp. 138–140, 143–144

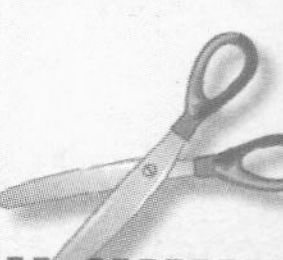

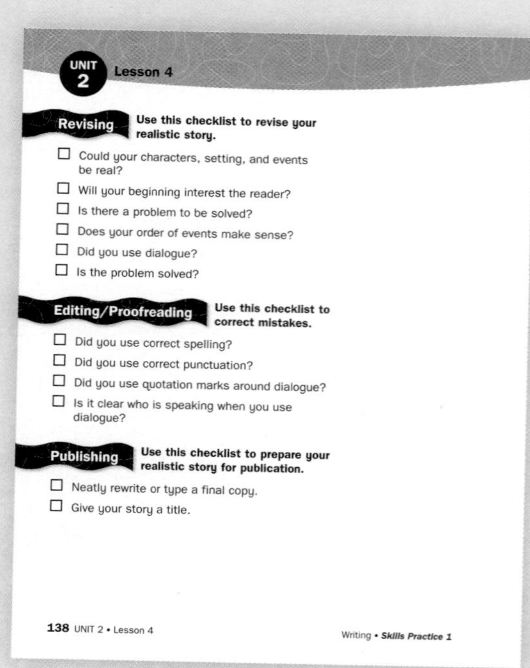

UNIT 2 Lesson 4

Revising Use this checklist to revise your realistic story.

- ☐ Could your characters, setting, and events be real?
- ☐ Will your beginning interest the reader?
- ☐ Is there a problem to be solved?
- ☐ Does your order of events make sense?
- ☐ Did you use dialogue?
- ☐ Is the problem solved?

Editing/Proofreading Use this checklist to correct mistakes.

- ☐ Did you use correct spelling?
- ☐ Did you use correct punctuation?
- ☐ Did you use quotation marks around dialogue?
- ☐ Is it clear who is speaking when you use dialogue?

Publishing Use this checklist to prepare your realistic story for publication.

- ☐ Neatly rewrite or type a final copy.
- ☐ Give your story a title.

138 UNIT 2 • Lesson 4 Writing • *Skills Practice 1*

Skills Practice 1, p. 138

Differentiating Instruction **English Learner**

IF. . . students have difficulty punctuating their dialogue, **THEN . . .** keep in mind that not all languages use the same quotation marks. French and Spanish, for example, often use angle quotation marks. «Hello!»

Writing Realistic Story

ROUTINE 16

Revising

Teach—Using Dialogue

- Use Routine 16 as you model revising. Tell students that during revision, they will make changes to characters, plot, and setting. In addition, they will work on creating dialogue with correct punctuation.
- Tell students that by having the characters speak, the story seems more real. This also helps the reader get to know the characters. Tell students that the words people use helps to define who they are, and that students should work on selecting words that will fit well with a character's personality.
- Remind students that as they revise they should make sure
  - the events, characters, and settings could all be real.
  - the story has a clear beginning, middle, and end.
  - the story has a sense of completeness or wholeness.
  - the plot includes a problem that is solved during the course of the story.
  - the story has details that make it seem real.
  - the descriptive language and vivid images keep the story interesting.

Guided Practice

Using the draft you created earlier, show students how to insert dialogue, deleting summary information as necessary. Explain to students why you chose the particular words for the character based on the character description.

Apply

Have students use the revising checklist on ***Skills Practice 1*** page 138 as they revise their realistic stories.

Traits of Good Writing

IDEAS The writer uses dialogue when writing a story to develop character, setting, and plot.

Spelling

Lesson Review and Homophones

Teach

- Tell students that homophones are words that sound alike but have different spellings and different meanings.
- Remind students that /ī/ can be spelled *igh, _y,* or *_ie.*
- Remind students that /ō/ can be spelled *_ow* or *oa_.*
- Remind students that consonant blends are groups of two or more consonants in which the sounds of all the letters are pronounced.
- Divide the class into two teams. Write the following word pairs on the board: *grone/groan, grown/gron, seam/seme, seim/seem, peice/piece, peece/peace, bi/by, bie/buy, toa/toe, tow/towe, howrse/horse, hoarse/haorse, meit/meet, meat/meight, and tale/tael.* Take turns calling on one student from each team to find the correctly spelled word and pronounce it. If the student is correct, give that student's team a point. The team with the most points wins.

Guided Practice

Have students turn to ***Skills Practice 1*** page 139. Read the instructions with them, and complete the first two questions as a class.

Apply

Have students complete ***Skills Practice 1*** pages 139–140 on their own. Remind students that challenge words are not used in ***Skills Practice*** exercises.

Monitor Progress to Differentiate Instruction

Formal Assessment

Spelling Note how well students are able to spell the lesson words.

APPROACHING LEVEL

IF . . .	THEN . . .
IF . . . students need to practice spelling this week's words,	THEN . . . instruct them to complete ***Reteach*** page 54.

ON LEVEL

IF . . .	THEN . . .
IF . . . students can spell this week's spelling words,	THEN . . . tell them to think of 3 pairs of homophones that were not in this week's lesson and write them on a separate sheet of paper.

ABOVE LEVEL

IF . . .	THEN . . .
IF . . . students are ready for a challenge,	THEN . . . have them complete ***Challenge Activities*** page 49.

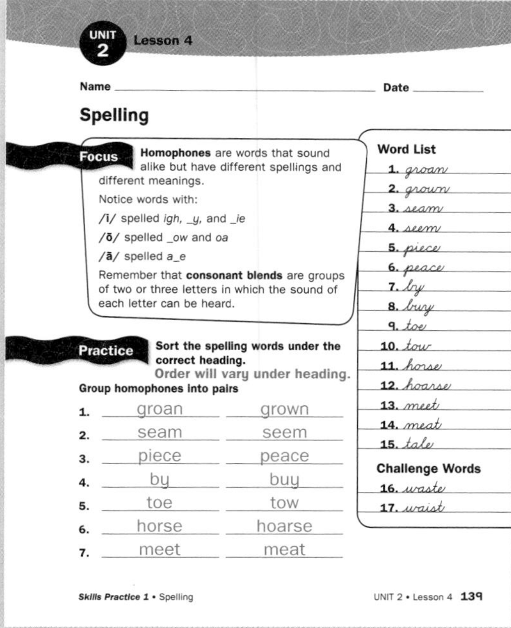
UNIT 2 Lesson 4

Name ______ Date ______

Spelling

Focus **Homophones** are words that sound alike but have different spellings and different meanings.

Notice words with:
/ī/ spelled *igh, _y,* and *_ie*
/ō/ spelled *_ow* and *oa*
/ā/ spelled *a_e*

Remember that **consonant blends** are groups of two or three letters in which the sound of each letter can be heard.

Word List
1. groan
2. grown
3. seam
4. seem
5. piece
6. peace
7. by
8. buy
9. toe
10. tow
11. horse
12. hoarse
13. meet
14. meat
15. tale

Challenge Words
16. waste
17. waist

Practice Sort the spelling words under the correct heading.
Order will vary under heading.

Group homophones into pairs

1.	groan	grown
2.	seam	seem
3.	piece	peace
4.	by	buy
5.	toe	tow
6.	horse	hoarse
7.	meet	meat

Skills Practice 1 • Spelling UNIT 2 • Lesson 4 139

Skills Practice 1, p. 139

UNIT 2 Lesson 4

/ā/ spelled *a_e*
8. tale

140 UNIT 2 • Lesson 4 Spelling • *Skills Practice 1*

Skills Practice 1, p. 140

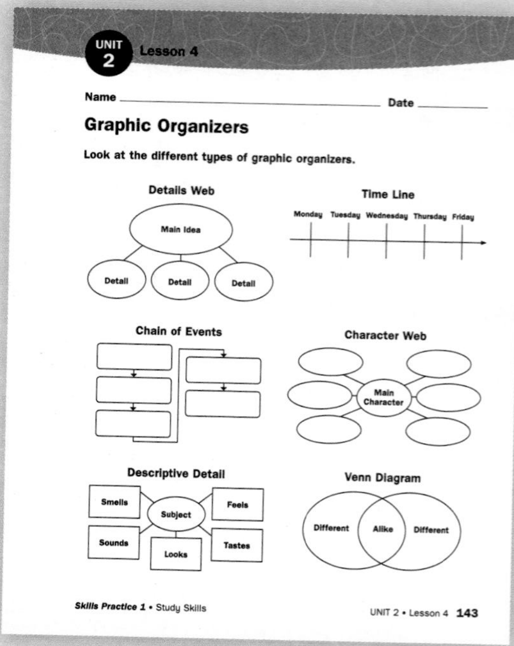

UNIT 2 Lesson 4

Name ______________________ Date ________

Graphic Organizers

Look at the different types of graphic organizers.

Details Web

Main Idea

Detail Detail Detail

Time Line

Monday Tuesday Wednesday Thursday Friday

Chain of Events

Character Web

Main Character

Descriptive Detail

Smells Subject Feels Sounds Looks Tastes

Venn Diagram

Different Alike Different

Skills Practice 1 • Study Skills UNIT 2 • Lesson 4 143

Skills Practice 1, p. 143

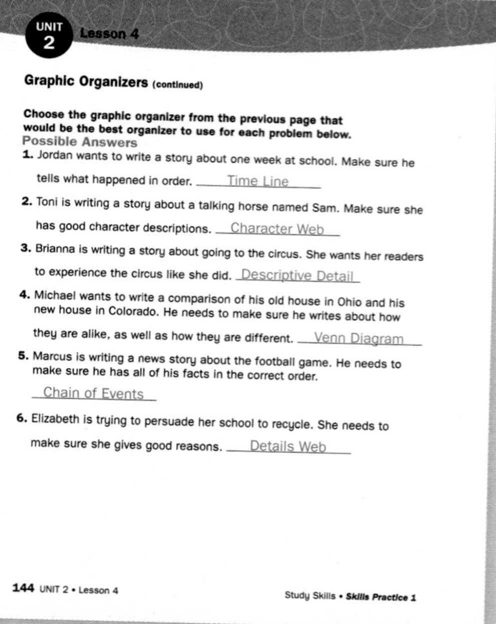

UNIT 2 Lesson 4

Graphic Organizers (continued)

Choose the graphic organizer from the previous page that would be the best organizer to use for each problem below.

Possible Answers

1. Jordan wants to write a story about one week at school. Make sure he tells what happened in order. Time Line
2. Toni is writing a story about a talking horse named Sam. Make sure she has good character descriptions. Character Web
3. Brianna is writing a story about going to the circus. She wants her readers to experience the circus like she did. Descriptive Detail
4. Michael wants to write a comparison of his old house in Ohio and his new house in Colorado. He needs to make sure he writes about how they are alike, as well as how they are different. Venn Diagram
5. Marcus is writing a news story about the football game. He needs to make sure he has all of his facts in the correct order. Chain of Events
6. Elizabeth is trying to persuade her school to recycle. She needs to make sure she gives good reasons. Details Web

144 UNIT 2 • Lesson 4 Study Skills • *Skills Practice 1*

Skills Practice 1, p. 144

Study Skills

Graphic Organizers

Teach

- Discuss the different graphic organizers students have used for their writing assignments and unit investigations. Discuss what was helpful about these organizers. If necessary, remind students about the importance of organizing information while taking notes on a writing assignment or for collecting ideas when researching an investigation or another type of assignment.
- Explain that most graphic organizers are suited for a particular purpose. For example, a story map is ideal when writing a narrative or fiction story. Time lines are helpful when writing nonfiction, because they keep events in chronological order. Idea webs can be used at the beginning of an assignment when the goal is to get ideas down quickly.

Guided Practice

Have students turn to ***Skills Practice 1*** page 143, and discuss the different graphic organizers. Help students complete the first couple of questions on page 144.

Apply

Have students complete ***Skills Practice 1*** page 144 on their own.

Monitor Progress to Differentiate Instruction

Formal Assessment 

Graphic Organization Note whether students know how to create and utilize graphic organizers.

APPROACHING LEVEL

IF . . . students need to practice creating and using graphic organizers,	**THEN . . .** have them create an organizer for their unit investigation during Workshop.

ON LEVEL

IF . . . students have an understanding of creating and using graphic organizers,	**THEN . . .** have them continue to work on their writing or unit investigations during Workshop.

ABOVE LEVEL

IF . . . students need a challenge,	**THEN . . .** have them help a peer create a graphic organizer during Workshop.

Grammar, Usage, and Mechanics

Subjects and Direct Objects

Teach

Ask students to explain the meaning of nouns as the subjects and objects of a sentence. If necessary, refer to Unit 2 Lesson 4 Day 2. Also, ask students to review how pronouns may be used to replace nouns as the objects of the sentence. Have students write several sentences on the board. Have them identify the subject and object and then replace the object with an object pronoun.

Apply

Have students review their realistic stories. Have them replace objects with object pronouns when the replacement will make the writing sound less repetitious.

Day 4

Preparing to Read

OBJECTIVES

Students will

- ✦ identify and know the meaning of homophones.
- ✦ build fluency.

MATERIALS

- ✦ ***Transparency*** 63

Daily Oral Practice

Daily News

Today!

I go to my aunt's house in the country to see wildlife. Many deer graze in her backyard. She feeds the deer in the winter when they have a hard time finding food. I love watching the deer roam freely in their natural habitat. I feel lucky to have found a window to their world.

- ✦ Write the daily news on the board or on chart paper. Then have students read the daily news in unison to practice fluency.
- ✦ As a review of yesterday's word structure lesson, ask a volunteer to identify any homophones in the daily news. *to (too/two), aunt (ant), see (sea), deer (dear), time (thyme), roam (Rome), through (threw), their (there/they're)*

Word Structure

Homphones

✦ Use ***Transparency*** 63 with the word lines from Day 3.

Line 1	deer	dear	one	won
Line 2	knew	new	tails	tales
Line 3	know	no	two	too
Line 4	there	their	blue	blew

✦ Review the meaning of homophones. If necessary, remind students that homophones are words like *whole* and *hole* that sound the same but have different meanings and different spellings.

✦ Have students read the words using normal intonation and expression.

Developing Oral Language

Use any of these activities to help students practice reading the words.

- Have a student choose a word from the word lines on the board and use the word in a sentence. **Possible Answer** *Our team* won *a game.* Point to the word *one* and ask another student what that word is in relation to the word *won*. *a homophone* Then have the student use both homophones in one sentence. **Possible Answer** *Our team has only* won one *game.*
- As a class, have students create a crossword puzzle on the board using all of the words on the word lines. They should write the questions and plot the answers on the board. Examples: Giraffes have long necks and short __*tails*__. Grandparents like to tell __*tales*__ about when they were young.
- If time permits, have students find other homophones from "Two Days in May," and add them to the words on the board. **Possible Answer** *I thought I had never seen such an amazing* sight. *The deer were looking for a new* site *in the city to live.*

Differentiating Instruction **English Learner**

IF . . . students have difficulty participating in the Developing Oral Language activities, **THEN . . .** define each word and use pictures, objects, or pantomime to help students understand the meanings of the words before beginning the activities.

Teacher Tip

BLENDING During Workshop, work with students who have difficulty blending words by using Routine 1 for sound-by-sound blending or Routine 3 for whole-word blending.

Monitor Progress 

to Differentiate Instruction
Formal Assessment

Word Structure Note how well students understand the words on the word lines.

APPROACHING LEVEL

IF . . . students do not understand the words on the word lines, **THEN . . .** use pictures, photos, objects, stick drawings, or pantomime to help them visualize the words during Workshop.

ON LEVEL

IF . . . students need practice with the words on the word lines **THEN . . .** have them form additional sentences using the same words on the lines during Workshop.

ABOVE LEVEL

IF . . . students understand the words on the word lines, **THEN . . .** have them make a list of other homophones and use them in a paragraph during Workshop.

When evening came, the crowd grew. We talked quietly and told jokes as we kept watch over our silent friends. We ordered pizza from Giuseppe's.

Ana Sánchez spoke to the animal control officer. "Would you like a slice of pizza?" she asked.

"Thanks so much," he said. "My name is Steve Scully, and I understand how hard this must be for all of you. This is the part of my job I dislike.

"The problem is population growth. We've built towns and highways where there were once forests and streams. Now there is very little habitat left for the deer. There is no easy solution." He shook his head sadly.

206

I begged Papa to let me sleep outside all night, since almost everyone was staying. Mama came out with my baby brother, Danny. She brought blankets, a quilt, a jacket, and even my stuffed dog, Hershey.

Mama sat close and draped her arm across my shoulders. "Are you sure you'll be warm enough, Sonia?" she asked.

"I'm sure," I said.

We sat silently together, admiring the deer.

Finally she said, "I have to go put Danny to bed." She kissed me on the top of my head. "Sweet dreams, pumpkin."

I slept like a bear cub, curled in a ball against Papa's broad back.

207

OBJECTIVES

Students will

- use the comprehension skill Cause and Effect.
- build fluency.
- check comprehension.

MATERIALS

- ***Student Reader,*** Book 1, pp. 206–215
- ***Skills Practice 1,*** pp. 135–136

Comprehension Skill

Cause and Effect

Continue to have students look for cause-and-effect relationships. Write the causes and effects on the board, and then have students create cause-and-effect sentences using causal indicator words.

Cause	Effect
People have built towns and highways where there used to be forests and streams.	The deer's habitat is disappearing.

Sentence: The deer's habitat is disappearing because people have built towns and highways where forests and streams used to be.

Next morning, I awoke with the sun in my eyes and city sounds buzzing in my ears. Papa hugged me and asked how I liked camping out.

"I dreamed I was sleeping with the deer in cool forests under tall trees."

"You were, Sonia!" he said, laughing. "But not in the forest."

I looked at the deer. "Has the wildlife rescuer called back?" I asked.

"Yes, Sonia. The organization called late last night and hopes to get someone out here this morning."

The group was quiet as we all continued to wait.

208

Later that morning, a rusty orange truck pulled up. The man who got out had a friendly, open face. All eyes were on him.

"Hi, folks. My name is Carl Jackson, and I'm with the wildlife rescue organization," he said. "I need to put the deer in crates in order to take them to our center. Don't be alarmed—I'm going to shoot them with a small amount of tranquilizer to make them sleep for a little while." Then, as they wobbled on unsteady legs, he grabbed them gently and guided them toward the wooden crates.

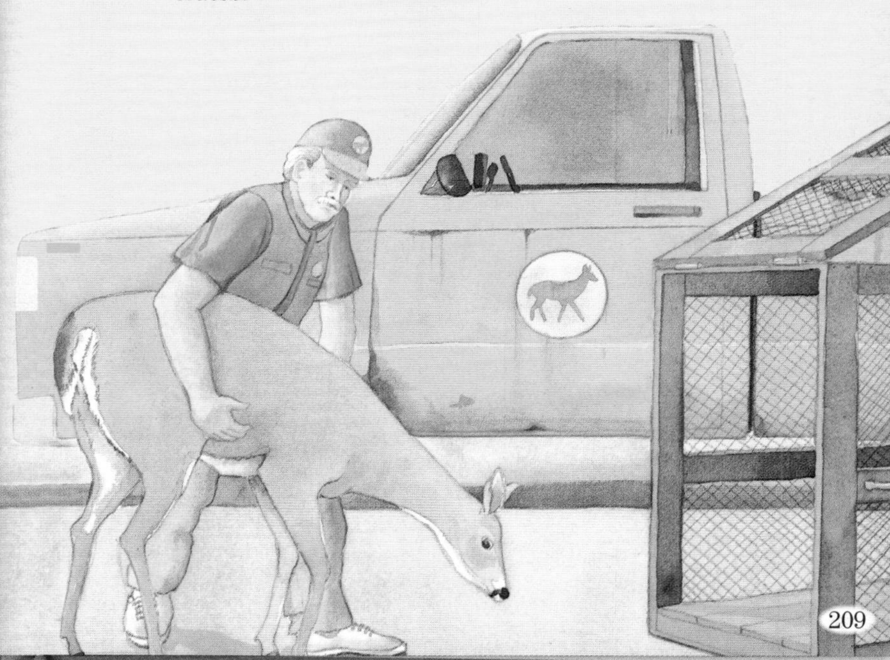

209

Reading with a Writer's Eye

Characterization

Writers say a lot about their characters through vivid description and dialogue. Readers have an insight into what the characters are really like when they pay close attention to how characters are described and how they speak. Ask students:

What clues does Harriet Peck Taylor give the reader about the character of Carl Jackson? **Possible Answer** *She describes him as having a friendly, open face. When he speaks, he seems friendly and tries to reassure the neighbors.*

Expanding Vocabulary

population (pop′ • ū • lā • shən) *n.* the number of people or animals living in a place (page 206)

As more people move to our town, the *population* of our school is growing, too.

Word Structure

Homophones: night (knight), bear (bare), sun (son), deer (dear), you (ewe), here (hear)

Carl turned to the crowd and smiled. "I'm an animal lover, too, and all of you should feel proud for helping save these deer. I'll find a home for them in the woods, where they'll be safe and happy and have plenty to eat."

Steve Scully came forward and extended his hand to Carl. "Glad you came, man."

A cheer went up from the crowd. People slapped each other on the back. Isidro high-fived everyone, including Mr. Donovan and the Pigeon Lady. Peach and I hugged each other, and Papa shook hands with Carl and Steve. I said goodbye to Teresa and Sandy Yasamura and to Mr. Benny.

I even saw Mr. Smiley shake the Pigeon Lady's hand. "Maybe you can feed the pigeons *behind* my Laundromat," he said. "I have a little space back there."

The Pigeon Lady smiled.

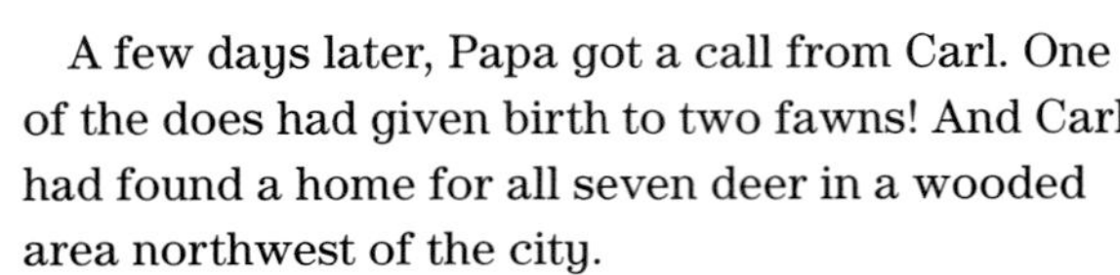

A few days later, Papa got a call from Carl. One of the does had given birth to two fawns! And Carl had found a home for all seven deer in a wooded area northwest of the city.

Sometimes, when I'm sitting on the fire escape, watching the flickering city lights, I think of the deer. In my mind, they're gliding silently across tall grass meadows all aglow in silver moonlight.

210 211

Word Structure

Homophones: to (too, two), too (to, two), deer (dear), you (ewe)

Teacher Tip

CHARACTERS Encourage students to remember to make vivid descriptions of their characters and to choose the dialogue of their characters carefully when writing their realistic stories.

Comprehension Skill

Cause and Effect

Encourage students to think about and discuss the cause-and-effect relationships after they finish reading this story. Practicing this skill will help them use it more automatically as they read other texts in the future.

Cause	Effect
The deer were rescued.	A cheer went up from the crowd.

Sentence: A cheer went up from the crowd because the deer were rescued.

Checking Comprehension

Ask students the following questions to check their comprehension of the story:

- *How did the deer end up in the city?* **Possible Answer** *They were looking for food in the city because their habitat had been taken over by towns and highways.*
- *What was so remarkable about what the neighbors did?* **Possible Answer** *They took the time to protect the wildlife. They made a difference by participating in a peaceful protest and by taking action to find someone to rescue the deer.*
- *How did the experience help the neighbors?* **Possible Answer** *The neighbors worked together as a team. Some of the neighbors who did not get along before had the chance to get to know each other and work out a compromise.*

Teacher Tip

WRITING Remind students to include a clear problem and resolution in their realistic stories.

Science Inquiry

Genre Advertisement 

Introduce the elements of an advertisement. If necessary, remind students that the purpose of advertisements is to persuade people to do something or to think and behave in a certain way.

Feature Maps

Point to the map in the advertisement. Tell students that **maps** show the location, size, and shape of an area.

Reading "A National Pleasure"

Have students read "A National Pleasure" silently. Ask them how this advertisement is related to the theme Animals and Their Habitats. **Possible Answer** *The advertisement lists some of the animals that inhabit Yellowstone National Park.* Make sure students look at the map and understand its significance in the advertisement.

Think Link

1. In what states is Yellowstone National Park located? *Yellowstone National Park is located in Wyoming, Montana, and Idaho.*
2. What is the purpose of the advertisement? **Possible Answer** *The purpose of this advertisement is to persuade people to visit Yellowstone National Park.*
3. Matter has three forms: solid, liquid, and gas. Find examples of each in the advertisement above. **Possible Answers** *Snow is a solid form of water. Water is a liquid. Air is made of gases. Steam (water vapor) is also a gas.*

Teacher Tips

SELECTION VOCABULARY Review the meaning of the highlighted selection vocabulary word *appreciate* in "A National Pleasure."

SILENT READ If some students are having difficulty comprehending the selection as they read silently, read the selection with them in small groups.

Science Inquiry

A National Pleasure

Genre

An **advertisement** tries to persuade people to do something, or to think or behave in a certain way.

Feature

A **map** shows the location, size, and shape of an area.

Are you a nature lover? Then Yellowstone National Park is the place for you! No other park can match the array of wildlife and land features found here.

Many members of the deer family make their home at the park. Elk, moose, and deer are a common sight on the ranges. Bears, wolves, and many kinds of birds might also be seen and heard.

Hiking trails offer a chance to get close to nature. Guests can hike on their own or with a park ranger who will guide them. Will you be visiting in the winter when the ground may be covered with snow? No problem! You can strap on cross-country skis and hit the trails.

More outdoor adventures await you at Yellowstone. You can fish, boat, and bike. At the end of the day, pitch a tent at one of the campgrounds. Do you not like sleeping outdoors? Then relax in one of the cabins, lodges, or inns at the park.

No trip to the park would be complete without seeing Old Faithful. This is the most famous geyser in the world. The park boasts six grand geysers that spew steam and hot water more than one hundred feet into the air.

Water from rain, melted snow, and ice seeps miles into the earth, where it comes in contact with molten rock. The superheated water sprays out of the ground as steam and boiling water.

Do you want even more water features? Then you will appreciate the park's hot springs and waterfalls. Many of these spots can be reached or viewed from marked trails.

Don't delay! Make plans now to visit Yellowstone.
It's more than a park—it's a national pleasure.

Think Link

1. In what states is Yellowstone National Park located?
2. What is the purpose of the advertisement?
3. Matter has three forms: solid, liquid, and gas. Find examples of each in the advertisement above.

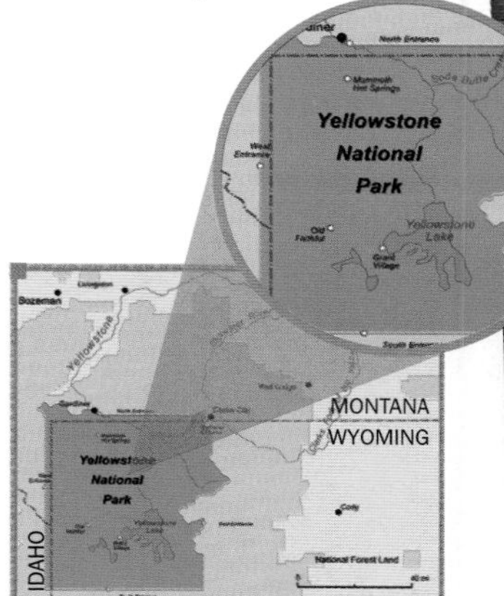

Try It!

As you work on your investigation, think about how you can use a map to show information in your final presentation.

Inquiry Connection

Have students discuss how using maps might be helpful in their investigation about animals and their habitats. For example, if students are describing a specific animal habitat, they might use a map to show its location and size. If students are showing the habitats of a specific species, they might want to show a map of the world highlighting that species' habitats.

Differentiating Instruction: English Learner

IF . . . students miss the play on words in the selection's title, **THEN . . .** explain that Yellowstone and other parks are often called "national treasures" because people in this country think the parks have great value. You may also need to explain that a *pleasure* is something that feels good or that people enjoy.

Inquiry Process

Step 5—Collecting Information

Whole-Group Time

Whole Group

- Students should practice the study skills they learned by creating tables, charts, and diagrams of information they collect. Seeing information in new arrangements may give students ideas about information they still need and what information they may not need for their presentations, which may help them evaluate their conjectures.
- Discuss questions or ideas students might have about the selection they have just read, "Two Days in May." Students should be asking themselves questions such as: *Does the selection tell me something about animals and their habitats that I didn't know before? Does the selection make me wonder about something? Has anything I've learned in this selection changed my ideas about animals or animal habitats?* Model taking notes and collecting information by recording their findings on the board. If possible, arrange student responses into a table, with column heads such as *New Information, New Questions/Wonderings,* and *Changed Ideas.* If students don't mention that there are wildlife rescue organizations dedicated to saving and protecting animals, share this in the discussion.
- As students come closer to their final presentations, hold a class discussion about the questions and ideas they had at the beginning of the unit. Discuss with students how their ideas have changed. Ask if any of their initial questions have been answered, and what they know now that they didn't know before.

Small-Group Time

Small Group

- Students should join their small groups. Have students record on ***Skills Practice 1,*** pages 135–136 any information from "Two Days in May" that might be useful for the unit investigation.

✦ Students should continue to collect the information they need to reevaluate their conjectures and work toward their final presentations. They should continue to record useful information for their investigation on ***Skills Practice 1*** pages 135–136.

✦ Have each group work to finalize how they want to present the results of their investigation. They should also start planning what contributions each group member will make to the group's presentation. Remind students to practice teamwork and give each group member equal responsibility.

Concept/Question Board

- Remind students to consult the **Concept/Question Board** for ideas about additional sources or information to collect for the unit investigation.
- Continue to have students contribute to the **Concept/Question Board.** Ask them how the Board helps them as they progress through the unit investigation. Encourage the use of the Board by recognizing and thanking students for their contributions. Incorporate discussion of those items into classroom discussions whenever possible. Remember to post your own questions, conjectures, pictures, articles, and summaries.

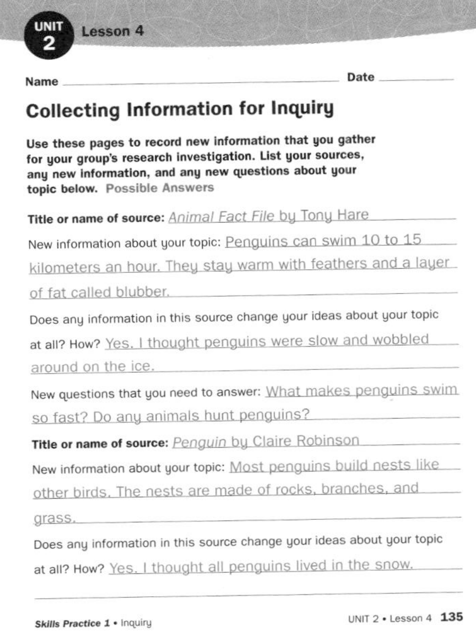
UNIT 2 Lesson 4

Name ______ Date ______

Collecting Information for Inquiry

Use these pages to record new information that you gather for your group's research investigation. List your sources, any new information, and any new questions about your topic below. Possible Answers

Title or name of source: *Animal Fact File* by Tony Hare

New information about your topic: Penguins can swim 10 to 15 kilometers an hour. They stay warm with feathers and a layer of fat called blubber.

Does any information in this source change your ideas about your topic at all? How? Yes. I thought penguins were slow and wobbled around on the ice.

New questions that you need to answer: What makes penguins swim so fast? Do any animals hunt penguins?

Title or name of source: *Penguin* by Claire Robinson

New information about your topic: Most penguins build nests like other birds. The nests are made of rocks, branches, and grass.

Does any information in this source change your ideas about your topic at all? How? Yes. I thought all penguins lived in the snow.

Skills Practice 1 • Inquiry UNIT 2 • Lesson 4 135

Skills Practice 1, pp. 135, 136

Teacher Tip

COLLECTING INFORMATION Remind students that they can use information they learned from "Two Days in May" in the unit investigation. Encourage them to use information from other selections in this unit as well.

Inquiry Rubric

To assess Collecting Information, see the Inquiry Rubrics in the Level Appendix.

OBJECTIVES

Students will
- ✦ edit/proofread their realistic stories.
- ✦ review previous lessons and learn homophones.
- ✦ exercise listening skills.
- ✦ learn to outline information.

MATERIALS
- ✦ Routine 16
- ✦ ***Student Reader,*** Book 1, pp. 214–215
- ✦ ***Transparencies*** 17, 17A
- ✦ ***Skills Practice 1,*** p. 138

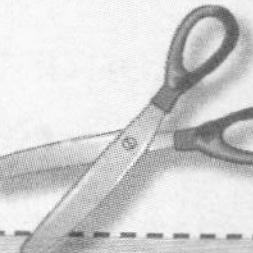

Writing Realistic Story

ROUTINE 16

Editing/Proofreading

Teach

- ✦ Tell students they will now edit/proofread the revised copy of their realistic stories. Use Routine 16.
- ✦ Remind students to look for errors in spelling, grammar, and punctuation.
- ✦ Tell students that as they read their stories to themselves or to a partner, they should make sure it is clear which character is speaking when using dialogue. Remind students to use quotation marks with dialogue and to start a new paragraph every time a different character begins to speak.
- ✦ Tell students to make sure the subject of each sentence is clear. This will clarify meaning for the reader. Suggest they also vary their sentences by adding objects and descriptions to further define the subject.
- ✦ Remind students of the proofreading marks by displaying ***Transparencies*** 17 and 17A.

Guided Practice

- ✦ Using the draft you created, show students how to edit grammar, spelling, and punctuation, as well as making changes to dialogue. Have students assist you in the editing process.
- ✦ Write a short two-character dialogue on the board, and have students insert the correct punctuation.

Differentiating Instruction — **English Learner**

IF . . . students need additional support during the editing/proofreading process,
THEN . . . pair them with proficient English speakers to help identify and correct errors in spelling, grammar, or punctuation.

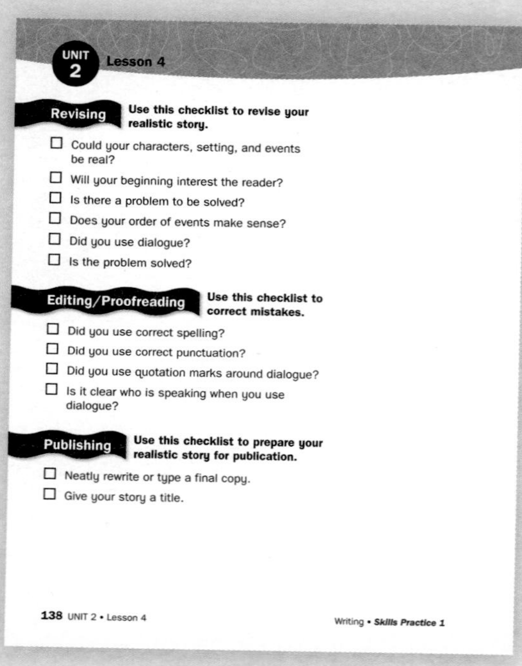
UNIT 2 Lesson 4

Revising Use this checklist to revise your realistic story.
- ☐ Could your characters, setting, and events be real?
- ☐ Will your beginning interest the reader?
- ☐ Is there a problem to be solved?
- ☐ Does your order of events make sense?
- ☐ Did you use dialogue?
- ☐ Is the problem solved?

Editing/Proofreading Use this checklist to correct mistakes.
- ☐ Did you use correct spelling?
- ☐ Did you use correct punctuation?
- ☐ Did you use quotation marks around dialogue?
- ☐ Is it clear who is speaking when you use dialogue?

Publishing Use this checklist to prepare your realistic story for publication.
- ☐ Neatly rewrite or type a final copy.
- ☐ Give your story a title.

138 UNIT 2 • Lesson 4 Writing • *Skills Practice 1*

Skills Practice 1, p. 138

Writing, continued

Apply

Composing — Publishing Have students refer to the editing/proofreading checklist on ***Skills Practice 1*** page 138 as they edit/proofread their realistic stories. Encourage them to begin working on their final drafts once they have completed the editing/proofreading process.

Monitor Progress to Differentiate Instruction

Formal Assessment 

Editing/Proofreading Note whether students are using correct grammar, spelling, and punctuation.

APPROACHING LEVEL

IF . . . students need to practice editing/proofreading,	**THEN . . .** have them work with a partner to edit their stories during Workshop.

ON LEVEL

IF . . . students have an understanding of editing/proofreading,	**THEN . . .** tell them to begin the final draft of their realistic stories during Workshop once they complete the editing/proofreading process.

ABOVE LEVEL

IF . . . students need a challenge,	**THEN . . .** have them work on incorporating more dynamic sentence structures into their writing during Workshop.

Spelling

Lesson Review and Homophones

Teach

- Students will learn homophones and review words with /ī/, /ō/, and consonant blends.
- **Consonant-Substitution Strategy** Tell students that some words retain the same vowel sound even if the consonants in the word are replaced.

Guided Practice

Write the following words on the board: *seam, tow, meet,* and *tale*. Then write the following sentences on the board:

1. The farmer had to feed his cows another bale of hay. *tale*

2. Would you like a beet sliced on your salad? *meet*

3. Please tie a bow on top of that present. *tow*

4. Kyoko excels on the balance beam. *seam*

Have students come to the board and identify which word from the list substitutes a consonant or consonants for the underlined word.

Study Skills

Graphic Organizers

Teach

Remind students of the usefulness of graphic organizers. Write the shell of an outline on the board.

Guided Practice

Have students turn to the science link advertisement on page 214 in ***Student Reader,*** Book 1. Ask volunteers to fill in the lines of an outline of the advertisement on Yellowstone National Park.

Title: Yellowstone National Park

1. *animal viewing*
    a. *deer*
    b. *elk*
    c. *moose*
    d. *bears*
    e. *wolves*
    f. *birds*
2. *hiking*
    a. *on your own*
    b. *with a guide*
    c. *cross-country ski*
3. *sightseeing*
    a. *Old Faithful*
    b. *hot springs*
    c. *waterfalls*

Apply

Create a story map graphic organizer on the board for students to see. Note the similarities between a story map and a basic outline. Have them copy and complete the organizer for the story "Two Days in May." Tell students that the author probably used a graphic organizer similar to this one before she began writing her story.

Listening/Speaking/Viewing

Recalling Information from Oral Presentations

Teach

- Explain that being able to recall a story is an important listening skill. If we are able to recall a story, we know that we have been listening carefully.
- Paraphrasing and retelling what we hear are good ways to practice recalling a story. If we can paraphrase a story in our own words and then retell it, we are able to share the story or the information we learned with others.

Guided Practice

- Have a volunteer read a short article to the class. Paraphrase and retell it to the class.
- Select a short fiction or nonfiction article, and have a student read it to the class. After it is read, have another student paraphrase and retell the main ideas in the article. Have other students add information as needed.

Apply

Have pairs read short fiction or nonfiction articles and then paraphrase and retell the articles to each other.

Preparing to Read

Review

OBJECTIVES

Students will

- review /ī/ spelled _igh, _y, and _ie; /ō/ spelled _ow and oa_; /ū/ spelled _ew and _ue.
- review consonant blends at the beginning or end of words.
- review homophones.
- build fluency.

MATERIALS

- ***Sound/Spelling Cards*** 29–31
- ***Transparencies*** 59, 63

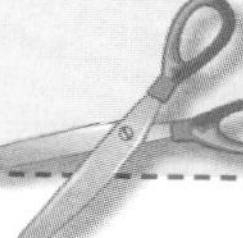

Phonics and Fluency

Use ***Transparency*** 59 with the blending lines and sentences from Days 1 and 2 to review /ī/ spelled *_igh*, *_y*, and *_ie;* /ō/ spelled *_ow* and *oa_;* /ū/ spelled *_ew* and *_ue;* and consonant blends at the beginning or end of words. Have students read the words and sentences on the blending lines. Then challenge students to think of words with consonant blends and /ī/, /ō/, or /ū/ sound/spellings.

Line 1	**highways**	**moonlight**	identify	replies
Line 2	**aglow**	**window**	throat	coastline
Line 3	**few**	pewter	**rescuer**	**continued**
Line 4	streets	slept	**except**	**protest**

Sentence 1: The glowing bright light <u>almost</u> made my <u>eyes</u> water.

Sentence 2: They rescued a few sheep and <u>part</u> of the lost goat herd.

Word Structure

Use ***Transparency*** 63 with the word lines from Days 3 and 4 to review homophones. Have students read the words on the word lines. Then have students use each homophone in a sentence that demonstrates its meaning.

Line 1	**deer**	dear	one	won
Line 2	knew	new	tails	tales
Line 3	know	no	two	too
Line 4	there	their	blue	blew

OBJECTIVES

Students will
- review selection vocabulary.
- review the comprehension strategies Asking Questions, Making Connections, and Summarizing.
- review the comprehension skill Cause and Effect.

MATERIALS
- ***Student Reader,*** Book 1, pp. 196–213
- ***Transparency*** 60

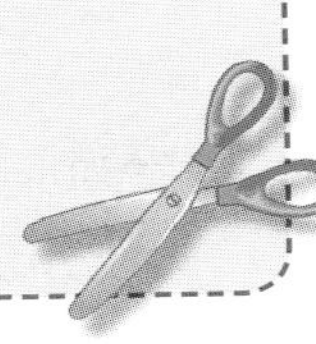

Selection Vocabulary

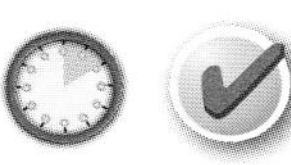

To review the selection vocabulary, organize students into small groups of three or four. Give each group 2–3 words. Ask each group to write a definition for each vocabulary word in their own words. When they are finished, have a volunteer from each group share their definition with the class.

Selection Vocabulary

relocates (rē • lō′ • kāts) *v.* a form of the verb **relocate:** to move to a new place (page 204)

stranded (strand′ • əd) *v.* a form of the verb **strand:** to leave in a helpless position (page 204)

exclaimed (eks • klāmd′) *v.* past tense of **exclaim:** to speak out (page 205)

sharp (shärp) *adj.* alert (page 205)

detect (də • tekt′) *v.* to find out (page 205)

cautiously (kosh′ • əs • lē′) *adv.* with close care (page 205)

appreciate (əp • prē′ • shē • āt′) *v.* to understand the value of (page 205)

extended (eks • tend′ • əd) *v.* past tense of **extend:** to reach out (page 210)

Day 5

Reading and Responding Review

Comprehension Strategies  

Review the following comprehension strategies with students. Then ask studen
to orally summarize "Two Days in May."

- **Asking Questions** helps readers focus attention on a text by asking and ther finding the answers to questions they have about the text. Have students loo at the **Concept/Question Board.** Ask students whether questions that they had about the theme Animals and Their Habitats were answered. If so, allow students time to post their answers on the Board.
- **Making Connections** requires readers to activate prior knowledge and connect what they know or have experienced to what they are reading. Have students review "Two Days in May" and share any connections they made to the story with the class. If students have difficulty, ask questions such as Have animals ever wandered near your home? If so, what did you do? Have you ev seen a deer? If so, did the deer match the description in the story on page 199? How would you describe the deer that you saw?
- **Summarizing** prompts readers to keep track of what they are reading and to focus their minds on important information. Ask students to review the story and give you a short summary of "Two Days in May." Use their information to create a time line on the board, and help students fill in any missing events o important information.

Comprehension Skill   

Review the following comprehension skill with students:

Cause and Effect is a skill readers use to put together logical explanations in th text once they understand what causes certain events to happen. Ask students to write three effects, or events, from "Two Days in May." Have students share their effects with the class, and have students supply the cause from the story.

Reading with a Writer's Eye  

eview the following literary elements with students:

Characterization is how the author describes and portrays his or her characters. Have students return to "Two Days in May," and find all of the characters in the story. List the characters on the board, and prompt students to ensure all characters are listed. Organize students into groups, and assign each group a character from the list. Have students complete a character web by finding descriptive words and dialogue from the story to add to their webs. Have students share their webs with the rest of the class.

Plot is what happens in the story. It tells about a problem and how it is solved. Place students into groups, and have them create a two-column chart with the headings *problems* and *solutions*. Have students fill in the chart by listing the problems faced by the characters, and then have them list how the problems were solved. Have groups take turns reading a problem from their chart, and have the other groups answer with the solution.

Fluency 

Review fluency by modeling expression for students. Remind students that expression, or reading with feeling and emotion, makes text easier to comprehend and enjoy. Read a passage from pages 204–206 from "Two Days in May." Make sure that the passage totals at least 160 words to ensure an appropriate practice length.

Have students read the passage chorally. Encourage students to read expressively. Also remind students to pause after commas and end punctuation.

OBJECTIVES

Students will
- ✦ publish their realistic stories.
- ✦ take the spelling posttest.
- ✦ practice cursive *p* and *j*.

MATERIALS

- ✦ Routine 17
- ✦ ***Language Arts Handbook,*** p. 42
- ✦ ***Skills Practice 1,*** p. 138
- ✦ ***Transparency*** 62

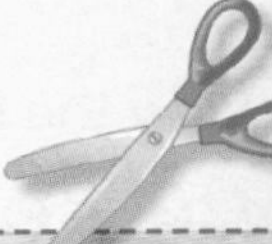

How Can I Share My Writing?

The last step in the writing process is **publishing.** At this stage, you are ready to share your writing with others. If you haven't already, you need to make a clean copy in your best handwriting or on the computer. The form in which you choose to publish your writing depends on what kind of writing it is and who your audience is. You should choose the best way to share what you have done for the audience that you have chosen.

Ways to Publish

If your writing is a story, you could make it a book and put it in the reading center.

How to Make a Book	
1. Fold some 8 ½ × 11-inch paper in half.	4. Draw pictures or add charts, tables, or diagrams.
2. Staple it in the middle.	5. Put a construction paper cover on it.
3. Write your story on the pages.	6. Write the title and your name on the cover.

If it is a letter, you should mail it.

If it is a play or a story, you could act it out.

If it is a description, you could illustrate it and put it on a bulletin board. That is what Charlie has decided for now. Later, she will include it in a letter to her pen pal. Then she will mail it to him.

42 How Can I Share My Writing? • The Writing Process

Language Arts Handbook, p. 42

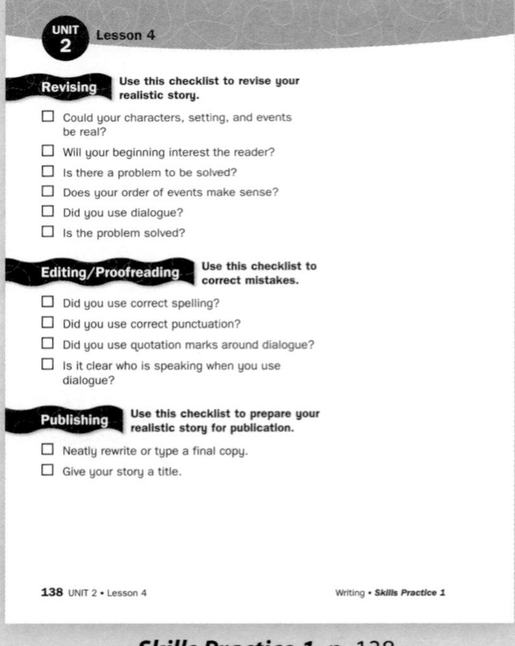

UNIT 2 Lesson 4

Revising Use this checklist to revise your realistic story.

- ☐ Could your characters, setting, and events be real?
- ☐ Will your beginning interest the reader?
- ☐ Is there a problem to be solved?
- ☐ Does your order of events make sense?
- ☐ Did you use dialogue?
- ☐ Is the problem solved?

Editing/Proofreading Use this checklist to correct mistakes.

- ☐ Did you use correct spelling?
- ☐ Did you use correct punctuation?
- ☐ Did you use quotation marks around dialogue?
- ☐ Is it clear who is speaking when you use dialogue?

Publishing Use this checklist to prepare your realistic story for publication.

- ☐ Neatly rewrite or type a final copy.
- ☐ Give your story a title.

138 UNIT 2 • Lesson 4 Writing • *Skills Practice 1*

Skills Practice 1, p. 138

Writing Realistic Story

ROUTINE 17

Publishing

Teach

- ✦ Use Routine 17 as students complete the publishing process. Refer students to ***Language Arts Handbook*** page 42 as a guide for making their stories into books.
- ✦ Students should decide on a method for publishing their realistic stories. Because each student has a different story to tell, you may decide to have students publish their stories as individual books.
- ✦ When students have bound their stories into books, have volunteers read their stories aloud to the class.
- ✦ Create a class library to display students' stories until the end of the year. Allow students to take the stories home to share with their families before returning them to the class library. Remind students that they may put this story in their Writing Portfolios.

Guided Practice

- ✦ Using the story you have been working on with students, show them how to fold or bind the papers to create a book. You may also want to add pictures, photos, or art to your work to model the use of visuals.
- ✦ Have students turn to ***Skills Practice 1*** page 138 and discuss the final publishing checklist with them.

Apply

- ✦ After students have completed the publishing process, encourage them to read the stories written by other students.

Assessment

Use the Writing Rubrics found in the Level Appendix to evaluate students' realistic stories. You may use any of the rubrics for Genre, Writing Process, and Writing Traits.

Spelling

Lesson Review and Homophone

Teach

Have students write Spelling and their names in the top margin of a clean piece of paper. Have them number the first fifteen lines 1–15, then skip a line and number the next two lines 1–2. Read each word, use it in a sentence, and give students time to spell it correctly. Encourage students to try to spell the challenge words, but assure them that misspelling a challenge word will not affect their test scores.

Spelling Words		**Challenge Words**
groan	toe	waste
grown	tow	waist
seam	horse	
seem	hoarse	
piece	meet	
peace	meat	
by	tale	
buy		

Guided Practice

✦ Have students proofread for any mistakes they made on the posttest. Tell them to categorize the mistakes as
- careless errors.
- errors in spelling words with /ī/.
- errors in spelling words with /ō/.
- errors in spelling words with consonant blends.
- errors in spelling homophones.

✦ Make certain students are correctly spelling homophones, words with /ī/ and /ō/, and words with consonant blends.

Penmanship

Cursive *p* and *j*

Teach

✦ Review cursive *p* and *j* with students using ***Transparency*** 62.

- **Letter *p*** Starting point, undercurve
  Slant, loop back
  Overcurve
  Curve back, undercurve: small *p*
- **Letter *j*** Starting point, undercurve
  Slant down
  Loop back
  Overcurve to endpoint
  Dot exactly above: small *j*

✦ To model proper letter formation, write the following sentence on the board: *James Patrick eats peanut butter and jelly in pajamas.*

Guided Practice

Tell students to hold up their index fingers in front of them. Say the strokes aloud as you trace the letters, and have students mimic your movements as if they were writing in the air.

Apply

✦ Have students practice writing each of the letters two times.

✦ After reviewing the sentence you wrote on the board, set a timer for three minutes and have students practice writing the sentence legibly and correctly. Have them circle the best sentence based on the proper formation of *p* and *j*.

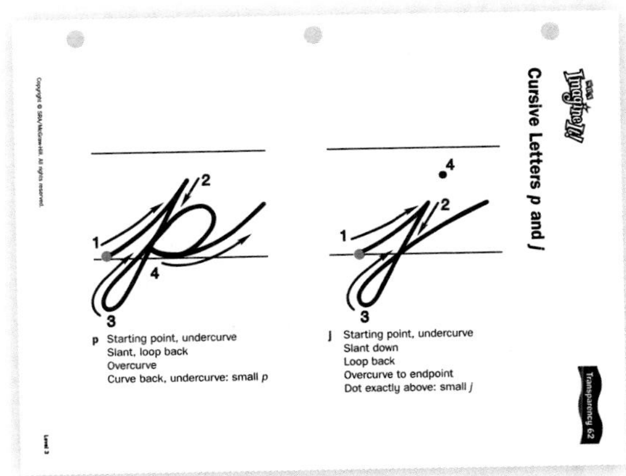

Transparency 62

Language Arts

Review

OBJECTIVES

Students will

- review the use of graphic organizers.
- review listening skills.
- review subjects and direct objects and object pronouns.

MATERIALS

- ***Lesson Assessment, Book 1,*** pp. 67–74

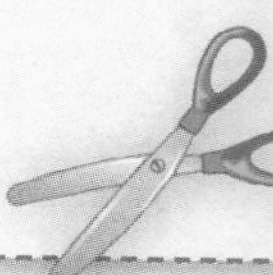

Study Skills

Graphic Organizers

Remind students how using graphic organizers to organize information can be helpful when writing and researching.

Ask students to name some graphic organizers. **Possible Answers** *time line, outline, idea web, spider map, Venn diagram*

Ask students how graphic organizers are helpful. **Possible Answer** *They organize information so it is easy to see the type of information, the amount of information, what might still be needed, and how the information relates to other information.*

For further practice using graphic organizers, have students create an organizer for the unit investigation.

Listening/Speaking/Viewing

Recalling Information from Oral Presenations

Remind students that listening to recall information is a good skill to learn and practice.

Ask students to give two reasons why it is important to listen carefully to recall information from a selection. **Possible Answers** *If you listen carefully to recall and retell information, then you are paying attention to the information and better understanding it. If you are able to paraphrase information from a story, then you are able to retell and share the story with others.*

Grammar, Usage, and Mechanics

Subjects and Direct Objects

Write the following sentences on the board. Then have students underline the subjects and circle the objects.

- The students gave an apple to Mrs. Lukas.
  subject: students; direct object: apple
- The students gave it to Mrs. Lukas.
  subject: students; direct object: it
- Rita visited the animals at the sanctuary.
  subject: Rita; direct object: animals
- Rita visited them at the sanctuary.
  subject: Rita; direct object: them

Have students write three more sentences on the board. Have others circle the subjects and underline the objects. Have students identify subjects and direct objects in their own writing.

Monitor Progress
Formal Assessment

Use pages 67–74 in ***Lesson Assessment Book 1*** to assess students' understanding of the skills taught in this lesson. Intervene with ***Reteach, Challenge Activities, Intervention Guide, eSkills, Leveled Readers,*** or activities in the ***Workshop Kit*** as needed.

Lesson Planner

Day 1

Day 2

Preparing to Read

MATERIALS
- ***Transparencies*** 65, 69
- ***Sound/Spelling Cards*** 31, 41
- Routines 2–9
- ***Skills Practice 1,*** pp. 145–148

Day 1

Daily News, p. T356
Phonics and Fluency
Review /ū/, /o͞o/, and Open and Closed Syllables, pp. T357–T359

Day 2

Daily News, p. T380
Phonics and Fluency, pp. T380–T381
Developing Oral Language, p. T381
Dictation, p. T381

Reading and Responding

MATERIALS
- ***Student Reader,*** Book 1, pp. 216–243
- ***Transparencies*** 23, 35, 66
- Routines 11, 13, 14, A
- ***Skills Practice 1,*** pp. 149–152
- Writer's Notebook
- ***Home Connection,*** pp. 23–24
- ***Listening Library CDs***
- ***Leveled Reader***

Day 1

Build Background, p. T360
Preview and Prepare, p. T361
Selection Vocabulary, pp. T362–T363
Reading the Selection, pp. T364–T367
Comprehension Skill
Classify and Categorize, p. T365
Comprehension Strategies

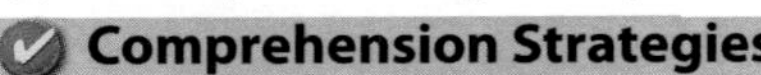

1st READ

- Clarifying, pp. T368, T372
- Making Connections, pp. T369, T371, T373
- Adjusting Reading Speed, pp. T370, T372

Inquiry, pp. T374–T375

Day 2

Comprehension Strategies
- Clarifying, p. T384
- Making Connections, pp. T383, T385
- Adjusting Reading Speed, p. T382

Discussing the Selection, p. T386
Review Selection Vocabulary, p. T387
Fluency, p. T387
Theme Connections, pp. T388–T389

Language Arts

MATERIALS
- ***Transparencies*** 67, 68, 70
- ***Skills Practice 1,*** pp. 153–160
- ***Language Arts Handbook,*** pp. 108–113
- Routines 15, 16, B
- ***Student Reader,*** Book 1, pp. 220–239
- ***Lesson Assessment Book 1,*** pp. 75–82

Day 1

Writing
Prewriting, p. T376
Spelling Pretest, p. T377
Penmanship, Cursive Letters *c* and *d,* p. T378

Day 2

Writing
Prewriting, pp. T390–T391
Spelling, p. T391
Grammar, Usage, and Mechanics
Subject Pronouns, pp. T392–T393

Monitor Progress

✓ = Formal Assessment

Day 1

✓ Phonics and Fluency, p. T359
✓ Comprehension Strategy, p. T364
✓ Comprehension Skill, p. T365
✓ Writing, p. T377
✓ Spelling Pretest, p. T377

Day 2

✓ Selection Vocabulary, p. T387
Fluency, p. T387
✓ Grammar, Usage, and Mechanics, p. T393

Literature Overview

Student Reader

Crinkleroot's Guide to Knowing Animal Habitats

written and illustrated by Jim Arnosky

Science Inquiry

Deserts Are Not Deserted

Haiku poems from If Not for the Cat

poem by Jack Prelutsky

illustrated by Ted Rand

Behind the Redwood Curtain

poem by Natasha Wing

illustrated by Lori Anzalone

Unit 2 • NAT-L3-U2-5-A

SRA
Imagine It!

★ Phonics ★ Fluency ★ Vocabulary ★ Comprehension

Day 3

Daily News, p. T394
Word Structure
Review Regular and Irregular Plurals, Homographs, and Homophones, pp. T394–T395

2nd READ

Comprehension Skill
- Author's Point of View, p. T396
- ☆ Classify and Categorize, pp. T398, T400

Reading with a Writer's Eye, pp. T397, T399, T401
Supporting the Reading
☆ Comprehension Skill: Classify and Categorize, p. T402
Fluency, p. T403
Inquiry, p. T403

Writing
Prewriting, p. T404
Spelling, p. T405
Study Skills
Index, p. T406
Grammar, Usage, and Mechanics, p. T407

Word Structure, p. T395
Comprehension Skill, p. T402
Fluency, p. T403
Spelling, p. T405
Study Skills, p. T406

Day 4

Daily News, p. T408
Word Structure, p. T409
Developing Oral Language, p. T409

Comprehension Skill
Classify and Categorize, pp. T410, T412
Reading with a Writer's Eye, p. T411
Inquiry, pp. T414–T415

Writing
Drafting, pp. T416–T417
Spelling, p. T417
Study Skills, p. T418
Listening/Speaking/Viewing
Chronological Order, p. T419

Day 5 Review

Phonics and Fluency, p. T420
Word Structure, p. T420

Selection Vocabulary, p. T421
Comprehension Strategies
- Making Connections, p. T422
- Adjusting Reading Speed, p. T422
- Clarifying, p. T422

Comprehension Skills
- Author's Point of View, p. T422
- ☆ Classify and Categorize, p. T422

Reading with a Writer's Eye, p. T423
Fluency, p. T423

Writing
Drafting, p. T424
Spelling Posttest, p. T425
Penmanship, p. T425
Study Skills, p. T426
Listening/Speaking/Viewing, p. T426
Grammar, Usage, and Mechanics, p. T427

Spelling Posttest, p. T425
***Lesson Assessment Book 1,* pp. 75–82**

Student Resources

Student Reader, Book 1, pp. 218–241

Phonics & Fluency

Decodable Stories, Book 3, Story 21, "A Visit"

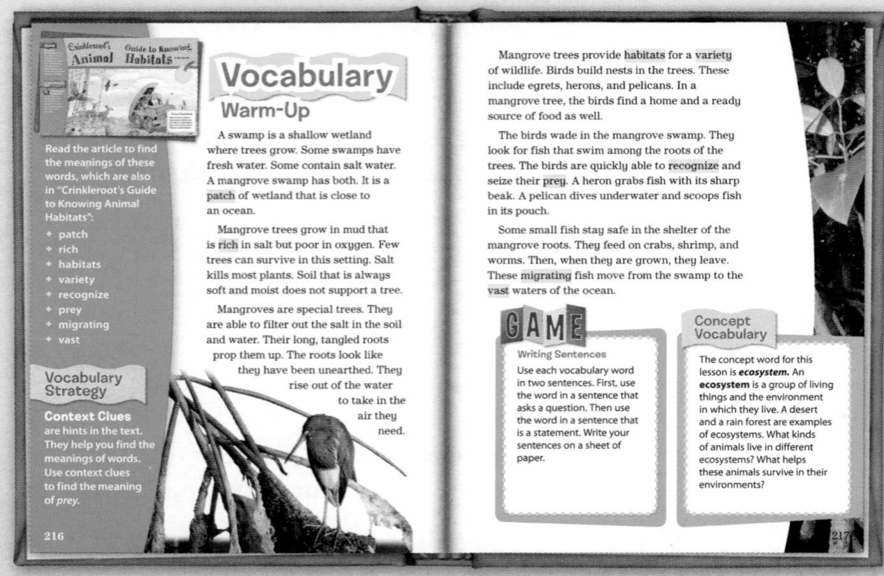

Student Reader, Book 1, pp. 216–217

Science

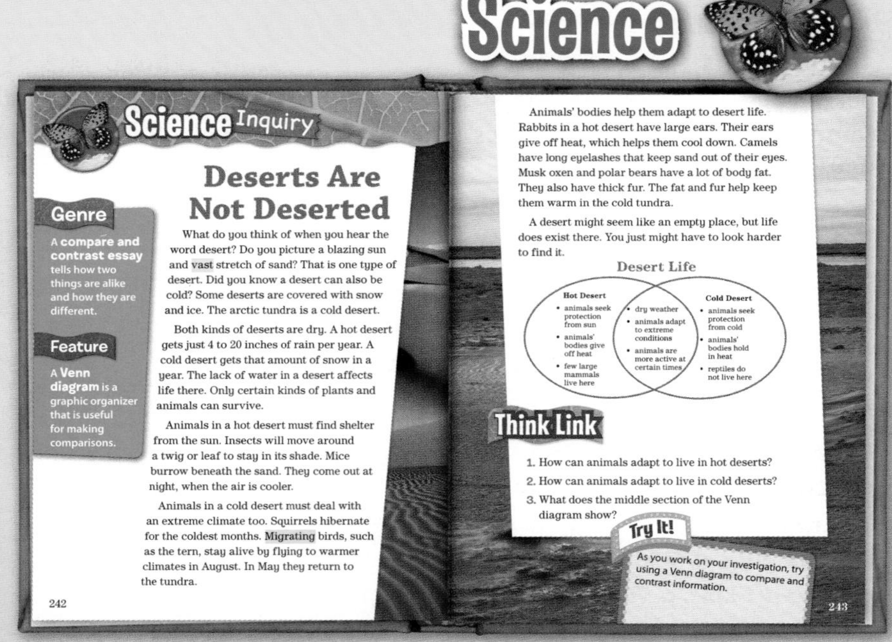

Student Reader, Book 1, pp. 242–243

Cross-Curricular Resources

Curriculum Connections

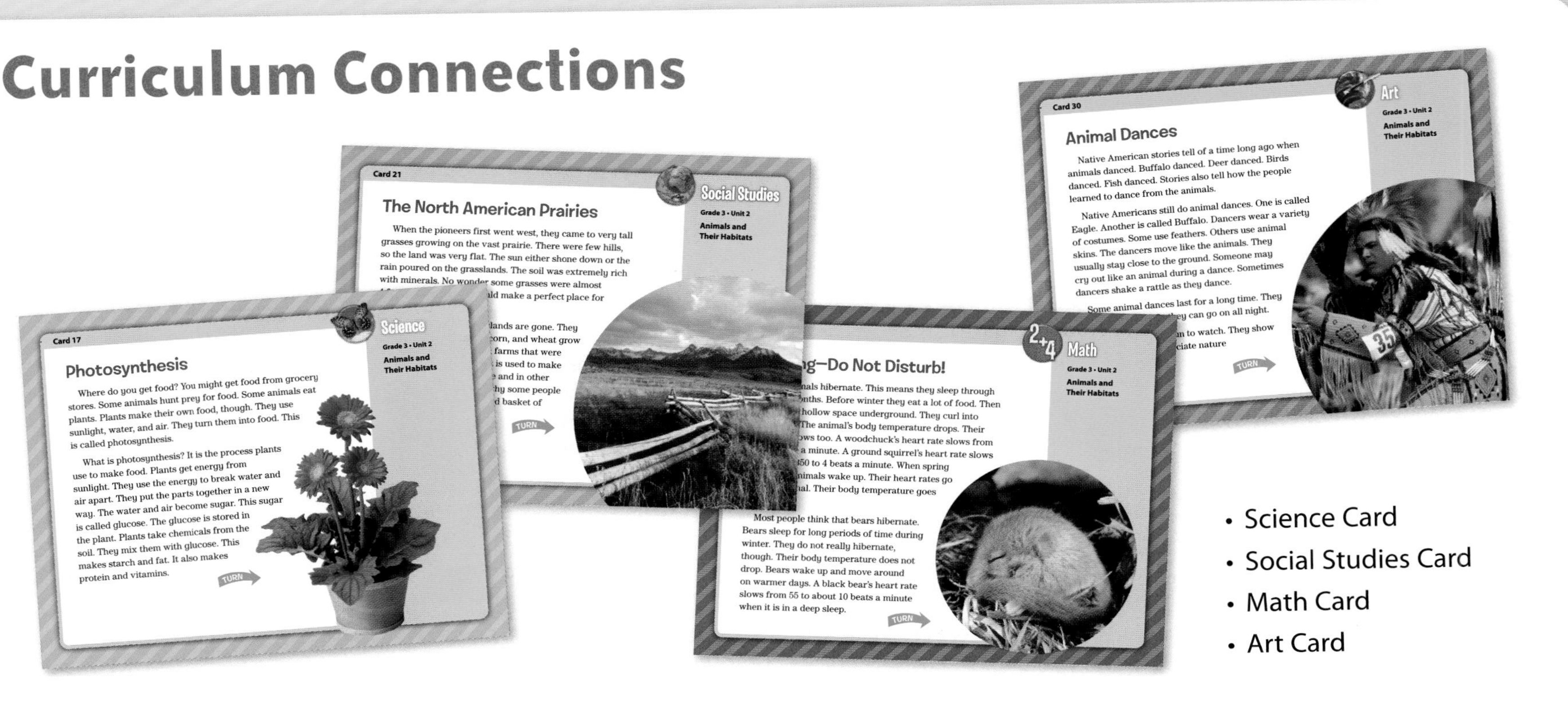

- Science Card
- Social Studies Card
- Math Card
- Art Card

Leveled Readers for Science

Approaching Level

On Level

English Learner

Above Level

Differentiating Instruction for Workshop

Day 1

	Approaching Level	On Level	English Learner	Above Level
Preparing to Read	**Phonics and Fluency:** Review the blending lines. Help students complete ***Reteach*** page 56, or work with them on the phonics activities in the ***Intervention Guide,*** Unit 2, Lesson 5. Then have students read ***Decodable Stories, Book 3,*** Story 21.	**Phonics and Fluency:** Have students make lists of words to add to the word lines.	**Phonics and Fluency:** Review the blending lines. Use the ***English Learner Support Guide*** for more phonics instruction. Then have students read ***Decodable Stories, Book 3,*** Story 21.	**Phonics and Fluency:** Have students complete ***Challenge Activities*** page 51. In pairs, students can scramble words from the word lines and give the words to a partner to unscramble.
Reading and Responding	**Vocabulary:** Have students create illustrations for the selection vocabulary words in their Writer's Notebooks. **Comprehension:** Have students write the Big Idea question in their Writer's Notebook. Have students write down possible answers for this story. **Inquiry:** Have students confirm and revise their conjectures based on new information they collected.	**Vocabulary:** Have students use the selection vocabulary words to write sentences. **Comprehension:** Have students begin a list of ideas about how this story relates to the unit theme. **Inquiry:** Have students confirm and revise their conjectures based on new information they collected.	**Vocabulary:** Use ***English Learner Support Guide*** to review vocabulary. **Comprehension:** Have students write a short paragraph about a connection they have to the selection. If students have difficulty expressing themselves, encourage them to illustrate their ideas. **Inquiry:** Have students confirm and revise their conjectures based on new information they collected.	**Vocabulary:** Have students find synonyms for the selection vocabulary words in a thesaurus. **Comprehension:** Have students add ideas and questions about animals and their habitats to the **Concept/Question Board.** **Inquiry:** Have students confirm and revise their conjectures based on new information they collected.
Language Arts	**Writing:** Have students browse reference book to gather ideas. **Spelling:** Have students proofread their informative report activity for spelling errors.	**Writing:** Have students begin to gather sources for their informative reports. **Spelling:** Have students write the spelling words for this lesson and circle the /o͞o/ sound spelling in each word.	**Writing:** Have students begin to gather sources for their informative reports. **Spelling:** Have students work in groups to decide four rules that will help them remember how to spell this lesson's words.	**Writing:** Have students gather sources for their informative reports. **Spelling:** Have students create a list of seven spelling words spelled incorrectly, trade papers with a partner, and correct the lists.

Day 2

	Approaching Level	On Level	English Learner	Above Level
Preparing to Read	**Phonics and Fluency:** Students can listen to the /ū/ and the /o͞o/ sounds on the Sound/Spelling Cards Stories CD. Then have students read ***Decodable Stories, Book 3,*** Story 21.	**Phonics and Fluency:** Students can read the selection looking for multisyllabic words with open syllables to add to the blending lines.	**Phonics and Fluency:** Have students write sentences using words from the blending lines. Then have them read ***Decodable Stories, Book 3,*** Story 21.	**Phonics and Fluency:** Have students play a game with ***Sound/Spelling Cards*** 31 and 41.
Reading and Responding	**Vocabulary:** Have students use ***Reteach*** page 58 or work with them using ***Intervention Guide,*** Unit 2, Lesson 5. **Comprehension:** Have students apply questions asked about the selection to the **Concept/Question Board.** **Fluency:** Have students listen to ***Listening Library CD.***	**Vocabulary:** Have students complete a game in the ***Workshop Kit.*** **Comprehension:** Have students create a list of words and passages they need clarified. Put students in groups, and let them help each other with their clarifications. **Fluency:** Have students reread a passage from the selection with a partner or individually.	**Vocabulary:** Help students create flash cards for the selection vocabulary words. Have students test themselves with the cards and use them to quiz a partner. **Comprehension:** Have students make connections between the story and other selections that they have read. **Fluency:** Have students read into a tape recorder at the beginning and end of the week. Have them listen to themselves at the end of the week so they can hear their progress.	**Vocabulary:** Have students complete ***Challenge Activities*** page 53. **Comprehension:** Have students write a journal entry about a connection that they can make to the story. **Fluency:** Have students engage in echo reading with passages from the selection.
Language Arts	**Writing:** Have students access materials from various sources. **Spelling:** Have students rewrite a paragraph from their selection. Remind them to pay special attention to the way the words are spelled. **Grammar, Usage, and Mechanics:** Have students complete ***Reteach*** page 62.	**Writing:** Have students access materials from various sources. **Spelling:** Working in pairs, have students think of and write a list of as many words with the /o͞o/ sound spellings as they can. **Grammar, Usage, and Mechanics:** Have students add subjects to their graphic organizers.	**Writing:** Have students access materials from various sources. **Spelling:** Have students write a list of as many words as they can think of that contain the /o͞o/ sound spellings. **Grammar, Usage, and Mechanics:** Refer to the ***English Learner Support Guide*** for support activities.	**Writing:** Have students access materials from various sources. **Spelling:** On a piece of paper, have students write five sentences that use two spelling words each. **Grammar, Usage, and Mechanics:** Have students complete ***Challenge Activities*** page 56.

Differentiating Instruction for Workshop

Day 3

	Approaching Level	On Level	English Learner	Above Level
Preparing to Read	**Word Structure:** Review the word lines. Then have students complete ***Reteach*** page 57, or work with them on the word structure activities in the ***Intervention Guide,*** Unit 2, Lesson 5.	**Word Structure:** Have students look for homographs and homophones as they reread "Crinkleroot's Guide to Knowing Animal Habitats."	**Word Structure:** Review the word lines. Have students write sentences using regular and irregular plural nouns.	**Word Structure:** Have students complete ***Challenge Activities*** page 52. Then students can scramble words from the word lines and give them to a partner to unscramble.
Reading and Responding	**Vocabulary:** Have students rewrite the definitions of three of the selection vocabulary words in their own words. **Comprehension:** Have students begin a list of ideas about how this selection relates to the theme Animals and Their Habitats. Place new ideas on the **Concept/Question Board.** **Fluency:** Have students use ***Leveled Readers.***	**Vocabulary:** Have students find words in the selection that are unfamiliar, find the meaning in the glossary, and use the words in sentences. **Comprehension:** Have students identify the genre and note examples of the genre from "Crinkleroot's Guide to Knowing Animal Habitats." **Fluency:** Have students discuss other books they have read that are similar to the selection.	**Vocabulary:** Help students create flash cards for the selection vocabulary words. Have students test themselves with the cards and use them to quiz a partner. **Comprehension:** Have students practice reading nonfiction by researching the various animals in the story using print and online resources. **Fluency:** Have students use ***Leveled Readers.***	**Vocabulary:** Have students write riddles for three of the expanding vocabulary words to share with the class. **Comprehension:** Have students use graphic organizers to organize the facts learned in "Crinkleroot's Guide to Knowing Animal Habitats." **Fluency:** Have students use ***Leveled Readers.***
Language Arts	**Writing:** Have students continue to take notes and to organize their ideas. **Spelling:** Have students complete ***Reteach*** page 61. **Grammar, Usage, and Mechanics:** Have students create a chart of gender-specific nouns and the pronouns that would replace them.	**Writing:** Have students continue to take notes and to organize their ideas. **Spelling:** Have pairs of students write a list of all the spellings of the /o͞o/ that they can think of. **Grammar, Usage, and Mechanics:** Have students continue to edit a piece of their writing.	**Writing:** Have students continue to take notes and to organize their ideas. **Spelling:** Have pairs of students think of as many words as they can with the /o͞o/ sound and make a list of these words. **Grammar, Usage, and Mechanics:** Have students continue to edit a piece of their writing.	**Writing:** Have students continue to take notes and to organize their ideas. **Spelling:** Have students complete ***Challenge Activities*** page 55. **Grammar, Usage, and Mechanics:** Have students review what they have written to make sure all of their replacement pronouns agree in number and gender to the original nouns.

Day 4

	Approaching Level	On Level	English Learner	Above Level
Preparing to Read	**Word Structure:** Have students write sentences using words from the word lines. Students can use the activities for plurals, homographs, or homophones in the ***Workshop Kit.*** Students can also use ***eSkills.***	**Word Structure:** Students can use the activities for plurals, homographs, or homophones in the ***Workshop Kit.*** Students can also use ***eSkills.***	**Word Structure:** Have students write sentences using words from the word lines. Students can use the activities for plurals, homographs, or homophones in the ***Workshop Kit.*** Students can also use ***eSkills.***	**Word Structure:** Students can use the activities for plurals, homographs, or homophones in the ***Workshop Kit.*** Students can also use ***eSkills.***
Reading and Responding	**Vocabulary:** Have students play a vocabulary on ***eGames.*** **Comprehension:** Have students write a summary for the selection. **Inquiry:** Have groups of students compare and revise their conjectures.	**Vocabulary:** Have students use the selection vocabulary words in extended sentences. **Comprehension:** Have students identify the genre and note examples of the genre characteristics from "Crinkleroot's Guide to Knowing Animal Habitats." **Inquiry:** Have groups of students compare and revise their conjectures.	**Vocabulary:** Have students create a list of words in the selection that need additional clarification. Have students research the words using a print or an online dictionary. **Comprehension:** Have students write a summary of "Crinkleroot's Guide to Knowing Animal Habitats." Encourage students to include illustrations if they have trouble expressing themselves. **Inquiry:** Have groups of students compare and revise their conjectures.	**Vocabulary:** Have students write a story using the selection vocabulary words. **Comprehension:** Have students use a Venn diagram to show how two selections from the same unit are alike and different. **Inquiry:** Have groups of students compare and revise their conjectures.
Language Arts	**Writing:** Have students continue to draft their informative reports. **Spelling:** Have students work in small groups to review the /o͞o/ sound spelling card. Then have them practice spelling words that contain the /o͞o/ sound.	**Writing:** Have students continue to draft their informative reports. Have students cite their sources. **Spelling:** Have students write a list of the five words that they hear most often that contain the /o͞o/ sound spellings.	**Writing:** Have students continue to draft their informative reports. **Spelling:** Have students write a list of the five words that they hear most often that contain the /o͞o/ sound spellings.	**Writing:** Have students continue to draft their informative reports. Have students use direct quotes in their reports. **Spelling:** Have students spell and misspell the spelling words on a piece of paper, trade papers with a partner, and circle which words are correct.

Differentiating Instruction for Workshop

Day 5

	Approaching Level	On Level	English Learner	Above Level
Preparing to Read	**Word Structure:** Review the word lines. Then have students read "A Visit" from ***eDecodable Stories***. Have the students read the ***High-Frequency Flash Cards*** with a partner.	**Word Structure:** Have pairs of students scramble the words from the word lines, and have a partner unscramble them.	**Word Structure:** Review the word lines. Then have students read "A Visit" from ***eDecodable Stories.*** Have students read the ***High-Frequency Flash Cards*** with a partner.	**Word Structure:** Have students make lists of other homographs and homophones to add to the word lines. Then have them write poems using words from their lists.
Reading and Responding	**Vocabulary:** Have students use a thesaurus to find words that are related to the expanding vocabulary words. **Comprehension:** Put students in small groups. Have them discuss a book they have read. **Fluency:** Have students write answers to comprehension questions from ***Leveled Readers.***	**Vocabulary:** Have students complete an activity on ***eSkills.*** **Comprehension:** Have students compare and contrast the selection with another story from Unit 2 using a Venn diagram. **Fluency:** Have students write answers to comprehension questions from ***Leveled Readers.***	**Vocabulary:** Have students use the expanding vocabulary words in extended sentences. **Comprehension:** Put students in groups to discuss "Crinkleroot's Guide to Knowing Animal Habitats." **Fluency:** Have students use vocabulary from ***Leveled Readers*** in extended sentences.	**Vocabulary:** Have students divide the vocabulary words into categories. Have students add the words to their Writer's Notebooks. **Comprehension:** Have students write about how the selection relates to the theme Animals and Their Habitats. **Fluency:** Have students create a play using the vocabulary words.
Language Arts	**Writing:** Have students make sure they use all of their sources in their drafts. Have students conference with peers. **Spelling:** Have students work in groups and read each other words aloud and attempt to spell those words on a piece of paper.	**Writing:** Have students continue to draft their informative reports. Have students conference with peers. **Spelling:** Have students find the sound spelling card that corresponds to each spelling word from this lesson.	**Writing:** Have students conference with peers. **Spelling:** Have students practice spelling by reading the spelling words to a partner and writing those words on a piece of paper.	**Writing:** Have students conference with peers. **Spelling:** Have students misspell this lesson's words on a piece of paper, trade with a partner, and write the skill that was misspelled next to each word.

Resources for

Differentiating Instruction 

Leveled Readers

Approaching Level

On Level

English Learner

Above Level

Additional Skills Practice

Approaching Level

Reteach

- The /o͞o/ and /ū/ Sounds and Syllables, p. 56
- Word Structure, p. 57
- Vocabulary, p. 58
- Classify and Categorize, pp. 59–60
- Spelling, p. 61
- Pronouns, p. 62

On Level

Skills Practice 1

- The /o͞o/ and /ū/ Sounds and Syllables, pp. 145–146
- Word Structure, pp. 147–148
- Vocabulary, pp. 149–150
- Classify and Categorize, pp. 151–152
- Writing a Report, pp. 153–154
- Spelling, pp. 155–156
- Pronouns, pp. 157–158

English Learner

English Learner Support Activities

English Learner Support Activities, Unit 2 Lesson 5

Above Level

Challenge Activities

- The /o͞o/ and /ū/ Sounds and Syllables, p. 51
- Word Structure, p. 52
- Vocabulary, p. 53
- Classify and Categorize, p. 54
- Spelling, p. 55
- Pronouns, p. 56

Lesson 5 Overview

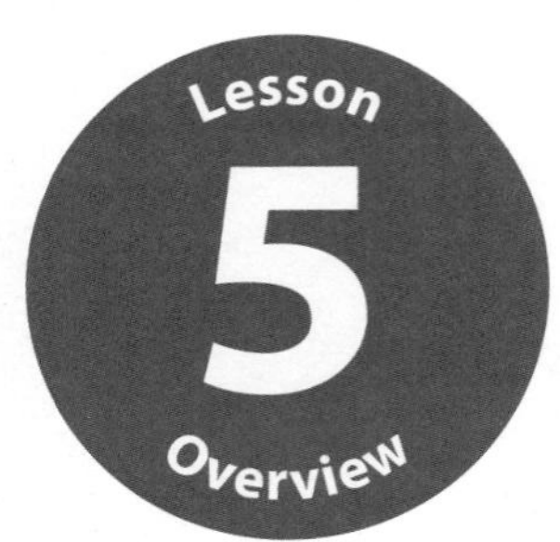

Additional Resources for Differentiating Instruction

RtI

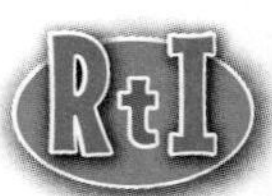

Workshop Kits

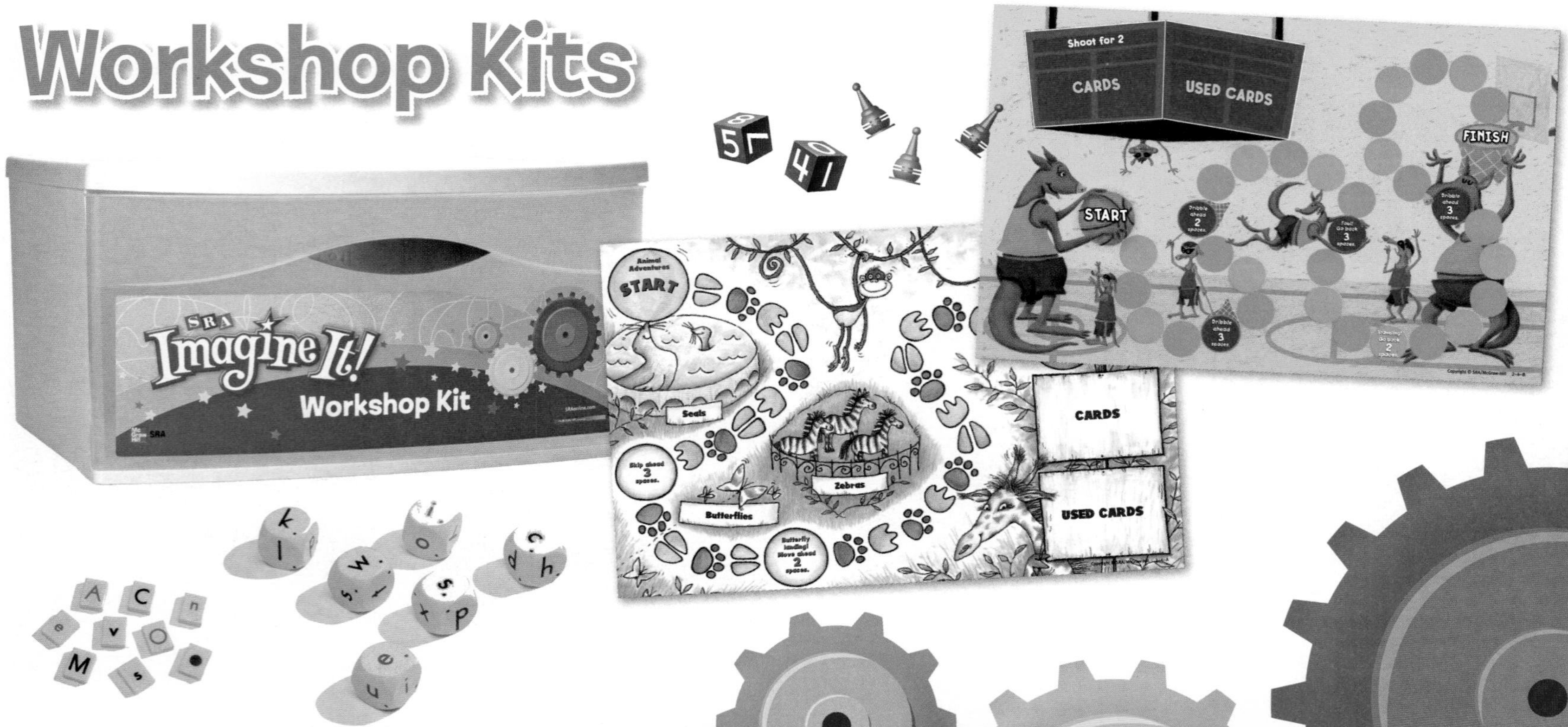

Technology

The following electronic resources are available for students:

- ***eStudent Reader***
- ***eDecodables***
- ***eSkills***
- ***eGames***
- ***Listening Library CD***

Electronic resources for the teacher include:

- ***ePlanner***
- ***eTeacher's Edition***
- ***eAssess***
- ***ePresentation***

All technology components are available online and on CD–ROM.

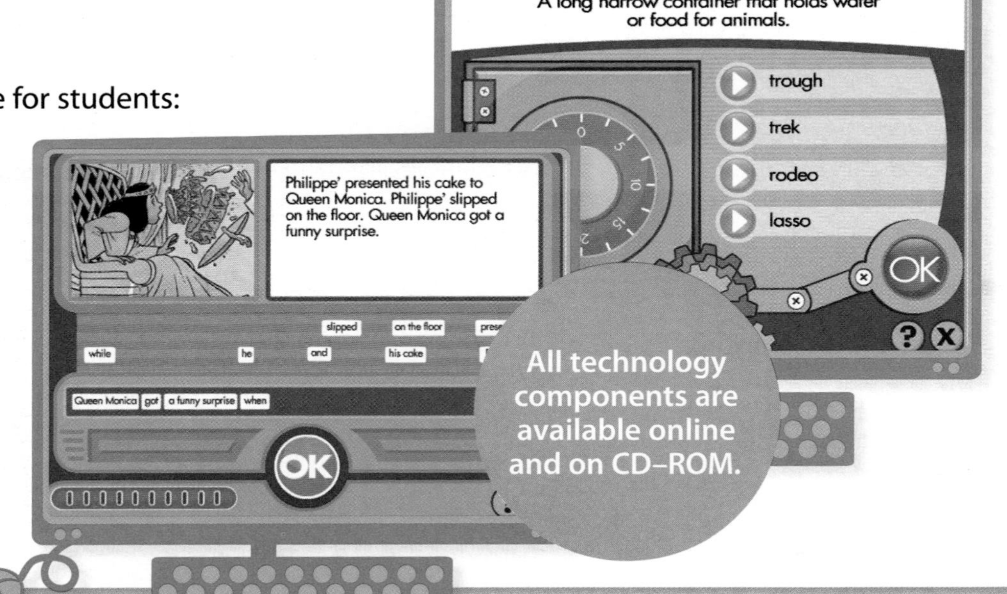

English Learner

Mountain Animals

by Allen Jacobs

Leveled Reader

English Learner Support Activities, Lesson 5

Listening Library Unit 2

English Learner Support Guide, Lesson 5

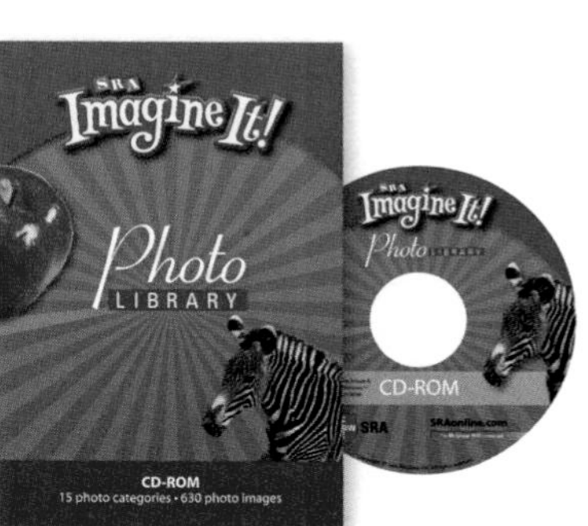

Photo Library

Approaching Level

Intervention

Intervention Workbook

Intervention Guide

Lesson 5 Overview

Lesson Assessment

Monitor Progress to Differentiate Instruction

Comprehension Strategies Rubrics

Use the Comprehension Strategies Rubrics to determine whether a student is using the strategies.

- ✦ Clarifying, p. T364
- ✦ Making Connections, p. T365
- ✦ Adjusting Reading Speed, p. T365

Inquiry Rubrics

Use the Inquiry Rubrics to assess a student's performance throughout the stages of the investigation for each unit. In addition, at the end of the unit you can use the rubrics to assess the groups' collaborative work as well as an individual's participation in that group.

- ✦ Confirming and Revising Conjectures, p. T415
- ✦ Presenting Inquiry Findings, p. T433
- ✦ Overall Research, p. T441
- ✦ Participation in Collaborative Inquiry, p. T441

Writing Rubrics

Use the writing rubrics in the Level Appendix to evaluate each student's informative report.

- ✦ Genre
- ✦ Writing Process
- ✦ Writing Traits

Lesson Assessments

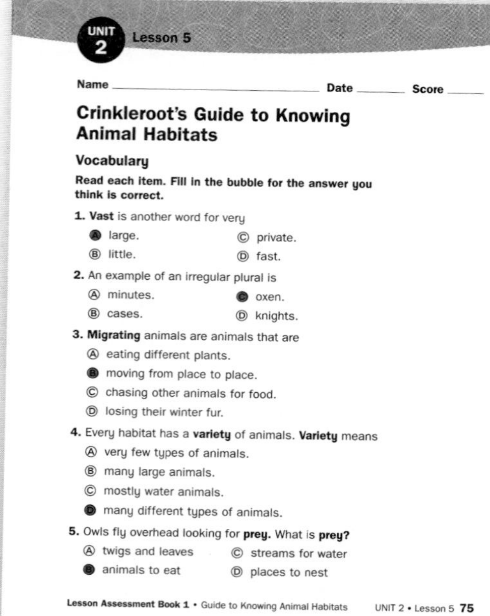

UNIT 2 Lesson 5

Name ______ Date ______ Score ______

Crinkleroot's Guide to Knowing Animal Habitats

Vocabulary

Read each item. Fill in the bubble for the answer you think is correct.

1. **Vast** is another word for very
   ● large. Ⓒ private.
   Ⓑ little. Ⓓ fast.
2. An example of an irregular plural is
   Ⓐ minutes. ● oxen.
   Ⓑ cases. Ⓓ knights.
3. **Migrating** animals are animals that are
   Ⓐ eating different plants.
   ● moving from place to place.
   Ⓒ chasing other animals for food.
   Ⓓ losing their winter fur.
4. Every habitat has a **variety** of animals. **Variety** means
   Ⓐ very few types of animals.
   Ⓑ many large animals.
   Ⓒ mostly water animals.
   ● many different types of animals.
5. Owls fly overhead looking for **prey.** What is **prey?**
   Ⓐ twigs and leaves Ⓒ streams for water
   ● animals to eat Ⓓ places to nest

Lesson Assessment Book 1 • Guide to Knowing Animal Habitats UNIT 2 • Lesson 5 75

Lesson Assessment Book 1, p. 75

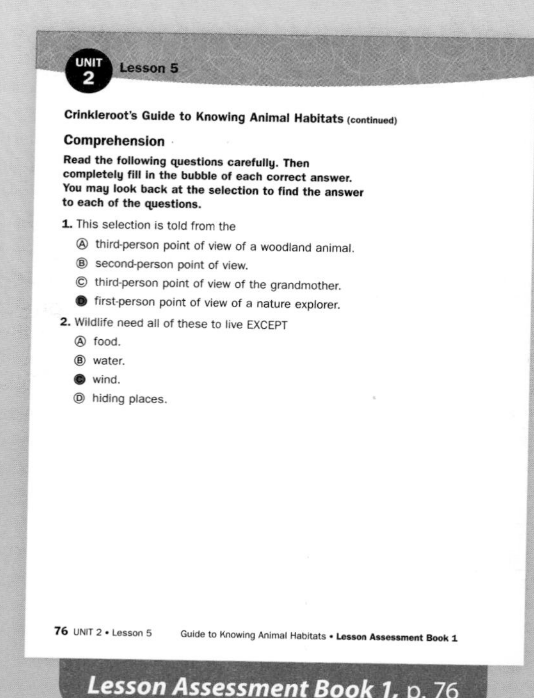

UNIT 2 Lesson 5

Crinkleroot's Guide to Knowing Animal Habitats (continued)

Comprehension

Read the following questions carefully. Then completely fill in the bubble of each correct answer. You may look back at the selection to find the answer to each of the questions.

1. This selection is told from the
   Ⓐ third-person point of view of a woodland animal.
   Ⓑ second-person point of view.
   Ⓒ third-person point of view of the grandmother.
   ● first-person point of view of a nature explorer.
2. Wildlife need all of these to live EXCEPT
   Ⓐ food.
   Ⓑ water.
   ● wind.
   Ⓓ hiding places.

76 UNIT 2 • Lesson 5 Guide to Knowing Animal Habitats • Lesson Assessment Book 1

Lesson Assessment Book 1, p. 76

Formal Assessment 

Use these summative assessments along with your informal observations to assess student mastery.

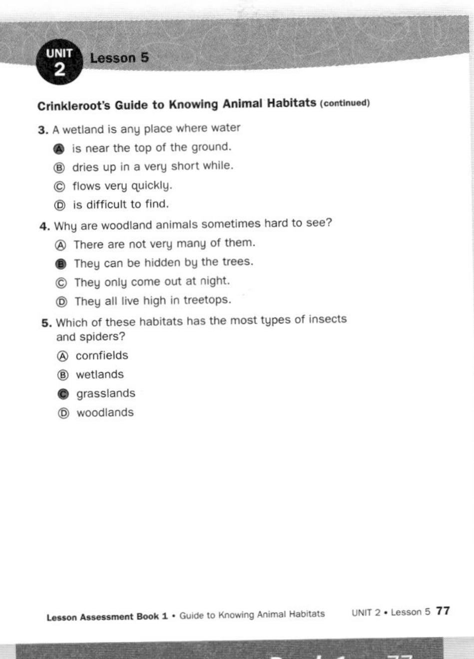

UNIT 2 Lesson 5

Crinkleroot's Guide to Knowing Animal Habitats (continued)

3. A wetland is any place where water
   - Ⓐ is near the top of the ground.
   - Ⓑ dries up in a very short while.
   - Ⓒ flows very quickly.
   - Ⓓ is difficult to find.
4. Why are woodland animals sometimes hard to see?
   - Ⓐ There are not very many of them.
   - Ⓑ They can be hidden by the trees.
   - Ⓒ They only come out at night.
   - Ⓓ They all live high in treetops.
5. Which of these habitats has the most types of insects and spiders?
   - Ⓐ cornfields
   - Ⓑ wetlands
   - Ⓒ grasslands
   - Ⓓ woodlands

Lesson Assessment Book 1 • Guide to Knowing Animal Habitats UNIT 2 • Lesson 5 77

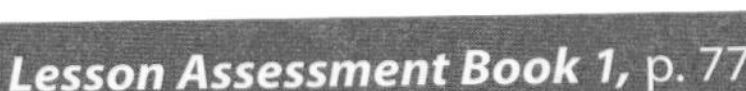

Lesson Assessment Book 1, p. 77

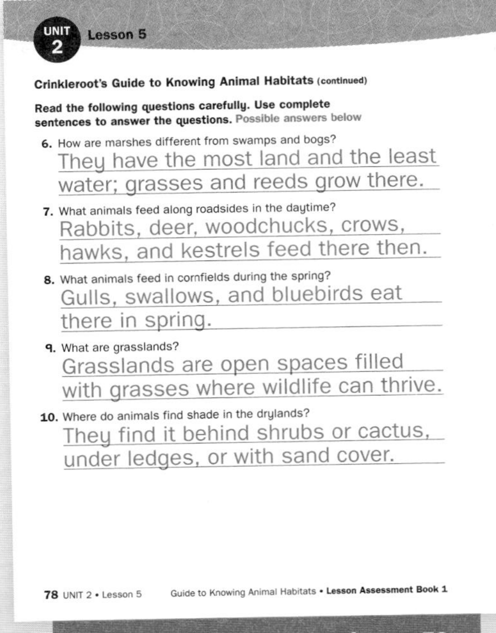

UNIT 2 Lesson 5

Crinkleroot's Guide to Knowing Animal Habitats (continued)

Read the following questions carefully. Use complete sentences to answer the questions. Possible answers below

6. How are marshes different from swamps and bogs?
   They have the most land and the least water; grasses and reeds grow there.
7. What animals feed along roadsides in the daytime?
   Rabbits, deer, woodchucks, crows, hawks, and kestrels feed there then.
8. What animals feed in cornfields during the spring?
   Gulls, swallows, and bluebirds eat there in spring.
9. What are grasslands?
   Grasslands are open spaces filled with grasses where wildlife can thrive.
10. Where do animals find shade in the drylands?
    They find it behind shrubs or cactus, under ledges, or with sand cover.

78 UNIT 2 • Lesson 5 Guide to Knowing Animal Habitats • Lesson Assessment Book 1

Lesson Assessment Book 1, p. 78

UNIT 2 Lesson 5

Crinkleroot's Guide to Knowing Animal Habitats (continued)

Read the question below. Write complete sentences for your answer. Support your answer with information from the selection.

Linking to the Concepts Why do different types of animals live in different habitats?

Read the question below. Your answer should be based on your own experience. Write complete sentences for your answer.

Personal Response Which habitat do you think is most interesting? Explain your answer.

Lesson Assessment Book 1 • Guide to Knowing Animal Habitats UNIT 2 • Lesson 5 79

Lesson Assessment Book 1, p. 79

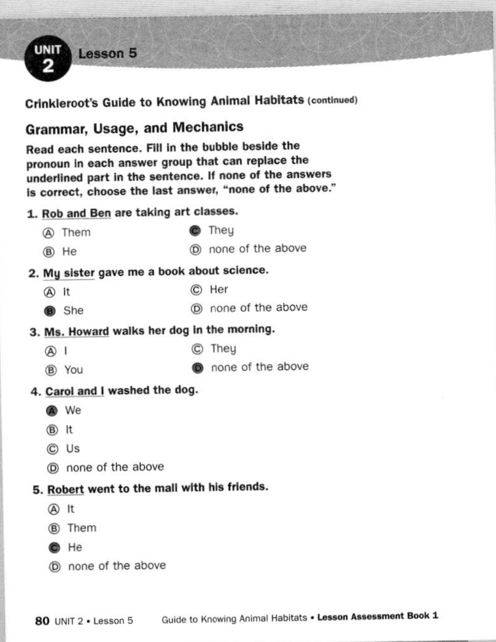

UNIT 2 Lesson 5

Crinkleroot's Guide to Knowing Animal Habitats (continued)

Grammar, Usage, and Mechanics

Read each sentence. Fill in the bubble beside the pronoun in each answer group that can replace the underlined part in the sentence. If none of the answers is correct, choose the last answer, "none of the above."

1. **Rob and Ben are taking art classes.**
   - Ⓐ Them
   - Ⓑ He
   - Ⓒ They
   - Ⓓ none of the above
2. **My sister gave me a book about science.**
   - Ⓐ It
   - Ⓑ She
   - Ⓒ Her
   - Ⓓ none of the above
3. **Ms. Howard walks her dog in the morning.**
   - Ⓐ I
   - Ⓑ You
   - Ⓒ They
   - Ⓓ none of the above
4. **Carol and I washed the dog.**
   - Ⓐ We
   - Ⓑ It
   - Ⓒ Us
   - Ⓓ none of the above
5. **Robert went to the mall with his friends.**
   - Ⓐ It
   - Ⓑ Them
   - Ⓒ He
   - Ⓓ none of the above

80 UNIT 2 • Lesson 5 Guide to Knowing Animal Habitats • Lesson Assessment Book 1

Lesson Assessment Book 1, p. 80

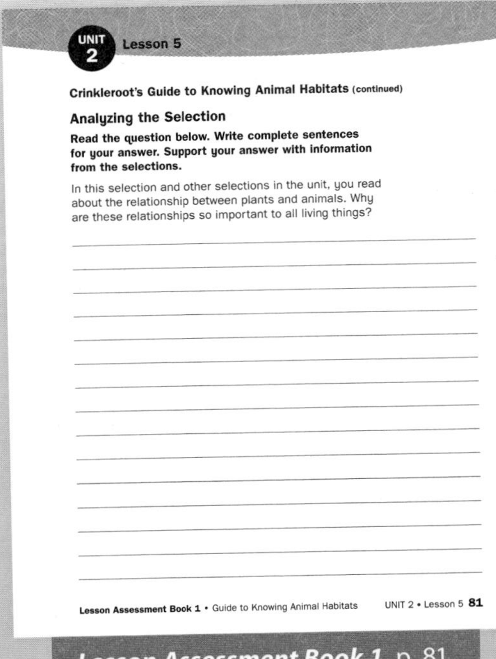

UNIT 2 Lesson 5

Crinkleroot's Guide to Knowing Animal Habitats (continued)

Analyzing the Selection

Read the question below. Write complete sentences for your answer. Support your answer with information from the selections.

In this selection and other selections in the unit, you read about the relationship between plants and animals. Why are these relationships so important to all living things?

Lesson Assessment Book 1 • Guide to Knowing Animal Habitats UNIT 2 • Lesson 5 81

Lesson Assessment Book 1, p. 81

UNIT 2 Lesson 5

Crinkleroot's Guide to Knowing Animal Habitats (continued)

Oral Fluency Assessment

Flying Spiders

Nature is filled with strange plants and animals. Some live in 1–11
far-off places. Others can be found right near your home. One 12–23
example is a special group of spiders. 24–30
Even though they do not have wings, these spiders can fly 31–41
though the air. They do this in an unusual way. The spiders 42–53
spin silk webs and use them like kites. They can do this 54–65
because a spider's web is very light and very strong. A web can 66–78
also be shaped in different ways. 79–84
The spider climbs to the top of a plant. It starts spinning 85–96
lines of silk. These silk lines seem to float in the air like sails. 97–110
The wind catches the lines and carries the spider away. 111–120
The spider cannot really steer through the air. It just lets the 121–133
wind carry it wherever. Spiders can travel miles on their kites 134–144
carried by the wind. After a while, the wind stops or the web 145–157
gets tangled in something. The spider climbs away from the 158–167
web and looks for a new home. 168–174

EVALUATING CODES FOR ORAL FLUENCY

sky (/) words read incorrectly

blue ^ sky (^) inserted word

( ]) after the last word

READING RATE AND ACCURACY

Total Words Read: ____

Number of Errors: ____

Number of Correct Words Read Per Minute (WPM): ____

Accuracy Rate: ____

(Number of Correct Words Read per Minute ÷ Total Words Read)

READING FLUENCY

	Low	Average	High
Decoding ability	○	○	○
Pace	○	○	○
Syntax	○	○	○
Self-correction	○	○	○
Intonation	○	○	○

Record student rates on the Oral Fluency Scores pages.

82 UNIT 2 • Lesson 5 Guide to Knowing Animal Habitats • Lesson Assessment Book 1

Lesson Assessment Book 1, p. 82

Day 1 **Preparing to Read**

OBJECTIVES

Students will

- ✦ review /ū/ spelled *_ew* and *_ue;* and /o͞o/ spelled *oo, _ue, u, _ew,* and *u_e.*
- ✦ review open and closed syllables.
- ✦ learn new high-frequency words.
- ✦ build fluency.

MATERIALS

- ✦ ***Transparency*** 65
- ✦ ***Sound/Spelling Cards*** 31, 41
- ✦ Routines 3, 4, 5, 6, 9
- ✦ ***Skills Practice 1,*** pp. 145–146

Daily Oral Practice

Daily News

Today!

I want to be an explorer, but I won't have to go too far from home. It's amazing how many animal habitats exist around me. The amount of different animal habitats surprised me. I bet some of them may even surprise you.

- ✦ Write the daily news on the board or on chart paper. Then have students read the daily news in unison to practice fluency.
- ✦ As a word structure review from Lesson 4, ask a volunteer to identify any homophones in the daily news. *be (bee), to (too/two), too (to/two), some (sum)*

Phonics and Fluency 

ROUTINE 3 ROUTINE 4

Review: /ū/ spelled _ew and _ue; /o͞o/ spelled oo, _ue, u, _ew, and u_e; open and closed syllables

Blending

✦ Write the following blending lines and sentences on the board or use ***Transparency*** 65. Show students one line at a time as you go through them by covering up the others. The boldface words are in the selection. The underlined words are new high-frequency words.

Line 1	few	nephew	cue	value
Line 2	**fooled**	**Crinkleroot**	**true**	**bluebirds**
Line 3	truth	**supermarket**	grew	**newt**
Line 4	rule	tube	flute	June
Line 5	human	cable	humble	candle

Sentence 1 We <u>should</u> rescue the few foxes who lost their habitat.

Sentence 2 A bluejay flew to the <u>end</u> of the lake to find food.

✦ Review ***Sound/Spelling Cards*** 31 and 41 with students. Using Routine 3, follow the whole-word blending process to have students blend the words in Lines 1–5.

✦ Follow Routine 4, the blending sentences process, to have students blend Sentences 1–2.

Line 1 /ū/ spelled _ew and _ue

As a review, ask students to identify the /ū/ sound/spelling in each word. */ū/ spelled* _ew *in* few, nephew; */ū/ spelled* _ue *in* cue, value Emphasize the difference between /o͞o/ and /ū/. Point out that even though /o͞o/ and /ū/ are different sounds, they may have the same spellings. Both /o͞o/ and /ū/ are sometimes spelled *_ue, _ew, u_e,* or *u.*

Line 2 /o͞o/ spelled oo and _ue

As you point to each word, have students read it aloud. Ask students to identify /o͞o/ spelled *oo* or *_ue* in each word. */o͞o/ spelled* oo *in* fooled, Crinkleroot; */o͞o/ spelled* _ue *in* true, bluebirds

Sound/Spelling Cards 31 and 41

Teacher Tip

SYLLABICATION To help students blend words and build fluency, demonstrate syllabication using the decodable, multisyllabic words in the word lines. Explain that we need to look at the vowel spellings in order to break words into syllables. Remind students that vowel spellings indicate the number of syllables in a word.

neph • ew	hu • man
val • ue	ca • ble
Crin • kle • root	hum • ble
blue • birds	can • dle
su • per • mar • ket	

✦ Use ***Transparency*** 65 with today's blending lines and sentences. Show students the lines one at a time as you go through them by covering up the other lines.

Line 3 **/o͞o/ spelled u and _*ew***

As you point to each word, have students read the word aloud in unison. Ask students to identify /o͞o/ spelled *u* or _*ew* in each word. */o͞o/ spelled* u *in* truth, supermarket; */o͞o/ spelled* _ew *in* grew, newt

Line 4 **/o͞o/ spelled *u_e***

As you point to each word in Line 4, have students read it aloud. Ask students to identify /o͞o/ spelled *u_e* in each word in Line 4. */o͞o/ spelled* u_e *in* rule, tube, flute, tune

Line 5 **Open and Closed Syllables**

Remind students that open syllables have syllables ending with vowel sounds; closed syllables have syllables that end with consonant sounds. Explain that open syllables usually have long vowels and closed syllables usually have short vowels. For example, in the word *tiger,* the first syllable is open and ends with /ī/. In the word *backpack,* both syllables are closed and have short vowels. Have students separate the words *human*, *cable, humble* and *candle* into syllables. *hu • man, ca • ble, hum • ble, can • dle* Have students point out the open syllables in *human* and *cable* and the closed syllables in *humble* and *candle*.

Sentences 1–2

Have students point to and read the new high-frequency words in Sentences 1–2. *should, end* Ask students to identify words in Sentence 1 with /ū/ spelled _*ew* or _*ue*. */ū/ spelled* _ew *in* few; */ū/ spelled* _ue in rescue Ask students to identify words in Sentence 2 with /o͞o/ spelled *oo,* _*ue,* or _*ew*. */o͞o/ spelled* oo in food; */o͞o/ spelled* _ue in bluejay; */o͞o/ spelled* _ew in flew Have students read the sentences in unison to practice fluency.

Animals and Their Habitats

Decodable Stories, Book 3, Story 20

Decodable Stories

Building Fluency

Decodable stories are used to help develop fluency for students who need extra practice. They are also used to practice the phonics and fluency elements being reviewed. Using Routine 9, reading a ***Decodable Story,*** have students who need additional support read ***Decodable Stories,*** Book 3, Story 21, "A Visit."

ROUTINE 5 ROUTINE 6

Syllabication

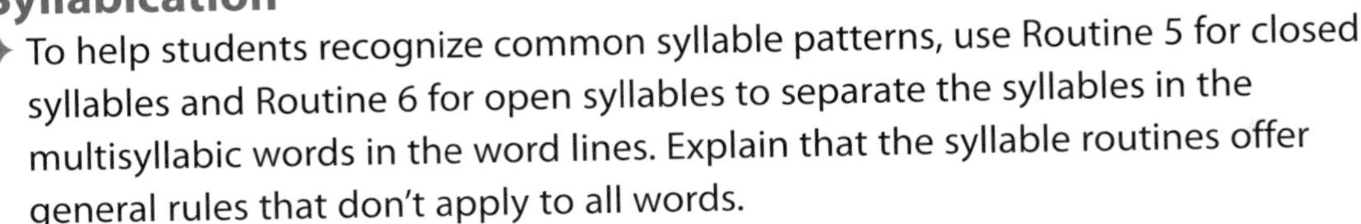

- To help students recognize common syllable patterns, use Routine 5 for closed syllables and Routine 6 for open syllables to separate the syllables in the multisyllabic words in the word lines. Explain that the syllable routines offer general rules that don't apply to all words.
- Using Routine 5 and Routine 6, have students identify the vowel spellings in *nephew, value, bluebirds, supermarket,* and *human*. Remind students that each vowel sound adds a syllable to a word. Ask students how many syllables there are in *supermarket*. *four* Remind students that open syllables end with vowel sounds and closed syllables end with consonant sounds. Have students identify the open and closed syllables in *nephew, value, bluebirds, supermarket,* and *human* and read them aloud, clapping for each syllable. If students divide the syllables incorrectly, they should notice that the word doesn't sound right and correct themselves. For example, splitting *value* into *va • lue* would make the word sound awkward, because it should be *val • ue*.
- Have students identify the *le* spelling in *Crinkleroot, cable, humble,* and *candle*. Explain that when only one consonant comes before the *le,* the first syllable has a long vowel and is open, as in *ca • ble*. When two consonants come before *le,* the first syllable has a short vowel and is closed, as in *hum • ble*. Have students split *Crinkleroot, cable, humble,* and *candle* into syllables and read them aloud, clapping for each syllable.
- Help students start the phonics activities in ***Skills Practice 1,*** pages 145–146. Read the focus box with them, and help them with the first few questions. Then have students complete the pages on their own.

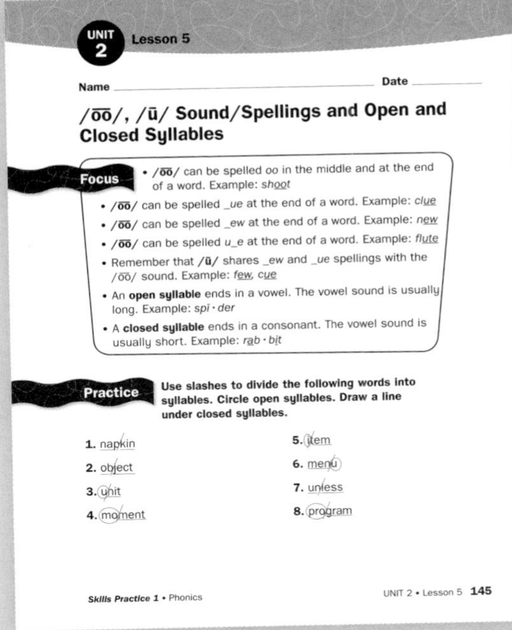

UNIT 2 Lesson 5

Name ______ Date ______

/o͞o/, /ū/ Sound/Spellings and Open and Closed Syllables

Focus

- **/o͞o/** can be spelled *oo* in the middle and at the end of a word. Example: *shoot*
- **/o͞o/** can be spelled *_ue* at the end of a word. Example: *clue*
- **/o͞o/** can be spelled *_ew* at the end of a word. Example: *new*
- **/o͞o/** can be spelled *u_e* at the end of a word. Example: *flute*
- Remember that **/ū/** shares *_ew* and *_ue* spellings with the /o͞o/ sound. Example: *few, cue*
- An **open syllable** ends in a vowel. The vowel sound is usually long. Example: *spī • der*
- A **closed syllable** ends in a consonant. The vowel sound is usually short. Example: *rab • bit*

Practice **Use slashes to divide the following words into syllables. Circle open syllables. Draw a line under closed syllables.**

1. napkin
2. object
3. unit
4. moment
5. item
6. menu
7. unless
8. program

Skills Practice 1 • Phonics UNIT 2 • Lesson 5 **145**

Skills Practice 1, p. 145

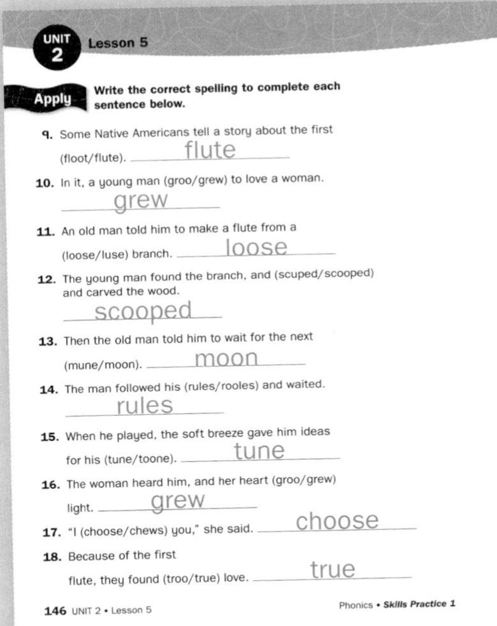

UNIT 2 Lesson 5

Apply **Write the correct spelling to complete each sentence below.**

9. Some Native Americans tell a story about the first (floot/flute). flute
10. In it, a young man (groo/grew) to love a woman. grew
11. An old man told him to make a flute from a (loose/luse) branch. loose
12. The young man found the branch, and (scuped/scooped) and carved the wood. scooped
13. Then the old man told him to wait for the next (mune/moon). moon
14. The man followed his (rules/rooles) and waited. rules
15. When he played, the soft breeze gave him ideas for his (tune/toone). tune
16. The woman heard him, and her heart (groo/grew) light. grew
17. "I (choose/chews) you," she said. choose
18. Because of the first flute, they found (troo/true) love. true

146 UNIT 2 • Lesson 5 Phonics • ***Skills Practice 1***

Skills Practice 1, p. 146

Monitor Progress to Differentiate Instruction

Formal Assessment

Phonics and Fluency During the blending activity, note how quickly students are reading the words.

APPROACHING LEVEL	**IF . . .** students need practice with open and closed syllables or today's sound/spellings for /o͞o/ or /ū/,	**THEN . . .** work with them on the phonics activities on ***Reteach*** page 56 during Workshop.
	IF . . . students need extra practice with open and closed syllables or today's sound/spellings for /o͞o/ or /ū/,	**THEN . . .** work with them on the phonics activities for Unit 2 Lesson 5 in the ***Intervention Guide*** during Workshop.
ON LEVEL	**IF . . .** students understand open and closed syllables and today's sound/spellings for /o͞o/ and /ū/,	**THEN . . .** have them make lists of words to add to the word lines during Workshop.
ABOVE LEVEL	**IF . . .** students are ready for a challenge with open and closed syllables or today's sound/spellings for /o͞o/ and /ū/,	**THEN . . .** have them complete the phonics activities on ***Challenge Activities*** page 51 during Workshop.

Day 1

Reading and Responding

OBJECTIVES

Students will
- ✦ activate prior knowledge to prepare to read the story.
- ✦ learn selection vocabulary.
- ✦ review the elements of narrative nonfiction.
- ✦ use the comprehension strategies Clarifying, Making Connections, and Adjusting Reading Speed.
- ✦ investigate the theme Animals and Their Habitats using the Inquiry process.

MATERIALS

- ✦ Routines 11, 13, 14
- ✦ ***Transparencies*** 35, 66
- ✦ ***Home Connection,*** pp. 23–24
- ✦ ***Student Reader,*** Book 1 pp. 216–231

Build Background

Activate Prior Knowledge

- ✦ Ask students to discuss the animal habitats already explored in this unit.
- ✦ Ask students to name the animal habitats that exist close to them, such as in nearby ponds, creeks, woods, schoolyards, or their own backyards.
- ✦ Discuss with students how habitats are different in different parts of the country or areas of the world, such as deserts, oceans, mountains, and so on.
- ✦ Remind students that while examining any form of animal habitat, it is important to observe without disturbing. We must respect and learn to appreciate the habitats that we encounter.

Background Information

The following information might help students understand the selection they are about to read:

- Tell students that the Crinkleroot character was inspired by the nineteenth-century naturalist and author John Burroughs.
- "Crinkleroot's Guide to Knowing Animal Habitats" is the eleventh book in the popular Crinkleroot series. Other books include *Crinkleroot's Guide to Walking in Wild Places, Crinkleroot's 25 Mammals Every Child Should Know,* and *Crinkleroot's 25 More Animals Every Child Should Know.*
- Crinkleroot finds animals because he knows where to look for them. This selection gives readers tips for finding habitats themselves.
- "Crinkleroot's Guide to Knowing Animal Habitats" gives lessons about nature and appreciating the natural world.

Preview and Prepare 

ROUTINE 13

Browse

Have students read the title and name of the author, and take a few minutes to browse the selection. Have students use features such as the story's title and illustrations to predict how this story might relate to animals and their habitats.

Follow Routine 13, the know, want to know, learned routine, to help students identify and share what they know before reading, what they want to know while reading, and what their purposes are for reading. Students will chart these on a transparency.

Tell students to look for interesting words they read. These words could be fun words to read, or words that are unfamiliar to them. They may be unfamiliar with the name *Crinkleroot*. Explain that *Crinkleroot* is the name of the explorer in the story.

Display ***Transparency*** 35 and model browsing for students. For example, students may "Know" that Crinkleroot looks like an explorer in search of animal habitats. Under "Want to Know," write *What animal habitats will the explorer find?* Record students' observations on the transparency as they browse the selection.

Set Purposes

Have students set their own purposes for reading this selection. Remind students that readers can set purposes for reading by picking up clues from the title, illustrations, and genre of the text. If students have trouble, suggest that they will learn about the many animal habitats around us as they read.

Where do animals live?

Before reading the selection, read the Big Idea question. Tell students to keep this question in mind as they read the selection.

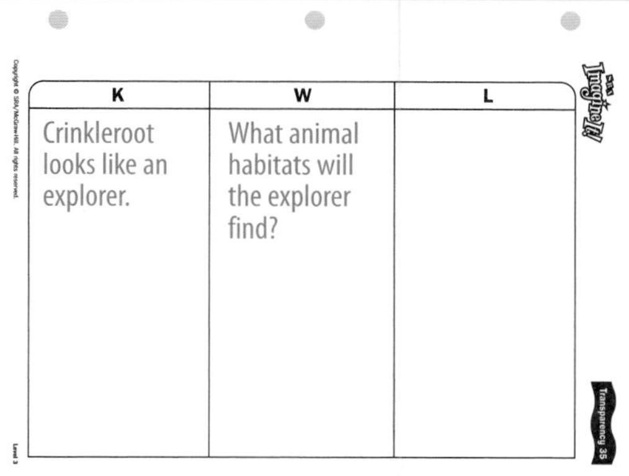

K	W	L
Crinkleroot looks like an explorer.	What animal habitats will the explorer find?	

Transparency 35

Give each student a copy of ***Home Connection*** page 23.The information is also available in Spanish on ***Home Connection*** page 24. Encourage students to discuss "Crinkleroot's Guide to Knowing Animal Habitats" with their families and complete the activity provided.

Selection Vocabulary

habitats (hab′ • it • ats′) *n.* plural form of **habitat:** the place where an animal or a plant naturally lives and grows (page 220)

rich (rich) *adj.* able to produce much; fertile (page 227)

variety (vər • ī′ • ə • tē′) *n.* a number of different things (page 228)

patch (pach) *n.* a small area (page 229)

migrating (mī′ • grāt′ • ing) *adj.* moving from one place to another (page 233)

vast (vast) *adj.* very great in size (page 234)

prey (prā) *n.* an animal that is hunted by another animal for food (page 236)

recognize (rek′ • əg • nīz′) *v.* to know and remember from before; to identify (page 239)

SRA Imagine It! Transparency 66

Selection Vocabulary

habitats (hab′ it ats′) *n.* plural form of **habitat:** the place where an animal or a plant naturally lives and grows (page 220)

rich (rich) *adj.* able to produce much; fertile (page 227)

variety (vər ī′ ə tē′) *n.* a number of different things (page 228)

patch (pach) *n.* a small area (page 229)

migrating (mī′ grāt′ ing) *adj.* moving from one place to another (page 233)

vast (vast) *adj.* very great in size (page 234)

prey (prā) *n.* an animal that is hunted by another animal for food (page 236)

recognize (rek′ əg nīz′) *v.* to know and remember from before; to identify (page 238)

 Unit 2, Lesson 5 Level 3

Transparency 66

Building Vocabulary

ROUTINE

Using Routine 11, the selection vocabulary process, have students read aloud the Vocabulary Warm-Up on ***Student Reader,*** Book 1 pages 216–217. As students read, have them stop to blend any difficult or unfamiliar words. Provide students with the pronunciations of words that are not decodable or that they cannot read automatically or fluently.

Guided Vocabulary Practice

Ask students to identify the highlighted vocabulary words they figured out using the vocabulary strategy context clues. **Possible Answers** *patch, rich, habitats* Have students explain how they figured out the meanings of the other vocabulary words as they read the Vocabulary Warm-Up.

Display ***Transparency*** 66, and have students read the words and definitions. Return to the Vocabulary Warm-Up, and read the sentences containing the vocabulary words with students. Then, if necessary, provide a brief in-context explanation of each word.

Use the vocabulary words on ***Transparency*** 66 to create fill-in-the-blank sentences. Have students fill in the appropriate vocabulary words. For example, "For Earth Day, my class planted flowers on a sunny ________ of land in front of our school." *patch*

Writer's Notebook

Have students copy the selection vocabulary and concept vocabulary words and definitions into the vocabulary section of their Writer's Notebooks. They can also include other words they think of that relate to the theme.

Read the article to find the meanings of these words, which are also in "Crinkleroot's Guide to Knowing Animal Habitats":

- patch
- rich
- habitats
- variety
- recognize
- prey
- migrating
- vast

Vocabulary Strategy

Context Clues are hints in the text. They help you find the meanings of words. Use context clues to find the meaning of *prey*.

Vocabulary Warm-Up

A swamp is a shallow wetland where trees grow. Some swamps have fresh water. Some contain salt water. A mangrove swamp has both. It is a patch of wetland that is close to an ocean.

Mangrove trees grow in mud that is rich in salt but poor in oxygen. Few trees can survive in this setting. Salt kills most plants. Soil that is always soft and moist does not support a tree.

Mangroves are special trees. They are able to filter out the salt in the soil and water. Their long, tangled roots prop them up. The roots look like they have been unearthed. They rise out of the water to take in the air they need.

Mangrove trees provide habitats for a variety of wildlife. Birds build nests in the trees. These include egrets, herons, and pelicans. In a mangrove tree, the birds find a home and a ready source of food as well.

The birds wade in the mangrove swamp. They look for fish that swim among the roots of the trees. The birds are quickly able to recognize and seize their prey. A heron grabs fish with its sharp beak. A pelican dives underwater and scoops fish in its pouch.

Some small fish stay safe in the shelter of the mangrove roots. They feed on crabs, shrimp, and worms. Then, when they are grown, they leave. These migrating fish move from the swamp to the vast waters of the ocean.

GAME

Writing Sentences

Use each vocabulary word in two sentences. First, use the word in a sentence that asks a question. Then use the word in a sentence that is a statement. Write your sentences on a sheet of paper.

Concept Vocabulary

The concept word for this lesson is ***ecosystem.*** An **ecosystem** is a group of living things and the environment in which they live. A desert and a rain forest are examples of ecosystems. What kinds of animals live in different ecosystems? What helps these animals survive in their environments?

Discuss the concept vocabulary word *ecosystem* with students. Ask students how they think the word *ecosystem* relates to the theme Animals and Their Habitats. As students read the selections in this unit, encourage them to think about other words that relate to the theme. Students can record these words in the vocabulary section of their Writer's Notebooks.

GAME

Have students play the Writing Sentences game during Small-Group Time.

Differentiating Instruction English Learner

IF . . . students have difficulty playing the Writing Sentences game, **THEN . . .** provide them with written yes-or-no questions, using the vocabulary words. Students should use the words in each question to write a complete answer. For example: *Do mangrove trees provide habitats for wildlife? Yes, mangrove trees provide habitats for wildlife.*

Concept/Question Board

As students read "Crinkleroot's Guide to Knowing Animal Habitats," encourage them to post questions, answers, comments, or other items related to the theme Animals and Their Habitats on the **Concept/ Question Board.**

Monitor Progress

Formal Assessment

Comprehension Observation Log Observe individual students as they read, and use the Comprehension Observation Log, located in ***Lesson Assessment Book 1,*** to record anecdotal information about each student's strengths and weaknesses.

Reading the Selection 

Genre Narrative Nonfiction

Have students identify the genre of "Crinkleroot's Guide to Knowing Animal Habitats." *narrative nonfiction* Tell students the elements of narrative nonfiction.

- Elements of fiction are blended with elements of nonfiction to make a more exciting story.
- Facts about real people, places, and events are included in narrative nonfiction.

1st READ

Comprehension Strategies

Model the use of the following comprehension strategies during the first reading of "Crinkleroot's Guide to Knowing Animal Habitats:"

- Clarifying
- Making Connections
- Adjusting Reading Speed

Comprehension Strategies Rubrics

Use the Informal Comprehension Strategies Rubrics to determine whether a student is using any of the strategies listed below. Note the strategies a student is using, instead of the degree to which a student might be using any particular strategy. In addition, encourage the student to tell of any strategies other than the ones being taught that he or she is using.

Clarifying

✦ The student recognizes when a word or idea is not making sense.

✦ The student uses decoding skills to read unfamiliar words.

✦ The student uses structural elements in words to read them.

✦ The student uses structural elements, context, and questioning to clarify the meanings of unfamiliar words.

Making Connections

- The student makes connections between prior knowledge and information in the text.
- The student makes connections between or relates personal experiences to what is read in the text (text-to-self connections).
- The student makes connections across or relates information from different selections (text-to-text connections).
- The student makes connections or relates information between what is happening in the text to what is happening in the world today (text-to-world connections).

Adjusting Reading Speed

- The student knows the text is not making sense and stops to reread.
- The student identifies the specific part of the text that is not making sense and rereads only that part.
- The student changes reading speed in reaction to the demands of the text.
- The student adjusts reading rate to skim or scan for specific information.

Informal Assessment 

Monitor Progress to Differentiate Instruction

Comprehension Skill Note students' understanding of the comprehension skill Classify and Categorize.

APPROACHING LEVEL

IF . . . students are having difficulty with the comprehension skill Classify and Categorize as they read,	**THEN . . .** have them practice classifying and categorizing items in the classroom, for example, types of books, writing instruments, furniture, and so on.

ON LEVEL

IF . . . students are gaining an understanding of the comprehension skill Classify and Categorize as they read,	**THEN . . .** have them identify groups of similar words in "Crinkleroot's Guide to Knowing Animal Habitats." Have students select a heading for each category.

ABOVE LEVEL

IF . . . students understand the comprehension skill Classify and Categorize,	**THEN . . .** have students extend their understanding of classifying and categorizing by researching additional habitats, animals, and so on and create new lists of facts that adds to the information taught by Crinkleroot in the selection.

Technology

eSTUDENT READER Students can access ***SRA Imagine It! Student Reader*** electronically by using the ***eStudent Reader*** online or on CD-ROM.

Comprehension Skills

Reread "Crinkleroot's Guide to Knowing Animal Habitats" using the following comprehension skills:

- Author's Point of View
- Classify and Categorize

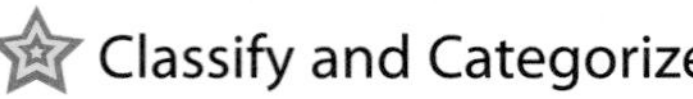

Reading with a Writer's Eye

When rereading "Crinkleroot's Guide to Knowing Animal Habitats," explain the following literary elements:

- Text Structure: Types
- Language Use

Focus Questions

Have students read aloud the Focus Questions on page 219. Encourage students to think about the Focus Questions when reading "Crinkleroot's Guide to Knowing Animal Habitats."

Reading Recommendation

Oral Reading

Use Routine 14, the reading the selection routine, as you read the story. While reading, model strategies and stop to ask and answer questions. Point out how the pictures reflect the story. Share the images that pop up in your mind as you read and how points in the reading relate to ideas you already know. Reread the text by applying comprehension skills. After reading, be sure to discuss the story using the "handing-off" procedure and have students discuss new information that they have learned.

Oral reading is recommended for the selection due to possible unfamiliarity of terms for some students and the abundant amount of information. Point out to students that in addition to reading the text, they should look at the illustrations and read the captions, which provide additional information. Remind students to adjust their reading speed accordingly if the text becomes confusing. Also, remind students that adjusting their reading speed while reading nonfiction will help them remember the facts they learn from the selection.

Genre

Narrative Nonfiction blends elements of fiction with elements of nonfiction to make a more exciting story. Facts about real people, places, and events are included in narrative nonfiction.

Comprehension Skill

Classify and Categorize
As you read, sort similar groups of information into categories to help you understand and remember what you read.

Crinkleroot's Animal Guide to Knowing Habitats

by Jim Arnosky

Focus Questions

What would it be like to study animal habitats as a job? Why is it important to learn about and to protect different animal habitats?

218 219

Students will read this story twice over a four-day period.

Day 1 **ORAL READ** Have students read the first half of the selection. Model the use of the comprehension strategies.

Day 2 **ORAL READ** Have students finish reading the selection. Continue to model the comprehension strategies.

Day 3 **SILENT READ** Have students reread the first half of the selection silently. Have students focus on the comprehension skills and Reading with a Writer's Eye.

Day 4 **SILENT READ** Have students finish rereading the selection.

Technology

Have students listen to "Crinkleroot's Guide to Knowing Animal Habitats" on the ***Listening Library CD.*** After students have listened, have them discuss what other things such as poetry, songs, or nonfiction they prefer to listen to on the radio or on CDs.

Reading and Responding

Hello! My name is Crinkleroot. I'm an explorer and a wildlife finder. I've found so many wild creatures sharing this sweet earth, I lost count somewhere around a billion!

I see so many wild critters because I know where they all live. The natural places where wild animals live are called habitats.

I'm going to visit lots of different wildlife habitats. You can come too! 1

220

221

Phonics and Fluency

One of the focuses of this lesson is /o͞o/ spelled *oo, _ew, u_e, _ue,* and *u.* Words with these spellings will be found in boxes similar to this one throughout the selection.

/o͞o/ sound spelled *oo:* Crinkleroot, too

Comprehension Strategies

This selection is broken into two parts. On the first day, read pages 220–231. On the second day, read pages 232–239.

1 Clarifying Teacher Modeling: *When we clarify, we are making the meanings of words, ideas, and passages easier to understand. I need to stop and clarify a couple of things. I wasn't sure what the word* Crinkleroot *was. As I read on, I realize that it is the name of the explorer. He's going to be our guide. The picture of the deer and the words with it also confused me at first. It is a part of the story, but it is more like an example set apart from the text. It gives us more information about what we are reading.*

Teacher Tip

CLARIFICATION Remind students to clarify all of the time. Tell students to use this strategy whenever they read any type of text.

The first place I want to show you is a watery place, or wetland.

A wetland is any place where water is near, at, or just above the surface of the ground. You may have a tiny wetland in your own backyard where the soil is always moist and the grass grows more lush. 

CROSS SECTION OF A WETLAND: mud
water table (water level in soil)
sand, pebbles, and stones.

NOTE: Some types of wetlands are not firm enough to walk on. The best way to observe most wetlands is in the company of an adult and from the safety of higher ground or a sturdy boardwalk.

222 223

2 Making Connections Teacher Modeling: *I can make a connection to this part of the story. Crinkleroot tells us what a wetland is and says that we may have a wetland in our own backyards. We have a spot in our yard that is always wet, even when the rest of the grass is dry. I guess we have a wetland habitat there. Can anyone else make a connection to this part of the story?*

Comprehension Check

Why would the grass be more lush near a wetland? **Possible Answer** *The grass would grow faster because there is more water.*

Teacher Tip

CLARIFICATION When a passage is confusing, prompt students to think about whether the meanings of some words are unknown or whether necessary information seems to be missing.

Differentiating Instruction English Learner

IF . . . students need help understanding the prepositions on page 223, **THEN . . .** demonstrate the meanings of the words by using gestures or sentences such as *I am near the board. Sue is sitting at her desk. The clock is just above the door.*

Reading and Responding

Differentiating Instruction **English Learner**

IF . . . students need extra help with vocabulary, **THEN . . .** use the ***English Learner Support Guide,*** or use pictures, objects, drawings, or pantomime to help them visualize the words.

IF . . . students would benefit from a review of numbers, **THEN . . .** review the numbers 1–24, and have students use them as they count the wildlife in this illustration.

Comprehension Strategies

③ **Adjusting Reading Speed** Teacher Modeling: *There is a lot of information on these pages. I'm going to reread these pages at a slower pace, just to make sure I understand everything I've read. I've learned about the three most common wetlands: marshes, swamps, and bogs.*

Comprehension Check

What are some examples of animals that live in the wetland habitat? **Possible Answer** *Great blue herons, painted turtles, mallards, alligators, and egrets are just some of the animals that live in the wetlands.* *How did you learn this information?* **Possible Answer** *The captions and the illustrations that go along with the text tell readers that these animals are examples of what you can find living in the wetlands.*

The shallow water of any wetland is a world of plants, rocks, sand, and sunken trees.

It is a rich weedy habitat for underwater wildlife. ④

sunfish
newt
damselfly larva
freshwater mussel
water boatman
crayfish
minnows
dragonfly larva
madtom
pickerel
snapping turtle

226 227

④ **Making Connections** Teacher Modeling: *I can make another connection to this selection. I went out in a canoe once with my uncle. I didn't know at the time that we were actually in a wetland habitat! He told me to look for some of the animals shown here in the illustrations and captions. I saw a crayfish, a pickerel, and a snapping turtle. Hey, we were habitat explorers and I didn't even know it! Can anyone make a connection to this part of the selection?*

Research in Action

Students need multiple exposures to words. Multiple exposures can occur through different learning experiences. Often the word may be used only one or two times in text in a grade level, so additional experiences need to be created. Preteaching and post-teaching vocabulary words, using vocabulary words during discussion and for writing, posting and revisiting vocabulary words on a regular basis, and making vocabulary words a part of a personal dictionary that students can refer to throughout the year will give students multiple exposures to new words.
(Marsha Roit)

Teacher Tips

INQUIRY Tell students that the information in this selection may be helpful as they continue the unit investigation.

COMPREHENSION Ask students the following questions to make sure they understand the story:

- *Can you summarize what you have read?*
- *Does what you are reading make sense?*

Vocabulary Tip

Point out the word *rich* on page 227 in the text. Ask students whether they know what the word *rich* means in other contexts, such as with money. Ask them how knowing the meaning in that context might help them understand how the underwater wildlife is a *rich* habitat. Have students find the word word *variety* on page 228 in the text. Ask students whether knowing that many animals are hidden in the woods on these pages helps them understand the word *variety*.

Comprehension Strategies

5 Clarifying Teacher Modeling: *I'm going to stop and clarify another point here. I'll reread the first sentence. OK, now I understand. We are in the woods now. Crinkleroot is telling us about some of the animal habitats found in the woods. He is saying that there are a lot of habitats in the woods, more than we can see and hear.*

6 Adjusting Reading Speed Teacher Modeling: *I'm going to slow down as I read these pages. I want to be sure I find all of the wildlife animals living in the woods. This is fun!*

Climb aboard my old jalopy! There are some interesting places I want to show you that are miles apart. Along the way, we're sure to spot some wildlife near the road.

crows

ring-necked pheasant

deer

woodchuck

230

Rabbits, deer, woodchucks, and other normally shy animals come out to the roadsides to feed on lush green plants growing in the open sunlight. 7

Roadsides are also hunting grounds for hungry crows, hawks, and kestrels.

red-tailed hawk

kestrel

35 MPH

NATURE

rabbit

231

7 Making Connections Teacher Modeling: *I have seen rabbits, woodchucks, and even deer on the side of the road. Mostly they are munching on grass or plants. I hope they're careful, though. The roadside can be a dangerous place.*

Comprehension Check

Why do you think that the normally shy animals would go to the roadside to eat grass and plants? **Possible Answer** *If they have eaten the grass and plants in the woods and are still hungry, they may have to go to the roadsides. We've also learned that highways and cities are moving closer to the woods, so their wooded areas are now roadsides.*

Teacher Tip

INQUIRY You may want students to record some of the animals they are learning about to use in their unit investigations or in future writing assignments.

STOP You have read the first half of the story. You will continue the story tomorrow on page T382.

Lesson 5 Inquiry Planner

STEP 6: Confirming or Revising Conjectures

Day 1 Students start gathering information together to evaluate conjectures.

Day 2 Students continue thinking about how the information collected relates to conjectures.

Day 3 Have a whole-group discussion about how the information in "Crinkleroot's Guide to Knowing Animal Habitats" relates to students' conjectures.

Day 4 Discuss new information about the theme in "Crinkleroot's Guide to Knowing Animal Habitats." Then students will revise their conjectures and start producing their presentations.

STEP 7: Sharing Your Answers

Day 5 With their groups, students will complete their presentations and rehearse them.

Day 6 Each group will give some kind of presentation about their investigation. Students will also discuss the presentations afterward.

STEP 8: Asking New Questions

Day 7 Students will ask new questions about their specific topics and the unit theme.

Teacher Tip

BACKYARD HABITATS A good project students may want to pursue is creating their own backyard habitats either at their homes, at a community center, or at school. Students can find information on establishing a backyard wildlife habitat and the requirements to be certified at the National Wildlife Federation. Once the requirements are met, the habitat will be certified by the NWF. For more information on this program or many other youth programs involving animals and their habitats, visit the National Wildlife Federation at www.nwf.org.

Inquiry Process

Step 6—Confirming or Revising Conjectures

Whole-Group Time

Whole Group

- Remind students that they have chosen an investigation question, have made conjectures about that question, and have gathered information about their topic. Now they will see how the information they have collected affects their conjectures and their understanding of their topic.

- Have students review the notes in their Writer's Notebooks and ***Skills Practice 1*** to remind them of the questions, ideas, and conjectures they had at the beginning of the unit. As they think about these initial questions and conjectures, they should be asking themselves questions like the following to help confirm or revise their conjectures: *What have I learned about my topic that I didn't know before? How has that changed how I think about animals and their habitats? How does the information our group has collected relate to my conjecture? What information confirms my conjecture? What information challenges my conjecture? How can I make my conjecture better with what I know now?*

- Have students reflect on their conjecture so that they can revise these conjectures. Model this process for students: *When I began, I thought that if people knew more about these animals losing their habitats, they would stop destroying their habitats. So my conjecture was that a campaign to raise awareness would solve the problem. I made a survey asking people about this problem, and I found out that some people don't think that this problem is an important one for the community. If people don't think the problem is important, then they probably won't take steps to solve it. My conjecture can't be fully correct because some people who know about the problem might not help solve it. I need to think more about my conjecture and how to change it. Protecting animal habitats takes more than just awareness.*

Small Group

Small-Group Time

- ✦ Students should join their investigation groups and continue collecting information to evaluate their conjectures.
- ✦ Each group should review all of its information. Remind them of the information they recorded about the selections in ***Skills Practice 1,*** in notes from class discussions, and any other notes from other sources they have, such as interviews, articles, surveys, or videos. Encourage students to make use of items on the **Concept/Question Board** as well as any graphic organizers, charts, or tables they have made in this unit.
- ✦ Circulate among the groups and help them think about how their information relates to their conjectures. If the information is leading them in a different direction than their original conjecture, they should consider revising their conjecture. Continue to model this process as needed. For example, a group may produce this conjecture: *Food, water, and shelter is what makes an animal habitat safe.* They learned from "Two Days in May," however, that some animals like deer need more than this to be safe. While food, water, and shelter are necessary for a safe animal habitat, a safe animal habitat may require more than this.

Concept/Question Board

Ask students to write information or questions on the **Concept/ Question Board.** Students might

- bring in pictures of animals and wildlife in their own backyard. (Remind students not to disturb the habitats of the animals while they are observing or photographing them.)
- bring in articles and/or pictures from magazines and newspapers of animals and their habitats.
- post interesting facts, quotes, or information that they have collected about animals.
- write a summary of a television program or film they have seen about animals and their habitats.
- respond to another group's question or conjecture.

Teacher Tips

REVISING CONJECTURES Remind students that revising conjectures is an important part of the investigation process. They have been collecting information along the way that has probably changed their initial conjecture. Now is the time to revise their conjectures before continuing on to their presentations. Explain that having to revise a conjecture means that something new has been learned.

STAYING FOCUSED Remind students that the goal of this unit's investigation is to come to a deeper understanding of some aspect of the theme Animals and Their Habitats. In order for this to happen, their questions, information, conjectures, and presentations should stay focused on the theme.

OBJECTIVES

Students will
- ✦ brainstorm ideas for report writing.
- ✦ take the spelling pretest.
- ✦ practice cursive *c* and *d*.

MATERIALS

- ✦ ***Skills Practice 1,*** p. 153
- ✦ ***Routine*** 15
- ✦ ***Transparencies*** 67, 68

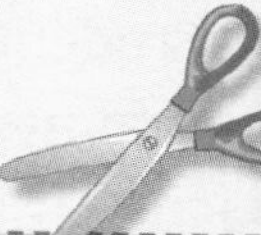

Teacher Tip

PLAN AHEAD Students will need to be able to access information via the school library, a classroom library, or the Internet.

Transparency 67

Informative Report

The Quarter by Shelly Combes

Quarters do not look the same as they did a long time ago. The pictures on them have changed. In this report I will tell you how quarters have changed.

The 1800s

The first quarters had an eagle on one side. On the other side, there was a woman called Lady Liberty. Some quarters only had her head on them. Some had her whole body.

The 1900s until 1999

In 1932, the quarter was changed. It was George Washington's 200th birthday. Washington's head was put on the quarter instead of Lady Liberty. Then, in 1976, it was America's 200th birthday. A picture of a drummer from 200 years ago was put on instead of the eagle.

1999 and the 2000s

Quarters changed again, starting in 1999. Instead of the drummer, the quarters have the names of states on them. Each state has a different picture that shows something special about that state. Quarters have changed a lot since the first quarters in the 1800s.

 Level 3

Transparency 67

UNIT 2 Lesson 5

Name ______ Date ______

Writing an Informative Report: Rough Draft

Think

Audience: Who will read your report?

Possible Answer my classmates

Purpose: What is your reason for writing this report?

Possible Answer I want to tell other people about tigers.

Prewriting Use this graphic organizer to prepare to write a rough draft of your report.

Expository Structure

Topic: Siberian Tigers	
Subtopic: How and where they live	Subtopic: Why they are endangered
Conclusion: We need to protect their habitats.	

Skills Practice 1 • Writing UNIT 2 • Lesson 5 153

Skills Practice 1, p. 153

Writing Informative Report

Prewriting

ROUTINE 15

Teach

- ✦ Ask students if they know what news reporters do. If necessary, tell students that news reporters convey information to a large audience. They give information about an event, and relay facts and statistics. Tell students that before a news reporter can report a story, he or she must first do research to make sure that all of the facts are accurate.
- ✦ Use Routine 15. Tell students that they will be writing a report. They will research the information and present it as facts and examples. If necessary, briefly discuss the difference between the report they will be writing and the reviews they wrote previously that contain opinion.
- ✦ Explain the criteria you will use to evaluate the informative reports.
- ✦ Display ***Transparency*** 67 and have a student read the report aloud. Explain the basic elements or the report: summary, direct quotes, author citation, and so on.

Guided Practice

- ✦ As a class, discuss some possible topics relating to the theme Animals and Their Habitats. Record their ideas on the board.
- ✦ Have them look at what you wrote. Ask students if they see any related topics on the board. Help students reorganize the information into separate categories such as endangered animals, zoos, circuses, tropical habitats, desert habitats, or farm animals. Tell students that categorizing is a way to organize information.
- ✦ Select a topic for which you can model researching, drafting, revising, editing/proofreading, and publishing.
- ✦ Have students turn to ***Skills Practice 1*** page 153. Discuss the Think questions as a class.

Writing, continued

Apply

Have students complete the Think questions on ***Skills Practice 1,*** page 153 as a getting started activity.

Assessment

You will use the Writing Rubrics found in the Level Appendix to evaluate students' informative reports. You may use any of the rubrics for Genre, Writing Process, and Writing Traits. Share with students what you will be looking for when assessing their informative reports.

Monitor Progress to Differentiate Instruction

Formal Assessment 

Brainstorming Note whether students have selected a topic.

APPROACHING LEVEL

IF . . . students need to brainstorm ideas,	**THEN . . .** during Workshop ask them which animals they like or what types of habitats they would like to visit.

ON LEVEL

IF . . . students have an understanding of brainstorming ideas,	**THEN . . .** have them complete ***Skills Practice 1*** page 153 and begin to select reference materials during Workshop.

ABOVE LEVEL

IF . . . students need a challenge,	**THEN . . .** have them do a computer search of their topic during Workshop.

Spelling

/o͞o/ Pretest

Teach

Say the sentences below. Have students write each spelling word on a separate sheet of paper. When they are finished, have them correct any misspelled words.

Pretest Sentences

1. Using a **clue,** the man solved the puzzle.
2. A **tuna** is a large ocean fish.
3. Do you like **root** vegetables?
4. My favorite month of the year is **June.**
5. My sister plays the **flute** in the school band.
6. My favorite color is steel **blue.**
7. Please take time to **chew** your food.
8. The teacher said we could **choose** any book.
9. We need more **glue** for the project.
10. If the **noodle** is soft, then it is cooked.
11. It is wise to always tell the **truth.**
12. The whistle **blew** when the game was over.
13. My grandmother likes to **stew** tomatoes.
14. The firefighter is about to go on **duty.**
15. The lightning crash was a **rude** awakening.

Challenge Sentences

16. The alexandrite is the **jewel** for June.
17. My brother and I sing a **duet.**

Diagnose any misspellings by determining whether students misspelled the /o͞o/ sound spellings or some other part of the word. Then have students use the pretest as a take-home list to study the spellings of words with the /o͞o/ sound spellings.

Teacher Tip

PENMANSHIP If students are having problems forming cursive *c* and *d,* or their letters are floating between the lines, then review proper paper position, check to make sure students are holding their pencils correctly, or review letter formation.

Penmanship

Cursive Letters *c* and *d*

Teach

✦ Remind students that cursive letters are made of four types of strokes (undercurve, overcurve, downcurve, and slant lines). Draw them on the board.

✦ Display ***Transparency*** 68. Introduce lowercase cursive *c* and *d* as downcurve letters. Say the strokes aloud as you trace the formations using your finger.

- **Letter *c*** Starting point, undercurve
Downcurve, undercurve: small *c*
- **Letter *d*** Starting point, undercurve
Downcurve, undercurve
Slant down, undercurve: small *d*

✦ On the board, write lowercase cursive *c* and *d,* saying the strokes aloud as you form the letters.

✦ To model proper letter formation, write the following words on the board: *dock, dance, candle, cuddle.*

Guided Practice

Have students practice forming the letters on the board.

Apply

✦ Have students practice writing each letter four times on a separate piece of paper. Ask them to circle the best formation of each of their letters.

✦ After reviewing the words you wrote on the board, ask students to write the words on their paper to practice letter formation. Have them circle the best formation of each word.

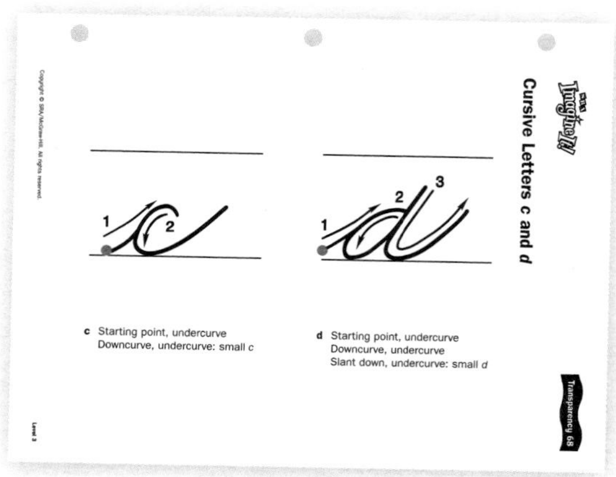

Transparency 68

Skills Traces

Preparing to Read

Word Structure: Irregular Plurals

Introduced in Grade 2, Unit 4, Lesson 5

Reviewed: Unit 2, Lesson 1
Practiced: Unit 2, Lesson 2
Unit 2, Lesson 5
Assessed: ***Lesson Assessment Book 1,*** p. 75

Phonics:

See Level Appendix

Reading and Responding

Comprehension Skill: Author's Point of View

Introduced in Grade 2, Unit 2, Lesson 4

Grade 3
Reviewed: Unit 1, Lesson 3
Practiced: Unit 2, Lesson 5
Assessed: ***Lesson Assessment Book 1,*** pp. 76–78

Reviewed in Grade 4, Unit 1, Lesson 1

Comprehension Skill: Classify and Categorize

Reviewed in Grade 2, Unit 2, Lesson 5

Grade 3
Reviewed: Unit 2, Lesson 5
Practiced: Unit 3, Lesson 1
Assessed: ***Lesson Assessment Book 1,*** pp. 76–78

Reviewed in Grade 4, Unit 2, Lesson 5

Comprehension Strategy: Adjusting Reading Speed

Introduced in Grade 2, Unit 1, Lesson 4

Grade 3
Reviewed: Unit 1, Lesson 2
Practiced: Unit 2, Lesson 5
Assessed: Unit 2, Lesson 5, p. T365

Reviewed in Grade 4, Unit 1, Lesson 4

Comprehension Strategy: Clarifying

Reviewed in Grade 2, Unit 1, Lesson 3

Grade 3
Reviewed: Unit 1, Lesson 2
Practiced: Unit 2, Lesson 5
Assessed: Unit 2, Lesson 5, p. T364

Reviewed in Grade 4, Unit 1, Lesson 4

Language Arts

Writing: Informative Report

Reviewed in Grade 2, Unit 2, Lesson 5

Grade 3
Reviewed: Unit 2, Lesson 5
Assessed: Unit 2, Lesson 5, p. T446

Reviewed in Grade 4, Unit 2, Lesson 4

Grammar, Usage, and Mechanics: Pronouns

Grade 3
Introduced: Unit 2, Lesson 5
Practiced: Unit 6, Lesson 2
Assessed: ***Lesson Assessment Book 1,*** p. 80

Reviewed in Grade 4, Unit 3, Lesson 1

Day 2

Preparing to Read

OBJECTIVES

Students will

- review /ū/ spelled _ew and _ue; and /o͞o/ spelled oo, _ue, u, _ew, and u_e.
- review open and closed syllables.
- build fluency.

MATERIALS

- ***Transparency*** 65
- ***Sound/Spelling Cards*** 31, 41
- Routines 2, 3, 4, 7, 8

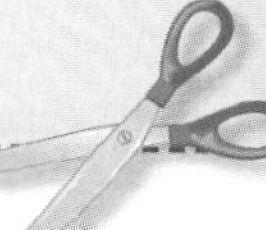

Daily Oral Practice

There is a small wetland habitat in my backyard. There's also a forest across the street that is home to many different animals. I never knew so many animal habitats existed so close to my home.

- Write the daily news on the board or on chart paper. Then have students read the daily news in unison to practice fluency.
- As a review of yesterday's phonics and fluency lesson, ask a volunteer to identify any words with /o͞o/ spelled _ew. *knew*

Phonics and Fluency

Review: /ū/ spelled *oo, _ue, u, _ew,* and *u_e;* /o͞o/ spelled *_ew* and *_ue;* open and closed syllables

Line 1	few	nephew	cue	value
Line 2	fooled	Crinkleroot	true	bluebirds
Line 3	truth	supermarket	grew	newt
Line 4	rule	tube	flute	June
Line 5	human	cable	humble	candle

Sentence 1	We <u>should</u> rescue the few foxes who lost their habitat.
Sentence 2	The bluejay flew to the <u>end</u> of the lake to find food.

Blending

- ✦ Use ***Transparency*** 65 with the blending lines and sentences from Day 1.
- ✦ Review ***Sound/Spelling Cards*** 31 and 41. Then use Routine 3, the whole-word blending process, to have students read Lines 1–5.
- ✦ Have students read the sentences using normal intonation and expression. If students have difficulty reading a sentence, stop and use Routine 4, the blending sentences process.

Developing Oral Language

Use one or both of these activities to help students practice reading the words from the blending lines.

- Give clues for each of the words in Lines 1–5, and ask students to identify the words. For example: It was a hot and *humid* day. Because the raccoon ate so much, it *grew* fat. After you have modeled a few examples, have students create clue sentences.
- Choose one of the lines on which students should focus. Have a volunteer choose a word and use it in a sentence to begin a story. Have another volunteer continue the story by supplying a sentence that uses a different word from the line. Continue until all of the words have been used.

Dictation

- ✦ Follow Routine 7 for whole-word dictation. When dictating words, say the word, use the word in a sentence, and then repeat the word.
- ✦ Follow Routine 8 for sentence dictation. When dictating sentences, say the sentence. Next, dictate one word at a time, following Routine 2 for sounds-in-sequence dictation or Routine 7 for whole-word dictation, depending upon your students. Have students proofread, checking for spelling, capitalization, and end punctuation.
- ✦ Dictate the following words and sentences for students to write.

Line 1	food	crew	June
Line 2	glue	tuna	hue
Challenge Word	raccoons		
Sentence	The raccoons and the bluebirds ate the food for the crew.		

Differentiating Instruction — English Learner

IF . . . students have difficulty writing the dictated words, **THEN . . .** before you dictate the words, write them on the board, pronounce them (emphasizing /ō/ or /ū/), and have students repeat the pronunciations.

Sound/Spelling Cards 31, 41

Teacher Tip

BLENDING During Workshop, work with students who have difficulty blending words by using Routine 1 for sound-by-sound blending or Routine 3 for whole-word blending.

Reading and Responding

Our first stop is a farmer's cornfield. Cornfields provide an ever-changing habitat for wildlife. In the spring gulls, swallows, and bluebirds feed on beetles, grubs, and earthworms unearthed by the farmer's plow.

By midsummer, when the corn stalks have grown high enough to provide cover, small animals move in to nest and raise their young.

At ripening time the cornfield becomes a supermarket for raiding raccoons.

By late fall, after the field of corn has been freshly cut and harvested, the scattered kernels are a feast for migrating geese. 8

232

233

OBJECTIVES

Students will

- use the comprehension strategies Adjusting Reading Speed, Making Connections, and Clarifying.
- discuss the selection using the handing-off process.
- review vocabulary, genre, and fluency.

MATERIALS

- ***Student Reader***, Book 1, pp. 232–241
- Routine A
- ***Transparency*** 35
- ***Skills Practice 1,*** pp. 149–150

Comprehension Strategies

8 Adjusting Reading Speed Teacher Modeling: *This is another good place to slow down my reading to understand all of the information. On these pages we learn about what cornfields are like in the spring, the summer, and the fall. Many animals use a cornfield as a habitat. It truly is "ever-changing."*

Most small grassland animals are birds or burrowers—or both!

From small hillside meadows to vast rolling plains, grasslands are wide open spaces where wildlife can thrive.

When walking in grassland, stop to check your clothes for ticks. Ticks are numerous in tall grass.

You'll find more kinds of insects and spiders in grasslands than in any other habitat.

234

The largest inhabitants of grasslands are grazing animals.

At first, grassland looks void of anything but waving green stems. But take time to really look and you will discover something wonderful. 9

The badger is a grassland predator that can dig down twelve feet to catch burrowing prey.

The coyote and red fox are open country predators that often share the same hunting grounds.

235

9 Making Connections Teacher Modeling: *My family has a picnic every May in a wide-open meadow. I've seen some of these animals and insects in the grasslands there. I've seen butterflies, spiders, and lots of grasshoppers. Fortunately, I've never seen a tick.*

Comprehension Check

In what habitat can you find more insects and spiders than any other? **Possible Answer** *There are more insects and spiders in grasslands than any other habitat.*
How can both large animals like buffalo and bison and small animals like voles share the same habitat? **Possible Answer** *Small animals can burrow into the ground, while large animals graze on the grasses.*

Phonics and Fluency

/o͞o/ spelled *oo, _ue:* bluebirds, raccoons

Differentiating Instruction **English Learner**

IF . . . students do not understand the metaphor on page 233, **THEN . . .** explain that a supermarket is a large store where people buy all kinds of food. The cornfield is a place where raccoons can find all kinds of food.

Teacher Tip

CLARIFY Some students may need to stop and clarify the meaning of *ripening time*. Tell them that this means "when the corn is ripe" or "fully grown."

Wherever the road leads, you will find wildlife living there. Even the hottest, driest places can be home to animals. In the drylands, wildlife find cover behind sage brush and cactus, beneath rock ledges, or for some, simply by digging
10 in and covering up with sand. Succulent plants provide both food and water. And for predators, there is prey.

vulture

Here is a sampling of the many wildlife species that inhabit drylands from sage brush country to desert sands.

mule deer
armadillo
kangaroo rat
jackrabbit
diamondback rattlesnake
roadrunner
collared lizard
broad-billed hummingbird
horned lizard
elf owl

236

237

Teacher Tips

CONCEPT/QUESTION BOARD As they read, tell students to add new information they have learned to the **Concept/Question Board.**

USING STRATEGIES Although Clarifying is the strategy being modeled, encourage students to use any strategy they have learned as they read the story.

Comprehension Strategies

10 **Clarifying** Teacher Modeling: *I need to stop and clarify a word. The text says that succulent plants provide both food and water. What does the word* succulent *mean? We know from the rest of the sentence that the plants provide both food and water, so these plants must have nutrients that are good for animals and they contain water for the animals, too. I'll look up the word in the dictionary just to make sure. The dictionary says* succulent *means "full of juice." That sounds like it would be good for the animals!*

Learn to recognize the different wildlife habitats, from lowlands to mountains, wetlands to drylands. Don't be fooled by how small a place may be. Some wild critters get by in surprisingly little space—a bit of brush, a swampy puddle, a pile of rocks, a tiny woodlot, or a lone cactus.

Well now! I told you we'd cover a lot of territory and we did! I counted over eighty different wildlife species on our trip. How many did you count? I hope you enjoyed the journey. I did. So did Sassafrass. She always likes riding in the old jalopy. We'll see you soon. Until then, remember, wherever you go, you share the world with wildlife. 11

11 **Making Connections** Teacher Modeling: *I've been on a wildlife journey before. I went on a bird-watching hike on a nature path. We had a guide like Crinkleroot, but we didn't see as many habitats as this story describes. You can go on a journey in a book. I learned a lot about nature on this journey.*

Comprehension Check

What does Crinkleroot mean when he says, "wherever you go, you share the world with wildlife"? **Possible Answer** *Animal habitats exist all around us, even when we don't notice them. People share Earth with animals.*

Vocabulary Tip

Point out the word *migrating* on page 233 in the text. Ask students whether they know that some groups of birds fly to other areas for warmth and food every fall. Ask students whether this helps them understand the word *migrating*. Point out the word *prey* on page 236 in the text. Ask students whether they know what the word *predators* means. Ask if knowing that *predators* are animals that hunt other animals for food helps them to understand the meaning of *prey*.

Phonics and Fluency

/o͞o/ spelled *oo*: food, fooled

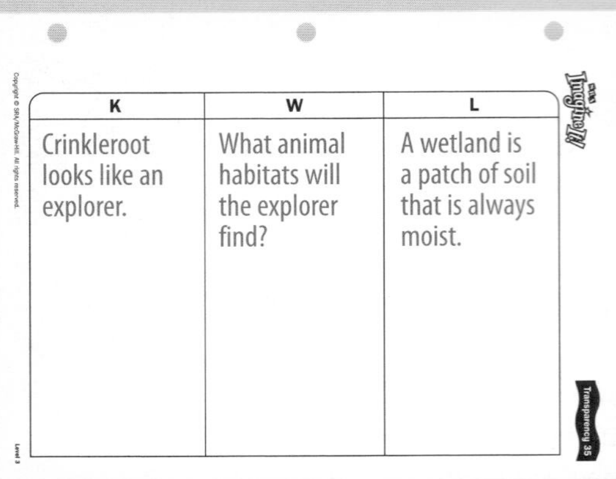

Transparency 35

Differentiating Instruction — English Learner

IF . . . students need help reading aloud,
THEN . . . have them first read along as they listen to the CD of "Crinkleroot's Guide to Knowing Animal Habitats." Then ask them to orally read along on a second listening.

Discussing the Selection

- ✦ It is important for students to see you as a contributing member of the group. Use Routine A, the handing-off process, to emphasize that you are part of the group. Actively participate in the handing-off process by raising your hand to be called on by the last speaker when you have a contribution to make. Point out unusual and interesting insights verbalized by students so that these insights are recognized and discussed. As the year progresses, students will take more responsibility for the discussion of the selections.
- ✦ Engage students in a discussion using the handing-off procedure to determine whether they have grasped the following ideas:
  - Crinkleroot is taking readers on a journey to learn about animal habitats.
  - Throughout the selection, readers learn about different animal habitats.
- ✦ Ask students how the story demonstrates the following key concepts:
  - Some animals take turns using a single habitat, depending on the season.
  - Crinkleroot teaches that "wherever you go, you share the world with wildlife."
- ✦ Return to the KWL chart on ***Transparency*** 35. Have students discuss whether the selection provided enough information to tell them what they wanted to know, and also have them discuss what they learned by reading the selection. Ask students if the predictions they made while browsing the story were confirmed or not confirmed.
- ✦ Also, have students return to the Focus Questions on ***Student Reader,*** Book 1 page 219. Select a student to read the questions aloud, and have students answer and discuss the questions. Have them return to the text as necessary.

Genre Review

Review the elements of narrative nonfiction with students on page T364. Then ask students how they know "Crinkleroot's Guide to Knowing Animal Habitats" is narrative nonfiction.

Where do different animals live?

After reading the selection, read the Big Idea question. Discuss with students how the selection helps answer this question.

Vocabulary Review

Review the selection vocabulary words and definitions students wrote in the Vocabulary section of the Writer's Notebook. Have students turn to pages 149–150 in ***Skills Practice 1.*** Read the first two questions aloud, and help students find the answers. Have students complete the rest on their own. Also, review the concept word *ecosystem*. Ask students if they can think of other words related to the theme Animals and Their Habitats. **Possible Answer** *environment, habitats, shelter, protection, wildlife, compassion*

Fluency

- Focus on pace when reading "Crinkleroot's Guide to Knowing Animal Habitats." Pace, or the speed at which a selection is read, is important when reading fluently. Point out that if reading is halted and contains inappropriate pauses, then the text is difficult to understand.
- Model pace as you read aloud pages 220–221 of "Crinkleroot's Guide to Knowing Animal Habitats." For example, point out the sentences *My name is Crinkleroot. I'm an explorer and a wildlife finder.* Point out that by using the correct pace, readers can easily hear who Crinkleroot is. Tell students that in order to read with correct pace, sometimes phrases or sentences need to be read more than once. Tell students that as they reread the selection, they should practice pace. Have students follow along in ***Student Reader,*** Book 1 and to raise their hands when you pause.

Formal Assessment

Monitor Progress to Differentiate Instruction

Selection Vocabulary Observe students' understanding of the vocabulary words and their definitions.

APPROACHING LEVEL

IF . . . students need extra help with the selection vocabulary,	**THEN . . .** use ***Intervention Guide,*** Unit 2 Lesson 5.
IF . . . students need extra help with the selection vocabulary,	**THEN . . .** use ***Reteach*** page 58

ON LEVEL

IF . . . students need practice using the selection vocabulary,	**THEN . . .** have students complete vocabulary activities on ***eSkills.***

ABOVE LEVEL

IF . . . students understand the selection vocabulary,	**THEN . . .** use ***Challenge Activities*** page 53.

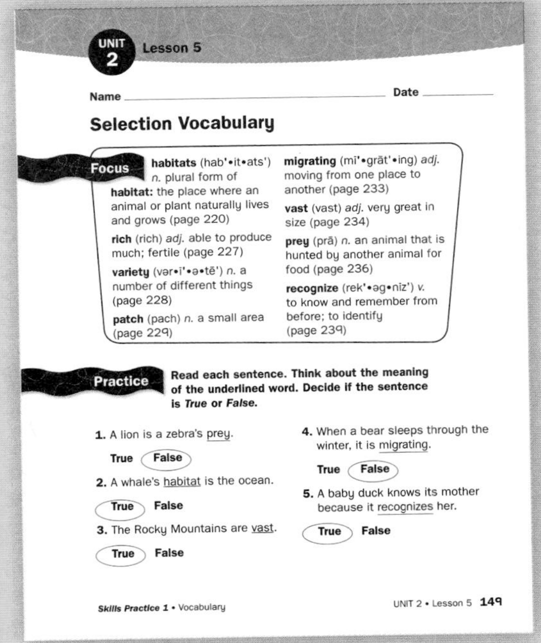

UNIT 2 Lesson 5

Name ______ Date ______

Selection Vocabulary

Focus

habitats (hab'•it•ats') *n.* plural form of **habitat:** the place where an animal or plant naturally lives and grows (page 220)

rich (rich) *adj.* able to produce much; fertile (page 227)

variety (var•ī'•a•tē') *n.* a number of different things (page 228)

patch (pach) *n.* a small area (page 229)

migrating (mī'•grāt'•ing) *adj.* moving from one place to another (page 233)

vast (vast) *adj.* very great in size (page 234)

prey (prā) *n.* an animal that is hunted by another animal for food (page 236)

recognize (rek'•ag•nīz') *v.* to know and remember from before; to identify (page 239)

Practice Read each sentence. Think about the meaning of the underlined word. Decide if the sentence is *True* or *False.*

1. A lion is a zebra's prey. True (False)
2. A whale's habitat is the ocean. (True) False
3. The Rocky Mountains are vast. (True) False
4. When a bear sleeps through the winter, it is migrating. True (False)
5. A baby duck knows its mother because it recognizes her. (True) False

Skills Practice 1 • Vocabulary UNIT 2 • Lesson 5 149

Skills Practice 1, pp. 149–150

Teacher Tip

WORD BANK If you created a Word Bank of key words related to the theme Animals and Their Habitats, remind students to find words from other resources, their activities, and family discussions and add them to the Word Bank. Organize the words according to parts of speech.

Fluency Tip

FLUENCY By this time in Grade 3, good readers should be reading approximately 99 words per minute with fluency and expression. The only way to gain this fluency is with practice. Have students reread the selection to you and to each other during Workshop to help build fluency. As students read, you may notice that some need work in building fluency. During Workshop, have these students choose a section of the text (a minimum of 160 words) to read several times to build fluency.

Teacher Tips

LISTENING During Workshop, have students listen to "Crinkleroot's Guide to Knowing Animal Habitats" for a model of oral reading. While students listen, have them list any new or unfamiliar words they encounter in the Writer's Notebooks, and instruct them to check the words using a dictionary or glossary. Also, instruct students to listen for the lesson's vocabulary words and to check that the words make sense within the reading.

WRITE ABOUT IT! Have students describe a habitat they visited away from their neighborhood in their Writer's Notebooks.

Meet the Author and Illustrator

After students read the information about the author, discuss the following questions with them:

- *Why do you think it is important for Jim Arnosky to take notes while he travels?* **Possible Answer** *His notes help him remember everything he sees so he can use specific details when he writes his stories.*
- *Why do you think Arnosky likes to write Crinkleroot guides?* **Possible Answer** *He likes to pass on information he has learned to others.*

Theme Connections

Within the Selection

1. Where does Crinkleroot look to find wildlife? **Possible Answer** *Crinkleroot looks many places to find wildlife: wetlands, woodlands, cornfields, grasslands, and dry lands.*
2. How many different species of wildlife did you count on this journey? *Answers will vary.*

Across Selections

3. How is this selection like "One Small Place in a Tree"? **Possible Answer** *"Crinkleroot's Guide to Knowing Animal Habitats" is like "One Small Place in a Tree" because both selections teach readers about many different kinds of animal habitats.*
4. How is it different? *Answers will vary.*

Beyond the Selection

5. What lessons have you learned about animals and their habitats? **Possible Answer** *This story gives a lot of facts and information about all of the different places that can be habitats for animals and what must be present for it to be a habitat. It teaches us that we need to share our world with all of the wildlife around us.*
6. What does Crinkleroot mean when he says, "…wherever you go, you share the world with wildlife"? **Possible Answer** *Crinkleroot means that people must share our Earth with all of the many different species of wildlife that exist all around us.*

Meet the Author and Illustrator

Jim Arnosky

Like his character Crinkleroot, Jim Arnosky loves to travel and explore new places. The details of the natural world fascinate him. When he travels, Arnosky takes pictures and notes to help him remember everything he sees. He then uses what he learns to write and illustrate his books. Arnosky's home is a farm in Vermont, where he likes to raise sheep and play his guitar.

240

Animals and Their Habitats

Theme Connections

Within the Selection

1. Where does Crinkleroot look to find wildlife?
2. How many different species of wildlife did you count on this journey?

Across Selections

3. How is this selection like "One Small Place in a Tree"?
4. How is it different?

Beyond the Selection

5. What lessons have you learned about animals and their habitats?
6. What does Crinkleroot mean when he says, ". . . wherever you go, you share the world with wildlife"?

Write about It!

Describe a habitat you visited away from your neighborhood.

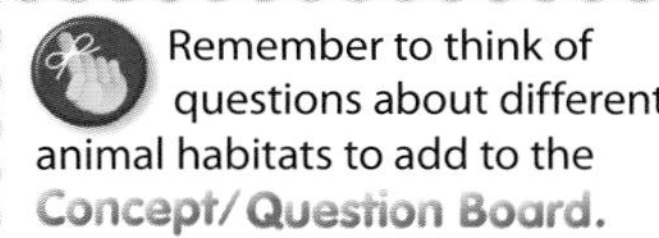

Remember to think of questions about different animal habitats to add to the **Concept/Question Board.**

241

Concept/Question Board

As students discuss "Crinkleroot's Guide to Knowing Animal Habitats," encourage them to post questions, answers, comments, or other items related to the theme Animals and Their Habitats on the **Concept/Question Board.**

Teacher Tip

BEYOND THE SELECTION Have students summarize what they have learned and tell how they might use this information in further investigations.

Writer's Notebook

- Have students use their Writer's Notebooks to list other nonfiction selections they have read in class or on their own.
- Have students compare the elements found in each selection.

OBJECTIVES

Students will
- ✦ learn to gather information to use in an informative report.
- ✦ learn to spell words with /o͞o/.
- ✦ learn pronouns used as subjects.

MATERIALS

- ✦ ***Transparency*** 70
- ✦ ***Skills Practice 1,*** pp. 157–158

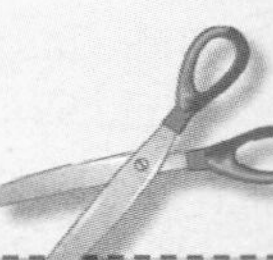

Teacher Tip:

PLAN AHEAD Have resources ready (school library, class library, or computers) for students to utilize. Select materials for your report, and have them ready to show students.

Imagine It! Transparency 70

Copyright Page for *Coyote Winter*

Copyright © 2007 by Daniel L. Fischer. All rights reserved. No part of this book may be reproduced or utilized in any form or by any means, without permission in writing from the Publisher. Inquires should be addressed to Egg Corn Publishing Company, 701 W. 34th Street, New York, NY, 10001.

Printed in the United States of America.

Library of Congress Cataloging-in-Publication Data

ISBN 0-153-09899-9

Bibliography

Arnold, Kingston. Animal Lives. New York, NY: K&T Publishers, 1999.

Fischer, Daniel L. Coyote Winter. New York, NY: Egg Corn Publishing Company, 2007.

Jambe, Lucy K. "Animals in the Den." Animal World Magazine January 2008: pp 16–20.

New Animal Habitats, accessed September 18, 2008. <http://animalhabitats.com>.

Copyright © SRA/McGraw-Hill. All rights reserved. Level 3

Transparency 70

Writing Informative Report

Prewriting

Teach—Accessing Reference Materials

- ✦ Have students write their topics on a piece of paper and give it to you. Briefly glance through the papers to make sure all students have selected a topic. Note those students who have not selected a topic or have selected a vague topic so that you can conference with them during Workshop.
- ✦ Tell students that the next step to writing an informative report is gathering the necessary resource materials.
- ✦ Using the topic you selected for yourself, show students how to gather resources to collect information. You may want to take them to the library and ask the librarian to discuss library searches, or you may want to show them how to do a key word search on the Internet. Show students how to gather visuals such as maps, charts, and graphs to add to their reports.
- ✦ Show students the index of one of the books you selected for your topic. Ask students if they can explain what they see. **Possible Answer** *a bunch of different topics* Explain that even though you have found a book on your topic, it does not mean the entire book will relate to it. Tell students that looking in the index will help you find only those pages that directly relate to your topic.
- ✦ Display ***Transparency*** 70. Ask students what the top half of the transparency looks like. **Possible Answer** *It looks like one of the pages in my book.* Explain the information on the copyright page.
- ✦ Next, tell students that the bottom half of ***Transparency*** 70 is a bibliography. Explain what a bibliography is and the function it serves. Using the transparency, show students how to set up a citation. Tell students that they will cite their sources in their informative report.
- ✦ Explain that even though they will gather information from other sources, it is still very important to give credit to the original author of each source. Explain *plagiarism,* and tell students that claiming others' ideas as your own is considered a form of theft.

Writing, continued

Guided Practice

- Using your book, create a bibliographical citation on the board, saying each step of the process aloud. If necessary, show this process with other print materials as well as Internet materials.
- Discuss different note-taking strategies with students. Remind them of the strategies they learned in Study Skills, Unit 2 Lesson 1.

Apply

If not already selected, have students select their materials, create a bibliography, and begin to read and take notes for their informative reports.

Traits of Good Writing

IDEAS The writer accesses reference materials for informative report writing.

Teacher Tip

LIBRARY SKILLS Make sure students are familiar with the areas of the library media center and how these resources can be beneficial to their writing assignments and unit investigations.

Spelling

/$\overline{\text{oo}}$/

Teach

Use a word sort to teach words with /$\overline{\text{oo}}$/ spelled *oo, _ew, _ue,* or *u*.

Guided Practice

Write the following headings on the board: /$\overline{\text{oo}}$/ spelled *oo,* /$\overline{\text{oo}}$/ spelled *_ew,* /$\overline{\text{oo}}$/ spelled *u_e,* /oo/ spelled *_ue,* and /$\overline{\text{oo}}$/ spelled *u*. Then write the following word list: *clue, tuna, root, June, flute, blue, chew, choose, glue, noodle, truth, blew, stew, duty,* and *rude*. Have volunteers write the words under the correct heading. After all spelling words have been used, ask for students to come to the board and underline the part of each word that reflects the category in which it was placed.

Word Sort Answers

Words with /$\overline{\text{oo}}$/ spelled *oo: root, choose, noodle*

Words with /$\overline{\text{oo}}$/ spelled *_ew: chew, blew, stew*

Words with /$\overline{\text{oo}}$/ spelled *u_e: June, flute, rude*

Words with /$\overline{\text{oo}}$/ spelled *_ue: clue, blue, glue*

Words with /$\overline{\text{oo}}$/ spelled *u: tuna, truth, duty*

Grammar, Usage, and Mechanics 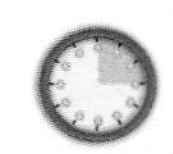

Subject Pronouns

Teach

- Ask students to review the previous grammar lesson. Ask them to explain the subject and direct object of a sentence. If necessary, refer them to Unit 2 Lesson 4.
- Write the following sentences on the board. Ask the students to read the sentences and explain the differences between the sentences in each pair.
    - Andy likes to swim and run.
      He likes to swim and run.
    - Kara and Henry prefer to bicycle.
      They prefer to bicycle.

  Possible Answer *In the first pair of sentences, the word* He *replaced the word* Andy; *in the second pair of sentences, the word* They *replaced the words* Kara and Henry.
- Explain reasons why subjects might be replaced with pronouns. For example, we can eliminate repetition when we are writing multiple sentences about the same people or characters.
- If the students did not note the fact that the pronouns agree in number with the nouns they replace, point this out. Discuss the subject pronouns *he, she, we,* and *they.*
- Write the following sentences on the board, and ask the students to explain the differences between the sentences in each pair. Explain gender agreement to the students.
    - Michael is going rafting this weekend.
      He is going rafting this weekend.
    - Maria is studying to be a veterinarian.
      She is studying to be a veterinarian.

Guided Practice

- Have a student write a sentence on the board. Have another student replace the subject noun with a pronoun and edit for number and gender agreement.
- Have students turn to ***Skills Practice 1*** page 157. Read the directions together and help students with the Practice questions.

Apply

Have students complete ***Skills Practice 1*** pages 157–158.

Formal Assessment 

Monitor Progress to Differentiate Instruction

Subject Pronouns Note whether students are replacing subject nouns with appropriate pronouns.

APPROACHING LEVEL

IF . . .	THEN . . .
IF . . . students need to practice subject pronouns,	**THEN . . .** have them complete ***Reteach*** page 62 during Workshop.
IF . . . students need more practice with subject pronouns,	**THEN . . .** refer them to Unit 2 Lesson 5 in the ***Intervention Guide.***

ON LEVEL

IF . . .	THEN . . .
IF . . . students have an understanding of subject pronouns,	**THEN . . .** have them work on inserting subject pronouns into their graphic organizers during Workshop.

ABOVE LEVEL

IF . . .	THEN . . .
IF . . . students need a challenge,	**THEN . . .** have them complete ***Challenge Activities*** page 56 during Workshop.

Differentiating Instruction: English Learner

IF . . . students are native Spanish speakers, **THEN . . .** keep in mind that unlike English, the Spanish pronoun for *they (ellos/ellas)* agrees in gender with the subjects it replaces. Remind students that they should use the same pronoun, *they,* for all plural subjects.

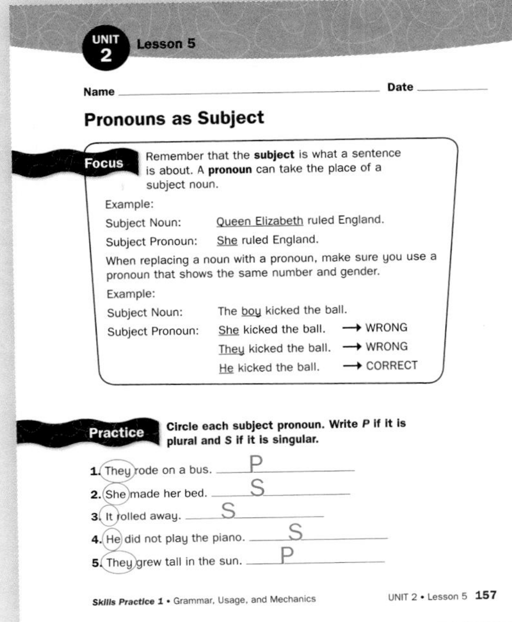

UNIT 2 Lesson 5

Name ______________________ Date __________

Pronouns as Subject

Focus Remember that the **subject** is what a sentence is about. A **pronoun** can take the place of a subject noun.

Example:

Subject Noun: Queen Elizabeth ruled England.

Subject Pronoun: She ruled England.

When replacing a noun with a pronoun, make sure you use a pronoun that shows the same number and gender.

Example:

Subject Noun: The boy kicked the ball.

Subject Pronoun: She kicked the ball. → WRONG

They kicked the ball. → WRONG

He kicked the ball. → CORRECT

Practice **Circle each subject pronoun. Write *P* if it is plural and *S* if it is singular.**

1. They rode on a bus. P
2. She made her bed. S
3. It rolled away. S
4. He did not play the piano. S
5. They grew tall in the sun. P

Skills Practice 1 • Grammar, Usage, and Mechanics UNIT 2 • Lesson 5 **157**

Skills Practice 1, p. 157

UNIT 2 Lesson 5

Apply **Read each pair of sentences. Write the subject pronoun that takes the place of the subject in the first sentence.**

6. Theodor Geisel wrote many books for children. He wrote them under the name *Dr. Seuss.*
7. His mother had the last name Seuss. She came to America from Germany.
8. Many publishers did not like his first book. They said his books did not teach and should not rhyme.
9. Dr. Seuss proved they were wrong. He wrote fun books about important ideas.
10. *The Lorax* is a book about pollution. It tells about a disappearing forest.
11. *The Sneetches* is a book about friendliness. It shows that how people look does not matter.
12. Now his books are very famous. They are still very popular.

158 UNIT 2 • Lesson 5 Grammar, Usage, and Mechanics • *Skills Practice 1*

Skills Practice 1, p. 158

Day 3

Preparing to Read

OBJECTIVES

Students will

- ✦ review regular plurals, irregular plurals, homographs, and homophones.
- ✦ build fluency.

MATERIALS

- ✦ ***Transparency*** 69
- ✦ ***Skills Practice 1,*** pp. 147–148

Daily Oral Practice

Daily News Today!

Animals share habitats in wetlands, woodlands, grasslands, and many more places. As we study different habitats, we can learn how animals survive and share the same spaces. Maybe we can learn how humans and wild animals can share the world better.

- ✦ Write the daily news on the board or on chart paper. Then have students read the daily news in unison to practice fluency.
- ✦ As a word structure review from Unit 1, have a volunteer identify any compound words in the message. *wetlands, woodlands, grasslands, maybe*

Word Structure

Review: Regular Plurals, Irregular Plurals, Homographs, and Homophones

- ✦ Write the following word lines on the board or use ***Transparency*** 69. Show students one line at time as you go through them by covering up the others. The words in boldface are in the selection.

Line 1	critters	marshes	grasses	branches
Line 2	oxen	deer	geese	sheep
Line 3	tie	bat	record	wound
Line 4	brake	break	where	wear

Line 1 **Regular Plurals**

Point to the words in Line 1, and ask students to read the words in unison. Ask students to tell you the singular form of each word and how the plural was formed. *critter: add s; marsh: add es; grass: add es; branch: add es*

Line 2 **Irregular Plurals**

Point to the words in Line 2, and ask students to read the words in unison. Ask students to tell you the singular form of each word. *ox, deer, goose, sheep*

Line 3 **Homographs**

Point to the words in Line 3, and ask students to read the words in unison. Ask students to tell what homographs are. If necessary, remind students that homographs are words that are spelled the same but have different meanings. Have students give two possible meanings of the words in Line 3. **Possible Answers** Tie *can be an article of clothing or something you do to make a knot.* Wound *can be a type of injury or what you do when you wrap something around something else.* Remind students that some homographs have different pronunciations for each meaning, like *record* and *wound;* but some homographs are pronounced the same for both meanings, like *tie* and *bat*.

Line 4 **Homophones**

Point to the words in Line 4, and ask students to read the words in unison. Ask students to tell what homophones are. If necessary, remind students that homophones are words that sound the same but are spelled differently and have different meanings. Ask students the meaning of each word in Line 4. **Possible Answers** *A* brake *is what you use to stop a car or bike.* Wear *is what you do with clothes.*

Help students start the word structure activities in ***Skills Practice 1*** pages 147–148. Read the Focus box with them, and help them with the first few questions. Then have them complete the pages on their own.

Teacher Tip

SYLLABICATION To help students blend words and build fluency, demonstrate syllabication using the decodable, multisyllabic words in the word lines.

crit • ters	bran • ches
mar • shes	ox • en
gras • ses	rec • ord or re • cord

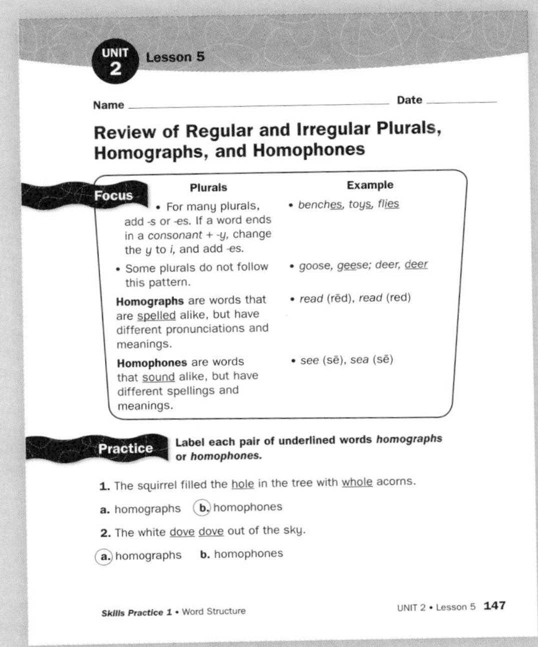

UNIT 2 Lesson 5

Name ______ Date ______

Review of Regular and Irregular Plurals, Homographs, and Homophones

Focus

Plurals	Example
• For many plurals, add -s or -es. If a word ends in a *consonant* + -*y*, change the *y* to *i*, and add -es.	• *benches, toys, flies*
• Some plurals do not follow this pattern.	• *goose, geese; deer, deer*
Homographs are words that are spelled alike, but have different pronunciations and meanings.	• *read* (rēd), *read* (red)
Homophones are words that sound alike, but have different spellings and meanings.	• *see* (sē), *sea* (sē)

Practice **Label each pair of underlined words *homographs* or *homophones.***

1. The squirrel filled the hole in the tree with whole acorns.

a. homographs (b.) homophones

2. The white dove dove out of the sky.

(a.) homographs b. homophones

Skills Practice 1 • Word Structure UNIT 2 • Lesson 5 **147**

Skills Practice 1, pp. 147–148

Monitor Progress to Differentiate Instruction

Formal Assessment 

Word Structure During the word structure activity, note how well students understand regular plurals, irregular plurals, homographs, and homophones.

APPROACHING LEVEL	**IF . . .** students need practice with regular and irregular plurals, homographs, or homophones,	**THEN . . .** work with them on the word structure activities on ***Reteach*** page 57 during Workshop.
	IF . . . students need extra practice with regular and irregular plurals, homographs, and homophones,	**THEN . . .** work with them on the word structure activities for Unit 2 Lesson 5 in the ***Intervention Guide*** during Workshop.
ON LEVEL	**IF . . .** students understand regular and irregular plurals, homographs, and homophones,	**THEN . . .** have them write sentences using words from the word lines during Workshop.
ABOVE LEVEL	**IF . . .** students are ready for a challenge with regular and irregular plurals, homographs, and homophones,	**THEN . . .** have them complete the word structure activities on ***Challenge Activities*** page 52 during Workshop.

Day 3 **Reading and Responding**

Hello! My name is Crinkleroot. I'm an explorer and a wildlife finder. I've found so many wild creatures sharing this sweet earth, I lost count somewhere around a billion!

I see so many wild critters because I know where they all live. The natural places where wild animals live are called habitats.

I'm going to visit lots of different wildlife habitats. You can come too!

220

221

OBJECTIVES

Students will

- use the comprehension skills Author's Point of View and Classify and Categorize.
- build fluency.

MATERIALS

- ***Student Reader***, Book 1 pp. 220–231
- ***Transparency*** 23
- ***Skills Practice 1***, pp. 151–152

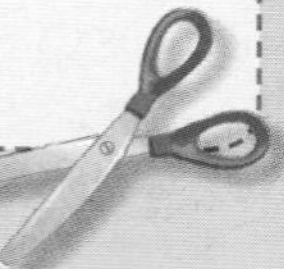

Comprehension Skill

Reread the selection using the comprehension skills Author's Point of View and Classify and Categorize.

Author's Point of View

Remind students that Author's Point of View refers to the narrator or speaker that the writer uses to tell the story. In a first-person narrative, the storyteller is a character in the story. Clue words used in the first-person narrative are *I, me, mine, my, we, our,* and *ours*. In the third-person narrative, the storyteller is not a character in the story. Clues used in the third-person narrative are *he, him, she, her, they,* and *theirs*.

- *What is the author's point of view in this story?* *first-person*
- *Can you find clue words on the first two pages?* *my, I'm, I've, I*
- *Why do you think Jim Arnosky wrote his story from the first-person point of view?* **Possible Answer** *Having Crinkleroot speak in the first person makes the story seem real.*

Reading with a Writer's Eye

Text Structure: Types

Explain that authors use certain types of text structure to tell their story. Even though he uses a fictional character as a guide, Jim Arnosky wants to present factual information in his story "Crinkleroot's Guide to Knowing Animal Habitats." Ask students:

- *How does the author present and organize facts on pages 222–223?* **Possible Answer** *Arnosky explains habitats with descriptive sentences, but he also chooses to give readers information by using diagrams and notes.*
- Why do you think a writer would use different types of text structure? **Possible Answer** *Sometimes writers have a lot of information to give their readers, and it can be easier to explain something technical using lists, diagrams, and so on.*

Expanding Vocabulary

explorer (eks • plor′ • ər) *n.* a person who travels in search of geographical or scientific information (page 220)

I want to explore our Earth, but my brother wants to be an *explorer* of the skies.

surface (sûr′ • fəs) *n.* the outside of a thing (page 223)

The science textbook says that there are craters on the *surface* of the moon.

moist (moist) *adj.* slightly wet; damp (page 223)

The *moist* ground behind my house is a wetland.

Reading and Responding

Word Structure

This lesson focuses on a review of the word structure lessons throughout this unit: regular plurals, irregular plurals, homographs, and homophones.
Regular plurals: wetlands, marshes, rocks, trees

Homophones: here (hear), where (wear)

Irregular plural: sand

Comprehension Skill

Classify and Categorize

Explain to students that grouping things that are alike in some way is called *classifying* or *categorizing*. Using the skill Classify and Categorize can help readers understand and remember the information they read in a story. On pages 224 and 225 of ***Student Reader,*** Book 1, have students search for items that can be classified under the headings "wetlands" and "marshes." You may want to track the categories and what is plotted under each throughout the selection on the board or in students' notebooks.

Wetlands	Marshes
marshes swamps bogs	tall grasses cattails reeds

The shallow water of any wetland is a world of plants, rocks, sand, and sunken trees.

It is a rich weedy habitat for underwater wildlife.

sunfish
newt
damselfly larva
freshwater mussel
water boatman
crayfish
pickerel
minnows
snapping turtle
dragonfly larva
madtom

226 227

Reading with a Writer's Eye

Language Use

Using vivid language and precise terminology is a skill used by expository writers. Using precise language helps readers understand exactly what is being explained. Using vivid language helps readers visualize what the author is explaining. Jim Arnosky uses both vivid language and precise terminology throughout "Crinkleroot's Guide to Knowing Animal Habitats." Ask students the following questions:

- What are some of the precise terms Jim Arnosky uses on pages 226–227? **Possible Answer** *shallow water; world of plants, rocks, sand and sunken trees*
- What is a vivid phrase used by Arnosky on these pages? **Possible Answer** *rich weedy habitat*

Expanding Vocabulary

swamps (swämps) *n.* plural form of **swamp:** an area of wet land that may have trees and shrubs growing in it (page 224)

I have read of alligators living in the *swamps* in Florida.

shallow (shal′ • lō) *adj.* not deep (page 226)

My little sister swims only in the *shallow* end of the pool.

Teacher Tip

WRITING Remind students to use precise terminology and vivid language when writing their reports and preparing their presentations for their unit investigations.

Day 3 Reading and Responding

two moths, red squirrel, deer, inchworm, box turtle, spider, five honeybees, two chickadees, fawn, chipmunk, wood thrush, woodpecker, bark beetle, skunk, oak worm (caterpillar), brown creeper, two bats

In a woodland, tree trunks, stems, and branches criss-cross and overlap. It takes sharp eyes to pick out even the noisiest creatures, like hammering woodpeckers or chirping red squirrels. But make no mistake! Any woodland is habitat for a variety of wildlife. For every animal you hear or see, there are many more hiding.

In the woods, animals may be living high in the treetops, in middle branches or trunks, or on the woodland floor.

See if you can find the wildlife living in this little patch of woods. (I'll give you a hint: there are twenty-four in all. Twenty-seven if you count walking stick, Sassafrass, and me.)

228 229

Word Structure

Regular plurals: trunks, stems, hawks, kestrels

Homophones: red (read), for (four), hear (here), see (sea), there (their, they're), you (ewe), way (weigh)

Irregular plural: deer

Comprehension Skill

Classify and Categorize

Remind students that Classify and Categorize is a skill that students can use to help them understand unfamiliar terms. It can also help them find new ways of looking at familiar terms. Writing and organizing items also helps readers remember what they have read and serves as a quick reminder of some of the important facts about what was read. Ask students to find items to place under the category "Where Wildlife Lives in the Woods."

Where Wildlife Lives in the Woods		
tree trunks	tree stems	tree branches
tree tops	woodland floor	

Climb aboard my old jalopy! There are some interesting places I want to show you that are miles apart. Along the way, we're sure to spot some wildlife near the road.

Rabbits, deer, woodchucks, and other normally shy animals come out to the roadsides to feed on lush green plants growing in the open sunlight.

Roadsides are also hunting grounds for hungry crows, hawks, and kestrels.

230

231

Reading with a Writer's Eye

Language Use

In addition to using descriptive language, writers of nonfiction and narrative nonfiction also use clue words to signal comparisons. Some of the clue words include *like, just as, both, also,* and *too.* These words are used to signal comparisons of people, places, or things within the text. Ask students:

- *What clue word is used on page 229 and what is it comparing? The word* also *compares how the roadsides are used both as feeding grounds and as hunting grounds.*
- *What descriptive language does Jim Arnosky use on page 229?* **Possible Answers** *lush green plants, open sunlight*

Teacher Tip

USING SKILLS As students continue to reread this selection, encourage them to find various categories and items they can include in those categories. Continue adding to the list created on the board or in students' notebooks throughout the selection.

STOP You have reread the first half of the story. You will continue the story tomorrow on page T410.

Teacher Tip

HOMEWORK To reinforce this skill, have students find an article from the newspaper or magazine as homework. They should follow the procedure they practiced in the Guided Practice portion of this lesson. In class, they can present the categories of the article. You may wish to post their articles around the room for students to read on their own later.

Three-Column Chart

wetlands	cornfields	dry lands

Transparency 23

UNIT 2 Lesson 5

Name ______ Date ______

Classify and Categorize

Focus Sometimes when you learn new ideas, it is helpful to place them into a group, or category. A **category** is the title for a group of things. When you put ideas into groups, you are **classifying and categorizing.**

Example: Category: Types of Flowers
Items to Classify: daisy, rose, daffodil, lilac

Practice **Think about the words in the box below. Then, answer the questions underneath it.**

bricks	cement	silk	clay
cotton	wood	stone	wool

1. Circle the category that all the words fit into.

a. Things People Should Eat
b. Materials to Make Things With
c. Materials Used to Make Clothes
d. Things That Grow

2. What two groups could be made from the group?

Possible Answer Materials for Houses and Materials for Clothes

Skills Practice 1 • Comprehension Skill UNIT 2 • Lesson 5 151

Skills Practice 1, pp. 151–152

Supporting the Reading

Comprehension Skill: Classify and Categorize

Teach

Tell students that categorizing new information is a natural process. Classifying and categorizing helps readers evaluate, understand, and remember information in the text. If put into writing, it can also serve as a source of important information learned from the reading.

Guided Practice

Bring an age-appropriate nonfiction article to class. Read the article to the class. Lead a class discussion by asking students to classify and categorize information in the article. You might start by having students name three of the headings or subtopics of the article. For example, in "Crinkleroot's Guide to Knowing Animal Habitats," headings could be *wetlands, woodlands, cornfields, grasslands,* and *dry lands.* Write the headings at the top of a three-column chart on ***Transparency*** 23. Then, have students fill in items to categorize under each heading.

Apply

Have students turn to pages 151–152 in ***Skills Practice 1.***

- Have students read aloud the Focus section of the lesson.
- Work through the Practice section of the lesson with students. Have students complete the Apply section on their own.
- Encourage students to think about the reports they are writing during Language Arts. Explain that classifying and categorizing information might help them group their information into subtopics and headings.

Monitor Progress to Differentiate Instruction

Formal Assessment

Comprehension Skill Note students' understanding of the comprehension skill Classify and Categorize.

APPROACHING LEVEL

IF . . . students need extra help with the comprehension skill Classify and Categorize, **THEN . . .** use ***Reteach*** pages 59–60.

ON LEVEL

IF . . . students need practice with the comprehension skill Classify and Categorize, **THEN . . .** have students play a game in the ***Workshop Kit.***

ABOVE LEVEL

IF . . . students understand the comprehension skill Classify and Categorize, **THEN . . .** use ***Challenge Activities*** page 54.

Fluency

A great deal of information is presented in "Crinkleroot's Guide to Knowing Animal Habitats." Additional information is provided in the captions of the illustrations. As students read orally, have them focus on the words in the text. Tell them they can read the captions and look at the illustrations later. Explain the importance of pace, or the speed at which a selection is read. Have students point out the commas and end punctuation. Tell them that whenever they come across commas and end punctuation when reading, they need to pause or stop appropriately.

- Model pace by reading pages 232–233 from "Crinkleroot's Guide to Knowing Animal Habitats." Have students follow along in their ***Student Readers,*** Book 1. Ask them to raise their hands if they hear an unfamiliar word or passage. Ask students how keeping a steady pace when reading helped them better understand and enjoy the story.
- After you have read through the passage, call on a volunteer to read the first paragraph. Before the student begins, clarify the pronunciations of any words in which students may be having difficulty. Have all students silently follow along, and note all commas and end punctuation while the volunteer reads.

LEVELED READERS To help students build fluency and strengthen their vocabulary and comprehension skills, have them read the ***Leveled Readers*** for this unit Use each student's Oral Fluency Assessment score from the previous lesson assessment to diagnose the appropriate ***Leveled Reader.***

Fluency Tip

FLUENCY For additional fluency practice, students can read the passage with a partner during Small-Group Time.

Inquiry

Confirming and Revising Conjectures

- Remind the groups that they are still collecting information about their investigation topics as they are evaluating their conjectures. Explain that they should try to understand how each new piece of information relates to their conjectures.
- Discuss how any information in "Crinkleroot's Guide to Knowing Animal Habitats" may relate to the investigations. If any group discovers relevant information from the selection, have the class discuss how that information affects their conjectures.
- Remind students that information can confirm a conjecture, challenge a conjecture, or both. Explain that this is because a conjecture can be partially right and partially wrong. Model this using the following example: *The conjecture that humans are bad for animal habitats is only partially right. In the selection, it says that farmers disrupt the habitats of grubs and worms by tilling the soil. This is bad for the habitats of grubs and worms, but it's good for the birds that eat them.*

OBJECTIVES

Students will

- ✦ create a graphic organizer for their reports.
- ✦ practice spelling words with /o͞o/.
- ✦ review replacing subject nouns with subject pronouns.
- ✦ learn the use of an index.

MATERIALS

- ✦ ***Language Arts Handbook,*** pp. 108–113
- ✦ Routine 16
- ✦ ***Skills Practice 1,*** pp. 153, 155–156, 159–160
- ✦ ***Transparency*** 70

Writing Informative Report

ROUTINE 16

Prewriting

Teach

✦ Use Routine 16. Ask students to review what they have done so far for their informative reports. **Possible Answers** *selected a topic, found reference materials, began to read and take notes*

✦ Ask students what the next step to the process might be. **Possible Answer** *organizing the information* Tell students that they will now organize the information they have gathered using an expository text graphic organizer.

✦ For further information on organizing and writing informative reports, see ***Language Arts Handbook*** pages 108–113.

Guided Practice

Have students turn to ***Skills Practice 1*** page 153. Copy the organizer from page 153 onto the board. Using the book you selected earlier and any notes you may have taken, show students how to put main topic and subtopic information into the boxes.

Apply

Composing—Prewriting Have students continue to take notes, and then transfer their notes to the graphic organizer on ***Skills Practice 1*** page 153. Also, have students create a bibliographical citation for each piece of additional information. Display ***Transparency*** 70 for students to refer to.

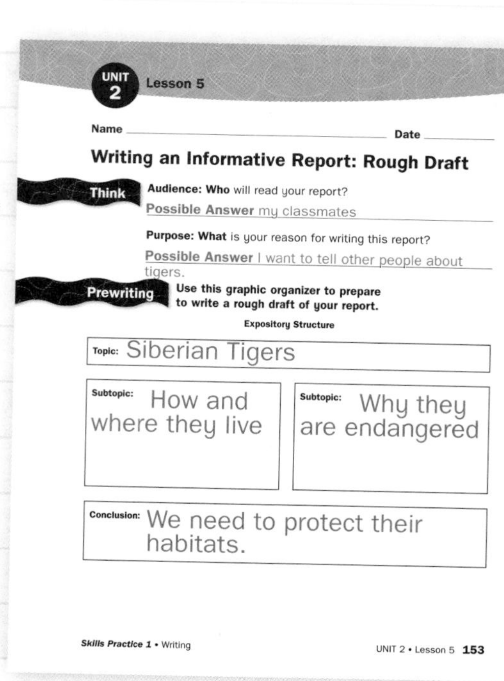

UNIT 2 Lesson 5

Name ______ Date ______

Writing an Informative Report: Rough Draft

Think

Audience: Who will read your report?

Possible Answer my classmates

Purpose: What is your reason for writing this report?

Possible Answer I want to tell other people about tigers.

Prewriting **Use this graphic organizer to prepare to write a rough draft of your report.**

Expository Structure

Topic: Siberian Tigers

Subtopic: How and where they live

Subtopic: Why they are endangered

Conclusion: We need to protect their habitats.

Skills Practice 1 • Writing UNIT 2 • Lesson 5 **153**

Skills Practice 1, p. 153

Informative Report

A good way to share what you know or have learned is through an **informative report.** The purpose of an informative research report is to give information about real facts, ideas, or events and explain what you think they mean. The information can be checked by looking in other sources, such as nonfiction books, magazine articles, encyclopedias, newspapers, or the Internet.

Informational text

- provides information
- is about real facts, ideas, or events
- gets straight to the point
- gives events in the order they happened
- may be divided into sections by topic, with headings
- may have photographs, diagrams, or illustrations with captions
- has information that can be checked in other sources

108 Informative Report • Expository Writing

Language Arts Handbook, p. 108

Differentiating Instruction **English Learner**

IF . . . students have difficulty completing the graphic organizer, **THEN . . .** allow them to describe their subtopics orally for a proficient English-speaking partner to record as key words or phrases.

Spelling

/o͞o/

Teach

Remind students that /o͞o/ can be spelled *oo, _ew, u_e, _ue,* and *u*.

Guided Practice

Write the word list on the board: *clue, tuna, root, June, flute, blue, chew, choose, glue, noodle, truth, blew, stew, duty,* and *rude.* Have a volunteer come to the board and choose one of the words to say aloud and use it in a sentence. Then have that student choose another volunteer to continue the activity. Continue until all words have been used.

Guided Practice

Have students turn to ***Skills Practice 1*** page 155. Read the instructions with them, and complete the first two questions as a class.

Apply

Have students complete ***Skills Practice 1*** pages 155–156 on their own. Remind students that challenge words are not used in ***Skills Practice*** exercises.

Monitor Progress 

to Differentiate Instruction

Formal Assessment

Spelling Note how well students are able to spell the lesson words.

APPROACHING LEVEL

IF . . . students need to practice spelling this week's words,	**THEN . . .** have them complete ***Reteach*** page 61.

ON LEVEL

IF . . . students can spell this week's spelling words,	**THEN . . .** have them use five spelling words to write five sentences. Have them spell the spelling word incorrectly, then trade sentences with a partner and have each student correct the other's sentences.

ABOVE LEVEL

IF . . . students are ready for a challenge,	**THEN . . .** have them complete ***Challenge Activities*** page 55.

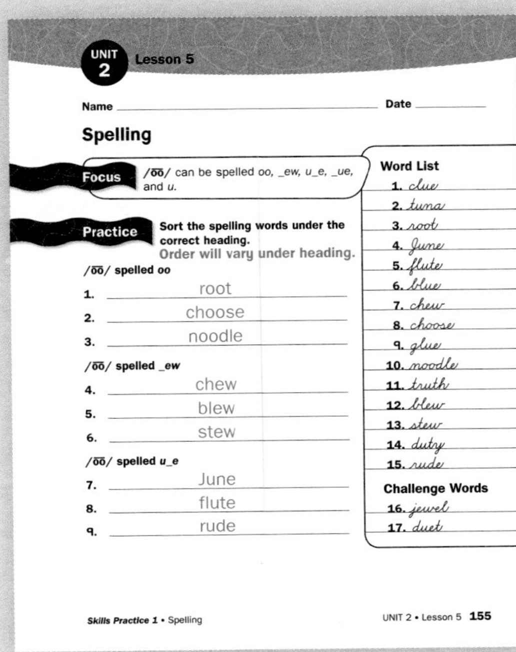

UNIT 2 Lesson 5

Name ________ Date ________

Spelling

Focus /o͞o/ can be spelled oo, _ew, u_e, _ue, and u.

Practice Sort the spelling words under the correct heading.
Order will vary under heading.

/o͞o/ spelled oo
1. root
2. choose
3. noodle

/o͞o/ spelled _ew
4. chew
5. blew
6. stew

/o͞o/ spelled u_e
7. June
8. flute
9. rude

Word List
1. clue
2. tuna
3. root
4. June
5. flute
6. blue
7. chew
8. choose
9. glue
10. noodle
11. truth
12. blew
13. stew
14. duty
15. rude

Challenge Words
16. jewel
17. duet

Skills Practice 1 • Spelling

UNIT 2 • Lesson 5 155

Skills Practice 1, p. 155

Teacher Tip

USING INDEXES Remind students that using indexes will help them as they conduct research for their writing assignments and unit investigations. They can use the indexes, in addition to tables of contents, to find particular information.

Monitor Progress

to Differentiate Instruction
Formal Assessment

Index Note whether students are able to access information using an index.

APPROACHING LEVEL

IF . . . students need to practice using an index, **THEN . . .** have them find theme-related topics using indexes during Workshop.

ON LEVEL

IF . . . students have an understanding of using an index, **THEN . . .** have them continue to research, take notes, and draft during Workshop.

ABOVE LEVEL

IF . . . students need a challenge, **THEN . . .** have them help a peer collect resources for the unit investigation during Workshop.

Study Skills

Index

Teach

Ask students to tell you what they know about using an index. Discuss the following points:

- An index is an alphabetical list of key words and topics in a given source.
- A topic may have a subtopic.
- An index may refer readers to other topics.
- Each key word may reference one or more pages in which the information can be found in the source.
- Indexes are found at the end of source books.

Guided Practice

✦ Select a book from the classroom or school library. Show the students the title, and ask them what information they might find in the book. Turn to the index and show the students the various topics and corresponding page numbers.

✦ Turn to ***Skills Practice 1*** page 159–160. Read the directions and the index page with students. Help students complete the first two questions on page 160.

Apply

Have students complete pages 159–160 in ***Skills Practice 1.***

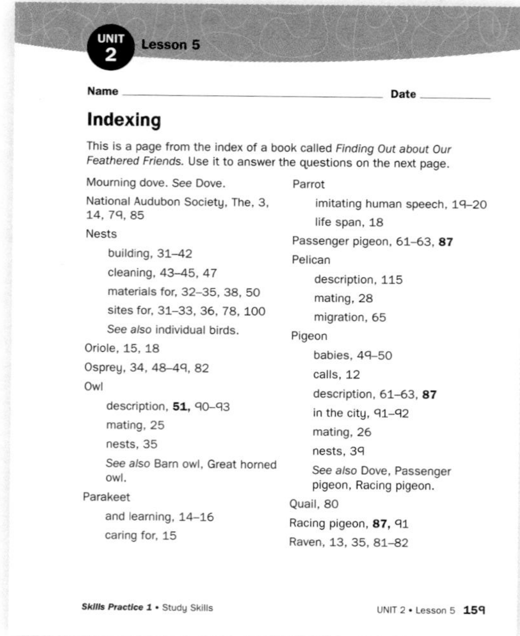

UNIT 2 Lesson 5

Name ______ Date ______

Indexing

This is a page from the index of a book called *Finding Out about Our Feathered Friends.* Use it to answer the questions on the next page.

Skills Practice 1 • Study Skills   UNIT 2 • Lesson 5 **159**

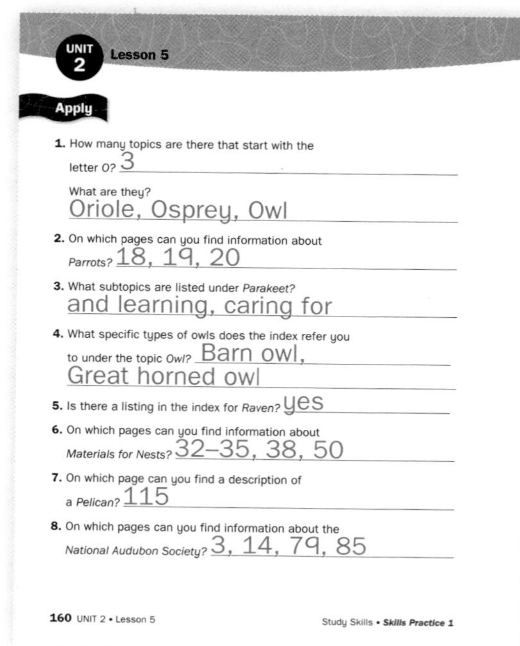

UNIT 2 Lesson 5

Apply

1. How many topics are there that start with the letter *O*? 3
   What are they? Oriole, Osprey, Owl
2. On which pages can you find information about *Parrots*? 18, 19, 20
3. What subtopics are listed under *Parakeet*? and learning, caring for
4. What specific types of owls does the index refer you to under the topic *Owl*? Barn owl, Great horned owl
5. Is there a listing in the index for *Raven*? yes
6. On which pages can you find information about *Materials for Nests*? 32–35, 38, 50
7. On which page can you find a description of a *Pelican*? 115
8. On which pages can you find information about the *National Audubon Society*? 3, 14, 79, 85

160 UNIT 2 • Lesson 5   Study Skills • ***Skills Practice 1***

Skills Practice 1, pp. 159–160

Grammar, Usage, and Mechanics 

Subject Pronouns

Teach

✦ Ask students to explain the use of pronouns as the subjects of sentences. If necessary, review subject pronouns.

✦ Write the following sentences on the board, and ask students to replace the subjects with pronouns.

- Sharon is investigating tropical rain forest habitats. She *is investigating tropical rain forest habitats.*
- Doris and Noah are traveling to Africa to study gorillas. They *are traveling to Africa to study gorillas.*
- Rick wants to investigate the habitats of big cats. He *wants to investigate the habitats of big cats.*

Guided Practice

Ask a volunteer to write a sentence on the board. Then have another student replace the subject noun with a subject pronoun that agrees in number and gender.

Apply

Have students edit a previous writing assignment to make sure that pronouns agree in number and gender with the nouns they replaced.

Differentiating Instruction **English Learner**

IF . . . students are having difficulty with subject pronouns, **THEN . . .** refer to the ***English-Learner Support Guide.***

Preparing to Read

OBJECTIVES

Students will

- ✦ review regular plurals, irregular plurals, homographs, and homophones.
- ✦ build fluency.

MATERIALS

- ✦ ***Transparency*** 69

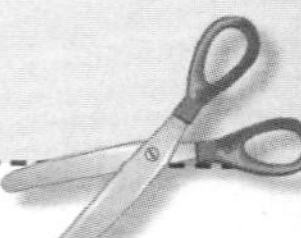

Daily Oral Practice

Daily News Today!

Wherever we go, nature surrounds us. Sometimes we hear birds singing in the trees or see squirrels gathering nuts. We are often unaware of all the habitats around us. Now we can be aware. Even if we don't see or hear any animals, we know some animals, big or small, are probably nearby.

- ✦ Write the daily news on the board or on chart paper. Then have students read the daily news in unison to practice fluency.
- ✦ As a review of yesterday's word structure lesson, ask a volunteer to identify any homophones in the daily news. *we (wee), hear (here), see (sea), are (our), be (bee), know (no), some (sum)*

Word Structure

Review: Regular Plurals, Irregular Plurals, Homographs, and Homophones

✦ Use ***Transparency*** 69 with the word lines from Day 3.

Line 1	critters	marshes	grasses	branches
Line 2	oxen	deer	geese	sheep
Line 3	tie	bat	record	wound
Line 4	brake	break	where	wear

✦ Ask students to state the rules for forming regular plural nouns and give definitions for homographs and homophones. If necessary, remind them of these rules and definitions.

✦ Have students read the words using normal intonation and expression.

Developing Oral Language

Use any of these activities to help students practice reading the words.

- Ask a volunteer to give the singular form of a noun from Lines 1–2. That student should select a volunteer to use the singular form of the word in a sentence. Then have the volunteer use the plural form in a sentence. **Possible Answers** *I know a farmer with fifty* sheep. *One* sheep *lost its flock.* Repeat the process for all the words in Lines 1–2.
- Ask the class what the words on Line 3 are. *homographs* Have a volunteer choose a word from Line 3 and choose a classmate to use the word in a sentence with one of its meanings. **Possible Answer** *I know how to tie a nice bow.* Then have the student choose a classmate to use the homograph in a sentence using the word's other meaning. **Possible Answer** *For Father's Day, my dad said he didn't want another* tie. Continue for all homographs in the line.
- Ask a student what the pairs of words are on Line 4. *homophones* Have the student choose a classmate to use a pair of homophones in a single sentence. **Possible Answer** Where *can I find the right clothes to* wear? Continue this activity with other homophones.

Teacher Tip

BLENDING During Workshop, work with students who have difficulty blending words by using Routine 1 for sound-by-sound blending or Routine 3 for whole-word blending.

Our first stop is a farmer's cornfield. Cornfields provide an ever-changing habitat for wildlife. In the spring gulls, swallows, and bluebirds feed on beetles, grubs, and earthworms unearthed by the farmer's plow.

232

By midsummer, when the corn stalks have grown high enough to provide cover, small animals move in to nest and raise their young.

At ripening time the cornfield becomes a supermarket for raiding raccoons.

By late fall, after the field of corn has been freshly cut and harvested, the scattered kernels are a feast for migrating geese.

233

OBJECTIVES

Students will

- use the comprehension skill Classify and Categorize.
- check comprehension.
- investigate the theme Animals and Their Habitats using the Inquiry process.

MATERIALS

- ***Student Reader,*** Book 1, pp. 232–239
- ***Skills Practice 1***, pp. 135–136

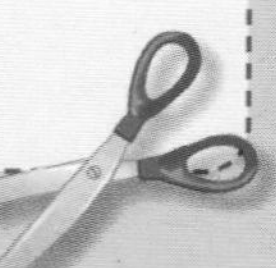

Comprehension Skill

Classify and Categorize

Explain to students that pages 232–233 are a good place to stop to classify and categorize information. The topic of these pages is "cornfields." Ask students to identify the categories they could use to categorize the animal inhabitants of a cornfield. *Spring, Midsummer, Ripening Time, Fall* Then have students put each animal in the appropriate category.

Spring		Midsummer	Ripening Time	Fall
gulls bluebirds grubs	swallows beetles earthworms	small animals	raccoons	geese

From small hillside meadows to vast rolling plains, grasslands are wide open spaces where wildlife can thrive.

At first, grassland looks void of anything but waving green stems. But take time to really look and you will discover something wonderful.

Reading with a Writer's Eye

Text Structure: Types

Remind students that writers of nonfiction and narrative nonfiction often compare information with things that are easy to understand in order to help readers form a clear understanding of the text. For example, Jim Arnosky has compared the animal habitats of wetlands, woodlands, and cornfields. Ask students:

- What words or phrases does the author use to compare grasslands on page 234? *He is comparing the grasslands on small hillside meadows to the grasslands on vast rolling plains.*
- How do they compare? *In either instance, they are wide open spaces where wildlife thrives.*

Expanding Vocabulary

provide (prō • vīd′) *v.* to give what is needed or wanted (page 232)
A bush can *provide* food and shelter for birds.

plains (plānz) *n.* plural form of **plain:** an area of flat, or almost flat, land (page 234)
The pioneers crossed the *plains* of the Midwest in covered wagons.

Teacher Tip

CATEGORIZE Students may choose other ways to categorize information, such as "types of birds in cornfields." Allow students to classify and categorize information as they see fit, as long as it is reasonable within the confines of the text.

Reading and Responding

Word Structure

Regular plurals: places, animals, dry lands, ledges, plants

Irregular plurals: cactus, sand, food, prey

Homographs: cover, brush

Homophones: you (ewe), there (their, they're), be (bee), to (too, two), by (buy), prey (pray)

Comprehension Skill

Classify and Categorize

On page 236, have students list the places wildlife can call home under the category "Drylands."

Drylands
sage brush
cactus
rock ledges
sand
plants

Checking Comprehension

Ask students the following questions to check their comprehension of the story.

- *Who is Crinkleroot?* **Possible Answer** *Crinkleroot is an explorer of animal habitats. He takes the readers on a journey through the habitats in this story.*
- *What does Crinkleroot teach us in this selection?* **Possible Answer** *He teaches readers about all of the different places where animal habitats can be found.*
- *What are some of the places animal habitats can be found?* **Possible Answer** *Animal habitats can be found in wetlands, woodlands, cornfields, grasslands, and drylands.*
- *If Crinkleroot is trying to teach readers a lesson, what is it?* **Possible Answer** *He teaches us that we should share the world with all of the wildlife habitats around us.*

Expanding Vocabulary

ledges (ledg′ • əz) *n.* plural form of **ledge:** a narrow shelf or surface like a shelf (page 236)

The window *ledges* provide resting spots for pigeons in the city.

Differentiating Instruction English Learner

IF . . . students do not know simple sequence words such as *beginning*, *middle*, *end*, *first*, *next*, and *last*, **THEN . . .** teach these words as you point to the frames of "Crinkleroot's Guide to Knowing Animal Habitats" in sequence.

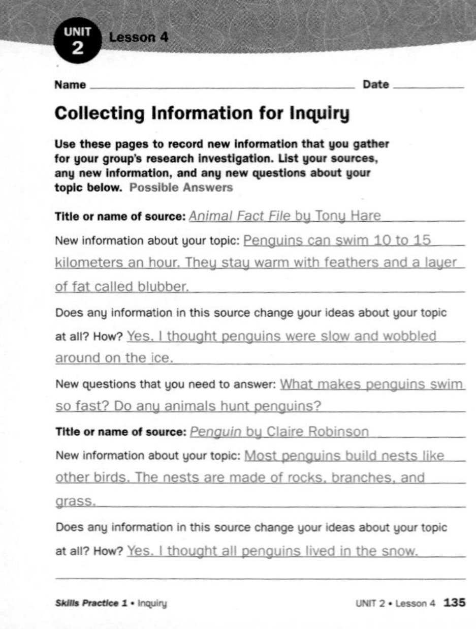

UNIT 2 Lesson 4

Name ______ Date ______

Collecting Information for Inquiry

Use these pages to record new information that you gather for your group's research investigation. List your sources, any new information, and any new questions about your topic below. Possible Answers

Title or name of source: *Animal Fact File* by Tony Hare

New information about your topic: Penguins can swim 10 to 15 kilometers an hour. They stay warm with feathers and a layer of fat called blubber.

Does any information in this source change your ideas about your topic at all? How? Yes. I thought penguins were slow and wobbled around on the ice.

New questions that you need to answer: What makes penguins swim so fast? Do any animals hunt penguins?

Title or name of source: *Penguin* by Claire Robinson

New information about your topic: Most penguins build nests like other birds. The nests are made of rocks, branches, and grass.

Does any information in this source change your ideas about your topic at all? How? Yes. I thought all penguins lived in the snow.

Skills Practice 1 • Inquiry UNIT 2 • Lesson 4 135

Skills Practice 1, p. 135

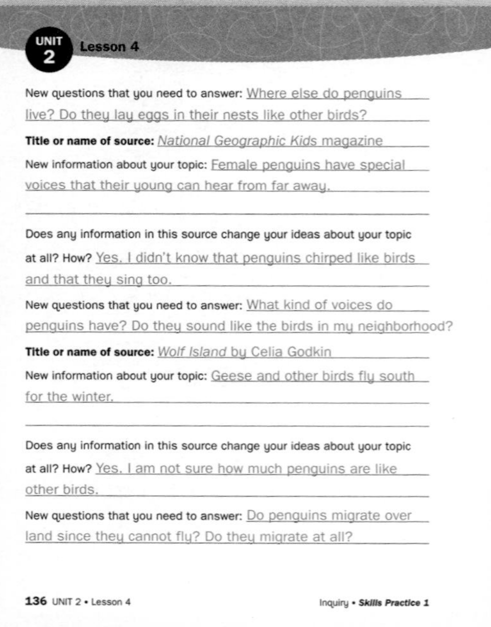

UNIT 2 Lesson 4

New questions that you need to answer: Where else do penguins live? Do they lay eggs in their nests like other birds?

Title or name of source: *National Geographic Kids* magazine

New information about your topic: Female penguins have special voices that their young can hear from far away.

Does any information in this source change your ideas about your topic at all? How? Yes. I didn't know that penguins chirped like birds and that they sing too.

New questions that you need to answer: What kind of voices do penguins have? Do they sound like the birds in my neighborhood?

Title or name of source: *Wolf Island* by Celia Godkin

New information about your topic: Geese and other birds fly south for the winter.

Does any information in this source change your ideas about your topic at all? How? Yes. I am not sure how much penguins are like other birds.

New questions that you need to answer: Do penguins migrate over land since they cannot fly? Do they migrate at all?

136 UNIT 2 • Lesson 4 Inquiry • *Skills Practice 1*

Skills Practice 1, p. 136

Inquiry Process

Step 6—Confirming or Revising Conjectures

Whole-Group Time

Whole Group

- Students have been collecting information about their investigation topic and conjectures. Now they should be getting ready to confirm or revise their conjectures based on what they've learned.
- Remind students that they may find that their conjectures are not confirmed or only partially confirmed as they find new information.
- Model confirming or revising your own conjecture, as: *My original conjecture was:* With a campaign to raise awareness, people will know not to destroy these animals' habitats. *After collecting information, I realize that some people don't think this problem is very important for our community. Now, I realize that raising awareness all by itself won't solve this problem. My conjecture may be partially right because I also found out from my survey that some people aren't aware of this problem but would be willing to help. I think I need to revise my orginal conjecture. My revised conjecture is:* A campaign not only needs to raise awareness about this problem but also convince people that this problem is important. *Now I wonder what I have to do to convince people that this problem is important.*
- Remind students that conjectures can be partially right and partially wrong, like the one you just modeled. In order to make conjectures better, they need to be revised.
- As much as time permits, each group should continue to collect information, which may help them improve their conjectures. "Crinkleroot's Guide to Knowing Animal Habitats" gives a lot of information about animal habitats. Conduct a discussion of what new things students learned about the theme from this selection. Have the students take notes, explaining that the new ideas could be useful for their group's Inquiry.

Small-Group Time

Small Group

- Students should join their small groups. Remind each group of the information they have recorded so far about their topic. If any new information from "Crinkleroot's Guide to Knowing Animal Habitats" is useful for their investigation, have them record it on ***Skills Practice 1*** pages 135–136.

- As necessary, continue to model how to revise conjectures for individual groups. If groups are having trouble seeing how their conjectures could be revised, point out places where more information could make their conjectures better. For example, consider the following conjecture: *Animals that don't like humans don't make good pets.* Challenge the group to think about animals that people typically have as pets, like cats. Although many stray cats don't like humans, cats do make good pets, usually. In such a case, you might suggest that sometimes certain animals make good pets, but sometimes not. Then encourage students to ask why this is the case.
- Help groups finalize how they will publish or present the results of their investigation. Have groups work on their presentations, dividing the work equitably. Encourage them to incorporate visual aids, tables, charts, graphs, or diagrams in their presentations. Allow groups enough time during Workshop to prepare and rehearse their presentations.

Concept/Question Board

Have students post revised conjectures next to their initial conjectures on the **Concept/Question Board.** Continue to encourage use of the Board by recognizing and thanking students for their contributions. Incorporate discussion of those items into classroom discussions whenever possible. Remember to post your own items on the Board.

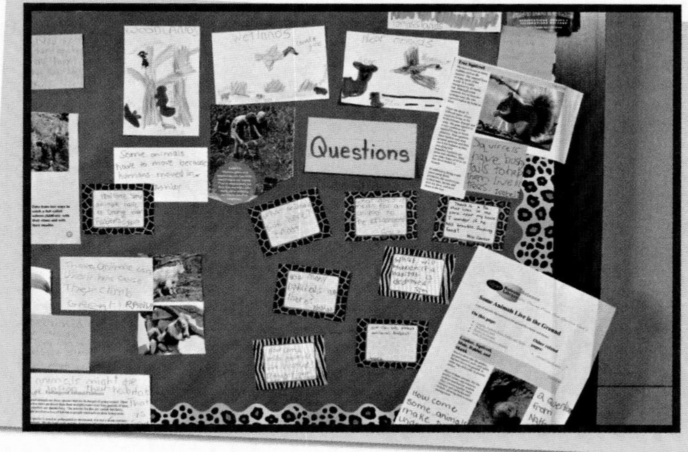

Inquiry Rubric

To assess Confirming and Revising Conjectures, see the Inquiry Rubrics in the Level Appendix.

Teacher Tip

FLEXIBILITY Remind students of the importance of sticking to their plans while still being flexible to change. Encourage students' changes of interest while keeping them on task.

OBJECTIVES

Students will

- ✦ draft their informative reports.
- ✦ learn to spell words with /o͞o/.
- ✦ learn the reasons for using chronological order.
- ✦ create an index.

MATERIALS

- ✦ ***Student Reader,*** Book 1, pp. 220–239

Writing Informative Report

Drafting

Teach

- ✦ Tell students that it is time for them to begin drafting their reports.
- ✦ Remind students that when writing drafts, it is most important to write ideas, words, passages, and so on. Students can fix spelling, grammar, and punctuation during editing/proofreading.
- ✦ Remind students to use reference materials to support their writing. They can continue accessing new sources of information as they work on their drafts.
- ✦ Tell students to keep track of the sources they are using by copying titles, copyright information, author or editor, publishing date, and page numbers on their bibliography page. They will put this information at the end of their reports. This will serve as proof that their information is factual, and others can check their sources if necessary.
- ✦ Remind students to use quotation marks if they are making a direct quote from a source.

Writing, continued

Guided Practice

- Use an article or book that most of the students have read, and show students how to write a brief summary of the information in the article. Then paraphrase the information, and have students discuss the difference. Show students how to cite the source, and explain that even though the words are your own, the ideas are not.
- Next, show students how to directly quote the author. Ask a student to explain what you are doing (adding quotes, commas, end punctuation, and in-text citations) as you go through the process.

Apply

Composing—Drafting Students will use their graphic organizers and notes to begin drafting their reports. They should also continue to access resources and take notes as needed.

Spelling

/o͞o/

Teach

Rhyming Strategy Tell students that words that rhyme with each other often have the same spelling pattern. Students can think of words that rhyme with a spelling word to get ideas about how that spelling word's sound might be spelled.

Guided Practice

Write the following words on the board: *June, noodle, blew,* and *rude*. Then write the following sentences on the board:

1. Jude is a wonderful gardener and cook. rude
2. Please play that tune again on the piano. June
3. The bird flew onto the feeder. blew
4. My cousin adopted a poodle from the animal rescue group. noodle

Have students come to the board and identify which spelling word rhymes with the underlined word in each sentence. Discuss how the spellings are alike and how they are different.

Study Skills

Index

Teach

Ask students to explain an index. **Possible Answer** *An index is the part of the book that gives information on which page a key word or topic can be found.* Ask a volunteer to explain how an index is helpful for doing research. **Possible Answer** *We can find specific information for our reports in the index.*

Guided Practice

Using "Crinkleroot's Guide to Knowing Animal Habitats," have students make a list of some of the topics that might be found in an index if this selection had one. Have students make an index of topics and their page numbers on the board.

Apply

Have students use an index to search for topics related to their informative reports.

Listening/Speaking/Viewing

Chronological Order

Teach

- Explain that chronological order is when events are listed in the order in which they happened.
- Explain that the chronological order of events is one way to present information in an oral presentation. The major events to be discussed are listed in the order in which they happened. Chronological order will make presentations easier to understand.

Guided Practice

- Have students turn to page 232 in "Crinkleroot's Guide to Knowing Animal Habitats." Have a volunteer tell what happens to the cornfields in the spring. Then have another volunteer tell what happens in the summer and so on. Write responses on the board. Explain how revealing these events in chronological order helps readers understand the growing cycle.
- Ask students what would happen if these events were told in a different order. **Possible Answer** *It would be more difficult to understand how the events relate to each other and how one event causes another event to happen.*

Apply

Have students create chronological-order charts for their school day from beginning to end and any after-school activities.

Differentiating Instruction **English Learner**

IF . . . students would benefit from additional practice describing events in chronological order, **THEN . . .** have them use the following linguistic patterns to describe events in their daily lives:

I ________ *before I* ________ .
I ________ *after I* ________ .

Preparing to Read

Review

OBJECTIVES

Students will

- review /o͞o/ spelled *oo, _ue, u, _ew,* and *u_e*; and /ū/ spelled *_ew* and *_ue*.
- review open and closed syllables.
- review regular and irregular plurals, homographs, and homophones.
- build fluency.

MATERIALS

- ***Sound/Spelling Cards*** 31, 41
- ***Transparencies*** 65, 69

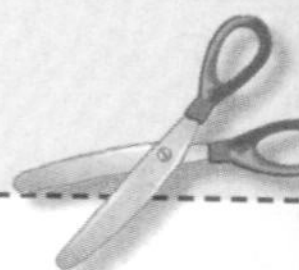

Phonics and Fluency

Use ***Transparency*** 65 with the blending lines and sentences from Days 1 and 2 to review /o͞o/ spelled *oo, _ue, u, _ew* and *u_e; /u/* spelled *_ew* and *_ue;* and open and closed syllables. Have students read the words and sentences on the blending lines. Then have students identify the open and closed syllables in the words on the lines.

Line 1	few	nephew	cue	value
Line 2	**fooled**	**Crinkleroot**	**true**	**bluebirds**
Line 3	truth	**supermarket**	grew	**newt**
Line 4	rule	tube	flute	June
Line 5	human	cable	humble	candle

Sentence 1	We should rescue the few foxes who lost their habitat.
Sentence 2	The bluejay flew to the end of the lake to find food.

Word Structure

Use ***Transparency*** 69 with the word lines from Days 3 and 4 to review regular and irregular plurals, homographs, and homophones. Have students read the words on the word lines. Then have volunteers choose two words from the lines and use them in a single sentence.

Line 1	**critters**	**marshes**	**grasses**	**branches**
Line 2	oxen	**deer**	**geese**	sheep
Line 3	tie	bat	record	wound
Line 4	brake	break	**where**	wear

Reading and Responding Review

OBJECTIVES

Students will

- ✦ review selection vocabulary.
- ✦ review the comprehension strategies Clarifying, Making Connections, and Adjusting Reading Speed.
- ✦ review the comprehension skills Author's Point of View and Classify and Categorize.

MATERIALS

- ✦ ***Student Reader,*** Book 1, pp. 218–241
- ✦ ***Transparency*** 66

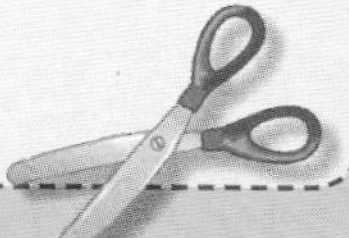

Selection Vocabulary 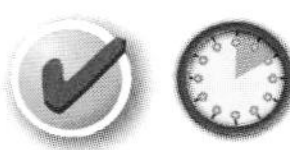

To review the selection vocabulary, organize the class into small groups, and divide the vocabulary words among them. Have each group give three examples for their vocabulary word. For example, three examples of *habitats* are *house, tree,* and *cave*. When they are finished, have each group share their answers with the class.

Selection Vocabulary

habitats (hab′ • it • ats′) *n.* plural form of **habitat:** the place where an animal or a plant naturally lives and grows (page 220)

rich (rich) *adj.* able to produce much; fertile (page 227)

variety (vər • ī′ • ə • tē′) *n.* a number of different things (page 228)

patch (pach) *n.* a small area (page 229)

migrating (mī′ • grāt′ • ing) *adj.* moving from one place to another (page 233)

vast (vast) *adj.* very great in size (page 234)

prey (prā) *n.* an animal that is hunted by another animal for food (page 236)

recognize (rek′ • əg • nīz′) *v.* to know and remember from before; to identify (page 239)

Comprehension Strategies  

Review the following comprehension strategies with students.

- **Clarifying** takes different forms, including clarifying the meaning of words and clarifying difficult ideas or passages. To clarify meanings, students can use context, structural analysis, apposition, rereading the text, charts or graphic organizers, or resources outside of the text. Ask students to point out a confusing idea or passage in "Crinkleroot's Guide to Knowing Animal Habitats." Have students clarify the passage and then explain which method they used.
- **Making Connections** requires readers to activate prior knowledge and connect what they know or have experienced to what they are reading. Ask students to return to "Crinkleroot's Guide to Knowing Animal Habitats" and share any connections they made as they read the text. If students have difficulty making connections, ask questions such as *Does Crinkleroot remind you of anyone you know? Have you ever gone exploring in the habitats that Crinkleroot visited?*
- **Adjusting Reading Speed** helps readers to slow down and reread to obtain all information. To review this comprehension strategy, ask students why readers might adjust their reading speed when reading page 228 of the text. **Possible Answer** *The paragraph on this page contains many descriptive words. There are also words on the side of the page that identify the animals in the illustration, which may confuse some readers.*

Comprehension Skill 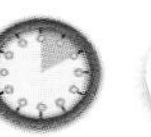  

Review the following comprehension skills with students:

- **Author's Point of View** tells readers who is telling the story. Ask students to find the clue words in the story that show that "Crinkleroot's Guide to Knowing Animal Habitats" is told in the first-person point of view. Have students select three sentences from the text and rewrite them to show third-person point of view.
- **Classify and Categorize** helps readers put like things or ideas together to make new ideas and information easier to understand. To review this comprehension skill, organize students into small groups. Assign each group a habitat from "Crinkleroot's Guide to Knowing Animal Habitats." Have each group choose a method of classifying or categorizing, such as a chart, outline, or web, and organize the information in the story using their method. Have each group present the information to the rest of the class.

Reading with a Writer's Eye

Review

eview the following literary elements with students:

Text Structure: Types is how an author presents facts in nonfiction and narrative nonfiction. An author can arrange information by comparing and contrasting information, classifying information, and by using organizing structures. Ask students how the author presents facts in "Crinkleroot's Guide to Knowing Animal Habitats."

Language Use is how an author uses words in a story. Point out how Jim Arnosky uses precise terminology and vivid descriptions to help explain the animal habitats on the journey throughout "Crinkleroot's Guide to Knowing Animal Habitats." Ask students to turn to the selection and find examples of Arnosky's vivid descriptions. Have students discuss how the fun, descriptive language mixed with precise, scientific language affected their reading of the selection.

Fluency

eview fluency by modeling pace for students. Remind students that pace, or ading with appropriate speed, makes text easier to comprehend and enjoy. ad a passage from pages 234–239 from "Crinkleroot's Guide to Knowing imal Habitats." Make sure that the passage totals at least 160 words to ensure appropriate practice length.

ave students read the passage chorally. Encourage students to pay careful tention to pace. Also remind students to pause after commas and end unctuation.

OBJECTIVES

Students will
- ✦ continue drafting their reports.
- ✦ take the spelling posttest.
- ✦ review cursive *c* and *d*.

MATERIALS

- ✦ Routine B
- ✦ ***Transparency*** 68

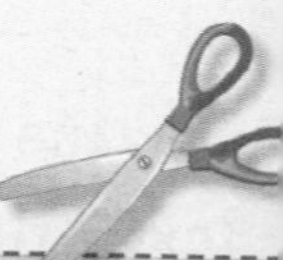

Teacher Tip

ASSESSMENT Use the Writing Rubrics found in the Level Appendix to evaluate students' informative reports. You may use any of the rubrics for Genre, Writing Process, and Writing Traits.

Traits of Good Writing

Vocabulary and Organization The writer uses transition words in expository writing.

Research in Action

Although students must write frequently and for many purposes, they also need to be explicitly taught critical writing skills, processes, and knowledge. The key is to create a balanced writing program that involves a judicious combination of writing, explicit instruction, and less formal techniques such as conferencing and capitalizing on teachable moments.
(Steve Graham and Karen Harris)

Writing Informative Report

ROUTINE B

Drafting

Teach—Using Transition Words

- ✦ Tell students they are going to continue to draft their reports. Use Routine B as you conference with students.
- ✦ Explain some of the features they can use in their reports, such as headings and subheadings, supporting details, examples, transition words, and visual aids.
- ✦ Tell students that transition words, such as *first, next, then, later,* and *finally* help readers understand the order of events in expository writing.
- ✦ Remind students that the supporting details of their reports should be factual. Facts should be presented without an opinion, and readers should be able to verify the research in other sources.
- ✦ Tell students to keep their audiences in mind while writing, and to write an effective, attention-getting beginning.

Guided Practice

Using the summary paragraph you created in the previous lesson, create another related paragraph, and then have students discuss ways to combine the two paragraphs using transition words.

Apply

Composing—Drafting Have students continue drafting their reports. They may also want to conference with peers.

Spelling

/$\overline{oo}$/

Teach

Have students write *Spelling* and their names in the top margin of a clean piece of paper. Have them number the first fifteen lines 1–15 and then skip a line and number the next two lines 1–2. Read each word, use it in a sentence, and give students time to spell it correctly. Encourage students to try to spell the Challenge words, but assure them that misspelling a Challenge word will not affect their test scores.

Spelling Words

clue
tuna
root
June
flute
blue
chew
choose
glue
noodle
truth
blew
stew
duty
rude

Challenge Words

jewel
duet

Guided Practice

- Have students proofread for any mistakes they made on the posttest. Tell them to categorize the mistakes as
  - careless errors.
  - errors in spelling words with /$\overline{oo}$/ spelled *oo, _ew, _ue,* or *u.*
- Make certain students are correctly spelling words with /$\overline{oo}$/ spelled *oo, _ew, _ue,* and *u.*

Penmanship

Cursive Letters *c* and *d*

Teach

- Review cursive *c* and cursive *d* with students. Display ***Transparency*** 68 and say the strokes aloud as you model writing letters.
  - **Letter *c*** Starting point, undercurve
    Downcurve, undercurve: small *c*
  - **Letter *d*** Starting point, undercurve
    Downcurve, undercurve
    Slant down, undercurve: small *d*
- Write the following sentence on the board to model proper letter formation: *The ducks cuddled on the deck.*

Guided Practice

- Have a student write the sentence on the board.

Apply

- After reviewing the sentence on the board, have students practice writing the sentence on a piece of paper. Have students circle the best formation of each letter and the best overall sentence.

Teacher Tip

PENMANSHIP If students are not using proper spacing between words, then check to make sure they are positioning their papers correctly, are holding their pencils correctly, and understand how to lift the pencil at the end of the word and reposition it for the next word.

Day 5

Language Arts

Review

OBJECTIVES

Students will

- review the use of an index.
- review the use of chronological order.
- review subject nouns and pronouns.

MATERIALS

- ***Lesson Assessment Book 1,*** pp. 75–82

Study Skills

Index

Remind students that an index helps readers locate information in a book.

Ask students what readers can find in an index. **Possible Answers** *key words, topic subtopics*

For further review, organize students into groups or pairs. Give them various topic having to do with the unit investigations; for example, endangered species, deser wildlife, farm animals, birds, and so on. Have the groups create a list of possible sources for their topic by looking in reference book indexes.

Listening/Speaking/Viewing

Chronological Order

Remind students that arranging items in chronological order means that items or events are listed in the order in which they happened.

Ask students why putting things in order is important. **Possible Answer** *Presentin things in chronological order helps listeners or readers understand information more clearly.*

Have students create a chronological order chart of the process followed for this unit's investigation.

Grammar, Usage, and Mechanics

Subject Pronouns

Write the following sentences on the board. Have students read the sentences aloud and then reread the sentences, replacing the subject noun with a subject pronoun.

- Lindsay is going to plant a tree in her yard. She *is going to plant a tree in her yard.*
- Daryl and Heather are going to volunteer at a wildlife reserve. They *are going to volunteer at a wildlife reserve.*
- Grant has a wildlife habitat in his own backyard. He *has a wildlife habitat in his own backyard.*

Have students write five sentences, and then have them rewrite the sentences using pronouns as substitutes for the subjects.

Have students discuss reasons why we replace subject nouns with pronouns in writing as well as speech. During their discussion, have them note instances when they automatically used a subject pronoun as a response to what someone else said and have them give a reason why.

Formal Assessment

Monitor Progress to Differentiate Instruction

Use pages 75–82 in ***Lesson Assessment Book 1*** to assess students' understanding of the skills taught in this lesson. Intervene with ***Reteach, Challenge Activities, Intervention Guide, eSkills, Leveled Readers,*** or activities in the ***Workshop Kit*** as needed.

Lesson Planner

MATERIALS

- ***Student Reader***, Book 1, pp. 242–251
- ***Transparencies*** 17, 17A, 62, 68, 71, 72, 72A
- ***Skills Practice 1***, p. 154
- Routines 16, 17
- ***Lesson Assessment Book 1***, pp. 43–84

Day 6

Reading and Responding

Science Inquiry, pp. T430–T431
Inquiry, pp. T432–T433

Language Arts

Writing
Revising, pp. T434–T435
Penmanship, p. T435

Workshop

Inquiry: Have students practice and rehearse their Inquiry presentations. Have the group provide feedback.
Writing: Have students read their informative reports quietly to themselves. Have them add details as needed.

Day 7

Reading and Responding

Poetry, pp. T436–T439
Inquiry, pp. T440–T441

Language Arts

Writing, Revising, p. T442
Writing, Editing/Proofreading, p. T443

Workshop

Inquiry: Have students work in a group to identify and list new questions about animals and animal habitats and post them on the **Concept/Question Board.**
Writing: Have students work on their final drafts after they complete editing and proofreading.

Monitor Progress

✓ = **Formal Assessment**
B = **Benchmark Assessment**

Day 8

Reading and Responding

Test Prep, pp. T444–T445

Language Arts

Writing, Publishing, pp. T446–T447
Penmanship, pp. T447

Writing: Have students share their reports.

***Expository Writing Prompt, Lesson Assessment Book 1,* pp. 83–84**

Day 9

Preparing to Read

Phonics and Fluency, Review, p. T448
Word Structure, Review, p. T448

Reading and Responding

Selection Vocabulary, Review, p. T449
Comprehension Strategies and Skills
Review, p. T450
Reading with a Writer's Eye
Review, p. T451
Fluency, Review, p. T451

Language Arts

Spelling, Review, p. T452
Study Skills, Review, p. T452
Listening/Speaking/Viewing
Review, p. T453
Grammar, Usage, and Mechanics
Review, p. T453

Day 10 Review

Unit Celebration, pp. T456–T457

***Lesson Assessment Book 1,* pp. 43–84**
Benchmark Assessment, Benchmark 3

Science Inquiry

Genre Compare and Contrast Essay 

Review the elements of a compare and contrast essay. If necessary, remind students that compare and contrast essays tell how two things are alike and how they are different.

Feature Venn Diagram

Point to the Venn diagram in the essay. Tell students that Venn diagrams are graphic organizers that are useful for making comparisons.

Ask students to point to the Venn diagram in "Deserts Are Not Deserted." Then ask students what is being compared and contrasted in the diagram. **Possible Answer** *It looks like how animals adapt to hot deserts and how animals adapt to cold deserts is being compared and contrasted.*

Reading "Deserts Are Not Deserted"

Have students read "Deserts Are Not Deserted" silently. Remind students how the author of "Crinkleroot's Guide to Knowing Animal Habitats" made comparisons. Make sure students understand that the Venn diagram is a way to organize information that is being compared and contrasted.

Think Link

1. How can animals adapt to live in hot deserts? **Possible Answer** *Animals in hot deserts must find shelter from the sun. They may move a twig or leaf to stay in its shade or burrow under the sand. Some animals come out at night when it is cooler. Hot desert animals' bodies help them adapt. Rabbits' large ears give off heat and camels' long eyelashes keep sand out of their eyes.*

OBJECTIVES

Students will
- read the Science Inquiry Link.
- investigate the unit theme Animals and Their Habitats by using the Inquiry process.

MATERIALS

- ***Student Reader,*** Book 1, pp. 242–243

Teacher Tips

SELECTION VOCABULARY Review the meaning of the highlighted selection vocabulary words *vast* and *migrating* in "Deserts Are Not Deserted."

SILENT READ If some students are having difficulty comprehending the selection as they read silently, read the selection with them in small groups.

Science Inquiry

Deserts Are Not Deserted

Genre

A **compare and contrast essay** tells how two things are alike and how they are different.

Feature

A **Venn diagram** is a graphic organizer that is useful for making comparisons.

What do you think of when you hear the word desert? Do you picture a blazing sun and vast stretch of sand? That is one type of desert. Did you know a desert can also be cold? Some deserts are covered with snow and ice. The arctic tundra is a cold desert.

Both kinds of deserts are dry. A hot desert gets just 4 to 20 inches of rain per year. A cold desert gets that amount of snow in a year. The lack of water in a desert affects life there. Only certain kinds of plants and animals can survive.

Animals in a hot desert must find shelter from the sun. Insects will move around a twig or leaf to stay in its shade. Mice burrow beneath the sand. They come out at night, when the air is cooler.

Animals in a cold desert must deal with an extreme climate too. Squirrels hibernate for the coldest months. Migrating birds, such as the tern, stay alive by flying to warmer climates in August. In May they return to the tundra.

242

Animals' bodies help them adapt to desert life. Rabbits in a hot desert have large ears. Their ears give off heat, which helps them cool down. Camels have long eyelashes that keep sand out of their eyes. Musk oxen and polar bears have a lot of body fat. They also have thick fur. The fat and fur help keep them warm in the cold tundra.

A desert might seem like an empty place, but life does exist there. You just might have to look harder to find it.

Desert Life

Hot Desert	Both	Cold Desert
• animals seek protection from sun • animals' bodies give off heat • few large mammals live here	• dry weather • animals adapt to extreme conditions • animals are more active at certain times	• animals seek protection from cold • animals' bodies hold in heat • reptiles do not live here

Think Link

1. How can animals adapt to live in hot deserts?
2. How can animals adapt to live in cold deserts?
3. What does the middle section of the Venn diagram show?

Try It!

As you work on your investigation, try using a Venn diagram to compare and contrast information.

243

2. *How can animals adapt to live in cold deserts?* **Possible Answer** *Some animals in cold deserts hibernate and some migrate. Cold desert animals' bodies help them adapt. Musk oxen and polar bears have a lot of body fat and thick fur to keep them warm.*
3. *What does the middle section of the Venn diagram show? The middle section shows that both hot deserts and cold deserts have dry weather. The animals must adapt to both extreme conditions and are more active at certain times of day.*

Inquiry Connection

Have students discuss how using Venn diagrams might be helpful in their investigations about animals and their habitats. For example, they might want to use Venn diagrams to compare and contrast different animal habitats they are investigating.

Inquiry Process

Step 7—Sharing Your Answers

Whole Group

Whole-Group Time

- Throughout the unit, groups of students have been researching their own questions and conjectures about animals and animal habitats. Now they will share the results of their investigations. Remind students that sharing knowledge is one main goal of Inquiry, and it can benefit the whole class.
- Consider allowing the groups to decide the order of the presentations.
- Review the listening, speaking, and viewing skills students have learned so that they can use them during the presentations. Encourage them to be good listeners, speak clearly, use visual aids, and present things in a chronological order.
- Remind students that the purpose of their Inquiry was not to learn the right answers, but rather to discover new things together.
- Allow time after each presentation for students to ask appropriate questions about each group's presentation and investigation. To encourage discussion, model asking simple questions after each presentation. You could ask any group what was most surprising or interesting about their topic or what they liked most about their investigation.

Teacher Tip

SHARING PRESENTATIONS Remind students of the flexible nature of the investigation process. Questions and answers change over the course of the process. Their presentations represent what they have learned about their conjecture so far.

Small Group

Small-Group Time

- Have students meet in their small groups to finalize their investigations and discuss how their presentation went.
- Have students discuss questions or ideas they might have about their investigations and their groups' investigations.
- As you circulate among the groups, ask them how the other groups' presentations affected their understanding of the theme Animals and Their Habitats.
- Allow time for each group to discuss other questions they have about the Inquiry process or the theme Animals and Their Habitats.

Concept/Question Board

Continue to encourage use of the **Concept/Question Board** by recognizing and thanking students for their contributions. Incorporate review of the posted items into classroom discussions whenever possible. Remember to post your own questions, ideas, conjectures, articles, summaries, and pictures.

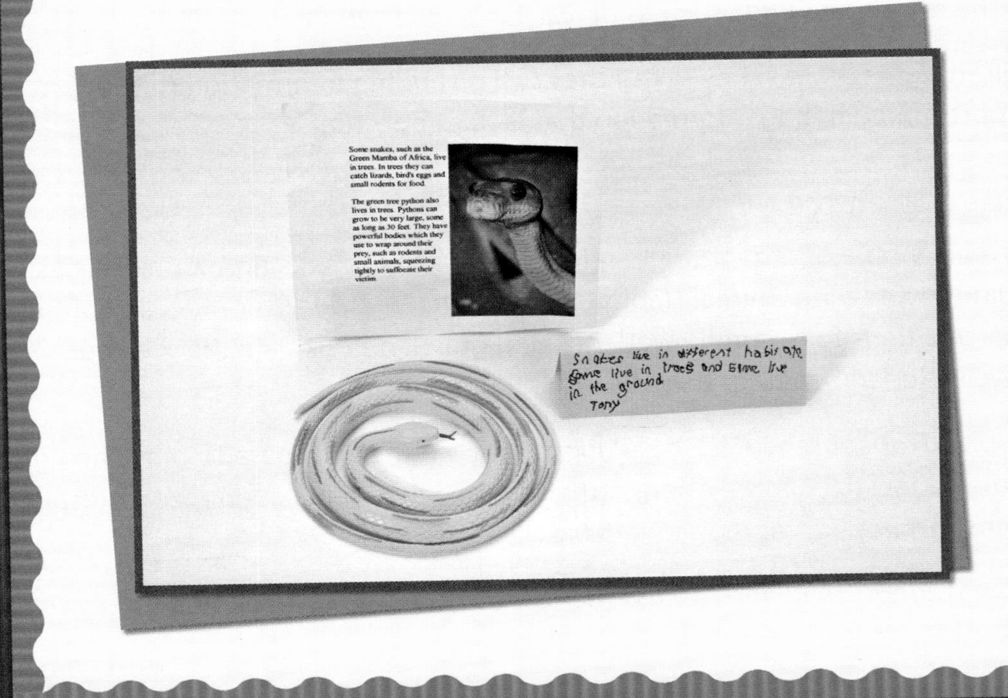

Inquiry Rubric

To assess Presenting Inquiry Findings, see the Inquiry Rubrics in the Level Appendix.

Teacher Tip

CONTINUING INQUIRY Remind students that unit investigations are meant to be open-ended. As some questions are answered, more will be asked. Encourage students to continue to ask and seek answers to questions they have about animals and their habitats.

OBJECTIVES

Students will
- ✦ revise their informative reports.
- ✦ review cursive *p, j, c,* and *d.*

MATERIALS

- ✦ Routine 16
- ✦ ***Transparencies*** 62, 72, 72A, 68
- ✦ ***Skills Practice 1,*** p. 154

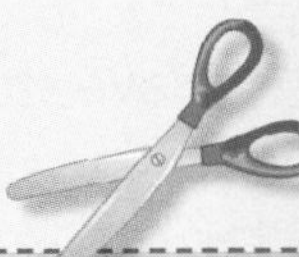

Transparency 72
72A

Revising Ideas and Details

Prairie dogs live in the southwestern United States and Mexico. ~~Prairie dogs live in Utah, New Mexico, and Texas.~~ Prairie dogs are small animals. ~~Prairie dogs are hairy. They have~~ short legs. They have a short tail. ~~They have~~ sharp claws. They bark like domestic dogs. ~~Some people keep them as pets. I have a pet dog but not a prairie dog.~~

Prairie dogs live in prairies. Prairie dogs burrow ~~underground. They~~ build nests underground. Prairie dogs eat grass. ~~They eat~~ roots. ~~They eat~~ seeds. ~~And they eat~~ leafy plants.

Final Draft

Prairie dogs live in the southwestern United States and Mexico. Prairie dogs are small, hairy animals with short legs. They have a short tail and sharp claws. They bark like domestic dogs.

Prairie dogs live in prairies. Prairie dogs burrow and build nests underground. Prairie dogs eat grass, roots, seeds, and leafy plants.

 SRA Imagine It! • Level 3 • Transparency 72 • 72A Level 3

Transparencies 72, 72A

Writing Informative Report

ROUTINE 16

Revising

Teach—Combine Ideas

- ✦ Students will revise their informative reports.
- ✦ Use Routine 16 as you model revising strategies. Tell students that as they revise their reports they should make sure that
  - the facts are correct.
  - the facts and examples are presented objectively.
  - the paragraphs are organized by topics.
  - the paper contains an introductory paragraph and a concluding paragraph.
  - the sentence structure and sentence length vary.
  - the transition words such as *at first, next, then, later,* and *finally* are used.
- ✦ Tell students that as they revise they will be adding information to their reports and deleting information that is not important.

Guided Practice

- ✦ As an example of organization, refer students to the selection "Crinkleroot's Guide to Knowing Animal Habitats." Point out how the author focused on one area at a time, for example wetlands and grasslands. Explain that he could have included headings above these sections.
- ✦ Display ***Transparency*** 72. Ask students to read the transparency and then give some suggestions for revision. After discussing students' suggestions, display ***Transparency*** 72A and discuss these revisions.
- ✦ Have students read and discuss the revising checklist ***Skills Practice 1*** page 154.

Writing, continued

Apply

Composing—Revising Students will begin revising their informative reports. Tell them to continue drafting, if necessary. Remind students to give credit to all of the original sources.

Assessment

You will use the Writing Rubrics found in the Level Appendix to evaluate students' informative reports. You may use any of the rubrics for Genre, Writing Process, and Writing Traits. Share with students what you will be looking for when assessing their informative reports.

UNIT 2 Lesson 5

Revising Use this checklist to revise your rough draft.

- ☐ Do you have a strong beginning?
- ☐ Are your ideas in the best order?
- ☐ Did you stick to your topic?
- ☐ Did you sum up your ideas in the conclusion?

Editing/Proofreading Use this checklist to correct mistakes.

- ☐ Did you use correct spelling?
- ☐ Did you use correct punctuation?
- ☐ Did you use quotation marks around dialogue?
- ☐ Are the names of people and places capitalized?

Publishing Use this checklist to prepare your report for publication.

- ☐ Write or type a neat final copy.
- ☐ Save it to use when making your finished report.

154 UNIT 2 • Lesson 5 Writing • *Skills Practice 1*

Skills Practice 1, p. 154

Traits of Good Writing

REVISING The writer combines ideas and deletes irrelevant ideas during revision.

Penmanship

Review Cursive Letters *p, j, c,* and *d*

Teach

- ✦ Remind students that cursive letters are made of four types of strokes (undercurve, overcurve, downcurve, and slant lines).
- ✦ Review lowercase cursive *p* and *j* as undercurve letters.
- ✦ Review lowercase cursive *c* and *d* as downcurve letters.
- ✦ For further instruction and letter formations, refer to Unit 2 Lessons 4 and 5, ***Transparencies*** 62 and 68, and the Appendix.
- ✦ On the board, write lowercase cursive *p, j, c,* and *d,* saying the strokes aloud as you form the letters.
- ✦ To model proper letter formation, write the following words on the board: *jiffy, decade, capital, jade*.

Guided Practice

Have students practice writing the letters and words on the board.

Apply

- ✦ Have students practice writing each of the letters four times on a piece of paper. Ask them to circle the best formation of each of their letters.
- ✦ After reviewing the words on the board, have students practice writing the words. Have them circle the best formation of each word based on the proper formation of *p, j, c,* and *d*.

Teacher Tip

PENMANSHIP Check students' handwriting for proper formation of *p, j, c,* and *d,* and make sure their letters do not "float" between the lines. Also check for alignment, spacing, and letter size. Have them pay attention to this while drafting and revising their reports.

Day 7

Reading and Responding

OBJECTIVES

Students will

- learn about haiku and word pictures.
- build fluency.
- understand literary devices and mood.
- continue investigating the unit theme Animals and Their Habitats.

MATERIALS

- ***Student Reader,*** Book 1, pp. 244–247

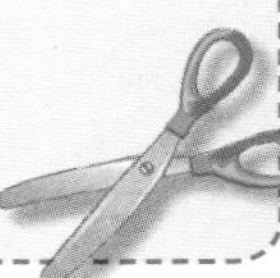

Poetry

Activating Prior Knowledge

- Ask students if they have read other poems about animals as a means of beginning discussion.
- Have students look at only the illustrations for the three poems. Ask students if they can guess what animal each poem is about.

Reading the Poem

Haiku

- Read the three haiku to the students. Have students listen closely to the rhythm of the haiku. Ask students whether the haiku rhyme and whether they notice the use of syllables in the haiku.
- Ask students if they notice what the three haiku have in common. *They are all about animals.* Ask a volunteer to explain personification. *a description of animals or things as if they were people* Have students describe how the animals' behavior personifies humans. **Possible Answers** *The ants are busy. The beaver is industrious. The kangaroo is protective of her baby.*

Fluency

Remind students to maintain a sense of rhythm when reading aloud, even if the lines do not rhyme. Encourage students to read the first haiku with a sense of urgency; the second with a proud sense of accomplishment; and the third with a nurturing, protective tone.

Focus Questions

Have students read aloud the Focus Questions on page 244. Ask students to think about the Focus Questions as they read the haiku from "If Not for the Cat."

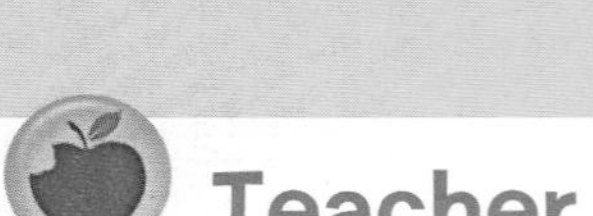

Teacher Tips

HAIKU Tell students that haiku originate from Japan and usually have three lines that do not rhyme. The first line has five syllables, the second has seven syllables, and the third line has five syllables.

POETRY Ask students whether they enjoyed listening to the poems. Do they usually like listening to poetry? Ask them to name other kinds of literature or material (such as nonfiction or songs) they like to listen to.

Listening, Speaking, Viewing

Literary Devices

- Explain to students that literary devices are techniques writers use to make writing more interesting, colorful, and meaningful.
- In the third poem, the writer uses tone to convey meaning to his readers. Explain that tone is the emotional state or attitude of a poem. Ask students if they detect the warm, protective, nurturing tone of this poem. Ask what words convey these feelings. **Possible Answers** *safe inside, sleeps, delicate, frail*

Theme Connection

- Have students read and discuss the Focus Questions on page 244.
- In the response section of the Writer's Notebooks, have students tell how these poems tell something about animals and their habitats. Encourage students to share their responses with a partner.

Reading and Responding

Poetry

Activating Prior Knowledge

- ✦ Ask students if they have ever seen a redwood tree or if they know anything about these trees. Tell students that redwoods are some of the oldest living things on Earth. Redwoods exist along the coast of California and Oregon. They are the tallest trees in the world.
- ✦ Ask students what animals might live in a redwood forest.

Reading the Poem

Word Pictures

- ✦ Have students close their eyes and listen as you read the poem "Behind the Redwood Curtain." Read the poem with a sense of wonder. Then have students read the poem silently to themselves. Ask students which words in the poem formed pictures in their minds. **Possible Answers** *The words* fingering the clouds *help readers see how tall the trees are as they stretch to the sky. The words* passing it from limb to limb *show the fog as it sweeps through the trees.*
- ✦ Explain that comparing the fog to a curtain shows readers the other world that lives behind the fog. Readers can see the deer leaping and the birds winging in the breeze.
- ✦ Point out the similes the author uses to describe the redwood forest. *redwood trees and skyscrapers, fog and a curtain* Explain that similes compare two different things using the words *like* or *as.* Ask students how similes help readers form pictures. *The redwood trees are very tall like skyscrapers. The fog is heavy and covers the stage like a curtain.*

Fluency

As students read the poem aloud, remind them to pause at punctuation. Model fluent reading when needed. Encourage students to read the poem with a sense of wonder and amazement.

Focus Questions

Have students read aloud the Focus Questions on page 246. Encourage students to think about the Focus Questions as they read the poem "Behind the Redwood Curtain."

Teacher Tip

POETRY Ask students whether they enjoyed listening to the poem. Do they usually like listening to poetry? What other kinds of literature or material (such as nonfiction or songs) do they like to listen to?

Focus Questions What might be happening in an animal habitat when we are not looking? What do wild animals do where you live? How long have they been doing those things?

Behind the Redwood Curtain

by Natasha Wing

illustrated by Lori Anzalone

Redwood trees rise like skyscrapers
Fingering the clouds in search of moisture
Pulling down the fog and passing it
From limb to limb
Into the deep of the forest.
The fog blankets the forest
Blocking out light, movement, and sound
Like a curtain
Draped across a stage.
Yet behind the redwood curtain
Black bear walk and stalk their prey
Deer sleep and leap away
Slugs climb and slime on leaves
Birds sing and wing in the breeze.
The show must go on
As it has for thousands of years
Behind the redwood curtain.

246

247

Listening/Speaking/Viewing

Mood

- Discuss the idea that every piece of writing should create a mood, tone, or attitude for the audience. Explain that listeners of poetry can develop an awareness of the mood by listening to key elements of the poem, such as vivid words and the speaker's voice.
- Read the poem again, and ask students what vivid word choices help set the mood for the poem. **Possible Answers** *Comparing the trees to skyscrapers sets the tone for something big and awe inspiring. Comparing the fog to a curtain on a stage makes the readers feel wonder as they see what is on the other side.*

Theme Connection

- Have students read and discuss the Focus Questions on page 246.
- In the response section of the Writer's Notebook, have students write about how these poems tell something about animals and their habitats.

Inquiry Process

Step 8—Asking New Questions

Whole Group

Whole-Group Time

Once student groups have completed their investigation inquiries:

- ✦ Tell students that just because their presentations are complete for this unit, this does not mean that there is nothing left to investigate about the theme Animals and Their Habitats. Explain that Inquiry is an ongoing process. Each answer raises new questions, and students should be continually raising new questions and forming new conjectures.
- ✦ Have students discuss what they learned and identify anything else they want or need to learn about animals and animal habitats. Model asking new questions: *After doing my investigation, I still need to know how people can be convinced to care about animals losing their habitats due to new land development. I also want to know why some people think that animals losing their habitats is not an important problem for our community.* Encourage students to raise other questions they have as a result of the investigation you modeled.
- ✦ Ask students whether they have changed any of the ideas or opinions they had about animals or animal habitats when they started the unit.
- ✦ Allow students to share anything else they would still like to know about the unit theme, especially given all that they have learned in their investigations.

Small Group

Small-Group Time

- Allow time for each group to informally discuss their Inquiry. Encourage them to talk about what they liked about their project as well as what they learned about the theme Animals and Their Habitats.
- Ask groups to think about and discuss what went well in their group and how well their group worked together.
- Get each group to think about what they found most challenging about the project, and remind them to keep this in mind for later group inquiries.
- Have each group post any additional questions they have about their topic on the **Concept/Question Board.**

Concept/Question Board

Have students post any new questions they have about animals and animal habitats on the **Concept/Question Board.** They can also post items from their presentations on the Board.

Teacher Tip

CONTINUING INQUIRY For more information about how students can become involved in saving and protecting animals and their habitats and for information on building your own wildlife backyard habitat, go to www.nwf.org or subscribe to National Wildlife Federation student magazines "Wild Animal Baby," "Your Big Backyard," and "Ranger Rick."

Inquiry Rubric

To assess Overall Research and Participation in Collaborative Inquiry, see the Inquiry Rubrics in the Level Appendix.

Day 7

Language Arts

OBJECTIVES

Students will

- ✦ continue to revise their informative reports.
- ✦ edit/proofread their informative reports.

MATERIALS

- ✦ Routine 16
- ✦ ***Skills Practice 1,*** p. 154
- ✦ ***Transparencies*** 17, 17A

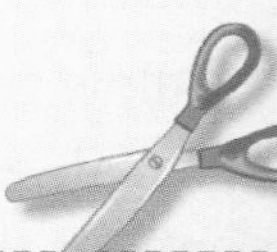

UNIT 2 Lesson 5

Revising Use this checklist to revise your rough draft.

- ☐ Do you have a strong beginning?
- ☐ Are your ideas in the best order?
- ☐ Did you stick to your topic?
- ☐ Did you sum up your ideas in the conclusion?

Editing/Proofreading Use this checklist to correct mistakes.

- ☐ Did you use correct spelling?
- ☐ Did you use correct punctuation?
- ☐ Did you use quotation marks around dialogue?
- ☐ Are the names of people and places capitalized?

Publishing Use this checklist to prepare your report for publication.

- ☐ Write or type a neat final copy.
- ☐ Save it to use when making your finished report.

154 UNIT 2 • Lesson 5 Writing • *Skills Practice 1*

Skills Practice 1, p. 154

Writing Informative Report

ROUTINE 16

Revising

Teach

- ✦ Use Routine 16. Tell students that they can continue to revise their informative reports, but they will also begin to edit/proofread their reports. Remind them to make sure their reports have an introductory paragraph, a paragraph for each subtopic, and a concluding paragraph.
- ✦ Ask students to state the difference between a report and a review. **Possible Answer** *A report gives facts about the topic from resources. A review has facts from resources, but it also gives the author's opinion about the topic.*
- ✦ Tell students that as they revise, they need to make sure they are not adding their own opinions to the text.

Guided Practice

Write a paragraph on the board. The paragraph should contain both fact and opinion. Ask students to read the paragraph and then help you revise it to delete the opinion. Show them how to replace opinion with fact.

Apply

Composing—Revising Have students continue to revise their informative reports. Remind them to refer to the revision checklist in ***Skills Practice 1*** page 154. Tell students that once they have completed their revisions, they should begin looking for errors in grammar, spelling, and punctuation.

Writing Informative Report

ROUTINE 16

Editing/Proofreading

Teach

- ✦ Tell students that they will now edit/proofread the revised copy of their reports.
- ✦ Use Routine 16. Remind students to look for errors in spelling, grammar, and end punctuation. Tell students to make sure all pronouns agree in number and gender with the nouns they replaced.
- ✦ Remind students to make sure their reports have an introductory paragraph, a paragraph for each subtopic, and a concluding paragraph. Tell students to make sure they have indented each new paragraph.
- ✦ Remind students that in Unit 2 Lesson 3 they learned about homographs, and in Unit 2 Lesson 4 they learned about homophones. Tell students that as they edit/proofread their reports, they need to make sure there are no errors in spelling that may relate to the use of a homograph or homophone.

Guided Practice

- ✦ Remind students of the proofreading marks they are to use by displaying ***Transparencies*** 17, 17A.
- ✦ Using the draft you have written for this assignment, or an editing nonfiction transparency, model editing and proofreading a report.
- ✦ Have students read and discuss the editing checklist on ***Skills Practice 1*** page 154.

Apply

Composing—Editing/Proofreading Have students refer to ***Skills Practice 1*** page 154 as they edit/proofread their informative reports.

Traits of Good Writing

VOCABULARY AND ORGANIZATION The writer uses transition words to organize information in expository writing.

OBJECTIVES

Students will

- recognize that there are important words in questions and answer choices.
- practice identifying and using important words.
- apply what they have learned about identifying and using important words.

MATERIALS

- ***Student Reader,*** Book 1, pp. 248–251

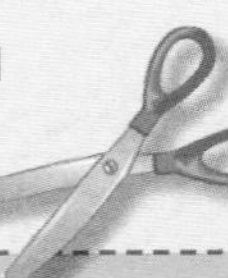

Teacher Tip

IDENTIFYING IMPORTANT WORDS Tell students to pay close attention to words that are underlined, are in all capitals, or are italicized. Suggest that students repeat any of these words in the question silently to themselves as they look for the best answer.

Differentiating Instruction English Learner

IF . . . students need additional support reading, "The Starling," **THEN . . .** read the story with them during Workshop.

Teaching Test-Taking Strategies

Teach

- Discuss with students how questions and answers on standardized tests often contain important words that will help them choose the correct answer. Tell students to pay close attention to words that are underlined, are in all capitals, or are italicized. These are often important words.
- Have students turn to ***Student Reader,*** Book 1 page 248. As a class, read the text on the far left side of the page as well as the first paragraph at the top of the page. Tell students that they should read carefully to look for important words that will help them choose the correct answer.

Guided Practice

- Have students read the sample directions, question, and answer choices in the box on page 248. Then ask a student to answer the question. Discuss with students which important words helped them choose the correct answer. Read and discuss the rest of the page with students.
- Before students begin reading "The Starling," point to the words "Go On" as well as the arrows at the bottom of pages 249 and 250. Tell them that when they see these words with the arrow on a test, they should go to the next page.
- Point to the stop sign at the bottom of page 251. Tell students that when they come to a stop sign on a test, they should go back and check their answers until they are told to stop.

Apply

- Have students silently read "The Starling" on pages 249–250. Then on a separate piece of paper, have them answer the questions about the story on page 251.
- Remind students to identify and use any important words when answering the questions. Encourage students to use the other test-taking strategies they have learned.
- When students are finished, discuss how following the directions helped them choose the correct answers.

Unit 2

Test Prep

Test-Taking Strategy: Identifying and Using Important Words

Pay attention to important words in directions and questions. These important words will help you find the right answer.

Identifying and Using Important Words

Each question or answer choice has important words. These words will help you answer the question correctly.

Read this item to yourself. Think about the important words in the question and answer choices.

According to this article, what should you do with a garden in the fall?

Ⓐ Use less water.
Ⓑ Use more fertilizer.
Ⓒ Pull all the plants out of the ground.
Ⓓ Cover the plants with plastic.

Important words in the question are *According to this article.* They tell you that you should use the information in the article, not other things that you might have heard or read. Another important word is *fall.* It tells you the time of year to think about. In the answer choices, some of the important words are *less*, *more*, and *all*. Even small words can help you understand the question and answer choices.

Test-Taking Practice

Read the selection "The Starling." Then answer numbers 1 through 4.

A bird that almost everyone knows is the starling. Most people think the starling is an American bird. It is not. A few dozen starlings were brought here from Europe more than a hundred years ago. They must have liked it. Now they are found all over the United States. There are millions of them.

Starlings are mostly black. They are about six inches long. Their feathers sometimes seem to change colors. You might see a little green or purple when the light shines on them.

Here is something strange about starlings. In the summer, the beak of a starling is yellow. In the winter, it is black.

You probably will not see just one or two starlings at a time. That is because starlings like to live in flocks of many birds. You will know when a flock of starlings is nearby. They will make a lot of noise. A flock of starlings can have more than one hundred birds.

GO ON

Some birds have beautiful songs. These songs often sound the same. People often know a bird by its song. This is not true about starlings. They can make many different sounds. They try to sound like other birds. In a city, starlings might even try to make sounds like horns honking.

Starlings are also very hungry birds. They eat seeds, berries, and bugs. Starlings do something that is not very nice. They eat so much that there is no food for other birds. When starlings come to an area, they often chase away other birds.

Just like other birds, starlings like to keep their babies safe. They make nests of sticks, feathers, and even trash. Starlings can live in trees and also buildings. Starlings sometimes make their nests in a person's house. Can you imagine waking up and finding a starling flying in your bedroom?

GO ON

Use what you learned from "The Starling" to answer Numbers 1 through 4. Write your answers on a piece of paper.

1. To learn more about starlings, you should
   Ⓐ look in a dictionary under "birds."
   Ⓑ look in an encyclopedia.
   Ⓒ ask a friend who has a big yard.
   Ⓓ find a book about pet birds.

2. Starlings are different from other birds because starlings
   Ⓐ sometimes sound like horns honking.
   Ⓑ build nests to keep their babies safe.
   Ⓒ live all over the United States.
   Ⓓ eat seeds, berries, and bugs.

3. What is the author's main purpose for writing "The Starling"?
   Ⓐ To tell why starlings are noisy
   Ⓑ To prove that starlings are beautiful
   Ⓒ To encourage people to feed starlings
   Ⓓ To share interesting facts about starlings

4. Why is it a problem that starlings are very hungry birds?
   Ⓐ It is not good for starlings to eat trash.
   Ⓑ Starlings eat food that people need.
   Ⓒ There is no food left for other birds.
   Ⓓ The starlings get fat and cannot fly.

Test Tips

- Read the story, but do not try to memorize it.
- Read each question carefully.
- If you do not know an answer, guess.

STOP

OBJECTIVES

Students will
- publish informative reports.

MATERIALS

- ***Skills Practice 1,*** p. 154
- Routine 17
- ***Transparencies*** 62, 68

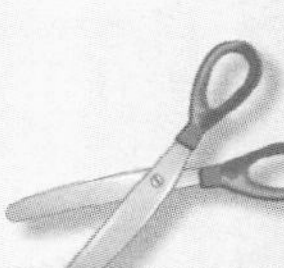

Writing Informative Report

Publishing

Teach—Using Multimedia to Illustrate Papers

- Use Routine 17. Tell students that they are at the final stage of the writing process: publishing.
- Students should decide on a method for publishing their informative reports. Since students have written information that they could share with other students, you may want to have students do an oral presentation in addition to their written reports. Encourage students to type their final drafts using a computer or other word processor.
- Tell students they can use the visual aids from their written reports as visual aids for the oral presentation.
- Students can also use multimedia forms of support, such as photographs, the Internet, portions of films or television programs, audio recordings, and so on.
- Create a special place in the class library to keep the reports until the end of the year. Allow students to take their reports home to share with their families before returning them to the class library.

Guided Practice

- Create a model of an informative report using the information you collected for your own paper. Show students how to incorporate a multimedia presentation for an oral report. Model presenting a report in front of the class and then discuss the various aspects of your report with the students. Make sure the students know that they have a role to play as your audience during your presentation.
- Have students read and discuss the publishing checklist on ***Skills Practice 1*** page 154.

UNIT 2 Lesson 5

Revising Use this checklist to revise your rough draft.
- ☐ Do you have a strong beginning?
- ☐ Are your ideas in the best order?
- ☐ Did you stick to your topic?
- ☐ Did you sum up your ideas in the conclusion?

Editing/Proofreading Use this checklist to correct mistakes.
- ☐ Did you use correct spelling?
- ☐ Did you use correct punctuation?
- ☐ Did you use quotation marks around dialogue?
- ☐ Are the names of people and places capitalized?

Publishing Use this checklist to prepare your report for publication.
- ☐ Write or type a neat final copy.
- ☐ Save it to use when making your finished report.

154 UNIT 2 • Lesson 5 Writing • *Skills Practice 1*

Skills Practice 1, p. 154

Writing, continued

Apply

- **Composing—Publishing** Have students create a clean, error-free copy of their informative papers. Have them also refer to the publishing checklist on page 154 in ***Skills Practice 1*** as a guide to completing their reports.
- If students wish, they can make a cover for their report. Remind students to include any tables, charts, diagrams, pictures, photographs, and so on.
- Remind students to include the bibliography that cites the sources they used in their reports.
- Have volunteers present their reports to the class, or allow time to have the entire class present their informative reports.

Traits of Good Writing

MULTIMEDIA PRESENTATION The writer uses multimedia sources to illustrate a paper and to accompany a presentation.

Teacher Tip

PORTFOLIOS Suggest that students add their published informative reports to the Writing Portfolio.

Penmanship

Cursive Letters *p, j, c,* and *d*

Teach

- Review cursive *p, j, c,* and *d* with students.
- Ask students what type of strokes are used to form letters *p* and *j* and what type of strokes are used to form letters *c* and *d*. *Letters p and j are undercurve letters, and letters c and d are downcurve letters.*
- For further instruction and letter formations, refer to Unit 2 Lessons 4 and 5, ***Transparencies*** 62 and 68; and the Appendix.
- To model proper letter formation, write the following sentence on the board: *The dog jumped across the pond.*

Guided Practice

Have students practice writing the sentence in the air. If necessary, show them how to hold and unsharpened pencil in front of them and form the words.

Apply

- Have students practice writing each of cursive *p, j, c*, and *d* two times.
- After reviewing the sentence you wrote on the board, have students practice writing the sentence on a piece of paper. Have them circle the best formation of each letter and their best overall sentence based on the proper formation of *p, j, c,* and *d.*

Unit 2

Unit Review

Write the bending lines on the board or use ***Transparency*** 71 to review phonics and fluency Lessons 1–5. Then use ***Decodable Stories, Book 3,*** Story 22, "Migrating Geese" to review the skills taught in Unit 2.

Phonics and Fluency

Whole Group

Write the blending lines on the board to review Lessons 1–5. Have students read the words on the blending lines. Then have volunteers identify the target sound/spellings or consonant blends in the words.

- **Lesson 1** /ī/ spelled *igh, _y, _ie;* consonant blends
- **Lesson 2** /ō/ spelled *_ow, oa_*
- **Lesson 3** /ū/ spelled *_ew* and *_ue*
- **Lesson 4** /ī/ spelled *igh, _y, _ie;* /ō/ spelled *_ow, oa_;* /ū/ spelled *_ew, _ue;* consonant blends
- **Lesson 5** /o͞o/ spelled *oo, _ue, u, _ew, u_e*
  /ū/ spelled *_ew, _ue*
  Open and Closed Syllables

flight	right	shy	tie	scratch
flow	window	boat	coach	road
curfew	nephew	cue	rescue	argue
moonlight	why	throat	tissue	protest
spooky	true	duty	grew	newest
pew	fewest	argue	value	barbeque
human	music	flavor	distant	wetlands

Word Structure

Whole Group

Write the blending lines on the board or use ***Transparency*** 71 to review word structure Lessons 1–5. Have students read the words on the word lines. Then have volunteers choose words from the lines and use them in sentences.

- **Lesson 1** Regular Plurals
- **Lesson 2** Irregular Plurals
- **Lesson 3** Homographs
- **Lesson 4** Homophones
- **Lesson 5** Review Lessons 1–4

claws	branches	calves	knights
children	feet	fish	fungi
fan	fly	bow	rose
deer	dear	there	their
foxes	cacti	dove	know/no

Selection Vocabulary

Small Group

To review some of the selection vocabulary words from Lessons 1–5, organize students into five teams. Have each team write definitions for their set of words. When they are finished, have the teams take turns sharing their definitions with the class. Their classmates should try to guess each word.

Lesson 1 Vocabulary

dwellers (dwel′ • ûrz) *n.* plural form of **dweller:** a person or animal that lives in a certain place (page 150)
hollow (hol′ • lō) *adj.* having a hole or an empty space inside (page 146)
maze (māz) *n.* a confusing series of paths or passageways through which people might get lost (page 142)

Lesson 2 Vocabulary

hatch (hach) *v.* to come out of an egg (page 164)
responsibility (ri • spon′ • sə • bi′ • li • tē) *n.* a duty (page 166)
beckoned (bek′ • ənd) *v.* past tense of **beckon**: to call someone by waving (page 168)

Lesson 3 Vocabulary

aboard (ə • bord′) *adv.* on or into a ship, train, or an airplane (page 181)
mild (mīld) *adj.* gentle or calm; not harsh or sharp (page 182)
balance (bal′ • əns) *n.* a steady, secure position (page 189)

Lesson 4 Vocabulary

appreciate (əp • prē′ • shē • āt′) *v.* to understand the value of (page 205)
cautiously (kosh′ • əs • lē′) *adv.* with close care (page 205)
relocates (rē • lō′ • kāts) *v.* a form of the verb **relocate:** to move to a new place (page 204)

Lesson 5 Vocabulary

habitats (hab′ • it • ats′) *n.* plural form of **habitat:** the place where an animal or a plant naturally lives and grows (page 220)
variety (vər • ī′ • ə • tē) *n.* a number of different things (page 228)
migrating (mī′ • grāt′ • ing) *adj.* moving from one place to another (page 233)

Unit 2

Unit Review

Comprehension Strategies and Skills

Small Group

Organize students into five teams. Have each team review one of the comprehension strategies or skills. Then have the teams share their strategy or skill and examples with the class.

Author's Purpose is the purpose the author had for writing the text. Readers can sort out what is important in a text from what is less important. Knowing the author's purpose gives readers an idea of what they can expect to find in the text. Have students review the selections in Unit 2. Ask students what the author's purpose was for writing each of the selections in this unit.

Predicting helps readers analyze information given about story events and characters in the context of how it may logically connect to the story's conclusion. Ask students what predictions they made as they read the selections in this unit.

Making Inferences is when readers use clues and suggestions from the text and their own background information to form a more complete picture of the story. Ask students what clues they found in the selections and what background information they used to help them understand the meaning of the selections.

Making Connections is when readers activate prior knowledge and connect what they know or have experienced to what they are reading. Ask students to share connections they made when reading the selections in this unit.

Classify and Categorize helps readers put like things or ideas together to make new ideas and information easier to understand. Ask students how they could classify and categorize the selections in this unit.

Reading with a Writer's Eye

Small Group

In their teams, have students review one of the following literary elements. When they are finished, ask each team to share their literary elements and examples with the class.

Text Structure: Technique is how an author explains and organizes facts and information. Ask students to review the selections in this unit and find examples of how authors organized their material.

Setting is the time and place or places where the story occurs. Ask students to review the text and find examples of settings in each of the selections in this unit. Have students list details provided by the writer that describe the settings.

Author's Purpose is the reason an author writes a story. Ask students what the author's purpose was for writing each of the selections in this unit. Have students find details in the selections which support the purpose or purposes they choose.

Characterization is how the author describes and portrays his or her characters. Ask students to describe the different characters in this unit's selections. Have students go back to the text and find details that support their descriptions.

Language Use is how an author uses words in a story. Ask students about the precise terminology and vivid descriptions found in this unit's selections. Have students review the selections and find examples to share with the class.

Fluency

Whole Group

Write the sentences on the board and model reading them aloud. Point out how you paused after the commas. Choose a few students to read the sentences aloud, pausing after the commas. Continue this process until students are reading the sentences fluently.

- The birds chirp, squawk, and sing.
- The chipmunks burrow, cuddle, and chew.
- The deer pranced through the meadow, bounded over the fence, and darted into the forest.

Unit 2

Unit Review

Spelling

Review spelling words from Lessons 1–5 with students. Say each word, and have students write it on a sheet of paper. When you are finished, have students exchange papers with a partner. Write each word on the board, and have students pick their partner's spelling.

Lesson 1		
fly	replies	knights
Lesson 2		
mice	oxen	float
Lesson 3		
ring	change	view
Lesson 4		
groan	grown	tale
Lesson 5		
clue	tuna	noodle

Study Skills

Review the following skills with students.

- **Taking Notes** Invite students to share how note taking has helped them in their research for unit investigations and writing assignments.
- **Tables and Charts** Have students share how they used tables and charts in their unit investigations and writing assignments.
- **Diagrams** Have students share how they used diagrams in their unit investigations and writing assignments.
- **Organizing Information** Invite students to share how they organized information when preparing for and presenting their unit investigations. Ask students to discuss how they organized information in their writing assignments.
- **Index** Ask students to locate the indexes in their textbooks. Ask students to discuss how this knowledge helps them during research projects.

Listening/ Speaking/ Viewing

Review the following skills with students.

- **Asking Questions** In pairs, have students take turns asking and answering questions. Have them take the time to carefully form their questions.
- **Listening and Responding** Remind students that listeners need to pay attention to get the most information from the speaker. When responding, speakers need to speak loudly and slowly with well informed questions and answers.
- **Using Visual Aids** Remind students that visual aids make oral presentations more informative and exciting. Visual aids help draw the attention of the audience to the additional information.
- **Recalling Information Presented Orally** Ask students to remind you why retelling and paraphrasing are good skills to practice. If we can paraphrase a story in our own words and then retell it, we are able to share the story or the information we learned with others.
- **Chronological Order** Ask students to remind you why the chronological order of events is one way to present information in an oral presentation. **Possible Answer** *We can select the major points or events we wish to discuss, and then list them in the order in which they happened.*

Grammar, Usage, and Mechanics

To review Lessons 1–5, write the following letter on the board. Ask students to identify possessive pronouns, regular plurals, nouns as subjects, pronouns as subjects, and pronouns as objects.

Dear Director Richards:

I would like to apply for a student volunteer position at the Wildlife Rescue and Rehabilitation Center. Mr. Amory, my social studies teacher, is recommending me for this position. He knows me well and thinks I would do well at the center. I love animals, the environment, and helping in the community. My goal is to be a veterinarian someday. I have attached my school report cards and a list of my activities. I hope I will be able to work for you. Thank you for your time.

Sincerely,
M. S. Bergh

possessive pronouns: my, your
regular plurals: animals, cards, activities
nouns as subjects: Mr. Amory, goal
pronouns as subjects: I, He
pronouns as objects: me, you

Unit 2

Benchmark Assessment

Day 9

Monitor Progress

Formal Assessment Options

You will need the following materials, along with your informal observations and ***Lesson Assessment*** results, to monitor student progress throughout the year.

Monitor student progress using ***SRA Imagine It!*** assessment tools.

Technology

- ***eAssess***
- ***eAssess CD-ROM***

Benchmark Assessment for Unit 2 addresses the following skills:

- **Phonics**
- **Vocabulary**
- **Comprehension**
- **Grammar, Usage, and Mechanics**
- **Spelling**

Results on ***Benchmark Assessment*** will serve as a performance indicator that shows how well students are prepared to take an end-of-the-year standardized test. ***Benchmark Assessment*** results also will allow you to intervene with students who are at risk for failure.

Monitor Progress with Benchmark Assessment

Below are two sets of ***Benchmark Assessment*** cutoffs that can be used for predicting student performance—one for Benchmark Skills Assessments and the other for Oral Fluency Assessments. Each cutoff begins with a baseline score under Benchmark 1, which is given at the beginning of the year and ends with Benchmark 7, which is given at the end of the year. The cutoffs are determined by finding the amount of growth a student must make over the course of the year to ensure he or she will not be at risk for reading failure.

Benchmark Skills Assessment

The Benchmark Skills Assessment is a 100-point test, consisting of questions covering phonics; vocabulary; comprehension; grammar, usage, and mechanics; and spelling. The table below shows how many points out of 100 third-grade students should score on a particular Benchmark Skills Assessment over the course of the year. The highlighted score indicates where your students should be at this time.

Benchmark 1	Benchmark 2	Benchmark 3	Benchmark 4	Benchmark 5	Benchmark 6	Benchmark 7
20	30	42	54	66	78	90

Oral Fluency Assessment

The Oral Fluency Assessment is an individually administered assessment, consisting of a passage that students read aloud to the teacher to assess how many words per minute students can read fluently. The table below shows how many words per minute third-grade students should read on a particular Oral Fluency Assessment over the course of the year. The highlighted score indicates where your students should be at this time.

Benchmark 1	Benchmark 2	Benchmark 3	Benchmark 4	Benchmark 5	Benchmark 6	Benchmark 7
44	60	75	91	106	122	137

Independent Tools to Monitor Progress

DIBELS and TPRI

Based on your DIBELS or TPRI scores, use the appropriate ***Leveled Reader*** or the fluency passages from the ***Workshop Resource Book.***

Unit 2

Unit Celebration

Day 10

BIG Idea

Where do animals live?

Write the Big Idea question on the board. Ask students what they learned about animals and their habitats. Which selections added something new to students' understanding of animals and their habitats? Encourage students to share their thoughts about the unit overall.

Theme Wrap-Up and Review

Small Group

Have students look in ***Student Reader,*** Book 1 at the five selections. Have students choose which selection they liked best. Organize students into small groups based on the selections they chose. Within their small groups, have students

- retell the selection.
- tell why they liked the selection.
- identify ways in which the selection related to the theme.
- share their ideas with the class.

Ask students to discuss their thoughts and feelings about the unit. To begin a discussion, ask the following questions:

- *What did you find most interesting about animal habitats?*
- *What is important about preserving animal habitats?*
- *What kinds of animal habitats do you often observe?*
- *How can you help preserve some animal habitats?*

Unit Review

Discuss with students how sharing knowledge helps us and others learn. Ask them how they would like to share what they have learned about animals and their habitats. For example, students may choose to

- tell a story or show pictures to the class or their friends and family about animal habitats they have observed or experienced.
- create a list of animal habitats they think need protection and preservation along with reasons why those habitats need protection.
- write and illustrate a story about an animal habitat they would like to study or be a part of.

Concept/Question Board

- ✦ Have students review items on the **Concept/Question Board.**
- ✦ Ask students to suggest other ideas related to animals and their habitats that they could learn more about.
- ✦ Discuss how students' ideas about animals and their habitats have changed over the course of the unit.

Pronunciation Key

a as in **a**t	**ô** as in b**ou**ght and r**aw**	**ə** as in **a**bout, chick**e**n, penc**i**l, cann**o**n, circ**u**s
ā as in l**a**te	**oi** as in c**oi**n	**ch** as in **ch**air
â as in c**a**re	**o͝o** as in b**oo**k	**hw** as in **wh**ich
ä as in f**a**ther	**o͞o** as in t**oo**	**ng** as in ri**ng**
e as in s**e**t	**or** as in f**or**m	**sh** as in **sh**op
ē as in m**e**	**ou** as in **ou**t	**th** as in **th**in
i as in **i**t	**u** as in **u**p	**t̸h** as in **th**ere
ī as in k**i**te	**ū** as in **u**se	**zh** as in trea**s**ure
o as in **o**x	**ûr** as in t**ur**n, g**er**m, l**ear**n, f**ir**m, w**or**k	
ō as in r**o**se		

The mark (´) is placed after a syllable with a heavy accent, as in **chicken** (**chik**´ ən).

The mark (´) after a syllable shows a lighter accent, as in **disappear** (**dis**´ əp pēr´).

Glossary

A

aboard (ə bord´) *adv.* On or into a ship, a train, or an airplane.

actually (ak´ shū əl lē´) *adv.* In fact; really.

adopt (əd opt´) *v.* To take and use as one's own.

affection (əf fek´ shən) *n.* A friendly feeling of liking or loving.

ancient (ān´ shənt) *adj.* Very old.

announced (ə nounst´) *v.* Past tense of **announce:** To make known.

apathetic (ap´ əth et´ ic) *adj.* Having or showing little interest, concern, or desire to act.

appointed (əp point´ əd) *v.* A form of the verb **appoint:** To name for an office.

appreciate (əp prē´ shē āt´) *v.* To understand the value of.

assure (əsh ûr´) *v.* To make certain or sure.

astonished (ə ston´ isht) *adj.* Greatly surprised.

bacteria (bak tēr´ ē ə) *n.* Plural form of **bacterium:** A tiny living cell that can be seen only through a microscope. Some cause disease; others help, such as making soil richer.

bacteria

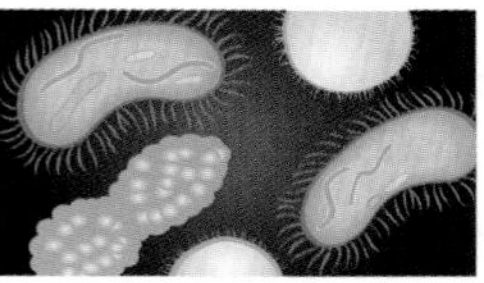

balance (bal´ əns) *v.* To make equal in weight, amount, or force. *n.* A steady, secure position.

barber (bär´ bûr) *n.* A person whose work is cutting hair, and shaving and trimming beards.

Pronunciation Key: **a**t; l**ā**te; c**â**re; f**ä**ther; s**e**t; m**ē**; **i**t; k**ī**te; **o**x; r**ō**se; **ô** in b**ou**ght; c**oi**n; b**o͝o**k; t**o͞o**; f**or**m; **ou**t; **u**p; **ū**se; t**û**rn; **ə** sound in **a**bout, chick**e**n, penc**i**l, cann**o**n, circ**u**s; **ch**air; **hw** in **wh**ich; ri**ng**; **sh**op; **th**in; **t̸h**ere; **zh** in trea**s**ure.

bargain (bär´ gən) *n.* An agreement to trade.

barter (bär´ dûr) *n.* The trade of one thing for another without using money.

beckoned (bek´ ənd) *v.* Past tense of **beckon:** To call someone by waving.

benefit (ben´ ə fit) *n.* Something that helps or that is good for a person.

blooming (blo͞om ing) *v.* A form of the verb **bloom:** To flower; to blossom.

boards (bordz) *n.* Plural form of **board:** A long, flat piece of sawed wood.

bore (bōr) *v.* To make a hole by digging or drilling.

bother (bot̸h´ ûr) *v.* To annoy.

break (brāk) *n.* A short rest period.

brightened (brī´ tənd) *v.* Past tense of **brighten:** To light up.

bringing up (bring´ ing up) *n.* Raising, as in children.

bundled (bun´ dəld) *v.* Past tense of **bundle:** To wrap together.

causes (koz´ əz) *n.* Plural form of **cause:** Something a person or group believes in.

cautiously (kosh´ əs lē´) *adv.* With close care.

certain (sûr´ tən) *adj.* Sure.

challenge (chal´ lənj) *v.* To question the truth of.

charged (chärjd) *v.* Past tense of **charge:** To ask a price.

chores (chorz) *n.* Plural form of **chore:** A small job.

chores

city limits (sit´ ē lim´ its) *n.* The points at which the city ends.

civil rights (siv´ əl rīts´) *n.* Plural form of **civil right:** The rights of every citizen of a country, including the right to vote and the right to equal protection under the law.

clung (klung) *v.* Past tense of **cling:** To stick closely.

collected (kəl lekt´ əd) *v.* A form of the verb **collect:** To gather together.

colony (kol´ ən ē) *n.* A group of animals or plants of the same kind that live together.

compete (kəm pēt´) *v.* To try to win.

competition (kom´ pə ti´ shən) *n.* The act of trying to win or gain something from another or others.

completely (kəm plēt´ lē) *adv.* Entirely.

condition (kən dish´ ən) *n.* Something needed for another event to happen.

consumer (kən so͞om´ ûr) *n.* A person who uses goods and services.

counterfeit (koun´ tûr fit´) *adj.* Fake.

county (coun´ tē) *n.* Part of a state.

cozy (cō´ zē) *adj.* Warm and comfortable.

curious (kyur´ ē əs) *adj.* Interested in knowing.

currency (kûr´ ren sē) *n.* Money—coins and paper—that people use.

customer (kus´ təm ûr´) *n.* A person who buys something at a store or uses the services of a business.

dawn (dôn) *n.* The first light that appears in the morning; daybreak.

deal (dēl) *n.* An agreement.

debts (dets) *n.* Plural form of **debt:** Something that is owed to another.

delayed (də lād´) *v.* Past tense of **delay:** To put off to a later time.

demand (də mand´) *n.* The desire for a product or service.

depended (də pend´ əd) *v.* Past tense of **depend:** To rely on; to trust.

deserted (də zûrt´ əd) *v.* A form of the verb **desert:** To leave alone.

Pronunciation Key: at; lāte; câre; fäther; set; mē; it; kīte; ox; rōse; ô in bought; coin; bo͝ok; to͞o; form; out; up; ūse; tûrn; ə sound in about, chicken, pencil, cannon, circus; chair; hw in which; ring; shop; thin; there; zh in treasure.

design (də zīn´) *n.* A drawing made to serve as a pattern.

design

despair (də spâr´) *n.* A complete loss of hope.

detect (də tekt´) *v.* To find out.

disappointed (dis əp point´ əd) *v.* A form of the verb **disappoint:** To make someone unhappy that something expected did not occur.

dither (dith´ ûr) *n.* A confused, upset feeling.

dwellers (dwel´ ûrz) *n.* Plural form of **dweller:** A person or an animal that lives in a certain place.

ecosystem (ek´ ō sis´ təm) *n.* A group of living things and the environment in which they live.

emblem (em´ bləm) *n.* A sign or figure that stands for something.

energy (en´ ûr jē) *n.* The strength or eagerness to do something.

enormous (ē nor´ məs) *adj.* Very big.

enthusiastic (en tho͞o´ zē ast´ ik) *adj.* Very excited about something.

environment (en vī´ rən mənt´) *n.* The surroundings that affect living things.

equal (ē´ kwəl) *n.* Someone who is at the same level as others.

equipment (ə kwip´ mənt) *n.* Tools and supplies used for a given purpose.

especially (is pesh´ əl lē) *adv.* Particularly.

eventually (ē ven´ chə lē´) *adv.* Finally.

examine (egz am´ in) *v.* To look at in detail.

examine

except (ek sept´) *prep.* Only.

exchange (eks chānj´) *n.* A trade of one thing for another.

exclaimed (eks klāmd´) *v.* Past tense of **exclaim:** To speak out.

expanded (eks pand´ əd) *v.* A form of the verb **expand:** To make larger or become larger.

expenses (eks pens´ əz) *n.* Plural form of **expense:** Money spent to buy or do something; cost.

explorer (eks plor´ ûr) *n.* A person who travels in search of geographical or scientific information.

extended (eks tend´ əd) *v.* Past tense of **extend:** To reach out.

F

factory (fak´ tûr ē) *n.* A building or group of buildings where things are manufactured; a plant.

factory

failing (fāl´ ing) *adj.* Losing money.

faith (fāth) *n.* Belief or trust in someone's ability or goodness.

farewell (fâr wel´) *adj.* Good-bye and good luck.

female (fē´ māl) *n.* A woman or girl.

flapped (flapt) *v.* Past tense of **flap:** To move up and down, as in wings.

flattered (fla´ tərd) *v.* A form of the verb **flatter:** To praise too much without meaning it.

foreign (for´ ən)) *adj.* Of or from another country.

Pronunciation Key: at; lāte; câre; fäther; set; mē; it; kīte; ox; rōse; ô in bought; coin; bo͝ok; to͞o; form; out; up; ūse; tûrn; ə sound in about, chicken, pencil, cannon, circus; chair; hw in which; ring; shop; thin; there; zh in treasure.

forms (formz) *n.* Plural form of **form:** Kind; type.

formula (for´ mū lə´) *n.* A set method for doing something.

freely (frē´ lē) *adv.* Without cost.

fungi (fun´ gī) *n.* Plural form of **fungus:** A large group of living things that have cell walls similar to those in plants, but that have no flowers, leaves, or green coloring. Fungi live on plant or animal matter.

gathered (gath´ ûr d) *v.* Past tense of **gather:** To bring together; to collect.

glum (glum) *adj.* Very unhappy or disappointed.

graduate (graj´ ū āt´) *v.* To finish at a school and be given a diploma.

graduation (graj´ ū ā´ shən) *n.* Ceremony for finishing at a school.

grateful (grāt´ fəl) *adj.* Thankful.

grazed (grāzd) *v.* Past tense of **graze:** To feed on grass or other plants.

grief (grēf) *n.* A very great feeling of being sad.

habitats (hab´ it ats´) *n.* Plural form of **habitat:** The place where an animal or a plant naturally lives and grows.

hatch (hach) *v.* To come out of an egg.

heartbroken (härt´ brō´ kən) *adj.* Filled with sorrow or grief.

hired (hîûr d) *v.* Past tense of **hire:** To give a job to; to employ.

hitched (hicht) *v.* Past tense of **hitch:** To tie up with a rope, strap, or hook.

hoes (hōz) *n.* Plural form of **hoe:** A tool used to loosen soil around plants and dig up weeds.

hoe

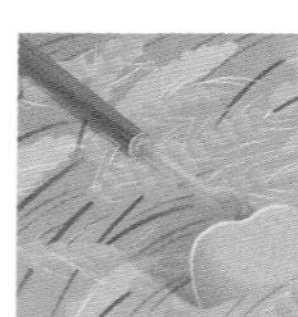

hollow (hol´ lō) *adj.* Having a hole or an empty space inside.

honesty (ôn´əs tē) *n.* Truthfulness.

hooves (ho͞ovz) *n.* Plural form of **hoof:** A hard covering on the feet of animals such as horses and cows.

host (hōst) *n.* A person who invites people to visit as guests.

humiliations (hū mil ē ā´ shənz) *n.* Plural form of **humiliation:** A feeling of shame or extreme embarrassment.

ignore (ig nor´) *v.* To pay no attention to.

insisted (in sist´ əd) *v.* Past tense of **insist:** To demand or say in a strong, firm manner.

inspect (in spekt´) *v.* To look at closely.

jealous (jel´ əs) *adj.* Being angry or upset because of what a person has or can do.

kindness (kīnd´ nəs) *n.* Showing gentle and caring behavior toward others.

kingdom (king´ dəm) *n.* A country that is ruled by a king or a queen.

lawyers (lô´ yərz´) *n.* Plural form of **lawyer:** A person who has studied the law and can give legal advice and represent people in court.

layer (lā´ ûr) *n.* One thickness of something.

layer

Student Reader Glossary

Pronunciation Key: at; lāte; câre; fäther; set; mē; it; kīte; ox; rōse; ô in bought; coin; bŏŏk; tōō; form; out; up; ūse; tûrn; ə sound in about, chicken, pencil, cannon, circus; chair; hw in which; ring; shop; thin; there; zh in treasure.

leagues (lēgz) *n.* Plural form of **league:** A group of teams.

ledges (ledg´ əz) *n.* Plural form of **ledge:** A narrow shelf or surface like a shelf.

legal tender (lē´ gəl ten´ dûr) *n.* Legally valid money that may be offered in payment of a debt.

line (līn) *v.* To cover the inside of.

lotion (lō´ shən) *n.* A special liquid for the skin that heals, soothes, softens, or cleans.

magnificent (mag nif´ is ənt´) *adj.* Very beautiful and grand; splendid.

mainland (mān´ lənd) *n.* The chief landmass of a country, or continent, as different from an island.

male (māl) *adj.* Of or having to do with men or boys.

managed (man´ ijd) *v.* Past tense of **manage:** To direct or control.

marbles (mär´ bəlz) *n.* Plural form of **marble:** A small, hard ball of glass used in games.

maze (māz) *n.* A confusing series of paths or passageways through which people might get lost.

maze

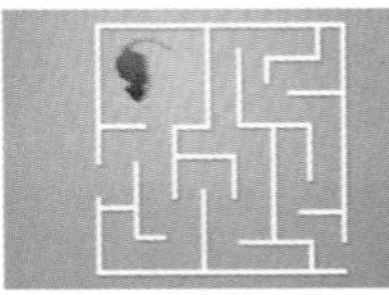

meadows (med´ ōz)) *n.* Plural form of **meadow:** A field of grassy land used as a pasture for animals.

mercy (mûr´ sē) *n.* Kindness or forgiveness greater than what is expected or deserved.

migrating (mī´ grāt´ ing) *adj.* Moving from one place to another.

mild (mīld) *adj.* Gentle or calm; not harsh or sharp.

millionaire (mil´ yə nâr´) *n.* A person who has money or property worth a million or more dollars.

miserable (miz´ ûr ə bəl´) *adj.* Very unhappy.

misfortune (mis for´ chən) *n.* Bad luck.

moist (moist) *adj.* Slightly wet; damp.

molt (mōlt) *v.* To lose or shed hair, feathers, skin, or a shell.

molt

mood (mōōd) *n.* The way a person feels at a certain time.

moped (mōp d) *v.* Past tense of **mope:** To act sad and gloomy.

nation (nā´ shən) *n.* A country.

nervous (nûr´ vəs) *adj.* Uneasy.

notes (nōts) *n.* Plural form of **note:** A piece of paper with a written promise to pay someone a sum of money.

operation (op´ ûr ā´ shən) *n.* Treatment on a person or an animal by surgery.

opponents (əp pō´ nəntz) *n.* Plural form of **opponent:** A person on the other side.

opportunity (op´ pûr tōō´ nə tē) *n.* A good chance to do something.

opposing (əp pōz´ ing) *adj.* Against something or someone.

organizations (or´ gən ə zā´ shənz) *n.* Plural form of **organization:** A group of people joined together for a purpose.

pale (pāl) *adj.* Not bright in color.

partners (pärt´ nûrz) *n.* Plural form of **partner:** A person who runs a business with one or more other persons.

Pronunciation Key: at; lāte; câre; fäther; set; mē; it; kīte; ox; rōse; ô in bought; coin; bŏŏk; tōō; form; out; up; ūse; tûrn; ə sound in about, chicken, pencil, cannon, circus; chair; hw in which; ring; shop; thin; there; zh in treasure.

pastel (pas tel´) *adj.* A pale, soft shade of a color.

patch (pach) *n.* A small area.

patient (pā´ shənt) *adj.* Willing to wait.

peculiar (pi kūl´ yər´) *adj.* Not usual; strange.

peer pressure (pēr´ presh´ ûr) *n.* Peers are people who are the same age or in the same group. Peer pressure is when one or more members of the group try to influence one another in the group.

permission (pûr mish´ ən) *n.* When an adult allows one to do something.

persuaded (pûr swād´ əd) *v.* Past tense of **persuade:** To convince.

picturing (pik´ shûr ing´) *adj.* Visualizing; making a picture in one's own mind.

plains (plānz) *n.* Plural form of **plain:** An area of flat, or almost flat, land.

plains

plumpest (plump´ əst) *adj.* Fullest and roundest.

pond (pond) *n.* A small lake.

population (pop´ ū lā´ shən) *n.* The number of people or animals who live in a place.

portrait (por´ trət) *n.* A picture of someone.

possess (pəz zes´) *v.* To have; to own.

prejudice (predj´ ə dis´) *n.* Hatred or unfair treatment of a particular group, such as members of a race or religion.

presses (pres´ əz) *n.* Plural form of **press:** A printing machine.

prey (prā) *n.* An animal that is hunted by another animal for food.

product (prod´ uct) *n.* Anything that is made or created.

profit (prof´ it) *n.* The amount of money left after all the costs of running a business have been paid.

protect (prə tekt´) *v.* To keep something or someone safe.

proud (proud) *adj.* Having a strong sense of satisfaction in a person or thing.

provide (prō vīd´) *v.* To give what is needed or wanted.

provoke (prə vōk´) *v.* To make angry.

pyramid (pē´ rəm id´) *n.* An object that has triangular sides that meet at a point at the top.

pyramid

raft (raft) *n.* A kind of flat boat made of logs or boards fixed firmly together.

recognize (rek´ əg nīz´) *v.* To know and remember from before; to identify.

relative (rel´ ə tiv) *n.* A person who belongs to the same family as someone else.

relocates (rē´ lō´ kāts) *v.* A form of the verb **relocate:** To move to a new place.

remained (rē mānd´) *v.* Past tense of **remain:** To be left.

remains (rē mānz´) *v.* A form of the verb **remain:** To be left.

resist (rə zist´) *v.* To keep from giving in to.

responded (rə spônd´ əd) *v.* Past tense of **respond:** To answer.

responsibility (ri spon´ sə bi´ li tē) *n.* A duty.

rich (rich) *adj.* Able to produce much; fertile.

ripest (rīp´ əst) *adj.* The readiest to be eaten; very ripe.

roost (rōōst) *v.* To rest or sleep as a bird does.

rule (rōōl) *v.* To have control over.

Pronunciation Key: at; lāte; câre; fäther; set; mē; it; kīte; ox; rōse; ô in bought; coin; bŏŏk; tōō; form; out; up; ūse; tûrn; ə sound in about, chicken, pencil, cannon, circus; chair; hw in which; ring; shop; thin; there; zh in treasure.

sacrifice (sak´ rə fīs´) *n.* Something a person gives up for the sake of someone else.

savings (sāv´ ingz´) *pl. n.* Money saved, or set aside, for use in the future.

seal (sēl) *n.* An official stamp.

secretary (sek´ rə tâ´ rē) *n.* A person whose job is to write letters and keep records for another person or a business.

segregated (seg´ rə gāt´ əd) *v.* A form of the verb **segregate:** To set apart.

segregation (se grə gā´ shən) *n.* The practice of setting one group apart from another.

serial numbers (sē´ rē əl num´ bûrz) *n.* Plural form of **serial number:** A number in a series used for identification.

serial numbers

series (sē´ rēz) *pl. n.* Several in a row.

settled down (set´ təld doun) *v.* Past tense of **settle down:** To make one's home.

several (sev´ ər əl) *adj.* More than two, but not many.

severe (səv ēr´) *adj.* Strict.

shallow (shal´ lō) *adj.* Not deep.

sharp (shärp) *adj.* Alert.

shelter (shel´ tûr) *n.* Something that covers or protects from weather or danger.

sighed (sīd) *v.* Past tense of **sigh:** To make a long, deep breathing sound because of sadness, tiredness, or relief.

splendor (splen´ dûr) *n.* A great display, as of riches or beautiful objects.

sold out (sōld out) *v.* A form of the verb **sell out:** To sell all of the items that were for sale.

solemnly (sol´ əm lē´) *adv.* Seriously.

solution (sə lōō´ shən) *n.* The answer to a problem.

stack (stak) *n.* A pile.

stack

stamped (stampt) *v.* Past tense of **stamp:** To mark with a tool that makes or prints a design, numbers, or letters.

stand (stand) *n.* A booth or counter where things are sold.

stations (stā´ shənz) *n.* Plural form of **station:** A place where a service is performed.

stored (stord) *v.* A form of the verb **store:** To put away for future use.

stranded (strand´ əd) *v.* A form of the verb **strand:** To leave in a helpless position.

strange (strānj) *adj.* Unusual.

streaked (strēkt) *v.* Past tense of **streak:** To mark with long, thin marks.

struggled (stru´ gəld) *v.* Past tense of **struggle:** To make a great effort.

sued (sōōd) *v.* Past tense of **sue:** To start a case against in a court of law.

suffer (suf´ fûr) *v.* To have pain or sorrow.

suited (sōōt´ əd) *v.* Past tense of **suit:** To meet the needs of.

supply (səp plī´) *n.* A quantity of something ready to be used.

suppose (səp pōz´) *v.* To imagine being possible.

surface (sûr´ fəs) *n.* The outside of a thing.

surrounding (sûr round´ ing) *adj.* Forming a circle around.

survive (sûr vīv´) *v.* To live through; to continue to exist.

swamps (swämps) *n.* Plural form of **swamp:** An area of wet land which may have trees and shrubs growing in it.

Pronunciation Key: at; lāte; câre; fäther; set; mē; it; kīte; ox; rōse; ô in bought; coin; bŏŏk; tōō; form; out; up; ūse; tûrn; ə sound in about, chicken, pencil, cannon, circus; chair; hw in which; ring; shop; thin; there; zh in treasure.

swarming (sworm´ ing) *adj.* Moving in a large group.

territory (ter´ rit or´ ē) *n.* Any large area of land, usually owned by someone or by a country.

thoughtfulness (thot´ fəl nəs´) *n.* Showing concern for others and their feelings.

timidly (tim´ id lē) *adv.* In a way that shows shyness or a lack of courage.

traders (trā´ dûrz) *n.* Plural form of **trader:** A person who buys and sells things as a business.

trainers (trā´ nûrz) *n.* Plural form of **trainer:** One who teaches people or animals.

trainer

translation (tranz lā´ shən) *n.* A changing of a speech or piece of writing into another language.

treated (trēt´ əd) *v.* A form of the verb **treat:** To act a certain way toward someone.

trusted (trust´ əd) *v.* Past tense of **trust:** To believe to be true, honest, or reliable.

unconscious (un kon´ shəs) *adj.* Not awake.

valuable (val´ ū bəl´) *adj.* Worth much money.

variety (vər ī´ ə tē´) *n.* A number of different things.

vast (vast) *adj.* Very great in size.

waddled (wä´ dəld) *v.* Past tense of **waddle:** To walk with short steps, swaying the body from side to side.

warned (wornd) *v.* Past tense of **warn:** To tell about something that may happen; put on guard.

wealth (welth) *n.* Riches.

weighs (wāz) *v.* A form of the verb **weigh:** To be of a certain heaviness.

weigh

whined (hwīnd) *v.* Past tense of **whine:** To cry in a soft, high, complaining voice.

wildlife (wīld´ līf) *n.* Living things, especially animals, in their natural environments.

worried (wûr´ rēd) *v.* A form of the verb **worry:** To think about troubles.

worth (wûrth) *prep.* Equal in value to. *n.* The money that someone is willing to pay for something.

Appendices

Unit 2 • NAT-L3-U2-6-A

SRA
Imagine It!

SRA Imagine It!

The Program Appendix includes a step-by-step explanation of procedures for research-based, effective practices in reading instruction that are repeatedly used throughout ***SRA Imagine It!*** These practices may also be used in other instructional materials.

Table of Contents

Phonological and Phonemic Awareness

The key to learning to read is the ability to identify different sounds and to connect those sounds to the letters of the alphabet. The basic purpose of providing structured practice in phonemic awareness is to help students hear and understand the sounds from which words are made. Before students can be expected to understand the sound/symbol correspondence that forms the base of written English, they need to have a strong working knowledge of the sound relationships that make up the spoken language. This understanding of spoken language lays the foundation for the transition to written language.

Phonological awareness is an umbrella term. It incorporates a range of oral language skills that involve the ability to notice, think about, and manipulate individual sounds in words. Phonological awareness involves working with sentences, words, rhyme, syllables, and sounds. The objective is for students to be able to manipulate words, word parts, and sounds without regard to meaning.

Phonological and phonemic awareness activities initially provide students with the opportunity to think about sentences and to break them into words and then to play with words and to break them into parts. It involves easy and fun activities that engage students in playing with and exploring the parts and sounds of language. The goal of these gamelike activities is to help students understand that speech is made of distinct, identifiable sounds. The playful nature of the activities makes them appealing and engaging, while giving students practice and support for learning about language. When students begin reading and writing, this experience with manipulating sounds will help them use what they know about sounds and letters to sound out and spell unfamiliar words when they read and write.

Developing phonological awareness engages students in activities that move from working with words and syllables — the larger units of language — to individual sounds (phonemes). Students progress by

- Identifying sentences
- Identifying words
- Working with rhymes
- Exploring compound words
- Listening for syllables
- Blending syllables
- Oral blending
- Deleting and substituting sounds
- Segmenting phonemes

As students progress through various phonemic awareness activities, they will become proficient at listening for and reproducing the sounds they hear. It is essential for their progression to phonics and reading that they are able to hear the sounds and the patterns used to make up recognizable words. The phonemic awareness activities support the phonics instruction. Initially students are not expected to read the words they are exploring and manipulating, so any consonant and vowel sounds may be used, even if students have not been formally taught the sounds and their spellings.

As students progress through various phonemic awareness activities, they will become proficient at listening for and reproducing the sounds they hear.

After students have an awareness of phonemes, they can begin to connect sounds to letters and to engage in a variety of activities in which sounds and letters are substituted to make new words. Students begin to understand that if a sound changes, a letter must change, and a new word is created. As students move into phonics, research suggests that connecting sounds to spellings actually heightens their awareness of language. Phonological and phonemic awareness is both a prerequisite for and a consequence of learning to read.

Research suggests that the majority of instructional time should be focused on two critical phonemic awareness formats: phoneme or oral blending and phoneme segmentation. These are supported by discrimination and elision activities (deleting and substituting sounds) and general wordplay. Oral blending encourages students to combine sounds to make words and lays the foundation for decoding and reading. Segmentation, conversely, requires students to break words into discrete sounds and lays the foundation for spelling. Other activities support discrimination, or recognition, of particular sounds. Sometimes simple songs, rhymes, or games engage students in wordplay. In these, students manipulate words in a variety of ways. From these playful activities, students develop serious knowledge about their language.

Oral Blending

Purpose

In oral blending, students are led through a progression of activities designed to help them hear how sounds are put together to make words.

Until students develop an awareness of the component parts of words, they have no tools with which to decode words or to put letters together to form words. Oral blending helps students understand these component parts of words, from syllables down to single sounds, or phonemes. Oral blending is not to be confused with the formal blending of specific sounds whose spellings students will be taught through phonics instruction. Oral blending does not depend on the recognition of written words; it focuses instead on hearing the sounds.

Oral blending focuses on hearing sounds through a sequence that introduces the most easily distinguished word parts and then systematically moves to oral blending of individual sounds that contains all the challenges of phonic decoding (except letter recognition). This sequence provides support for the least-prepared student—one who comes to school with no concept of words or sounds within words. At the same time, the lively pace and playful nature of oral blending activities hold the interest of students who already have some familiarity with words and letters.

Oral blending prepares students for phonics instruction by developing an awareness of the separate sounds that make up speech. Oral blending activities then continue in concert with phonics instruction to reinforce and extend new learning. And because these activities involve simply listening to and reproducing sounds, oral blending need not be restricted to the sounds students have been or will be taught in phonics.

The tone of the activities should be playful and informal and should move quickly. Although these activities will provide information about student progress, they are not diagnostic tools. Do not expect mastery. Those students who have not caught on will be helped more by varied experiences than by more drilling on the same activity.

Procedure

The following is a description of the progression of oral blending activities.

Word-Part Blending

Syllables are easier to distinguish than individual sounds (phonemes), so students can quickly experience success in forming meaningful words. Tell students that you are going to say some words in two parts. Tell them to listen carefully so they can discover what the words are. Read each word, pronouncing each part distinctly with a definite pause between syllables. The lists of words that follow are arranged in sequence from easy to harder. They cover different types of cues. Whenever they fit into the sequence, include multisyllabic names of students in the class.

Model

Teacher: dino . . . saur. What's the word?
Students: dinosaur

Example Words

- First part of the word cues the whole word:
  vita . . . min
  vaca . . . tion
  hippopot . . . amus
  ambu . . . lance
- Two distinct words easily combined:
  butter. . . fly
  straw. . . berry
  surf . . . board
  basket . . . ball
- Two distinct words, but first word could cue the wrong ending:
  tooth . . . ache
  tooth . . . paste
  water . . . fall
  water . . . melon
- First part, consonant + vowel, not enough to guess whole word:
  re . . . member
  re . . . frigerator
  bi . . . cycle
  bi . . . ology
- Identifying cues in second part:
  light . . . ning
  sub . . . ject
  in . . . sect
- Last part, consonant + vowel sound, carries essential information:
  yester . . . day
  rain . . . bow
  noi . . . sy
  pota . . . to
- Changing the final part changes the word:
  start . . . ing
  start . . . er
  start. . . ed

Initial Consonant Sounds

Initial consonant blending prepares students for consonant replacement activities that will come later. Tell students that you will ask them to put some sounds together to make words. Pronounce each word part distinctly, and make a definite pause at the breaks indicated. When a letter is surrounded by slash marks, pronounce the letter's sound, not its name. When you see /s/, for example, you will say "ssss," not "ess." The words that follow are arranged from easy to harder. Whenever they fit into the sequence, include names of students in the class.

Model

Teacher: /t/ . . . iger. What's the word?
Students: tiger

Example Words

- Separated consonant blend, with rest of word giving strong cue to word identity:
  /b/ . . . roccoli */k/ . . . racker*
  /f/ . . . lashlight */k/ . . . reature*
- Held consonant that is easy for students to hear, with rest of word giving strong cue:
  /s/ . . . innamon */l/ . . . adybug*
  /s/ . . . eventeen */n/ . . .* ewspaper
- Stop consonant that is harder for students to hear preceding vowel, with rest of word giving strong cue:
  /t/. . . adpole */p/ . . . iggybank*
  /d/ . . . ragonfly */b/ . . . arbecue*
- Single-syllable words and words in which the second part gives a weaker cue:
  /s/ . . . ing */l/ . . . augh* */v/ . . . ase*

Final Consonant Sounds

In this phase of oral blending, the last sound in the word is separated.

Model

Teacher: cabba . . . /j/. What's the word?
Students: cabbage

Example Words

- Words that are easily recognized even before the final consonant is pronounced:
  bubblegu . . . /m/ *Columbu . . . /s/*
  crocodi . . . /l/ *submari . . . /n/*
- Multisyllabic words that need the final consonant for recognition:
  colle . . . /j/ (college) *come . . . /t/ (comet)*
- Single-syllable words:
  sa . . . /d/ *gra . . . /s/ (grass)* *snai . . . /l/*

Initial Consonant Sound Replacement

This level of oral blending further develops awareness of initial consonant sounds. The activity begins with a common word then quickly changes its initial consonant sound. Most of the words produced are nonsense words, which helps keep the focus on the sounds in the word. Note that the words are written on the board, but students are not expected to read them. The writing is to help students see that when the sounds change, the letters change, and vice versa.

Model

Teacher: [Writes word on board.] This word is *magazine*. What is it?
Students: magazine
Teacher: Now I'm going to change it. [Erases initial consonant.] Now it doesn't start with /m/; it's going to start with /b/. What's the new word?
Students: bagazine
Teacher: That's right . . . [Writes *b* where *m* had been.] It's *bagazine*. Now I'm going to change it again. . . .

Repeat with different consonant sounds. Then do the same with other words such as *remember, Saturday, tomorrow, lotion,* and *million*. Continue with single-syllable words such as *take, big, boot, cot, seat, look, tap, ride,* and *late*. There are two stages in using written letters:

- The replacement letter is not written until ***after*** the new "word" has been identified.

- Later, the replacement letter is written at ***the same time*** the change in the initial phoneme is announced. For example, erase *d* and write *m* while you say, "Now it doesn't start with /d/; it starts with /m/."

When the consonants used have already been introduced in phonics, you may wish to alter the procedure by writing the replacement letter and having students sound out the new word. Feel free to switch between the two procedures within a single exercise. If students are not responding orally to written spellings that have been introduced in phonics, do not force it. Proceed by saying the word before writing the letter, and wait until another time to move on to writing before pronouncing.

One-Syllable Words

Students now begin blending individual phonemes to form words. This important step can be continued well into the year. Continued repetitions of this activity will help students realize how they can use the sound/spellings they are learning to read and write real words.

At first, the blended words are presented in a story context that helps students identify the words. They soon recognize that they are actually decoding meaningful words. However, the context must not be so strong that students can guess the word without listening to the phonemic cues. Any vowel sounds and irregularly spelled words may be used because there is no writing involved.

Model

Teacher: When I looked out the window, I saw a /l/ /ī/ /t/. What did I see?
Students: A light.
Teacher: Yes, I saw a light. At first I thought it was the /m/ /o͞o/ /n/. What did I think it was?
Students: The moon.
Teacher: But it didn't really look like the moon. Suddenly I thought, maybe it's a space /sh/ /i/ /p/. What did I think it might be?
Students: A spaceship!

When students are familiar with this phase of oral blending, they can move to blending one-syllable words without the story context.

Example Words

- CVC (consonant/vowel/consonant) words beginning with easily blended consonant sounds (/sh/, /h/, /r/, /v/, /s/, /n/, /z/, /f/, /l/, /m/):
  nip nap
- CVC words beginning with any consonant:
  ten bug lip
- Add CCVC words:
  flap step
- Add CVCC words:
  most band went
- Add CCVCC words:
  stamp grand scuffs

Final Consonant Sound Replacement

Final consonant sounds are typically more difficult for students to use than initial consonants.

- Begin with multisyllabic words, and move to one-syllable words.
- As with initial consonants, first write the changed consonant after students have pronounced the new word.
- Then write the consonant as they pronounce it.
- For sound/spellings introduced in phonics instruction, write the new consonant spelling, and have students identify and pronounce it.

Model

Teacher: [Writes word on board.] This word is *teapot*. What is it?
Students: teapot
Teacher: Now I'm going to change it. [Erases final consonant.] Now it doesn't end with /t/; it ends with /p/. What's the word now?
Students: teapop
Teacher: That's right . . . [Writes *p* where *t* had been.] It's *teapop*. Now I'm going to change it again. . . .

Example Words

- Words that are easily recognized even before the final consonant is pronounced:
  picnic picnit picnis picnil picnid
  airplane airplate airplabe airplafe
- Multisyllabic words that need the final consonant for recognition:
  muffin muffil muffim muffip muffit
  amaze amate amake amale amade
- Single-syllable words:
  neat nean neap neam neaj nead neaf
  broom broot brood broof broop broon

Initial Vowel Replacement

Up to now, oral blending has concentrated on consonant sounds because they are easier to hear than vowels. As you move to vowel play, remember that the focus is still on the sounds, not the spellings. Use any vowel sounds.

Model

Teacher: [Writes word on board.] This word is *elephant*. What is it?
Students: elephant
Teacher: Now I'm going to change it. [Erases initial vowel.] Now it doesn't start with /e/; it starts with /a/. What's the word now?
Students: alephant
Teacher: That's right . . . [Writes *a* where *e* had been.] It's *alephant*. Now I'm going to change it again. . . .

Example Words

- Multisyllabic words:
  angry ingry oongry ungry engry
  ivy avy oovy evy ovy oivy
- One-syllable words:
  ink ank oonk unk onk oink
  add odd idd oudd edd udd

Segmentation

Purpose

Segmentation and oral blending complement each other: Oral blending puts sounds together to make words, while segmentation separates words into sounds. Oral blending will provide valuable support for decoding when students begin reading independently.

Procedure

Syllables

The earliest segmentation activities focus on syllables, which are easier to distinguish than individual sounds, or phonemes. Start with students' names, and then use other words. As with the oral blending activities, remember to move quickly through these activities. Do not hold the class back waiting for all students to catch on. Individual progress will vary, but drilling on one activity is less helpful than going on to others. Return to the same activity often. Frequent repetition is very beneficial and allows students additional opportunities to catch on.

- Say, for example, "Let's clap out Amanda's name. A-man-da."
- Have students clap and say the syllables along with you. Count the claps.
- Tell students that these word parts are called syllables. Don't try to explain; the idea will develop with practice. After you have provided the term, simply say, "How many syllables?" after students clap and count.
- Mix one-syllable and multisyllabic words: *fantastic* *tambourine* *good* *imaginary* *stand* *afraid*

Oral blending will provide valuable support for decoding when students begin reading independently.

Comparative Lengths of Words

Unlike most phonemic awareness activities, this one involves writing on the board or on an overhead transparency. Remember, though, that students are not expected to read what is written. They are merely noticing that words that take longer to say generally look longer when written.

- Start with students' names. Choose two names, one short and one long, with the same first letter (for example, *Joe* and *Jonathan*).
- Write the two names on the board, one above the other, so that the difference is obvious.
- Tell students that one name is *Jonathan* and that one is *Joe*. Have them pronounce and clap each name. Then have them tell which written word they think says *Joe*.
- Move your finger under each name as students clap and say it syllable by syllable.
- Repeat with other pairs of names and words such as *tea/telephone, cat/caterpillar, and butterfly/bug.* Be sure not to give false clues. For example, sometimes write the longer word on top, sometimes the shorter one; sometimes ask for the shorter word, sometimes the longer; sometimes ask for the top word, sometimes the bottom; and sometimes point to a word and ask students to name it, and sometimes name the word and ask students to point to it.

Listen for Individual Sounds

Activities using a puppet help students listen for individual sounds in words. Use any puppet you have on hand. When you introduce the puppet, tell students that it likes to play word games. Each new activity begins with the teacher speaking to and for the puppet until students determine the pattern. Next, students either speak for the puppet or correct the puppet. To make sure all students are participating, alternate randomly between having the whole group or individuals respond. The activities focus on particular parts of words, according to the following sequence:

1. Repeating last part of word. Use words beginning with easy-to-hear consonants such as *f, l, m, n, r, s,* and *z.* The puppet repeats only the rime, the part of the syllable after the initial consonant.

Model

Teacher: farm
Puppet: arm
After the pattern is established, students respond for the puppet.
Teacher: rope
Students: ope

Example Words

Use words such as the following:
mine . . . ine *soup . . . oup* *feet . . . eet*

2. Restoring initial phonemes. Now students correct the puppet. Be sure to acknowledge the correction.

Model

Teacher: lake
Puppet: ake
Teacher: No, lllake. You forgot the /l/.
Teacher: real
Puppet: eal
Teacher: What did the puppet leave off?
Students: /r/. It's supposed to be *real.*
Teacher: That's right. The word is *real.*

Example Words

Use words such as the following:
look . . . ook *mouse . . . ouse*
sand . . . and

3. Segmenting initial consonants. The puppet pronounces only the initial consonant.

Model

Teacher: pay
Puppet: /p/

Example Words

Use words such as the following:
moon . . . /m/ *nose . . . /n/* *bell . . . /b/*

4. Restoring final consonants. Students correct the puppet. Prompt if necessary: "What's the word? What did the puppet leave off?"

Model

Teacher: run
Puppet: ru
Students: It's run! You left off the /n/.
Teacher: That's right. The word is *run.*

Example Words

Use words such as the following:
meet. . . mee *cool . . . coo* *boot. . . boo*

5. Isolating final consonants. The puppet pronounces only the final consonant.

Model

Teacher: green
Puppet: /n/

Example Words

Use words such as the following:
glass . . . /s/ *boom . . . /m/* *mice . . . /s/*

6. Segmenting initial consonant blends. The sounds in blends are emphasized.

Model

Teacher: clap
Puppet: lap
Next have students correct the puppet.
Teacher: stain
Puppet: tain
Students: It's stain! You left off the /s/.
Teacher: That's right. The word is *stain.*

Example Words

Use words such as the following:
blaze . . . laze *draw. . . raw*
proud . . . roud

Discrimination

Purpose

Discrimination activities help students focus on particular sounds in words.

Listening for long-vowel sounds is the earliest discrimination activity. Vowel sounds are necessary for decoding, but young students do not hear them easily. This is evident in students' invented spellings, where vowels are often omitted. Early in the year, students listen for long-vowel sounds, which are more easily distinguished than short-vowel sounds:

- ✦ Explain to students that vowels are special because sometimes they say their names in words.
- ✦ Tell students which vowel sound to listen for.
- ✦ Have them repeat the sound when they hear it in a word. For example, if the target-vowel sound is long *e,* students will say long *e* when you say *leaf,* but they should not respond when you say *loaf.*
- ✦ Initially students should listen for one long vowel sound at a time. Later they can listen for two vowel sounds. All Example Words, however, should contain one of the target vowels.

Procedure

Listening for short-vowel sounds

These discrimination activities should be done after the short vowels /a/ and /i/ have been introduced. Short vowels are very useful in reading. They are generally more regular in spelling than long vowels, and they appear in many short, simple words. However, their sounds are less easily distinguished than those of long vowels. Thus, the activities focus only on /a/ and /i/. All the words provided have one or the other of these sounds. Either have students repeat the sound of a specified vowel, or vary the activity as follows: Write an *a* on one side of the board and an *i* on the other. Ask students to point to the *a* when they hear a word with the /a/ sound and to point to the *i* when they hear a word with the /i/ sound. Use words such as the following:

bat mat sat sit spit
pit pat pan pin spin

Consonant sounds in multisyllabic words

Discriminating these sounds helps students attend to consonant sounds in the middle of words.

- ✦ Say the word *rib,* and have students repeat it. Ask where they hear the /b/ in *rib.*
- ✦ Then say *ribbon,* and ask students where they hear the /b/ in *ribbon.*
- ✦ Tell students that you will say some words and that they will repeat each word.
- ✦ After they repeat each word, ask what consonant sound they hear in the middle of that word. Use words such as the following:
  famous message picky
  jogger flavor zipper

Phonemic Play

Purpose

Wordplay activities help students focus on and manipulate sounds, thus supporting the idea that words are made of specific sounds that can be taken apart, put together, or changed to make new words. Through wordplay, students gain important knowledge about language.

Procedure

Producing rhymes

Many phonemic play activities focus on producing rhymes. A familiar or easily learned rhyme or song is introduced, and students are encouraged to substitute words or sounds. An example is "Willaby Wallaby Woo," in which students change the rhyming words in the couplet "Willaby Wallaby Woo/An elephant sat on you" so that the second line ends with a student's name and that the first line ends with a rhyme beginning with *W;* for example, "Willaby Wallaby Wissy/An elephant sat on Missy."

Generate alliterative words

Students can also say as many words as they can think of that begin with a given consonant sound. This is a valuable complement to discrimination activities in which the teacher produces the words and students identify them.

The Alphabetic Principle: How the Alphabet Works

The Alphabetic Principle

Purpose

A major emphasis in the kindergarten program is on letter recognition and attending to sounds. Students need to learn the alphabetic principle: that letters work together in a systematic way to connect spoken language to written words. This understanding is the foundation for reading. Students are not expected to master letter/sound correspondence at the beginning of kindergarten, nor are they expected to blend sounds into words themselves. They are expected to become an "expert" only on their Special Letters as they learn how the alphabet works. Through this introduction to the alphabetic principle, students will have the basic understanding required to work through the alphabet letter by letter, attaching sounds to each.

Key concepts of the alphabetic principle include the following:

- A limited number of letters combine in different ways to make many different words.
- Words are composed of sounds, and letters represent those sounds.
- Anything that can be pronounced can be spelled.
- Letters and sounds can be used to identify words.
- Meaning can be obtained by using letters and sounds to determine words.

Procedures for Kindergarten

The following steps can be used for introducing letters and sounds in kindergarten. These steps may be adapted for students at other grades if they do not understand the alphabetic principle. The tone of these activities should be informal, fun, and fast-paced. The purpose of these activities is to familiarize students with how the alphabet works by having them participate in group play with letters and sounds.

I Can Spell Anything

- Reinforce the idea that anything that can be pronounced can be spelled with the letters of the alphabet.
- Tell students that you can spell any word. Have them give you words to spell.
- Write the words on the board, naming each letter as you write it. This shows students that the words contain the letters displayed on the ***Alphabet Sound Wall Cards.***
- Have students help you spell the words again by pointing to letters as you say them.
- Encourage students to spell each word letter by letter.

The alphabetic principle is the understanding that speech sounds can be mapped onto print.

Letter Expert Groups

- Have ***Alphabet Letter Cards*** (Levels K and 1) available for the following set of letters: *b, d, f, h, l, m, n, p, s, t*. You will need two or three cards for each letter. (You will not need the ***Alphabet Sound Cards*** until later.)
- You will be the letter expert for the vowels.
- Organize the class into groups of two or three, and assign each group a letter. Give each student the appropriate ***Alphabet Letter Card.***
- Tell students that they are now in their Letter Expert groups and that they are going to become experts on their Special Letter's name, shape, and sound.

Making Words

- Begin each lesson with a rehearsal of each group's letter name.
- Demonstrate how letters work by writing a word in large letters on the board.
- Tell students the experts for each letter in the word should hold up their ***Alphabet Letter Cards*** and name the letter. One member of the group should stand in front of their letter on the board.
- Continue until all letters in the word are accounted for. Remember that you are responsible for the vowels.
- Demonstrate that you can make different words by changing a letter or by changing the letter order.

Identifying Sounds in Words

- Use the ***Alphabet Sound Cards*** to demonstrate that every letter has at least one sound.
- Give each student the ***Alphabet Sound Card*** for his or her Special Letter.
- Point out the pictures on the cards. Explain that each card has a picture of something that makes the letter's sound. The picture will help them remember the sound.
- Tell each group the sound for its letter. (Remember, you are the expert for the vowels.)
- Quickly have each group rehearse its letter's name and sound.
- Write a word on the board in large letters. First say the word sound by sound, and then blend the word.
- For each letter/sound in the word, have one student from each Letter Expert group come forward, stand in front of the appropriate letter, and hold his or her card. Although only one member of the group may come forward with the ***Alphabet Letter Card*** or ***Alphabet Sound Card,*** all students in a Special Letter group should say the name or sound of their letter when it occurs in words.
- Say the word again, pointing to the ***Alphabet Sound Cards.***
- Ask students who are not already standing to help you hold the vowel cards.
- Vary the activity by changing one letter sound and having an expert for that letter come forward.

- End the activity for each word by saying the sounds in the words one by one and then saying the entire word. Encourage students to participate.

Tips

- Remind students to use the picture on the ***Alphabet Sound Card*** for their Special Letter to help them remember the letter's sound. Students are expected to "master" only their own Special Letter and to share the information with their classmates. At this point in the year, they are not expected to blend and read the words by themselves. These are group activities in which you work with students to help them gain insight into the alphabet.
- Be sure to connect what students learn about the letters and words to the words they work with in ***Big Book*** selections.
- Occasionally, have students find their special letters in a ***Big Book*** selection. Play some of the letter replacement and rearrangement games with words encountered in the ***Big Books.***

Developing the Alphabetic Principle

Purpose

The alphabetic principle is the understanding that speech sounds can be mapped onto print. It is the association of sounds with letters and the understanding that speech can be turned into print and that print can be turned into speech sounds. Activities associated with the alphabetic principle help kindergarten students develop a more thorough understanding of how sounds "work" in words. In this group of activities, students are introduced to specific letter/sound correspondences, consonants, and short vowels. While students have previously been introduced to vowels and their special characteristics, students' understanding is extended by introducing students to the convention that a vowel has a short sound in addition to its long sound. With this information and a carefully structured set of activities, students can begin to explore and understand the alphabetic principle in a straightforward and thorough manner. Students not only listen for sounds in specified positions in words, they also link sounds to their corresponding letters. The activities in this group of lessons lay the groundwork for students to work their way through the entire alphabet as they learn letter-sound associations and to understand the purpose and the value of this learning.

Move students quickly through these activities. Do not wait for all students to master each letter/sound correspondence before going on. They will have more opportunities to achieve mastery. The goal of these activities is for students to obtain a basic understanding of the alphabetic principle.

> *Students need to learn the alphabetic principle: that letters work together in a systematic way to connect spoken language to written words. This understanding is the foundation for reading.*

Procedures

Introducing Consonant Letters and Sounds

- Point to the ***Alphabet Sound Wall Card*** and ask students what they know about the card (the letter name, the capital and lowercase letter, and so on).
- Turn the card, and point to the picture. Name the picture, and point to and name the letter. Tell students the sound of the letter and how the picture helps them remember the sound. Repeat the sound several times.
- Tell students you will read them the short story or an alliterative sentence to help them remember the sound of the letter. Read the story several times, emphasizing the words with the target sound. Have students join in and say the sound.
- After introducing and reviewing a letter/sound correspondence, summarize the information on the ***Alphabet Sound Wall Card:*** the name of the card, the sound, and the letter.

Generating Words with the Target Sound

Brainstorm to create a list of words that begin with the target sound. Write the words on the board or on a chart. Include any of the students' names that begin with the target sound.

Listening for Initial Sounds

- Give each student an ***Alphabet Letter Card*** for the target sound.
- Point to the picture on the ***Alphabet Sound Wall Card,*** and have students give the sound.
- Tell students to listen for the first sound in each word you say. If it is the target sound, they should hold up their cards. Establish a signal so that students know when to respond.
- Read the list of words, some beginning with the target sound and some beginning with other sounds.

Listening for Final Sounds

The procedure for listening for the final sound of a word is the same as that for listening for the initial sound. Students may need to be reminded throughout the activity to pay attention to the final sound.

Read a list of words, some ending with the target sound and some ending with other sounds. Avoid words that begin with the target sound.

Linking the Sound to the Letter

- **Word Pairs (initial sounds).** Write pairs of words on the board. One of each pair should begin with the target sound. Say the word beginning with the target sound, and ask students to identify it. Remind them to listen for the target sound at the beginning of the word, to think about which letter makes that sound, and to find the word that begins with that letter. For example,
  Target sound: /s/
  Word pair: *fit sit*
  Which word is *sit?*
- **Word Pairs (final sounds).** Follow the same procedure used for initial sounds, and direct students to think about the sound that they hear at the end of the word. Because it is often more difficult

for students to attend to the ending sound, you may need to lead them through several pairs of words. Remind students to listen for the target sound and to think about which letter makes that sound.

- **Writing Letters.** Using either of the handwriting systems outlined in this Program Appendix or the system in use at your school, have students practice writing uppercase and lowercase letters. Remind students about the letter sound, and have them repeat it.

Other activities that support the development of the alphabetic principle include the following:

Comparing Initial Consonant Sounds

This activity is exactly like Listening for Initial Sounds except that students must discriminate between two sounds. They are given ***Alphabet Letter Cards*** for both sounds and must hold up the appropriate card when they hear the sound.

Comparing Final Consonant Sounds

This activity is exactly like Listening for Final Sounds except that students must discriminate between two sounds. They are given ***Alphabet Letter Cards*** for both sounds and must hold up the appropriate card when they hear the sound.

Linking the Consonant Sound to the Letter

In these activities students will link beginning and ending sounds and letters.

- **I'm Thinking of Something That Starts (Ends) with ___ Game.** Begin with the target sound, and add clues until students guess the word. If students give a word that does not begin with the target sound, emphasize the beginning sound, and ask if the word begins with the target sound.
- **Silly Sentences.** Make silly sentences with students that include many words with the target sound. Encourage students to participate by extending the sentences: Mary mopes. Mary mopes on Monday. Mary and Michael mope on Monday in Miami. For older students, have them make silly sentences using the sound at the beginning of their first name. Have them use the dictionary to find more words beginning or ending with the target sound.

Introducing Short-Vowel Sounds

- Tell students that the vowels are printed in red to remind them that they are special letters. (They are not special because they are printed in red.) They are special because they have more than one sound, and every word in English must have a vowel sound.
- Point to the long *Aa* ***Alphabet Sound Wall Card,*** and remind students that this letter is called a vowel. Tell them vowels sometimes say their names in words (for example, *say, day, tray).* When the vowel says its name, the sound is long. Tell them this vowel sound is called long *a*.
- Have students repeat the sound.
- Tell students sometimes vowels say different sounds. Point to the picture of the lamb on the short *Aa* card, and tell students that *a* also makes the sound heard in the middle of *lamb*. This is the short *a*. Read the short vowel story to help students remember the short *a*.
- Have all students join in saying/a/ /a/ /a/.

Listening for Short-Vowel Sounds Versus Long-Vowel Sounds

- Tell students that you will read words with long *a* and short *a*. Review the two sounds.
- Give students a signal to indicate when they hear the vowel sound. You may want one signal for short *a,* such as scrunching down, and another for long *a,* such as stretching up tall.
- Continue with lists of words such as *add, back, aid, tan, bake,* and *tame.*

Linking the Vowel Sound to the Letter

- **Writing Letters.** Have students practice writing the letter and review the sound of the letter.
- In this activity to help students link sounds and letters, students will make words either by adding initial consonants to selected word parts or by adding a different final consonant to a consonant-vowel-consonant combination. Change the beginning of the word or the word ending, but retain the vowel sound to make new words:

at	hat	mat	pat
ap	map	tap	sap
am	Sam	Pam	ham

Comparing Short-Vowel Sounds

This activity requires students to discriminate between short-vowel sounds in the middle of words. Review the short-vowel sounds.

- Say a word, and have students repeat it. Establish a signal to indicate whether they hear short *a* or short *o* in the middle of the word. For example, they can hold up the appropriate ***Alphabet Letter Card*** when they hear a sound. Sample words: *cap, cot, rat, rot, rack,* and *rock.*

Linking the Sound to the Letter

- In this activity, write a word on the board, and help students say it.
- Change the word by changing the vowel. Help students say the new word, for example, *map, mop; hot, hat; pot, pat.*
- For a variation of this activity, write the pairs of words, and simply have students say which word is the target word. For example, students see *tap* and *top.* Ask which word *top* is, directing students' attention to the vowel.

Introducing Long-Vowel Sounds

The introduction of short vowels and consonants helps students internalize the alphabetic principle—a sound can be mapped onto a letter. In English, however, some sounds are represented by more than one letter, for example, the /ē/ can be represented by the letter *e* as in *me* but also represented by e_e as in *Pete*. Toward the end of kindergarten, students will be introduced to long vowels and two common representations of those sounds. These include the single vowel such as *a* or *e* and the vowel consonant silent *e* (VCe). The introduction of the VCe pattern or unit gives students a wide range of common words to read by the end of kindergarten and sets a solid foundation for first grade.

- If necessary, remind students that vowels are written in red. Point to the long *Aa* card, and tell students that the sound of long *a* is /ā/.

- ✦ Have students say the sound with you.
- ✦ Tell students that long *a* can be written in more than one way; it can be written as *a* just like short *a* but it can also be written as *a_e*. When we see the blank, it is a clue that another sound and letter needs to be put on the blank or line to make a word.
- ✦ Write a_e, and have students give the sound: /ā/. Then write a *t* on the blank, say the sound, and blend the word: *ate*.
- ✦ The goal is to have students see the *a_e* or any of the other VCe patterns as a unit.
- ✦ While students have been blending and reading short-vowel words, long vowels create a shift in thinking: Combinations of letters can be used to represent a sound. Here are some easy tips when you are first working with the VCe patterns:
  - The VCe patterns are not written on the ***Alphabet Sound Cards.*** You may want to write the *a_e, e_e, i_e, o_e,* and *u_e* units on the respective long-vowel cards as a reminder for students. Do this as you introduce each long vowel unit. Use an erasable marker so you can reintroduce these special patterns each year.
  - Provide maximum support when first using the long-vowel units in blending.
  - Write the letter for the first sound, for example, /m/, and have students give the sound.
  - Write the unit for /ā/: *a_e*. Tell students this says /ā/. Be sure to write the whole unit.
  - Write the final letter ON the blank, for example, *k*. Give the sound for the *k*, and then blend the word.
  - Let students hear your voice during the blending, but gradually reduce it so they are doing more of the thinking.
  - Help students blend long vowel words as they are reading their ***Decodables.***

Tips

- ✦ Model and support the activities as necessary until students begin to catch on and can participate with confidence.
- ✦ To keep students focused on the various activities, have them tell you the task for each activity. For example, after telling students to listen for final sounds, ask students what they will be listening for.
- ✦ Actively involve students by giving them opportunities to tell what they know rather than supplying the information for them. *What is the letter name? What is the sound? What words begin with the sound?*
- ✦ Keeping students focused on the idea that they are learning about sounds and letters so they can read books themselves makes the lessons more relevant for students.

Introducing Sounds and Letters

Purpose

In ***SRA Imagine It!*** students learn to relate sounds to letters in kindergarten through the use of thirty-one ***Alphabet Sound Wall Cards.*** In the upper grade levels, ***Sound/Spelling Wall Cards*** (Levels 1–3) are used to relate sounds and spellings. The purpose of the ***Alphabet Sound Wall Cards*** is to remind students of the sounds of the English language and their letter correspondences. These cards are a resource for students to use to remember sound-letter associations for both reading and writing.

Each card contains the capital and small letter and a picture that shows the sound being produced. For instance, the Sausage card introduces the /s/ sound and shows sausages sizzling in a pan. The sound the sausages make sizzling in the pan is /s/ /s/ /s/. The name of the picture on each card contains the target sound at the beginning of the word for the consonants and in the middle for the vowels. Vowel letters are printed in red, and consonants are printed in black. In addition, the picture associates a sound with an action. This action-sound association is introduced through a short, interactive story found in the ***Teacher's Edition,*** in which the pictured object or character "makes" the sound of the letter. Long vowels are represented by a tall—or "long"—picture of the letters themselves rather than by a picture for action-sound association. Short vowels have a green background, and long vowels have a yellow background.

Procedures

- Display Cards 1–26 with the picture sides to the wall. Initially post the first twenty-six cards in alphabetical order so that only the alphabet letters on the back show. The short-vowel cards may be posted as they are introduced later. As you introduce the sound of each letter, you will turn the card to show the picture and the letter on the other side. Because students will be referring to these cards for reading and writing, post them where all students can easily see them.
- Before turning a card, point to the letter. Ask students to tell what they know about the letter. For example, they are likely to know its name if the letter is one with which they have already worked. They might also note that there is an upper- and lowercase for the letter or that the letter is a consonant or a vowel.
- Turn the card, and point to the picture. Tell students the name of the picture (card), and explain that it will help them remember the sound the letter makes.
- Tell students the name and the sound of the letter.
- Read the story that goes with the card. Read it expressively, emphasizing the words with the target sound and the isolated sound when it occurs. Have students join in to produce the sound.

*The purpose of the **Alphabet Sound Wall Cards** is to remind students of the sounds of the English language and their letter correspondences.*

- Repeat the story a few times, encouraging all students to say the sound along with you.
- Repeat the name of the letter and the sound.
- Follow the story with the cards for the target sound. (These are listed within the lessons.)
- Name each picture, and have students listen for the target sound at the beginning of the word. Ask students to repeat the words and the sound.
- Listening for the sound in different positions in words provides additional work with phonemic awareness. Give each student the letter card for the introduced sound and letter. Read the words from Listening for the Sound, and have students raise their letter card if they hear the target sound at the beginning of the word. For many letters, students will also listen for the sound at the end of words as well.
- To link the sound and the letter, demonstrate how to form the uppercase and lowercase letters by writing on the board or on an overhead transparency. Have students practice forming the letter and saying the sound as they write.

Alphabet Sound Cards

The pictures and letters on the ***Alphabet Sound Wall Cards*** also appear on the small sets of individual ***Alphabet Sound Cards.*** The ***Teacher's Edition*** specifically suggests that you use the individual ***Alphabet Sound Cards*** for Workshop and small-group activities for review, reteaching, and practice sessions. Place sets of the cards in the appropriate Workshop area for students to use alone or with partners. Add each small card to the Activity Center after you have taught the lesson in which the corresponding individual ***Alphabet Sound Card*** is introduced. Here are some suggestions for activities using the individual ***Alphabet Sound Cards:***

1. **Saying sounds from pictures.** The leader flashes pictures as the others say the sound each picture represents.
2. **Saying sounds.** The leader flashes the letters on the cards as the others say the sound that the letters represent.
3. **Naming words from pictures.** The leader flashes pictures. The others say the sound and then say a word beginning with that sound.
4. **Writing letters from the pictures.** Working alone, a student looks at a picture and then writes the letter for the sound that picture represents.
5. **Making words using the pictures.** A student uses the pictures (Sausages, Pig, Timer for *sit*) or the letters to make words.

Tips

- Throughout the beginning lessons, help students remember that vowels are special by reminding them that vowels sometimes say their names in words. For example, tell them the picture of the *a* on the long *a* ***Alphabet Sound Wall Card*** is long because the long *a* says its name. The short *a* ***Alphabet Sound Wall Card*** pictures the lamb because the lamb makes the short *a* sound, and you can hear the sound in the word *lamb*.
- From the very beginning, encourage students to use the ***Alphabet Sound Wall Cards*** as a resource to help them with their work.
- Mastery of letter recognition is the goal students should reach so that they will be prepared to link each letter with its associated sound. If students have not yet mastered the names of the letters, it is important to work with them individually in Workshop, or at other times during the day.
- Both the *Cc* and the *Kk* cards have the same picture—a camera. A camera makes the /k/ sound when it clicks, and the word *camera* begins with the /k/ sound. However, the word *camera* is not spelled with a *k*. Remember, the first sound of the word helps students remember the sound of the letter.
- The picture on the *Qq* card depicts quacking ducks. Make sure that students consistently call them quacking ducks, not ducks, and that they focus on the /kw/ sound.

Explicit, Systematic Phonics

The purpose of phonics instruction is to teach students the association between the sounds of the language and the written symbols—spellings—that have been chosen to represent those sounds.

As with all alphabetic languages, English has a limited number of symbols—twenty-six—that are combined and recombined to make the written language. These written symbols are a visual representation of the speech sounds we use to communicate. This is simply a code. The faster students learn the code and how it works, the faster the whole world of reading opens up to them.

Beginning at the kindergarten level, students are introduced to sounds and letters. Students learn that sounds can be mapped onto letters and that those sounds and letters can be blended to read words.

In Grade 1, students make the shift from mapping sounds onto letters to mapping sounds onto spellings. The introduction of both sounds and letters in kindergarten and the sounds and spellings in Grade 1 is done in a very systematic, sequential manner. This allows students to continually build on what they learned the day before. As each sound/symbol relationship is introduced, students learn about and practice with words containing the target sound and letter in kindergarten and sound/spelling in Grade1. This new knowledge is then reinforced through the use of engaging text specifically written for this purpose.

It can be very difficult for students to hear the individual sounds, or phonemes, that make up words. When phonics instruction is explicit—students are told the sounds associated with the different written symbols—there is no guesswork involved. They know that the sound /b/ is spelled *b*. Therefore, students in an ***SRA Imagine It!*** classroom spend time learning to discriminate individual speech sounds, and then they learn the spellings of those sounds. This systematic, explicit approach affords students the very best chance for early and continuing success.

Sound/Spelling Wall Cards

(Grade 1 on) See The Alphabetic Principle for information on the introduction of sounds and letters in pre-kindergarten and kindergarten.

Purpose

The purpose of the ***Sound/Spelling Wall Cards*** (Levels 1–3) is to remind students of the sounds in English and their spellings. The name of the picture on each card contains the target sound at the beginning of the name for consonants and in the middle for the short vowels. Long vowels are represented by elongated pictures of the vowel. The variant vowels such as /aw/ and /oi/ contain the vowel sound in the name as well. In addition, the picture associates a sound with an action. This association is introduced through an interactive story in which the pictured object or character "makes" the sound. This "action" cue is particularly helpful for students whose primary language is not English. In some cases, the name of the card and the initial sound may be similar to words in other languages. For example, the word for *lion* in Spanish is *león,* which begins with the same sound as the English word. This is not true for other languages. In Russian the word for *lion* is *лев* and in Japanese it is *raion*. The word for *zipper* in Spanish is *cremallera,* in Russian it is *застежка-молния* and in Japanese it is *jippa*. But all students can remember the actions and sounds and use them as a resource for both reading and writing.

The faster students learn the code and how it works, the faster the whole world of reading opens up to them.

Procedure

Posting the Cards

In Grade 1, initially post the first twenty-six cards with the picture to the wall so that only the alphabet letters on the backs show. As you introduce each card, you will turn it to show the picture and the spellings on the front of the card. Some Grade 1 teachers who have students who are familiar with the cards from kindergarten choose to place the first twenty-six cards (the alphabet) with the pictures facing the class. Because students are familiar with the cards and how to use them, this provides support for writing. Even these first-grade teachers, however, cover the spellings not introduced in kindergarten. In second- or third-grade classrooms in which students are reviewing what they learned the year before, place all the cards with the pictures and the spellings facing forward so students can use these as a resource from the beginning of the school year. Make sure that the cards are positioned so that you can touch them with your hand or with a pointer when you refer to them and so that all students can see them easily. The cards should be placed where students can readily see and reference them throughout the day.

Special Devices

- ✦ Vowel spellings are printed in red to draw attention to them. It is the vowels and their different spellings that challenge us all. Consonants are printed in black. The blank line in a spelling indicates that a letter will take the place of the blank in a word. For example, the replacement of the blank with *t* in the spelling *a_e* makes the word *ate*. The blank lines may also indicate the position of a spelling in a word or a syllable. The blank in *h_*, for example, means that the sound /h/ spelled *h_* occurs at the beginning of a word or a syllable.
- ✦ The blanks in *_ie_* indicate that the *ie* spelling will not come at the beginning or the end of a word or a syllable as in *babies,* while the blank in *_oy* shows that the *oy* spelling comes at the end of a word or a syllable as in *toy*. Uses of blanks in specific spellings are discussed in the lessons. Please note now, however, that when you write a spelling of a sound on

the board or an overhead transparency, you should include the blanks.

- The color of the background behind the spellings also has a meaning. Consonants have a white background. The colors behind vowel spellings are pronunciation clues. Short-vowel spellings have a green background, which corresponds to the green box that appears before some consonant spellings. Thus, before *ck, tch,* or *x,* you will see a green box, which indicates that a short vowel always precedes that spelling. Long-vowel spellings have a yellow background; other vowel spellings such as *r*-controlled vowels, diphthongs, and variant vowels have a blue background. The color code reinforces the idea that vowels are special and have different pronunciations.

Introducing the Sound/Spelling Wall Cards

In first grade, each sound and spelling is introduced by using a see/hear/say/write sequence. In Grades 2 and 3 the same sequence is used in the review of the cards.

1. *See:* Students see the spelling or spellings on the ***Sound/Spelling Wall Card*** and the board or an overhead transparency.
2. *Hear:* Students hear the sound used in words and in isolation in the story. The sound is, of course, related to the picture (and the action) shown on the ***Sound/Spelling Wall Card.***
3. *Say:* Students say the sound.
4. *Write:* Students write the spelling(s) for the sound.

There are a number of important points to remember about this routine.

- Take down the ***Sound/Spelling Wall Card,*** tell the class the name of the card, the sound, and the spelling.
- Read the alliterative story so students hear the sound used in words as well as in isolation, and say the sound.
- After you present the sound and spelling, have several students go to the board to write the spelling. Have them say the sound as they write the spelling. After they have written the spelling of the sound, give them an opportunity to proofread their own work. Then give the other students the opportunity to help with proofreading by noting what is good about the spelling and then suggesting how to make it better.
- Difficulty in blending may be the result of not knowing the sounds or not being able to pronounce the sounds. Teach the sounds thoroughly during the introduction of the ***Sound/Spelling Wall Card*** and during initial sounding and blending. To help ensure success for all students, make certain that every student is able to see the board or screen.

Introducing the Sound /s/ spelled *s*

- Point to the back of ***Sound/Spelling Wall Card*** 19—Sausages, and have students tell you what they know about the card: it is a consonant and there is an upper and lowercase *s* on the card. Turn the card, and tell the class the name of the card: Sausages. Point to the sausages in the picture, and say the word *sausages,* emphasizing the initial consonant sound—*ssssssausages.* Note: teachers usually place a sticky note over the other spellings of /s/—the *ce, ci_,* and *cy*—in order to help students focus on the single spelling being introduced in the lesson.
- Point to the spelling *s.* Tell students that /s/ is spelled *s.*
- Read the alliterative story. In Grades 2 and 3, the stories for the card are printed in the Level Appendix of the ***Teacher's Edition.*** If your students in Grades 2 and 3 are familiar with the cards, have them tell you the name of the card, the sound, and the spelling and tell the story.
- If students had ***SRA Imagine It!*** before, you can ask them if they learned an action to help them remember the sound. If your students do not already have an action they associate with the sound, make some up with your students. They will have fun, and it will be another way for them to remember the sound/spelling relationships.
- Write *s* on the board or on an overhead transparency, and say the sound. Write the spelling again and ask students to say the sound with you as they write the spelling on slates, on paper, or with their index fingers in the air or in the palm of their hands. Repeat this activity several times.
- Have several students come to the board and write the upper- and lowercase spelling while the others continue to write them on slates or with their fingers. Be sure to encourage students to say the sound as they make the spelling. For students writing at the board, take time to have them proofread their work.
- Have students listen for words beginning with /s/, indicating by some signal, such as thumbs-up or thumbs-down, whether they hear the /s/ sound and saying /s/ when they hear it in a word. Repeat with the sound in various positions in words. Encourage students to tell you and the class words with /s/ at the beginning, as well as at the ends of words.
- Check students' learning by pointing to the card. Have students identify the sound, name the spelling, and discuss how the card can help them remember the sound.

Remember that saying the sound, listening to the alliterative story, and listening for the sound (discriminating it from other sounds) in different positions in words are all phonemic awareness activities that have been integrated into phonics.

Individual Sound/Spelling Cards

Use the individual ***Sound/Spelling Cards*** for review and for small-group reteaching and practice sessions. Students can use them alone or with partners. Here are some suggestions for activities using the individual ***Sound/Spelling Cards:***

1. **Saying sounds from pictures.** The leader flashes pictures as the others say the sound each picture represents.
2. **Saying sounds.** The leader flashes the spellings on the cards as the others say the sound that the spellings represent.
3. **Naming spellings from pictures.** The leader flashes pictures. The others name the card, say the sound, and then name as many spellings as they can.
4. **Writing spellings from the pictures.** Working alone, a student looks at a picture and then writes as many spellings for that ***Sound/Spelling Card*** as he or she can remember.
5. **Saying words from pictures.** The leader presents a series of individual cards, for example, Sausages, Lamb, Timer. The others tell the word by blending the sounds represented—*sat.*

Blending

Purpose

The purpose of blending is to teach students a strategy for figuring out unfamiliar words. Initially students will be blending sound by sound as they learn how to blend. After they understand the process, they will move to whole-word blending and develop the strategy they will use to read unfamiliar words. Ultimately students will sound and blend only those words that they cannot read. Eventually the blending process will become quick and comfortable for them.

Procedure

Learning the sounds and their spellings is only the first step in learning to read and write. The second step is learning to blend the sounds into words.

Blending Techniques

Blending lines are written on the board or an overhead transparency as students watch and participate. The lines and sentences should not be written out before class begins. It is through the sound-by-sound blending of the words and the sentences that students learn the blending process.

Sound-by-Sound Blending

- Write the spelling of the first sound in the word. Point to the spelling, and say the sound. For example, the word students will be blending is *sat*.
- Have students say the sound with you as you say the sound again. Write the spelling of the next sound. Point to the spelling, and say the sound. Have students say the sound with you as you say the sound again. After you have written the vowel spelling, blend through the vowel (unless the vowel is the first letter of the word), making the blending motion—a smooth sweeping of the hand beneath the sounds, linking them from left to right, for example, *sa*. As you make the blending motion, make sure that your hand is under the letter that corresponds to the sound you are saying at the moment.
- Write the spelling of the next sound—*t*. Point to the spelling, and have students, say the sound with you as you touch the spelling. If this is the last sound and spelling in the word, then have students blend and read the word—*sat*. If this is not the final sound and spelling, continue pointing to the spelling and asking for the sound. For example, in the word *sand,* you would blend through the vowel then ask for the sounds for the spellings *n* and *d* before blending the word. After pronouncing the final sound in the word, make the blending motion from left to right under the word as you blend the sounds. Then have students blend the word. Let them be the first to pronounce the word normally.
- Ask a student to read the word again naturally, as he or she would say or speak it. Then have a student use it in a sentence. Ask another student to extend the sentence, that is, make it more interesting by giving more information. Help the student by asking an appropriate question about the sentence, using, for example, *How? When? Where?* or *Why?* Continue blending the rest of the words in the blending line. At the end of each line, have students reread the words naturally.

Blending is the heart of phonics instruction and the key strategy students must learn to open the world of written language.

Whole-Word Blending

When students are comfortable with sound-by-sound blending, they are ready for whole-word blending.

- Write the whole word to be blended on the board or display the overhead transparency.
- Ask students to blend the sounds as you point to each spelling.
- Then have students say the whole word.
- Ask students to use the word in a sentence and then to extend the sentence.
- After blending each line, have students read the words naturally, as they would say them.
- When all of the words have been blended, point to words randomly, and ask individuals to read them.

Blending Syllables

In reading the ***Student Readers,*** students will often encounter multisyllabic words. Some students are intimidated by long words, yet many multisyllabic words are easily read by reading and blending the syllables rather than the individual sounds. Beginning in first grade, students will learn about different syllable generalizations, open and closed syllables, consonant *-le*, and the like. Following a set of rules for syllables is difficult because so many of the rules have exceptions. Students need to remember that each syllable in a word contains one vowel sound. Early in the process, you will need to provide support.

- Have students identify the vowel sounds and spellings in the word.
- Have students blend the first syllable sound by sound if necessary or read the first syllable.
- Handle the remaining syllables the same way.
- Have students blend the syllables together to read the word.

Blending Sentences

Blending sentences is the logical extension of blending words. Blending sentences helps students develop fluency, which is critical to comprehension. Encourage students to reread sentences with phrasing and natural intonation.

Write the sentence on the board, underlining any high-frequency sight words—words that students cannot decode either because they are irregular or because they contain sounds or spellings that students have not yet learned or reviewed—or display the transparency. High-frequency sight words are taught before blending. Write the word or words on the board or the overhead transparency, and introduce them before writing the sentence. Read the word, and have students repeat the word then spell the word. Use each word in a sentence. Point to the word or words, and have students read them again. These words should not be blended but read as whole words.

Tips

- The goal of blending in first grade is not to have students blend words sound by sound for the whole year. Sound-by-sound instruction should begin with maximum instructional support—with teachers and students blending together. As students understand the sound-by-sound blending routine, drop the verbal cues (sound, sound, blend, sound, blend), and simply point to the spellings after they are written, and have the class give the sounds.

- ✦ How do you know when to move from sound-by-sound to whole-word blending? When you are writing the final spelling and students are reading the word, it is time to move on to whole-word blending. This often occurs around Unit 3 in first grade.
- ✦ Keep in mind, however, that when you introduce more complex long-vowel and variant vowel spellings, you can always drop back to sound-by-sound blending for the first couple of blending lines in the lesson.
- ✦ Even though the entire class may be doing whole-word blending, sound-by-sound blending is an excellent preteaching tool for students needing extra help. After all the sounds and spellings have been introduced, students may be ready to move just to reading the words in the blending line. Have them read the words, stopping to blend only words they cannot read fluently and automatically.
- ✦ In Grades 2 and 3, teachers often begin the phonics review in the Getting Started lessons with sound-by-sound blending and then quickly move into whole-word blending. Again, the goal is to have students reading the words as quickly and automatically as possible. If the majority of the class can do this, then use whole-word blending. Use sound-by-sound blending to preteach the blending lines with students who need more support.

Building for Success

A primary cause of students' blending failure is their failure to understand how to use the ***Sound/Spelling Cards.*** Students need to practice sounds and spellings when the ***Sound/Spelling Cards*** are introduced and during initial blending. They also need to understand that if they are not sure of how to pronounce a spelling, they can check the cards. You may need to lead the group almost constantly. Soon, however, leaders in the group will take over. Watch to see whether any students are having trouble during the blending. Include them in small-group instruction sessions. At that time you may want to use the vowel-first procedure to reteach blending lines.

Extra Help

In working with small groups during Workshop, you may want to use some of the following suggestions to support students who need help with blending.

Vowel-First Blending

Vowel-first blending is an alternative to sound-by-sound and whole-word blending for students who need special help. Used in small-group sessions, this technique helps students who have difficulty with the other two types of blending focus on the most important part of each word—the vowels—and do only one thing at a time. These students are not expected to say a sound and blend it with another at virtually the same time. The steps to use in vowel-first blending follow:

1. Across the board or on an overhead transparency, write the vowel spelling in each of the words in the line. For a short vowel, the line may look like this:
   a a a
   For a long vowel, the line may look like this: *ee ea ea*
2. Point to the spelling as students say the sound for the spelling.
3. Begin blending around the vowels. In front of the first vowel spelling, add the spelling for the beginning sound of the word. Make the blending motion, and have students blend through the vowel, adding a blank to indicate that the word is still incomplete. Repeat this procedure for each partial word in the line until the line looks like this:
   ma__ sa__ pa__
   see__ mea__ tea__
4. Have students blend the partial word again as you make the blending motion, and then add the spelling for the ending sound.
5. Make the blending motion, and have students blend the completed word—for example, *mat* or *seed.*
6. Ask a student to repeat the word and to use it in a sentence. Then have another student extend the sentence.
7. Repeat steps 4, 5, and 6 for each word in the line, which might look like this:
   mat sad pan
   or
   seed meat team

Tips

- ✦ In the early lessons, blend with as much direction and dialogue as is necessary for success. Reduce your directions to a minimum as soon as possible. You have made good progress when you no longer have to say, "Sound—Sound—Blend," because students automatically sound and blend as you write.
- ✦ Blending is more than just reading words; it is an opportunity to build vocabulary and to develop oral language.

Always ask students to use less familiar words in sentences and then to extend the sentences. This sentence extension is a technique that can be applied to writing as well. Students will naturally extend sentences by adding phrases to the ends of the sentences. Encourage them to add phrases at the beginning or in the middle of the sentence as well.

- ✦ Use the vowel-first procedure in small-group preteaching or reteaching sessions with students who are having a lot of trouble with blending. Remember that you must adapt the blending lines in the lessons to the vowel-first method.
- ✦ The sight words in the sentences cannot be blended. Students must approach them as sight words to be memorized. If students are having problems reading sight words, tell them the words.
- ✦ Cue marks written over the vowels may help students.
  - Straight line cue for long vowels
    EXAMPLES: āpe, mē, fīne, sō, ūse
  - Curved line cue for short vowels
    EXAMPLES: căt, pĕt, wĭn, hŏt, tŭg
  - Tent cue for variations of *a* and *o*
    EXAMPLES: âll, ôff
  - Dot cue for schwa sound with multisyllabic words
    EXAMPLES: salȧd, planėt, pencil, wagȯn

Dictation and Spelling

Purpose

The purpose of dictation is to teach students to segment words into individual sounds and to spell words by connecting sounds to spellings. In addition, learning dictation gives students a new strategy for reflecting on the sounds they hear in words to help them with their own writing.

As students learn about sounds and spellings, they begin to learn the standard spellings that will enable others to read their writing. As students learn to encode, they develop their visual memory for spelling patterns and words (spelling ability) and hence increase their writing fluency. Reinforcing the association between sounds and spellings and words through dictation gives students a spelling strategy that provides support and reassurance for writing independently. Reflecting on the sounds they hear in words will help students develop writing fluency as they apply the strategy to writing unfamiliar words.

A dictation activity is a learning experience; it is not a test. Students should be encouraged to ask for as much help as they need. The proofreading technique is an integral part of dictation. Students' errors lead to self-correction and, if need be, to reteaching. The dictation activities must not become a frustrating ordeal. Students should receive reinforcement and feedback.

There are two kinds of dictation: Sounds-in-Sequence Dictation and Whole-Word Dictation. The two types differ mainly in the amount of help they give students in spelling the words. The instructions vary for each type.

Procedure

Sounds-in-Sequence Dictation

Sounds-in-Sequence Dictation gives students the opportunity to spell words sound by sound, left to right, checking the spelling of each sound as they write. (Many students write words as they think they hear and say the words, not as the words are actually pronounced or written.)

- Pronounce the first word to be spelled. Use the word in a sentence, and say the word again (word/sentence/word). Have students say the word.
- Tell students to think about the sounds they hear in the word. Ask, "What's the first sound in the word?"
- Have students say the sound.
- Point to the ***Sound/Spelling Card,*** and direct students to check the card. Ask what the spelling is. Students should say the spelling and then write it.
- Proceed in this manner until the word is complete.
- **Proofread.** You can write the word on the board as a model, or have a student do it. Check the work by referring to the ***Sound/Spelling Cards.*** If a word is misspelled, have students circle the word and write it correctly, either above the word or next to it.

Whole-Word Dictation

Whole-Word Dictation gives students the opportunity to practice this spelling strategy with less help from the teacher.

- Pronounce the word, use the word in a sentence, and then repeat the word (word/sentence/word). Have students repeat the word. Tell students to think about the word and each sound in the word. Remind students to check the ***Sound/Spelling Cards*** for spellings and to write the word.
- **Proofread.** Write or have a volunteer write the word on the board as a model. Check the word by referring to the ***Sound/Spelling Cards.***

Sentence Dictation

Writing dictated sentences. Help students apply this spelling strategy to writing sentences. Dictation supports the development of fluent and independent writing. Dictation of a sentence will also help students apply conventions of written language, such as capitalization and punctuation.

- Say the complete sentence aloud.
- Dictate one word at a time, following the procedure for Sounds-in-Sequence Dictation.

Continue this procedure for the rest of the words in the sentence. Remind students to put a period at the end. Then proofread the sentence sound by sound or word by word. When sentences contain sight words, the sight words should be dictated as whole words, not sound by sound. Students should be encouraged to check the high-frequency sight words posted in the room if they are unsure how to spell them. As students learn to write more independently, the whole sentence can be dictated word by word.

Proofreading

Whenever students write, whether at the board or on paper, they should proofread their work. Proofreading is an important technique because it allows students to learn by self-correction, and it gives them an immediate second opportunity for success. It is the same skill students will use as they proofread their writing. Students should proofread by circling—not by erasing—each error. After they circle an error, they should write the correction beside the circle. This type of correction allows you and students to see the error as well as the correct form. Students also can see what needs to be changed and how they have made their own work better.

You may want to have students use a colored pencil to circle and write in the correction. This will make it easier for them to see the changes.

Procedure for Proofreading

- Write—or have a student write—the word or sentence on the board or on an overhead transparency.
- Have the other students tell what is good; for example, it is spelled correctly.
- Have students check their words and identify whether anything can be made better, the word needs to be spelled differently, or the handwriting needs to be improved.
- If there is a mistake, have the student circle it and write it correctly—make it better.
- Have the rest of the class proofread their own work.

The Word Building Game (Grades K and 1)

The major reason for developing writing alongside reading is that reading and writing are complementary communicative processes. Decoding requires that students blend the phonemes together into familiar cohesive words. Spelling requires that students segment familiar cohesive words into separate phonemes. Both help students develop an understanding of how the alphabetic principle works.

The Word Building game gives students a chance to exercise their segmentation abilities and to practice using the sounds and spellings they are learning. The game is a fast-paced activity in which students spell related sets of words with the teacher's guidance. (Each successive word in the list differs from the previous one by one sound.)

For the Word Building game, students use their ***Alphabet Letter Cards*** (Levels K and 1) to build the words. (As an alternative they can use pencil and paper.) You will be writing at the board.

Give students the appropriate ***Alphabet Letter Cards.*** For example, if the list for the Word Building game is *am, at,* and *mat,* they will need their *a, m,* and *t* ***Alphabet Letter Cards.***

- Say the first word, such as *am.* (Use it in a sentence if you wish.) Have students repeat the word. Say the word slowly sound by sound. Tell students to look at the ***Alphabet Sound Cards*** to find the letters that spell the sounds. Touch the first sound's card, in this case the Lamb card, and have students say the sound. Continue the process with the second sound. Write the word on the board while students use their ***Alphabet Letter Cards*** to spell it. Have students compare their words with your word, make changes as needed, and then blend and read the word with you.
- Students will then change the first word to make a different word. Say the next word in the list, (at). Segment the sounds of the word, and have students find the ***Alphabet Letter Cards*** that correspond. Write the new word *(at)* under the first word *(am)* on the board, and have students change their cards to spell the new word. Have them compare their words to yours and make changes as needed. Blend and read the word with students. Continue in a like manner through the word list.

Word Structure

Purpose

As students move into the upper grades, there is a shift from Phonics to Word Structure. Phonology is the study of the sounds that make up words. In the early grades, students learn to map sounds with spellings to read words. However, as students move into the upper grades and encounter more complex and longer words, the understanding of morphology and the morphological units that make up words is important for fluent reading, vocabulary development, and comprehension.

Morphology is the study of Word Structure. Word Structure activities support the development of fluency as students learn to identify and read meaningful chunks of words rather than individual spellings. Word Structure also supports the development of vocabulary as students learn how inflectional endings change a word's tense, number, and so on and how affixes can be added to a base word to create or derive a new but related meaning.

Morphemes are the smallest units that have semantic meaning. Morphemes may be free or bound. A free morpheme can stand alone, such as the words *dog, man,* or *woman.* A bound morpheme, on the other hand, is a unit of meaning that must be combined with another morpheme to make a meaningful word. For example, in *rewrite* the prefix *re-* means "to do again", and in *dogs* the *-s* changes the meaning to plural. Both *re-* and *-s* are bound morphemes because they must combine with other words to create new words.

Learning about word structure helps the reader on several levels. Being able to identify key-word parts not only helps with the pronunciation of longer, unfamiliar words but it also helps with meaning. In Word Structure, students learn how to deconstruct words—to identify the root of the word as well as the affixes. When affixes occur at the beginning of a word, they are called prefixes, and when they occur at the end of a word they are called suffixes. The prefix, root word, and suffix are all morphemes.

In the word *restatement,* there are three morphemes: the prefix *re-,* the root *state* and the suffix *-ment.*

prefix	*root*	*suffix*
re-	*state*	*-ment*

Suffixes, in particular, can impact the root word in different ways. Suffixes such as *-s* and *-ed* can change the tense of a verb; suffixes such as *-s* can change the number of a noun to make it a plural. Deviational morphemes, in contrast, can be added to words to create or derive another word, for example the addition of *-ness* to *sad* creates the new word *sadness,* or the addition of *-ly* changes *sad* to an adverb, *sadly.*

Word structure includes the study of the following:

- **Compound words** are made of two words that combine to form a new word. Compounds can be open or closed.
- **Root words** focus on learning about the basic element of words. Root words are the foundations upon which the meaning of a word is formed. A root may be a real word as in *audio,* meaning "sound," but it can also used with a suffix to become *audible,* changing the noun to an adjective. Although *audible* can have other elements, it does not need other elements to be complete. Most roots, however, do need other elements. Roots such as *duct, anthrop,* and *cred* require affixes to form the words *deduct, anthropology,* and *incredible,* respectively. Knowledge of root words and affixes provides students with critical tools for understanding derived words.
- **Prefixes** include any morpheme that is attached to the beginning of a root or word and changes the meaning of that word. Prefixes do not change the form of the word, only the meaning. Common prefixes include: *con-, com-, ad-, de-, di-, dis-, per-, re-, sub-, hyper-, un-,* and so on as well as numbers *(bi-, tri-, uni-, mono-, octo-,* and so on.)
- **Suffixes** include any morpheme that is attached to the end of a word or root and that changes the meaning of that word. Suffixes often change the function of the word and often require a spelling change in the root as well. For example, the addition of *-ial* to *colony* changes a noun to an adjective.

Common Latin Roots

Aud: auditory, auditorium, inaudible, audible, audition
Dict: dictate, predict, contradict, prediction
Ject: reject, inject, project, object, projection, objection
Port: transport, import, export, portable, support, report
Rupt: rupture, erupt, eruption, disrupt, interruption
Scrib/script: scribe, describe, manuscript, inscription, transcript, description, prescription
Spect: spectator, inspect, inspector, respect, spectacle, spectacular
Struct: structure, construct, instruct, destruction, reconstruction
Tract: tractor, traction, attract, subtraction, extract, retract, attractive
Vis: vision, visual, visit, supervisor, invisible, vista, visualize, visionary

Common Greek Roots

Auto: automatic, autograph, autobiography, automobile
Bio: biology, biography
Graph: graphite, geography, graphic, photograph, phonograph
Hydr: hydrogen, hydrant
Meter: speedometer, odometer, thermometer, metronome
Ology: geology, zoology, phonology
Photo: photography, photocopy, photosynthesis, photogenic
Scope: telescope, stethoscope, microscope, microscopic, periscope
Tele: telephone, television, telegraph
Therm: thermos, thermostat

Other examples of suffixes that change the word form include the following:

- Noun suffixes: *-age, -al, -ance, -ant, -ate, -ee, -ence, -ent, -er, -or, -ar, -ese, -ess, -hood, -ice, -isn, -ist, -ment, -ness, -sion, -tain, -tion, -ure*
- Suffixes that form adjectives: *-able, -al, -er, -est, -ette, -let, -ful, -fully, -ible, -ic, -ical, -ish, -ive, -less, -ous, -some, -worthy*
- Suffixes that form adverbs: *-ly, -wards, -ways, -wide, -wise*
- Suffixes that create verb forms: *-ate, -ed, -en, -ing, -ise, -ize, -yze*
- Inflectional endings are a special set of suffixes that change the number (singular to plural), case, or gender when added to nouns and change tense when added to verbs.

Teaching Word Structure

- *Have students read the words in a line.
- Tell students that words can be made of several individual parts.
- Examine the words in each line for meaningful parts, roots, and affixes.
- Identify the root or base word, and discuss the meaning.
- Underline and discuss the meaning of the prefix or suffix or both. If there is a prefix and a suffix, begin with the prefix. Tell students a prefix is a group of letters that is attached to the beginning of a base or root word. These letters have a specific meaning. For example, *un-* means "not" or "the opposite of," *non-* means "not," and *re-* means "again." A suffix is a group of letters that comes at the end of the base or root word and changes the meaning of the word. For example, *-er* changes a verb to a noun or the person doing the action as in *sing* and *singer,* or *-al* or *-ial* change nouns to adjectives as in *colony* and *colonial.*
- Reassemble the word, thinking about the meaning of the word parts.
- Say the word.
- Use the word in the sentence.

*Sometimes students are intimidated by longer words. Understanding syllable breaks helps when reading these longer words. The following chart includes information on syllable "generalizations." These may help your students when reading longer words during Word Structure activities and in the reading.

Word	Break into Syllables	Syllable Generalizations
Puppet	Pup-pet	Closed. If a word has two consonants in the middle, divide the word between the two consonants. The first syllable is closed, and the vowel pronunciation is short.
Music	Mu-sic	Open. If a word has a VCV pattern, break the syllables before the consonant, which makes the first syllable an open syllable and the first vowel long.
Closet	Clos-et	Some VCV patterns have the break after the consonant, which makes the first syllable a closed syllable and the vowel pronunciation short.
Hundred	Hun-dred	When there is a VCCCV pattern, the break is usually between the consonants. The first syllable is closed, and the vowel pronunciation is short.
Coward	Cow-ard	When there are two diphthongs, the syllable break comes between them.
Chaos	Cha-os	When there is a VV pattern, the syllable break comes between the vowels, and the first vowel is usually long.
Handle	Han-dle	Consonant plus *-le.* If a word has an *-le* (or *-el*) at the end, it usually forms a separate syllable and is pronounced with the consonant and /ə/ /l/.
Excitement Reform	Ex-cite-ment Re-form	Prefixes and suffixes are separate syllables.
Entertain Hurdle	En-ter-tain Hur-dle	*R*-controlled vowels. In most syllables where the vowel is followed by an *r,* the vowel sound is *r*-controlled.
Complete	Com-plete	Final *e.* When there is a vowel, consonant, and then an *e* at the end, the vowel before the consonant is pronounced long, and the *e* is silent.

Developing Vocabulary

For students to develop a deeper understanding of words, they should have multiple experiences with them. There are any number of activities that students can do to help them use words and internalize their meanings. The following activities can be used with the whole class or in small groups during Workshop.

- Give a word, and ask the student to find it in the line and to give a definition.
- Give a word, and ask the student to add a prefix or a suffix and to tell the meaning of the new word and the new part of speech.
- If the word is a multiple-meaning word, have the student point to the word, and then have the student give one meaning and use it in a sentence. Then have a second student give another meaning and use it in a sentence. (Be sure that the words that are used are truly multiple-meaning words and not words that can be used as different parts of speech, for example, a verb and a noun that have the same basic meaning.)
- Give two words, and have the student point to them. Ask what is the difference between these two words. For example, *hot* and *cold* are antonyms. The same could be done for synonyms, homonyms,

and homophones. This gets students to use the vocabulary and do the thinking. Point to two words, and have students tell how they are alike and different. For example, *history, historical,* and *historian* all have the same roots. All three words have a common root, but *history* and *historian* are nouns, and *historical* is an adjective.

- Give students a word, and have them point to the word. If it is a singular noun, have them change it to a plural or vice versa. If it is a verb, have students change the tense, or if it is an adjective, change it into an adverb if appropriate. In all cases, be sure that students spell the new word.
- Give students a word, have them point to and read the word, and then give the part of speech.
- Give a student a word, and have him or her use the word in a sentence. Have the class decide if the sentence truly shows the meaning of the word. For example, if the word is *camouflage,* and the student says, "Animals use camouflage," have the class add to the sentence to show the meaning: "Animals use camouflage to protect themselves from predators."
- Give students a word with a base word, and ask them to point to the word and read it and then to tell the root of the word.
- Give students a word with a Greek or Latin root. Have them point to and read the word, and then have them identify the root. Challenge students to think of other words that have the same root.
- Give students a word with a prefix or suffix. Have a student point to and read the word and then identify the prefix or suffix and tell the meaning of the affix. Then, if appropriate, have the student or a different student replace the affix with a different one and tell the meaning of the new word.
- When appropriate, give students a word, and have them give a synonym or antonym. When appropriate, work on gradations of words. For example, if the word is *hot* then the opposite is *cold*. Gradations would be *hot, warm, tepid, cool, cold*. These kinds of activities expand vocabulary.
- Give two words that are connected in some way, for example, *colony* and *colonial*. Have students come to the board, point to the words, and read them. Then have them tell why or how the words are connected.
- Have students find other words that follow comparable patterns to those taught in the lesson. If *colony, colonial, colonist* is a line in Word Structure, many students could find related nouns and use them with affixes, *(history, historical, historian)*. Challenge students to think more about words.

Tips

- Be sure students understand the limits of structural analysis. The *un-* in *unhappy* is a prefix, but the *un* in *under* and *uncle* is not.
- Help students realize that many words are related and that using their knowledge of a word can help them understand related words.
- Encourage students to use their knowledge of word structure during all reading to clarify unfamiliar words.

Fluency

Fluency is the ability to read or access words effortlessly with seemingly little attention to decoding. Fluent readers decode words not only automatically but accurately. In addition, fluent readers group words into meaningful units, utilize punctuation to guide their voices, and use expression appropriately to help them comprehend what they are reading. Fluent readers also adjust their reading rate as necessary.

To become proficient readers who fully understand what they read, the whole process of decoding must become automatic. Readers need to be so familiar with the sound/spellings, with common meaningful units like prefixes and suffixes and with the most common nondecodable sight words that they automatically process the spellings and word chunks. This enables them to read the word effortlessly and expend most of their energy on comprehending the meaning of the text. Automaticity is a key component of fluency.

The concept of fluency is introduced in the early grades, even before students are reading. When reading aloud, teachers are modeling fluency and using expression and intonation to support meaning. In pre-kindergarten and kindergarten, emergent readers learn about concepts of print that support fluency: learning about spaces and ending punctuation, reading from left to right, and automatically recognizing high-frequency sight words. Students apply this knowledge to reading ***Pre-Decodables.*** These skills are then applied to reading ***Decodables.*** While fluency begins in first grade, many students will continue to need practice in building fluency in second and third grades. Initially students can use the ***SRA Imagine It! Decodable Stories*** in Grades 2 and 3, but fluency practice should include using materials from a variety of different sources, including selections from the ***Student Readers, Leveled Readers,*** and the ***Leveled Science*** and ***Social Studies Readers.*** At all grade levels using ***Pre-Decodables, Decodables, Readers,*** or any other materials, students need to appreciate that fluency is about meaning. Take time to ask questions after students have read, talk about new and interesting words, and discuss any problems students encountered.

Building Fluency: Reading Pre-Decodables (K–1)

Purpose

Pre-Decodables play an important role in students' early literacy development by providing them with meaningful "reading" experiences before they are actually reading on their own and by expanding their awareness of the forms and uses of print. By following along as you read aloud a ***Pre-Decodable,*** students learn about the left-to-right and top-to-bottom progression of print on a page, the clues that indicate the beginnings and endings of sentences, the connections between pictures and words, and important book conventions such as front and back covers, authors' and illustrators' names, title pages, and page numbers.

The ***Pre-Decodables*** provide students with opportunities to apply their growing knowledge of letter names, shapes, and sounds and to become familiar with individual words. In addition, students practice reading high-frequency sight words. The automatic recognition of these words, the identification of ending punctuation, and reading with expression support the development of foundational fluency skills.

Through retelling the story in a ***Pre-Decodable,*** predicting or wondering about what will happen, and asking and responding to questions about the book, students not only learn about the relationship between spoken and written language, they learn to think about what they have read.

About the Pre-Decodables

Each ***Pre-Decodable*** contains a story that engages students' interest as it provides them with opportunities to practice what they are learning in their lessons. These "pre-decodable" stories each contain several high-frequency words that most students already have in their spoken vocabularies and that are a basic part of all meaningful stories. Learning to identify high-frequency words quickly, accurately, and effortlessly is a critical part of students' development as fluent, independent readers. The inside back cover of each ***Pre-Decodable*** contains a list of high-frequency words.

How to Use the Pre-Decodables

- Before reading a ***Pre-Decodable,*** take time to familiarize students with any new high-frequency words in the book and to review previously introduced words. To reinforce the idea that it is important to know these words because they are used so often in print, always point out the words in context. For example, focus students' attention on the words in ***Big Book*** selections or on signs and posters around the classroom.
- Give each student a copy of the book. Tell students that you will read the book together. Hold up your book. Read the title. If the title has a rebus picture, point to it, and tell students what it is. Then point to the word beneath it, and explain that the picture represents that word. Point to and read the names of the author and illustrator, reminding students that an author writes a book, and an illustrator draws the pictures. Page through the book, pointing to and naming the rebus pictures. Have students say the name of each rebus. To avoid confusion, always tell them the exact word that a rebus represents. Do not encourage them to guess at its meaning.
- Allow students time to browse through the book on their own, commenting on what they see in the illustrations and making predictions about what they think the book will be about. Encourage them to comment on anything special they notice about the story, the illustrations, or the words in the book.
- Help students find page 3. Read the book aloud without stopping. As you read, move your hand beneath the words to show the progression of print. Pause at each rebus as you say the word it represents, pointing first to the rebus then to the word beneath it.
- Reread the book. This time, ask students to point to and read the high-frequency words.
- Tell students to follow along in their books as you read the story again. Read the title aloud, and then have students read it with you. Reread page 3. Point to each rebus picture, and ask a volunteer

to "read" it. Point to the word beneath the picture, and remind students that the picture shows what the word is. Continue through each page of the book, calling on volunteers to "read" and stopping as necessary to clarify and help students with words.

- After reading, answer any questions students might have about the book. Encourage them to discuss the illustrations and to explain what is happening in each one.

Building Fluency: Reading Decodables (K–3)

Purpose

The most urgent task of early reading instruction is to make written thoughts intelligible to students. This requires a balanced approach that includes systematic instruction in phonics as well as experiences with authentic literature. Thus, from the very beginning, ***SRA Imagine It!*** includes the reading of literature. At the beginning of first grade, when students are learning phonics and blending as a tool to access words, the teacher reads aloud. During this time students are working on using comprehension strategies and skills and discussing stories. As students learn to code and blend words, recognize critical sight words, and develop some level of fluency, they take more responsibility for the actual reading of the text.

This program has a systematic instruction in phonics that allows students to begin reading independently. This instruction is supported by ***SRA Imagine It! Decodables.***

About the Decodables

The ***SRA Imagine It! Decodables*** are designed to help students apply, review, and reinforce their expanding knowledge of sound/spelling correspondences. Each story supports instruction in new phonic elements and incorporates elements and words that have been learned earlier. There are eight-page and sixteen-page ***Decodables.*** Grade K has eight-page ***Decodables.*** In Grade 1, the eight-page books focus on the new element introduced in the lesson, while the sixteen-page books review and reinforce the elements that have been taught since the last sixteen-page book. They review sounds from several lessons and provide additional reading practice. Grades 2–3 have eight-page ***Decodable Stories*** in Getting Started, and eight- and sixteen-page stories in Units 1–3 in Grade 3 and Units 1–6 in Grade 2. The primary purpose is to provide practice reading the words. It is important that students also attach meaning to what they are reading. Questions are often included in the ***Teacher's Edition*** to check both understanding and attention to words.

How to use Decodables

Preparing to Read

- Introduce and write on the board or cards any nondecodable high-frequency or story words introduced or reviewed in the story. Tell students how to pronounce any newly introduced high-frequency words. Then point to each new word, and have students spell and say it. Have them read any previously introduced sight words in the Word Bank list. All the ***SRA Imagine It! Decodables*** contain high-frequency words that may not be decodable. For example, the word *said* is a common high-frequency word that is not decodable. Including words such as *said* makes the language of the story flow smoothly and naturally. Students need to be able to recognize and read these words quickly and smoothly.
- Read the title. At the beginning of the year, you may need to read the title of the book to students, but as the year goes on, you should have a student read it whenever possible. In Grade 1, selected sixteen-page ***SRA Imagine It! Decodables*** contain two related chapters, each using the same sounds and spellings. In such cases, read the title of the ***Decodable,*** and then point out the two individual chapter titles. Have volunteers read the title of the chapter you are about to read.
- Browse the story. Have students look through the story, commenting on whatever they notice in the text or illustrations and telling what they think the story will tell them.

Reading the Story

After this browsing, students will read the story a page at a time. Again, these stories are designed to support the learning of sounds and spellings. The focus should not be on comprehension. Students should understand what they are reading, and they should feel free to discuss anything in the story that interests them. Any areas of confusion are discussed and clarified as they arise, as described below.

- Have students read a page to themselves. Then call on one student or groups of students to read the page aloud, or have the entire group read it aloud.
- If a student has difficulty with a word that can be blended, help her or him blend the word. Remind the student to check the ***Sound/Spelling Cards*** for help. If a word cannot be blended using the sound/spellings learned so far, pronounce the word for the student.
- If a student has trouble with a word or sentence, have the reader call on a classmate for help and then continue reading after the word or sentence has been clarified. After something on a page has been clarified or discussed, have a different student reread that page before moving on to the next page.
- Repeat this procedure for each page.
- Reread the story twice more, calling on various students to read or reading it in unison. These readings should go more quickly, with fewer stops for clarification.

Responding to the Story

After the story has been read aloud a couple of times, have students respond as follows:

- Ask students which difficult words they found in the story and how they figured them out. They may mention high-frequency words they did not recognize, words they had to blend, and words whose meanings they did not know.
- Have students tell about the story, retelling it in their own words, describing what they liked about it, or citing what they found interesting or surprising. Specific suggestions to use are listed in the ***Teacher's Edition.***
- Questions are often provided in the ***Teacher's Edition.*** They are designed to focus students' attention on the words and not just the pictures. Ask students the questions, and have all students point to the answer in the story rather than having one student respond orally. Having students point to the answers is important. First, it ensures that all students are engaged in finding

the answer, not just one. Second, by pointing to the answer, you know that students know the answer from reading and not just from having heard it read. Third, locating information in a text is an important skill. Finally, by pointing to the answer, you can quickly monitor who is understanding the story and who may still need more support during Workshop.

- Have students reread the story with partners. Circulate among the pairs, listening to individual students read. This allows you to monitor students' reading and to identify any students who may need additional help during Workshop.

Building Fluency beyond Decodables (middle of grade 1 on)

For some students, fluency develops naturally, seemingly without instruction. Other students, however, can benefit from more explicit instruction. There are students who can decode and read words but lack the critical phrasing, intonation, and expression that support meaning. Teach the text characteristics that support fluency, model them for students, and then provide students regular opportunities to practice fluency. Instruction can focus on any or all of the following areas:

- Discuss and model ending punctuation and what this means in terms of expression and intonation. This should be modeled and then discussed with students. Begin with ending punctuation, and then move to internal punctuation such as commas and semicolons. During modeling,
    - pause longer at a period or other ending punctuation.
    - raise your voice at a question mark.
    - use expression when you come to an exclamation point.
    - pause at commas or other internal punctuation such as semicolons.
    - when you come to quotation marks, think of the character and how he or she might say his or her words.
    - pause at an ellipsis.
    - pause at dashes.
- Discuss and model words written in a special way—typographical signals such as underlined words, boldfaced words, or those in all caps—need to be read with expression and changed in intonation for emphasis.
- Talk about reading rate. Oral reading should be done at a normal speaking rate. Students should not be reading so fast that someone listening could not hear the individual words and make sense of what is being read.
- Discuss and model intonation. Let students hear how voices change with different ending punctuation, how voices change when reading dialogue, and how intonation changes with cues from the author. In dialogue, think of the difference between "screamed Jennifer" versus "pleaded Jessie."
- Work on phrase cue boundaries. A good way to teach this is by using an overhead of what students are reading. Mark natural phrase boundaries—for example, clauses, prepositional phrases, subject phrases, verb phrases, and so on, with slashes. For example, *In the summertime,/Josh likes to play baseball/ at the park/down the street from his house.* Have students listen to you read the text, noticing how you paused at the markers. Then have students read the sentences naturally, using the markers as guides. Scaffold the instruction. In the beginning, mark the boundaries, and have students practice reading using the already marked passages. As students become comfortable, have them mark what they are reading with boundary markers. Gradually fade out the markers or slashes.

Fluency develops over time, and students should be given repeated opportunities to practice fluency with a variety of different texts. After students have read a text, take time to go back and discuss any new vocabulary or interesting words that students encountered while reading. Fluency is not an isolated activity; it is about supporting comprehension.

There are a number of techniques for practicing fluency: repeated readings, partner reading, tape-assisted reading, and Reader's Theater. All of these techniques can be done with a variety of different reading materials, including selections from the ***Student Readers,*** the ***Leveled Readers,*** and the ***Science*** and ***Social Studies Leveled Readers.***

- Repeated readings increase reading rate, accuracy, and comprehension by providing students with multiple exposures to words and spelling patterns. In addition, it helps students improve their ability to break sentences into meaningful phrases and to use intonation. It is effective with both older and younger students. Repeated readings involve the students reading segments of text between 50 to 200 words, depending upon students' ability. Students should practice repeated readings with a variety of different text types. While repeated readings can be done with materials from ***SRA Imagine It!*** using segments from science and social studies texts helps students in the upper grades apply their reading knowledge across the curriculum. The goal is to have students read the text fluently and automatically at a per-minute rate commensurate with grade-level norms.
- CD-assisted readings help build confidence and are excellent support for second-language learners. Tape-assisted reading allows students to hear good models of reading and to develop their awareness of phrasing and prosody, or expressive reading. Tapes should provide students with experiences from a variety of text types. Tape selections should be read at approximately 80–100 words per minute by fluent readers with natural intonation, phrasing, and expression. Students read along with the text, aloud or subvocalizing. When the student is comfortable with the text, the student should practice reading the text independently and then read a portion of it to the teacher. The CDs in ***SRA Imagine It!*** can help students develop fluency with selections in the ***Student Readers.***
- Reader's Theater legitimizes practicing fluency because it involves reading a script. While students do not memorize the script the way actors do in a play, they must be able to read the script fluently so the audience—the rest of the class—can enjoy the play. Several students can work together on a single play or playlet. They will need to practice reading the script several times before presenting it to the class. Reader's Theater also provides students with a writing opportunity. They can use a selection from their ***Student Readers,***

write a playlet, and then practice it for Reader's Theater.

- Radio Reading, like Reader's Theater, connects reading aloud to real-life situations. Students, with copies of the text, read aloud in front of the class as if they were news broadcasters. Expository text works particularly well for this. Students can practice, and then once a week, several students can be the radio announcers. Students can also write weekly news reports and read them.
- Partner Reading involves students reading with a partner. They can take turns reading pages or the entire selection. While one student reads, the listening-partner should note misread words and then discuss them with the partner after the reading. If the pairs are reading for one-minute-fluency checks, the nonreading partner can be responsible for timing the reading. Selections should be read multiple times with the goal being that students achieve a higher fluency rate on successive readings.

Assessing Fluency

Fluency should be assessed periodically to determine students' growth and to monitor progess. Listening to students read regularly is key. Fluency assessment should include not just reading rate but decoding accuracy, prosody (phrasing and intonation), and expression. In addition, checks should be done using various text types.

Generally accepted procedures for assessment include the following:

- Use a passage of approximately 250 words at student's reading level. In the first half of first grade, use the appropriate ***Decodable*** in the Practice set. Have two copies—one for the student and one for you to mark.
- Have the student read the passage for one minute. Use a timer, if possible, so you do not have to keep watching a stopwatch or the minute hand on a clock. You can also tape-record the reading. The goal is to have students read the text aloud in a natural way, the way they would speak the words. This is not a race! Use the following scoring conventions. Mark any errors made by the reader.
- Draw a line through any misread word, and count it as an error.
- Circle any words the student omits or refuses to read, and count them as errors.
- Indicate with a caret any extra words the student inserts.
- Draw an arrow between words that student reverses, and count as one error.
- Put two check marks above a word that a student repeats, but do not count it as an error.
- Draw a box around the last word student reads in the one-minute time frame.

To calculate the student's accuracy rate, count the total number of words read in one minute. Subtract the number of errors from the total number of words read, and use that number to find the number of correct words read per minute.

For example, to calculate the rate:

Total words read – errors = words correct per minute

75 words read – 10 errors = 65 words per minute

For example, to calculate the accuracy:

Number of words ÷ the total number of words = percent of accuracy

145 (words correct) ÷ 156 (total number of words) = 93%

Descriptive Statistics for Oral Reading Fluency by Season for Grades 1–6 (Medians)

		Fall	Winter	Spring
Grade	Percentile	WCPM[2]	WCPM	WCPM
1	75		46.75	82
	50		23	53
	25		6	15
2	75	79	100	117
	50	51	72	89
	25	25	42	61
3	75	99	120	137
	50	71	92	107
	25	44	62	78
4	75	119	139	152
	50	94	112	123
	25	68	87	98
5	75	139	156	168
	50	110.25	127	139
	25	85	99	109
6	75	153	167	177
	50	127	140	150
	25	98	111	122

[2]WCPM = words correct per minute

SOURCE
From "Curriculum-Based Oral Reading Fluency Norms for Students in Grades 1 Through 6" (2005) by Jan E. Hasbrouck and Gerald Tindal. *Behavioral Research and Teaching.*

In addition, watch for and note the following:

- Expression
- Ability of the reader to read words in natural syntactic clusters

Assessing accuracy, pace or rate, and expression provide information for instruction.

In addition to the qualitative information, some teachers like to use rubrics in their evaluation of fluency.

- **Level 1:** Reads basically word by word with limited phrasing, little expression. Reading is labored with difficulty in reading words automatically and fluently.
- **Level 2:** Reads in limited phrases of two words, but grouping of words is not natural. There is little or no appropriate expression or intonation.
- **Level 3:** Reads in phrases with most having appropriate breaks. Most of the reading has appropriate expression and intonation. There is limited comprehension.
- **Level 4:** Reads with appropriate phrasing, intonation, and expression and demonstrates understanding of the piece.

Interpreting Fluency Data

First compare the student's number of correct words per minute with accepted fluency norms.

Then examine the student's accuracy percentage. Reading accuracy should remain constant or gradually increase within and between grades until it stabilizes at 90 percent or higher. Compare the student's accuracy percentage after each assessment to ensure that his or her accuracy percentage is holding constant or improving.

Next examine the types of errors the student made, and consider what they mean for instruction.

- Inserting extra words suggest that the student understands what is being read but is reading perhaps impulsively or carelessly.
- Refusing to attempt to read words suggests that the student may be uncertain of his or her abilities, unwilling to take risks, or needs additional work with decoding at the sound/spelling or morpheme level. Look at the words the student does not read. Are they one-syllable words or multisyllabic words?
- Misreading routine CVC and CVCe words suggest that the student may need more work with the sounds and spellings. In some cases, a student may be able to read words with common sounds and spellings but needs more work with long vowels, diphthongs, and diagraphs.
- Looking for patterns in errors is key.
- Using or not using intonation, expression, and phrasing but reading quickly and accurately suggests that students need to think about how words combine to make meaning and how our expression can support understanding.

Tips

- Use Workshop time for building fluency. Introduce different ways to practice fluency one at a time.
- Set up a listening area for Workshop that students can use for tape-assisted instruction.
- Make sure ***Pre-Decodables, Decodables,*** and ***Leveled Readers*** are available to students.
- Have simple timers available for students to check their fluency rate.
- Encourage students to chart their fluency growth. If students are doing repeated reading, have them chart the number of words read each day for several days so they can see their fluency improving.
- When students have developed some degree of fluency with a ***Pre-Decodable, Decodable,*** or ***Leveled Reader,*** send the materials home for additional practice.
- Use a range of materials to practice building fluency throughout the day. Remember, fluency practice can be as short as one minute several times a day.

Reading Aloud

Purpose

Adults read aloud a variety of materials to students. In this program there are ***Big Books,*** picture books, novels, and excerpts for reading aloud. Research has shown that students who are read to are more likely to develop the skills they need to read successfully on their own.

In kindergarten and Grade 1, there are ***Big Books.*** In every grade level of ***SRA Imagine It!*** there are opportunities for teachers to read aloud to students. At the beginning of each unit is a Read Aloud selection tied to the unit theme. This Read Aloud selection allows students the opportunity to think about the unit theme before reading selections on their own.

Reading aloud at any age serves multiple purposes. Reading aloud

- provokes students' curiosity about text.
- conveys an awareness that text has meaning.
- demonstrates the various reasons for reading text (to find out about the world, to learn useful new information and new skills, or simply for pleasure).
- exposes students to the "language of literature," which is more complex than the language they ordinarily use and hear.
- provides an opportunity to teach the problem-solving strategies that good readers employ. As students observe you interacting with the text, expressing your own enthusiasm, and modeling your thinking aloud, they perceive these as valid responses and begin to respond to text in similar ways.

Procedures

The following set of general procedures for reading aloud is designed to help you maximize the effectiveness of any Read Aloud session.

- **Read-Aloud sessions.** Set aside time each day to read aloud.
- **Introduce the story.** Tell students that you are going to read a story aloud to them. Tell its title, and briefly comment on the topic. To allow students to anticipate what will happen in the story, be careful not to summarize.
- **Activate prior knowledge.** Ask whether anyone has already heard the story. If so, ask them to see if this version is the same as the one they have heard. If not, activate prior knowledge by saying, "First, let's talk a little about ______." If the story is being read in two (or more) parts, before reading the second part, ask students to recall the first part.
- **Before reading.** Invite students to interrupt your reading if there are any words they do not understand or ideas they find puzzling or to ask questions. Throughout the reading, encourage them to do this.
- **Read the story expressively.** Occasionally react verbally to the story by showing surprise, asking questions, giving an opinion, expressing pleasure, or predicting events. Expressive reading not only supports comprehension but serves as a model for fluency. Think-aloud suggestions are outlined below.
- **Use Comprehension Strategies.** While reading aloud to students, model the use of comprehension strategies in a natural, authentic way. Remember to try to present a variety of ways to respond to text. These include visualizing, asking questions, predicting, making connections, clarifying, and summarizing.
- **Retell.** When you have finished reading the story, call on volunteers to retell it.
- **Discuss.** After reading, discuss with students their own reactions: how the story reminded them of things that have happened to them, what they thought of the story, and what they liked best about the story.
- **Reread.** You may wish to reread the selection on subsequent occasions, focusing the discussion on the unit theme.

Think-Aloud Responses

The following options for modeling thinking aloud will be useful for reading any story aloud. Choose responses that are most appropriate for the selection you are reading.

- React emotionally by showing joy, sadness, amusement, or surprise.
- Ask questions about ideas in the text. This should be done when there are points or ideas that you really do wonder about.
- Identify with characters by comparing them to yourself.
- Show empathy with or sympathy for characters.
- Relate the text to something you already know or something that has happened to you.
- Show interest in the text ideas.
- Question the meaning or clarity of the author's words and ideas.

Questions to Help Students Respond

At reasonable stopping points in reading, ask students general questions to get them to express their own ideas and to focus their attention on the text. These types of generic questions will help students discuss their reactions to the reading and demonstrate their comprehension.

- What do you already know about this?
- What seems really important here? Why do you think so?
- Was there anything that you did not understand? What?
- What did you like best about this?
- What did you not like about this?
- What new ideas did you learn from this?
- What does this make you wonder about?
- What surprised you in the story?

Vocabulary

Purpose

Strong vocabulary skills are correlated to achievement throughout school. The purpose of vocabulary instruction is to introduce students to new words (and ideas) and to teach students a range of strategies for learning, remembering, and incorporating unknown vocabulary words into their existing reading, writing, speaking, and listening vocabularies.

Words chosen for inclusion in ***SRA Imagine It!*** are based upon the vocabulary research of Andrew Biemiller, who has developed a comprehensive database of words students with large vocabularies know by the end of sixth grade. Biemiller's work identifies words that all students need to know and provides evidence that students from various backgrounds acquire these word meanings in roughly the same order. It appears that for students with small vocabularies, improving vocabulary mainly means moving them through the sequence faster. Because vocabulary knowledge is so critical to comprehension, vocabulary instruction is integrated throughout ***SRA Imagine It!***

Vocabulary is taught throughout every part of the lesson.

Part 1: Preparing to Read

- In Grades 2–6, Word Structure develops vocabulary and the understanding that words can be deconstructed and related through known elements to determine meaning. In addition, students are learning about Greek and Latin roots, antonyms, synonyms, and multiple-meaning words. The emphasis on root words and affixes, in particular, serves to expand students' knowledge of words and their vocabulary.
- In Grades K–1, students are using words they blend in sentences to develop vocabulary and oral language. Learning about inflectional endings also helps children see the relationship between root words and various forms of the root. Reviews of blending lines focus on using words based on teacher clues as well as finding synonyms and antonyms.

Part 2: Reading and Responding

- The selection vocabulary instruction in this part of the lesson focuses on teaching specific vocabulary necessary for understanding the literature selection more completely.
- In kindergarten and the first half of Grade 1, the teacher introduces the selection vocabulary orally before reading the selection. Suggestions are made throughout the reading to discuss new and interesting words as the class reads the ***Big Books.*** Work from Biemiller suggests that clarifying words in the context of reading is an effective technique for expanding student vocabulary. Suggestions for which words to stop and clarify are suggested throughout the lessons. Vocabulary review activities are found throughout the lesson.
- From the middle of Grade 1 on, critical word meanings needed to understand the story are pre-taught as students read the Vocabulary Warm-Up in the ***Student Reader.*** This provides an initial exposure to the selection vocabulary. This is followed by guided vocabulary practice in which students discuss the definitions of critical words; learn to apply critical skills such as context, structure and apposition; use the vocabulary words in a variety of activities, and then return to the Vocabulary Warm-Up to reread the sentences containing the vocabulary words and to discuss the words. The clarification of additional vocabulary words is highlighted throughout the reading of each selection. Vocabulary review activities are found throughout the lesson.
- Students write the words and their definitions in their Writer's Notebooks.
- Vocabulary words, along with any other words students find interesting, are posted on charts to remind students to use these words in discussion of their reading as well as in their writing.

Part 3: Language Arts

During writing, students are encouraged to use their new vocabulary.

General Strategies

There is no question that having students read and reading to students are effective vocabulary instructional strategies. Most word learning occurs through exposure to words in listening and reading. Multiple exposures to words, particularly when students hear, see, say, and write words, is also effective. Wordplay, including meaning and dictionary games, helps develop a word consciousness as well.

Vocabulary Strategies for Unknown Words

Different strategies have been shown to be particularly effective for learning completely new words. These strategies are included in the Vocabulary Warm-Up lessons and ***Skills Practice*** activities.

Key Word This strategy involves providing or having students create a mnemonic clue for unknown vocabulary. For example, the word *mole* is defined in chemistry as a "gram molecule." By relating *mole* to *molecule,* students have a key to the meaning of the word.

Definitions Copying a definition from a dictionary is somewhat effective in learning new vocabulary. Combining this with using the word in writing and speaking adds to the effectiveness of this strategy. Requiring students to explain a word or to use it in a novel sentence helps ensure that the meaning is understood. It is not uncommon when students use words in sentences that the meaning of the vocabulary word is not clear. For example, a typical sentence a student might give for the word *camouflage* is "The octopus uses camouflage." The word *camouflage* is correctly used, but there is no real indication that the student knows the meaning of the word. Having students extend the sentence to explain why or how in the sentence helps: "The octopus uses camouflage to protect itself from predators." Or "The camouflage an octopus uses when it is in danger is to change its shape and color."

Context Clues Some words can be inferred from context and can be learned with repeated exposure to words in reading and listening. While using context can be useful, it is not the most effective way to learn new words. Also, as students move into content area reading, context becomes a less effective tool for determining the meaning of unfamiliar words.

- **Syntax** How a word is used in a sentence may provide some clue as to its meaning. This is particularly effective with homographs. "The lead pipe is a hazard to the community." Here lead is an adjective and is pronounced with a short e. In the sentence "He will lead the troops into battle," *lead* has a very different meaning, is a verb, and is pronounced with a long e.
- **Apposition** Sometimes the word is actually defined within the text. In an appositive, the definition of a word is often set off by commas for the reader.

Word Structure Examining the affixes and roots of a word often provides clues to its meaning. Knowing the meaning of at least part of the word can provide a clue as to its meaning. For example, *unenforceable* can be broken down into meaningful word parts. This is a particularly important tool in content area reading.

Developing Vocabulary

Purpose

Vocabulary is closely connected to comprehension. Considerable vocabulary growth occurs incidentally during reading. A clear connection exists between vocabulary development and the amount of reading a person does, and there are strong indications that vocabulary instruction is important and that understanding the meanings of key words helps with comprehension.

In ***SRA Imagine It!*** vocabulary is addressed before, during, and after reading. Before reading, the teacher presents vocabulary words from the selection. Students use skills such as context clues, apposition, and structural analysis to determine the meanings of the words. These selection vocabulary words are not only important to understanding the text but are also high-utility words that can be used in discussing and writing about the unit theme.

During reading, students monitor their understanding of words and text. When they do not understand something, they stop and clarify what they have read. Students will use these same skills—context clues, apposition, structural elements, and so on—to clarify the meanings of additional words encountered while reading. Determining the meanings of words while reading prepares students for the demands of independent reading both in and out of school.

After reading, students review the vocabulary words that they learned before reading the selection. They also review any interesting words that they identified and discussed during reading. Students record in their Writer's Notebooks both the selection vocabulary words and the interesting words they identified during their reading and are encouraged to use both sets of words in discussion and in writing.

Procedure

Before students read the selection, they read the Vocabulary Warm-Up in the ***Student Reader.*** As they read, students use context clues, word structure, or apposition to figure out the highlighted selection vocabulary. If students cannot determine the meaning of a word using one of the skills, they can consult the glossary or dictionary. After reading the Vocabulary Warm-Up, the teacher displays an overhead transparency to review the selection vocabulary.

Below are suggestions for modeling the use of context clues, apposition, or word structure to determine the meaning of a word.

Modeling Using Context Clues

Write the following sentences on the board or on a transparency. Explain to students that they will use context clues, or other words in the sentence, to determine the meaning of the underlined word.

1. Mrs. Frisby must undertake a <u>treacherous</u> journey to take her son some medicine.
2. We took a <u>treacherous</u> walk near a swamp filled with crocodiles.

Have students look for clues in the sentences that might help them understand the meaning of the underlined word. Point out that a good clue in the second sentence is "near a swamp filled with crocodiles." This clue should help them understand that *treacherous* probably has something to do with danger. Guide students until they can give a reasonable definition of *treacherous.* To consolidate understanding of the word, ask another student to use the definition in a sentence.

Modeling Using Apposition

Write the following sentences on the board or on a transparency. Explain to students that they will use apposition to determine the meaning of the underlined word. In apposition, the word is followed by the definition, which is set off by commas.

1. The conductor thought he was an <u>abolitionist,</u> a person who wanted to end slavery.
2. John Brown was a famous <u>abolitionist</u>, a person who wanted to end slavery.

It should be clear to students using apposition that the definition of the word *abolitionist* is "a person who wanted to end slavery."

Modeling Using Word Structure

Write the following sentences on the board or on a transparency. Explain to students that they will use word structure, or parts of the word, to determine the meaning of the underlined word.

1. The strong wind blew Ivan's ship away into <u>uncharted</u> seas.
2. The explorers Lewis and Clark went into <u>uncharted</u> territory.

Have students look at the word *uncharted* and break it into parts: the prefix *un-*, *chart,* and the suffix *-ed.* Students should know that the suffix *un-* means "not" and that the suffix *-ed* usually indicates the past tense of a verb. However, you may need to remind students about the meanings of these affixes. Ask students for the meaning of the word *chart.* Students should know that a chart could be a map or a table. Guide them as they put together the definitions of the word parts: *un-* (not), *charted* (mapped or tabled). They should be able to come up with the definition "not mapped" or "unmapped" or even "unknown." Have them substitute their definition in the sentences to see if the definition makes sense. For instance, the first sentence would read, "The strong wind blew Ivan's ship away into unmapped (or unknown) seas." Confirm with students that the new sentence makes sense, and then repeat the same process for the second sentence.

Everything students learn about phonemic awareness, phonics, word structure and decoding has one primary goal—to help them understand what they are reading. Without comprehension, there is no reading.

Take time to review words and their meanings. Help students connect new words to familiar words. Each unit in ***SRA Imagine It!*** revolves around a theme, and there are key words. In every lesson, there is a concept.

Semantic Mapping Having students create a semantic map of an unknown word after learning its definition helps them learn it. Have students write the new word and then list in a map or web all words they can think of that are related to it.

Semantic Feature Analysis A semantic feature analysis helps students compare and contrast similar types of words within a category to help secure unknown words. Have students chart, for example, the similarities and differences between various types of sports, including new vocabulary such as *lacrosse* and *cricket.*

Reading Comprehension

Purpose

The primary aim of reading is comprehension. Without comprehension, neither intellectual nor emotional responses to reading are possible—other than the response of frustration. Reading is about problem solving. Expert readers bring their critical faculties to bear on everything they read. They generally understand most of what they read, but just as importantly, they recognize when they do not understand, and they have at their command an assortment of strategies for monitoring and furthering their understanding.

The goal of comprehension strategy instruction is to turn responsibility for using strategies over to students as soon as possible. Research has shown that students' comprehension and learning problems are not a matter of mental capacity but rather their inability to use strategies to help them learn. Expert readers use a variety of strategies to help them make sense of the text and to get the most out of what they read. Trained to use a variety of comprehension strategies, students dramatically improve their learning performance. To do this, the teacher models strategy use and gradually incorporates various kinds of prompts and possible student think-alouds as examples of the types of thinking students might do as they read to comprehend what they are reading.

Setting Reading Goals

Even before they begin reading and using comprehension strategies, good readers set reading goals and expectations. Readers who have set their own goals and have definite expectations about the text they are about to read are more engaged in their reading and notice more in what they read. Having determined a purpose for reading, they are better able to evaluate a text and to determine whether it meets their needs. Even when the reading is assigned, the reader's engagement is enhanced when he or she has determined ahead of time what information might be gathered from the selection or how the selection might interest him or her.

Comprehension Strategies

Descriptions of strategies expert readers use to comprehend the text follow.

Good readers continually monitor their speed and ability to understand throughout reading.

Summarizing

Periodically it is important to summarize and check our understanding as we read. Sometimes readers reread to fill in gaps in their understanding. They use the strategy of summarizing to keep track of what they are reading and to focus their minds on important information. The process of putting the information in one's own words not only helps good readers remember what they have read but also prompts them to evaluate how well they understand the information. Sometimes the summary reveals that one's understanding is incomplete, in which case it might be appropriate to reread the previous section to fill in the gaps. The strategy of summarizing is particularly helpful when readers are reading long or complicated text. When to stop and summarize depends on the difficulty of the text as well as the type of text. Often in content area reading, it makes sense to stop and summarize the key ideas after each section. In narratives, the reader often stops to summarize after an episode has been read. Many of us will automatically summarize what has happened if we have put down a book and are about to continue reading it again. Students should think to themselves the following:

- ✦ Does this make sense? What is this selection about?
- ✦ What are the big ideas the writer is trying to get at?
- ✦ What can I delete from my summary? What is not important?
- ✦ Have I said the same thing more than once in my summary?
- ✦ How can I put what I just read into my own words?
- ✦ What is unclear? What is the meaning of the word or sentence? How can I determine this?

Clarifying

Monitoring understanding is key to reading. It allows readers to make sure they understand what they read. They note the characteristics of the text, such as whether it is difficult to read or whether some sections are more challenging or more important than others are. In addition, when readers become aware that they do not understand, they stop and take appropriate action, such as rereading, to understand the text better. As they read, good readers stay alert for problem signs such as loss of concentration, unfamiliar vocabulary, or lack of sufficient background knowledge to comprehend the text. This ability to self-monitor and identify aspects of the text that hinder comprehension is crucial to becoming a proficient reader. Clarifying may occur at the word, the sentence, the paragraph, or at the whole-text level. Students should think to themselves the following:

- ✦ What does not make sense? If it is a word, how can I figure it out? Do I use context, structure, or apposition, or do I need to ask someone or look it up in the dictionary or glossary?
- ✦ What does not make sense? The paragraph is long and full of details. What can I do? I can take some notes, I can reread it more slowly; I can discuss it with someone.
- ✦ These sentences are endless. How can I deal with long, complicated sentences?
- ✦ What is the main idea of what I just read?
- ✦ Can I summarize what I just read?

Asking Questions

Asking questions allows the reader to constantly check his or her understanding and to follow the writer's train of thought. Good readers ask questions that may prepare them for what they will learn. If their questions are not answered in the text, they may try to find answers elsewhere and thus add even more to their store of knowledge. Certain kinds of questions occur naturally to a reader, such as to clear up confusion or to wonder why something in the text is as it is. Intentional readers take this somewhat informal questioning one step further by formulating questions with the specific intent of checking their understanding. They literally test themselves by thinking of questions a teacher might ask and then by determining answers to those questions. Students should think to themselves the following:

- Why is this the way it is? What else is there to know about this?
- What question can I ask to check if I have understood what I just read?
- How does this connect to the unit theme? What new information will I learn?
- What questions do I think the author will answer as I read this selection?
- Do I understand the author? What is not making sense?
- What is interfering with my understanding?

Predicting

Predicting what will happen in the story allows the reader to summarize what has been read so far, to identify clues and events in the text, and to use prior knowledge and personal experience to make inferences about what will happen next. When reading fiction, readers make predictions about what they are reading and then confirm or revise those predictions as they go. Predictions are not wild guesses. They are made based on information provided by the author as well as the reader's background knowledge. Students should think to themselves the following: What do I already know that will help me predict? What are the clues in the text that will help me predict?

- Why was my prediction confirmed?
- Why was my prediction not confirmed?
- What clues did I miss that would have helped me make a better prediction?

The responsibility for using strategies by students should begin as soon as they understand that reading is about problem solving and making sense of text and that these strategies will help them do both.

Making Connections

Making connections between the text and what is known from personal experience or previous reading deepens our understanding of text and expands our understanding. Comprehension is enhanced when we relate what is read to what is known. Students should think to themselves the following:

- What does this remind me of? What else have I read like this?
- What does this remind me of in my own life? In my own experiences?
- How does this connect with other selections I have read?
- How does this connect with what is going on in the world today?

Visualizing

Creating a mental image about the text involves not just the literal interpretation of the author's word but going beyond the literal to incorporating prior knowledge and experiences that deepen understanding. Readers form mental images as they read. They picture the setting, the characters, and the action in a story. Visualizing can also be helpful when reading expository text. Visualizing helps readers understand descriptions of complex activities or processes. When a complex process or an event is being described, the reader can follow the process or the event better by visualizing each step or episode. Sometimes an author or an editor helps the reader by providing illustrations, diagrams, or maps. If no visual aids have been provided, it may help the reader to create one. Creating mental images helps the reader create pictures that can be stored efficiently in his or her long-term memory. Students should think to themselves the following:

- What picture does the words create in my mind? How do the words suggest feelings, actions, and settings?
- Would a drawing help me understand the process?
- How does my mental picture extend beyond the words in the text?
- How did this picture help me understand what I am reading?

Adjusting Reading Speed

Some texts are easy to read; others are more challenging. How difficult a text is to read depends on both author and reader variables. Good readers understand that not all text is equal. Because of this, they continuously monitor what they are reading and adjust their reading speed accordingly. Efficient readers skim parts of the text that are not important or relevant to their reading goals, and they purposely slow down when they encounter difficulty in understanding the text. Students should think to themselves the following:

- When I reread does this make sense?
- This is a long and involved sentence. Rereading may help.

Procedures

Modeling and Thinking Aloud

One of the most effective ways to help students understand and use critical comprehension is to make strategic thinking public. Modeling these behaviors and encouraging students to think aloud as they attempt to address comprehension problems and to understand text can demonstrate for everyone in a class how these behaviors are put into practice. Suggestions for think-alouds are provided throughout the ***Teacher's Edition.***

The most effective models you can offer will be those that come from your own reading experiences. What kinds of questions did you ask yourself? What kinds of things surprised you the first time you read a story? What kinds of new information did you learn? What kinds of things were confusing until you reread or read further? Drawing on these questions and on your students' questions and comments as they read will make the strategic reading process more meaningful to students. Below are suggestions for modeling each of the comprehension strategies.

Before Reading

✦ **Modeling Setting Reading Goals.** To model setting reading goals, engage students in the following:

- **Activate prior knowledge.** As you approach a new text, consider aloud what you already know about the subject or what your experiences have been in reading similar material.
- **Browse the text.** To get an idea of what to expect from a text, look at the title and the illustrations. When students are reading fiction, they will browse the text to look for Clues, Problems and Wonderings. Possible clues will support comprehension—for example, genre, content, author, setting, and so on—potential problems might include things such as difficult words or dense paragraphs as well as unfamiliar concepts; and wonderings are the things students are curious to find out about from their reading— questions about the selection. Wonderings are students' purposes for reading. When students read nonfiction, they will use a KWL chart— this is what I know (K), this is what I want to find out (W), and this is what I have learned (L). Both these activities— Clues, Problems, and Wonderings and KWL—engage students in thinking before reading the selection by having them activate their own background knowledge, identify potential problems, and set purposes for reading. Have students glance quickly at the selection, looking briefly at the illustrations and the print. Have them tell what they think they might be learning about as they read the selection. Early in the year, model the thinking involved with these activities and then begin to turn the responsibility for completing them over to students.

During Reading

Modeling— or thinking aloud— about how to use strategies to solve problems is a powerful tool for teaching comprehension. While think-aloud models are included in all lessons, relate your own thinking and experiences to the lesson and the think-alouds. Early in the process you will need to model thinking about how, when, and why to use the strategies. Encourage students to stop and use them as well; engage them in thinking!

✦ **Modeling Summarizing.** Just as the strategy of summarizing the plot and then predicting what will happen next can enhance a student's reading of fiction, so too can the same procedure be used to the student's advantage in reading nonfiction. In expository text, it is particularly logical to stop and summarize at the end of a chapter or section before going on to the next. One way to model the valuable exercise of making predictions and at the same time to expand knowledge is to summarize information learned from a piece of expository writing and then to predict what the next step or category will be. Appropriate times to stop and summarize include the following:

- When a narrative text has covered a long period of time or a number of events
- When many facts have been presented
- When an especially critical scene has occurred
- When a complex process has been described
- Any time there is the potential for confusion about what has happened or what has been presented in the text
- When returning to a selection

✦ **Modeling Clarifying.** A reader may need clarification at any point in the reading. Model this strategy by stopping at points that confuse you or that may confuse your students. Indicate that you are experiencing some confusion and need to stop and make sure you understand what is being read. Difficulty may arise from a challenging or unknown word or phrase. It may also stem from the manner in which the information is presented. Perhaps the author did not supply needed information. As you model this strategy, vary the reasons for stopping to clarify so that students understand that good readers do not simply skip over difficult or confusing material—they stop and determine what they do not understand.

✦ **Modeling Asking Questions.** Learning to ask productive questions is not an easy task. Students' earliest experiences with this strategy take the form of answering teacher-generated questions. However, students should be able to move fairly quickly to asking questions like those a teacher might ask. Questions that can be answered with a simple *yes* or *no* are not typically very useful for helping them remember and understand what they have read. Many students find it helpful to ask questions beginning with *Who? What? When? Where? How?* and *Why?* As students become more accustomed to asking and answering questions, they will naturally become more adept at phrasing their questions. As their question asking becomes more sophisticated, they progress from simple questions that can be answered with explicit information in the text to questions that require making inferences based on the text.

✦ **Modeling Predicting.** Predicting can be appropriate at the beginning of a selection—on the basis of the titles and the illustrations—or at any point while reading a selection. At first, your modeling will take the form of speculation about what might happen next, but tell students from the start what clues in the text or illustrations helped you predict to make it clear that predicting is not just guessing. When a student makes a prediction—especially a far-fetched one—ask on what in the selection or in his or her own experience the prediction is based. If the student can back up the prediction, let the prediction stand; otherwise, suggest that the student make another prediction on the basis of what he or she already knows. Often it is appropriate to summarize before making a prediction. This will help students consider what has come before as they make their predictions about what will happen next. When reading aloud, stop whenever a student's prediction has been confirmed or contradicted. Have students tell whether the prediction was correct. If students seem comfortable with the idea of making predictions but rarely do so on their own, encourage them to discuss how to find clues in the text that will help them.

- **Modeling Making Connections.** To model making connections, share with students any thoughts or memories that come to mind as you read the selection. Perhaps a character in a story reminds you of a childhood friend, allowing you to better identify with interactions between characters. Perhaps information in an article on Native American life in the Old West reminds you of an article that you have read on the importance of the bison to Native Americans. Sharing your connections will help students become aware of the dynamic nature of reading and show them another way of being intentional, active learners.
- **Modeling Visualizing.** Model visualizing by describing the mental images that occur to you as you read. A well-described scene is relatively easy to visualize, and if no one does so voluntarily, you may want to prompt students to express their own visualizations. If the author has not provided a description of a scene, but a picture of the scene would make the story more interesting or comprehensible, you might want to model visualizing as follows: "Let's see. The author says that the street was busy, and we know that this story is set during the colonial period. From what I already know about those times, there were no cars, and the roads were different from the roads of today. The street may have been paved with cobblestones. Horses would have been pulling carriages or wagons. I can almost hear the horses' hoofs going clip-clop over the stones." Remind students that different readers may picture the same scene quite differently, which is fine. Every reader responds to a story in her or his own way.
- **Modeling Adjusting Reading Speed.** Just as readers need to monitor for problems, they need to be aware that various texts can be approached in various ways. For example, if reading a story or novel for enjoyment, the reader will typically read at a relaxed speed that is neither so fast as to miss information nor as slow as they might read a textbook. If on the other hand, the reader is reading a textbook, he or she will probably decrease speed to assure understanding and make sure that all important information is read and understood. When modeling this strategy, be sure you indicate why you, as the reader, have chosen to slow down or speed up. Good readers continually monitor their speed and ability to understand throughout reading.

If your students have not previously engaged in the sort of strategic thinking aloud that is promoted throughout ***SRA Imagine It!,*** you will have to do all or most of the modeling at first, but encourage students to participate as soon as possible. Remember, however, the goal is for students to use these strategies independently as they read both in and out of school. In addition to the think-alouds for the teachers, there are also prompts to encourage students to do the thinking. The responsibility for using strategies by students should begin as soon as they understand that reading is about problem solving and making sense of text and that these strategies will help them do both.

Reading Aloud

At the beginning of the year, students should be encouraged to read selections aloud. This practice will help you and them understand some of the challenges posed by the text and how individual students approach these challenges.

Reading aloud helps students build fluency, which in turn will aid their comprehension. Students in Grades K–3 can use ***Decodables*** to build fluency, while students in Grades 4–6 can use the literature from the ***Student Readers. Leveled Readers*** are also available for Grades 1–6. Fluent second graders read between 79 and 117 words per minute with accuracy and understanding, depending on the time of the year (fall/spring). Fluent third graders can be expected to read between 99 and 137 words per minute; fourth (119/152); fifth (139/168); sixth (123/177).

Make sure that you set aside time to hear each student read during the first few days of class—the days devoted to Getting Started are perfect for this—so that you can determine students' abilities and needs. Workshop is also a good time to listen to any students who do not get to read aloud while the class is reading the selection together.

As the year progresses, students should continue reading aloud often, especially with particularly challenging text. Model your own use of strategies, not only to help students better understand how to use strategies but also to help them understand that actively using strategies is something that good, mature readers do constantly.

Most students are unaccustomed to thinking aloud. They will typically stand mute as they try to determine an unfamiliar word or to deal with a confusing passage. When this happens, students should be encouraged to identify specifically with what they are having difficulty. A student might identify a particular word, or he or she may note that the individual words are familiar but that the meaning of the passage is unclear.

Active Response

Not only are good readers active in their reading when they encounter problems, but they respond constantly to whatever they read. In this way they make the text their own. As students read they should be encouraged to

- make as many connections as they can between what they are reading and what they already know.
- visualize passages to help clarify their meanings or simply to picture appealing descriptions.
- ask questions about what they are reading. The questions that go through their minds during reading will help them examine, and thus better understand, the text. Doing so may also interest them in pursuing their own investigations. The questions may also provide a direction for students' research or exploration.
- summarize and make predictions as a check on how well they understand what they are reading.

Tips

- Remember that the goal of all reading is comprehension. If a story or article does not make sense, the reader needs to choose whatever strategies will help make sense of it. If one strategy does not work, the reader should try another.
- Always treat problems encountered in text as interesting learning opportunities rather than something to be avoided or dreaded.
- Encourage students to think aloud about text challenges.
- Encourage students to help each other build meaning from text. Rather than telling each other what a word is or what

a passage means, students should tell each other how they figured out the meanings of challenging words and passages.

- Assure students that these are not the only strategies that can be used while reading. Any strategy that they find helpful in understanding text is a good, useful strategy.
- Encourage students to freely share strategies they have devised on their own. You might want to write these on a large sheet of paper and tape them onto the board.
- An absence of questions does not necessarily indicate that students understand what they are reading. Be especially alert to students who never seem to ask questions. Be sure to spend tutorial time with these students occasionally, and encourage them to discuss specific selections in the context of difficulties they might have encountered and how they solved them as well as their thoughts about unit concepts.
- Observing students' responses to text will enable you to ascertain not only how well they understand a particular selection but also their facility in choosing and applying appropriate strategies. Use the strategy rubrics to evaluate students' understanding of and ability to use the different reading strategies. Take note of the following:
  - Whether the strategies a student uses are effective in the particular situation.
  - Whether the student chooses from a variety of appropriate strategies or uses the same few over and over.
  - Whether the student can explain to classmates which strategies to use in a particular situation and why.
  - Whether the student can identify alternative resources to pursue when the strategies she or he has tried are not effective.
  - Whether students' application of a given strategy is becoming more effective over a period of time.
- Encourage students to use the reading strategies throughout the day in all their reading activities.

Becoming familiar and comfortable with these self-monitoring techniques gives readers the confidence to tackle material that is progressively more difficult. A good, mature reader knows when understanding what he or she is reading is becoming a problem and can take steps to correct the situation. He or she has internalized the strategies, values them, and uses strategies automatically.

Comprehension Skills

Purpose

An important purpose of writing is to communicate thoughts from one person to another. The goal of instruction in reading comprehension skills is to make students aware of the logic behind the structure of a written piece. If the reader can discern the logic of the structure, he or she will be more able to understand the author's logic and to gain knowledge both of the facts and the intent of the selection. By keeping the organization of a piece in mind and considering the author's purpose for writing, the reader can go beyond the actual words on the page and make inferences or draw conclusions based on what was read. Strong, mature readers utilize these "between the lines" skills to get a complete picture of not only what the writer is saying but what the writer is trying to say.

Effective comprehension skills include the following:

Author's Point of View

Point of view involves identifying who is telling the story. If a character in the story is telling the story, that one character describes the action and tells what the other characters are like. This is first-person point of view. In such a story, one character will do the talking and use the pronouns *I, my,* and *me.* All other characters' thoughts, feelings, and emotions will be reported through this one character.

If the story is told in third-person point of view, someone outside the story who is aware of all of the characters' thoughts, feelings, and actions is relating them to the reader. All of the characters are referred to by their names or the pronouns *he/she, him/her,* and *it.*

If students stay aware of who is telling a story, they will know whether they are getting the full picture or the picture of events as seen through the eyes of only one character.

Sequence

The reader cannot make any decisions about relationships or events if he or she has no idea in which order the events take place. The reader needs to pay attention to how the writer is conveying the sequence. Is it simply stated that first this happened and then that happened? Does the writer present the end of the story first and then go back and let the reader know the sequence of events? Knowing what the sequence is and how it is presented helps the reader follow the writer's line of thought.

Fact and Opinion

Learning to distinguish fact from opinion is essential to critical reading and thinking. Students learn what factors need to be present for a statement to be provable. They also learn that an opinion, while not provable itself, should be based on fact. Readers use this knowledge to determine for themselves the validity of the ideas presented in their reading.

Main Idea and Details

An author always has something specific to say to his or her reader. The author may state this main idea in different ways, but the reader should always be able to tell what the writing is about.

To strengthen the main point or main idea of a piece, the author provides details to help the reader understand. For example, the author may use comparison and contrast to make a point, to provide examples, to provide facts, to give opinions, to give descriptions, to give reasons or causes, or to give definitions. The reader needs to know what kinds of details he or she is dealing with before making a judgment about the main idea.

Compare and Contrast

Using comparison and contrast is one of the most common and easiest ways a writer gets his or her reader to understand a subject. Comparing and contrasting unfamiliar thoughts, ideas, or things with familiar thoughts, ideas, and things gives the reader something within his or her own experience base to use in understanding.

Cause and Effect

What made this happen? Why did this character act the way he or she did? Knowing the causes of events helps the reader see the whole story. Using this information to identify the probable outcomes (effects) of events or actions will help the reader anticipate the story or article.

Classify and Categorize

The relationships of actions, events, characters, outcomes, and such in a selection should be clear enough for the reader to see the relationships. Putting like things or ideas together can help the reader understand the relationships set up by the writer.

Author's Purpose

Everything is written for a purpose. That purpose may be to entertain, to persuade, or to inform. Knowing why a piece is written—what purpose the author had for writing the piece—gives the reader an idea of what to expect and perhaps some prior idea of what the author is going to say.

If a writer is writing to entertain, then the reader can generally just relax and let the writer carry him or her away. If, on the other hand, the purpose is to persuade, it will help the reader understand and keep perspective if he or she knows that the purpose is to persuade. The reader can be prepared for whatever argument the writer delivers.

Drawing Conclusions

Often, writers do not directly state everything—they take for granted their audience's ability to "read between the lines." Readers draw conclusions when they take from the text small pieces of information about a character or event and use this information to make a statement about that character or event.

Reality and Fantasy

Students learn to distinguish reality from fantasy as they read different genres, including expository text, realistic fiction, fables, fairy tales, and so on. As students read, they note that a fantasy contains people, animals, and objects that do things that could not happen in the real world. Reality contains people, animals, and objects that can exist and do things in the real world.

Making Inferences

Readers make inferences about characters and events to understand the total picture in a story. When making inferences, readers use information from the text, along with personal experience or knowledge, to gain a deeper understanding of a story event and its implications.

Procedures

Read the Selection

First, have students read the selection using whatever skills they need to help them make sense of the selection. Then discuss the selection to assure that students did, indeed, understand what they read. Talk about any confusion they may have, and make any necessary clarifications.

Reread

Revisiting or rereading a selection allows the reader to note specific techniques that authors use to organize and present information in narratives and expository genres. When students have a basic understanding of the piece, have them reread the selection in whole or in part, concentrating on selected skills. Students learn to appreciate that writers use different structures, for example, cause and effect or compare/contrast, to organize their work and that recognizing these structures can help readers understand what they have read. It is these same structures that students will use in their own writing.

Limit this concentration on specific comprehension/writing skills to one or two that can be clearly identified in the piece. Trying to concentrate on too many things will just confuse students and make it harder for them to identify any of the organizational devices used by the writer. If a piece has many good examples of several different aspects, then go back to the piece several times over a span of days.

Write

Solidify the connection between how an author writes and how readers make sense of a selection by encouraging students to incorporate these organizational devices into their own writing. As they attempt to use these devices, they will get a clearer understanding of how to identify them when they are reading.

Remind students often that the purpose of any skill exercise is to give them tools to use when they are reading and writing. Unless students learn to apply the skills to their own reading—in every area of reading and study—then they are not gaining a full understanding of the purpose of the exercise.

Writing is a complicated process. A writer uses handwriting, spelling, vocabulary, grammar, usage, genre structures, and mechanics skills with ideas to create readable text. In addition, a writer must know how to generate content, or ideas, and understand genre structures to effectively present ideas in writing. Many students never progress beyond producing a written text that duplicates their everyday speech patterns. Mature writers, however, take composition beyond conversation. They understand the importance of audience and purpose for writing. They organize their thoughts, eliminating those that do not advance their main ideas, applying what they have learned in reading, and elaborating on those that do so that their readers can follow a logical progression of ideas in an essay or story. Mature writers also know and can use the conventions of grammar, usage, spelling, and mechanics. They proofread and edit for these conventions, so their readers are not distracted by errors.

Reading Big Books

Purpose

Many students come from homes where they are read to often, but a significant number of other students have not had this valuable experience. ***Big Books*** (Levels K and 1) offer all students crucial opportunities to confirm and expand their knowledge about print and reading, to develop vocabulary, and to enjoy literacy experiences. They are especially useful for shared reading experiences in the early grades.

The benefits of reading ***Big Books*** include engaging even nonreaders in

- unlocking the books' messages.
- developing print awareness.
- participating in good reading behaviors.
- observing what a good reader does: remarking on the illustrations and the title, asking questions about the content and what might happen, making predictions, and clarifying words and ideas.
- promoting the insights about print, for example, that a given word is spelled the same way every time it occurs as high-frequency words are identified.
- reinforcing the correspondence between spoken and written words and spelling patterns.
- enjoying the illustrations and connecting them to the text to help students learn to explore books for enjoyment and information.
- learning about different genre and the language of print.
- developing vocabulary and academic language.
- interpreting and responding to literature and expository text before they can read themselves.

Procedure for Reading Big Books

During the first reading of the ***Big Books,*** you will model reading behaviors and comprehension strategies similar to those that will later apply to their own reading. This focus on strategies encourages students to think about the ideas in the stories, to ask questions, and to learn new vocabulary. During the second reading, you will address print awareness and teach comprehension skills such as classifying and categorizing or sequencing, which help the reader organize information and focus on the specifics in the selection. In addition, you will teach skills such as making inferences and drawing conclusions, which help the reader focus on the deeper meaning of the text. At first, teachers should expect to do all of the reading but should not prevent students from trying to read on their own or from reading words they already know.

- **Activate Prior Knowledge.** Read the title of the selection and the author's and illustrator's names. At the beginning of each ***Big Book,*** read the title of the book and discuss what the whole book is about before going on to reading the first selection. Initiate a brief discussion of any prior knowledge students have that might help them understand the selection.

> **Big Books** *offer all students opportunities to confirm and expand their knowledge about print and reading.*

- **Browse the Selection.** Explain to the class that browsing means to look through the pages of the story to get a general idea of what the story is about, to see what interests them, and to ask questions. Ask students to tell what they think the story might be about just from looking at the illustrations. This conversation should be brief so that students can move on to a prereading discussion of print awareness.
- **Develop Print Awareness.** The focus of browsing the ***Big Books*** is to develop awareness of print. Urge students to tell what words or letters they recognize rather than what they expect the selection to be about.

  To develop print awareness, have students look through the selection page by page and to comment on whatever they notice in the text. Some students may know some of the words, while others may recognize only specific letters or sounds. The key is to get students to look at the print separately from the illustrations even before they have heard the actual text content. This process isolates print awareness so that it is not influenced by content. It also gives you a clearer idea of what your students do or do not know about print.
- **Read Aloud.** Read the selection aloud expressively, using intonation and pauses at punctuation. Not only does this enable students to hear and enjoy the text as it is read through once, it serves as an early model for fluency. Good fluency and expression support comprehension. As you read, you will stop periodically to model behaviors and comprehension strategies that all students will need to develop to become successful readers—for example, asking questions; clarifying unfamiliar words, first by using the pictures and later by using context; or predicting what might happen next.
- **Reread.** Read the selection expressively again. During the second reading of the stories, you will focus on teaching comprehension skills. Also, to develop print awareness, point to each word as it is read, thus demonstrating that text proceeds from left to right and from top to bottom and helping advance the idea that words are individual spoken and written units. Invite students to

identify the rhyming words in a poem or to chime in on repetitive parts of text as you point to the words. Or students can read with you on this second reading, depending on the text. As students' knowledge of words and phonics grows, they can participate in decoding words and reading high-frequency sight words.

- **Discuss Print.** Return to print awareness by encouraging discussion of anything students noticed about the words. Young students should begin to realize that you are reading separate words that are separated by spaces. Later, students will begin to see that each word is made of a group of letters. Students should be encouraged to discuss anything related to the print. For example, you might ask students to point to a word or to count the number of words on a line. Or you might connect the words to the illustrations by pointing to a word and saying it and then asking students to find a picture of that word.
- **Responding.** Responding to a selection is a way of insuring comprehension. Invite students to tell about the story by asking them what they like about the poem or story or calling on a student to explain in his or her own words what the poem or story tells about. Call on others to add to the telling as needed. For nonfiction selections, this discussion might include asking students what they learned about the topic and what they thought was most interesting.

Tips for Using Big Books

- Make sure the entire group is able to see the book clearly while you are reading.
- If some students are able to read words, encourage them to do so during the rereading.
- Encourage students to use their knowledge of print.
- Encourage students' use of academic language as they talk about reading. Students should be comfortable using strategic reading words such as *predict* and *clarify* and book and print words such as *author* and *illustrator.*
- Allow students to look at the ***Big Books*** whenever they wish.
- Provide small versions of the ***Big Books*** for students to browse through and to try to read at their leisure.
- The reader of the ***Big Book*** should try to be part of the collaborative group of learners rather than the leader.

Strategic Reading

Purpose

Reading is a complex process that requires students not only to decode automatically and correctly what they read but also to understand and respond to it. The purpose of this section is to help you identify various reading behaviors used by good readers and to encourage those behaviors in your students.

Reading Behaviors and Comprehension Strategies

There are four basic behaviors that good readers engage in during reading: Setting Reading Goals and Expectations, Responding to Text, Checking Understanding, and Monitoring and Clarifying Unfamiliar Words and Passages. Engaging in these behaviors involves the application of certain comprehension strategies. These strategies are initially modeled while reading the ***Big Books*** (Level K and the first half of Level 1) and ***Student Readers*** (Levels 1–6). The goal of strategy instruction, however, is to ultimately turn over responsibility for using strategies to students so they set their own goals for reading, respond to text, and check their own understanding and solve problems while reading. Students need to take responsibility for doing the thinking and making sense of text.

Setting Reading Goals and Expectations

Good readers set reading goals and expectations before they begin reading. This behavior involves a variety of strategies that will help students prepare to read the text.

- **Activate prior knowledge.** When good readers approach a new text, they consider what they already know about the subject or what their experiences have been in reading similar material.
- **Browse the text.** To get an idea of what to expect from a text, good readers look at the title and the illustrations. They may look for potential problems, such as difficult words. When browsing a unit, have students glance quickly at each selection, looking briefly at the illustrations and the print. Have them tell what they think they might be learning about as they read the unit.
- **Decide what they expect from the text.** When reading for pleasure, good readers anticipate enjoying the story or the language. When reading to learn something, they ask themselves what they expect to find out.

Responding to Text

Good readers are active readers. They interact with text by using the following strategies:

- **Making connections.** Good readers make connections between what they read and what they already know. They pay attention to elements in the text that remind them of their own experiences. Readers make connections to personal experiences, to other stories they have read, and to world knowledge.
- **Visualizing, or picturing.** Good readers visualize what is happening in the text. They not only form mental images as they read but make inferences based on their own experiences. Visualizing goes beyond the words in text. They imagine the setting and the emotions it suggests, they picture the characters and their feelings, and they visualize the action in a story. When reading expository text, good readers picture the objects, processes, or events described. Visualizing helps readers understand descriptions of complex activities or processes.
- **Asking questions.** Good readers ask questions that may prepare them for what they will learn. If their questions are not answered in the text, they may try to find answers elsewhere and thus add even more to their store of knowledge.
- **Predicting.** Good readers predict what will happen next. When reading fiction, they make predictions about what they are reading and then confirm or revise those predictions as they go.
- **Thinking about how the text makes you feel.** Well-written fiction touches readers' emotions; it sparks ideas.

Checking Understanding

One of the most important behaviors good readers exhibit is the refusal to continue reading when something fails to make sense. Good readers continually assess their understanding of the text with strategies such as the following:

- **Interpreting.** As they read, good readers make inferences that help them understand and appreciate what they are reading.
- **Summarizing.** Good readers summarize to check their understanding as they read. Sometimes they reread to fill in gaps in their understanding.
- **Adjusting reading speed.** Good readers monitor their understanding of what they read. They slow down as they come to difficult words and passages. They speed up as they read easier passages.

Monitoring and Clarifying Unfamiliar Words and Passages

Monitoring understanding involves knowing when meaning is breaking down. The reader needs to stop and identify what the problem or source of confusion is. It might be an unfamiliar word, complex and hard-to-understand sentences or unfamiliar concepts that need clarifying. At the word level, the reader might

- apply decoding skills to sound out unknown words.
- apply context clues in text and illustrations to figure out the meanings of words.
- use structural elements to figure out the meaning of the word.
- ask someone the meaning of the word.
- reread the passage to make sure the passage makes sense.
- check a dictionary or the glossary to understand the meanings of words not clarified by clues or rereading.

Complex sentences may require the reader to look for the main idea in the sentence, to pull out clauses that may interfere with the main idea, or to ask for help. When faced with unfamiliar concepts, readers often ask for clarification from someone.

These cognitive activities engage the reader in thinking about text before, during, and after reading. Readers think about text before they read by activating background knowledge, anticipating content, setting purposes, and wondering about the text and what they will learn. During reading, the reader is constantly checking understanding—asking whether what is being read makes sense and constructing conclusions or summary statements. When the text is not making sense, the reader uses strategies to clarify words, ideas, and larger units of text or may reread more slowly for clarification. After reading, the reader reflects on what was read, connecting new information to prior knowledge, evaluating purposes, and connecting the relevance of the new information to the purpose.

Procedures

Modeling and Thinking Aloud

Modeling and encouraging students to think aloud as they attempt to understand text can demonstrate for everyone how reading behaviors are put into practice. Modeling and thinking aloud helps students learn how to process information and learn important content. It is more than asking students questions; it is letting students in on the thinking that helps readers make sense of text, solve problems while reading, and use strategies differentially and intentionally. The most effective models will be those that come from your own reading. As you model the different strategies, let students know what strategy you are using and why you are using it.

Model comprehension strategies in a natural way, and choose questions and comments that fit the text you are reading. Present a variety of ways to respond to text.

- Pose questions that you really do wonder about.
- Identify with characters by comparing them with yourself.
- React emotionally by showing joy, sadness, amusement, or surprise.
- Show empathy with or sympathy for characters.
- Relate the text to something that has happened to you or to something you already know.
- Show interest in the text ideas.
- Question the meaning or clarity of the author's words and ideas.

Encourage Students' Responses and Use of Strategies

Most students will typically remain silent as they try to figure out an unfamiliar word or a confusing passage. Encourage students to identify specifically with what they are having difficulty. When the problem has been identified, ask students to suggest a strategy for dealing with the problem. Remind students to

- treat problems encountered in text as interesting learning opportunities.
- think aloud about text challenges.
- help each other build meaning. Rather than tell what a word is, students should tell how they figured out the meanings of challenging words and passages.
- consider reading a selection again with a partner after reading it once alone. Partner reading provides valuable practice in reading for fluency.
- make as many connections as they can between what they are reading and what they already know.
- visualize to clarify meanings or enjoy descriptions.
- ask questions about what they are reading.
- notice how the text makes them feel.

In addition, using open-ended questions such as the following, as well as your students' questions and comments, will make both the text and the strategic reading process more meaningful to students.

- What kinds of things did you wonder about?
- What kinds of things surprised you?
- What new information did you learn?
- What was confusing until you reread or read further?

Discussion

The more students are able to discuss what they are learning, to voice their confusions, and to compare perceptions of what they are learning, the deeper and more meaningful their learning becomes.

Purpose

Through discussions, students are exposed to points of view different from their own and learn how to express their thoughts and opinions coherently. Through discussion, students add to their own knowledge that of their classmates and learn to explain themselves coherently. They also begin to ask insightful questions that help them better understand what they have read and all that they are learning through their inquiry/research and explorations. The purpose of classroom discussion is to provide a framework for learning.

Procedure

Reflecting on the Selection

After students have finished reading a selection, provide an opportunity for them to engage in discussion about the selection. Students should

- check to see whether the questions they asked before reading as part of Clues, Problems, and Wonderings and KWL (What I Know, What I Want to Know and What I Have Learned) have been answered. Encourage them to discuss whether any unanswered questions should still be answered. If unanswered questions are related to the theme, add those questions to the **Concept/ Question Board.**
- discuss any new questions that have arisen because of the reading. Encourage students to decide which of these questions should go on the **Concept/ Question Board.**
- share what they expected to learn from reading the selection and tell whether expectations were met.
- talk about whatever has come to mind while reading the selection. This discussion should be an informal sharing of impressions of, or opinions about, the selection; it should never take on the aspects of a question-and-answer session about the selection.
- give students ample opportunity to ask questions and to share their thoughts about the selection. Participate as an active member of the group, making your own observations about information in a selection or modeling your own appreciation of a story. Be especially aware of unusual and interesting insights suggested by students so that these insights can be recognized and discussed. To help students learn to keep the discussion student-centered, have each student choose the next speaker instead of handing the discussion back to you.

The purpose of classroom discussion is to provide a framework for learning.

Recording Ideas

As students finish discussions about their reactions to a selection, they should be encouraged to record their thoughts, feelings, reactions, and ideas about the selection or the subject of the selection in their Writer's Notebooks. This will not only help keep the selections fresh in students' minds; it will strengthen their writing abilities and help them learn how to write about their thoughts and feelings.

Students may find that the selection gave them ideas for their own writing, or it could have reminded them of some person or incident in their own lives. Perhaps the selection answered a question that has been on their minds or raised a question they had never thought before. Good, mature writers—especially professional writers—learn the value of recording such thoughts and impressions quickly before they fade. Students should be encouraged to do this also.

Handing Off

Handing off (Levels 1–6) is a method of turning over to students the primary responsibility for controlling discussion. Often, students who are taking responsibility for controlling a discussion tend to have all "turns" go through the teacher. The teacher is the one to whom attention is transferred when a speaker finishes, and the teacher is the one who is expected to call on the next speaker—the result being that the teacher remains the pivotal figure in the discussion.

Having students "hand off" the discussion to other students instead of the teacher encourages them to retain complete control of the discussion and to become more actively involved in the learning process. When a student finishes his or her comments, that student should choose (hand off the discussion to) the next speaker. In this way, students maintain a discussion without relying on the teacher to decide who speaks.

When handing off is in place, the teacher's main roles are to occasionally remind students to hand off, to help students when they get stuck, to encourage them to persevere on a specific point, and to get them back to a discussion, and to monitor the discussion to ensure that everyone gets a chance to contribute. The teacher may say, for example, "Remember, not just boys (or girls)." or "Try to choose someone who has not had a chance to talk yet." It is not unusual early in the process for students to roam from the topic and selection. To bring the discussion back to the topic and selection, be a participant, raise your hand, and ask a question or make a statement that refocuses students' thinking and discussion.

For handing off to work effectively, a seating arrangement that allows students to see one another is essential. It is hard to hold a discussion when students have their backs to each other. A circle or a semicircle is effective. In addition, all students need to have copies of the materials being discussed.

Actively encourage this handing-off process by letting students know that they, not you, are in control of the discussion.

If students want to remember thoughts about, or reactions to, a selection, suggest that they record these in the Response Journal section of their Writer's Notebooks.

Encourage students to record the thoughts, feelings, or reactions that are elicited by any reading they do.

Exploring Concepts within the Selection

To provide an opportunity for collaborative learning and to focus on the concepts, you may want to have students form small groups and spend time discussing what they have learned about the concepts from this selection. Topics may include new information that they have acquired, new ideas that they have had, or new questions that the selection raised.

Students should always base their discussions on postings from the **Concept/ Question Board** as well as on previous discussions of the concept. The small-group discussions should be ongoing throughout the unit; during this time, students should continue to compare and contrast any new information with their previous ideas, opinions, and impressions about the concepts. How does this selection help confirm their ideas? How does it contradict their thinking? How has it changed their outlook?

As students discuss the concepts in small groups, circulate around the room to make sure that each group stays focused upon the selection and the concepts. After students have had some time to discuss the information and the ideas in the selection, encourage each group to formulate some statements about the concept that apply to the selection.

Sharing Ideas about Concepts

Have a representative from each group report and explain the group's ideas to the rest of the class. Then have the class formulate one or more general statements related to the unit concepts and write these statements on the **Concept/Question Board.** As students progress through the unit, they will gain more and more confidence in suggesting additions to the **Concept/Question Board.**

- **Visual Aids** During this part of the discussion, you may find it helpful to use visual aids to help students as they build the connections to the unit concepts. Not all units or concepts will lend themselves to this type of treatment; however, aids such as time lines, charts, graphs, and pictographs may help students see how each new selection adds to their growing knowledge of the concepts.

Encourage students to ask questions about the concepts that the selection may have raised. Have students list on the **Concept/Question Board** those questions that cannot be answered immediately and that they want to explore further.

Through discussions, students are exposed to points of view different from their own and learn how to express their thoughts and opinions coherently.

Exploring Concepts across Selections

As each new selection is read, encourage students to discuss its connection with the other selections and with the unit concepts. Also encourage students to think about selections that they have read from other units and how they relate to the concepts for this unit.

Ultimately, this ability to make connections between past knowledge and new knowledge allows any learner to gain insights into what is being studied. The goal of the work with concepts and the discussions is to help students to start thinking in terms of connections—how is this like what I have learned before? Does this information confirm, contradict, or add a completely different layer to that which I already know about this concept? How can the others in the class have such different ideas than I do when we just read the same selection? Why is so much written about this subject?

Learning to make connections and to delve deeper through self-generated questions and substantive discussions give students the tools they need to become effective, efficient, lifelong learners.

Tips

- Create an environment that facilitates discussion. Have students sit in circles or some other configuration so everyone can see each other.
- When students are discussing the selection, they should have their books with them, and students should feel free to refer to them throughout the discussion.
- Discussions offer a prime opportunity for you to introduce, or seed, new ideas about the concepts. New ideas can come from a variety of sources: Students may draw on their own experiences or on the books or videos they are studying; you may introduce new ideas into the discussion; or you may at times invite experts to speak to the class.
- If students do not mention an important idea that is necessary to the understanding of some larger issue, you may "drop" that idea into the conversation and, indeed, repeat it several times to make sure that it does get picked up. This seeding may be subtle ("I think that might be important here") or quite direct ("This is a big idea, one that we will definitely need to understand and one that we will return to regularly").
- To facilitate this process for each unit, you must be aware of the unit concepts and be able to recognize and reinforce them when they arise spontaneously in discussions. If central unit concepts do not arise naturally, then, and only then, will you seed these ideas by direct modeling. The more you turn over discussions to students, the more

involved they will become, and the more responsibility they will take for their own learning. Make it your goal to become a participant in, rather than the leader of, class discussions.

- Help students see that they are responsible for carrying on the discussion. After a question is asked, always wait instead of jumping in with a comment or an explanation. Although this wait time may be uncomfortable at first, students will come to understand that the discussion is their responsibility and that you will not jump in every time there is a hesitation.
- As the year progresses, students will become more and more adept at conducting and participating in meaningful discussions about what they have read. These discussions will greatly enhance students' understanding of the concepts that they are exploring.

Discussion Starters and Questions

The following examples of discussion starters can be modeled initially, but then the responsibility for using them should be turned over to students. The starters provide the opportunity for open-ended discussions by students.

- I didn't know that . . . .
- Does anyone know . . . .
- I figured out that . . . .
- I liked the part where . . . .
- I'm still confused about . . . .
- This made me think . . . .
- I agree with ______________ because . . . .
- I disagree with ______________ because . . . .
- The reason I think ________ is . . .
- I found _______ interesting because. . . .
- I learned . . .
- What I learned in this selection reminds me of what we read in ________ because . . .
- This author's writing reminds me of . . .
- I had problems understanding _______ because . . .
- I wonder why the author chose to . . .
- I still do not understand . . .
- I was surprised to find out . . .
- I like the way the author developed the character by . . .
- The author made the story really come alive by . . .

In addition to these open-ended discussion starters, students should be encouraged to ask open-ended questions. When students ask questions, other students should respond to the question before moving on to another idea or topic. One student asking a question often helps to clarify something for the whole class and places a value on asking questions as a critical part of learning.

- Why did the author . . .?
- What did the author mean when he or she wrote . . . ?
- Who can help me clarify . . . ?
- Who can help me figure out . . . ?
- How does this piece connect to the unit theme?
- What does this section mean?

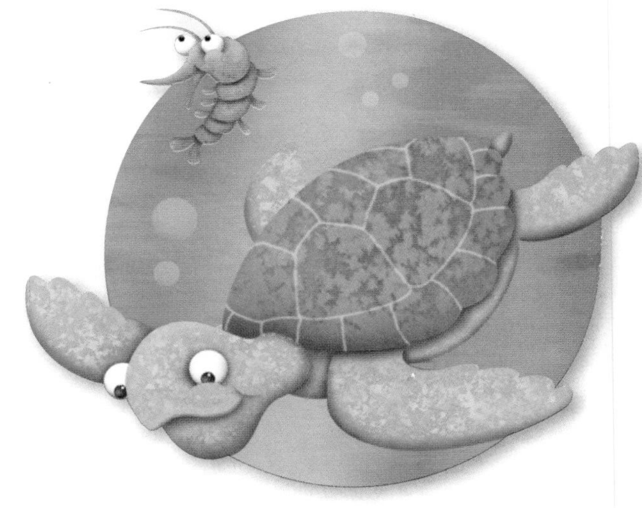

Writing

Purpose

The writing program in ***SRA Imagine It!*** teaches students how to write skillfully. This is essential, as writing is a powerful tool that fosters learning, communication, creativity, and self-discovery. ***SRA Imagine It!*** writing teaches students how to use writing effectively for these purposes.

Writing is a complex process. It involves deftly juggling a variety of skills, strategies, and knowledge. Writers must make plans, consider the reader, draw ideas from memory, develop new ideas, organize thoughts, consider the conventions of the genre, translate ideas into words, craft sentences, evaluate decisions, make needed revisions, transcribe words into correctly spelled print, and monitor the writing process, among other things.

SRA Imagine It! writing is designed to ensure that students acquire the skills, knowledge, strategies, and dispositions they need to become skilled writers. This includes the following:

- Knowledge about the qualities of good writing, characteristics of different genres, intended audience, and writing topics. Skilled writers know how to obtain information about their topics, are familiar with basic features of different genres, and possess basic schemas or frameworks for accomplishing common writing tasks.
- The writing strategies involved in basic composing processes such as prewriting, drafting, monitoring, evaluating, revising, editing/proofreading, and publishing. Skilled writers flexibly employ these strategies to create text.
- Command of basic writing skills such as handwriting, spelling, sentence construction, grammar, and usage. Skilled writers execute these basic writing skills with little conscious effort.
- Interest and motivation to write as well as perceptions of competence as a writer. Skilled writers possess an "I can do" attitude.

Procedures

With ***SRA Imagine It!*** writing, evidence-based practices are used to teach students to write skillfully. These evidence-based practices are drawn from research on the effectiveness of specific writing interventions that show that the quality of students' writing can be improved by

- explicitly teaching strategies for prewriting, drafting, revising, editing/proofreading, and publishing.
- modeling effective use of writing strategies.

*Children start school wanting to learn how to write and enjoying writing. The goal of **SRA Imagine It!** writing is for children to become lifelong writers—people who enjoy writing and use writing effectively at work as well as in their personal lives.*

- having students work together to prewrite, draft, revise, edit/proofread, and publish their compositions.
- using prewriting tools such as graphic organizers to gather information.
- involving students in inquiry activities designed to help them further develop their ideas for writing.
- making the goals for writing assignments clear and specific.
- teaching students how to construct more sophisticated sentences.
- providing students with the opportunity to read, evaluate, and emulate models of good writing.
- teaching students how to use word processing as a tool for composing.

The evidence-based practices in ***SRA Imagine It!*** are also based on the study of expert teachers who

- make sure their students are engaged, spending most of their writing time doing something that involves thoughtfulness, such as crafting a story or learning how to construct a complex sentence.
- teach basic writing skills, strategies, and knowledge balanced by ample opportunity to apply what is learned.
- involve students in writing for a variety of different purposes.
- create a writing classroom environment that is supportive, pleasant, and motivating.
- encourage students to accomplish as much as possible on their own (to act in a self-regulated fashion), but who are ready to offer support and instruction as needed.
- use reading to support writing development and vice versa.
- monitor students' growth in writing and encourage students to monitor their own growth.
- provide extra assistance to students who experience difficulty.
- are passionate about writing.

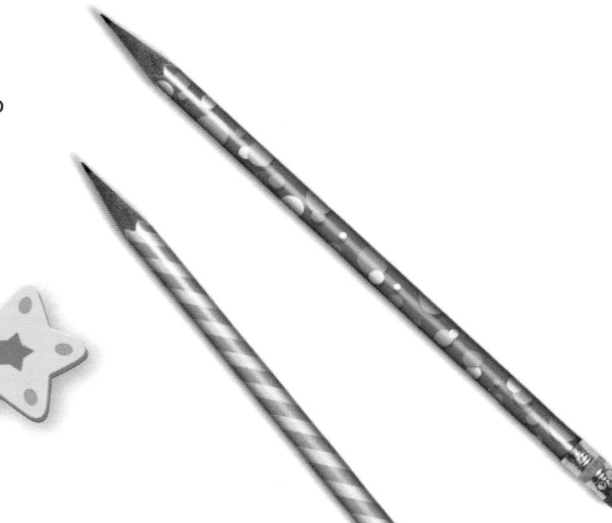

Knowledge about Writing

Purpose

Writing can be used to communicate, entertain, inform, reflect, persuade, and learn. To take full advantage of this flexible tool, students must acquire knowledge about the qualities of good writing and the various purposes and forms of writing. They must also carefully consider their audience and be knowledgeable about the topics they write about.

Procedures

Qualities of Good Writing

One way students learn about the qualities of good writing is by directly teaching them that good writing is characterized by the following seven traits:

- Clearly presented and fully developed ideas
- Writing that is easy to follow and logically organized
- Effective and precise word choice
- Varied use of sentence structure to promote fluency, rhythm, and natural speech patterns
- Writing that captures appropriate tone or mood to make the desired impact on the reader
- Correct spelling, usage, and grammar
- A written product that is legible, attractive, and accessible

For each writing assignment, teachers concentrate on one or more of these traits, teaching students strategies for enhancing the trait(s) in their writing. For example, students are taught to circle words that are vague in their writing and to replace them with more precise ones.

Another way that students learn about the qualities of good writing is through reading. The reading material in ***SRA Imagine It!*** provides concrete models that illustrate the characteristics of good writing, such as how authors

- present, develop, and organize ideas.
- use words to evoke specific images and feelings.
- manipulate sentences to speed up or slow down the flow of text.
- set and change the mood to match the action of the characters.
- use illustrations to reinforce and sharpen readers' understanding.

This knowledge is fostered in ***SRA Imagine It!*** through Reading with a Writer's Eye. Teachers and students discuss what the author of a reading selection did to achieve certain purposes. For example, after reading a mystery, the class discusses how the author planted a false lead to make the story more interesting and complex. Students are then encouraged to use the same technique in a mystery they write.

Different Purposes and Forms of Writing

Students learn the purposes and forms of a wide range of genres they need to master for success both in and out of school. This includes using writing to do the following:

- Communicate with others (personal letters, business letters, notes, cards, and e-mail)
- Create personal narratives (journal writing, autobiography, writing about a personal event, and so on)
- Entertain (stories, plays, poems, and so on)
- Learn (learning logs, reports, journal entries, summarizing, and biographies)
- Inform (writing lists, explaining how to do something, describing objects or places, describing events, news reports, reports, and biographies)
- Respond to literature (book evaluations, book reports, and book reviews)
- Persuade (advertisements, opinions about controversial topics)
- Demonstrate knowledge (for example, traditional classroom tests, high-stakes tests involving writing, high-stakes tests involving multiple-choice answers)

In ***SRA Imagine It!*** writing, students learn to write stories, poetry, plays, journal entries, summaries, book reviews, informative reports, descriptions, explanations, letters, critiques, and e-mail. They also use these various forms of writing to gather, think about, and report what they have learned when doing extended Inquiry projects.

One way they learn about the purposes and forms of these various genres is through the use of models of each type of writing. As students begin working on a new genre, the class analyzes an exemplary model of this type of writing to determine its characteristics and functions. They are encouraged to incorporate these features in their writing. In addition, what they write is frequently tied to what they read, so their reading material provides a model and source of information on the purpose and form of their writing.

Students are also asked to carefully consider the purpose for each of their compositions and include this determination as part of the planning process. As they plan, the form and purpose of their compositions is further emphasized through the use of graphic organizers, in which students typically generate and organize ideas for each of the basic elements included in the type of composition they are composing.

Knowledge of Writing Topics

To write well, students must have something to write about. Good writers typically know a lot about their topics or have strategies for acquiring such information. With ***SRA Imagine It!*** writing, students are taught effective strategies for gathering information to write about. This includes how to

- locate information in written and electronic sources.
- obtain information through interviews or surveys.
- summarize information in notes.
- reference informational sources.

Developing a Sense of Audience

While writing is often viewed as a solitary activity, it is typically meant to be read by others. Children and adults most often use writing to communicate, persuade, or inform others. Because the writer is usually not present when the composition is read, he or she must carefully consider the needs of the readers. ***SRA Imagine It!*** writing helps students develop a sense of audience by asking them to identify their audience when they write collaboratively or independently. Students are also encouraged to share what they write with their peers and others. The following are procedures for presenting and sharing:

- Before presenting, have the writer
  - decide what will be shared.
  - practice what will be shared.
- During presenting,
  - have the writer tell what is to be shared and why.

- have the writer read aloud his or her work or idea.
- remind students to listen carefully.

✦ After presenting,

- have students tell what they like.
- have students offer the writer helpful suggestions.
- take notes of students' comments to share with the writer.

Tips

✦ Have students keep a log of new information they have learned about the attributes of good writing.

✦ Develop wall charts that specify the purpose and attributes of specific writing genres.

✦ Ask students to evaluate their writing and the writing of others based on seven traits of good writing.

✦ Before students begin work on a writing assignment, hold a class discussion on the topic to share information, clarify misperceptions, and identify information students still need to locate.

Mastering the Writing Process

Purpose

To write skillfully, young writers must master the basic processes involved in writing. These processes include the strategic "know-how" involved in writing and include the following:

✦ **Prewriting:** Writers spend time thinking about and planning their topics. They consider their purposes, audience, and the focus of their topics. Writers make plans to guide the composing process, establishing goals for what to do and say. They gather possible ideas for their writing, drawing on memory and external sources such as books, interviews, articles, and the Internet. Writers make decisions about which information to include and how to organize it.

✦ **Drafting:** Writers draft or put their ideas into words, using the initial plans they developed as a guide. These plans are expanded, modified, and even reworked as writers create a first draft of their composition, often in a rough form.

✦ **Revising:** While some revising may occur during prewriting and drafting, writers revisit and revise their first drafts. They reread them to see whether the drafts say what the writers intended. Writers check to be sure the drafts make sense and that the meaning is clear for the audience. They consider whether their writing will have the desired impact on the audience. As they make changes in their text, they discover new things to say and new ways to present their ideas.

Writers need feedback throughout the writing process. Feedback is one of our most powerful tools for helping developing writers.

✦ **Editing/Proofreading:** Writers edit/proofread their work. They recognize that spelling, grammar, and usage errors make it harder for others to understand and enjoy their published work. Writers know that readers are more likely to value their message when they correct these mistakes.

✦ **Publishing:** Writers share their writing by reading their entire work, or part of their work, to others. They publish their work in books, newspapers, magazines, anthologies, and so on.

Skilled writers move back and forth through these processes—from prewriting to drafting to revising and back—to create their final pieces.

Procedures

Much of what happens during writing is not visible. It occurs inside the writer's head. ***SRA Imagine It!*** writing makes the processes involved in writing concrete and visible in the following four ways:

✦ Establishing a predictable writing routine during which students are expected to prewrite, draft, revise, edit/proofread, and publish.

✦ Using graphic organizers and revising, editing/proofreading, and publishing checklists that help developing writers carry out basic writing processes.

✦ Teaching strategies for prewriting, drafting, revising, editing/proofreading, and publishing.

✦ Providing feedback throughout the writing process through writing conferences and students' presentation of their works in progress and completed compositions.

Establishing a Predictable Writing Routine

One way to make the basic writing processes more concrete is to create a predictable classroom writing routine, during which students plan, draft, revise, edit, proofread, and publish their work. This establishes that these processes are important and ensures that time is provided for each process. It also allows students to work with minimum teacher direction and at their own pace.

Tips

✦ Guide students through the steps of the writing routine. Model each step of prewriting, drafting, revising, editing/proofreading, and publishing.

✦ Make sure students learn that the processes of writing do not always occur in the same order but are recursive. For example, revising may occur at any stage of the composing process. You should not only model this by showing how this is done, but the predictable routine should vary at times to reflect this flexibility.

Using Graphic Organizers and Revising, Editing/Proofreading, and Publishing Checklists

Graphic organizers and revising, editing/proofreading, and publishing checklists provide students with assistance in carrying out the thinking activities involved in a writing assignment. They provide structure and information for how to carry out the process. The graphic organizer typically includes a series of prompts that ask the student to think about the purpose for writing a particular piece and the intended audience. It also provides prompts designed to help the student generate and organize possible writing ideas. This frequently involves generating possible content for each part of the target composition. The revising, editing/proofreading, and publishing checklists direct students' attention to specific features or aspects of text that would be useful to consider while writing.

Tips

It is important to be sure that students understand how to use graphic organizers and revising, editing/proofreading, and publishing checklists. Be sure to

- explain the purpose of the graphic organizer or revising, editing/proofreading, and publishing checklist.
- describe how students are to use the graphic organizer or revising, editing/proofreading, and publishing checklist.
- model aloud how to carry out the basic activities on the graphic organizer or revising, editing/proofreading, and publishing checklist.
- make sure students understand each part of the graphic organizer or revising, editing/proofreading, and publishing checklist.

Teaching Strategies for Carrying Out Basic Writing Processes

A strategy involves a series of actions a writer undertakes to achieve a desired goal. In ***SRA Imagine It!*** students are taught strategies to help them carry out each of the basic writing processes—prewriting, drafting, revising, editing/proofreading, and publishing. Each strategy is also designed to enhance one or more of the seven traits of good writing. These include clearly presented and fully developed ideas; writing that is easy to follow and logically organized; effective and precise word choice; varied use of sentences to promote fluency, rhythm, and natural speech patterns; writing that captures appropriate tone or mood to make maximum impact on readers; correct spelling, usage, and grammar; and a written product that is legible, attractive, and accessible.

The goal is for students to be able to use the strategy independently and to make it part of their writing tool kit. The steps for teaching writing strategies are to

- describe the strategy.
- tell why the strategy is important.
- tell students when they should use the strategy.
- model how to use the strategy when writing, making your thoughts visible by saying aloud each thing you are doing and thinking.
- make sure students understand why the strategy is important, when to apply it, and how to use it.
- provide students with assistance in applying the strategy until they can do it on their own.
- remind students to use the strategy when they write.

Tips

- Ask students to evaluate their progress and how the strategy improved their writing.
- Be enthusiastic about learning the strategy.
- Establish the importance of effort in learning and using the strategy.
- Provide opportunities for students to see how the strategy improves their writing.
- Praise and reinforce students' use of the strategy.
- Foster students' ownership of the strategy.

Providing Feedback through Conferencing and Presentation

Writers need feedback throughout the writing process. They need reactions to ideas, drafts, and revisions. Feedback is one of our most powerful tools for helping developing writers. Writers want to know how their works-in-progress sound to someone else, whether their compositions make sense, whether they contain any incorrect or misleading information, and where and how to make changes.

Regular feedback encourages developing writers to solve problems and make meaningful changes throughout the writing process.

One way of providing feedback is through conferences. Teachers may initiate conferences, but students should also be encouraged to call conferences on an as-needed basis. Because conferences can be held at various times throughout the writing process, the focus will vary. Conferences held during the early stages of the writing process help students identify and refine a topic or identify research references. During the revision process, conferences help students learn to elaborate and reorganize their writing. During the final stages, students learn to edit and proofread stories before they are published. Conferences offer an excellent opportunity for the teacher and student to evaluate jointly the student's progress and set goals for future growth.

The basic procedures for writing conferences are as follows:

- Have the student read aloud his or her work.
- Review any feedback the student has received so far.
- Identify positive elements of the work.
- Use one or more of these strategies to help the student improve his or her work.
    - Have the student explain how he or she got his or her ideas.
    - Have the student think aloud about how he or she will address the feedback he or she has received.
    - Ask the student to help you understand any confusion you may have about his or her writing.
    - Have the student add, delete, or rearrange something in the work, and ask how it affects the entire piece.
    - Think aloud while you do a part of what the student was asked to do. Then ask the student to compare what you did to what he or she did.
    - Have the student prescribe as if to a younger student how to revise the work.
- Ask two or three questions to guide the student through revising (see below).
- Conclude the conference by having the student state his or her plan for continuing work on the piece of writing.

Tips

- Set aside a special area of the classroom for you to work with students or for students to work with each other.
- You don't have to meet with every student every day.
- Conferences should be brief; don't overwhelm students with too many comments or suggestions. Several short conferences are often more effective than one long one.
- If appropriate, suggest that students take notes to help them remember where changes are to be made.

- Don't take ownership of the students' work. Encourage students to identify what is good and what needs to be changed, and let the students make the changes.
- Focus on what is good about the students' work; discuss how to solve problems rather than telling students what to do.
- Peer conferencing should be encouraged during Workshop.
- As students engage in peer conferencing, note which students are participating, the types of questions they ask, and the comments they make. Use this information to help students become more effective in peer conferencing.
- You may need to structure peer conferences by asking students to first explain what they liked about the composition, and then teaching them how to give constructive feedback.

Having students present or share their work provides another opportunity for them to receive feedback about their writing. Student presentations can involve

- presenting an initial idea or plan for a writing assignment.
- sharing a first draft of a paper.
- presenting orally part or all of a final piece of writing.

Tips

- Everyone must listen carefully and provide constructive feedback. Focus on what is good about a piece and ways to make it better.
- The student author has ownership and can decide which suggestions to use. The author does not have to incorporate all suggestions from the audience.
- Have a chair designated as the "Author's Chair" from which the student author can read his or her work or share ideas. This lends importance to the activity.
- The student author should be encouraged to give a bit of background, including where he or she is in the process, why he or she chose a particular part, or what problem he or she is having. This helps orient the audience.
- Short pieces of writing can be read in their entirety. As students become more proficient and write longer papers, they should be encouraged to read just a part of their writing; for example, a part they need help with, a part that has been revised, or a part they particularly like.
- Take notes during the presentations, and encourage older students to do the same.
- Be sensitive to the attention span of the class and the feedback being given. Students have a tendency to repeat the same comments to each author.

Word Processing and Other Aspects of Electronic Composing

Using a word processor to compose a piece of writing makes many aspects of the writing process easier. Text can easily be changed, deleted, or moved during drafting or revising. Software such as spell-checkers or word prediction provides assistance with basic writing skills. Information for writing can be obtained on-line or through other electronic sources, such as encyclopedias. Students can use publishing software to develop a more polished and attractive final product by adding pictures to their composition, developing a cover, changing fonts, and so on. ***SRA Imagine It!*** supports the use of these technologies.

Teaching Basic Writing Skills

Purpose

Young writers need to learn many basic writing skills to the point that the skills can be executed with minimal effort so they do not interfere with other writing processes. Correct handwriting, spelling, and grammar should be mastered to the point that they require little attention on the part of the writer. While sentences cannot and should not be constructed without conscious attention and effort, developing writers need to become familiar with different sentence types, and they need to become proficient at building them.

Procedures

Sentence Construction

SRA Imagine It! teaches sentence construction skills through the use of sentence frames, sentence expansion, and sentence combining.

- **Sentence Frames** With sentence frames, students are given part of a sentence and asked to generate the rest of it. For example, students can be taught to write a simple sentence, with a single subject and predicate, by giving them a frame containing the subject (The dog ______ ______.) and asking them to complete the sentence by telling what happened (The dog ran.).
- **Sentence Expansion** With sentence expansion, students are given a kernel sentence and asked to expand it by adding additional words. For example, students can be taught to make sentences more colorful by adding descriptive words to a kernel sentence: *Rewrite **The cat and dog like the toy** so the sentence tells more about the cat and dog and the toy — The big dog and gray cat like the fuzzy little toy.*
- **Sentence combining** With sentence combining, students learn how to combine two or more kernel sentences into a more complex single sentence. For example, you can lead students to produce sentences with relative clauses by combining the following two sentences:

  John will win the race.

  John is very fast. (who)

  John, who is very fast, will win the race.

When teaching sentence construction skills, the following three steps should be followed:

- Describe the skill, establish why it is important, and model how to use it.
- Provide students with assistance until they can apply the skill correctly and independently.
- Ask students to apply the skill when they write.

Tips

- Use more than one method to teach a sentence construction skill.
- Ask students to monitor how often they use the sentence construction skill.
- Encourage students to set goals to use sentence construction skills in their writing.

Handwriting

Students need to develop both legible and fluent handwriting. An important aspect of meeting this goal is to teach them an efficient pattern for forming individual letters (both lowercase and uppercase letters). Effective teaching procedures include

- modeling how to form the letter.
- describing how the letter is similar to and different from other letters.
- using visual cues, such as numbered arrows, as a guide to letter formation.
- providing practice tracing, copying, and writing the letter from memory.
- keeping instructional sessions short, with frequent review and practice.
- asking students to identify or circle their best formed letter or letters.
- encouraging students to correct or rewrite poorly formed letters.
- monitoring students' practice to ensure that letters are formed correctly.
- reinforcing students' successful efforts and providing corrective feedback as needed.

In addition to learning how to write the letters of the alphabet correctly, students must be able to produce them quickly. Fluency generally develops as a consequence of writing frequently, but it can also be fostered by having students copy short passages several times, and trying to write them a little faster each time.

Tips

- Make sure that each student develops a comfortable and efficient pencil grip.
- Encourage students to sit in an upright position, leaning slightly forward, as they write.
- Show students how to place or position their papers when writing.
- Implement appropriate procedures for left-handed writers, such as how to properly place or position their papers when writing.
- Monitor students' handwriting, paying special attention to their instructional needs in letter formation, spacing, slant, alignment, size, and line quality.
- Encourage students to make all final drafts of their papers neat and legible.

Spelling

Purpose

To become good spellers, students must learn to spell correctly and easily the words they are most likely to use when writing. They need to be able to generate and check plausible spellings for words whose spellings are uncertain. They also need to learn to use external sources such as spell-checkers to ensure correct spelling during writing. In ***SRA Imagine It!*** students are taught how to spell words they frequently use when writing as well as spelling patterns that help them spell untaught words.

Tips

- Teach students an effective strategy for studying spelling words.
- Reinforce the correct spelling of taught words in students' writing.
- Have students build words from letters or letters and phonograms, for example, c - at.
- Teach strategies for determining and checking the spelling of unknown words.
- Model the use of correct spelling and how to correct spelling errors when you write in front of the class.
- Encourage students to correct misspelled words in all final drafts of their writing.
- Provide instruction and practice in proofreading.
- Encourage students to use spell-checkers, dictionaries, and so on to determine the correct spelling of unknown words.

Grammar and Usage

Traditional methods of teaching grammar and usage skills are not effective. With such instruction, students are initially provided with an abstract definition, such as an adjective is a word that describes a noun or pronoun. This is often followed by asking students to practice applying the skill correctly without actually generating any textual material longer than a word or a phrase. For example, students might be asked to complete the following sentence: The ___________ wagon rolled through the ___________ town. It is not surprising that many students do not understand the rules they are taught or how to use them in their writing, because such instruction is abstract and decontextualized.

To make grammar instruction effective, ***SRA Imagine It!*** applies the following five principles. To make these principles concrete, the program illustrates each as it would apply to the rule for capitalizing the first letter in a person's name.

- Grammar and usage skills need to be defined in a functional and concrete manner. The rule of capitalizing the first letter in a person's name can be introduced by writing a sentence with two or three familiar names on the board. With the students' help, identify each name in the sentence, and ask them what they notice about the first letter in each name—They are capital letters. Repeat this process with a second sentence, and then establish the "capitalization rule" with students' help.
- As soon as the skill is functionally described or defined, establish why it is important—Capitalizing the first letter in a person's name makes the name stand out and shows respect for the person named. This is an important rule for writing.
- Show students how to use the skill when writing. Generate a sentence using the names of students in the class, or have your students help you generate such a sentence. Write it on the board, capitalizing the first letter while simultaneously telling the class what you are doing.

- Provide students with guided practice in applying the skill when writing. Generate with the class another sentence that includes three of your students' names. Tell the class you will write the sentence on the board, but they will need to tell you when to capitalize a word. Next, have students work together in pairs to generate two sentences using names of their friends, capitalizing the first letter in each name. Provide support as needed. Finally, have each student generate one sentence of his or her own containing two names. Monitor to ensure that students capitalize the first letter in each name. Have them share their sentences with a peer.
- Ask students to apply the skill in their compositions. Have students look at one of the papers in their writing portfolio and correct any capitalization mistakes involving people's names. Remind students to capitalize people's names when writing and revising subsequent writing assignments.

Tips

- Ask students to correct other students' papers, focusing on specific grammar and usage rules and mistakes.
- Encourage students to read their papers aloud when revising. This will help them spot grammar and usage mistakes.

Fostering Motivation

Purpose

Children start school wanting to learn how to write and enjoying writing. Too quickly, however, many begin to view writing as a chore or something to be avoided. The goal of ***SRA Imagine It!*** writing is for children to become lifelong writers—people who enjoy writing and use writing effectively at work as well as in their personal lives.

Procedures

One way to foster an interest in writing is to have students write for real purposes and audiences. This includes having students identify why they are writing and what they hope to accomplish. Likewise, students need to share their writing with others. They are more likely to do their best writing when there is an audience. Students can share their plans, an initial draft, a portion of their composition, or the completed paper with you, their peers, or other children or adults.

Students are also likely to give their best effort when the writing environment is supportive and pleasant. This can be accomplished by the following:

- Establishing clear rules for student behavior during the writing period. Keep the rules simple and reasonable in number and consistently reinforce them. Students are not likely to enjoy writing, or learn well, if the classroom environment is chaotic.
- Creating a low-risk environment in which students feel comfortable taking risks with their writing. This means being accepting and encouraging of students' efforts and encouraging them to act in the same manner. For example, make it a rule in your class that when someone shares his or her writing, the first thing that you or other students do is say what you liked most about it.
- Supporting students as they begin to apply the knowledge, skills, or strategies you teach them. This can include reteaching, providing hints and reminders, giving useful feedback, and initially helping students apply what was taught.
- Having students help each other as they plan, draft, revise, edit/proofread, and publish their work. This is most effective when the process of working together is structured. For instance, students are more likely to give good advice for revising if they are asked to focus on specific aspects of the composition, such as identifying places where the writing is unclear or more detail is needed.
- Celebrating student success by displaying their work. This can be done by prominently displaying student work in the classroom or in other places in the school. Students can also be asked to publish their work in a class or school newspaper or to read their compositions aloud to younger children, in other classes, or at a special event.
- Fostering an "I can do" attitude among your students. Consistently emphasize that the key to good writing is effort and the use of what they have learned.
- Setting a positive mood during writing time. Be enthusiastic about writing and what your students write.

Tips

- Allow students to make their own decisions and to accomplish as much on their own as possible.
- Increase students' ownership of a writing topic by allowing them to develop unique interpretations of the topic.
- Encourage students to take ownership of their writing. This includes allowing them to arrange a suitable writing environment, construct a personal plan for accomplishing the writing task, to work at their own pace when possible, and to decide what feedback from you and their peers is most pertinent for revising their writing.
- Look for opportunities to give students positive feedback about their work. Let them know when they have done something well in their writing.
- Encourage students to monitor their progress. For example, have students select their best writing to keep in a writing portfolio, identifying why they selected each piece.
- Show your students that you are a writer too. Share your writing with them. Talk about the various ways you use writing each day.
- Connect writing to students' lives and the world in general. Have them document the types of writing they do outside school. Develop a wall chart on which the class can identify how they use writing away from school.
- Provide incentives for writing at home. For example, have parents document that their child writes for twenty minutes at home a set number of nights for a month. Provide a special party for these children, allowing each one to select a book to keep from an array of books donated by parents or a sponsoring business partner.

Spelling Strategies

Spelling

Many people find English difficult, because English sound/spelling patterns seem to have hundreds of exceptions. The key to becoming a good speller, however, is not just memorization. The key is recognizing and internalizing English spelling patterns. Some people do this naturally as they read and develop large vocabularies. They intuitively recognize spelling patterns and apply them appropriately. Others need explicit and direct teaching of vocabulary and spelling strategies and spelling patterns before they develop spelling consciousness.

Purpose

Spelling is a fundamental skill in written communication. Although a writer may have wonderful ideas, he or she may find it difficult to communicate those ideas without spelling skills. Learning to spell requires much exposure to text and writing. For many it requires a methodical presentation of English spelling patterns.

English Spelling Patterns

A basic understanding of English spelling patterns will help provide efficient and effective spelling instruction. Just as the goal of phonics instruction is to enable students to read fluently, the goal of spelling instruction is to enable students to write fluently so they can concentrate on ideas rather than spelling.

Sound Patterns Many words are spelled the way they sound. Most consonants and short vowels are very regular. When a student learns the sound/spelling relationships, he or she has the key to spelling many words.

Structural Patterns Structural patterns are employed when adding endings to words. Examples of structural patterns include doubling the final consonant, adding *-s* or *-es* to form plurals, and dropping the final *e* before adding *-ing, -ed, -er,* or *-est.* Often these structural patterns are very regular in their application. Many students have little trouble learning these patterns.

Meaning Patterns Many spelling patterns in English are morphological; in other words, the meaning relationship is maintained regardless of how a sound may change. Prefixes, suffixes, and root words that retain their spellings regardless of how they are pronounced are further examples of meaning patterns.

Foreign Language Patterns Many English words are derived from foreign words and retain those language patterns. For example, kindergarten (German), boulevard (French), and ballet (French from Italian) are foreign-language patterns at work in English.

Developmental Stages of Spelling

The most important finding in spelling research in the past thirty years is that students learn to spell in a predictable developmental sequence, much as they learn to read. It appears to take the average student three to six years to progress through the developmental stages and emerge as a fairly competent, mature speller.

Prephonemic The first stage is the prephonemic stage, characterized by random letters arranged either in continuous lines or in wordlike clusters. Only the writer can "read" it, and it may be "read" differently on different days.

Semiphonemic As emergent readers learn that letters stand for sounds, they use particular letters specifically to represent the initial consonant sound and sometimes a few other very salient sounds. This marks the discovery of phonemic awareness that letters represent speech sounds in writing.

Phonemic When students can represent most of the sounds they hear in words, they have entered the phonemic stage of spelling. They spell what they hear, using everything they know about letter sounds, letter names, and familiar words. Many remedial spellers never develop beyond this stage and spell a word the way it sounds whenever they encounter a word they cannot spell.

Transitional or Within-Word Pattern As they are exposed to more difficult words, students discover that not all words are spelled as they sound. They learn that they must include silent letters, spell past tenses with *-ed,* include a vowel even in unstressed syllables, and remember how words look. The transitional stage represents the transition from primarily phonemic strategies to rule-bound spelling.

Derivational The derivational stage occurs as transitional spellers accumulate a large spelling vocabulary and gain control over affixes, contractions, homophones, and other meaning patterns. They discover that related or derived forms of words share spelling features even if they do not sound the same. As spellers gain control over these subtle word features and spell most words correctly, they become conventional spellers.

Procedures

The spelling lessons are organized around different spelling patterns, beginning with phonetic spelling patterns and progressing to other types of spelling patterns in a logical sequence. Word lists including words from the literature selection focus on the particular patterns in each lesson. In general, the sound patterns occur in the first units at each grade, followed by structural patterns, meaning patterns, and foreign-language patterns in the upper grade levels.

- As you begin each new spelling lesson, have students identify the spelling pattern and how it is like and different from other patterns.
- Give the pretest to help students focus on the lesson pattern.
- Have students proofread their own pretests immediately after the test, crossing out any misspellings and writing the correct spelling.
- Have them diagnose whether the errors they made were in the lesson pattern or in another part of the word. Help students determine where they made errors and what type of pattern they should work on to correct them.
- As students work through the spelling pages from ***Skills Practice,*** encourage them to practice the different spelling strategies in the exercises.

Sound Pattern Strategies

Pronunciation Strategy As students encounter an unknown word, have them say the word carefully to hear each sound. Encourage them to check the ***Sound/Spelling Cards.*** Then have them spell each sound. (/s/ + /i/ + /t/: sit). This strategy builds directly on the Dication and Spelling introduced in kindergarten and taught in Levels 1–3.

Consonant Substitution Have students switch consonants. The vowel spelling usually remains the same. (bat, hat, rat, flat, splat) This is a natural extension of Phonemic Awareness activities begun in prekindergarten and kindergarten.

Vowel Substitution Have students switch vowels. The consonant spellings usually remain the same. (CVC: hit, hat, hut, hot; CVCV: mane, mine; CVVC: boat, beat, bait, beet) This is a natural extension of Phonemic Awareness activities begun in prekindergarten and kindergarten.

Rhyming Word Strategy Have students think of rhyming words and the rhymes that spell a particular sound. Often the sound will be spelled the same way in another word. (cub, tub, rub) This is a natural extension of Phonemic Awareness activities begun in prekindergarten and kindergarten.

Structural Pattern Strategies

Conventions Strategy Have students learn the rules and exceptions for adding endings to words (dropping *y*, dropping *e*, doubling the final consonant, and so on).

Proofreading Strategy Many spelling errors occur because of simple mistakes. Have students check their writing carefully and specifically for spelling.

Visualization Strategy Have students think about how a word looks. Sometimes words "look" wrong because a wrong spelling pattern has been written. Have them double-check the spelling of any word that looks wrong.

Meaning Pattern Strategies

Family Strategy When students are not sure of a spelling, have them think of how words from the same base word family are spelled. (critic, criticize, critical; sign, signal, signature; nation, national, nationality)

Meaning Strategy Have students determine a homophone's meaning to make sure they are using the right word. Knowing prefixes, suffixes, and base words will also help.

Compound Word Strategy Tell students to break apart a compound and to spell each word. Compounds may not follow convention rules for adding endings. (homework, nonetheless)

Foreign-Language Strategy Have students think of foreign-language spellings that are different from English spelling patterns. (ballet, boulevard, sauerkraut)

Dictionary Strategy Ask students to look up the word in a dictionary to make sure their spelling is correct. If they do not know how to spell a word, have them try a few different spellings and look them up to see which one is correct. (fotograph, photograph) Have students use the ***Sound/Spelling Cards*** to help them look up words. This develops a spelling consciousness.

Use the post test to determine understanding of the lesson spelling pattern and to identify any other spelling pattern problems. Encourage student understanding of spelling patterns and use of spelling strategies in all their writing to help transfer spelling skills to writing.

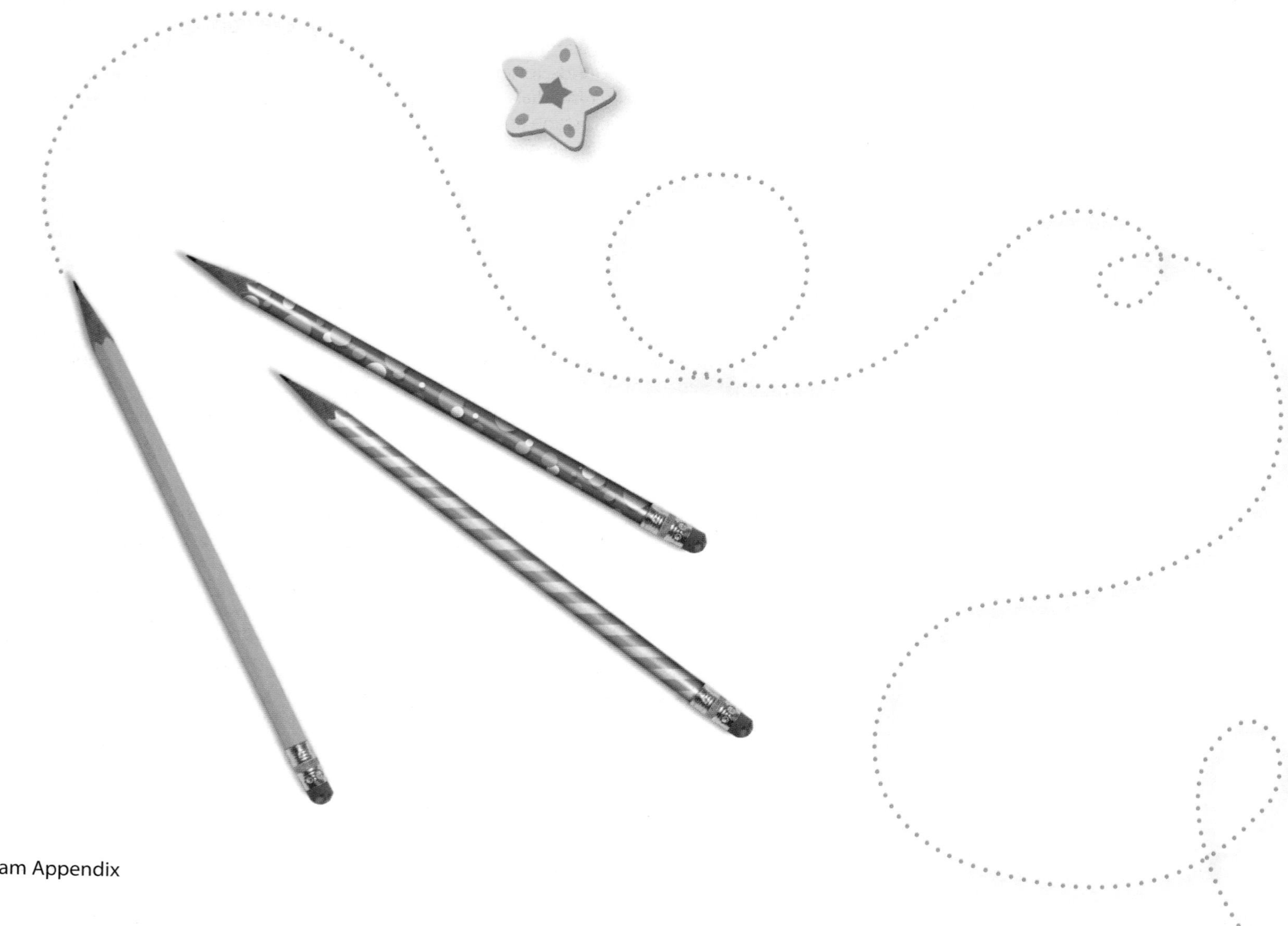

Grammar, Usage, and Mechanics

Purpose

The Study of English Conventions

Over the years the study of grammar, usage, and mechanics has gone in and out of favor. In the past century much research has been done to demonstrate the effectiveness of traditional types of instruction in the conventions of English. Experience and research have shown that learning grammatical terms and completing grammar exercises have little effect on the student's practical application of these skills in the context of speaking or writing. These skills, in and of themselves, do not play a significant role in the way students use language to generate and express their ideas—for example, during the prewriting and drafting phases of the writing process. In fact, emphasis on correct conventions has been shown to have a damaging effect when it is the sole focus of writing instruction. If students are evaluated only on the proper use of spelling, grammar, and punctuation, they tend to write fewer and less complex sentences.

Knowledge of English conventions is, however, vitally important in the editing and proofreading phases of the writing process. A paper riddled with mistakes in grammar, usage, or mechanics is quickly discounted. Many immature writers never revise or edit. They finish the last sentence and turn their papers in to the teacher. Mature writers employ their knowledge of English language conventions in the editing phase to refine and polish their ideas.

The study of grammar, usage, and mechanics is important for two reasons.

1. Educated people need to know and understand the structure of their language, which in large part defines their culture.
2. Knowledge of grammar gives teachers and students a common vocabulary for talking about language and makes discussions of writing tasks more efficient and clearer.

Procedure

The key issue in learning grammar, usage, and mechanics is how to do it. On the one hand, teaching these skills in isolation from writing has been shown to be ineffective and even detrimental if too much emphasis is placed on them. On the other hand, not teaching these skills and having students write without concern for conventions is equally ineffective. The answer is to teach the skills in a context that allows students to directly apply them to a reading or writing activity. Students should be taught proper use of punctuation or subject/verb agreement at the same time they are taught to proofread for those conventions. As they learn to apply their knowledge of conventions during the final stages of the writing process, they will begin to see that correcting errors is an editorial rather than a composition skill.

A paper riddled with mistakes in grammar, usage, or mechanics is quickly discounted.

History of English

A basic understanding of the history and structure of the English language helps students understand the rich but complex resource they have for writing.

Old English

The English language began about A.D. 450 when the Angles, Jutes, and Saxons––three tribes that lived in northern Europe–– invaded the British Isles. Much of their language included words that had to do with farming (*sheep, dirt, tree, earth*). Many of their words are the most frequently used words in the English language today. Because of Latin influences, English became the first of the European languages to be written.

Middle English

In 1066 William the Conqueror invaded England and brought Norman French with him. Slowly Old English and Norman French came together, and Middle English began to appear. Today forty percent of Modern English comes from French. With the introduction of the printing press, English became more widespread.

Modern English

With the Renaissance and its rediscovery of classical Greek and Latin, many new words were created from Greek and Latin word elements. This continued intensively during the Early Modern English period. This rich language was used in the writings of Shakespeare and his contemporaries and profoundly influenced the nature and vocabulary of English. With dictionaries and spelling books, the English language became more standardized, although it continues to be influenced by other languages and new words and trends. These influences continue to make English a living, dynamic language.

Punctuation

Early writing had no punctuation or even spaces between words. English punctuation had its beginning in ancient Greece and Rome. Early punctuation reflected speaking rather than reading. By the end of the eighteenth century, after the invention of printing, most of the rules for punctuation were established, although they were not the same in all languages.

The Structure of English

Grammar is the sound, structure, and meaning system of language. People who speak the same language are able to communicate because they intuitively know the grammar system of that language, the rules to make meaning. All languages have grammar, and yet each language has its own grammar.

Traditional grammar study usually involves two areas:

- **Parts of speech** (nouns, verbs, adjectives, adverbs, pronouns, prepositions, conjunctions) are typically considered the content of grammar. The parts of speech involve the form of English words.
- **Sentence structure** (subjects, predicates, objects, clauses, phrases) is also included in grammar study. Sentence structure involves the function of English.

Mechanics involves the conventions of punctuation and capitalization. Punctuation helps readers understand writers' messages. Proper punctuation involves marking off sentences according to grammatical structure. In speech students can produce sentences as easily and unconsciously as they can walk, but in writing they must think about what is and what is not a sentence.

In English there are about fourteen punctuation marks (period, comma, quotation mark, question mark, exclamation point, colon, semicolon, apostrophe, hyphen, ellipsis, parenthesis, bracket, dash, and underscore). Most immature writers use only three: period, comma, and question mark. The experienced writer or poet with the command of punctuation adds both flexibility and meaning to his or her sentences through his or her use of punctuation.

Usage is the way in which we speak in a given community. Language varies over time, across national and geographical boundaries, by gender, across age groups, and by socioeconomic status. When the variation occurs within a given language, the different versions of the same language are called dialects. Every language has a prestige dialect associated with education and financial success. In the United States, this dialect is known as Standard English and is the language of school and business.

Usage involves the word choices people make when speaking certain dialects. Word choices that are perfectly acceptable in conversation among friends may be unacceptable in writing. Usage is often the most obvious indicator of the difference between conversation and composition. Errors in word usage can make a writer seem ignorant and thus jeopardize his or her credibility, no matter how valid or important his or her overall message might be. Usage depends on a student's cultural and linguistic heritage. If the dialect students have learned is not the formal language of school settings or if it is not English, students must master another dialect or language in order to write Standard English.

The Grammar, Usage, and Mechanics lessons in ***SRA Imagine It!*** are structured to focus on skills presented in a logical sequence. A skill is introduced with appropriate models and then practiced in reading and writing on subsequent days to ensure that skills are not taught in isolation. Encourage students to use the focused English language convention presented in each lesson as they complete each Writing Process Strategies activity. Also encourage them to reread their writing, checking for proper use of the conventions taught. With practice, students should be able to apply their knowledge of conventions to any writing they do.

Tips

- Some of the errors students make in writing are the result simply of not carefully reading their final drafts. Many errors occur because the writer's train of thought was interrupted and a sentence is not complete or a word is skipped. These may look like huge errors that a simple rereading can remedy. Most often the writer can correct these types of errors on his or her own. A major emphasis of any English composition program should be to teach the editing and proofreading phases of the writing process so students can eliminate these types of errors themselves. This involves a shift in perception—from thinking of grammar as a set of discrete skills that involve mastery of individual rules to understanding grammar as it applies to the act of communicating in writing.
- As students learn English language conventions, they should be expected to incorporate them into their written work.
- Sometimes, students write sentences that raise grammatically complex problems that require a deep understanding of English grammar. Use the Sentence Lifting strategies outlined in the Proofreading part of the Appendix to identify and discuss these more sophisticated types of errors that can include the following:
- **Faulty Parallelism.** Parts of a sentence parallel in meaning are not parallel in structure.
- **Nonsequiturs.** A statement does not follow logically from something said previously.
- **Dangling Modifiers.** A phrase or clause does not logically modify the word next to it.
- **Awkwardness.** Sentences are not written simply.
- **Wordiness.** Thoughts are not written in as few words as possible. Precise words are not used.

Listening/Speaking/Viewing

Some people are naturally good listeners, and others have no trouble speaking in front of groups. Many people, however, need explicit instruction on how to tune in for important details and how to organize and make an oral presentation. While some people naturally critique what they read, hear, and see, many others need specific guidance to develop skills for analyzing what they encounter in images and the media. The abilities to listen appropriately and to speak in conversations and in groups, as well as to critically evaluate the information with which they are presented, are fundamental skills that will serve students throughout their lives.

Purpose

In addition to reading and writing, listening, speaking, and viewing complete the language arts picture. Through the development of these language arts skills, students gain flexibility in communicating orally, visually, and in writing. When speaking and listening skills are neglected, many students have difficulty speaking in front of groups, organizing a speech, or distinguishing important information they hear. A top anxiety for many adults is speaking in front of groups. Much of this anxiety would not exist if listening, speaking, and viewing skills were taught from the early years.

The Listening/Speaking/Viewing instruction focuses on the literature selection or the Writing Process Strategies to provide context, to reinforce other elements of the lesson, and to integrate the other language arts. Many of the listening, speaking, and viewing skills are very similar to reading or writing skills. For example, listening for details is the same type of skill as reading for details. Preparing an oral report employs many of the same skills as preparing a written report. Learning to use these skills effectively gives students flexibility in how they approach a task. Furthermore, listening and speaking are naturally integrated into all aspects of learning as students listen and respond to each other during discussions, writing, and Inquiry.

Procedure

Listening, speaking, and viewing skills are presented with increasing sophistication throughout every grade level of ***SRA Imagine It!*** in the Language Arts part of each lesson. Every unit includes at least one lesson on each of the following skills so that students encounter the skills again and again throughout a grade level:

- ✦ **Listening.** Listening skills include comprehending what one hears and listening for different purposes, such as to identify sequence or details, to summarize or draw conclusions, or to follow directions.
- ✦ **Speaking.** Speaking skills include speaking formally and conversationally, using appropriate volume, giving oral presentations, and using effective grammar. Speaking skills also include using descriptive words, figurative language, and formal and informal language.
- ✦ **Viewing.** Viewing skills include comprehending main ideas and messages in images, mass media, and other multimedia.
- ✦ **Interaction.** Interaction instruction focuses on a combination of listening and speaking skills. These include asking and responding to questions; nonverbal cues such as eye contact, facial expression, and posture; and contributing to and interacting in group settings.
- ✦ **Presenting Information.** The last Listening/Speaking/Viewing lesson in every unit usually focuses on presentation skills. These include sharing ideas, relating experiences or stories, organizing information, and preparing for speeches. These lessons often parallel the Writing Process Strategies instruction so that students can prepare their information in written or oral form. These skills are an integral part of the Inquiry process as students share their ideas, questions, conjectures, and findings.

Tips

- ✦ Identify the parallels among the language arts skills: providing written and oral directions, telling or writing a narrative, and so on. Encourage students to see that they have choices for communicating. Discuss the similarities and differences between different forms of communication, and determine whether one is preferable in a given situation.
- ✦ Ensure that all students have opportunities to speak in small groups and whole-class situations.
- ✦ Provide and teach students to allow appropriate wait time before someone answers a question.
- ✦ Encourage students (when they are able) to take notes to help them remember what they heard so they can better respond.
- ✦ Remind students to use visuals when appropriate in their presentations to support their presentations and to help keep the listeners' attention.
- ✦ Set up simple class rules to show respect for the listener and speaker. These rules should be used during Inquiry or handing off or any time of the day and should foster respect for the speaker and listeners.
    - Students should speak in a voice loud and clear enough for everyone in the class to hear.
    - Students should raise their hands and not interrupt.
    - If someone asks a question, then the person who responds should address the question before going on to another idea or topic.
    - The speaker should look at the audience, and the audience should look at the speaker.

Inquiry

Even in elementary school, students can produce works of genuine research—research that seeks answers to real questions or solutions to real problems.

Inquiry—research, investigation, and exploration—forms the heart of the ***SRA Imagine It!*** program. To encourage students to understand how reading and writing are tools for learning that can enhance their lives and help them become mature, educated adults, they are asked in each unit to use the content they are learning in the unit as the basis for further inquiry, exploration, and research. The unit information is simply the base for their investigations.

There are two types of units in the ***SRA Imagine It!*** program—units based on universal topics of interest such as friendship, heritage, and courage and content units that provide students a very solid base of information upon which they can begin their own inquiry and research. Units delving into science-related areas such as camouflage, energy, and ecology or into social studies units that address American history, geography, or money invite students to become true researchers by exploring personal areas of interest driven by problems or questions raised by students. Based upon common areas of interest, students conduct Inquiry in small collaborative groups and then present their findings to their classmates. In this way, students recognize the importance of sharing knowledge and gain much more knowledge of the unit theme than they would have simply by reading the selections in the unit.

The selections in the units are organized so that each selection will add more information or a different perspective to students' growing bodies of knowledge.

Inquiry through Reflective Activities

Purpose

The units in ***SRA Imagine It!*** that deal with universal topics tend to be explored through reflective activities. These units—such as Courage, Friendship, and Risks and Consequences—are organized to help students expand—perhaps even change—their perspectives of familiar concepts. As they explore and discuss the concepts that emerge from reading selections related to each unit topic, students are involved in activities that extend their experiences and offer opportunities for reflection. Such activities include writing, drama, art, interviews, debates, and panel discussions. Students will choose the activities and presentation format best suited to explore or investigate their research questions. Throughout each unit, students may be involved in a single ongoing investigative activity, or they may participate in a number of different activities. They may choose to produce a final written project or a multimedia presentation. They will share with the rest of the class the new knowledge that they have gained from their investigations. Workshop provides an ideal time for students to work individually or in collaborative groups on their investigation and/or projects.

The Inquiry activities will be those of students' own choosing, thereby allowing them to explore the unit concepts more fully. They are free, of course, to make other choices or to devise activities of their own.

Procedure

Choosing an Area to Investigate

Students may work on activities alone, in pairs, or in small groups. They have the option of writing about or using other methods for presenting their findings to the entire group. Students should decide what concept-related question or problem they wish to explore. Generally, it is better for students to generate wonderings, questions, or problems after they have engaged in some discussion at the beginning of each unit. This should be done, however, before they have had a chance to consult source materials. The goal is to have students ask questions that will drive their inquiry. This approach is more likely to bring forth ideas that students actually wonder about or wish to understand. Students may also look at the questions posted on the **Concept/Question Board** or introduce fresh ideas inspired by material they have just finished reading.

Inquiry pairs or groups are developed based upon common areas of interest or common questions that appear on the **Concept/Question Board.** Students who share a common interest for inquiry should work together to develop a common question to explore. Some of students may need your assistance in deciding upon, or narrowing down, a question or a problem so that it can be explored more easily. A good way to model this process for students is to make webs for a few of your own ideas on the board and to narrow down these ideas to a workable question or problem.

Organizing the Group

After a question or a problem has been chosen, students may choose an activity that will help them investigate that problem or question. For example, if students in Grade 3 are exploring the question "What are the common characteristics that define friendship?" they may want to develop and conduct a survey of classmates, friends, and so on. To develop the survey, group participants may want to do some additional reading about friendship, explore resources on the Internet, and so on to have a sense of the kinds of questions to include in the survey. Students' next responsibility is to decide who is going to investigate which facet of the question or the problem (when they are conducting a literature search, for example) or who is going to perform which activity related to the particular reflective activity (when they are writing and performing an original playlet or puppet show, for example). Lastly, students need to decide how, or if, they want to present their findings. For instance, after conducting a literature search, some students may want to read and discuss passages from a book with a plot or theme that relates to a unit concept. Other students may prefer performing and discussing scenes from the book.

Deciding How to Investigate

The following suggestions may help you and your students choose ways in which to pursue their investigations. For units on universal topics that are more literary in nature, students may want to do one of the following activities to pursue answers to their questions.

- Conduct a literature search to pursue a question or a problem. Discussion or writing may follow.

- Write and produce an original playlet or puppet show based on situations related to the concepts.
- Play a role-playing game to work out a problem related to the concepts.
- Stage a panel discussion with audience participation on a question or problem.
- Hold a debate on an issue related to the concept.
- Write an advice column dealing with problems related to the concepts.
- Write a personal-experience story related to the concepts.
- Invite experts to class. Formulate questions to ask.
- Conduct an interview with someone on a subject related to the concepts.
- Produce and carry out a survey on an issue or a question related to the concept.
- Produce a picture or photo-essay about the concept.

You may want to post this list in the classroom so that groups have access to it as they decide what they want to investigate and how they want to proceed. Encourage students to explore other possibilities as well and to add these ideas to the list.

EXAMPLE: In the Heritage unit in Grade 5 of ***SRA Imagine It!,*** students read "In Two Worlds: A Yup'ik Eskimo Family." This selection is about how three generations of Eskimos living in Alaska near the Arctic strive to adopt the best of modern ways without abandoning their traditional values. During the class discussion, some students may note that Alice and Billy Rivers want their students to learn both the new and the old ways of living. As the discussion continues, many students may conclude from the story that the older generations hope that future generations will continue to value their roots and their cultural traditions. Students then relate this story to their own heritage. Some students may share information about their customs or traditions.

Students choose some reflective activities that will help them learn more about family heritage and that will answer some of their questions about the unit concepts. These questions may relate to the value of maintaining traditional customs and values versus. adopting contemporary ones. Other students may ask exploring questions related to how to maintain traditional values in the face of contemporary changes. Some students may be interested in interviewing family members or close family friends about their cultural traditions and heritages or interviewing students in their class about their cultural heritage and then looking for commonalities and differences. These students review what they know about interviewing. They should proceed by performing the following:

- Researching examples of interviews to see what they might look like and how to build in space to write answers
- Preparing a list of questions to ask
- Preparing a list of subjects to interview, deciding how to record the interview (by audiotape, videotape, or taking notes)
- Contacting in advance the person(s) they want to interview
- Deciding whether to photograph the person and, if so, getting permission to do so in advance—collecting the equipment necessary for conducting the interview
- After they conduct the interviews, students decide how they wish to present the information that they have collected.

EXAMPLE: Another group of students in the same fifth-grade class may be more interested in planning a photo-essay about one family or about a neighborhood with many families belonging to a particular culture. These students may decide to reexamine "In Two Worlds" in terms of how the text and the photographs complement each other and what information is conveyed in each photograph. They may also decide to examine some photo-essays listed in the unit bibliography. These students will need to make some advance preparations as well. They should proceed by performing the following:

- Determining which neighborhood and which family or families to photograph
- Contacting in advance the persons to be interviewed and photographed
- Touring the neighborhood in advance of the photo shoot
- Making a list of questions to ask the family or families about their heritage or about their neighborhood
- Thinking about what information to include in their essay so that they can determine what photographs to take
- Collecting the equipment necessary for conducting interviews and photographing subjects

After students collect the information and take photographs, they may write and organize the photo-essay and present it to the class. The teacher should remind students of the phases of the writing process and encourage them to plan, draft, revise, and edit/proofread their work until they are completely satisfied with it.

Not all questions on the **Concept/Question Board** will be explored in depth. Throughout the unit, students can continue discussing family heritage and raising and posting new questions. The teacher should remind them that as they read further, they may think of additional ways to explore the unit concepts. Students should sign or initial their questions or ideas so that they can identify classmates with similar interests and exchange ideas with them. The teacher should encourage students to feel free to write an answer or a note on someone else's question or to consult the Board for ideas for their own explorations. From time to time, the teacher should post his or her own questions on the **Concept/Question Board.**

Tips

- The ***Leveled Readers*** contain books related to the unit concepts. Remind students that these are good sources of information and that they should consult them regularly—especially when they are investigating concept-related ideas and questions.
- Some students work better within a specified time frame. Whenever they are beginning a new activity, discuss with students a reasonable period of time within which they will be expected to complete their investigations. Post the completion date somewhere in the classroom so that students can refer to it and pace themselves accordingly. At first, you may have to help them determine a suitable deadline, but eventually they should be able to make this judgment on their own.
- Some teachers like to do the Inquiry for the first unit with a common question decided upon by the whole class. Then students break into small groups and work on different ways to explore the question. One group may do a literature search while another might conduct a survey. The end results in students sharing new knowledge that addresses

the common research question.

Inquiry through Research

Purpose

Students come to school with a wealth of fascinating questions. Educators need to capitalize on this excitement for learning and natural curiosity. A classroom in which the teacher is the only person who asks the questions and defines the assignments, only correct answers are accepted, and students are not allowed to make errors and consider alternative possibilities to questions can quickly deaden this natural curiosity and enthusiasm. The purpose of the inquiry and research aspect of this program is to capitalize on students' questions and natural curiosity by using a framework or structure based upon the scientific method. This structure helps students ask questions and preserve the open-ended character of real research, which can lead to unexpected findings and to questions that were not originally considered.

The conventional approach to school research papers can be found, with minor variations, in countless textbooks and instructional resources. This approach consists of a series of steps such as the following: Select a topic or choose a topic from a list suggested by the teacher, narrow the topic to something of interest, collect materials, take notes, outline, and write. By following these steps, a student may produce a presentable paper, but the procedure does not constitute research in a meaningful sense. Indeed, this restrictive approach gives students a distorted notion of what research is about. We see students in universities and even in graduate schools still following this procedure when they do library research papers or literature reviews; we see their dismay when their professors regard such work as mere cutting and pasting and ask them where their original contribution is.

Elementary school students can produce works of genuine research—research that seeks answers to real questions or solutions to real problems—when they are provided the opportunity, taught how to ask good questions and develop conjectures, and work collaboratively to find information or data that will support or refute their conjecture. Being able to collect, analyze, and evaluate information are critical twenty-first century skills. In the adult world, as knowledgeable consumers, productive members of a sophisticated workforce, and lifelong learners, students will be expected to constantly identify problems, raise questions, analyze new information, and make informed decisions on the basis of this information. Preparing students for the analytic demands of adult life and teaching them how to find answers to their questions are goals of education.

Procedure

To make the research productive, the following important principles are embodied in this approach:

1. Research is focused on problems, not topics.
2. Questions and wonderings are the foundation for inquiry and research.
3. Conjectures—opinions based on less than complete evidence or proof—are derived from questions and guide the research; the research does not simply produce conjectures.
4. New information and data are gathered to test and revise conjectures.
5. Discussion, ongoing feedback, and constructive criticism are important in all phases of the research but especially in the revising of problems and conjectures.
6. The cycle of true research is essentially endless, although presentations of findings are made from time to time; new findings give rise to new problems and conjectures and thus to new cycles of research.

Following a Process

While working with the science and social studies units, students are encouraged to use this framework to keep their research activities focused and on track. Within this framework, there is flexibility. Students may begin with a question, develop a conjecture, and begin collecting information only to find that they need to redefine their conjecture. Like the writing process, there is a recursive nature to this framework. Students may go through these steps many times before they come to the end of their research. Certainly for adult researchers, this cycle of question, conjecture, research, and reevaluation can go on for years and, in some cases, lifetimes.

This cycle uses the following process:

1. Decide on a problem or question to research. Students should identify a question or problem that they truly wonder about or wish to understand and then form research groups with other students who have the same interests.
   - My problem or question is _________.
2. Formulate an idea or conjecture about the research problem. Students should think about and discuss with classmates possible answers to their research problems or questions and meet with their research groups to discuss and record their ideas or conjectures.
   - My idea/conjecture/theory about this question or problem is _________.
3. Identify needs and make plans. Students should identify knowledge needs related to their conjectures and meet with their research groups to determine which resources to consult and to make individual job assignments. Students should also meet periodically with the teacher, other classmates, and research groups to present preliminary findings and to make revisions to their problems and conjectures on the basis of these findings.
   - I need to find out _________.
   - To do this, I will need these resources: _________
   - My role in the group is _________.
   - This is what I have learned so far: _________
   - This is what happened when we presented our findings ___________
4. Reevaluate the problem or question based on what we have learned so far and the feedback we have received.
   - My revised problem or question is ___________.
5. Revise the idea or conjecture.
   - My new conjecture about this problem is _________.
6. Identify new needs and make new plans.
   - Based on what I found out, I still need to know _________.
   - To do this, I will need these resources: _________
   - This is what I have learned: _________
   - This is what happened when we presented our new findings: _________

Procedure for Choosing a Problem to Research

1. Discuss with students the nature of the unit. Explain to students that the

unit they are reading is a research unit and that they will produce and publish in some way the results of their explorations. They are free to decide what problems or questions they wish to explore, with whom they want to work, and how they want to present their finished products. They may publish a piece of writing, produce a poster, write and perform a play, or use any other means to present the results of their investigations and research. They may work individually, with partners, or in small groups.

2. Discuss with students the schedule you have planned for their investigations: how long the project is expected to take, how much time will be available for research, when the first presentation will be due. This schedule will partly determine the nature of the problems that students should be encouraged to work on and the depth of the inquiry students will be encouraged to pursue.
3. Have students talk about things they wonder about that are related to the unit subject. For example, in the Grade 3 unit Money, students might wonder where money in the money machine comes from or how prices are determined. Conduct a free-floating discussion of questions about the unit subject.
4. Brainstorm possible questions for students to think about. It is essential that students' own ideas and questions be the starting point of all inquiry. Helpful hint: For the first research unit, you might wish to generate a list of your own ideas, having students add to this list and having them choose from it.
5. Using their wonderings, model for students the difference between a research topic and a research problem or question by providing several examples. For example, have them consider the difference between the topic *California* and the problem *Why do so many people move to California?* Explain to them that if they choose to research the topic *California,* everything they look up under the subject heading or index entry *California* will be related in some way to their topic. Therefore, it will be quite difficult to choose which information to record. This excess of information also creates problems in organizing their research. Clearly, then, this topic is too broad and general. Choosing a specific question or problem, one that particularly interests them, helps them narrow their exploration and advance their understanding. Some possible ideas for questions can be found in the unit introduction. Ideas can also be generated as you and your students create a web of their questions or problems related to the unit concept. For example, questions related to the topic *California* might include the following: Why do so many people move to California? How have the different groups of people living in California affected the state?
6. A good research problem or question not only requires students to consult a variety of sources but is engaging and adds to the groups' knowledge of the concepts. Furthermore, good problems generate more questions. Help students understand that the question *Why do so many people move to California?* is an easy one to research. Many sources will contribute to an answer to the question, and all information located can be easily evaluated in terms of usefulness in answering the question. Helpful hint: Students' initial responses may indeed be topics instead of problems or questions. If so, the following questions might be helpful: What aspect of the topic really interests you? Can you turn that idea into a question?
7. Remember that this initial problem or question serves only as a guide for research. As students begin collecting information and collaborating with classmates, their ideas will change, and they can revise their research problem or question. Frequently, students do not sufficiently revise their problems until after they have had time to consider their conjectures and to collect information.
8. As students begin formulating their research problems, have them elaborate on their reasons for wanting to research their stated problems. They should go beyond simple expressions of interest or liking and indicate what is puzzling, important, or potentially informative, and so forth about the problems they have chosen.
9. At this stage, students' ideas will be of a very vague and limited sort. The important thing is to start them thinking about what really interests them and what value it has to them and the class.
10. Have students present their proposed problems or questions, along with reasons for their choices, and have an open discussion of how promising proposed problems are. As students present their proposed problems, ask them what new things they think they will be learning from their investigations and how that will add to the group's growing knowledge of the concepts. This constant emphasis on group knowledge building will help set a clear purpose for students' research.
11. Form research groups. To make it easier for students to form groups, they may record their problems on the board or on self-sticking notes. Final groups should be constituted in the way you find best for your class—by self-selection, by assignment on the basis of common interests, or by some combination of methods. Students can then meet during Workshop to agree on a precise statement of their research problem, the nature of their expected research contributions, and lists of related questions that may help later in assigning individual roles. They should also record any scheduling information that can be added to the planning calendar.

Using Technology

Students and teachers can access the Web site **www.SRAonline.com** to find information about the themes in their grade level.

What does Inquiry look like in the classroom?

Inquiry is a new concept for many students and is performed over an extended period of time. The following series of vignettes are an example of what Inquiry might look like in a third-grade classroom that is studying the third-grade unit Money.

Lesson 1

Developing questions

For the unit on money, Ms. Hernandes introduced the theme through "A New Coat for Anna" and now is focusing on having her students generate some questions. To maximize the number of resources available to her students to do their inquiry, she talked with the librarian at her local library as well as local high school teachers who are knowledgeable in the area. Both were able to provide resources for the class. Ms. Hernandes began with a discussion of money. She had prepared some basic questions to get the class started.

- Why do you think it is important to have a system of money like ours?
- What is money?
- Why do you think we have both paper money and coins?
- How have you learned about money?
- How would your life change if suddenly there were no money in the world?
- When people are using credit cards to pay for something, are they paying with real money?
- When someone writes a check, are they paying with real money?
- What is the difference between credit cards and checks and cash, or actual money?
- Why do you think people use credit cards and checks instead of cash?

The teacher felt that using open-ended questions like these would help get her students talking about what they know about money as well as give her an opportunity to informally assess students' background knowledge.

Students were able to provide some basic information such as the following:

- Money is used to buy things.
- There was not always money in the world.
- Some people used things such as animals instead of money.
- Sometimes people traded things to get something they wanted.
- Coins are made of metal.
- Some things cost more than other things.
- Sometimes you need to determine ways to get things when you do not have money.

But there were some basic misunderstandings that arose during the conversation, such as the following:

- All countries use dollars and cents.
- Everything costs the same no matter where you live.
- Money is made of paper.
- You can use credit cards whenever you want.

By discussing money in such general terms, students were able to share basic information.

To move students to the next level—asking questions—Ms. Hernandes began by thinking aloud about things related to the unit that interested her.

"I really am curious about how money is made. And another thing I've wondered about is how the government knows how much money to print." Ms. Hernandes encouraged her students to share some of their wonderings or things they are curious about. Some student wonderings included the following:

- What kind of money do people in other countries use?
- Does everyone make the same amount of money?
- What would happen if there were only credit cards and no money?
- How much money do people make?
- Does ripped money get thrown away?
- How come we cannot make our own money?

Lesson 2

Forming groups based on shared interest

Developing good research questions

Ms. Hernandes and her class have been reading about money for the past week. Many students read different trade books during Workshop to learn more about money. Every day at the end of Workshop, they shared some of their new questions. Some students even started bringing in articles from newspapers and magazines and posting them on the **Concept/Question Board.**

By now there are a number of questions on the **Concept/Question Board** and Ms. Hernandes wants to work with the class to generate more questions that will help students connect what they are learning in school to the real world. She began by modeling or thinking aloud and sharing some of her own thoughts: "I know that at the checkout stand in stores, you can buy plastic cards that have a dollar amount printed on them. I wonder how might this change our whole idea about money. Maybe instead of getting cash from the automatic money machines, we'll get a coded card."

The focus is on asking questions. She recognized that students' questions needed to be refined to lead to functional conjectures. The class discussed what makes a good question.

- Questions or wonderings should be things that students are truly curious about.
- Questions should be generated without consulting an encyclopedia or a reference source.
- Good questions cannot be answered with a simple *yes* or *no.*
- Questions should help students deepen their understanding of the unit theme rather than focus on a character or incident in a specific story.
- A good research question often begins with *how.*

Ms. Hernandes and the class talked about their questions and how to refine them. For example, one question the class raised earlier was "Does money change?" The class decided to change the question to "How does money change over time?"

- What possible changes might we see in the future?
- Given the changes in technology today, how might our use of money change over time?

Based on the selections the class has read, students generated the following questions to add to their existing ones on the **Concept/Question Board:**

- I wonder when and how the government decided to change coins and bills.
- I wonder if the government can ever run out of money.
- What happens when people make fake money?
- How do people choose the metals they use to make coins?
- How can money be made so people cannot copy it or make counterfeits?
- What do other countries use for money?
- Where do you save money?

To help move students toward developing some good questions for inquiry, the class reviewed all the questions and grouped them together. They discussed these groups of questions and decided to think of a good representative question. The class worked over the next couple of days to think of a question they were all interested in.

Lesson 3

Forming Conjectures

Identifying Needs and Making Plans

A goal of Inquiry is to have students move from asking questions to forming conjectures. Ms. Hernandes explained to the class that they were now going to take their question and develop a conjecture. Developing a conjecture simply means thinking of what they think the best answer is, given what they know now and have read so far.

Ms. Hernandes modeled this by using one of the questions students raised in the earlier lesson. The question was "How do people choose the metals to make coins?" Ms. Hernandes thought aloud about possible answers to this question: "I think that people choose a strong metal that will last a long time but that is not too heavy for people to carry."

Then Ms. Hernandes wrote the question the class thought of last week. They discussed the question and talked about what possible answers they might find. The question the class decided to focus on was "How is money made so that people cannot copy it?"

The class conjecture was "Special paper and really detailed pictures are used so no one can copy it." However, Ms. Hernandes realized that there could be other conjectures for the same question. She arranged the class into small groups and had them think about other possible conjectures. Some additional conjectures included the following:

- Every dollar has a different number that is recorded in a computer.
- Special ink is used so colors cannot be duplicated.
- When you hold up a bill to the light, you can see a special band in it that maybe only a special government machine can make.

At the end of the lesson, Ms. Hernandes created a chart with the question and all the conjectures students developed.

During the week, Ms. Hernandes continued working with the class on Inquiry. To help the group get started on identifying needs and materials related to their conjecture, Ms. Hernandes asked the following questions:

- What information will we need to help us decide if our conjecture is accurate?
- Where can we find this information?
- Who can help us find information related to our conjecture?
- What people in our school might be able to help us?
- What family members might know something about this?
- What words could we plug in on the Internet to help us get more information?

During the rest of this week, students started collecting different resources and reading various books during Workshop. Students were encouraged to take notes and to share with their groups each day.

Lesson 4

Revising Plans as Necessary

Collecting Data and Information

Now that students have started collecting material, they need to identify individual job assignments so they are not duplicating efforts. At the beginning of this week, Ms. Hernandes took time to have students meet in their groups. During this time she met with the small groups to track their progress, discuss any problems, and help them focus their research efforts.

The group working with the conjecture "Every dollar has a different number that is recorded in a computer" was having trouble finding information to support or refute their conjecture. They had looked in books but did not really find anything. As they talked with the teacher, someone mentioned the term *mint.* As they discussed what happened in the mint, someone suggested that they write the mint with their question to see if they could get some help. This simple activity led students to the Internet to find out the address of the mint. They then spent the rest of that period composing a letter.

At the end of Inquiry that day, Ms. Hernandes made time for each group to present a summary of what it had done. If the group had any unsolved problems, it shared them with the class to get possible suggestions on how to solve the problems. When the group who wrote to the mint shared its problem and solution, several other groups realized that the Internet would be a good resource for them to use as well.

Lesson 5

Continuing Working and Planning Final Presentation

At this point students are beginning to conclude their investigations. Several of the groups realized as they collected information that they really needed to change or revise their conjectures. Ms. Hernandes asked in what ways their ideas have changed—what do they know now that they did not know before? For example, the group that had the conjecture that special ink was used so colors cannot be duplicated revised its conjecture by broadening it. After doing some research, their new conjecture was that there are many different things that the government does in addition to using special ink to protect money from being copied.

As groups presented their conjectures and progress, Ms. Hernandes modeled constructive comments such as the following: "Your points are clearly made." "Your charts and graphs help us understand each of your points." "Each one of you presented different pieces of information that all connect to your conjecture." "How was your conjecture supported?" After the lesson, Ms. Hernandes took time to reflect and realized that it was very hard for her students to give constructive feedback. She knew that this is an area they would need to work on. She would have to continue modeling but also thought about having groups exchange conjectures and provide feedback in writing to each other. This might reduce anxiety as well as give students time to reflect on the questions and conjectures and to develop some thoughtful feedback.

During this week, Ms. Hernandes took time to discuss possible ways that students could present their findings. The class brainstormed other ideas including the following:

- Writing a series of articles on their information for a magazine
- Creating a poster with diagrams of a process
- A panel discussion
- A computer presentation

Students returned to their groups to decide how they wanted to present their findings.

Final Presentation

Students have been busy working on completing their investigations and developing their presentations. While the class decided on a single research question at the beginning of the unit, different groups developed their own conjectures. Because their conjectures guided their research, each group will be presenting different information. Ms. Hernandes has created a simple web with the class's research question in the center and circles around the question. After groups present their work, the class will discuss what information was found to address the research question. As presentations are made, students will also be encouraged to make connections not only to the question but to each other's findings.

Throughout the unit, Ms. Hernandes recognized that students need more work on asking questions of each other and providing constructive feedback. She plans on modeling questions and comments as groups complete their presentations. Some examples include the following:

- How does what you presented support or refute your conjecture?
- Would you clarify . . .
- It would be helpful if . . .
- Have you thought about . . .
- Your visuals really helped me better understand your ideas.
- That was a great idea. Where can we find more information on it so we can learn more about it?
- What other questions did you think of as you were researching your conjecture?

Overall, Ms. Hernandes felt that this first attempt at Inquiry with the entire class focusing on a single question but generating multiple conjectures made Inquiry manageable for students and herself. Ms. Hernandes is now thinking about how to plan the next Inquiry unit so there are multiple questions as well as multiple conjectures. From the final presentations, she has really begun to appreciate how Inquiry incorporates all the reading and writing skills she has been teaching and how it takes students to the next level of learning—delving deeper into ideas that personally interest them, taking time and responsibility to learn about something, working collaboratively, and sharing new ideas and information.

Tips

- ✦ Inquiry takes time to develop. You may want to do the first unit as an entire class.
- ✦ Provide time throughout the unit for students to work on Inquiry. Use Workshop as well as computer and library time to support Inquiry.
- ✦ If students are careful about the problems or questions they choose to research, they should have few problems in following through with the research. If the problem is too broad or too narrow, they will have problems.
- ✦ Have students take sufficient time in assessing their needs—both knowledge needs and physical needs in relation to their research. Careful preplanning can help the research progress smoothly with great results.
- ✦ Encourage students to reevaluate their needs often so they are not wasting time finding things they already have or ignoring needs that they have not noticed.
- ✦ Interim presentations of material are every bit as important, if not more so, than final presentations. It is during interim presentations that students have the opportunity to rethink and reevaluate their work and change direction or to decide to carry on with their planned research.
- ✦ Connect Inquiry to learning in the content areas. Have students apply their Inquiry skills to learning science, social studies, and the arts.

Assessment

Assessment can be your most effective teaching tool if it is used with the purpose of informing instruction and highlighting areas that need special attention.

Purpose

The assessment components of ***SRA Imagine It!*** are designed to help you make informed instructional decisions, make adequate yearly progress, and help ensure you meet the needs of all your students. The variety of assessments is intended to be used continuously and formatively. That is, students should be assessed regularly as a follow-up to instructional activities, and the results of the assessment should be used to inform subsequent instruction.

You can use assessment as a tool to monitor students' progress, to diagnose students' strengths and weaknesses, to prescribe forms of intervention as necessary, and to measure student outcomes. Both formal and informal assessment can be used, though formal assessment will be your main assessment tool. Formal assessment of student learning consists of performance assessment (both reading and writing), objective tests (multiple choice, short answer, and essay), progress assessment (through students' everyday oral and written work), and assessment rubrics (used for writing, inquiry, and comprehension strategies). Informal assessment can be done by observing or listening to students as they work and jotting down notes either in the Comprehension Observation Log or in a notebook.

Procedure

Formal Assessment

Formal assessment is addressed in ***SRA Imagine It!*** in the form of ***Benchmark Assessments*** and ***Lesson Assessments.*** Both will help you use the results to differentiate instruction, especially for students needing some type of intervention to ensure they will not be at risk for reading failure.

Benchmark Assessments

The ***Benchmark Assessments*** are a form of general outcome measurement that offer an overall framework for assessment and serve as a predictor of how well students will perform at the end of the school year. Each ***Benchmark Assessment*** has material that students will learn over the course of the school year, and each ***Benchmark Assessment*** is of equivalent difficulty. Students are not expected to score high on the initial screening benchmark; instead, students are expected to show growth as they move on to each subsequent benchmark. Only at the end of the year are students expected to have mastered the materials on these assessments.

> *Observing students as they go about their regular classwork can be an effective way to learn your students' strengths and areas of need.*

One ***Benchmark Assessment*** will be administered at the beginning of the year for screening. This can serve as a baseline score against which you can measure students' progress throughout the year. Subsequent benchmarks will also be given at regular intervals—at the end of every other unit in grades K–1, for a total of six assessments, and at the end of each unit for students in grades 2–6, for a total of seven assessments. Since the tests are of equivalent difficulty and contain the same types of items, students' higher scores will reflect their increasing mastery of the curriculum over the course of the year. Use the data from the ***Benchmark Assessments*** to identify students who are at risk for reading failure, to identify strengths and weaknesses of students, and to gauge student progress toward high-stakes tests.

Depending upon the grade level, tested benchmark skills include the following:

- letter recognition,
- phonemic/phonological awareness,
- phonics,
- high-frequency word recognition,
- vocabulary,
- spelling,
- grammar, usage, and mechanics,
- comprehension,
- oral fluency, and
- maze fluency.

In addition, a writing assessment is given in the initial screening, at midyear, and also again at the end of the year for students in grades 3–6. This assessment is the type of on-demand writing performance students will encounter in high-stakes tests. Each writing assessment is of equal difficulty, and student outcomes should reflect an increased mastery of writing convention and genre expectations.

Lesson Assessments

The ***Lesson Assessments*** cover the most important skills featured in the lesson of a given unit—skills that are closely related to reading success and are typically in state and national standards. These assessments will help you determine how well students are grasping the skills and concepts as they are taught and will help inform you about any additional instruction they might need.

The ***Lesson Assessments*** are easily administered and scored. They feature the same language used in the instructional components of ***SRA Imagine It!*** and correspond to its sequence of instruction. The format of these weekly assessments range from multiple choice questions to short answer to an extended writing response. Depending upon the grade level, skills assessed include the following:

- letter and number recognition
- phonological and phonemic awareness
- phonics
- print and book awareness
- high frequency words

- selection vocabulary
- spelling
- grammar, usage, and mechanics skills
- comprehension skills
- oral fluency
- writing

The ***Lesson Assessments*** are offered in several formats so that students can demonstrate their knowledge of content in a number of developmentally appropriate ways. Wherever possible, the assessments are designed to be administered to the whole class or small groups of students. In some cases, however, individually administered assessments are included, such as the oral fluency assessments, as well as critical pre-literacy skills such as phoneme blending or segmentation as well as letter and number recognition.

The ***Lesson Assessments*** will allow you to monitor students' progress as they are assessed on the specific skills taught in a given lesson. The results will provide instructionally relevant information that you can use to differentiate instruction for students who may need additional learning opportunities.

Progress Assessment

Written Practice

Students work on several different skills throughout the day. Each of these assignments can provide you with valuable information about your students' progress. One very helpful resource that students will work in daily is the ***Skills Practice Book*** (Levels K–6). The ***Skills Practice Books*** include lessons that act as practice and reinforcement for the skills lessons taught before and during the reading of the lesson as well as in conjunction with the Language Arts lesson. These skills pages give you a clear picture of students' understanding of the skills taught. Use them as a daily assessment of student progress in the particular skills taught through the program.

Also included in the ***Skills Practice Books*** are lessons that help students with their Inquiry activities. Students can record what they know about the concepts and what they learn, they can keep a record of their research, and they can practice study and research skills that will help them in all of their schooling. You will be able to monitor their growing ability to make connections, find resources, and enhance their knowledge base as they find the answers to the research questions they have posed.

Dictation

In grades 1–3, students use dictation to practice the sound/spelling associations they are learning and/or reviewing. Collect the dictation papers and look through them to see how the students are doing with writing and with proofreading their words. Record notes on the papers and keep them in the student portfolios.

Portfolios

Portfolios are more than just a collection bin or gathering place for student projects and records. They add balance to an assessment program by providing unique benefits to teachers, students, and families.

- ✦ Portfolios help build self-confidence and increase self-esteem as students come to appreciate the value of their work. More importantly, portfolios allow students to reflect on what they know and what they need to learn. At the end of the school year, each student will be able to go through their portfolios and write about their progress.
- ✦ Portfolios provide the teacher with an authentic record of what students can do. Just as important, portfolios give students a concrete example of their own progress and development. Thus, portfolios become a valuable source of information for making instructional decisions.
- ✦ Portfolios allow families to judge student performance directly. Portfolios are an ideal starting point for discussions about a student's achievements and future goals during teacher/family conferences.

You will find that there are many opportunities to add to students' portfolios.

Fluency

- ✦ During partner reading, during Workshop, or at other times of the day, invite students, one at a time, to sit with you and read a story from an appropriate ***Decodable*** (grades 1–3), ***Leveled Readers*** (grades 1–6), ***Leveled Readers for Science*** or ***Social Studies*** (grades 1–6), or the ***Student Reader.***
- ✦ As each student reads to you, follow along and make note of any recurring problems the student has while reading. Note students' ability to decode unknown words as well as any attempt—successful or not—to use strategies to clarify or otherwise make sense of what they are reading. From time to time, check students' fluency by timing their reading and noting how well they are able to sustain the oral reading without faltering.
- ✦ If a student has trouble reading a particular ***Decodable*** or ***Leveled Reader,*** encourage the student to read the story a few times on her or his own before reading it aloud to you. If the ***Decodable*** has two stories, use the alternate story to reassess the student a day or two later.
- ✦ If after practicing with a particular Decodable Book or Leveled Reader and reading it on his or her own a few times, a student is still experiencing difficulty, try the following:
  - Drop back two ***Decodables***. (Continue to drop back until the student is able to read a story with no trouble.) If the student can read that book without problems, move up one book. The same is true for ***Leveled Readers.***
  - Continue the process until the student is able to read the current ***Decodable*** or ***Leveled Readers.***

Assessment Rubrics

In addition to the formal assessment opportunities available in ***Benchmark Assessments, Lesson Assessments,*** and progress assessment, ***SRA Imagine It!*** provides rubrics for you to evaluate students' performance in comprehension, Inquiry, and writing. Rubrics provide criteria for different levels of performance. Rubrics established before an assignment is given are extremely helpful in evaluating the assignment. When students know what the rubrics for a particular assignment are, they can focus their energies on the key issues. Rubrics can be found in the Level Appendix.

Informal Assessment

Observation

Informal assessment is a part of the everyday classroom routine. Observing students as they go about their regular classwork can be an effective way to learn your students' strengths and areas of need. The more students become accustomed to you jotting down informal notes about their work, the more it will become just another part of classroom life that they accept and take little note of. This gives you the opportunity to assess their progress constantly without the interference and possible drawback of formal testing situations.

One tool that will help you make

informal assessment of student progress a part of your everyday classroom routine is the Comprehension Observation Log. You can record information quickly on this observation sheet and even extend your observations over several days, until you have had a chance to observe each student's performance in a particular area.

- Enter students' names in the Comprehension Observation Log, found in the ***Lesson Assessment Books.***
- Before each day's lesson begins, decide which students you will observe.
- Keep the Comprehension Observation Log available so that you can easily record your observations.
- Decide what aspect of the students' learning you wish to monitor.
- During each lesson, observe this aspect in the performances of several students.
- When observing students, do not pull them aside; rather, observe students as part of the regular lesson, either with the whole class or in small groups.
- Record your observations.
- It may take four to five days to make sure you have observed and recorded the performance of each student. If you need more information about performance in a particular area for some of your students, you may want to observe them more than once.

Responding to Assessment Results

The point of assessment is to monitor progress in order to inform instruction, diagnose students' strengths and weaknesses, and differentiate instruction for students who need extra practice in certain skills or an extra challenge. ***SRA Imagine It!*** offers you opportunities to diagnose areas that may cause problems for students, differentiate instruction according to their abilities, monitor their progress on an ongoing basis, and measure student outcomes through ***Lesson Assessments*** or ***Benchmark Assessments,*** in addition to high-stakes state assessments. ***SRA Imagine It!*** also provides several ways to differentiate instruction based on the results of the various assessments. These include the following:

- Reteach lessons are available for students who are approaching level and appear to grasp a given concept but need more instruction and practice to solidify their learning. Many skills taught in the ***Skills Practice Books*** are available in a ***Reteach*** format.
- Intervention lessons provide options for you to use with students who need more intensive support and who are struggling to understand the on-level material. In addition to the support for the weekly lesson, controlled vocabulary lessons and specific skills lessons can help bring students up to grade level.
- ***English Learner Support*** lessons are available for students who are having difficulty with the concepts because they lack the necessary English language background. These resources will provide English Learners with the vocabulary, phonics, comprehension, grammar, and writing support they need to access the ***SRA Imagine It!*** lessons.
- ***Challenge Activities*** provide continued stimulation for those students who are doing well and working above grade level. Many skills covered in the ***Skills Practice Books*** are also available in ***Challenge Activities.***
- ***Workshop Resource Book*** activities give students alternative activities to strengthen or extend their skills in areas such as letter recognition, phonics, vocabulary, comprehension, fluency, word structure, and grammar.
- ***Leveled Readers*** provide students at all different levels of instruction—Approaching Level, On Level, Above Level, and English Learners—with additional opportunities to practice fluency, vocabulary, and comprehension skills. Besides the general ***Leveled Readers, Leveled Readers for Science*** and ***Leveled Readers for Social Studies*** provide students cross-curricular opportunities.

These materials, along with formal and informal assessments, help ensure that assessment and instruction work together to meet every student's needs.

Workshop

Every teacher and every student needs time during the day to organize, to take stock of work that is done, to make plans for work that needs doing, and to finish up incomplete projects. In addition, teachers need time for differentiating instruction, for holding conferences with students, and for doing fluency checks.

Purpose

Workshop is the period of time each day in which students work independently or collaboratively to practice and review material taught in the lessons.

A variety of activities may occur during this time. Students may work on a specific daily assignment, complete an ongoing project, work on unit inquiry activities, focus on writing, or choose from a wide range of possibilities. With lots of guidance and encouragement, students gradually learn to make decisions about their use of time and materials and to collaborate with their peers.

A goal of Workshop is to get students to work independently and productively. This is essential because Workshop is also the time during which the teacher can work with individuals or groups of students to reinforce learning, to provide extra help for those having difficulties, to extend learning, or to assess the progress of the class or of individuals.

Procedure

Initially for many students you will need to structure Workshop carefully. Eventually students will automatically go to the appropriate areas, take up ongoing projects, and get the materials they will need. Workshop will evolve slowly from a very structured period to a time when students make choices and move freely from one activity to the next.

Setting up Workshop guidelines is key. By the time students have completed the first few weeks of school, they should feel confident during Workshop. If not, continue to structure the time and limit options. For young students, early periods of Workshop may run no more than five to eight minutes. The time can gradually increase to fifteen minutes or longer as students gain independence. Older students may be able to work longer and independently from the very beginning of the school year.

Introducing Workshop

Introduce Workshop to students by telling them that every day there will be a time when they are expected to work on activities on their own or in small groups. For younger students explain that in the beginning there may be just a couple of activities but that gradually new ones will be introduced and that students can choose what they want to do. With older students and for those who have experienced Workshop in early grades, you may want to introduce the concept of Workshop and discuss the range of Workshop options from working on fluency to completing their writing.

Workshop is the period of time each day in which students work independently or collaboratively to practice and review material taught in the lessons.

Establish and discuss rules for Workshop with students. Keep them simple and straightforward. You may want to write the finalized rules on the board or on a poster. You may want to review these rules each day at the beginning of Workshop for the first few lessons or so. You may also wish to revisit and revise the rules from time to time. Suggested rules include the following:

- Share.
- Use a quiet voice.
- Take only the materials you need.
- Return materials.
- Always be working.
- When the teacher is working with a student or small group, do not interrupt.

Early in the process, review rules routinely, and discuss how Workshop is going. Is the class quiet enough for everyone to work on his or her own? Are there any rules that need changing? What problems are students having with materials?

For young students in the beginning you will assign the Workshop activities to help them learn to work on their own. Point out the shelf or area of the classroom where Workshop materials are stored. Tell students that when they finish working with the materials for one activity, they will choose something else from the Workshop shelf. New activity materials will be added to the shelf from time to time. Make sure students know that they may always look at books during Workshop.

Tell older students that they will have an opportunity each day to work on their unit inquiry activities, their writing, and other projects. Students will be working independently and collaboratively during this time.

Guidelines

- ✦ Make sure each student knows what he or she needs to do during Workshop.
- ✦ Demonstrate for the entire group any activity or game assigned for Workshop, for example, teaching students a new game, introducing new materials or projects, or explaining different areas.
- ✦ For young students, it is essential to introduce and demonstrate different activities and games before students do them on their own. With games, you may want to have several students play while the others watch. Make sure that all students know exactly what is expected of them.
- ✦ In the beginning, plan to circulate among students, providing encouragement and help as necessary.
- ✦ When students are engaged in appropriate activities and can work independently, meet with those students who need your particular attention. This may include individual students or small groups.
- ✦ Let students know that they need to ask questions and to clarify assignments during Workshop introduction so that you are free to work with small groups.
- ✦ Be sure that students know what they are to do when they have finished an activity and where to put their finished work.

Setting Up Your Classroom for Workshop

Carefully setting up your classroom to accommodate various Workshop activities will help assure that the Workshop period progresses smoothly and effectively. While setting up your classroom, keep the primary Workshop activities in mind. During Workshop, students will be doing independent and collaborative activities. In kindergarten and first grade, these activities may include letter recognition and phonemic awareness activities and writing or illustrating stories or projects. In addition, they will be working on individual or small-group projects.

Many classrooms have areas that students visit on a regular or rotating basis. Unlike traditional centers, all students do not rotate through all the areas each day.

The following are suggestions for space and materials for use during Workshop:

1. Reading Area supplied with books and magazines. The materials in the Reading Area should be dynamic—changing with students' abilities and reflecting unit themes they are reading. You may wish to add books to your classroom library.
2. Writing Area stocked with various types and sizes of lined and unlined paper, pencils, erasers, markers, crayons, small slates, and chalk. The area should also have various ***Letter Cards*** and other handwriting models for those students who want to practice letter formation or handwriting. Students should know that this is where they come for writing supplies. In addition to the supplies described above, the Writing Area can also have supplies to encourage students to create and write on their own:
   - Magazines and catalogs to cut up for pictures; stickers, paint, glue, glitter, and so on to decorate books and book covers; precut and stapled blank books for students to write in (Some can be plain and some cut in special shapes.)
   - Cardboard, tag board, construction paper, and so on for making book covers (Provide some samples.)
   - Tape, scissors, yarn, hole punches for binding books
   - Picture dictionaries, dictionaries, thesauruses, word lists, and other materials that may encourage independence
3. Listening Area supplied with tape recorder, CD player, optional headphones, and CDs of stories, poems, and songs for students to listen to and react to. You might also want to provide blank tapes and encourage students to retell and record their favorite stories or to make up and tell stories for their classmates to listen to on tape. You may also want to make available the Listening Library CDs that are available with the program.
4. Phonics Activities supplied with ***Alphabet Flash Cards,*** individual ***Alphabet Sound Card*** sets (Kindergarten), individual ***Sound/Spelling Cards*** and ***High-Frequency Flash Cards*** (Grades K, 1, 2, and 3), and other materials that enhance what students are learning. Other commonly used classroom materials that enhance reading can be included, for example, plastic letters, puzzles, and games.
5. Fluency Area supplied with ***Pre-Decodables and Decodables, Leveled Readers, Leveled Science Readers*** and ***Leveled Social Studies Readers,*** and other resources for practicing fluency. Some teachers have folders for each student with materials to practice during the week. In addition, some Fluency areas have timers and tape recorders as well.

Because students will be working on their inquiry/investigations during Workshop, make sure there are adequate supplies to help them with their research. These might include dictionaries, encyclopedias, magazines, newspapers, and computers—preferably with Internet capability.

Students thrive in an environment that provides structure, repetition, and routine. Within a sound structure, students will gain confidence and independence. This setting allows you to differentiate instruction to provide opportunities for flexibility and individual choice. This will allow students to develop their strengths, abilities, and talents to the fullest.

Suggestions for English Learners

Workshop affords students who are English Learners a wealth of opportunities for gaining proficiency in English. It also encourages them to share their backgrounds with peers. Since you will be working with all students individually and in small groups regardless of their reading ability, students who need special help with language will not feel self-conscious about working with you. In addition, working in small groups made of students with the same interests rather than the same abilities will provide them with the opportunity to learn about language from their peers during the regular course of Workshop activities.

Some suggestions for meeting the special needs of students with diverse backgrounds are as follows:

- ✦ Preread a selection with English Learners to help them identify words and ideas they wish to talk about. This will prepare them for discussions with the whole group.
- ✦ Preteach vocabulary and develop selection concepts that may be a challenge for students.
- ✦ Negotiate the meaning of selections by asking questions, checking for comprehension, and speaking with English Learners as much as possible.
- ✦ Draw English Learners into small-group discussions to give them a sense that their ideas are valid and worth attention.
- ✦ Pair English Learners with native English speakers to share their experiences and to provide new knowledge to other students.
- ✦ Have English Learners draw or dictate to you or another student a description of a new idea they may have during Workshop activities.

Book Review

Sessions can be small or large. Workshop is a good time for students to share the reading they do on their own. They can discuss a book they have all read, or one person can review a book for the others and answer questions from the group.

During Workshop, students can discuss and review a variety of books:

- ✦ Full-length versions of ***Student Reader*** selections
- ✦ Books that students learn about when discussing authors and illustrators
- ✦ Books related to the investigations of unit concepts that can be shared with others who might want to read them
- ✦ Interesting articles from magazines, newspapers, and other sources

When a student reviews a book others have not read, he or she can use some of the sentence starters to tell about the book. These may include "This book is about . . . ," "I chose this book because . . . ," "What I really like/don't like about this book is . . ., " and so on.

- When several students read the same book and discuss it during Workshop, they can use discussion starters.

Encouraging Reading

- Read aloud to your students regularly. You can read from your classroom library or full-length versions of ***Student Reader*** selections.
- Provide a time each day for students to read silently. This time can be as short as 10–15 minutes but should be strictly observed. You should stop what you are doing and read. Students should be allowed to choose their own reading materials during this time and record their reactions in the response journal section of their Writer's Notebooks.
- Establish a classroom library and reading center with books from the school or local library, or ask for donations of books from students, parents, and community members.
- Take your students to the school library or to the public library.

Workshop Management Tips

Use the following Workshop management tips to ensure that Workshop runs smoothly.

Note that these suggestions for a weekly unit/lesson may not exactly correspond to a particular unit/lesson in a given grade level but will give you a sense of how Workshop should progress. All of the time suggestions depend upon the needs of the class and their readiness to work independently.

Kindergarten through Grade 1

Unit 1, Week 1 Introduce Workshop as whole-class workshop. Explain Workshop and its rules. Give the class an activity to do, for example, putting letters in alphabetical order (Grade 1) or copying their names (kindergarten). Tell the class that they will be doing Workshop today. As they do their activity, you will walk around, observing students and noting how well Workshop is going. The class is working quietly and independently. Workshop may last only a few minutes in kindergarten and about ten minutes in first grade.

Unit 1, Weeks 2 and 3 Depending upon your class, you can move to whole-group Workshop with two activities. Give half the class one activity and the other half the other. Explain to the class that for the next few Workshop sessions, there will be two different activities but that the class is supposed to work quietly and independently. Switch activities for the next day, and repeat this format for the next few days or so. Introduce the concept of "debriefing." Take a few minutes at the end, have several students share what they did or learned during Workshop. You may want to have students tell what they like about Workshop and if any changes need to be made.

Unit 2, Week 1 Begin introducing Workshop Areas, explaining the materials and how they can be used. Explain to students that the materials in these areas will be changing regularly so students will be able to practice and use their new reading and writing skills. Workshop activities should change routinely and reflect the changing nature of the curriculum. Often, during the early weeks of Workshop, teachers assign students to different activities and, as students become ready, turn over to students the responsibility for choosing activities.

Unit 3 Add new activities for students. Encourage them to do a couple of Workshop activities each day, perhaps working on their writing in progress and fluency practice (reading a Pre-Decodable or Decodable). Other options might include on-line phonemic awareness and phonics activities, phonics activities such as word sorts, using blended words in written sentences, practicing high-frequency sight words, and so on.

Unit 4 By this time, students should be making choices and working independently. Each Workshop session may be fifteen minutes long with the teacher working with small groups. Take time to review Workshop activities to be sure they are being used and that students are learning from the activities. If activities become stale, vary them, or change them altogether.

Grades 2–6

Unit 1, Lesson 1 Introduce Workshop to students. Make sure they know where materials are located. Post the rules on the board or other prominent place in the classroom. Keep Workshop time short (less than thirty minutes) and very directed during the first few weeks until students can work independently.

Unit 1, Lesson 2 Discuss using small groups for pre-/reteaching purposes and how you will indicate who will be in the groups. Start by forming one small group randomly and having other students do something specific such as a writing assignment. When you have finished with the small group, send them to do independent work. Call another small group of students to work with you. Continue this each day until students are accustomed to forming groups and working independently.

Unit 1, Lesson 3 Reading Roundtable is a student-formed and student-run book discussion. Encourage students participating in Reading Roundtable to choose a book that they all will read and discuss. Several different Reading Roundtable groups may form on the basis of the books students choose.

Unit 1, Lesson 4 For the first few weeks of the school year, make sure each student has a plan for using Workshop time.

Unit 1, Lesson 5 (Days 1–5) Allow time for presentation and discussion of research activities. Use an entire Workshop day, and have all groups present their findings, or split the presentations over several days, depending on the small-group needs of your class.

Unit 1, Lesson 5 (Days 6–10) Review how students have used Workshop during this unit. Have they used their time well? Do they have the materials they need? Discuss suggestions for improving their use of this time. Take a few minutes at the beginning of each Workshop to make sure students know what they will be doing.

Unit 2, Lesson 1 Form small extra-practice groups with the more advanced students from time to time, as they also need special attention.

Unit 2, Lesson 2 To keep the entire class informed about the independent research being done, every other day or so invite a research group to explain what it is doing, how the research is going, and any problems they are encountering.

Unit 2, Lesson 3 Discuss the use of Workshop time for doing Inquiry and research projects, and share ***eInquiry*** with different research activities.

Unit 2, Lesson 4 Make sure small extra-practice groups are formed based on your observations of students' work on the different daily lessons. Small groups should be fluid and based on demonstrated need rather than become static and unchanging.

Unit 2, Lesson 5 (Days 1–5) One purpose of Workshop is to help students learn independence and responsibility. Assign students to monitor Workshop materials. They should alert you whenever materials are running low or missing, and they can be responsible for checking on return dates of library books and making sure the books are either returned or renewed.

Unit 2, Lesson 5 (Days 6–10) Students sometimes have difficulty starting discussions in Reading Roundtable. Try some of these discussion starters with students, and print them on a poster for student use.

I didn't know that . . .
I liked the part where . . .
Does anyone know . . .
I'm still confused by . . .
I figured out that . . .
This made me think . . .
I agree/disagree with because . . .

Unit 3, Lesson 1 By this time students should be accustomed to the routines, rules, expectations, and usage of Workshop time and be moving smoothly from small teacher-led groups to independent work. Monitor small groups occasionally to see that they are on task and making progress on their activities.

Unit 3, Lesson 2 Make a practice of reading aloud to students. All students enjoy being read to, no matter their age or grade. Encourage them to discuss the shared reading in groups and to bring books and read them aloud to their classmates.

Unit 3, Lesson 3 Encourage cooperation and collaboration by providing students with opportunities to engage in small groups.

Unit 3, Lesson 4 Spend a few minutes each day circulating around the room and monitoring what students are doing independently or in small groups. Students can then share with you on a timely basis any questions or problems they are having.

Unit 3, Lesson 5 (Days 1–5) Take note of various small groups. Make sure that quieter students are able to participate in the discussions. Often the stronger, more confident students dominate such discussions. Encourage them to give all participants an opportunity to share their ideas.

Unit 3, Lesson 5 (Days 6–10) If students are not productive during Workshop, keep them in the small group you are working with until they can successfully benefit from independent work. Discuss strategies they could use to become more independent.

Unit 4, Lesson 1 Individual students can monitor Workshop materials and alert you when materials or supplies are running low or missing and can check that library books are either returned or renewed.

Unit 4, Lesson 2 From time to time, join a Reading Roundtable group, and take part in their discussion. Make sure students lead the discussion.

Unit 4, Lesson 3 Encourage responsibility and independence by reminding students to show respect for each other and the materials provided.

Unit 4, Lesson 4 Be sure students discuss during Reading Roundtable what they like or dislike about a book, why they wanted to read it, and how the book either lived up to their expectations or disappointed them. Discussions should not be about basic comprehension but should help students think more deeply about the ideas presented in the book.

Unit 4, Lesson 5 (Days 1–5) Make sure students continue to use the activities provided for use with this unit at **SRAonline.com.**

Unit 4, Lesson 5 (Days 6–10) If students are not productive in Workshop, keep them in the small group you are working with until they can successfully benefit from independent work. Discuss strategies they could use to become more independent.

Unit 5, Lesson 1 Students often make great tutors for other students. They are uniquely qualified to understand problems that others might be having. Encourage students to pair up during Workshop to help each other with their daily lessons.

Unit 5, Lesson 2 Form small extra-practice groups with the more advanced students from time to time, as they also need special attention.

Unit 5, Lesson 3 To keep the entire class informed about the independent research being done, every other day or so, invite a research/investigation group to explain what it is doing, how the research is going, and any problems they are encountering.

Unit 5, Lesson 4 Most of the authors of the ***Student Reader*** selections are well known and have written many, many pieces of fine literature. Encourage students who enjoy the selections to find other books by the same author. Encourage them to think about and discuss what about that particular author's work attracts them.

Unit 5, Lesson 5 (Days 1–5) Share your impressions of books from your classroom library or other readings during Reading Roundtable. Note which students initiate sharing and which are reluctant to share.

Unit 5, Lesson 5 (Days 6–10) Review with students the time they have used in Workshop. Have they used their time well? Do they have the materials they need? Discuss suggestions for improving the use of this time.

Unit 6, Lesson 1 Spend a few minutes each day circulating and monitoring what students are doing independently or in small groups. Students can share with you on a timely basis any questions or problems they are having.

Unit 6, Lesson 2 Students should be accustomed to the routines, rules, expectations, and usage of Workshop time and be moving smoothly from small teacher-led groups to independent work. Make sure to monitor small groups occasionally to see that they are on task and making progress with their activities.

Unit 6, Lesson 3 Make sure students continue to use the activities provided for use with this unit at **SRAonline.com.**

Unit 6, Lesson 4 If the reading selection is an excerpt from a longer piece, encourage students to read the book from which the excerpt is taken and to discuss how the excerpt fits into the larger work.

Unit 6, Lesson 5 (Days 1–5) Students often make great tutors for other students. The fact that they, too, are just learning the materials makes them uniquely qualified to understand problems that others might be having. Encourage students to pair up during Workshop to help each other on their daily lessons.

Unit 6, Lesson 5 (Days 6–10) Allot time for presentation and discussion of research activities. You may want to use a whole Workshop day and have all groups present their findings or split the presentations over several days, depending on the urgency of the small-group instruction your class needs.

Scope and Sequence

Reading

	K	1	2	3	4	5	6
Print/Book Awareness (Recognize and understand the conventions of print and books)							
Capitalization	X	X					
Constancy of Words		X					
Differentiate between Letter and Word	X						
Differentiate between Word and Sentence	X						
End Punctuation	X	X					
Follow Left-to-Right, Top-to-Bottom	X	X					
Letter Recognition and Formation	X	X					
Page Numbering	X	X					
Parts of a Book	X	X					
Picture/Text Relationship	X	X					
Punctuation	X	X					
Quotation Marks	X	X					
Relationship Between Spoken and Printed Language	X	X					
Sentence Recognition	X	X					
Spacing Between Sentences	X	X					
Spacing Between Words	X	X					
Table of Contents	X	X					
Text Features		X					
Text Relationships		X					
Word Length	X	X					
Word Boundaries		X					
Write Left-to-Right, Top-to-Bottom	X	X					
Phonemic Awareness (Recognize Discrete Sounds in Words)							
Oral Blending: Words/Word Parts	X	X					
Oral Blending: Onset and Rime	X	X					
Oral Blending: Syllables	X	X					
Oral (Phoneme) Blending: Initial Sounds	X	X					
Oral (Phoneme) Blending: Final Sounds	X	X					
Oral Blending: Initial Vowels		X					
Oral Blending: Vowel Replacement		X					
Rhyming	X	X					
Phoneme Matching: Initial Sounds	X	X					
Phoneme Matching: Final Sounds	X	X					
Phoneme Matching: Medial Sounds	X	X					
Phoneme Manipulation: Initial Sounds	X	X					
Phoneme Manipulation: Final Sounds	X	X					
Phoneme Manipulation: Medial Sounds	X	X					
Segmentation: Final Consonants	X	X					
Segmentation: Initial Consonants/Blends		X					
Segmentation: Words/Word Parts	X	X					
Segmentation: Syllables	X	X					
Segmentation: Identifying the Number and Order of Sounds in Words	X	X					

Reading (continued)

	K	1	2	3	4	5	6
How the Alphabet Works							
Letter Knowledge (Alphabetic Knowledge)	X	X					
Letter Order (Alphabetic Order)	X	X					
Letter Sounds	X	X					
Sounds in Words	X	X					
Phonics (Associate Sounds and Spellings to Read Words)							
Blending Sounds into Words	X	X	X	X			
Consonant Clusters		X	X	X			
Consonant Digraphs		X	X	X			
Phonograms		X	X	X			
Schwa			X	X			
Silent Consonants			X	X			
Syllables		X	X	X			
Vowel Diphthongs		X	X	X			
Vowels: Long Sounds and Spellings	X	X	X	X			
Vowels: r-controlled		X	X	X			
Vowels: Short Sounds and Spellings	X	X	X	X			
Comprehension Strategies							
Adjusting Reading Speed			X	X	X	X	X
Asking Questions/Answering Questions	X	X	X	X	X	X	X
Clarifying	X	X	X	X	X	X	X
Making Connections	X	X	X	X	X	X	X
Predicting/Confirming Predictions	X	X	X	X	X	X	X
Summarizing		X	X	X	X	X	X
Visualizing	X	X	X	X	X	X	X
Comprehension Skills							
Author's Point of View			X	X	X	X	X
Author's Purpose			X	X	X	X	X
Cause and Effect	X	X	X	X	X	X	X
Classify and Categorize	X	X	X	X	X	X	X
Compare and Contrast	X	X	X	X	X	X	X
Drawing Conclusions	X	X	X	X	X	X	X
Fact and Opinion			X	X	X	X	X
Main Idea and Details	X	X	X	X	X	X	X
Making Inferences		X	X	X	X	X	X
Reality and Fantasy	X	X	X	X			
Sequence	X	X	X	X	X	X	X
Vocabulary							
Apposition		X	X	X	X	X	X
Concept Words		X	X	X	X	X	X
Context Clues		X	X	X	X	X	X
Expanding Vocabulary		X	X	X	X	X	X
High-Frequency Words	X	X	X	X			
Idioms				X	X	X	X
Multiple-Meaning Words		X	X	X	X	X	X
Selection Vocabulary	X	X	X	X	X	X	X
Time and Order Words (Creating Sequence)	X	X	X	X	X	X	X
Utility Words (Colors, Classroom Objects, etc.)	X	X					

Reading (continued)

	K	1	2	3	4	5	6
Reading with a Writer's Eye							
Author's Purpose	X		X	X	X	X	
Alliteration			X		X		X
Captions and Headings			X	X		X	X
Characterization	X	X	X	X	X	X	X
Choosing Good Examples				X	X		
Description		X	X	X	X	X	X
Diagrams							X
Dialect						X	
Dialogue		X	X	X	X	X	X
Effective Beginnings					X	X	
Effective Endings					X		
Event Sequence	X	X	X	X		X	
Expository Writing Techniques					X	X	
Fable Characteristics					X		
Figurative Language		X	X	X	X	X	X
Flashback							X
Genre Knowledge	X		X	X	X	X	X
Idiom						X	X
Irony					X		
Language Use	X		X	X	X	X	X
Mood and Tone		X	X	X			X
Onomatopoeia			X	X	X		X
Personification			X	X		X	X
Persuasive Techniques					X	X	
Plot (Problem/Solution)	X	X	X	X	X	X	X
Point of View					X	X	
Punctuation					X	X	
Quoting Sources					X		
Rhyme	X		X			X	X
Sensory Details		X		X		X	
Sentence Variety						X	
Setting	X	X	X	X	X	X	X
Sidebars							X
Similes and Metaphors				X	X		X
Stage Directions					X		
Style							X
Suspense and Surprise				X		X	
Text Structure	X		X	X	X	X	X
Theme	X		X	X	X	X	X
Transitions					X		X
Using Comparisons		X	X	X		X	
Voice					X	X	X
Word Choice				X			X
Word Structure							
Antonyms			X	X	X	X	X
Comparatives/Superlatives			X	X	X	X	
Compound Words	X	X	X	X	X	X	X
Contractions			X	X	X	X	
Connotation and Denotation							X
Content/Concept Words							X

Reading (continued)

	K	1	2	3	4	5	6
Foreign Words and Phrases						X	X
Gerunds							X
Greek and Latin Roots				X	X	X	X
Homographs			X	X	X	X	X
Homonyms/Homophones			X	X	X	X	X
Inflectional Endings			X	X	X	X	X
Irregular Plurals			X	X	X	X	
Multiple-Meaning Words					X	X	X
Multisyllabic Words			X	X	X	X	
Plurals			X	X	X	X	
Position Words	X	X					
Prefixes			X	X	X	X	X
Root or Base Words			X	X	X	X	X
Shades of Meaning/Levels of Specificity						X	X
Suffixes			X	X	X	X	X
Synonyms			X	X	X	X	X
Word Families			X	X	X	X	X
Word Origins					X	X	X

Inquiry and Study Skills

Study Skills	K	1	2	3	4	5	6
Comparing Information across Sources		X		X		X	
Charts, Graphs, and Diagrams/Visual Aids	X	X	X	X	X	X	X
Collaborative Inquiry	X	X	X	X	X	X	X
Communicating Research Progress Results		X	X	X	X	X	X
Compile Notes			X		X	X	X
Conducting an Interview		X	X	X	X	X	X
Finding Needed Information	X	X	X	X	X	X	X
Follow Directions	X		X	X	X		X
Formulate Questions for Inquiry and Research	X	X	X	X	X	X	X
Give Reports	X		X	X	X	X	X
Make Outlines			X	X	X	X	X
Making Conjectures	X	X	X	X	X	X	X
Maps	X	X	X	X	X	X	
Note Taking		X	X	X	X	X	X
Parts of a Book	X	X	X	X	X		
Planning Inquiry		X	X	X	X	X	X
Recognizing Information Needs		X	X	X	X	X	X
Revising Questions and Conjectures	X	X	X	X	X	X	X
Summarize and Organize Information		X	X	X	X	X	X
Time Lines			X	X	X	X	
Use Appropriate Resources (Media Sources, Reference Books, Experts, Internet)		X	X	X	X	X	X
Using a Dictionary/Glossary		X	X	X	X		
Using a Media Center/Library		X	X	X	X		
Using a Thesaurus			X	X	X	X	
Using an Encyclopedia		X	X	X	X		
Using Newspapers and Magazines		X	X		X		X
Using Technology	X	X	X	X	X	X	X

Language Arts

Writing/Composition

	K	1	2	3	4	5	6
Approaches							
Collaborative Writing	X	X	X	X	X	X	X
Individual Writing	X	X	X	X	X	X	X
Writing Process							
Brainstorming/Prewriting	X	X	X	X	X	X	X
Drafting	X	X	X	X	X	X	X
Revising	X	X	X	X	X	X	X
Editing	X	X	X	X	X	X	X
Proofreading	X	X	X	X	X	X	X
Publishing	X	X	X	X	X	X	X
Writing Genres							
Action Tale			X				
Autobiography/Biography	X	X	X	X	X	X	X
Book Review		X	X	X	X	X	
Business Letter			X	X		X	X
Describe a Process		X	X	X	X	X	X
Descriptive Writing	X	X	X	X	X	X	X
Expository/Informational Text	X	X	X	X	X	X	X
Fantasy		X	X	X			
Folklore (Folktales, Fairy Tales, Tall Tales, Legends, Myths)		X	X	X	X	X	
Friendly Letter	X	X	X	X	X	X	X
Historical Fiction					X		X
Invitation		X		X		X	
Journal Writing			X	X	X		
Magazine Article						X	X
Making a List	X	X	X	X	X	X	X
Mystery				X			
Narrative	X	X	X	X	X	X	X
News Story		X	X	X	X		
Personal Writing	X	X	X	X	X	X	X
Persuasive Writing	X	X	X	X	X	X	X
Play/Dramatization			X	X	X	X	X
Poetry	X	X	X	X	X	X	X
Realistic Fiction		X	X	X	X	X	X
Summary		X	X	X	X	X	X
Timed Writing		X	X	X	X	X	X
Writing Traits							
Audience		X	X	X	X	X	X
Conventions	X	X	X	X	X	X	X
Elaboration		X	X	X	X	X	X
Focus		X	X	X	X	X	X
Ideas/Content	X	X	X	X	X	X	X
Organization		X	X	X	X	X	X
Presentation	X	X	X	X	X	X	X
Purpose		X	X	X	X	X	X
Sentence Fluency	X	X	X	X	X	X	X
Sentence Variety		X			X	X	X
Vocabulary		X	X	X	X	X	X
Voice	X	X	X	X	X	X	X
Word Choice	X	X	X	X	X	X	X

Language Arts

Writing/Composition (continued)

Writing Strategies	K	1	2	3	4	5	6
Action and Describing Words	X	X	X	X			
Adding Details	X	X	X	X	X	X	X
Addressing Audience Needs		X	X	X	X	X	X
Brainstorming	X	X	X	X	X	X	X
Categorizing Ideas							X
Cause and Effect					X	X	X
Character Sketch					X	X	
Choosing a Topic	X	X	X	X	X	X	X
Compare and Contrast			X			X	X
Conveying a General Mood				X	X	X	
Creating Suspense				X			X
Creating Vivid Images		X		X	X	X	
Dialogue	X	X	X	X	X	X	X
Effective Beginnings					X	X	X
Elements of a Letter		X	X	X	X	X	X
Elements of Persuasion			X	X	X	X	
Eliminating Irrelevant Information		X	X	X	X	X	X
Eliminating Wordiness			X	X	X	X	X
Evaluate Personal Growth as a Writer			X	X	X	X	
Explanatory Paragraphs		X					
Figurative Language			X	X	X	X	X
Formality of Language		X	X	X	X	X	
Format		X			X	X	X
Generate Additional Ideas		X	X	X	X		
Highlight a Memorable Event		X			X		
Identifying Best Feature of Something Written			X	X			
Illustrations and Drawings	X	X	X	X			
Information from Multiple Sources				X	X	X	X
Main Idea and Details					X	X	
Making Connections							X
Organizing a Multi-Paragraph Composition					X	X	X
Planning		X			X	X	X
Plot Structure—Beginning, Middle, Climax, and End		X		X	X	X	X
Point of View						X	X
Presenting Facts and Examples Objectively				X	X	X	X
Proofreading	X	X	X	X	X	X	X
Purpose		X	X	X	X	X	X
Realism					X	X	X
Referencing a Source					X	X	
Revising	X	X	X	X	X	X	X
Rhythm and Rhyme		X	X			X	
Sensory Details				X	X	X	X
Sentence Combining			X	X	X	X	X
Sequence	X	X	X	X		X	
Setting		X	X	X	X	X	X
Story Elements		X	X	X	X	X	
Style							X
Summary			X	X	X	X	X
Taking Notes		X	X	X	X	X	X

Language Arts

Writing/Composition (continued)

	K	1	2	3	4	5	6
Timed Writing		X	X	X	X	X	X
Time Line			X	X		X	
Transition Words/Devices			X	X	X	X	X
Using a Checklist		X	X	X	X	X	
Using a Graphic Organizer		X	X	X	X	X	X
Using a Model as a Guide to Writing			X	X		X	
Using Outlines to Organize Information				X	X	X	X
Using Multimedia Sources			X	X	X	X	X
Vary Sentence Beginnings			X	X	X	X	
Vary Sentence Length		X	X			X	
Vary Sentence Types	X	X	X	X	X	X	
Voice				X		X	
Voicing an Opinion		X				X	X
Word Choice		X	X	X	X	X	X
Working Collaboratively						X	X
Writing Coherent Paragraphs		X	X	X	X	X	X

Language Arts

Grammar

	K	1	2	3	4	5	6
Parts of Speech							
Adjectives (Describing Words)	X	X	X	X	X	X	X
Adverbs			X	X	X	X	X
Conjunctions			X	X	X	X	X
Nouns	X	X	X	X	X	X	X
Prepositions				X	X	X	X
Pronouns	X	X	X	X	X	X	X
Verbs	X	X	X	X	X	X	X
Sentences							
Complete and Incomplete Sentences		X	X	X	X	X	X
Fragments			X	X	X	X	X
Independent and Dependent Clauses							X
Parts (Subjects and Predicates)			X	X	X	X	X
Run-on Sentences					X		X
Sentence Combining			X	X	X	X	X
Structure (Simple, Compound, Complex, Compound-Complex)			X	X	X	X	X
Subject/Verb Agreement		X	X	X	X	X	X
Types (Declarative, Interrogative, Exclamatory, Imperative)	X	X	X	X	X	X	X
Usage							
Adjectives		X	X	X	X	X	X
Adverbs			X	X	X	X	X
Antonyms		X	X				
Articles			X	X		X	X
Contractions			X	X	X		
Nouns		X	X	X	X	X	X
Pronouns		X	X	X	X	X	X
Regular and Irregular Plurals					X	X	X
Synonyms		X	X				
Verb Tenses		X	X	X	X	X	X
Verbs (Action, Helping, Linking, Regular/Irregular)		X	X	X	X	X	X

Language Arts

Grammar (continued)

	K	1	2	3	4	5	6
Mechanics							
Capitalization (Sentence, Proper Nouns, Titles, Direct Address, Pronoun "I")	X	X	X	X	X	X	X
Punctuation (End Punctuation, Comma Use, Quotation Marks, Apostrophe, Colon, Semicolon, Hyphen, Parentheses)	X	X	X	X	X	X	X
Spelling							
Antonyms					X	X	X
Base or Root Words					X	X	
Comparatives/Superlatives				X	X	X	X
Compound Words				X	X	X	
Connotation and Denotation							X
Content/Concept Words							X
Contractions				X	X		X
Foreign Words and Phrases							X
Gerunds							X
Greek and Latin Roots				X	X	X	X
Homographs				X	X	X	X
Homonyms/Homophones				X	X	X	X
Inflectional Endings		X		X	X	X	X
Irregular Plurals		X		X	X	X	
Irregular Verbs						X	
Long Vowel Patterns		X	X	X	X		
Multiple-Meaning Words					X	X	X
Multisyllabic Words		X	X	X	X		X
Phonograms		X					
Prefixes				X	X	X	X
r-Controlled Vowel Spellings		X	X				
Shades of Meaning					X		X
Short Vowel Spellings		X	X	X	X		
Silent Letters			X	X	X		
Sound/Letter Relationships	X	X	X				
Special Spellings Patterns/Rules		X	X	X	X	X	
Special Vowel Spellings		X	X	X			
Suffixes		X		X	X	X	X
Synonyms					X	X	X
Word Families		X		X		X	X

Listening/Speaking/Viewing

	K	1	2	3	4	5	6
Listening							
Analyze/Evaluate Intent and Content of Speaker's Message		X	X	X		X	X
Ask Questions		X	X	X	X	X	X
Determine Purposes for Listening		X	X	X	X	X	X
Drawing Conclusions and Making Inferences						X	
Follow Directions	X	X		X	X	X	X
Learn about Different Cultures through Discussion				X	X		
Listen for Poetic Language (Rhythm/Rhyme)	X	X			X		X
Listening for Details			X	X	X		
Listening for Information				X	X		
Participate in Group Discussions	X	X	X	X	X	X	X
Recalling What Was Heard				X			
Recognizing Fact and Opinion				X			
Respond to Speaker	X	X	X	X	X	X	X
Use Nonverbal Communication Techniques		X		X	X	X	X
Speaking							
Answer Questions	X	X	X	X	X	X	X
Asking Questions		X		X	X		
Describe Ideas and Feelings	X	X	X				X
Effective Word Choice/Voice			X	X	X	X	
Engaging the Audience					X	X	
Give Directions		X			X	X	X
Learn About Different Cultures through Discussion		X		X			X
Listen and Respond		X		X	X		
Making Announcements and Introductions		X					
Organizing Presentations				X	X	X	X
Paraphrasing			X	X			
Participate in Group Discussion	X	X	X	X	X	X	X
Present Oral Reports		X	X	X	X	X	X
Purposes of Speech			X				
Read Fluently with Expression, Phrasing, and Intonation		X	X	X	X	X	X
Read Orally	X	X	X	X	X	X	X
Share Information		X	X	X	X	X	X
Small Group Discussion			X	X	X	X	X
Speak Clearly at Appropriate Volume		X	X	X	X	X	X
Speaking Strategies				X	X		
Staying on Topic		X					
Summarize/Retell Stories	X	X	X	X	X	X	X
Understand Formal and Informal Language		X		X	X	X	X
Use Appropriate Language for Audience		X		X	X	X	X
Use Nonverbal Communication Techniques		X	X	X	X	X	X

Listening/Speaking/Viewing (continued)

	K	1	2	3	4	5	6
Viewing							
Analyze Purposes and Techniques of the Media			X	X	X	X	X
Appreciate/Interpret Artist's Techniques		X					
Compare Visual and Written Material on the Same Subject		X					X
Culture in Media		X			X	X	
Describe Pictures			X				
Gather Information from Visual Images		X	X	X	X	X	X
Interpreting Media				X	X		
Language Development							X
Literary Devices				X			X
Relating to Content				X	X		
Understanding Gestures				X	X		
Using Multimedia				X	X	X	
View Critically		X		X	X	X	X
Penmanship							
Cursive Letters			X	X			
Manuscript Letters	X	X					
Numbers	X	X					

Unit Themes

	Level K	Level 1	Level 2
Unit 1	Off to School	Back to School	Kindness
Unit 2	Patterns	Where Animals Live	Let's Explore
Unit 3	Finding Friends	I Am Responsible!	Around the Town
Unit 4	By the Sea	Our Neighborhood at Work	Look Again
Unit 5	Stick to It	What's the Weather?	Courage
Unit 6	My Shadow	North, South, East, West	America's People
Unit 7	Teamwork	I Think I Can	
Unit 8	Ready, Set, Grow!	Away We Grow!	
Unit 9	Red, White, and Blue	Home, Sweet Home	
Unit 10	Windy Days	I Am Brave	

Level 3	Level 4	Level 5	Level 6
Friendship	Risks and Consequences	Heritage	Taking a Stand
Animals and Their Habitats	Nature's Delicate Balance	Energy at Work	Ancient Civilizations
Money	A Changing America	Making a New Nation	Ecology
Earth, Moon, and Sun	Science Fair	Our Corner of the Universe	Great Expectations
Communities across Time	America on the Move	Going West	Earth in Action
Storytelling	Dollars and Sense	Call of Duty	Art and Impact

Glossary of Reading Terms

This glossary includes linguistic, grammatical, comprehension, and literary terms that may be helpful in understanding reading instruction.

acronym a word formed from the initial letter of words in a phrase, **scuba (self-contained underwater breathing apparatus)**.

acrostic a kind of puzzle in which lines of a poem are arranged so that words or phrases are formed when certain letters from each line are used in a sequence.

adjective a word or group of words that modifies or describes a noun.

adventure story a narrative that features the unknown or unexpected with elements of excitement, danger, and risk.

adverb a word or group of words that modifies a verb, adjective, or other adverb. An adverb answers questions such as **how, when, where,** and **how much.**

affective domain the psychological field of emotional activities such as interests, attitudes, opinions, appreciations, values, and emotional sets

affix a word part, either a prefix or a suffix, that changes the meaning or function of a word root or stem.

affricate a speech sound that starts as a stop but ends as a fricative, the /ch/ in **catch.**

agreement the correspondence of syntactically related words; subjects and predicates are in agreement when both are singular or plural.

alliteration the repetition of the initial sounds in neighboring words or stressed syllables.

alphabet the complete set of letters representing speech sounds used in writing a language. In English there are twenty-six letters.

alphabet book a book for helping young children learn the alphabet by pairing letters with pictures whose sounds they represent.

alphabetic principle the association between sounds and the letters that represent them in alphabetic writing systems.

alveolar a consonant speech sound made when the tongue and the ridge of the upper and lower jaw stop to constrict the air flow, as /t/.

anagram a word or phrase whose letters form other words or phrases when rearranged, for example, **add** and **dad.**

analogy a likeness or similarity.

analytic phonics also deductive phonics, a whole-to-part approach to phonics in which a student is taught a number of sight words and then phonetic generalizations that can be applied to other words.

antonym a word that is opposite in meaning to another word.

appositive a word that restates or modifies a preceding noun, for example, **my daughter, Charlotte.** Appositives are also definitions of words usually set off by commas.

aspirate an unvoiced speech sound produced by a puff of air, as /h/ in **heart.**

aspirated stop a stop consonant sound released with a puff of air, as /k/, /p/, and /t/.

auditory discrimination the ability to hear phonetic likenesses and differences in phonemes and words.

author's purpose the motive or reason for which an author writes; includes to entertain, inform, persuade, and explain how.

automaticity fluent processing of information, requiring little effort or attention.

auxiliary verb a verb that precedes another verb to express time, mood, or voice; includes verbs such as **has, is,** and **will.**

ballad a narrative poem, composed of short verses to be sung or recited, usually containing elements of drama and often tragic in tone.

base word a word to which affixes may be added to create related words.

blank verse unrhymed verse, especially unrhymed iambic pentameter.

blend the joining of the sounds of two or more letters with little change in those sounds, for example, /spr/ in **spring;** also **consonant blend** or **consonant cluster.**

blending combining the sounds represented by letters or spellings to sound out or pronounce a word; contrast with **oral blending.**

breve the symbol placed above a vowel to indicate that it is a short vowel.

browse to skim through or look over in search of something of interest.

canon in literature, the body of major works that a culture considers important at a given time.

case a grammatical category that indicates the syntactic/semantic role of a noun phrase in a sentence.

cause-effect relationship a stated or implied association between an outcome and the conditions that brought it about; also the comprehension skill associated with recognizing this type of relationship as an organizing principle in text.

chapter book a book long enough to be divided into chapters, but not long or complex enough to be considered a novel.

characterization the way in which an author presents a character in a story, including describing words, actions, thoughts, and impressions of that character.

choral reading oral group reading to develop oral fluency by modeling.

cinquain a stanza of five lines, specifically one that has successive lines of two, four, six, eight, and two syllables.

cipher a system for writing in code.

clarifying a comprehension strategy in which the reader rereads text, uses a dictionary, uses decoding skills, or uses context clues to comprehend something that is unclear.

clause a group of words with a subject and a predicate used to form a part of or a whole sentence, a dependent clause modifies an independent clause, which can stand alone as a complete sentence.

collaborative learning learning by working together in small groups.

command a sentence that asks for action and usually ends with a period.

common noun in contrast to **proper noun,** a noun that denotes a class rather than a unique or specific thing such as **girl** versus **Susan.**

comprehension the understanding of what is written or said.

comprehension skill a skill that aids in understanding text, including identifying **author's purpose, author's point of view,** comprehending **cause-and-effect** relationships, **clarifying, comparing and contrasting** items and events, **drawing conclusions,** distinguishing **fact from opinion,** identifying **main ideas, making inferences,** distinguishing **reality from fantasy,** and understanding **sequence.**

comprehension strategy a sequence of steps for monitoring and understanding text, includes adjusting reading speed, asking questions, clarifying, making connections, predicting, summarizing, and visualizing.

conjugation the complete set of all possible inflected forms of a verb.

conjunction a part of speech used to connect words, phrases, clauses, or sentences, including the words **and, but,** and **or.**

consonant a speech sound, and the alphabet letter that represents that sound, made by partial or complete closure of part of the vocal tract, which obstructs air flow and causes audible friction.

context clue information from the immediate and surrounding text that helps identify a word.

contraction a short version of a written or spoken expression in which letters are omitted, for example, **can't.**

convention an accepted practice in spoken or written language, usually referring to spelling, mechanics, or grammar rules.

cooperative learning a classroom organization that allows students to work together to achieve their individual goals. Related term is **collaboration.**

creative writing prose and poetic forms of writing that express the writer's thoughts and feelings imaginatively.

cueing system any of the various sources of information that help identify an unrecognizable word in reading, including phonetic, semantic, and syntactical information.

cumulative tale a story, such as "The Gingerbread Man," in which details are repeated until the climax.

dangling modifier usually a participle that because of its placement in a sentence modifies the wrong object.

decodable text text materials controlled to include a majority of words whose sound/spelling relationships are known by the reader.

decode to analyze spoken or graphic symbols for meaning.

diacritical mark a mark, such as a breve or macron, added to a letter or graphic character to indicate a specific pronunciation.

dialect a regional variety of a particular language with phonological, grammatical, and lexical patterns that distinguishes it from other varieties.

dialogue a piece of writing written as conversation, usually punctuated by quotation marks.

digraph two letters that represent one speech sound, for example, /sh/ or /ch/.

diphthong a vowel sound produced when the tongue glides from one vowel sound toward another in the same syllable, for example, /oi/ or /ou/.

direct object the person or thing that receives the action of a verb in a sentence, for example, the word **cake** in this sentence: **Madeline baked a cake.**

drafting the process of writing ideas in rough form to record them.

drama a story in the form of a play, written to be performed.

edit in the writing process, to revise or correct a manuscript. Often this is part of the final step in the process with a focus on correcting grammar, spelling, and mechanics rather than content, structure, and organization.

emergent literacy the development of the association of meaning and print that continues until a child reaches the stage of conventional reading and writing.

emergent reading a child's early interaction with books and print before the ability to decode text.

encode to change a message into symbols, for example, to change speech into writing.

epic a long narrative poem, usually about a hero.

exclamatory sentence a sentence that shows strong emotion and ends with an exclamation point.

expository writing or **exposition** a composition in writing that explains an event or process.

fable a short tale that teaches a moral.

fantasy a highly imaginative story about characters, places, and events that cannot exist.

fiction imaginative narrative designed to entertain rather than to explain, persuade, or describe.

figure of speech the expressive, nonliteral use of language usually through metaphor, simile, or personification.

fluency freedom from word-identification problems that hinder comprehension in reading. Fluency involves rate, accuracy, and expression.

folktale a narrative form of genre such as an epic, myth, or fable that is well-known through repeated storytellings.

foreshadowing giving clues to upcoming events in a story.

free verse verse with irregular metrical pattern.

freewriting writing that is not limited in form, style, content, or purpose; designed to encourage students to write.

genre a classification of literary works, including tragedy, comedy, novel, essay, short story, mystery, realistic fiction, and poetry.

grammar the study of the classes of words, their inflections, and their functions and relations in sentences; includes phonological, morphological, syntactic, and semantic descriptions of a language.

grapheme a written or printed representation of a phoneme, such as **c** for /k/.

guided reading reading instruction in which the teacher provides the structure and purpose for reading and responding to the material read.

handing off a method of turning over to students the primary responsibility for controlling discussion.

indirect object in a sentence, the person or thing to or for whom an action is done, for example, the word **dog** in this sentence: **Madeline gave the dog a treat.**

inference a conclusion based on facts, data, or evidence.

infinitive the base form of a verb, usually with the infinitive marker, for example, **to go.**

inflectional ending an ending that expresses a plural or possessive form of a noun, the tense of a verb, or the comparative or superlative form of an adjective or adverb.

interrogative word a word that marks a clause or sentence as a question, including **interrogative pronouns who, what, which, where.**

intervention a strategy or program designed to supplement or substitute instruction, especially for those students who fall behind.

invented spelling the result of an attempt to spell a word based on using the sounds in the letter names to determine the sound the letter names. Gradually sounds are connected to letters, which leads to conventional spelling..

irony a figure of speech in which the literal meanings of the words is the opposite of their intended meanings.

journal a written record of daily events or responses.

juvenile book a book written for children or adolescents.

legend a traditional tale handed down from generation to generation.

leitmotif a repeated expression, event, or idea used to unify a work of art such as writing.

letter one of a set of graphic symbols that forms an alphabet and is used alone or in combination to represent a phoneme, also **grapheme.**

linguistics the study of the nature and structure of language and communication.

literary elements the elements of a story such as **setting, plot,** and **characterization** that create the structure of a narrative.

macron a diacritical mark placed above a vowel to indicate a long vowel sound.

main idea the central thought or chief topic of a passage.

making connections a reading strategy used to connect information being read to one's own experiences to other reading materials or to one's knowledge of the world. Making connections fosters engagement, while reading helps the reader make sense of the text and connect information.

mechanics the conventions of capitalization and punctuation.

metacognition awareness and knowledge of one's mental processes or thinking about what one is thinking about.

metaphor a figure of speech in which a comparison is implied but not stated; for example, **She is a jewel.**

miscue a deviation from text during oral reading in an attempt to make sense of the text.

modeling an instructional technique in which the teacher makes public the thinking needed to use critical reading and writing behaviors.

mood the literary element that conveys the emotional atmosphere of a story.

morpheme a meaningful linguistic unit that cannot be divided into smaller units, for example, **word**; **a bound morpheme** is a morpheme that cannot stand alone as an independent word, for example, the prefix **re-**; a **free morpheme** can stand alone, for example, **dog.**

myth a story designed to explain the mysteries of life.

narrative writing or **narration** a composition in writing that tells a story or gives an account of an event.

nonfiction prose designed to explain, argue, or describe rather than to entertain with a factual emphasis; includes biography and autobiography.

noun a part of speech that denotes persons, places, things, qualities, or acts.

novel an extended fictional prose narration.

onomatopoeia the use of a word whose sound suggests its meaning, for example, **purr.**

oral blending the ability to fuse discrete phonemes into recognizable words; oral blending puts sounds together to make a word, **see also segmentation.**

orthography correct or standardized spelling according to established usage in a language.

oxymoron a figure of speech in which contrasting or contradictory words are brought together for emphasis.

paragraph a subdivision of a written composition that consists of one or more sentences, deals with one point, or gives the words of one speaker, usually beginning with an indented line.

participle a verb form used as an adjective, for example, **the skating party.**

personification a figure of speech in which animals, ideas, or things take on human characteristics.

persuasive writing a composition intended to persuade the reader to adopt the writer's point of view.

phoneme the smallest sound unit of speech, for example, the /k/ in **book.**

phonemic awareness the ability to recognize that spoken words are made of discrete sounds and that those sounds can be manipulated.

phonetic spelling the respelling of entry words in a dictionary according to a pronunciation key.

phonetics the study of speech sounds.

Glossary of Reading Terms, continued

phonics a way of teaching reading that addresses sound/symbol relationships, especially in beginning instruction.

phonogram a letter or symbol that represents a phonetic sound.

phonological awareness the ability to attend to the sound structure of language; includes sentence, word, syllable rhyme and phonological awareness.

plot the literary element that provides the structure of the action of a story, which may include rising action, climax, and falling action leading to a resolution or denouement.

plural a grammatical form of a word that refers to more than one in number; an irregular plural is one that does not follow normal patterns for inflectional endings.

poetic license the liberty taken by writers to ignore conventions.

poetry a metrical form of composition in which language is chosen and arranged to create a powerful response through meaning, sound, or rhythm.

possessive showing ownership either through the use of an adjective, an adjectival pronoun, or the possessive form of a noun.

predicate the part of the sentence that expresses something about the subject and includes the verb phrase; a **complete predicate** includes the principal verb in a sentence and all its modifiers or subordinate parts.

predicting a comprehension strategy in which the reader attempts to anticpate what will happen, using clues from the text and prior knowledge, and then confirms predictions as the text is read.

prefix an affix attached before a base word that changes the meaning of the word.

preposition a part of speech in the class of function words such as **of, on,** and **at** that precede noun phrases to create prepositional phrases.

prewriting the planning stage of the writing process in which the writer formulates ideas, gathers information, and considers ways to organize them.

print awareness in emergent literacy, a child's growing recognition of conventions and characteristics of written language, including reading from left to right and from top to bottom in English and that words are separated by spaces.

pronoun a part of speech used as a substitute for a noun or noun phrase.

proofreading the act of reading with the intent to correct, clarify, or improve text.

pseudonym an assumed name used by an author; a pen name or nom de plume.

publishing the process of preparing written material for presentation.

punctuation graphic marks such as commas, periods, quotation marks, and brackets used to clarify meaning and to give speech characteristics to written language.

question an interrogative sentence that asks a question and ends with a question mark.

realistic fiction a story that attempts to portray characters and events as they actually are.

rebus a picture or symbol that suggests a word or syllable.

revise in the writing process, to change or correct a manuscript to make its message more clear.

rhyme identical or very similar recurring final sounds in words, often at the ends of lines of poetry.

rime a vowel and any following consonants of a syllable.

segmentation the ability to break words into individual sounds; **see also oral blending.**

semantic mapping a graphic display of a group of words that are meaningfully related to support vocabulary instruction.

semantics the study of meaning in language, including the meanings of words, phrases, sentences, and texts.

sentence a grammatical unit that expresses a statement, question, or command; a **simple sentence** is a sentence with one subject and one predicate; a **compound sentence** is a sentence with two or more independent clauses usually separated by a comma and conjunction, but no dependent clause; a **complex sentence** is a sentence with one independent and one or more dependent clauses.

sentence combining a teaching technique in which complex sentence chunks and paragraphs are built from basic sentences.

sentence lifting the process of using sentences from children's writing to illustrate what is wrong or right to develop children's editing and proofreading skills.

sequence the order of elements or events.

setting the literary element that includes the time, place, and physical and psychological background in which a story takes place.

sight word a word that is taught to be read as a whole word, usually words that are phonetically irregular.

simile a figure of speech in which a comparison of two things that are unlike is directly stated, usually with the words **like** or **as**; for example, **She is like a jewel.**

spelling the process of representing language by means of a writing system.

statement a sentence that tells something and ends with a period.

study skills a general term for the techniques and strategies that help readers comprehend text with the intent to remember; includes following directions, organizing, locating, and using graphic aids.

style the characteristics of a work that reflect the author's particular way of writing.

subject the main topic of a sentence to which a predicate refers, including the principal noun; a **complete subject** includes the principal noun in a sentence and all its modifiers.

suffix an affix attached at the end of a base word that changes the meaning and the function of the word.

summarizing a comprehension strategy in which the reader constructs a brief statement that contains the essential ideas of a passage.

syllable a minimal unit of sequential speech sounds comprised of a vowel sound or a vowel-sound combination.

symbolism the use of one thing to represent something else to represent an idea in a concrete way.

synonym a word that means the same as another word.

syntax the grammatical pattern or structure of word order in sentences, clauses, and phrases.

tense the way in which verbs indicate past, present, and future time of action.

text structure the various patterns of ideas that are built into the organization of a written work.

theme a major idea or proposition that provides an organizing concept through which, by study, students gain depth of understanding.

topic sentence a sentence intended to express the main idea of a paragraph or passage.

tragedy a literary work, often a play, in which the main character suffers conflicts and which presents a serious theme and has an unfortunate ending.

usage the way in which a native language or dialect is used by the members of the community.

verb a word that expresses an action or state that occurs in a predicate of a sentence; an irregular verb is a verb that does not follow normal patterns of inflectional endings that reflect past, present, or future verb tense.

visualizing a comprehension strategy in which the reader constructs a mental picture of a character, setting, or process.

vowel a voiced speech sound and the alphabet letter that represents that sound, made without stoppage or friction of the air flow as it passes through the vocal tract.

vowel digraph a spelling pattern in which two or more letters represent a single vowel sound.

word calling proficiency in decoding with little or no attention to word meaning.

writing also **composition** the process or result of organizing ideas in writing to form a clear message; includes persuasive, expository, narrative, and descriptive forms.

writing process the many aspects of the complex act of producing a piece of writing, including prewriting, drafting, revising, editing/proofreading, and publishing.

Penmanship

SRA Imagine It! develops handwriting skills through weekly Penmanship lessons. The instruction for these lessons appears in the Language Arts part of the lesson in Levels 2 and 3. The purpose of these lessons is to develop important handwriting skills that are necessary for producing legible, properly spaced documents.

In addition to the board, the overhead projector can be a very effective device for teaching penmanship. Students can move their pencils at the same time you form letters on the transparency. It also helps to recite the descriptions or chants that go with each letter.

Penmanship in Levels K and 1

Beginning in kindergarten, the Penmanship lessons expand on the sound/letter instruction by introducing letters that students study in Sounds and Letters. Students learn that those letters are made of four basic lines: curved lines, horizontal lines, vertical lines, and slanted lines.

Next, students learn letter and number formations. Students practice letter formation by writing the letter that is being studied and then by writing words that contain that particular letter. This instruction continues in Level 1 and is tied to the letter formation instruction in Phonics and Fluency.

Cursive Handwriting Models

Penmanship is developed and practiced through Level 3, with cursive instruction beginning in the first unit of Level 2. Students are taught that most cursive letters are comprised of four strokes: undercurve, downcurve, overcurve, and slanted lines. These lessons teach students the essentials of cursive handwriting, such as proper slant; loop; joining; and spacing between letters, words, and sentences. As in the earlier levels, students practice letter formation by writing the letters and then by writing words that contain the particular letter.

The writing exercises progress with each level. Students begin writing words in kindergarten and graduate to writing sentences by the end of Level 1. Level 2 eases students into cursive by having them practice letters, words, and sentences. By Level 3, students are writing complete paragraphs in cursive.

Hand and Paper Positioning

The hand and paper positioning models are for your reference and enhance the written instruction of positioning lessons. The diagrams give you a visual aid so you may better understand and demonstrate an effective technique of positioning.

A right-handed student should hold the pencil loosely about one inch above the point, between the thumb and middle finger. A left-handed student should hold the pencil the same way, but up to one half inch farther away from the point. The index fingers of both writers should rest lightly on the top of the pencil. The wrist should be level and slightly raised from the desk.

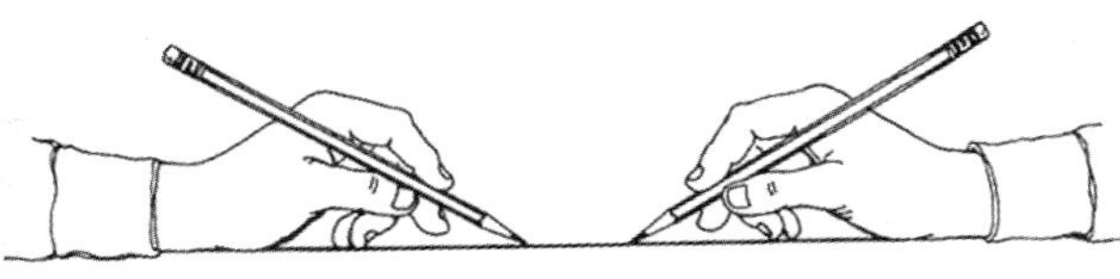

Left-handed writers Right-handed writers

For both kinds of writers, the paper should lie straight in front of the student with the edges parallel to the edges of the desk. A left-handed writer may find it easier to slant the paper slightly to the right and parallel to the left forearm. A right-handed writer's writing hand should be kept well below the writing. The left hand should hold down the paper.

Left-handed writers

Right-handed writers

Cursive Handwriting Models

The models of cursive handwriting provide you with a systematic method for teaching the formation of uppercase and lowercase letters of the alphabet. The dots on the letters indicate starting points. The numbered arrows show the order and direction the lines should go to form the particular letter. You may use the chants to give a step-by-step description of the formation of the letter as you model the formation on the board. Students may also say the chants in unison as they practice the formation, whether they are writing the letter or tracing it on the board.

The four basic cursive strokes diagram provides examples of the strokes that recur frequently in cursive handwriting. Students can form most cursive letters by using one or more of these strokes. The letters in the Penmanship lessons are grouped according to the strokes that are particular to each letter.

undercurve downcurve overcurve slant

Undercurve Letters

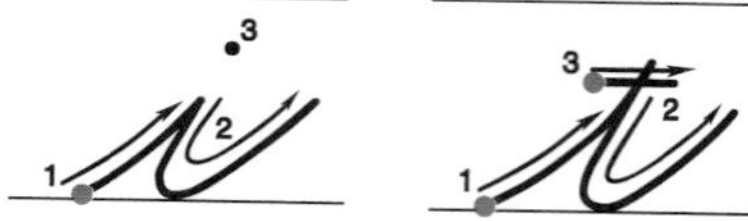

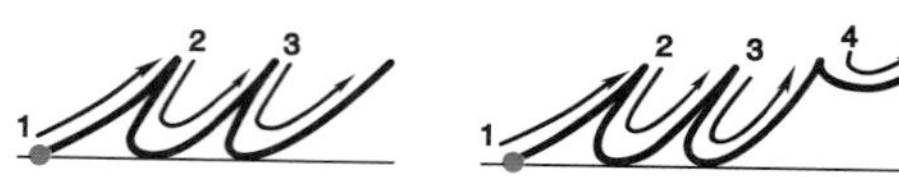

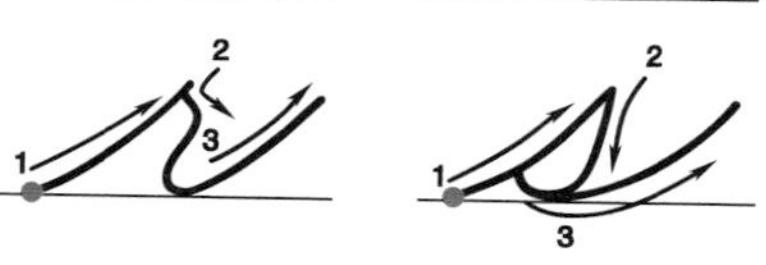

i Starting point, undercurve
Slant down, undercurve to endpoint, dot exactly above: small *i*

t Starting point, undercurve
Slant down, undercurve to endpoint
Starting point, straight across: small *t*

u Starting point, undercurve
Slant down, undercurve
Slant down, undercurve: small *u*

w Starting point, undercurve
Slant down, undercurve, slant down, undercurve, small curve to right: small *w*

r Starting point, undercurve
Slant right
Slant down, undercurve: small *r*

s Starting point, undercurve
Curve down and back, undercurve: small *s*

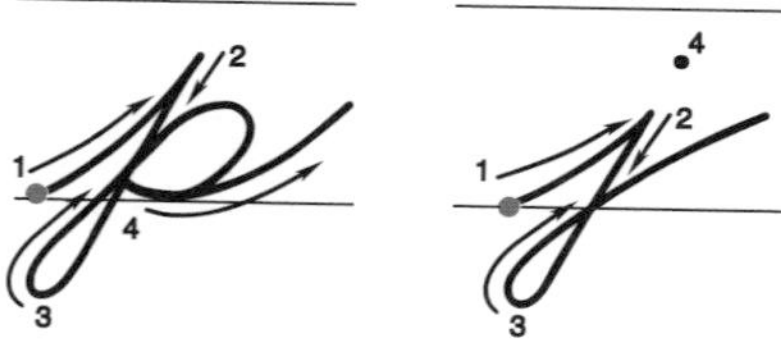

p Starting point, undercurve
Slant, loop back
Overcurve
Curve back, undercurve: small *p*

j Starting point, undercurve
Slant down
Loop back
Overcurve to endpoint
Dot exactly above: small *j*

Downcurve Letters

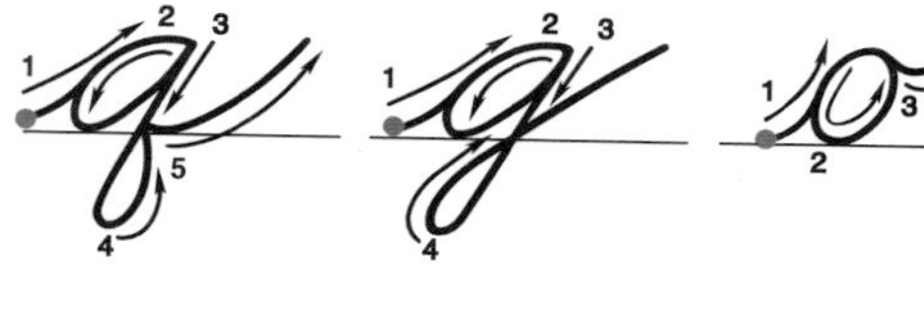

a Starting point, undercurve
Downcurve, undercurve
Slant down, undercurve: small *a*

c Starting point, undercurve
Downcurve, undercurve: small *c*

d Starting point, undercurve
Downcurve, undercurve
Slant down, undercurve: small *d*

q Starting point, undercurve
Downcurve, undercurve
Slant down and loop forward,
Undercurve: small *q*

g Starting point, undercurve
Downcurve, undercurve
Slant down and loop back,
Overcurve: small *g*

o Starting point, undercurve
Downcurve, undercurve
Small curve to right: small *o*

Cursive Handwriting Models

Overcurve Letters

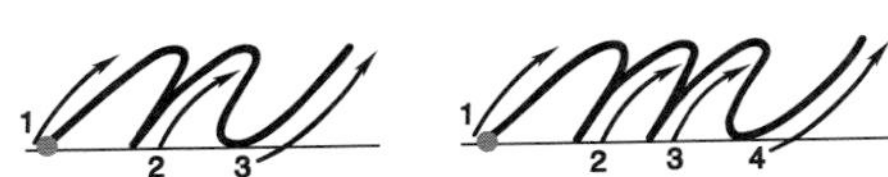

n Starting point, overcurve
Slant down, overcurve
Slant down, undercurve: small *n*

m Starting point, overcurve
Slant down, overcurve
Slant down, overcurve
Slant down, undercurve: small *m*

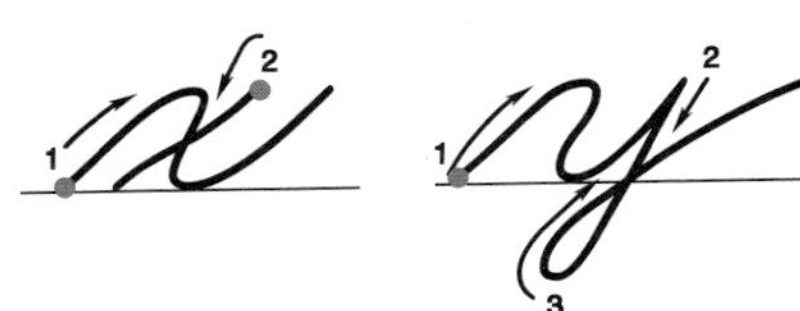

x Starting point, overcurve
Slant down, undercurve to endpoint
Starting point slant down: small *x*

y Starting point, overcurve
Slant down
Undercurve, slant down
Loop back into overcurve: small *y*

z Starting point, overcurve
Slant down, overcurve, down
Loop into overcurve: small *z*

v Starting point, overcurve
Slant down
Undercurve
Small curve to right: small *v*

Letters with Loops

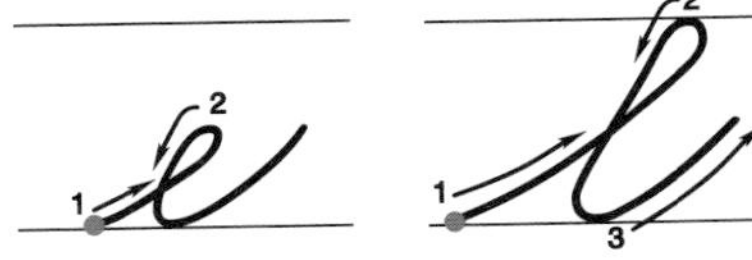

e Starting point, undercurve
Loop back, slant down
Undercurve: small *e*

l Starting point, undercurve
Loop back, slant down
Undercurve: small *l*

h Starting point, undercurve
Loop back, slant down
Overcurve, slant down
Undercurve: small *h*

k Starting point, undercurve
Loop back, slant down
Overcurve, curve forward and under
Slant down, undercurve: small *k*

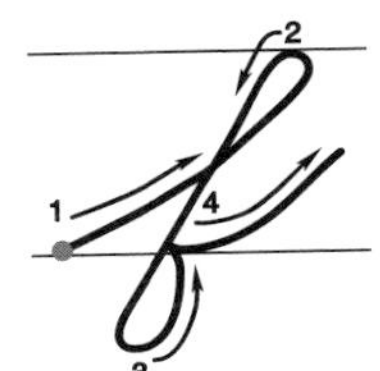

f Starting point, undercurve
Loop back, slant down
Loop forward into undercurve:
small *f*

b Starting point, undercurve
Loop back, slant down
Undercurve, small curve to right:
small *b*

Cursive Handwriting Models

Downcurve Letters

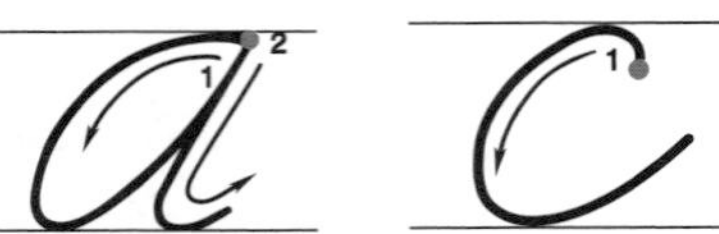

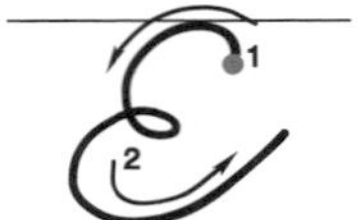

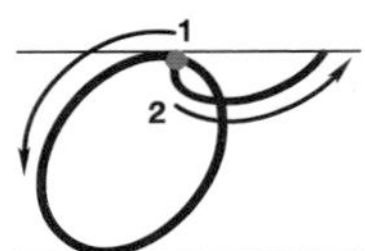

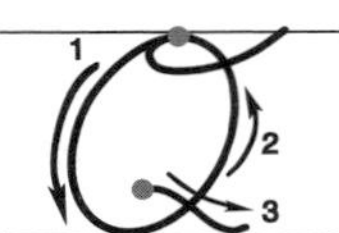

A Starting point, downcurve
Undercurve to starting point
Slant down, undercurve: capital *A*

C Starting point, downcurve
Undercurve: capital *C*

E Starting point, downcurve
Loop back, downcurve
Undercurve: capital *E*

O Starting point, downcurve
left into undercurve
Loop and curve right: capital *O*

Q Starting point, downcurve
Left into undercurve
Loop and curve right
Starting point, slant down right: capital *Q*

Overcurve Letters

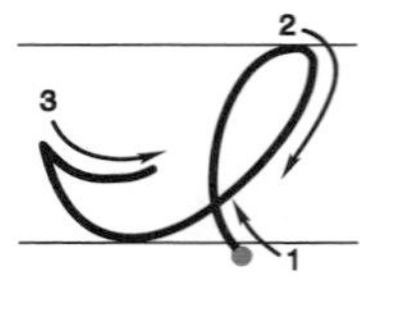

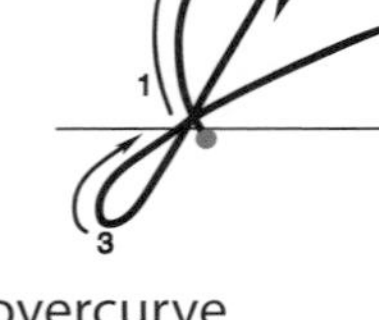

I Starting point, overcurve
Curve down and up
Curve right, capital *I*

J Starting point, overcurve
Slant down and loop back
Overcurve: capital *J*

Letters with Loops

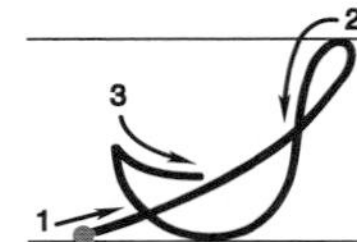

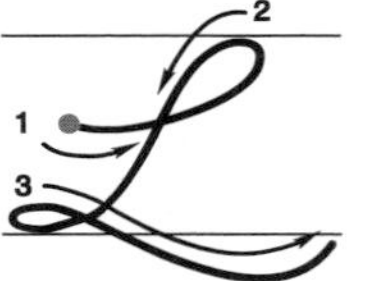

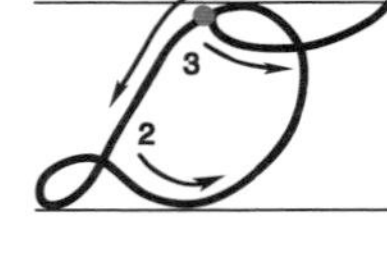

G Starting point, undercurve
Loop, curve up
Double curve, curve up
Curve right: capital *G*

S Starting point, undercurve
Loop, curve down and up
Curve right: capital *S*

L Starting point, undercurve
Loop, curve down and loop
Curve under: capital *L*

D Starting point, slant down
Loop, curve down and up
Loop and curve right: capital *D*

Cursive Handwriting Models

Undercurve-Slant Letters

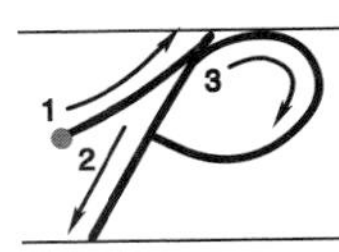
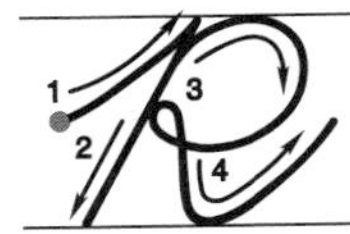

P Starting point, undercurve
Slant down, retrace up
Curve forward and back: capital *P*

R Starting point, undercurve
Slant down, retrace up
Curve forward to slant
Curve forward
Undercurve: capital *R*

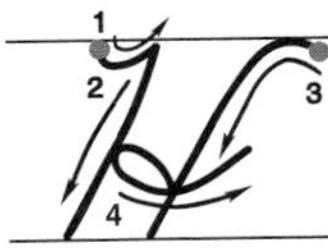
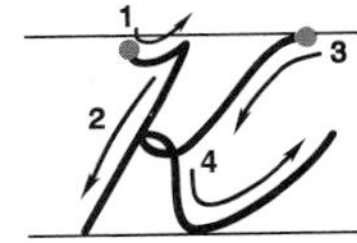

H Starting point, undercurve
Slant down to end point
Starting point
Curve back and slant down
Retrace up slant, loop left and curve right: capital *H*

K Starting point, undercurve
Slant down to end point
Starting point
Doublecurve back to slant
Curve forward
Undercurve up: capital *K*

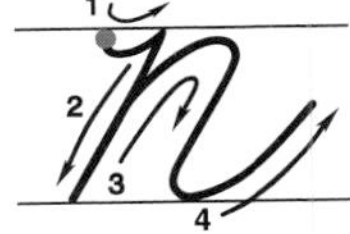

M Starting point, undercurve
Slant down
Retrace up slant, overcurve
Slant down, retrace up slant
Overcurve down into undercurve: capital *M*

N Starting point, undercurve
Slant down
Retrace up slant
Overcurve down into undercurve: capital *N*

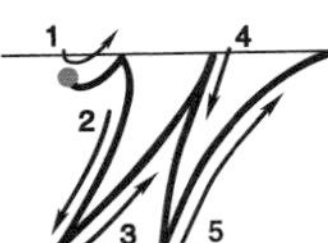

U Starting point, undercurve
Slant down into undercurve
Slant down, undercurve: capital *U*

W Starting point, undercurve
Curve forward, slant down into undercurve
Slant down into undercurve
Overcurve: capital *W*

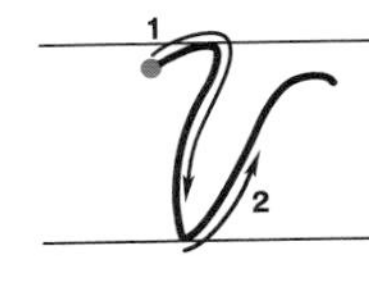
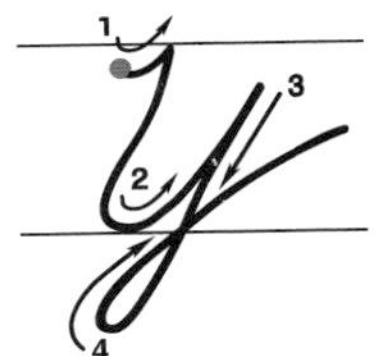

V Starting point, undercurve
Curve forward and slant down, undercurve up and overcurve: capital *V*

Y Starting point, undercurve
Slant down, undercurve up
Slant down, loop back
Overcurve: capital *Y*

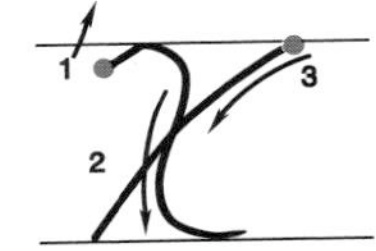

X Starting point, undercurve
Curve forward, slant down
Undercurve
Starting point, slant down: capital *X*

B Starting point, undercurve
Slant down, retrace up
Curve forward, loop
Curve forward and back
Curve right: capital *B*

Doublecurve Letters

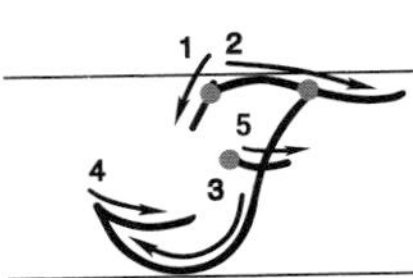

F Starting point, slant down
Curve up and right to end point
Starting point
Slant down, curve up and right
Starting point, across: capital *F*

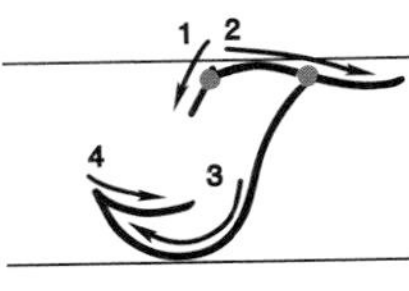

T Starting point, slant down
Curve up and right to end point
Starting point
Slant down, curve up and right: capital *T*

Curve Forward Letter

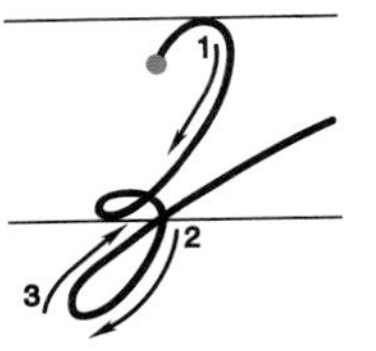

Z Starting point, curve forward
Slant down
Overcurve, curve down
Loop into overcurve: capital *Z*

Numbers

0 Starting point, curving left all the way around to starting point: *0*

1 Starting point, straight down: *1*

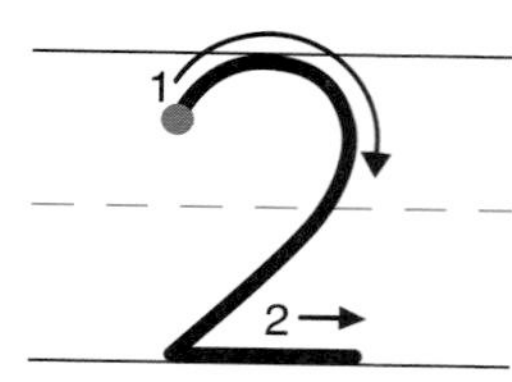

2 Starting point, around right, slanting left and straight across right: *2*

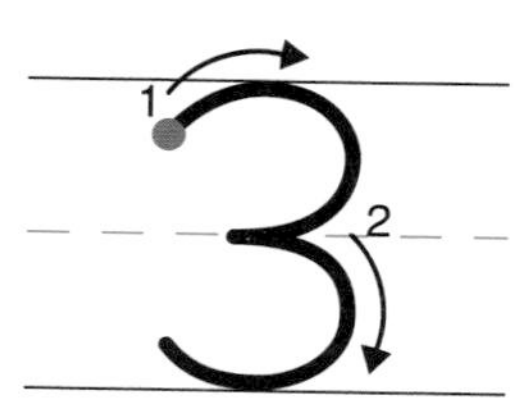

3 Starting point, around right, in at the middle, around right: *3*

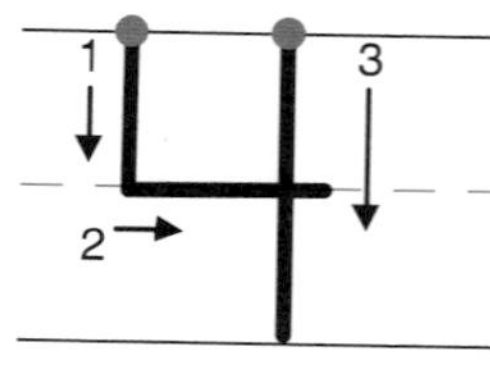

4 Starting point, straight down
Straight across right
Starting point, straight down, crossing line: *4*

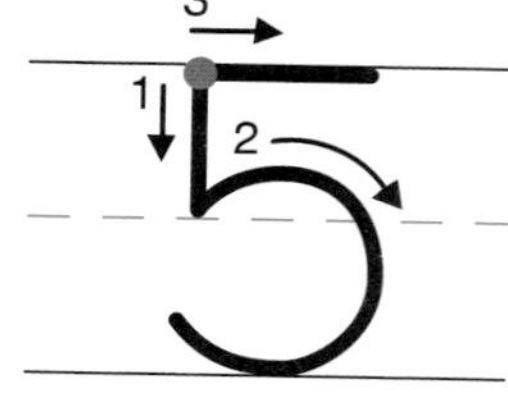

5 Starting point, straight down, curving around right and up
Starting point, straight across right: *5*

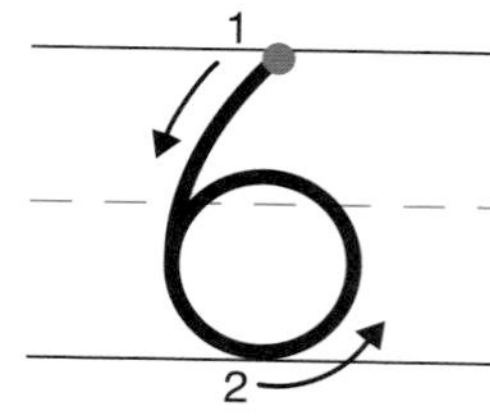

6 Starting point, slanting left, around the bottom curving up around right and into the curve: 6

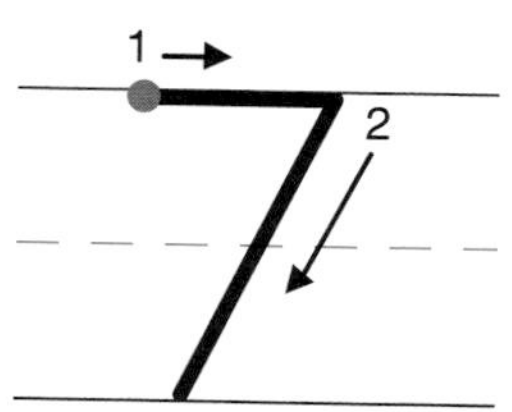

7 Starting point, straight across right, slanting down left: *7*

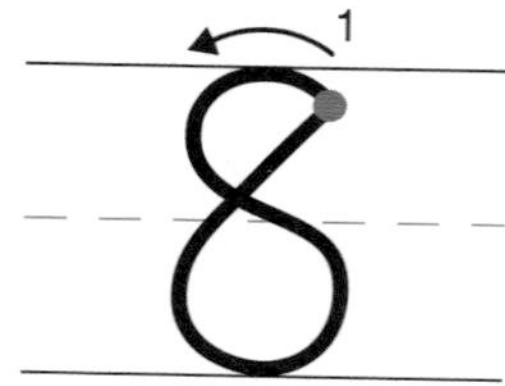

8 Starting point, curving left, curving down and around right, slanting up right to starting point: *8*

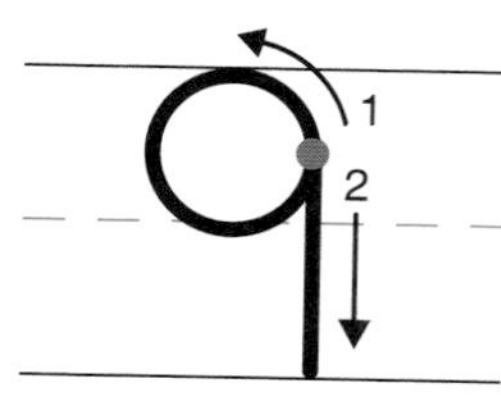

9 Starting point, curving around left all the way, straight down: *9*

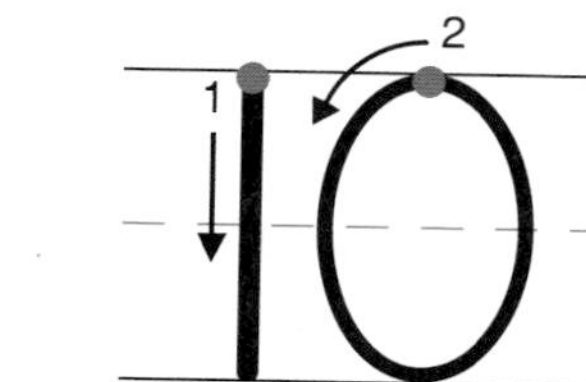

10 Starting point, straight down
Starting point, curving left all the way around to starting point: *10*

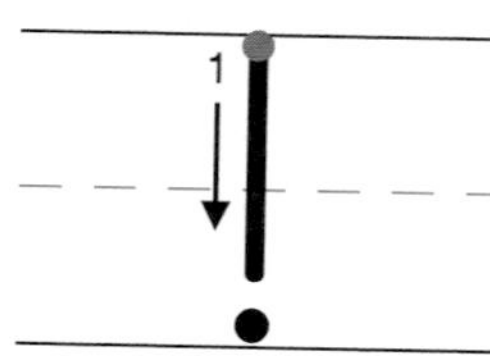

! Starting point, straight down
Dot exactly below: exclamation point

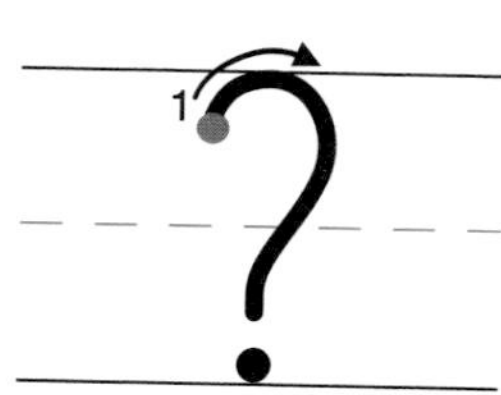

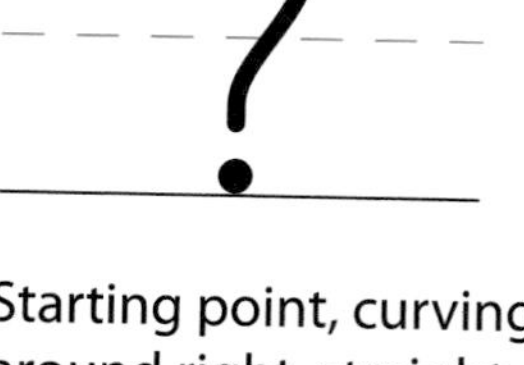

? Starting point, curving around right, straight down
Dot exactly below: question mark

High-Frequency Word List

Level 2 High-Frequency Words

again	done	grow	new	say	try
always	draw	has	off	seven	under
animal	drink	hold	once	show	upon
another	eight	hurt	only	sing	us
ate	fall	keep	open	together	use
because	far	kind	our	small	warm
been	fast	laugh	own	soon	wash
best	find	learn	people	sound	water
better	first	light	pick	start	which
black	fly	live	picture	stop	white
both	found	made	place	tell	who
bring	full	many	play	ten	why
buy	funny	may	please	thank	wish
carry	gave	much	pull	these	work
clean	give	must	read	those	write
cold	goes	myself	round	three	
does	great	never	run	today	

Level 3 High-Frequency Words

above	close	head	name	second	took
air	each	hear	near	set	trees
almost	earth	high	need	should	turned
along	end	home	next	side	until
also	enough	house	night	still	watch
answer	even	land	often	story	while
back	ever	large	other	such	without
began	eyes	last	paper	talk	words
between	face	letters	part	than	world
book	feet	might	plants	things	years
change	following	more	point	thought	
children	hand	most	same	through	
city	hard	move	school	time	

Introduction to Sounds

Lesson	Phonics and Word Structure Skills	Decodable Book/Story
Getting Started		
Day 1	/s/ spelled *s, ss*; /m/ spelled *m;* /t/ spelled *t, tt;* /d/ spelled *d;* /n/ spelled *n;* /h/ spelled *h_*; /a/ spelled *a*	1 Nat, Nan, and Sam
Day 2	/l/ spelled *l* and *ll;* /b/ spelled *b;* /p/ spelled *p;* /k/ spelled *c, k;* /r/ spelled *r;* /i/ spelled *i;* /f/ spelled *f* and *ff;* /g/ spelled *g;* /j/ spelled *j;* /ks/ spelled ■*x;* /o/ spelled *o;* /e/ spelled *e, _ea_*	2 A Pal 3 Help
Day 3	/w/ spelled *w_*; /kw/ spelled *qu_*; /v/ spelled *v;* /y/ spelled *y_*; /z/ spelled *z, zz, _s;* /u/ spelled *u;* /ch/ spelled *ch;* /th/ spelled *th;* /sh/ spelled *sh;* /hw/ spelled *wh_*; /ar/ spelled ar; closed syllables	4 Fast Sam 5 Stars
Day 4	/j/ spelled ■*dge;* /k/ spelled ■*ck;* /ch/ spelled ■*tch;* /ng/ spelled ■*ng;* /nk/ spelled ■*nk;* /ks/ spelled ■*x;* Short Vowels; Closed Syllables; /er/ spelled *er, ir,* and *ur, ear*	6 Midge 7 Fran and Ann
Day 5	/or/ spelled *or, ore;* /ar/ spelled *ar;* Syllable *-le;* ə + /l/, including words with *el, il, al;* Review	8 Tell Your Pals 9 Riddles 10 Fran's Story
Unit 1		
Lesson 1	/ā/ spelled *a* and *a_e;* /ē/ spelled *e* and *e_e;* /ī/ spelled *i* and *i_e;* /ō/ spelled *o* and *o_e;* /ū/ spelled *u* and *u_e;* Antonyms and Synonyms	11 Vic's Big Chore
Lesson 2	/s/ spelled *ce, ci_*; /j/ spelled *ge, gi_*; Compound Words	12 Gem Is Missing
Lesson 3	Review; Related Words	13 More Clover
Lesson 4	/ā/ spelled *ai_, _ay;* /ē/ spelled *ee, ea, _y, _ie_, ey;* Related words	14 On a Train
Lesson 5	/n/ spelled *kn_*; /r/ spelled *wr_*; /f/ spelled *ph;* /m/ spelled *_mb;* /s/ spelled *cy;* Review	15 Bike Races 16 Too Cold?
Unit 2		
Lesson 1	/ī/ spelled *igh, _ie, _y;* Plurals	17 Bats
Lesson 2	/ō/ spelled *oa_, _ow;* Irregular Plurals	18 More Bats
Lesson 3	/ū/ spelled *_ew , _ue;* Homographs	19 Condors
Lesson 4	Review; Homophones	20 Strange Stuff
Lesson 5	/o͞o/ spelled *oo, u, u_e, _ew, _ue;* Review	21 A Visit 22 Migrating Geese
Unit 3		
Lesson 1	/oo/ spelled *oo;* Inflectional Ending *-ing*	23 A Trade
Lesson 2	/ow/ spelled *ow, ou_*; Inflectional Ending *-ed*	24 A Brief History of Money
Lesson 3	/aw/ spelled *au_, aw, augh, ough, al, all;* Comparative and Superlative Adjectives	25 Collecting Baseball Cards
Lesson 4	/oi/ spelled *oi, _oy;* Irregular Comparative and Superlative Adjectives	26 Money Stories
Lesson 5	Contrast /ō/ spelled *_ow* and /ow/ spellings; Contrast /o͞o/ spellings and /ū/ spellings; Review	27 Seven Bank Facts 28 Dad Is Back

Lesson	Word Structure Skills
Unit 4	
Lesson 1	Suffixes *-ly*, *-y*, *-ment*, *-tion*
Lesson 2	Suffixes *-ful*, *-able;* Inflectional Endings *-ed* and *-ing*
Lesson 3	Suffixes *-ity*, *-less*, *-ness*, *-sion*
Lesson 4	Greek and Latin Roots
Lesson 5	Review
Unit 5	
Lesson 1	Prefixes *re-*, *un-*, *pre-*, *mis-*
Lesson 2	Prefixes *bi-*, *mid-*, *dis-*, *auto-*
Lesson 3	Affixes as Syllables; Affixes Used to Change Word Meaning
Lesson 4	Word Families; Multisyllabic Words and Silent Consonants
Lesson 5	Review
Unit 6	
Lesson 1	Unit 1 Review
Lesson 2	Unit 2 Review
Lesson 3	Unit 3 Review
Lesson 4	Unit 4 Review
Lesson 5	Unit 5 Review

Sound/Spelling Card Stories

Card 1: /a/ Lamb

I'm Pam the Lamb, I am.
This is how I tell my Mommy where
I am: /a/ /a/ /a/ /a/ /a/.

I'm Pam the Lamb, I am.
This is how I tell my Daddy where
I am: /a/ /a/ /a/ /a/ /a/.

I'm Pam the Lamb, I am.
That young ram is my brother Sam.
This is how I tell my brother where
I am: /a/ /a/ /a/ /a/ /a/.

I'm Pam the Lamb; I'm happy where
I am.

Can you help me tell my family where
I am?
(Have the children respond.) /a/ /a/ /a/ /a/ /a/

Card 2: /b/ Ball

Bobby loved to bounce his basketball.
He bounced it all day long.
This is the sound the ball made:
/b/ /b/ /b/ /b/ /b/.

One day, while Bobby was bouncing
his basketball,
Bonnie came by on her bike.

Bonnie said, "Hi, Bobby. I have a little
bitty ball.
May I bounce my ball with you?"

Bobby said, "Sure!" and Bonnie
bounced her little bitty ball.
What sound do you think Bonnie's ball
made?
(Encourage a very soft reply.) /b/ /b/ /b/ /b/ /b/

Soon Betsy came by. "Hi, Bobby. Hi, Bonnie," she said.
"I have a great big beach ball. May I bounce my ball with you?"

Bobby and Bonnie said, "Sure!" and Betsy bounced her
big beach ball.
What sound do you think the beach ball made?
(Encourage a louder, slower reply.) /b/ /b/ /b/ /b/ /b/

(Designate three groups, one for each ball sound.)

Now when Bobby, Bonnie, and Betsy bounce their balls
together, this is the sound you hear:
(Have all three groups make their sounds in a chorus.)
/b/ /b/ /b/ /b/ /b/

Card 3: /k/ Camera

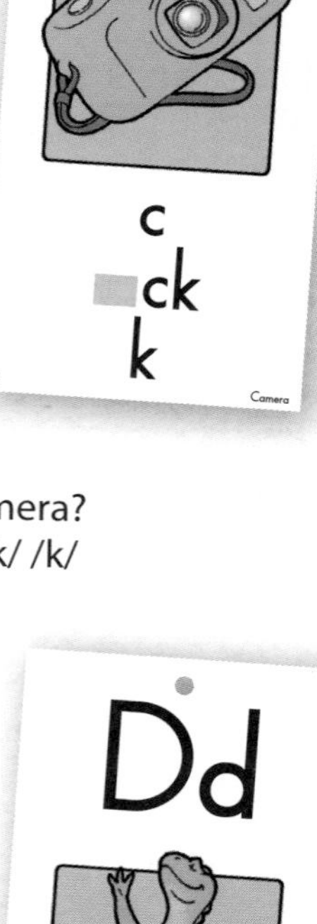

Carlos has a new camera. When he
takes pictures, his camera makes a
clicking sound like this:
/k/ /k/ /k/ /k/ /k/.

In the garden, Carlos takes pictures of
caterpillars crawling on cabbage:
/k/ /k/ /k/ /k/ /k/.

At the zoo, Carlos takes pictures of a
camel, a duck, and a kangaroo:
/k/ /k/ /k/.

In the park, Carlos takes pictures of his
cousin flying a kite: /k/ /k/ /k/ /k/ /k/.

In his room, Carlos takes pictures of his
cute kitten, Cozy: /k/ /k/ /k/ /k/ /k/.

Can you help Carlos take pictures with his camera?
(Have the children join in.) /k/ /k/ /k/ /k/ /k/ /k/ /k/

Card 4: /d/ Dinosaur

Dinah the Dinosaur loves to dance.
She dances whenever she gets the chance.
Whenever that dinosaur dips and whirls,
this is the sound of her dancing twirls:
/d/ /d/ /d/ /d/ /d/ /d/!

Dinah the Dinosaur dances all day.
From dawn to dark, she dances away.
And when Dinah dances, her dinosaur feet
make a thundering, thudding, extremely
loud beat:
(loudly, with an exaggerated rhythm)
/d/ /d/ /d/ /d/ /d/ /d/!

Now if you were a dinosaur just like Dinah,
you would certainly dance just as finely as she.
And if you were a Dino, and you had a chance,
what sound would your feet make when you did a dance?
(Have the children join in.) /d/ /d/ /d/ /d/ /d/ /d/

Card 5: /e/ Hen

Jem's pet hen likes to peck, peck, peck.
She pecks at a speck on the new red deck.
This is how her pecking sounds:
/e/ /e/ /e/ /e/ /e/.

Jem's pet hen pecks at corn in her pen.
She pecks ten kernels, then pecks again.
This is how her pecking sounds:
/e/ /e/ /e/ /e/ /e/.

Jem's hen pecks at a cracked egg shell.
She's helping a chick get out, alive and well.
This is how her pecking sounds:
/e/ /e/ /e/ /e/ /e/.

Can you help Jem's hen peck?
(Have children say:) /e/ /e/ /e/ /e/ /e/.

Card 6: /f/ Fan

/f/ /f/ /f/ /f/ /f/ /f/—What's that funny sound?
It's Franny the Fan going round and round,
and this is the sound that old fan makes:
/f/ /f/ /f/ /f/ /f/.

When it gets too hot, you see,
Franny cools the family: /f/ /f/ /f/ /f/ /f/.
She fans Father's face
and Foxy's fur
and Felicity's feet.
Hear the Fan whir: /f/ /f/ /f/ /f/ /f/.

Can you make Franny the Fan go fast?
(Have the children say quickly:)
/f/ /f/ /f/ /f/ /f/.
Faster? /f/ /f/ /f/ /f/ /f/
Fastest? /f/ /f/ /f/ /f/ /f/

Card 7: /g/ Gopher

Gary's a gopher.
He loves to gulp down food.
/g/ /g/ /g/ /g/ /g/, gulps the gopher.

Gary the Gopher gulps down grass
because it tastes so good.
/g/ /g/ /g/ /g/ /g/, gulps the gopher.

Gary the Gopher gulps down grapes—
gobs and gobs of grapes.
/g/ /g/ /g/ /g/ /g/, gulps the gopher.

Gary the Gopher gobbles green beans
and says once more,
/g/ /g/ /g/ /g/ /g/. He's such a hungry gopher!

Gary the Gopher gobbles in the garden
until everything is gone.

What sound does Gary the Gopher make?
(Ask the children to join in.) /g/ /g/ /g/ /g/ /g/

Card 8: /h/ Hound

Harry the Hound dog hurries around.
Can you hear Harry's hurrying hound-
dog sound?
This is the sound Harry's breathing
makes when he hurries:
/h/ /h/ /h/ /h/ /h/ /h/!

When Harry the Hound dog sees a
hare hop by,
he tears down the hill, and his four
feet fly.
Hurry, Harry, hurry! /h/ /h/ /h/ /h/ /h/ /h/!

How Harry the Hound dog loves to hunt
and chase!
He hurls himself from place to place.
Hurry, Harry, hurry! /h/ /h/ /h/ /h/ /h/ /h/!

When Harry the Hound dog sees a big skunk roam,
he howls for help and heads for home.

What sound does Harry make when he hurries?
(Have the children answer.) /h/ /h/ /h/ /h/ /h/ /h/

Card 9: /i/ Pig

This is Pickles the Pig.
If you tickle Pickles, she gets the giggles.
This is the sound of her giggling:
/i/ /i/ /i/ /i/ /i/.

Tickle Pickles the Pig under her chin.
Listen! She's giggling: /i/ /i/ /i/ /i/ /i/.
Wiggle a finger in Pickles' ribs.
Listen! She's giggling: /i/ /i/ /i/ /i/ /i/.

Give Pickles the Pig a wink,
and what do you think? First comes a grin.
Then listen!
She's giggling again: /i/ /i/ /i/ /i/ /i/.

Quick! Tickle Pickles the Pig. What will she say?
(Have the children join in.) /i/ /i/ /i/ /i/ /i/

Card 10: /j/ Jump

When Jenny jumps her jump rope,
it sounds like this: /j/ /j/ /j/ /j/ /j/.
When Jackson jumps his jump rope,
it sounds like this: /j/ /j/ /j/ /j/ /j/.

The judges generally agree
that Jenny jumps most rapidly:
(quickly) /j/ /j/ /j/ /j/ /j/.

When Jenny jumps, she jumps to this jingle:
"Jump, jump, jump so quick.
Whenever I jump, I like to kick."
/j/ /j/ /j/ /j/ /j/

The judges generally agree
that Jackson jumps most quietly:
(quietly) /j/ /j/ /j/ /j/ /j/.

When Jackson jumps, he jumps to this jingle:
"Jump, jump, nice and quiet.
See what happens when you try it." /j/ /j/ /j/ /j/ /j/

(to the children) Jump rope like Jenny.
(quickly) /j/ /j/ /j/ /j/ /j/
(to the children) Jump rope like Jackson.
(quietly) /j/ /j/ /j/ /j/ /j/

Card 11: /k/ Camera

Carlos has a new camera. When he takes pictures,
His camera makes a clicking sound like this:
/k/ /k/ /k/ /k/ /k/.

In the garden, Carlos takes pictures of caterpillars crawling on cabbage:
/k/ /k/ /k/ /k/ /k/.

At the zoo, Carlos takes pictures of a camel, a duck, and a kangaroo:
/k/ /k/ /k/.

In the park, Carlos takes pictures of his cousin flying a kite: /k/ /k/ /k/ /k/ /k/
In his room, Carlos takes pictures of his cute kitten, Cozy. /k/ /k/ /k/ /k/ /k/

Can you help Carlos take pictures with his camera?
(Have the children join in.) /k/ /k/ /k/ /k/ /k/ /k/ /k/

Card 12: /l/ Lion

Look! It's Leon the Lion.
Leon loves to lap water from lakes,
and this is the sound the lapping lion makes: /l/ /l/ /l/ /l/ /l/.

Let's join Leon. Quick!
Take a little lick: /l/ /l/ /l/ /l/ /l/.

Are you a thirsty lass or lad?
Then lap until you don't feel bad:
/l/ /l/ /l/ /l/ /l/.

What sound do you make when you lap like Leon the Lion?
(Have the children say:) /l/ /l/ /l/ /l/ /l/.

Card 13: /m/ Monkey

For Muzzy the Monkey, bananas
are yummy.
She munches so many, they fill up
her tummy.
When she eats, she says:
/m/ /m/ /m/ /m/ /m/!

Bananas for breakfast, bananas
for lunch.
Mash them up, mush them up,
munch, munch, munch, munch!
What does Muzzy the Monkey say?
(Have the children say:) /m/ /m/ /m/ /m/ /m/.

Bananas at bedtime? I have a hunch
Muzzy will mash them up, mush them up,
munch, munch, munch, munch!
Then what will Muzzy the Monkey say?
(Have the children say:) /m/ /m/ /m/ /m/ /m/.

Card 14: /n/ Nest

Nine feet up in a neighbor's tree
is a noisy, noisy nest.
I cannot see what's in there,
but it's a noisy pest!
/n/ /n/ /n/ /n/

What is in that noisy nest?
A nervous night owl crying?
A nosy nuthatch chatting?
A nightingale that's sighing?
/n/ /n/ /n/ /n/

I think it's time we take a look,
but please, do not start yapping.
Now I see what's in that nest!
A snoring bluebird napping!
/n/ /n/ /n/ /n/

Card 15: /o/ Fox

Bob the Fox did not feel well at all.
He jogged to the doctor's office.
"Say /o/ Mr. Fox! /o/ /o/ /o/."

"My head is hot, and my throat hurts a lot,"
said the fox.
"Say /o/, Mr. Fox!
"/o/ /o/ /o/ /o/."

"Yes, you've got a rotten cold," said
the doctor.
"Say /o/, Mr. Fox!
"/o/ /o/ /o/."

"Find a spot to sit in the sun," said the doctor.
"Say /o/, Mr. Fox!
"/o/ /o/ /o/."

He sat on a rock in the sun.
Soon he felt much better.
(with a satisfied sigh) "/o/," said Mr. Fox.
/o/ /o/ /o/

Card 16: /p/ Popcorn

Ping and Pong liked to pop corn. As
it cooked, it made this sound:
/p/ /p/ /p/ /p/ /p/ /p/ /p/.

One day Ping poured a whole package of
popcorn into the pot. It made this sound:
/p/ /p/ /p/ /p/ /p/ /p/ /p/.

The popcorn popped and popped. Ping filled
two pots, and still the popcorn popped:
/p/ /p/ /p/ /p/ /p/ /p/ /p/.

Pong filled three pails with popcorn, and still
it kept popping: /p/ /p/ /p/ /p/ /p/ /p/ /p/.

"Call all your pals," said their pop. "We'll have a party."
And the popcorn kept popping.

(Have the children say the /p/ sound very fast.)

Card 17: /kw/ Quacking ducks

Quincy the Duck couldn't quite quack
like all the other quacking ducks.
Oh, he could say /kw/ /kw/ /kw/ /kw/,
but it never seemed just right.

When Quincy tried to quack quietly,
(softly) /kw/ /kw/ /kw/ /kw/
his quack came out loudly.
(loudly) /kw/ /kw/ /kw/ /kw/!

When he tried to quack slowly,
(slowly) /kw/ . . . /kw/ . . . /kw/ . . . /kw/
his quack came out quickly.
(quickly) /kw/ /kw/ /kw/ /kw/!
Quincy just couldn't quack right!

One day Quincy was practicing quacks.
His friend Quip quacked along with him.
"Repeat after me," said Quip.
(quietly) /kw/ /kw/ /kw/ /kw/
But Quincy quacked back,
(in normal voice) /kw/ /kw/ /kw/ /kw/ /kw/!

Quincy still couldn't quack quite right.
But Quincy kept quacking. He said, "I won't quit until I quack
like the best quackers around."
Can you show Quincy how quacking ducks quack?
(Have the children join in.)
/kw/ /kw/ /kw/ /kw/ /kw/ /kw/ /kw/ /kw/

Card 18: /r/ Robot

Little Rosie Robot just runs and runs and runs.
She races round and round to get her chores
all done.
Here's how Rosie sounds when she's working:
/r/ /r/ /r/ /r/ /r/!

Rosie can rake around your roses.
Here comes that running robot!
/r/ /r/ /r/ /r/ /r/!

Rosie can repair your wrecked radio.
Here comes that racing robot!
(softly) /r/ /r/ /r/ /r/ /r/

Rosie can mend your round red rug.
Here comes that roaring robot!
(loudly) /r/ /r/ /r/ /r/ /r/!

Rosie rarely does anything wrong.
But there are two things that Rosie can't
do: rest and relax.
Here comes that roaring robot!

What does she say?

(Have the children call out the answer:)
/r/ /r/ /r/ /r/ /r/.

Card 19: /s/ Sausages

Sue and Sammy had a nice place in
the city.
On Saturday, Sue and Sammy decided
to have sausages for supper.
Sammy put seven sausages in
a skillet. /s/ /s/ /s/ /s/ /s/ /s/ /s/

Soon the smell of sausages filled
the air.
/s/ /s/ /s/ /s/ /s/, sizzled the sausages.

"Pull up a seat, Sue," said Sammy.
"The sausages are almost ready to serve."
/s/ /s/ /s/ /s/ /s/, sizzled the sausages.

Sue and Sammy ate the delicious sausages.
Soon they wanted more, so Sam put six more sausages
in the frying pan.
/s/ /s/ /s/ /s/ /s/ /s/, sizzled the sausages.

If you were cooking sausages with Sammy and Sue,
what sound would the sausages make as they sizzled?
(Have the children join in:) /s/ /s/ /s/ /s/ /s/ /s/

Card 20: /t/ Timer

When Tom Tuttle cooks, he uses
his timer.
Tom Tuttle's timer ticks like this:
/t/ /t/ /t/ /t/ /t/ /t/ /t/

Tonight Tom Tuttle wants tomatoes
on toast.
Tom turns on the oven.
Tom puts tomatoes on toast in the oven.
Tom sets the timer.
The timer will Ding! when Tom's toast
and tomatoes are done.
Until the timer dings,
it ticks: /t/ /t/ /t/ /t/ /t/ /t/ /t/.

Tomatoes on toast takes ten minutes.
/t/ /t/ /t/ /t/ /t/ /t/ /t/
Tom can hardly wait. /t/ /t/ /t/ /t/ /t/ /t/ /t/
He taps out the time: /t/ /t/ /t/ /t/ /t/ /t/ /t/.

What is the sound of Tom Tuttle's ticking timer?
(Have the children join in.) /t/ /t/ /t/ /t/ /t/ /t/ /t/
Ding! Time for dinner, Tom Tuttle!

Card 21: /u/ Tug

Tubby the Tugboat can huff and puff
and push and pull to move big stuff.
/u/ /u/ /u/ /u/ /u/ /u/ /u/
That's the sound of Tubby the Tug.

If a boat is stuck and will not budge,
Tubby the Tugboat can give it a nudge.
/u/ /u/ /u/ /u/ /u/ /u/ /u/
It's Tubby the Trusty Tug.

If a ship is caught in mud and muck,
Tubby the Tugboat can get it unstuck.
/u/ /u/ /u/ /u/ /u/ /u/ /u/
It's Tubby the Trusty Tug.

Can you help Tubby push and pull?
(Have the children join in.)
/u/ /u/ /u/ /u/ /u/ /u/ /u/

Card 22: /v/ Vacuum

Vinny the Vacuum is cleaning again.
Before visitors visit, he always begins.
This is the sound of his very loud voice:
/v/ /v/ /v/ /v/ /v/!
If only that Vinny could clean without noise!

Vinny sucks up the crumbs baby Vicki dropped.
/v/ /v/ /v/ /v/ /v/!
He visits nearly everywhere except the tabletop.
/v/ /v/ /v/ /v/ /v/!
Three vine leaves, two vitamins, part of a vase—
all vanish when Vinny goes over the place!
/v/ /v/ /v/ /v/ /v/

As Vinny vacuums the velvety rug
a van full of visitors starts to drive up.
But Vinny's not done with the very last room!
Will you help Vinny the Vacuum vacuum?
(Ask groups of children to say /v/ in a round to make the continuous sound of a vacuum cleaner.)

Card 23: /w/ Washer

Willie the Washer washed white
clothes all week.
When he washed, he went:
/w/ /w/ /w/ /w/ /w/ /w/ /w/.

All winter, Willie worked well.
/w/ /w/ /w/ /w/ /w/ /w/ /w/
But last Wednesday, Willie was weak.
(softly) /w/ /w/ /w/ /w/ /w/ /w/ /w/
This week, he got worse.
(slower and slower) /w/. . . /w/. . . /w/. . .
Poor Willie was worn out.
(slowly) /w/

Then a worker came and fixed Willie's wires.
Willie felt wonderful.
(more loudly) /w/ /w/ /w/ /w/ /w/ /w/ /w/!
Now Willie can wash and wash wildly!
(quickly) /w/ /w/ /w/ /w/ /w/ /w/ /w/!

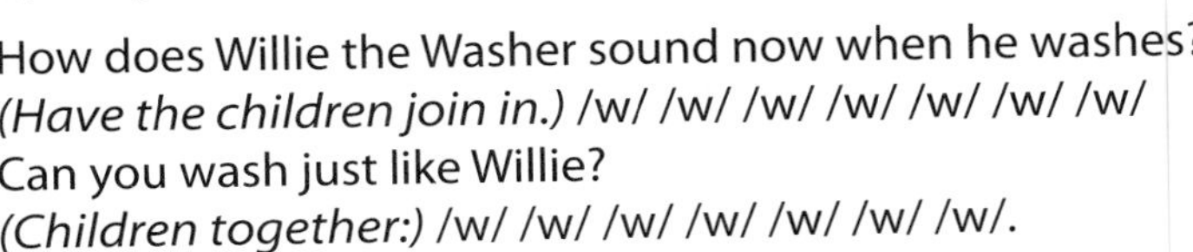

How does Willie the Washer sound now when he washes?
(Have the children join in.) /w/ /w/ /w/ /w/ /w/ /w/ /w/
Can you wash just like Willie?
(Children together:) /w/ /w/ /w/ /w/ /w/ /w/ /w/.

Card 24: /ks/ Exit

Rex is called the Exiting X;
he runs to guard the door.
To get past Rex, make the sound of X:
/ks/ /ks/ /ks/ /ks/.
That is what Rex expects!

The ox knows the sound of X,
so she says /ks/ /ks/ /ks/ /ks/
and gets past Rex.

The fox knows the sound of X,
so he says /ks/ /ks/ /ks/ /ks/
and gets past Rex.

Can you say /ks/ /ks/ /ks/ /ks/
and get past Rex the Exiting X?
(Have the children respond:) /ks/ /ks/ /ks/ /ks/!
Did we get past Rex?
(Have the children say:) Yes!

Card 25: /y/ Yaks

Yolanda and Yoshiko are yaks.
They don't yell.
They don't yelp.
They don't yodel.
They don't yawn.
These young yaks just yak.
Yakety-yak, yakety-yak!
Can you hear the sound they make?
/y/ /y/ /y/ /y/ /y/ /y/ /y/

Yolanda and Yoshiko yak in the yard.
/y/ /y/ /y/ /y/ /y/ /y/ /y/
They yak on their yellow yacht.
/y/ /y/ /y/ /y/ /y/ /y/ /y/
They yak in the yam patch.
/y/ /y/ /y/ /y/ /y/ /y/ /y/
These yaks yak all year!
/y/ /y/ /y/ /y/ /y/ /y/ /y/

Do you think these yaks like to yak?
(Have the children answer:) Yes!
(Ask the children to yak like Yolanda and Yoshiko.)

Card 26: /z/ Zipper

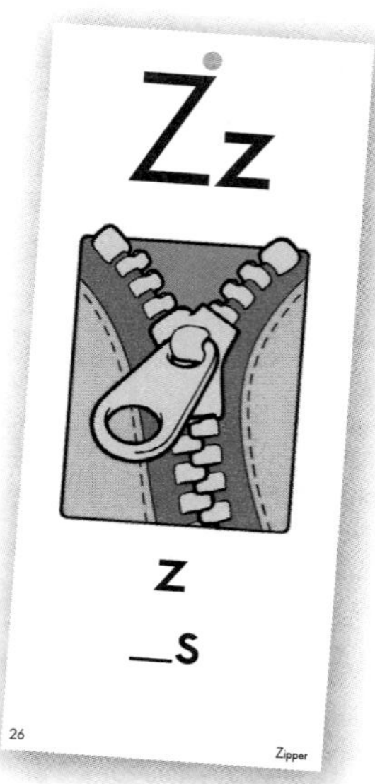

Zack's jacket has a big long zipper.
The zipper zips like this: /z/ /z/ /z/ /z/.

When little Zack goes out to play,
he zips the zipper up this way:
/z/ /z/ /z/ /z/.
Later, when he comes back in,
Zack zips the zipper down again.
/z/ /z/ /z/ /z/

Can you help Zack zip his jacket zipper?
(Have the children join in.) /z/ /z/ /z/ /z/

Card 32: /sh/ Shell

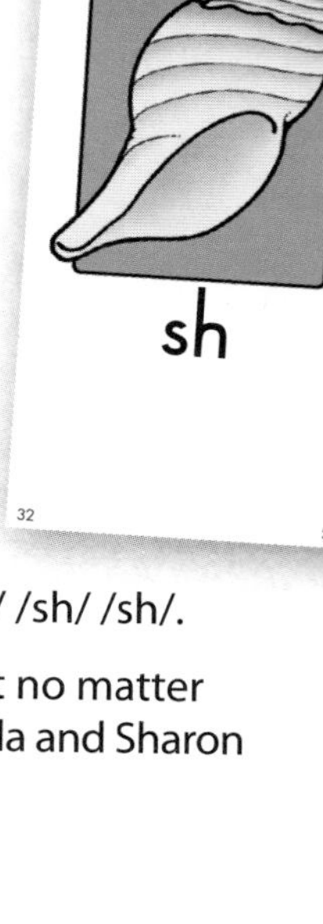

Sheila and Sharon went to the seashore.
They saw lots of shells.
Sheila rushed from shell to shell.
Sharon held a shell to Sheila's ear.

"Do you hear anything?" asked Sharon.
"Yes, it sounds like the ocean crashing on
the shore," shouted Sheila,
"/sh/ /sh/ /sh/ /sh/ /sh/."

"Let's try different-shaped shells," said Sharon.
She found a big shell. It made a loud
/sh/ /sh/ /sh/ /sh/.
Sheila found a small shell.
It made a soft /sh/ /sh/ /sh/ /sh/.
They found a thin shell.
It made a high /sh/ /sh/ /sh/ /sh/.
They found a fat shell. It made a deep /sh/ /sh/ /sh/ /sh/.

Sheila and Sharon listened to lots of shells. But no matter what the size and shape, what do you think Sheila and Sharon heard in every shell?
(Have the children join in.) /sh/ /sh/ /sh/ /sh/

Card 33: /th/ Thimble

Theodore Thimble is a thinker.
Theodore thinks and thinks and thinks.
And when he thinks, he rubs his head.
/th/ /th/ /th/ /th/ /th/ /th/ /th/ /th/ /th/

Theodore thinks of thumbs—
thin thumbs,
thick thumbs,
all different kinds of thumbs.
/th/ /th/ /th/ /th/ /th/ /th/ /th/ /th/ /th/

Theodore thinks of thread—
red thread,
blue thread,
all different-colored thread.
/th/ /th/ /th/ /th/ /th/ /th/ /th/ /th/ /th/

Thread and thumb,
thumb and thread.
These are the thoughts
in Theodore's head.
/th/ /th/ /th/ /th/ /th/ /th/ /th/ /th/ /th/

Card 34: /ch/ Chipmunk

Chipper the chipmunk is cheerful and chubby.
He chats and he chatters all day:
/ch/ /ch/ /ch/ /ch/ /ch/ /ch/
He sits on a chimney.
Can you hear him chat?
He chats and he chatters this way:
/ch/ /ch/ /ch/ /ch/ /ch/ /ch/.

Chipper stuffs cherries into his cheek.
Then he chatters /ch/ /ch/ /ch/ /ch/ /ch/ /ch/.
Chipper likes chestnuts and acorns to eat.
Then he chatters /ch/ /ch/ /ch/ /ch/ /ch/ /ch/.

Can you children chatter like Chipper?
(Have the children answer.)
/ch/ /ch/ /ch/ /ch/ /ch/ /ch/

Now chat with the chipmunk child beside you.
(Ask partners to have chipmunk conversations.)
/ch/ /ch/ /ch/ /ch/ /ch/ /ch/

Card 35: /hw/ Whales

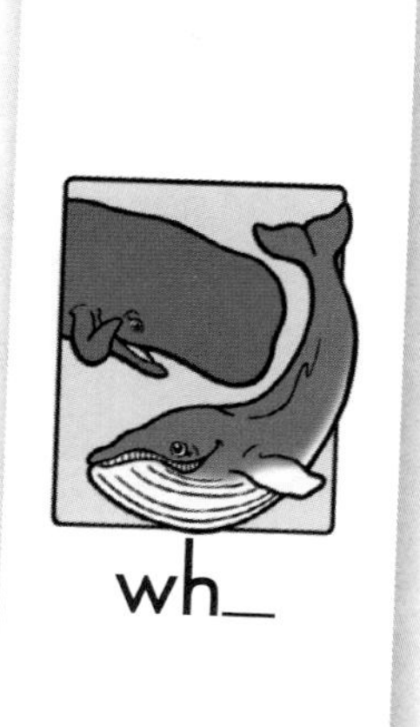

Look! It's Whitney the Whispering Whale!
Listen to her whisper: /hw/ /hw/ /hw/ /hw/ /hw/.

When Whitney meets with other whales,
she entertains them, telling tales.
She whispers: /hw/ /hw/ /hw/ /hw/ /hw/.
She's Whitney the Whispering Whale.

What ocean wonders does Whitney relate?
Does she whisper of whirlpools or whales
that are great?
We're only people, so we'll never guess.
She's Whitney the Whispering Whale!
/hw/ /hw/ /hw/.

Whatever Whitney whispers must be fun.
The other whales whistle when she's done.
They whoop and whack the white-capped waves.
They love Whitney the Whispering Whale! /hw/ /hw/ /hw/

If you were Whitney, what sounds would you whisper
to your whale friends as they gathered to listen?
(Have the children whisper:) /hw/ /hw/ /hw/ /hw/ /hw/

Card 36: /ng/ Gong

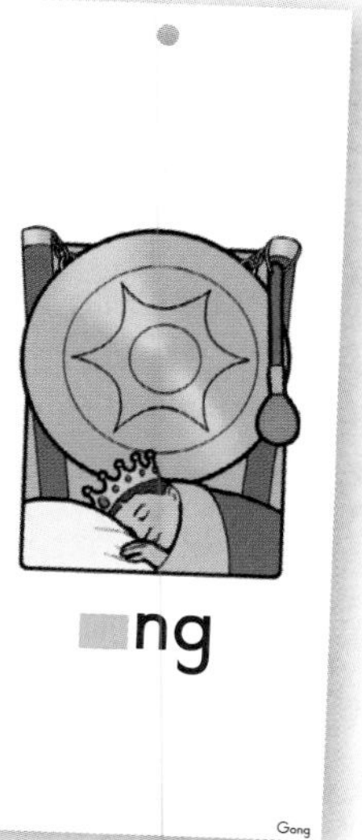

The young king has slept much
too long.
Let's go and awaken the king with
a gong.

A pinging gong? It makes a quiet song:
(softly) /ng/ /ng/ /ng/ /ng/ /ng/.

That gong is wrong.
(softly) /ng/ /ng/ /ng/ /ng/
We need a louder gong!

A dinging gong? It makes this song:
(a bit louder) /ng/ /ng/ /ng/ /ng/ /ng/ /ng/.

That, too, is wrong.
(as before) /ng/ /ng/ /ng/ /ng/
We need an even louder gong!

A clanging gong?
It makes this song:
(loudly) /ng/ /ng/ /ng/ /ng/ /ng/!

That's just the thing! /ng/ /ng/ /ng/ /ng/ /ng/!
That's the gong we needed all along!

Now, which gong should we bring to awaken the King?
(Have children make the /ng/ sound loud enough to wake the king.) /ng/ /ng/ /ng/ /ng/ /ng/!

Card 37: /nk/ Skunk

Sammy the Skunk
finds his skates in the trunk.
He thinks he'll go skating today.
Once at the rink,
poor Sammy does think
his pink nose feels funny some way.
/nk/ /nk/ /nk/

Home from the rink
he gets hot soup to drink.
Sammy hopes his cold slinks away.
/nk/ /nk/ /nk/ /nk/

Then the poor skunk
spends the night in his bunk.
Sammy's sneezes and honks do stay.
/nk/ /nk/ /nk/ /nk/ /nk/

Now the sun winks,
the skunk's eyes start to blink.
Sammy gets up and feels okay!
Sammy the Skunk finds his skates in the trunk.
He thinks he'll go skating today.

Can you make the sound Sammy the Skunk makes when he has a cold?

(Have the students join in.) /nk/ /nk/ /nk/ /nk/ /nk/

Card 38: /or/ Stork

Orville McCormick was quite a stork.
He liked to eat pork while holding a fork.
He also ate corn while blowing a horn:
/or/ /or/ /or/ /or/ /or/ /or/ /or/ /or/

Orville ran out of corn and needed more pork.
So he flew to the store and tore through the door
before the rain came and started to pour.
/or/ /or/ /or/ /or/ /or/ /or/ /or/

He was so happy now with his pork and his corn
that all he could say was "/or/ /or/ /or/ /or/!"

Card 39: /ar/ Armadillo

Arthur Armadillo likes to whistle,
hum, and sing.
But when he gets a head cold,
his voice won't do a thing.

To sing and still sound charming—
and not sound so alarming—
Arthur has thought up the thing
of very often gargling.

Then Arthur Armadillo sounds like this:
/ar/ /ar/ /ar/ /ar/ /ar/.
Arthur gargles in the park.
/ar/ /ar/ /ar/ /ar/ /ar/
He gargles in the dark.
/ar/ /ar/ /ar/ /ar/ /ar/
He gargles on the farm.
/ar/ /ar/ /ar/ /ar/ /ar/
He gargles in the barn.
/ar/ /ar/ /ar/ ar/ /ar/_
Arthur is great at gargling!
/ar/ /ar/ /ar/ /ar/ /ar/

What does Arthur Armadillo's gargling sound like?
(Have the children respond.) /ar/ /ar/ /ar/ /ar/ /ar/

Card 40: /er/ Bird

Bertie the Bird is the oddest bird
that anyone has ever heard.
He doesn't caw like a crow or a gull,
or tweet like a robin or a wren.
Instead, he makes a chirping sound—
over and over again!
/er/ /er/ /er/ /er/ /er/ /er/!

Bert can't fly, since his wings are too short.
He arranges his feathers in curls.
He admits, "I've short wings and I don't really sing,
but I still am an interesting bird!"
/er/ /er/ /er/ /er/ /er/ /er/

Can you chirp like Bertie the Bird?
(Have children say:) /er/ /er/ /er/ /er/ /er/ /er/!

Card 41: /o͞o/ Goo

What can be making that sound?
Could it be a new flute playing a tune?
No. It's goo!
/o͞o/ /o͞o/ /o͞o/ /o͞o/

The goo is oozing all over my hand.
/o͞o/ /o͞o/ /o͞o/ /o͞o/
The goo is oozing on my boots.
/o͞o/ /o͞o/ /o͞o/ /o͞o/

The goo is oozing off the roof.
The goo is oozing everywhere!
/o͞o/ /o͞o/ /o͞o/ /o͞o/
The goo is as sticky as glue.
It is as thick as stew.
/o͞o/ /o͞o/ /o͞o/ /o͞o/

Soon the goo will fill the school!
/o͞o/ /o͞o/ /o͞o/ /o͞o/
Soon the goo will reach the moon!
/o͞o/ /o͞o/ /o͞o/ /o͞o/

What sound does the oozing goo make?
(Have the children join in.) /o͞o/ /o͞o/ /o͞o/ /o͞o/

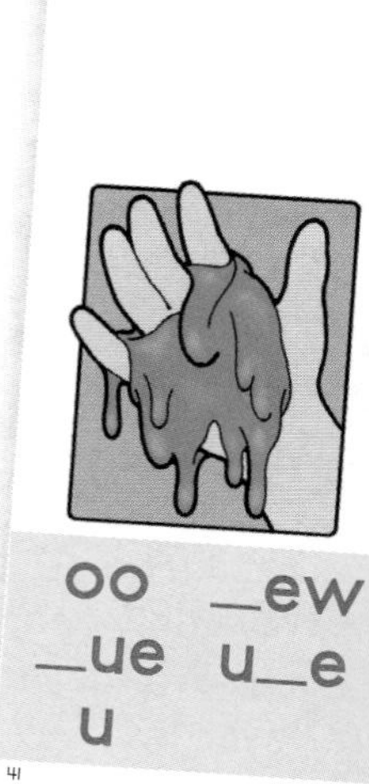

Card 42: /o͝o/ Foot

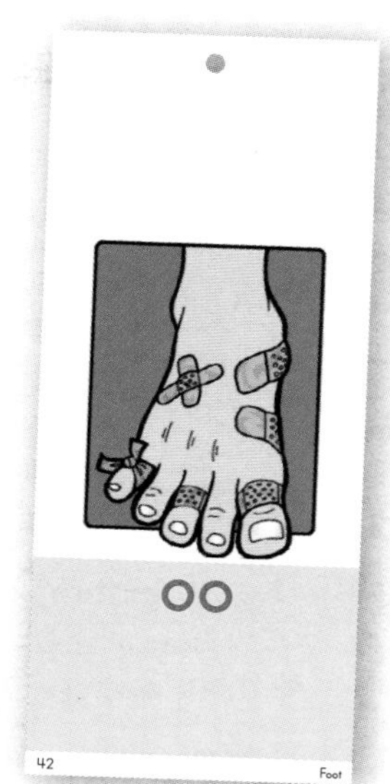

Mr. Hood took off his shoes and socks
and went out walking in the woods.
He kicked a rock and hurt his foot.
/o͝o/ /o͝o/ /o͝o/ /o͝o/

"Look, look!" said Mr. Hood. "There's a
babbling, bubbling brook. I'll walk
in the brook, so I won't hurt my foot."

So he stepped in the water, and guess what?
/o͝o/ /o͝o/ /o͝o/ /o͝o/
Mr. Hood stepped on a hook!
/o͝o/ /o͝o/ /o͝o/ /o͝o/
Mr. Hood stood. He shook his foot.
/o͝o/ /o͝o/ /o͝o/ /o͝o/

"This isn't good," said Mr. Hood.
"I think I'll go home and read a book.
At least that won't hurt my foot."
(Have the children join in.) /o͝o/ /o͝o/ /o͝o/ /o͝o/

Card 43: /ow/ Cow

Wow! Can you see poor Brownie
the Cow?
She got stung by a bee, and look at
her now!
She jumps up and down with an
/ow/ /ow/ /ow/ /ow/.

Poor Brownie found that a big
buzzing sound
meant bees all around—in the air,
on the ground.
Just one little bee gave Brownie a sting.
Now you can hear poor Brownie sing:
/ow/ /ow/ /ow/ /ow/.

Now if you were a cow and a bee found you,
you'd probably jump and shout out too!
(Have the children join in.) /ow/ /ow/ /ow/ /ow/

Card 44: /aw/ Hawk

Hazel the Hawk never cooks her food;
instead, she eats it raw.
And when she thinks of dinnertime
she caws: /aw/ /aw/ /aw/ /aw/.

Hazel the Hawk likes rabbits and mice
and catches them with her claws.
In August, she flies high above the fields
and spies them below, in the straw.
Sometimes she even snatches a snake!
And when she's caught one, she caws:
/aw/ /aw/ /aw/ /aw/.

If you were a hawk thinking of dinnertime,
what do you think you'd say?
(Have the children answer.) /aw/ /aw/ /aw/ /aw/

Card 45: /oi/ Coil

Boing! Boing! Boing! Boing!
Roy the Coil is a bouncing toy,
and this is the sound of his bounce:
/oi/ /oi/ /oi/ /oi/ /oi/.

Doing! Doing! Doing! Doing!
Roy the Coil just dances for joy.
This is the sound of his dance:
/oi/ /oi/ /oi/ /oi/ /oi/.

Ke-boing! Ke-boing!
Roy the Coil springs over a boy.
What springing sound does he make?
(Have the children join in.)
/oi/ /oi/ /oi/ /oi/ /oi/

Rubrics

Comprehension Strategy Rubrics

The following rubrics can be used to gauge students' growing knowledge of the comprehension strategies and how adept they are becoming in their use. Use the rubrics as a guide because students will probably develop strategies of their own. The important thing to consider is whether students are becoming strategic, active readers—do they employ these and other strategies, or do they continue to simply plow through text, unaware of any problems they might be having? The rubrics indicate the types of behaviors strategic readers use and will help you identify the growing facility your students can gain in dealing with text of all sorts.

Adjusting Reading Speed

- The student knows the text is not making sense and stops to reread.
- The student identifies the specific part of the text that is not making sense and rereads only that part.
- The student changes reading speed in reaction to the demands of the text.
- The student adjusts reading rate to skim or scan for specific information.

Asking Questions

- The student stops to ask questions—any question.
- The student asks questions directly related to the text.
- The student asks *who, what, why, when, where,* or *how* questions as opposed to yes or no questions.
- The student asks questions that help clarify information in the text.

Clarifying

- The student recognizes when a word or idea is not making sense.
- The student uses decoding skills to read unfamiliar words.
- The student uses structural elements in words to read them.
- The student uses structural elements, context, and questioning to clarify the meanings of unfamiliar words.

Making Connections

- The student makes connections between prior knowledge and information in the text.
- The student makes connections between or relates personal experiences to what is read in the text (text-to-self connections).
- The student makes connections across or relates information from different selections (text-to-text connections).
- The student makes connections or relates information between what is happening in the text to what is happening in the world today (text-to-world connections).

Predicting

- The student stops to make a prediction about the text.
- The student identifies the clues in the text used to make a prediction.
- The student uses clues in the text and prior knowledge to make a prediction.
- The student recognizes when a prediction is or is not confirmed by the text.

Summarizing

- The student retells information from the story.
- The student paraphrases or puts the main ideas and details in his or her own words.
- The student gives a summary that includes only the important or main ideas.
- The student recognizes when the same ideas are included more than once in a summary and deletes them.

Visualizing

- The student recognizes appropriate places in the text to stop and visualize.
- The student visualizes literal ideas or scenes described by the author.
- The student makes inferences while visualizing to show understanding of characters' feelings, mood, and setting. The visualizations go beyond the author's literal words.
- The student uses visualizing differently depending on the type of text (for example, characters, setting, and actions in narratives or a process description in nonfiction).

Inquiry Rubrics

Throughout each unit, students engage in Inquiry activities based on the unit concepts. They will present the findings of their research to the class. In this way they exhibit the wealth of knowledge and understanding they have gained about that particular concept. In addition to gaining knowledge about the concepts, students will be honing their research skills. With each unit, they will progress with their research in the same manner that professional researchers do. With each new unit of study, students should also become more sophisticated in their ability to formulate questions, make conjectures about those questions, recognize their own information needs, conduct research to find that information, reevaluate their questions and conjectures as new information is added to their knowledge base, and communicate their findings effectively. In addition, they will become more adept at working as a team and being aware of the progress being made as individuals and as a group. The Inquiry Rubrics will help you assess students' progress as researchers and as members of collaborative teams.

SRA Imagine It! provides four-point rubrics for each step in the Inquiry process. This enables you to clearly distinguish among different levels of performance.

1 Point score indicates that a student is performing below basic level.
2 Point score indicates that a student's abilities are emerging.
3 Point score indicates that a student's work is adequate and achieving expectations.
4 Point score indicates that a student is exceeding expectations.

Generating Ideas and Questions

1 With much teacher assistance, the student identifies or articulates an idea, though the idea may not be on topic.
2 With teacher assistance, the student uses some relevant background knowledge and vocabulary to identify or articulate an idea.
3 With little teacher assistance, the student identifies information and ideas to develop research questions about the topic.
4 The student independently identifies information and ideas in relation to a topic and contributes research questions.

Identifying a Question to Investigate

1 With help, the student identifies an idea or asks a question related to a particular topic.
2 With help, the student expresses curiosity about topics and translates this curiosity into a basic research question or problem.
3 With help, the student poses a problem or question for research and refines it into a researchable question.
4 The student independently identifies an interesting problem and translates it into a researchable question.

Making a Conjecture

1 The student makes a conjecture based on personal opinions or well-known facts.
2 The student makes a conjecture based on somewhat relevant background knowledge.
3 The student makes a conjecture based on relevant background knowledge and begins to address the research question.
4 The student makes a conjecture based on relevant background knowledge and addresses the research question.

Identifying Information Needs

1 The student identifies an overly broad range of information needs.
2 The student identifies information needs that are relevant but not essential to the research question.
3 The student identifies information needs that are clearly related to the specific research question.
4 The student identifies information needs that will allow for a deeper understanding of the research question.

Collecting Information

1 The student collects information that is not related to the topic.
2 The student collects information loosely related to the topic.
3 The student collects information clearly related to the topic.
4 The student collects useful information, reviews it critically, and pays attention to the reliability of sources.

Confirming and Revising Conjectures

1 Even with much teacher guidance, the student minimally participates in confirming or revising a conjecture.
2 With teacher guidance, the student recognizes whether information confirms a conjecture or requires a revision of the conjecture.
3 With some teacher guidance, the student recognizes whether new information confirms a conjecture or causes the conjecture to be revised.
4 With little teacher guidance or independently, the student revises or confirms a conjecture based on new knowledge.

Presenting Inquiry Findings

1 The student explains a key fact or idea to the teacher.
2 The student shares some new ideas with the teacher.
3 With teacher support, the student risks sharing new ideas and information with a small group of peers.
4 With teacher support or independently, the student shares new ideas and information in an organized fashion to a small group of peers or to the entire class.

Overall Research

1 With much teacher guidance, the student shows a limited understanding that research has led to new knowledge about the research question.
2 With teacher guidance, the student shows some understanding that research efforts have led to new knowledge about the research question.
3 The student understands that research efforts have led to new knowledge related to the research question.
4 The student understands that ideas change and develop and explains how (for example: *I used to think* X, *but now I know* Y).

Participation in Collaborative Inquiry

1 With much teacher prompting, the student works collaboratively with peers throughout the Inquiry process.
2 With some teacher prompting, the student works collaboratively with peers throughout the Inquiry process.
3 With little teacher prompting, the student works collaboratively with peers to share questions, ideas, and information sources.
4 With no teacher prompting, the student works collaboratively with peers to share questions, conjectures, and information. The student gains more knowledge by working with a group than by working independently.

Writing Rubrics

Rubrics are particularly effective for writing assignments, which do not have simple right or wrong answers. Different sets of rubrics cover various elements of the writing, including genre, writing process, and writing traits. They are intended to help teachers provide criteria and feedback to students.

SRA Imagine It! provides four-point rubrics for writing in each of four areas. This enables teachers to clearly distinguish among different levels of performance.

1 Point score indicates that a student is performing below basic level.
2 Point score indicates that a student's abilities are emerging.
3 Point score indicates that a student's work is adequate and achieving expectations.
4 Point score indicates that a student is exceeding expectations.

Writing Genres

Genre	1 Point	2 Points	3 Points	4 Points
Descriptive Writing	The writing includes little or no description of setting, character, or motivations.	The writing includes minimal description.	The writing includes adequate detail description.	The writing includes sensory details, motivations, and scenery details that add depth of understanding.
Narrative	The narrative has missing details or elements (characterization, plot, setting). Logical order is not apparent.	The narrative includes plot outline but does not elaborate on the details of character, plot, or setting.	The narrative adequately develops plot, character, and setting.	The narrative fully develops and elaborates on plot, character, and setting.
Personal	Personal writing is seen as an assignment rather than as an aid to the writer. Minimal effort is made, and the writing does not reflect the writer's ideas.	Some elements of personal writing reflect the writer's thoughts and ideas.	The writer uses personal writing to record or develop his or her thoughts.	The writer relies on personal writing to record, remember, develop, or express his or her thoughts.
Poetry	Little effort is made to select and arrange words to express a particular thought or idea. The main idea of the poem is not evident.	Some effort is made to work with word choice and arrangement to develop a thought in poetry form.	The writer has a clear idea and has attempted to use poetic form to express it. Poetry form may reflect established forms.	The writer has expressed an idea in an original or established poetic form. The writer has carefully selected words and arranged them for poetic effect.
Persuasive	The writer's position is absent or confusing. There is insufficient writing to show that criteria are met.	The writer's position is vague or lacks clarity. Unrelated ideas or multiple positions are included.	An opening statement identifies the writer's position. The writing may develop few or more points than delineated in the opening. The focus may be too broad.	The writer sets the scope and purpose of the paper in the introduction. The writer maintains his or her position throughout, supports his or her arguments, and includes an effective closing.
Persuasive Letter	The letter shows little audience awareness. The writer's viewpoint is not clear and/or not supported with facts, reasons, and examples.	The letter is written to a certain reader and is not likely to appeal to others. The letter begins with the writer's viewpoint but includes few facts, reasons, or examples to support that viewpoint.	The letter is written to a certain group of people and is likely to influence those readers to think, feel, or act in a certain way. The letter begins with the writer's viewpoint and includes some facts, reasons, and examples to support that viewpoint.	The letter is written to appeal to a wide audience and is likely to influence most readers to think, feel, or act in a certain way. The letter begins with the writer's viewpoint and includes concrete facts, logical reasoning, and specific examples to support that viewpoint.

Expository Writing Genres

Genre	1 Point	2 Points	3 Points	4 Points
Expository Structure	The main points and supportive details can be identified, but they are not clearly marked.	The composition is clearly organized around the main points with supportive facts or assertions.	The writer presents adequate, appropriate evidence to make a point or support a position. The positions are compared and contrasted while the main point is developed. The main points and supportive details can be identified, but they are not clearly marked.	The writer traces and constructs a line of argument, identifying part-to-whole relations. The main points are supported with logical and appropriate evidence.
Book Review (Fiction Book)	Information about the title, author, illustrator, and copyright date is missing. A sketchy description of characters, setting, and plot suggests the reviewer did not finish reading the book. The reviewer's opinion about the book is vague and unsupported.	Some basic information about the book is missing. The characters are named but not described; the time or place of the story is unclear. The plot summary is confusing. The author's main point is not mentioned. The reviewer offers an opinion about the book without supporting it.	The review includes basic information about the book and describes the main characters and setting. The plot is summarized, but parts of it may be unclear. The reviewer may not explain the author's main point. The reviewer offers an opinion about the book but may not support it strongly.	The review includes the book's title, author, illustrator, and copyright date. It briefly describes the main characters and setting and summarizes the plot. The writer explains the author's main point. The reviewer also gives an opinion about the book and supports it with examples from the story.
Compare and Contrast Essay	The subjects being compared are not clear. The writer briefly describes people, events, or objects without making connections between them. The essay lacks a summary.	The writer names the subjects being compared but does not clearly explain how they are similar and different. The essay has few clue words (such as also, like, but, although) and lacks a summary.	The writer names the subjects being compared and describes some things they have in common and some ways they are each unique. The writer uses some clue words (such as *also, like, but, although*) but mixes some comparisons with contrasts, creating confusion. The summary may not be strong	After introducing the subjects, the writer describes what they have in common using clue words such as *also, like,* and *too.* The writer also describes how each subject is unique using clue words such as *but, however,* and *although.* The essay concludes with a summary of the main points.
Explaining a Process	The process being described is not clear. The steps are sketchy, incomplete, and/or out of order. There is no awareness of the audience's needs.	The introduction names the process but lacks a needed list of materials and definition of terms. Several steps are missing, described incorrectly, or placed out of order. Too much or too little explanation is included.	The introduction names the process but lacks a needed list of materials or a definition of terms. A step may be missing, described incorrectly, or placed out of order. An explanation is included.	The introduction names the process, lists materials (if applicable), and defines the terms. Every step in the process is described accurately and in the correct order. The explanation shows an awareness of what the audience needs to know.
Informative Report	The report has no introduction or clear topic. It offers a group of loosely related facts or a series of poorly written steps. No graphic or conclusion is included.	The report has no clear introduction, but its topic is identifiable. However, it includes many facts unrelated to the topic, or it describes things in a disorganized way. No graphic or conclusion is included.	The report has an introduction and offers facts about the topic. Some facts may be irrelevant, or some ideas may be vague or out of order. A chart, diagram, or map is included. The report is fairly well-organized but doesn't have a strong conclusion.	The report begins with an introduction and offers relevant facts about the topic or describes the topic appropriately. A chart, diagram, map, or other graphic is well-integrated. The report is organized using cause/effect, comparison/contrast, or another pattern. It ends with a strong conclusion.
News Story	The topic of the story is vague. It lacks a headline and/or byline. The lead paragraph provides little accurate information.	The story describes a recent event and includes a headline and/or byline. The lead paragraph answers two or three of the five *Ws (who, what, when, where, why)* and *how* but includes many inaccuracies. The information is collected mainly by observation.	The story describes a recent event and includes a headline and byline. The lead paragraph answers four of the five *Ws* and *how* but may have slight inaccuracies. The information is collected mainly through research or observation.	The story describes a recent event or development and includes a headline and byline. The lead paragraph accurately answers the five *Ws* and *how*. Information and quotations are collected through interviews, research, or observation.

Expository Writing Genres

Genre	1 Point	2 Points	3 Points	4 Points
Summary	Sentences and phrases are taken from the original document with little attempt to identify the main ideas. The writer adds his or her own opinions.	The summary includes some of the main ideas, a few important details, and a number of minor details. Much of the wording is from the original document. The writer includes his or her own opinions.	The summary includes most main ideas and important details. Some minor details are also included. Some wording is from the original document. The writer may change the meaning of the original document slightly or add his or her own opinion.	The summary includes only the main ideas and most important details, organized by the key points. The writer uses his or her own words without changing the meaning of the original document or inserting his or her opinions or comments.

Narrative Writing Genres

Genre	1 Point	2 Points	3 Points	4 Points
Narrative: Character	The writer describes the characters in increasing detail in original stories, including the physical and mental qualities, such as *strong* or *kind*.	The writer describes the internal mental world of the story characters by explicitly describing their thoughts, feelings, and desires.	The writer creates life-like characters whose action and speech reflect unique qualities that are integral to the plot.	The writer creates complex characters, identifying psychological traits that are represented throughout the narrative.
Narrative: Plot	The plot includes a problem, failed attempts, sub-problems, and a resolution. There is evidence of coherence and cohesion, but it may depend on formulaic structure. The subject and theme are clear and maintained.	The plot is elaborated with descriptive details and elements that add excitement or color. The narrative structure is clear. The subject and theme are clear and developed throughout.	The plot is well-developed with subplots and complications that are integrated into the resolution.	The writer includes more complicated plot lines with varied time lines, flashbacks, or dual story lines.
Narrative: Setting	The writer creates settings that include simple descriptions of time, character, and place.	The writer describes the settings in ways that contribute to the mood, suspense, humor, or excitement of the story.	The writer identifies how the settings influence the story problems and their resolutions or contribute to other story elements, such as character and plot.	The writer creates settings that include metaphoric or symbolic elements that help to develop the story elements.
Narrative: Theme	No theme is apparent.	The superficial theme is included but not integrated.	A theme is expressed but not well developed.	The narrative fully develops a theme that expresses an underlying message beyond the narrative plot.
Biography/Autobiography	The events included are sketchy and do not clearly describe the life of the subject. The time line of events is not clear.	The writing describes a few events in the life of the subject but leaves unexplained gaps. Several events in the life of the subject are described out of chronological order.	The writer describes many important events in the subject's life, perhaps including family, education, early influences, and accomplishments. A few gaps remain. Most events are described chronologically.	The writer describes the most important events in the subject's life (family, education, early influences, accomplishments) and summarizes the rest. All events are described chronologically.
Play	The play does not list and describe the characters or describe all the scenes. Sketchy, confusing dialogue and stage directions do not result in life-like characters. The roles of several characters are unclear. Most stage directions are missing or confused with dialogue.	The play does not begin with a list and description of the characters and does not describe all the scenes. The dialogue and stage directions are vague and do not create unique characters. The roles of some characters in the plot are unclear. Many stage directions are missing or confused with the dialogue.	The play either does not begin with a list and description of the characters or does not describe all the scenes. The actions and speech of some characters may be inconsistent. Some of their traits are overly exaggerated. One or two characters may be superfluous to the plot. Some stage directions are confused with the dialogue.	The play begins with a list and description of its characters. The script describes the time and place of each scene or setting. The dialogue and stage directions create unique, believable characters with consistent actions and speech. All the characters are important to the plot. The stage directions are set off from the dialogue with italics, parentheses, and/or brackets.

The Writing Process

The Writing Process	1 Point	2 Points	3 Points	4 Points
Getting Ideas	The composition consists of statements that are loosely related to a topic, with no evident order or organization. Extraneous material may be present.	The statements not only relate to a topic but have an evident purpose (to describe, explain, argue, and so on).	The main points and supportive details can be identified, but they are not clearly marked.	The composition is clearly organized around the main points with supportive facts or assertions.
Prewriting—Organizing Writing	The writer makes little or no attempt to develop a plan for writing.	The writer uses a given model to plan his or her writing.	The writer elaborates on the model for planning his or her writing.	The writer develops his or her own plan based on the model.
Drafting	The writer writes without attention to a plan or is unable to write.	The writer writes a minimal amount with some attention to his or her plan.	The writer uses a plan to draft.	The writer elaborates on a plan to draft.
Revising	The writer quickly finishes his or her writing activities and does not seek feedback.	The writer pays attention as you provide feedback about his or her written work.	The writer welcomes feedback and advice from you or other students.	The writer actively seeks feedback from you or other students.
Editing	The writer demonstrates no attention to correcting grammar, usage, mechanics, or spelling errors.	Some errors in English language conventions are corrected. Many are not corrected.	The writer corrects many errors in English language conventions.	The writer corrects most errors in English language conventions and uses resources or seeks assistance to address uncertainties.
Presentation/Publishing	The writer presents his or her revised and edited draft as the final version.	The writer recopies his or her final draft with no extra presentation.	The writing includes adequate presentation efforts with illustration, format, and style.	The writer completes an impressive presentation of his or her written work with attention to format, style, illustration, and clarity.
Self-Management	The writer does not have a plan for writing and does not use graphic organizers or checklists when writing.	The writer employs an unclear plan for writing and sometimes uses graphic organizers to plan his or her writing or checklists to revise/proofread his or her writing.	The writer employs a plan for writing and often uses graphic organizers to plan his or her writing or checklists to revise/proofread his or her writing.	The writer employs a clear plan for writing and uses graphic organizers to plan his or her writing and checklists to revise/proofread his or her writing.
Time Management	The writer puts off the writing tasks to the last minute and seldom finishes his or her work on time.	The writer allows some, but often not enough, time for the writing task.	The writer allows time for writing but not enough for revising or proofreading.	The writer listens to advice about time requirements and plans accordingly.

Writing Traits

Writing Traits	1 Point	2 Points	3 Points	4 Points
Audience	The writer displays little or no sense of the audience and does not engage the audience.	The writer displays some sense of the audience	The writer writes with the audience in mind throughout.	The writer displays a strong sense of the audience and engages the audience.
Citing Sources	The writer demonstrates little commitment to the quality and significance of research and to the accuracy of the written document. There is no documentation of the sources.	The writer demonstrates limited commitment to the quality and significance of research and to the accuracy of the written document. The documentation is sometimes used to avoid plagiarism and to enable the reader to judge how believable or important a piece of information is by checking the source.	The writer demonstrates a commitment to the quality and significance of research and to the accuracy of the written document. Documentation is used to avoid plagiarism and to enable the reader to judge how believable or important a piece of information is by checking the source.	The writer demonstrates an exceptionally strong commitment to the quality and significance of research and to the accuracy of the written document. Documentation is used to avoid plagiarism and to enable the reader to judge how believable or important a piece of information is by checking the source.
Conventions Overall	Numerous errors in usage, grammar, spelling, capitalization, and punctuation repeatedly distract the reader and make the text difficult to read. The reader finds it difficult to focus on the message.	The writing demonstrates limited control of standard writing conventions (punctuation, spelling, capitalization, grammar, and usage). Errors sometimes impede readability.	The writing demonstrates control of standard writing conventions (punctuation, spelling, capitalization, grammar, and usage). Minor errors, while perhaps noticeable, do not impede readability.	The writing demonstrates exceptionally strong control of standard writing conventions (punctuation, spelling, capitalization, grammar, and usage) and uses them effectively to enhance communication. Errors are so few and so minor that the reader can easily skim over them.
Conventions: Sentence Structure	Some sentences are standard, but many are run-on sentences or sentence fragments. The writer may use repetitive sentence patterns.	The writer primarily uses simple sentences. The writing has some run-on sentences or sentence fragments. The writer may use repetitive sentence patterns.	The writer uses standard sentence construction throughout with a variety of simple and complex sentence patterns. The writing may have a few run-on sentences or sentence fragments.	The writer uses standard sentence construction throughout. The sentence pattern and length are varied, effective, and enhance what is said. The writing has no unintentional run-on sentences or sentence fragments.
Conventions: Spelling	The writer uses sound spelling as a primary strategy. Many words are misspelled.	The writer uses many correct sound spellings and some structural spelling patterns.	The writer uses mostly correct sound spellings and structural patterns.	The writer uses correct sound spelling patterns and structural patterns and understands affixes, homophones, and meaning patterns.
Conventions: Grammar and Usage	The writing shows a lack of awareness of standard usage and has many errors in subject-verb agreement.	The writing demonstrates some awareness of standard usage and proper sentence structure.	The writing includes mainly standard usage and correct sentence structures	The writer uses a variety of sentence structures appropriately for effect and demonstrates an understanding of standard usage.
Conventions: Punctuation	The writer uses periods correctly but makes little use of other punctuation.	The writer uses end punctuation correctly.	The writer uses most punctuation correctly.	The writer uses end punctuation, commas, quotation marks, parentheses, ellipses, and other forms of punctuation correctly and appropriately.
Conventions: Capitalization	The writer uses capital letters correctly at the beginnings of sentences but inconsistently in other places.	The writer consistently uses capital letters at the beginnings of sentences and for some proper nouns.	The writer uses capitalization correctly most of the time.	The writer uses capitalization correctly in sentences, proper nouns, and titles and demonstrates an awareness of capitalization rules in unique situations.
Elaboration (Supporting Details and Examples that Develop the Main Idea)	The writer states his or her ideas or points with minimal detail to support them	The writing includes sketchy, redundant, or general details; some may be irrelevant. Support for the key ideas is very uneven.	The writer includes a mix of general statements and specific details/examples. The support is mostly relevant but may be uneven and lack depth in places.	The writing includes specific details and supporting examples for each key point/idea. The writer may use compare/contrast to support those ideas.

Writing Traits

Writing Traits	1 Point	2 Points	3 Points	4 Points
Focus	The topic is unclear or wanders and must be inferred. Extraneous material may be present.	The topic/position/direction is unclear and must be inferred.	The topic/position is stated, and the direction/purpose is previewed and maintained. The writing stays mainly on topic.	The topic/position is clearly stated, previewed, and maintained throughout the paper. The topics and details are tied together with a central theme or purpose that is maintained/threaded throughout the paper.
Ideas/Content	Superficial and/or minimal content is included.	The main ideas are understandable, although they may be overly broad or simplistic, and the results may not be effective. The supporting details are limited, insubstantial, overly general, or off the topic.	The writing is clear and focused. The reader can easily understand the main ideas. Support is present, although it may be limited or rather general.	The writing is exceptionally clear, focused, and interesting. The main ideas stand out and are developed by strong support and rich details.
Organization	The writing lacks coherence; the organization seems haphazard and disjointed. The plan is not evident. Facts are presented randomly, and no transitions are included. The beginning is weak, and the ending is abrupt. There is no awareness of paragraph structure or organization.	An attempt has been made to organize the writing; however, the overall structure is inconsistent or skeletal. A plan is evident but loosely structured, or the writer overuses a particular pattern. The writing may be a listing of facts or ideas with a weak beginning or conclusion. The transitions are awkward or nonexistent. The writing includes a beginning use of paragraphs.	The organization is clear and coherent. Order and structure are present but may seem formulaic. A plan is evident. Reasons for the order of the key concepts may be unclear. A beginning or conclusion is included but may lack impact. The transitions are present. Paragraph use is appropriate.	The organization enhances the central idea and its development. The order and structure are compelling and move the reader through the text easily. The plan is evident, and the key concepts are logically sequenced. The beginning grabs the reader's attention, and the conclusion adds impact. The writing uses a variety of transitions that enhance the meaning. The writer uses paragraphs appropriately.
Sentence Fluency	The writing is difficult to follow—either choppy or rambling. The sentences are incomplete, or their awkward constructions force the reader to slow down or reread.	The writing tends to be mechanical rather than fluid. Occasional awkward constructions may force the reader to slow down.	The writing flows; however, connections between the phrases or sentences may be less than fluid. The sentence patterns are somewhat varied, contributing to an ease in oral reading.	The writing has an effective flow and rhythm. The sentences show a high degree of craftsmanship, with consistently strong and varied structure that makes expressive oral reading easy and enjoyable.
Voice	The writing provides little sense of involvement or commitment. There is no evidence that the writer has chosen a suitable voice. It does not engage the audience.	The writer's commitment to the topic seems inconsistent. A sense of the writer may emerge at times; however, the voice is either inappropriately personal or inappropriately impersonal.	A voice is present. The writer demonstrates commitment to the topic. In places, the writing is expressive, engaging, or sincere. The words and expressions are clear and precise.	The writer has chosen a voice that is appropriate for the topic, purpose, and audience. Unique style comes through. The writing is expressive, engaging, or sincere. The writer demonstrates a strong commitment to the topic.
Word Choice	The writer exhibits less than minimal word usage. The writing shows an extremely limited vocabulary and frequent misuse of words. The language is monotonous. The writing includes no interesting words. The words and expressions are simple and may be repetitive, inappropriate, or overused.	The writer exhibits minimal word usage. The language is ordinary; lacks interest, precision, and variety; or may be inappropriate to the audience and purpose in places. The writing is filled with familiar words and phrases and contains only a few interesting words. The words and expressions are clear but usually more general than specific.	The writer exhibits adequate word usage. The words effectively convey the intended message. The writer employs a variety of words that are functional and appropriate to the audience and purpose. The writing contains some interesting words and some vivid descriptive language.	The writer exhibits exceptional word usage. The words convey the intended message in an exceptionally interesting, precise, and natural way that is appropriate to the audience and purpose. The writer employs a rich, broad range of words, which have been carefully chosen and thoughtfully placed for impact. The writing contains many interesting words. The writer uses literary devices effectively.

G

M

Use this page to record lessons or elements that work well or need to be adjusted for future reference.

Lessons that work well.

Lessons that need adjustments.